The Holy Spirit and Ethics in Paul

The Holy Spirit and Ethics in Paul

Transformation and Empowering for Religious-Ethical Life

SECOND REVISED EDITION

Volker Rabens

Fortress Press

Minneapolis

THE HOLY SPIRIT AND ETHICS IN PAUL
Transformation and Empowering for Religious-Ethical Life, Second Revised Edition

Fortress Press Edition © 2014

Copyright © 2010 Mohr Siebeck Tübingen.

Cover image © DeA Picture Library / Art Resource, NY
Cover design: Tory Herman

Library of Congress Cataloging-in-Publication Data available

ISBN 978-1-4514-7220-2

Manufactured in the U.S.A.

Preface to the Fortress Press Second Edition

How, according to the apostle Paul, does the Spirit enable religious-ethical life? By way of answer, the first part of this book challenges the "infusion-transformation" approach to Pauline pneumatology and ethics, which builds on a Stoic concept of the Spirit as a material substance. The second part of the book advances the idea that it is primarily through initiating and sustaining an intimate relationship with God the Father, Jesus Christ, and with the community of faith that the Spirit transforms and empowers people for ethical living.

I am very happy that the two chief theses of this monograph[1] have been received with so much interest and positive feedback that the book has already gone into a second edition (WUNT II/283, Mohr Siebeck, 2013,[2] containing a number of corrections but the same pagination as the first edition). To my great joy this second edition is now published by Fortress Press as a paperback. I would like to express my gratitude to Neil Elliott and the editorial team at Fortress Press for their effort in bringing this edition of the book on its way.

One of the first responses to this study was a comparative review of Troels Engberg-Pedersen's 2010 monograph *Cosmology and Self in the Apostle Paul: The Material Spirit* and my monograph.[2] Troels Engberg-Pedersen's study appeared the same month that I was completing the manuscript of this book,

---

1. Cf. the two summary articles: V. Rabens, 'Ethics and the Spirit in Paul (1): Religious-Ethical Empowerment through Infusion-Transformation?', *ExpTim* 125.5 (2014), forthcoming, published OnlineFirst, June 5, 2013, DOI: 10.1177/0014524613492668; and 'Ethics and the Spirit in Paul (2): Religious-Ethical Empowerment through the Relational Work of the Spirit', *ExpTim* 125.6 (2014), forthcoming, published OnlineFirst, June 5, 2013, DOI: 10.1177/0014524613492672.

2. P. Orr, 'Review of T. Engberg-Pedersen, *Cosmology and Self in the Apostle Paul*, and V. Rabens, *The Holy Spirit and Ethics in Paul*', *Them* 35 (2010), 452–55.

so I was able to start interacting immediately with this part of his work. Both studies appear to propose opposite approaches to Paul, particularly with regard to the apostle's view of the nature of the Spirit. As the subtitle of his monograph indicates, Troels Engberg-Pedersen reads Paul in a Stoic context and ascribes a material concept of pneu/ma to the apostle. The first part of my study critically examines this reading. For this reason, one or two reviews have interpreted my work as arguing the opposite, namely that Paul had an immaterial concept of the Spirit.[3] However, while I was indeed subconsciously operating with a Platonist notion of pneu/ma during the initial stage of my research, I soon realized that this approach to Paul is inadequate. I have dealt with this interpretative option in detail in my excursus 'The Alleged Concept of the Spirit as Immaterial Substance', in which I argue that Paul's letters provide no evidence that the apostle operated with an immaterial concept of pneu/ma (pp. 82–86). As Paul does not discuss or evidently presuppose a particular ontology of the Spirit, I maintain that it is best to refrain from such claims regarding the nature of pneu/ma in Paul – whether immaterial or material.[4]

Likewise, I do not argue that all of Paul's statements regarding the reception of the Spirit are metaphorical.[5] In section 2.1.1. I have discussed in great

---

3. E.g., M.P. O'Reilly concludes his review with the words: 'Rabens's relational approach is carefully argued and will be of particular use to specialists in Pauline pneumatology and ethics, although the implications of an immaterial Spirit will cause this study to be of interest to other specializations within Pauline studies in particular and biblical studies in general (e.g., cosmology, anthropology, soteriology)' (O'Reilly, 'Review of V. Rabens, *The Holy Spirit and Ethics in Paul*', *RelSRev* 38 [2012], 21). Cf. G. Buch-Hansen, 'Review of V. Rabens, *The Holy Spirit and Ethics in Paul*', *TRev* 108 (2012), 118; and M.D. Litwa, *We Are Being Transformed: Deification in Paul's Soteriology*; BZNW 187 (Berlin: de Gruyter, 2012), 131–33, who appears to misinterpret my treatment of 1 Cor. 15:35–54 as suggesting that σῶμα πνευματικόν signifies an immaterial body (however, see 3.1 below, esp. p. 96 n.71).

4. Cf. Engberg-Pedersen's approach to Paul's view of God, which is almost identical to what I say about the nature of πνεῦμα in Paul: 'Then we can ask: if Paul accepted the Stoic argument for God's existence, did he also accept the specifically Stoic *ontology* of God, which connects God directly with the pneuma? No. There is no indication of this in Romans 1. Nor can I find any such indication elsewhere. It appears, therefore, that although he knew the Stoic argument for the existence of God, Paul simply understood God as an acting person without engaging in any further speculation about his ontological status. Or differently put: Paul's God was just the Jewish God. If that is the correct conclusion, it is probably also unlikely that there is any ontological underpinning in Paul for his understanding of the functional relationship of the pneuma with God' (Engberg-Pedersen, *Cosmology*, 61). However, with regard to Paul's pneumatology, Engberg-Pedersen seems to buy into an 'either Platonic or Stoic' approach to Paul (e.g., *Cosmology*, 19) without considering the option that Paul does not discuss or clearly presuppose a particular ontology of πνεῦμα – although a detailed investigation of the relevant texts shows exactly this (see ch. 3 below, esp. pp. 119–20, and ch. 7, esp. p. 249).

5. *Pace* Buch-Hansen, 'Review of Rabens, *Spirit*', 118.

detail how one can detect and interpret figurative language in a given text. I have applied this methodology to a number of relevant passages throughout the monograph (esp. 1QH^a 15.6–7: pp. 43–54; Rom. 8:9, 1 Cor. 3:16, 6:19: pp. 82–86; 1 Cor. 12:13: pp. 96–119) – with different results! In the aforementioned excursus I explicitly oppose a binary interpretation of Paul's Spirit-language as being necessarily *either* literal *or* metaphorical (pp. 85–86).

The history of interpretation of the New Testament, and especially that of Paul, is saturated with 'either–or' approaches: either Stoic or Platonic, either literal or metaphorical, and: either substance-ontological or relational. In the second part of my study I develop a fresh approach to Paul which is 'relational' but which is designed to overcome this latter dichotomy between 'substantial' and 'relational'.[6] 'Relational transformation' as we see it in Paul implies a 'substantive' dimension. I have argued that 'believers can "hardly fail to be transformed by a living relationship with the life-giving God"[7] which implies that Paul's more "substantive language" has a place in our concept of the relational work of the Spirit in Paul's ethics too. The adjacent pairs which are often conceived as opposites (i.e. relational versus substance-ontological transformation; [functional] empowering versus [ontological] transformation; new self-understanding versus a completely new self) thus converge in our concept of *transforming relationships*' (p. 143). In a forthcoming publication I discuss in more detail what this implies for the current debate[8] on theosis and deification in Paul.[9]

This monograph addresses the question of how the Spirit enables believers to live according to the values of Paul's gospel. However, it does not provide an in-depth discussion of how the 'form and content' of Paul's paraenesis is shaped by his pneumatology (although, see, e.g., pp. 237–39). For this reason, Stefan Schreiber makes the valid point in his otherwise positive review that my preliminary statement that the transferral into the realm of the Spirit would mean '*freedom from* sin, the flesh, the law, the enslaving powers, etc., . . .' (p. 172) is

---

6. See esp. pp. 138–44. *Pace* F. Blischke, 'Review of V. Rabens, *The Holy Spirit and Ethics in Paul*', *ThLZ* 137 (2012), 682.

7. J.D.G. Dunn, *The Theology of Paul the Apostle* (Edinburgh: T. & T. Clark, 1998), 344.

8. With regard to this discussion, see, e.g., B.C. Blackwell, *Christosis: Pauline Soteri-ology in Light of Deification in Irenaeus and Cyril of Alexandria*; WUNT II/314 (Tübingen: Mohr Siebeck, 2011), who categorizes the different approaches to the role of πνεῦμα in human transformation of Engberg-Pedersen and me as 'essential-transformative' and 'attributive' deification respectively (p. 104). Cf. V. Rabens, 'Review of D.M. Litwa, *We Are Being Transformed*', *ThLZ* 138 (2013), 446–48. I also look forward to the dialogue at the sixth conference organized by the Studiorum Novi Testamenti Societas' Eastern Europe Liaison Committee, to be held in Belgrade (25–31 August 2013), where we will discuss 'The Holy Spirit and the Church according to the New Testament' from 'Eastern' and 'Western' perspectives.

9. V. Rabens, '*Pneuma* and the Beholding of God – Reading Paul in the Context of Philonic Mystical Traditions', in J. Frey and J.R. Levison (eds.), *Historical Contexts of the Early Christian Notion of the Spirit*; Ekstasis (Berlin/New York: De Gruyter, 2014), forthcoming.

an unsatisfactory answer to the question of how ethical life relates to the Jewish Torah.[10] This is particularly true given that Paul says that 'the just requirement of the law might be fulfilled in us, who walk not according to the flesh but according to the Spirit' (Rom. 8:4). However, as this book has a slightly different focus, I provide a nuanced discussion of the believers' relation to sin and flesh but not with regard to the law. The question raised by Schreiber is an issue for further research.[11]

Finally, I am thankful that the theologian Mark Saucy has published a review article of the monograph which brings the results of this exegetical study into fruitful dialogue with the *topoi* of systematic and practical theology.[12] Such dialogue was also one of the aims of the recent *Festschrift* for Max Turner, who supervised the research which has been distilled into this monograph.[13] Max was the first one to introduce me to the academic study of New Testament pneumatology nearly two decades ago (during an undergraduate course at London School of Theology), and I have been grateful for his model of dedicated scholarship ever since.

Jena, June 2013   Volker Rabens

---

10. S. Schreiber, 'Review of V. Rabens, *The Holy Spirit and Ethics in Paul*', *BN* 152 (2012), 142.

11. The development of my thoughts on the relationship between Spirit and law in Paul can be seen in a forthcoming article on 'The Spirit in Paul's First Epistle to the Thessalonians', in K. Warrington and T.J. Burke (eds.), *A Biblical Theology of the Spirit* (London: SPCK, 2013), section 2.1., esp. n.10 where I draw on the work of my colleague at Ruhr University Bochum, J.-C. Maschmeier, *Rechtfertigung bei Paulus: Eine Kritik alter und neuer Paulusperspektiven*; BWANT 189 (Stuttgart: Kohlhammer, 2010).

12. M. Saucy, 'How Does the Holy Spirit Change Us? – A Review Essay', *JBPR* 4 (2012), 109–22. I too have pointed out some further theological implications of my model in V. Rabens, '"Indicative and Imperative" as Substructure of Paul's Theology-and-Ethics in Galatians? A Discussion of Divine and Human Agency in Paul's Letter to the Churches in Galatia', in N.T. Wright, S.J. Hafemann and M.W. Elliott (eds.), *Galatians and Christian Theology* (Grand Rapids: Baker Academic, 2014), forthcoming. Apart from that, it is worth noting that this relational model of ethical enabling in Paul shares significant parallels with the theology-and-ethics of John's Gospel and 1 John, as I have tried to show in V. Rabens, 'Johannine Perspectives on Ethical Enabling in the Context of Stoic and Philonic Ethics', in J. van der Watt and R. Zimmermann (eds.), *Re-thinking the Ethics of John: "Implicit Ethics" in the Johannine Writings*; Contexts and Norms of New Testament Ethics III; WUNT I/291 (Tübingen: Mohr Siebeck, 2012), 114–39.

13. I.H. Marshall, V. Rabens, and C. Bennema (eds.), *The Spirit and Christ in the New Testament and Christian Theology: Essays in Honor of Max Turner* (Cambridge/Grand Rapids: Eerdmans, 2012). My own essay in this volume provides a hermeneutical reflection on the experiential nature of Paul's pneumatology ('Power from In Between: The Relational Experience of the Holy Spirit and Spiritual Gifts in Paul's Churches', pp. 138–55).

Preface to the First Edition

This study, submitted as a Ph.D. dissertation at London School of Theology in 2007, is not just the result of my own efforts but it owes thanks to the support of many 'significant others'. First of all, I would like to express my gratitude to my *Doktorvater*, Professor Max Turner, who first directed my attention to the need for a study of Spirit and ethics in Paul and for his friendly and insightful advice at the various stages of the research. I am also grateful for the encouraging feedback of my examiners Professor James D. G. Dunn and Professor Steve Walton. Additional thanks goes to Professor Jörg Frey for accepting my thesis into the WUNT monograph series. I am also grateful to Dr. Henning Ziebritzki and the Mohr Siebeck team for their helpful assistance as well as patience – due to a busy lecturing job and then a change to a new position at Bochum University (which involved moving with the family to a different part of the country) this book appears two years later than originally intended. A number of important publications have appeared in the meantime, most significantly Troels Engberg-Pedersen's *Cosmology and Self in the Apostle Paul: The Material Spirit*, which came out in the very month of the completion of the present book. In the light of this recent discussion I am thankful for the fresh perspectives on religious dynamics which I have gained in the context of my work with the International Consortium for Research in the Humanities 'Dynamics in the History of Religions' at Bochum University, which have inspired me to expand my treatment of the dynamics between Stoic ethics and Paul in the course of updating the manuscript of this book in April 2010.

Furthermore, I would like to thank those who have financially supported this research project. Thanks goes to my parents, Heike† and Jürgen Rabens, who have supported me – not just financially – both during my undergraduate studies as well as the at early stages of research life. I thank the Rufford Maurice Laing Foundation for various scholarship awards and the *Deutsche Forschungsgemeinschaft* and the Theological Faculties of the University of Tübingen for a full scholarship during the years of my work with the interdisciplinary *Graduiertenkolleg* 'Die Bibel – ihre Entstehung und ihre Wirkung' (2002–2005). Finally, I extend my thanks to the British New Testament Society travel fund committee for sponsoring my attendance at various British New Testament Conferences. It was there, at the 2000 meeting at King's College London, that I first had the chance of presenting in a seminar paper my focal theory and several parts of the argument of this dissertation.

Since then I have had the privilege of being able to present the material of this thesis at a number of national and international theological conferences. Here particular thanks goes to the New Testament research seminars of Professor Hans-Joachim Eckstein, the bilingual Colloquium for Graduates (Prof. Otto Betz†, Prof. Hermann Lichtenberger and Dr. Scott Caulley), and the New Testament research conferences at London School of Theology.

Several scholars have taken the time to interact with my ideas on a personal level. I would like to thank Prof. John Barclay, Prof. Hartmut Gese, Prof. Friedrich Wilhelm Horn, Prof. Carsten Lehmkühler and Prof. Peter Stuhlmacher.

Special thanks goes to Dr. Annette Glaw and Dr. Helen Shephard for proof-reading the manuscript of this book, and to Dr. Cor Bennema, Dr. Annette Glaw, Dr. Burkhard Reis and Dr. Johannes Woyke for engaging with different parts of the thesis.

It is a great blessing to have close friends with whom I am able to share both my academic interests as well as the other aspects of my life. These friends include Dr. Cor Bennema, Dr. Annette Glaw, Dr. Desta Heliso, Dr. André Munzinger, Drs. Ester & Viktor Petrenko and Dr. Chris Tilling. Other friends who have been a great source of encouragement and support include Johannes Euhus, Detlef Garbers, Volkmar Kuhmann, and many others. Special gratitude goes to my 'English families' who have overwhelmed me and my wife Heike with hospitality and friendship during the past years: Hazel & Michael Gammage, Kath & Brian Taylor, Kathy & Andy Coomar, and Val & Dr. Steve Motyer.

Finally, most important has been the love and friendship of my wife Heike. She has walked with me through the majority of this part-time project, and she has not shrunk back from giving a lot of her time and energy so that this book could see its completion. I dedicate this study to her and to our two children, Lena and Thilo, who often have lit up my day.

Bochum, April 2010   Volker Rabens

Acknowledgements

Citations from the Bible are usually taken from the New Revised Standard Version (NRSV); references to and citations from the Dead Sea Scrolls are taken from F. García Martínez and E.J.C. Tigchelaar (eds.), *The Dead Sea Scrolls Study Edition*, 2 vols. (Leiden/Cambridge: Brill/Eerdmans, 2000), unless otherwise indicated; those from the Pseudepigrapha are taken from J.H. Charlesworth (ed.), *The Old Testament Pseudepigrapha*, 2 vols. (New York: Doubleday, 1983, 1985); those from the Rabbis are taken from J. Israelstam, *Midrash Rabbah: Leviticus I–XIX. Translated under the Editorship of Rabbi H. Freedman and M. Simon* (London: Soncino, 1957) *et alii*; those from Philo are taken from the Loeb Classical Library (Cambridge: Havard University Press, various dates), unless it is indicated that the translation is by C.D. Yonge, *The Works of Philo* (Peabody: Hendrickson, 1995³).

Citations from Graeco-Roman literature are taken from A.A. Long and D.N. Sedley, *The Hellenistic Philosophers*; 2 vols. (Cambridge: Cambridge University Press, 1998, 2001), referenced, where available, in square brackets, e.g. '[*LS* 61M]'; from the relevant editions of the Loeb Classical Library; and from I. ab Arnim, *Stoicorum Veterum Fragmenta*, 4 vols. (Stuttgart: Teubner, 1964). Further sources include, P. de Lacy (ed.), *Galen, On the Doctrines of Hippocrates and Plato. Vol. 1* (Berlin: Akademie-Verlag, 1984³); J. Mau (ed.), *Plutarchi Moralia. Vol. 5.2/1* (Leipzig: Teubner, 1971); W. Scott, *Hermetica: The Ancient Greek and Latin Writings which contain Religious or Philosophic Teachings Ascribed to Hermes Trismegistus*, *Vol. 1* (Oxford: Clarendon, 1924); R.B. Todd, *Alexander of Aphrodisias on Stoic Physics: A Study of the De Mixtione with Preliminary Essays, Text, Translation and Commentary* (Leiden: Brill, 1976); T. Mommsen and A. Watson (eds.), *The Digest of Justinian*, 4 vols. (Philadelphia: University of Pennsylvania Press, 1985).

Citations from any of these sources, especially from the Pauline epistles, sometimes appear in an edited form without comment, or the translation is entirely that of the author wherever it is considered to provide a clearer or more literal rendering than suggested by the translations cited above.

Table of Contents

Part II
Religious-Ethical Empowerment by the Relational Work of the Spirit
A New Approach

Part III
Conclusions

Abbreviations

The abbreviations in this book are taken from P.H. Alexander et al. (eds.), *The SBL Handbook of Style for Ancient Near Eastern, Biblical and Early Christian Studies* (Peabody: Hendrickson, 1999), with the exception of the abbreviations of the Dead Sea Scrolls which are taken from F. García Martínez and E.J.C. Tigchelaar (eds.), *The Dead Sea Scrolls Study Edition*, 2 vols. (Leiden/Cambridge: Brill/Eerdmans, 2000). Abbreviations not found in the *SBL Handbook of Style* are noted below.

References to particular sections in this book usually start with the number of the chapter. For example, when one is referred to 4.4.1., one should turn to chapter 4 and look for section 4.1.

General Abbreviations:

art.	article of an unnamed author in a dictionary
DSS	Dead Sea Scrolls
ET	English translation
KJV	King James Version (Bible Translation)
NIV	New International Version (Bible Translation)
NRSV	New Revised Standard Version (Bible Translation)
NT	New Testament
orig. publ.	original publication (usually of a translated work)
OT	Old Testament (used interchangeably with 'Hebrew Bible')
RSV	Revised Standard Version (Bible Translation)

Journals, Major Reference Works, Series, etc.:

AASF.DHL	Annales Academiae Scientiarum Fennicae: Dissertationes Humanarum Litterarum
ABG	Arbeiten zur Bibel und ihrer Geschichte
AC	*Acta Classica*
AJEC	Ancient Judaism and Early Christianity
AS	Ausgewählte Schriften
AThD	Acta theologica Danica
AUU.HR	Acta Universitatis Upsaliensis: Historia Religionum
AYBRL	The Anchor Yale Bible Reference Library
BECNT	Baker Exegetical Commentary on the New Testament
BEvTh	Beiträge zur evangelischen Theologie
BIS	Biblical Interpretation Series
BISPUL	Bibliothèque de l'Institut Supérieur de Philosophie, Université de Louvain
BRLAJ	The Brill Reference Library of Ancient Judaism
BSGRT	Bibliotheca Scriptorum Graecorum et Romanorum Teubneriana
BsR	Beck'sche Reihe

BThSt	Biblisch-theologische Studien
CCWJCW	Cambridge Commentaries on Writings of the Jewish and Christian World 200 BC to AD 200
CMG	Corpus Medicorum Graecorum
CR.BS	*Currents in Research: Biblical Studies*
CS	Collected Studies Series
CSLS	Current Studies in Linguistics Series
CThM	Calwer Theologische Monographien
DHR	Dynamics in the History of Religions
DJBP	J. Neusner and W.S. Green (eds.), *Dictionary of Judaism in the Biblical Period: 450 B.C.E. to 600 C.E.*, 2 vols. (New York: Macmillan, 1996)
DNTB	C.A. Evans and S.E. Porter (eds.), *Dictionary of New Testament Background* (Leicester/Downers Grove: IVP, 2000)
ECC	Early Christianity in Context
EMSP	European Monographs in Social Psychology
EQ	*Evangelical Quarterly*
EREAMA	Ekstasis: Religious Experience from Antiquity to the Middle Ages
EUS	European University Studies
EWNT[2]	H. Balz and G. Schneider (eds.), *Exegetisches Wörterbuch zum Neuen Testament*, 3 vols. (Stuttgart: Kohlhammer, 1992[2])
FSÖT	Forschung zur systematischen und ökumenischen Theologie
FTS	Frankfurter theologische Studien
GAP	Guides to Apocrypha and Pseudepigrapha
GGA	*Göttingische Gelehrte Anzeigen*
GlLern	*Glaube und Lernen*
GSPR	The Guildford Series on Personal Relationships
HCS	Hellenistic Culture and Society
HLSLNT	Historical and Linguistic Studies in Literature related to the New Testament
HPWh	J. Ritter (ed.), *Historisches Wörterbuch der Philosophie*, 13 vols. (Darmstadt: Wissenschaftliche Buchgesellschaft, 1971–2007)
HTA	Historisch-Theologische Auslegung
HThKAT	Herders theologischer Kommentar zum Alten Testament
H.UAN	Hypomnemata: Untersuchungen zur Antike und zu ihrem Nachleben
HUTh	Hermeneutische Untersuchungen zur Theologie
ILLCDS	Institute for Logic, Language and Computation Dissertation Series
IPS	International Plato Studies
ISPCK	Indian Society for Promoting Christian Knowledge
JAAC	*Journal of Aesthetics and Art Criticism*
JBPR	*Journal of Biblical and Pneumatological Research*
JBTh	*Jahrbuch für Biblische Theologie*
JCCP	*Journal of Consulting and Clinical Psychology*
JCR	*The Journal of Conflict Resolution*
JIG	Jahrbuch für internationale Germanistik
JPsyChr	*Journal of Psychology and Christianity*
JPT	*Journal of Pentecostal Theology*
JPTS	Journal of Pentecostal Theology Supplement Series
JWJ	*Neue Jahrbücher für Wissenschaft und Jugendbildung*
KTAH	Key Themes in Ancient History
LCL	Loeb Classical Library (Cambridge, Mass.: Havard University Press)

LCT	Library of Constructive Theologie
LHB	Library of Hebrew Bible
LHD	The Library of History and Doctrine
LNTS	Library of New Testament Studies
LS	A.A. Long and D.N. Sedley, *The Hellenistic Philosophers*, 2 vols. (Cambridge: Cambridge University Press, 1998, 2001)
LTh	Leitfaden Theologie
MTS	Major Thinkers Series
MPG	J.-P. Migne (ed.), *Patrologiae Cursus Completus: Series Graeca*, 161 vols. (Paris 1857–66)
NCBC	New Cambridge Bible Commentary
N-HLS	North-Holland Linguistic Series
NSBT	New Studies in Biblical Theology
NTA	Neutestamentliche Abhandlungen
NTSR	New Testament for Spiritual Reading
OED²	J.A. Simpson and E.S.C. Weiner (eds.), *The Oxford English Dictionary*, 20 vols. (Oxford: Clarendon, 1989²)
O.SSSC	Origins: Studies in the Sources of Scientific Creativity
OTM	Oxford Theological Monographs
OTPNT	The Old Testament Pseudepigrapha and the New Testament
PBM	Paternoster Biblical Monographs
PH	Papyrusinstitut Heidelberg
PhA	Philosophia Antiquia
PS	Pauline Studies
PSPB	*Personality and Social Psychology Bulletin*
PW.TS	Philosophie und Wissenschaft: Transdisziplinäre Studien
RBL	*Review of Biblical Literature*
REPh	E. Craig (ed.), *Routledge Encyclopedia of Philosophy*, 10 vols. (London: Routledge, 1998)
RGG²	H. Gunkel et al. (eds.), *Die Religion in Geschichte und Gegenwart: Handwörterbuch für Theologie und Religionswissenschaft*, 5 vols. (Tübingen: J.C.B. Mohr (Paul Siebeck), 1927–1931²)
RGG⁴	H.D. Betz et al. (eds.), *Religion in Geschichte und Gegenwart*, 8 vols. (Tübingen: Mohr Siebeck, 1998–2005⁴)
RMCS	Routledge Monographs in Classical Studies
RPSP	Review of Personality and Social Psychology
SAM	Schriften der Académie du Midi
SAPERE	Scripta Antiquitatis Posterioris ad Ethicam Religionemque pertinentia
SBEC	Studies in the Bible and Early Christianity
SBL	Society of Biblical Literature
SBL	Studies in Biblical Literature (Peter Lang)
SBTS	Sources for Biblical and Theological Study
SF	Studia Friburgensia
SFEG	Schriften der Finnischen Exegetischen Gesellschaft
SGBS	Sprache in der Gesellschaft: Beiträge zur Sprachwissenschaft
SGKA	Studien zur Geschichte und Kultur des Altertums
SJTOP	Scottish Journal of Theology Occasional Papers
SLAG	Schriften der Luther-Agricola-Gesellschaft
SNTG	Die Schriften des Neuen Testaments neu übersetzt und für die Gegenwart erklärt

SNTW	Studies of the New Testament and its World
SPA	The Studia Philonica Annual
SPB	Studia Post-Biblica
StANT	Studien zum Alten und Neuen Testament
STI	Studies in Theological Interpretation
TANZ	Texte und Arbeiten zum neutestamentlichen Zeitalter
TBT	Theologische Bibliothek Töpelmann
TDOT	G.J. Botterweck et al. (eds.), *Theological Dictionary of the Old Testament*, 15 vols. (Grand Rapids/Cambridge: Eerdmans, 2004)
TGSG	Tesi Gregoriana: Serie Teologia
ThBNT²	L. Coenen and K. Haacker (eds.), *Theologisches Begriffslexikon zum Neuen Testament* (Wuppertal: Brockhaus, 1997²)
THNTC	The Two Horizons New Testament Commentary
UTB	Uni-Taschenbücher
UTBW	Uni-Taschenbücher für Wissenschaft
VLAR	Veröffentlichungen der Luther-Akademie Ratzeburg
VoxEv	*Vox Evangelica*
VSOD	Veröffentlichungen der Stiftung Oratio Dominica
WB.KK	Die Welt der Bibel: Kleinkommentare zur Heiligen Schrift
WdF	Wege der Forschung
ZNT	*Zeitschrift für Neues Testament*
ZS	Zur Sache
ZVS	*Zeitschrift für Völkerpsychologie und Sprachwissenschaft*

Chapter 1

Introduction

1. Rationale

Every student of Paul is at some point confronted with the question: how is it possible to put Paul's ethic into practice? What is the apostle's basis for thinking that believers will be able to live according to the moral standards set forth by him? In trying to find an answer to this central question one first of all needs to acknowledge that Paul's moral reasoning evidences more than one enabling factor for religious-ethical living. In fact, various aspects that enable ethical conduct have been singled out throughout the history of scholarship. These include, among others, justification-sanctification; baptism and the 'new creation'; the Christ-event and its narrative impact; Christian gratitude for God's forgiveness; *imitatio Christi* and *imitatio Pauli*; the church and its formative power; the moral 'imperative' (and its performative power); the believer's will to obey; and motivation through the prospect of potential reward or punishment in the eschaton.[1] This study, however, will focus on one prime factor which makes Paul believe in the feasibility of his ethic. This factor is perhaps *the* central one, namely, the Holy Spirit.[2]

The question of this book is how Paul, the 'theologian of the Holy Spirit',[3] comprehends religious-ethical life to be empowered by the Spirit. How does the Spirit help the believer to overcome sin, to be strengthened in temptation and to display the 'fruit of the Spirit'?

---

[1] For a discussion of a number of these aspects, see V.P. Furnish, *Theology and Ethics in Paul* (Nashville: Abingdon, 1968), 11, 212–24; R.B. Hays, *The Moral Vision of the New Testament: Community, Cross, New Creation. A Contemporary Introduction to New Testament Ethics* (Edinburgh: T. & T. Clark, 1997), 19–41; F. Blischke, *Die Begründung und die Durchsetzung der Ethik bei Paulus*; ABG 25 (Leipzig: Evangelische Verlagsanstalt, 2007), 466–69. On the *Forschungsgeschichte* of Pauline ethics, see the Appendix, n.2.

[2] According to Furnish's judgement, the majority of scholarship thinks that Paul's pneumatology is the touchstone of his ethics (Furnish, *Theology*, 11). For a recent example, see D.A. Campbell, *The Quest for Paul's Gospel: A Suggested Strategy* (London: T. & T. Clark, 2005), 60, 68.

[3] J.D.G. Dunn, 'Geist/Heiliger Geist: III. Neues Testament', *RGG⁴*, III, 566.

The most straightforward answer to this question would be that 'the resident Spirit is... God present as effective power, controlling ("leading") the way one lives – that is, it generates obedience.'[4] However, it is to be expected that an in-depth study devoted to this matter will be able to generate a more nuanced picture of the interplay of Spirit and ethics in the theology of Paul. This monograph is intended to provide such an investigation into this complex issue that has provoked vigorous discussion throughout the history of Pauline scholarship.

2. Overview of Contemporary Scholarship with Specific Reference to the 'Infusion-Transformation Approach' to Spirit and Ethics in Paul

The history of research evidences a broad interest in the interplay of theology and ethics in Paul. Particularly the role of the Spirit in Paul's ethics has received a lot of attention, although only once in a separate monograph.[5] Since a comprehensive presentation and critical analysis of the various positions has thus far not been provided, one objective of the present work is to fill this gap. However, as the past 140 years of research on both pneumatology and ethics in Paul has produced such a wealth of viewpoints (partly guided by the philosophical concepts current at the time), we reserve this detailed, chronological *Forschungsgeschichte* for the Appendix of this book.[6] In the present section we aim to give a brief thematic summary and systematisation of the different approaches to the matter of inquiry. The focus will be on one particular view that we will define in 1.3. as the 'infusion-transformation' approach and which will be the object of scrutiny in the first half of the study.

2.1. Diverging Explanations

The past 140 years of Pauline scholarship have generated diverging explanations of the ethical work of the Spirit. At one end of the spectrum one finds the conviction that the Spirit guarantees ethical life by 'driving' the believer. This is the position of H. Gunkel, and, without the notion of

---

[4] L.E. Keck, *Romans*; ANTC (Nashville: Abingdon, 2005), 206–207.

[5] K. Stalder, *Das Werk des Geistes in der Heiligung bei Paulus* (Zürich: EVZ-Verlag, 1962). However, Stalder's study on sanctification and pneumatology in Paul is heavily influenced by the *topoi* of systematic theology. He will thus not be our main dialogue partner. See our full discussion of his work in Appendix 2.2.

[6] For our rationale of providing a comprehensive, chronological overview of 140 years of scholarship at the end of this study, see further the introduction to the Appendix.

overpowering, that of T. Deidun and G.D. Fee.[7] These scholars stress the pneumatological indicative. On the other end of the spectrum we meet with a stronger emphasis on the will and the decision of the believer. K. Stalder, following in the steps of R. Bultmann, understands the work of the Spirit predominantly as making believers aware of their salvation by which they are enabled to realize the ethical imperative by their *own* power.[8] When one looks at these two opposite lines of interpretation from a different perspective, one could say that life in the Spirit is on the one hand seen by Fee as being without internal struggle (although not without sin). On the other hand, J.D.G. Dunn – while recognizing the Spirit as a powerful end-time gift to enable obedience from the heart – places strong emphasis on the intense battle with the flesh introduced to the believer through Spirit-reception.[9]

As might be expected, there are mediating positions between these two poles. O. Pfleiderer sought to encompass both lines of thought by pro-pounding that they are found unconnectedly in Paul. However, he was not followed by the majority of Pauline scholars.[10] F.W. Horn could be under-stood as arguing for both positions on a micro-scale. In his article 'Wandel im Geist', Horn contends that Paul's thought developed from the first position in Galatians (i.e. a stronger emphasis on the work of the Spirit) to the second in Romans (i.e. a stronger emphasis on the decision of the believer).[11] However, the main thesis of Horn's monograph *Das Angeld des Geistes* seems to side with the pneumatological indicative (though with a strong anthropological dimension). That is, Horn's model of human trans-formation through the reception of the *stofflich* πνεῦμα comes close to an automatism of ethical life as the result.[12]

Horn's main thesis on the ethical work of the Spirit has thus far been left unchallenged. As Horn is neither the first nor the only one to propound that believers are substance-ontologically transformed by the infusion of the (physical) Spirit, we need to look at this view more closely.

---

[7] See the Appendix: 1.3., n.94, and 3.2. However, while Fee believes in the primacy of the Spirit, he differs from Deidun in that he gives stronger weight to the believer's own doing, particularly in Rom. 8:16 (G.D. Fee, *God's Empowering Presence: The Holy Spirit in the Letters of Paul* (Peabody: Hendrickson, 1994), 569).

[8] See Appendix 2.1.–2.2.

[9] See Appendix 2.3., 3.2. However, although Dunn's view of Christian life can be un-derstood as anti-triumphalistic, he nevertheless does not major on the ethical imperative but appears to hold both aspects in balance.

[10] See Appendix 1.2. Other *viae mediae* will be presented in the course of this study.

[11] See F.W. Horn, 'Wandel im Geist: Zur pneumatologischen Begründung der Ethik bei Paulus', *KD* 38 (1992), 149–70, as discussed in Appendix 3.1.

[12] See F.W. Horn, *Das Angeld des Geistes: Studien zur paulinischen Pneumatologie*; FRLANT 154 (Göttingen: Vandenhoeck & Ruprecht, 1992), as summarized in 1.2.2.3.

2.2. The 'Infusion-Transformation Approach' to Spirit and Ethics in Paul

A major area of discussion in the history of scholarship on Pauline pneumatology and ethics concerns the nature of the believer's transformation
accomplished by the Spirit. A number of mainly German scholars argue
that the ethical life of believers derives from an ontic change achieved by
the Spirit at baptism.[13] R. Asting's statement is somewhat typical for the
whole generation of scholars from H. Ernesti to A. Schweitzer as well as
for many modern scholars (so, e.g., J. Becker):[14] 'On the basis of the fact
that he receives the Holy Spirit, the Christian becomes a different person.
The content of his soul is from now on divine... and the Spirit brings forth
a new, divine way of life.'[15]

However, since the days of Pfleiderer and Gunkel an additional concept
has influenced Pauline scholars in their thinking about the Spirit's work of
ethical transformation. W. Wrede, for whom salvation 'is an *ontic transformation of humanity* which produces ethical transformation as its result',[16] expresses this presupposition clearly. He argues that in a number of
places Paul 'appears to understand him [the Spirit] as a heavenly substance
that transforms the human being substantially'.[17] These two concepts,
namely that of the *stofflich* nature of the ontically renewing Spirit (although criticized by H.H. Wendt, H. Bertrams, et al.)[18] and that of the ontic
nature of the renewal itself (although criticized by Bultmann, Stalder, et
al.)[19] still hold sway over modern scholarship, as the publications of Horn

---

[13] The terms 'ontic' and 'substance-ontological' are used more or less interchangeably.
See the definitions in 1.3.

[14] See Appendix 1.1.–1.4.; J. Becker, 'Geschöpfliche Wirklichkeit als Thema des Neu-
en Testaments', in H.C. Knuth and W. Lohff (eds.), *Schöpfungsglaube und Umweltver-
antwortung: Eine Studie des Theologischen Ausschusses der VELKD*; ZS 26 (Hannover:
Lutherisches Verlagshaus, 1985), 68–71; J. Becker, 'Die Erwählung der Völker durch das
Evangelium: Theologiegeschichtliche Erwägungen zum 1. Thessalonicherbrief', in W.
Schrage (ed.), *Studien zum Text und zur Ethik des Neuen Testaments*; BZNW 47; FS H.
Greeven (Berlin/New York: W. de Gruyter, 1986), 88–89.

[15] R. Asting, *Die Heiligkeit im Urchristentum*; FRLANT 46 (Göttingen: Vandenhoeck
& Ruprecht, 1930), 215.

[16] W. Wrede, 'Paulus', in K.H. Rengstorf (ed.), *Das Paulusbild in der neueren deutschen Forschung*; WdF 24 (Darmstadt: Wissenschaftliche Buchgesellschaft, 1969), 61.

[17] Ibid., 58–59. Wrede builds this assumption on Paul's description of the transition of
the individual from ἐν σαρκί to ἐν πνεύματι (e.g. Rom. 8:9).

[18] H.H. Wendt, *Die Begriffe Fleisch und Geist im biblischen Sprachgebrauch* (Gotha:
Berthes, 1878), see Appendix 1.2.; H. Bertrams, *Das Wesen des Geistes nach der An-
schauung des Apostels Paulus: Eine biblisch-theologische Untersuchung*; NTA 4.4
(Münster: Aschendorff, 1913), *passim*.

[19] See Appendix 2.1.–2.2.

and Engberg-Pedersen in particular demonstrate.[20] An important step on the way to this development is the work of the early Käsemann and Stuhlmacher who have argued with great erudition that the concept of the *stofflich* nature of the Spirit is an integral part of Paul's ethics, and that it is through this Spirit that God transforms human beings *substance-ontologically*.

Both Käsemann and Stuhlmacher also acknowledge the relational aspect of the Spirit's work in drawing the believer closer to God. However, this aspect does not play a major role in their view of ethical enabling by the Spirit.[21] Rather, with their detailed substantiation of a substantial view of πνεῦμα and its work, the early Käsemann and Stuhlmacher have confirmed previous emphases of German scholarship and paved the way for further scholars. For this reason we will take a closer look at how Käsemann, Stuhlmacher and Horn comprehend the Spirit's enabling of religious-ethical life.

2.2.1. Ernst Käsemann

Being both influenced by and critical of his teacher Bultmann,[22] and in reaction to idealism, Käsemann stresses (a) that the Holy Spirit is a real, divine power that *transforms the historical person*, and (b) that it is the *Holy Spirit* who enacts ethical life within the believer. For Käsemann, this ethical work of the Spirit is founded upon the sacraments. He explains that the conjunction of Spirit and sacraments is due to the fact that 'im Sakrament ein Kraftstrom stofflich in den Menschen dringt'.[23] In other words,

---

[20] On Horn, see below; T. Engberg-Pedersen, 'A Stoic Understanding of *Pneuma* in Paul', in T. Engberg-Pedersen and H. Tronier (eds.), *Philosophy at the Roots of Christianity*; Working Papers 2 (Copenhagen: The Faculty of Theology, University of Copenhagen, 2006), esp. 121–22; T. Engberg-Pedersen, 'The Material Spirit: Cosmology and Ethics in Paul', *NTS* 55 (2009), 179–97; T. Engberg-Pedersen, 'Complete and Incomplete Transformation in Paul – A Philosophic Reading of Paul on Body and Spirit', in T.K. Seim and J. Økland (eds.), *Metamorphoses: Resurrection, Body and Transformative Practices in Early Christianity*; EREAMA 1 (Berlin/New York: W. de Gruyter, 2009), 123–46; T. Engberg-Pedersen, *Cosmology and Self in the Apostle Paul: The Material Spirit* (Oxford: Oxford University Press, 2010), *passim*.

[21] This is particularly true for their early writings. More on this below.

[22] For a helpful overview of the discussion between Bultmann, Käsemann and Stuhlmacher with regard to salvation in Paul, see S.J. Hafemann, 'Paul and His Interpreters', *DPL*, 676–77. On the agreements and disagreements between the early Käsemann and the early Bultmann in particular, see D.V. Way, *The Lordship of Christ: Ernst Käsemann's Interpretation of Paul's Theology*; OTM (Oxford: Clarendon, 1991), 45–59. On Bultmann, see further Appendix 2.1.

[23] E. Käsemann, *Leib und Leib Christi: Eine Untersuchung zur paulinischen Begrifflichkeit*; BHT 9 (Tübingen: J.C.B. Mohr (Paul Siebeck), 1933), 125.

the sacramental elements are 'pneumatic' in that they convey heavenly power-substance.[24]

How does Käsemann reach this conclusion? In his 1947/48 essay 'The Pauline Doctrine of the Lord's Supper'[25] Käsemann maintains with regard to 1 Corinthians 10:3–4 that

βρῶμα and πόμα πνευματικόν undoubtedly mean "food and drink which convey πνεῦμα". This is why it is immediately suggested that the rock which follows was spiritual, i.e. Christ himself, who is again identified with πνεῦμα in II Cor. 3.17. The gift takes on the character of the Giver and through the gift we become partakers of the Giver himself.[26]

However, it is debatable whether what is said in verses 3–4 of the food and drink in the wilderness can be applied in every single detail to the Lord's Supper in verses 16–17. In fact, just a few months before the publication of Käsemann's essay, K. Stürmer had argued that 'Paul never describes the elements in the Lord's Supper as πνευματικὸν βρῶμα and πόμα but reserves this description for the miraculous food and drink given to the people of Israel in the wilderness.'[27] Käsemann deals with this potential counter-argument by showing that 10:3–4 does not merely speak of historical Israel but of Israel as a τύπος of the Christian people of God, to whom a warning example is being held up. Käsemann is convinced that the entire thrust of the passage is designed to present not merely similarities between, but the identity of, the old and the new saving events (e.g. being 'baptised into Moses' and 'baptised into Christ'). It is on these grounds that Paul applies the saving events of the journey through sea and wilderness to baptism and the Lord's Supper. 'Because the Lord is the *Pneuma* and because in the sacrament the exalted Lord conveys, along with his gift, participation in himself as the Giver, therefore the gift of the sacrament must also be *Pneuma*.'[28] This is also the sense of those passages which explicitly characterise the πνεῦμα as the baptismal gift (i.e. 1 Cor. 6:11; 12:13; 2 Cor. 1:22).[29]

---

[24] E. Käsemann, 'Das Abendmahl im Neuen Testament', in H. Asmussen, et al. (eds.), *Abendmahlsgemeinschaft?*; BEvTh 3 (Munich: Kaiser, 1937), 90.

[25] E. Käsemann, 'The Pauline Doctrine of the Lord's Supper', in E. Käsemann, *Essays on New Testament Themes*; SBT (London: SCM Press, 1964), 108–135; orig. publ.: E. Käsemann, 'Anliegen und Eigenart der paulinischen Abendmahlslehre', *EvT* 7 (1947/48), 263–83. Where the wording of the quotations from this essay differs from the ET we have used our own translation of the German original.

[26] Käsemann, 'Doctrine', 113.

[27] K. Stürmer, 'Das Abendmahl bei Paulus', *EvT* 7 (1947/48), 58 n.34.

[28] Käsemann, 'Doctrine', 114.

[29] Ibid., 113, 134. Cf. E. Käsemann, *Commentary on Romans* (London: SCM Press, 1980), 222–23; Käsemann, 'Abendmahl', 75, 80; Käsemann, *Leib*, 126: 'In den Pneuma-Aeon wird man durch die Taufe hineingestellt, in ihm befestigt durch Abendmahl und Wortverkündigung.'

Käsemann raises the question as to the nature of the background against which one would have to interpret Paul's sacramental pneumatology. By way of answer he points out that Paul is here falling back on traditions familiar from the world of Hellenistic Gnosis. There, too, the doctrine of the transformation of human beings through the power of πνεῦμα is proclaimed. In fact, this transformation is presented as a kind of naturalistic process. 'For *pneuma* is seen in Hellenistic thought as the finest heavenly matter (*Stofflichkeit*) which has the capacity to penetrate man's being and, in doing so, to endow him with a new nature.'[30]

Before we go on to delineate how Käsemann continues his argumentation in his 1947/48 article, we will briefly turn to Käsemann's 1933 dissertation *Leib und Leib Christi* and his 1937 article on the Lord's Supper. In both publications Käsemann maintains that Paul adheres to the kind of Hellenistic pneumatology outlined above. It is in the context of his concept of the Spirit as a *stofflich* and substance-like power that Paul's naturalism and the *religionsgeschichtlich* influence upon his thought is particularly obvious.[31] This dependence on Hellenism is also evident in Paul's conception of the resurrection body (1 Cor. 15:42–50), because, like the writers of antiquity, Paul knows no energy without substratum. The Spirit thus appears substantially as radiance.[32]

In his publications of the 1930s Käsemann further argues that believers are changed in their substance upon the reception of the Spirit at baptism. Σάρξ has been extinguished and a new creation has been brought into being (2 Cor. 5:17; Gal. 6:15; Rom. 6:6). Drawing on Bousset, Käsemann highlights that 'damit ist allerdings gegeben, daß "der von Gottes Geist erfüllte Pneumatiker und der alte Mensch völlig von einander getrennte, verschiedene Wesen" sind, daß ["]von dem einen zum anderen... nur der Weg göttlichen Wunders" führt.'[33] How radical this transformation was for Paul can easily be demonstrated by the example of 1 Corinthians 12:13 and Galatians 3:28: national, social and even sexual distinctions are abolished, the person is thus de-individualised (*entindividualisiert*).[34]

---

[30] Käsemann, 'Doctrine', 115; cf. 116.

[31] Käsemann, *Leib*, 125, 127–28, 161–62; Käsemann, 'Abendmahl', 75, 90. Apart from Gnostic influences, Käsemann likewise identifies similarities in Paul's pneumatology with the Stoic concept of the immanence of the Spirit. However, Käsemann points out that Pauline pneumatology does diverge from Stoicism in a number of places since for Paul the Spirit is dualistically opposed to the flesh and is comprehended as an aeon which is at once power, person and substance (Käsemann, *Leib*, 126).

[32] Käsemann, *Leib*, 135. Cf. Käsemann, *Romans*, 212.

[33] Käsemann, *Leib*, 127, quoting W. Bousset, *Kyrios Christos: A History of the Belief in Christ from the Beginnings of Christianity to Irenaeus* (New York: Abingdon, 1970), 122.

[34] Käsemann, *Leib*, 127, 134, 161.

It is only logical that this Spirit-wrought new creation will determine the character of Paul's sacramental ethics. Since the nature of this renewal is so radical, Käsemann is convinced that it is characteristic for Paul's ethic to talk of a 'must' of the believer rather than of a 'can' or 'should'.[35]

With assertions like these, Käsemann's ethics sounds somewhat reminiscent of Gunkel's work. Nevertheless, while Gunkel did also believe in the importance of the Spirit-wrought new creation for Paul's ethics, for him this was not based on the idea of sacramental infusion with πνεῦμα-*Stoff* but on ecstatic experiences. Käsemann, however, was the first to provide an exegetical foundation for the logical chain of infusion with a physical Spirit, ontological renewal and ethical life in Paul.[36]

Nonetheless, for the sake of completeness it should be mentioned that Käsemann was aware of a tension in Paul between the concept elucidated above and what Käsemann calls the historical dialectic, the 'Geschichtlichkeit' of Paul's ethics. This second aspect is evident in the eschatological character of the Spirit. Käsemann expresses this tension in his interpretation of 1 Thessalonians 5:19 when he says that it is possible to *quench* the 'doch zugleich naturhaft vorgestellten Geist'.[37]

Finally, we need to return to Käsemann's 1947/48 article. For after describing the Hellenistic naturalism on which Paul falls back, Käsemann eventually says that Paul actually *distances himself* from a number of the features of this philosophy. The views summarized above are thus those of the *early* Käsemann. In his later work, *per contra*, Käsemann maintains that it was the *Corinthians* who adhered to a naturalistic view of the sacramental Spirit. Paul does speak of the Spirit and of pneumatological transformation of human beings in exactly the same terms as his Hellenistic environment and even gives πνεῦμα a corporeal substratum.[38] However,

---

[35] Ibid., 127.

[36] However, without an exegetical foundation this train of thought had been presented to scholarship three decades before Käsemann by W. Heitmüller. Without giving textual evidence Heitmüller claims that 'we can see especially from the way in which... Paul pictures the effects of the Spirit, that the Spirit is naturally a physical entity, that he cannot imagine the Spirit without an immaterial-material basis' (W. Heitmüller, *Taufe und Abendmahl bei Paulus: Darstellung und religionsgeschichtliche Beleuchtung* (Göttingen: Vandenhoeck & Ruprecht, 1903), 19). Heitmüller believes that one can see this concept of the Spirit in the background of 1 Cor. 7:14, where sanctification (which is worked by the Spirit) is physically/sexually transferred. Likewise, Heitmüller thinks that 'physisch-hyperphysische... auch die Naturgrundlage umfassende' transformation and recreation of the entire being by the Spirit leads to transformation into a higher (divine) existence (δόξα, 2 Cor. 3:18) (Heitmüller, *Paulus*, 20–21; cf. W. Heitmüller, *Taufe und Abendmahl im Urchristentum* (Tübingen: J.C.B. Mohr (Paul Siebeck), 1911), 25–26). On Käsemann's dependence on Heitmüller, see Way, *Lordship*, 68.

[37] Käsemann, *Leib*, 128.

[38] Käsemann, 'Doctrine', 117.

this emphasis disappears behind another, a more dominant one. Referring to his exegesis of 1 Corinthians 10 (see above), Käsemann now maintains that for Paul the sacramental Spirit is not some substance which enters a person in an impersonal manner. Rather, this gift brings with it its Giver. It is the epiphany of the exalted Lord who comes with it.

> [W]herever he [Paul] describes the *Pneuma* as a sacramental gift, there he is speaking most radically of the revelation of Christ himself, his self-manifestation and his presence... Therefore the Lord's Supper dispenses πνευματικὸν βρῶμα and πόμα... Therefore the sacrament effects the transformation of man.[39]

This change of emphasis with regard to the Spirit in Käsemann's thought is of interest for the present study because the weight that the later Käsemann gives to the relational work of the Spirit supports the new approach to the ethical work of the Spirit that will be put forward in the second part of this book. It is particularly fascinating to see how Käsemann's change of emphasis in his concept of the Spirit in Paul influences his view of Paul's ethics. In his earlier work, Käsemann spoke of the Spirit as 'die dem Menschen in der Taufe neu zugeeignete Substanz, die "Christusnatur", in der die menschliche Individualität ausgerottet, die Vielzahl der Subjekte zu "einem" wird, zum Christus und seinem Leibe.'[40] This *Pneuma*- or Christ-Body is comprehended as a more or less impersonal sphere of domination.[41] The ethics that follows from this substantial view of the Spirit is one of compulsion.[42] In his later work, by contrast, Käsemann stresses the personal nature of the Spirit's work. The Spirit reveals Christ's presence and lordship and, as one's existence is determined by whoever is one's Lord at a given time, in this way mediates a new existence.[43] This (Spirit of the) Lord 'does not reign as Necessity, but, according to II Cor. 3.18 [*sic*], dispenses freedom: the freedom to decide between obedience and disobedience.'[44]

The fact that Käsemann's concept of the Spirit has so clearly determined his comprehension of the Spirit's ethical work shows the need for a critical study of the alleged physical nature of the Spirit. Käsemann did not with-

---

[39] Ibid., 118; cf. 125.

[40] Käsemann, *Leib*, 162.

[41] Ibid., 175, 168, 165, 176, 184–85.

[42] Ibid., 127; cf. Käsemann, 'Abendmahl', 77–78.

[43] Käsemann, 'Doctrine', 118; cf. 124 where Käsemann appears to recognise his change of emphasis himself. That a person is relationally determined by who is her Lord was already put forward in Käsemann, *Leib*, 112–13 (cf. the analysis of P.F.M. Zahl, *Die Rechtfertigungslehre Ernst Käsemanns*; CThM 13 (Stuttgart: Calwer Verlag, 1996), 7–9). However, the theme of lordship was not prominent in Käsemann's early work (so Way, *Lordship*, 56).

[44] Käsemann, 'Doctrine', 119.

draw his *stofflich* view of the Spirit even in his later work, and his (early) pneumatology has had considerable influence upon scholarship after him.

2.2.2. Peter Stuhlmacher

Käsemann's immediate influence on the scholars after him is particularly obvious in the work of Stuhlmacher. Stuhlmacher's concepts of the Spirit and of baptism clearly bear the mark of the early views of his teacher.[45] Nevertheless, Stuhlmacher is also critical of his instructors. He disagrees with Bultmann's criticism of Paul's ancient (substance-ontological) concept of being (*Seinsbegriff*) and his eschatology. Bultmann has set up a false antithesis (which was also followed by the late Käsemann) when he constitutes the new creation as a 'historical' (*geschichtlich*) and not an 'ontic' (*naturhaft*) entity. For Stuhlmacher, *per contra*, the *nota creaturae* is both.[46] With this innovative combination Stuhlmacher's work has led biblical research out of the cul-de-sac of previous scholarship, as Hafemann appreciates.[47]

A major reason for Stuhlmacher to argue for the ontic character of the καινὴ κτίσις is Paul's supposed concept of the nature and work of the Spirit. In a tradition-historical analysis Stuhlmacher identifies Paul's concept of the Spirit as being derived from both Hellenism and apocalyptic Judaism.[48] Like a Hellenist, Paul thinks of the Spirit as a mighty substance

---

[45] However, Stuhlmacher's pneumatology has perhaps to some extent developed over the years in a way slightly similar to that of Käsemann. In his early works Stuhlmacher emphasizes on the one hand – like the early Käsemann – that Paul understands the Spirit as *Stoff* and the Spirit's renewing work as a substance-ontological change (e.g. P. Stuhlmacher, 'Erwägungen zum ontologischen Charakter der καινὴ κτίσις bei Paulus', *EvT* 27 (1967), 24–25), and, on the other hand – like the late Käsemann – that the Spirit is the *praesentia Christi* which inaugurates believers into a doxological relationship to God (e.g. P. Stuhlmacher, *Gerechtigkeit Gottes bei Paulus*; FRLANT 87 (Göttingen: Vandenhoeck & Ruprecht, 1966[2]), 224–25; Stuhlmacher, 'Erwägungen', 31). However, in his more recent work Stuhlmacher no longer mentions the supposedly substantial nature of the Spirit. Instead, he refers to the Spirit exclusively as the presence of Christ and states explicitly that there is no material transferral of the Spirit in the sacraments (P. Stuhlmacher, *Biblische Theologie des Neuen Testaments. Vol. 1: Grundlegung. Von Jesus zu Paulus* (Göttingen: Vandenhoeck & Ruprecht, 2005[3] [1992[1]]), 355, 370). Nevertheless, in contrast to Käsemann's development, Stuhlmacher does not contradict his earlier writings.

[46] Stuhlmacher, 'Erwägungen', 23–25. Cf. Stuhlmacher, *Gerechtigkeit*, 222. Stuhlmacher, *Theologie. I*, 334: new creation is both forensic and effective justification.

[47] Hafemann, 'Paul', 676–77.

[48] Stuhlmacher, *Gerechtigkeit*, 230; Stuhlmacher, 'Erwägungen', 20. Stuhlmacher thus combines the emphases of the early and late Käsemann. However, in the context of his more recent 'biblical-theology' approach to the NT, Stuhlmacher no longer mentions the influence of Hellenistic religiosity upon Paul's theology.

which eliminates ἀδικία within a person in a powerful act of ontic change (so, e.g., *Corp. Herm.* 13.9).[49] Like a Second Temple Jew, Paul thinks of the Spirit as a 'seinshafte, seinsstürzende und zugleich auf den Weg der Erneuerung... stellende Segensmacht'.[50] That Jews could view the Spirit in such terms is clear, for instance, from *Joseph and Aseneth* where the ethical Spirit (19.11), which is transferred through heavenly food and Joseph's kiss, bestows celestial beauty upon Aseneth (18.9–11). According to Stuhlmacher, beauty is here an expression of the 'spiritual-ontic new creation' (*geistlich-ontische Neuerschaffung*).[51] Likewise, at Qumran, conversion to the community is an act of new creation (*Neuschöpfung*) by the Holy Spirit (1QH[a] 11.19–22; 19.10–14). The convert is made to share in the purifying and forgiving gift of the Holy Spirit (cf. 1QH[a] 15.6–7), a Spirit that bears the characteristics of a substance.[52]

Stuhlmacher believes that these concepts of the Spirit and of Spirit-wrought transformation are evidently present in Paul, particularly in his theology of baptism. Following the majority of German commentators, Stuhlmacher assumes that 'the ἐν Χριστῷ of 2 Cor. 5:17 is realized through baptism. Since baptism imparts the Spirit according to the early Christian and Pauline view (cf. Rom. 6:3 with 1 Cor. 12:13 and Rom. 8:10–11), καινὴ κτίσις in 2 Cor. 5:17 has to mean the incorporation into the sphere of the Spirit.'[53] That baptism is thus more than just an ethical change is due, in particular, to the very nature of the Spirit, a Spirit that is 'neuschaffende Kraft' and a mighty substance.[54] According to Stuhlmacher this is also clear from the fact that Paul draws in Romans 8:29–30 on a 'für

---

[49] Stuhlmacher, *Gerechtigkeit*, 218; cf. 221, 230. Stuhlmacher defines ontic transformation as 'Wiedereinsetzung in den schöpfungsmäßigen Urstand der Gottebenbildlichkeit' (Stuhlmacher, 'Erwägungen', 2).

[50] Stuhlmacher, 'Erwägungen', 19.

[51] Ibid., 18–19; 29–30.

[52] Ibid., 13, drawing on O. Betz, *Offenbarung und Schriftforschung in der Qumransekte*; WUNT 6 (Tübingen: J.C.B. Mohr (Paul Siebeck), 1960), 119–35; O. Betz, 'Geistliche Schönheit', in O. Michel and U. Mann (eds.), *Die Leibhaftigkeit des Wortes*; FS A. Köberle (Hamburg: Furche, 1958), 75; O. Betz, 'Die Geburt der Gemeinde durch den Lehrer', *NTS* 3 (1956/57), 325.

[53] Stuhlmacher, 'Erwägungen', 28. Cf. Stuhlmacher, *Gerechtigkeit*, 222, 230, 233. However, in Stuhlmacher, *Theologie. I*, 353, he admits at least once that baptismal Spirit-transferral cannot be played off against the giving of the Spirit ἀκοὴ πίστεως (Gal. 3:2). Cf. P. Stuhlmacher, *Der Brief an die Römer*; NTD 6 (Göttingen: Vandenhoeck & Ruprecht, 1998[2]), 112. Nevertheless, in most of his other references to the reception of the Spirit Stuhlmacher presupposes that it takes place at baptism (e.g. Stuhlmacher, *Gerechtigkeit*, 217–18, 350).

[54] Stuhlmacher, *Gerechtigkeit*, 221–22. Cf. Stuhlmacher, 'Erwägungen', 24–25, 27, 33.

unsere Begriffe wohl massiv-naturalistische Taufanschauung'.[55] Baptism is here understood as a substance-ontological change (*seinswandelnd*) as is principally indicated by the verb δοξάξειν.[56]

However, Stuhlmacher does not proclaim the Spirit-wrought new creation as *ex opere operato*. For Paul, the transforming gift of the Spirit needs to be answered by thanksgiving. The new being drives towards doxology (e.g., in Rom. 8:15–16), and it is only there that the new being comes to its full fruition.[57] While this latter emphasis finds echoes in the second half of our study where we will expound our relational approach to Spirit and ethics in Paul, Stuhlmacher's main thesis will need to undergo closer examination in the first part of the monograph. There it will be asked whether ethical renewal by the Spirit is indeed understood by Paul as a substance-ontological transformation.

2.2.3. Friedrich Wilhelm Horn

The reasoning that led the early Käsemann and Stuhlmacher to believe in a substance-ontological transformation by the Spirit still prevails in modern scholarship, as Horn's *Das Angeld des Geistes* clearly demonstrates.[58] Horn endorses the thesis that both Judaism (e.g. 1QH^a 4.26; 15.6–7; 20.11–13; 1QS 3.3–9; *Jos. Asen.* 8.5, 9; 15.5; 16.16; 19.5; 21.13–14) and Hellenism (e.g. Chrysipp., *Frag.* 1027; Seneca, *Ep.* 66.12) thought of the Spirit as a material substance. He freely presupposes that what he believes to be true for the history of religions also applies to Hellenistic Christianity, namely that the Spirit is thought to utilise assistant materials ('Hilfsstoffe') like water or food for the Spirit-transferral. Paul picked up from the Corinthians this sacramental theology and the resultant concept of the Spirit as a material substance.[59]

Horn provides further details of Paul's view of πνεῦμα and its substantially transforming effects. He argues that at the outset of the development of his pneumatology Paul starts with a functional view of the Spirit (as evident from 1 Thess.). Towards the end of his career (particularly in Rom. 8) Paul begins to think of the Spirit as a hypostasis. However, in the middle phase of Paul's development, from 1 Corinthians onwards, a different concept of the Spirit strikes the reader: Paul adopts the Corinthians' idea of

---

[55] Stuhlmacher, 'Erwägungen', 28.

[56] Ibid., 28.

[57] Ibid., 31: Stuhlmacher speaks of an 'in die Doxologie ausströmenden Seinsbewegung', and 'von einem kreatürlichen Sein..., daß erst in der Doxologie gegenüber dem creator zu seiner bergenden Eigentlichkeit kommt.' Cf. Stuhlmacher, *Gerechtigkeit*, 258.

[58] On Horn, see further Appendix 3.1. and V. Rabens, 'The Development of Pauline Pneumatology: A Response to F.W. Horn', *BZ* 43 (1999), 161–79.

[59] Horn, *Angeld*, 43–48, 57–59, 430.

the Spirit as a material substance. Horn explains that the Spirit is under-stood as a *substance* 'when the Spirit takes up residence within the be-liever as "forma substantialis" (1 Cor. 3:16; 6:19; Rom. 8:9; 1 Thess. 4:8)'.[60] Furthermore, one can speak of a *material* ('stofflich') concept of the Spirit when the Spirit, through this 'qualification as substance ["sub-stanzhafte Bestimmung"], enters into such close junction with matter that the Spirit becomes bound to it', as in the sacraments (1 Cor. 10:4; 12:13; etc.), amalgamation with fire (Acts 2:3) and light (1 Cor. 15:43; 2 Cor. 3:8) or in connection with water (Rom. 5:5; 2 Cor. 1:21–22).[61]

Horn points out that Paul does not drop his functional view of the Spirit during his middle phase, nor does he cease to think of the Spirit as a sub-stance when the hypostatical concept comes into view. Horn is also careful to emphasize that Paul is critical of the magical impact that the Corinthians attributed to the *stofflich* gift. For example, Paul is positive that the Spirit provides a material basis for the resurrection body (1 Cor. 15:46) because it is transferred sacramentally (2 Cor. 1:22; 5:5). Nevertheless, according to Horn, Paul makes clear that

as one is concerned here with a down payment, the new nature is not yet perfect in a magical sense; on the other hand, the down payment motif is only then meaningful (from the point of its own *Begriffsgeschichte*), when, together with the juridical, a material aspect is also ascribed to it.[62]

With regard to his apocalyptic-eschatological conception of history, Paul thus aligns himself with the Jewish tradition. However, with regard to the sacramental transferral of the material, ontically renewing Spirit, Paul is part of his Hellenistic context.[63]

How does Paul understand this ontically renewing work of the Spirit in detail? Horn elucidates the fact that when Paul says that 'we were all made to drink of one Spirit' (1 Cor. 12:13), he tries to suggest that the Spirit has become 'the substance of the new being'. This means that 'Paul... presup-poses that the church is familiar with the fact that the Spirit is comparable to a substance or fluid which has been incorporated sacramentally into the believer; it has thus become the new substance of his existence.'[64] Horn

---

[60] Ibid., 60.

[61] Ibid., 60; 405, 429–30.

[62] Ibid., 393–94.

[63] Ibid., 400. On Paul's eschatological reservation, see further, Horn, *Angeld*, 423, 427; F.W. Horn, 'Holy Spirit', *ABD*, III, 273. On the impartation of the Spirit through the sacraments, see further, Horn, *Angeld*, 142–46, 151, 298, 399–400, 429–30; 169: 'Es kann schwerlich bestritten werden, daß Pl hierbei [i.e. when he refers to the Lord's Supper as πνευματικὸν βρῶμα (1 Cor. 10:3)] ein realistisches Sakramentsverständnis bekundet, daß also der Geist substanzhaft mit der Speise übereignet wird.'

[64] Horn, *Angeld*, 175; cf. 400.

explains further that 'with the sacramental transferral of the Spirit *an ontic basis of the new being is given, from which conduct in harmony with the Spirit is to be expected.*'[65] While Horn points out that the church's orientation towards the Spirit will follow from the Spirit's own instruction to believers,[66] he nevertheless puts special emphasis on the fact that through the Spirit holiness is *effectively* passed on ('effektiv übereignet') to the believer.[67] 'The holiness of the church is settled by the gift of the spirit (1 Thess. 4:8; 1 Cor. 3:16; 6:19) because it is sacramentally transferred (1 Cor. 6:11).'[68] It is Paul's expectation and demand that the church will now also live in accordance with the sanctified, Spirit-created new nature.[69]

2.3. Conclusion

At the heart of the view of ethical living set out above is a concept that is well summarized in the words of E. Brandenburger: 'What is proposed... is the idea of the original rootedness of righteous or... sinful behaviour before God in a substance which exercises power. A change of behaviour in the broadest sense (thinking, wanting, acting) is based on an exchange of the underlying being ["zugrundeliegenden Wesens"].'[70] We have seen

---

[65] Ibid., 388, italics added. Horn has reiterated this point in F.W. Horn, 'Zwischen Redaktionsgeschichte und urchristlicher Religionsgeschichte', in E.-M. Becker (ed.), *Neutestamentliche Wissenschaft: Autobiographische Essays aus der Evangelischen Theologie*; UTB 2475 (Tübingen/Basel: Francke, 2003), 210: 'Da Paulus aber im Geist Gottes nicht allein eine Kraft versteht, die in die Lebenswirklichkeit eingreift und zugleich Glaubende zu besonderen Taten befähigt, sondern vielmehr eine Substanz, die – metaphorisch gesprochen – in den Christen wohnt, weisen die Geistaussagen auf eine substanzhaft gedachte Grundlage christlicher Existenz hin.' We will argue in chs. 2–3 that the concept of metaphors evidenced in this statement is problematic.

[66] Horn, *Angeld*, 386–88.

[67] Ibid., 124. Horn admits that the striking use of the present tense (διδόντα) in 1 Thess. 4:8 is in tension with a 'one-off sacramentally mediated ontic interpretation of the transferral of the Spirit' (which is part and parcel of Paul's pneumatology in 1 Cor.). 'Vollzieht diese [i.e. the Spirit-transferral] sich seit der Berufung ständig wiederholend in der Zeit im Zusammenhang zunehmender Heiligung (3,12f.; 5,23), so ist wohl die neue Natur der Gläubigen in einem ontischen Sinn mit dieser Gabe im Blick, aber eben nicht als einmalige Heiligung im Taufakt (so 1.Kor 6,11; 1,30).' Horn's interpretation of 1 Thess. 4:8 thus seems to endorse Ernesti's idea of the bestowal of an 'ontic and growing ἁγιωσύνη' (H.F.T.L. Ernesti, *Die Ethik des Apostels Paulus in ihren Grundzügen dargestellt* (Braunschweig: Leibrod, 1880[3] [1868[1]]), 41–42; cf. Appendix 1.1.). Nevertheless, Horn qualifies his rendering of this verse by highlighting the possibility that Paul used the present tense purely in order to convey that the OT promise which is here in the background (Ezek. 36:27: future tense) has been fulfilled (Horn, *Angeld*, 126–27).

[68] Horn, *Angeld*, 387.

[69] Ibid., 387, 298.

[70] E. Brandenburger, *Fleisch und Geist: Paulus und die dualistische Weisheit*; WMANT 29 (Neukirchen-Vluyn: Neukirchener Verlag, 1968), 227.

that the three scholars described above have derived this view of the 'mechanics' of ethical living from their concept of the Spirit. Because πνεῦμα is a mighty (physical) substance, it transforms substance-ontologically.[71]

In order to evaluate this position, it will be necessary, first of all, to scrutinize one of its main components, namely, the concept of the Spirit as a physical substance. In this context it will also be necessary to look at the language of how the Spirit enters the believer. Are formulations like 'the Spirit has been poured out on us' metaphorical, and if so, what does that imply for our interpretation of such phrases?

Another aspect of this question regards Paul's religious and philosophical background. Is Paul's pneumatology predominantly influenced by Hellenism (so Pfleiderer, the early Käsemann, Horn et al.)? Or was his thinking on Spirit and ethics mainly based on the Old Testament (so Wendt et al.) or early Judaism (so Gunkel et al.)[72] – or on both or all three? Against the background of the history of research it seems that the answer that is given to this question partly determines how one comprehends Paul's concepts of the Spirit and of ethical transformation. Therefore, it needs to be asked whether the concept of substance-ontological transformation based on a physical Spirit was current in Paul's Jewish and Hellenistic context.

Finally, the inhomogeneous usage of 'substance' and 'ontology' language has led to equivocation among biblical scholars.[73] For this reason we will suggest using the term 'infusion-transformation' in order to describe the approach outlined above. It will be defined in more detail in the next section.

3. Definition of Terms

A number of concepts that will be used in this study need to be defined in order to avoid misinterpretation. Further terms will be defined in 4.1.

---

[71] Cf., most recently, Engberg-Pedersen, 'Understanding', 121–22: 'I propose that we read all of Paul's references to the *pneuma*... as drawing on the distinctly cosmological idea of a concrete, physicalistic power from heaven that... is infused into believers at baptism, informs their bodies and directs their lives here on earth... Here too belongs the connection with the ethical dimension of possessing the *pneuma*. And here too belongs the question of the precise function of Pauline paraenesis when he also had the two ideas of a physical takeover of believers by the *pneuma* and of the concomitant state of sinlessness into which they had thereby been transported. The real insight in all this is that there is no inconsistency. Rather, these ideas all fit intimately together.'

[72] Cf. Appendix 1.2.–1.3., and ch. 2, esp. 2.2.1.

[73] See, e.g., the discussion in J. Ashton, *The Religion of Paul the Apostle* (London: Yale University Press, 2000), 146 n.9.

Ethics/Religious-Ethical: According to Schrage, the subject matter of New Testament ethics 'is the question of what was the enabling and grounds, criteria and content of the early Christian way of acting and living.'[74] Within this broad area the present study focuses on the *enabling* of the early Christian way of acting and living as presented in the letters of Paul. This aspect of Paul's ethics (which as such is not a systematic ethic)[75] will be described in the context of the pneumatology of Paul and his context. In the light of the above definition of Schrage it is presupposed that Paul's ethical concerns cannot be separated from his basic theological convictions (*contra* Rosner, who defines Paul's ethics as being about Christian conduct, rather than Christian belief[76]).[77] As a group's religious life and ethical conduct are interrelated,[78] we use the slightly broader term 'religious-ethical'[79] more or less synonymously with 'ethical'. Both terms

---

[74] W. Schrage, *Ethik des Neuen Testaments*; NTD 4 (Göttingen: Vandenhoeck & Ruprecht, 1989[2]), 9. Cf. S. Schulz, *Neutestamentliche Ethik* (Zürich: Theologischer Verlag, 1987), 5; G. Theissen, *A Theory of Primitive Christian Religion* (London: SCM, 1999), 337, 63, 78–79 (endorsed by J.G. Lewis, *Looking for Life: The Role of "Theo-Ethical Reasoning" in Paul's Religion*; JSNTSup 291 (London: T. & T. Clark, 2005), 19); D.G. Horrell, *Solidarity and Difference: A Contemporary Reading of Paul's Ethics* (London: T. & T. Clark, 2005), 95–97 (helpfully discussing W.A. Meeks, *The Origins of Christian Morality: The First Two Centuries* (New Haven: Yale University Press, 1993), 3–5, and P.F. Esler, 'Social Identity, the Virtues, and the Good Life: A New Approach to Romans 12:1–15:13', *BTB* 33 (2003), 51–63). Recently also Blischke has endorsed such a broad definition of Pauline ethics as 'Lebensführung' (Blischke, *Begründung*, 13).

[75] See, e.g., Furnish, *Theology*, 208–12. Zimmerman suggests for this reason that it is better to speak of Paul's 'implicit ethics' (R. Zimmermann, 'Jenseits von Indikativ und Imperativ: Zur "impliziten Ethik" des Paulus am Beispiel des 1. Korinterbriefs', *TLZ* (2007), 272–74).

[76] B.S. Rosner, '"That Pattern of Teaching": Issues and Essays in Pauline Ethics', in B.S. Rosner, *Understanding Paul's Ethics: Twentieth-Century Approaches* (Grand Rapids: Eerdmans, 1995), 4.

[77] Cf. the discussion in Furnish, *Theology*, 211–12; Lewis, *Life*, 18–20; L.T. Johnson, *Among the Gentiles: Greco-Roman Religion and Christianity*; AYBRL: Yale University Press, 2009), 160–61. Moreover, ethics as a concept was not part of Paul's terminological world, so that one should try to avoid absolutizing concepts like these as if there were, for instance, an independent field of discourse in Paul that one might identify as constituting his ethics (cf. Engberg-Pedersen, 'Spirit', 184 n.26).

[78] On this see further M. Wenk, *Community-Forming Power: The Socio-Ethical Role of the Spirit in Luke-Acts*; JPTSS 19 (Sheffield: Sheffield Academic Press, 2000), 51–52; T. Engberg-Pedersen, 'The Logic of Action in Paul: How Does He Differ from the Moral Philosophers on Spiritual and Moral Progression and Regression?', in J.T. Fitzgerald (ed.), *Passions and Moral Progress in Greco-Roman Thought*; RMCS (London: Routledge, 2008), 242.

[79] On the usage of the term, cf. G. Schneider, *Neuschöpfung oder Wiederkehr? Eine Untersuchung zum Geschichtsbild der Bibel* (Düsseldorf: Patmos, 1961), 30. See already

refer to the *quality of personal and communal life before God* (and hence also include ministry and witness to the world[80]).

Empowering: see 4.1.

Transformation: see 4.1.

Relationship: see 4.1.

Spirit as Substance/Matter: In order to define what is meant by the notion of the Spirit being a 'substance', one ought to go back to the scholars who introduced this terminology to Pauline studies. Although they rarely give evidence of their precise understanding of 'substance', it seems that the majority of these writers think of some kind of 'matter' when they use this terminology for the Spirit.[81] For example, shortly after saying that Paul thought of the Spirit as a substance, Heitmüller continues that 'dasselbe von Haus aus eine physische Größe ist'.[82] This judgement is confirmed by the dictionary that might reflect most accurately the concept of 'substance' that was held by the writers of the *religionsgeschichtliche Schule* (who were the ones to make this view a major position in Pauline scholarship), namely, the second edition of *Die Religion in Geschichte und Gegenwart*.[83] This dictionary was even edited by one who himself proposed such a view of the Spirit, namely by Gunkel. Here Steinmann writes that in common usage 'substance' is synonymous with 'Stoff oder Masse' ('matter or mass').[84]

However, this definition of 'substance' could be criticized for being too narrow.[85] And, in fact, Steinmann further explains that in a second, phil-

---

J. Gloël, *Der heilige Geist in der Heilsverkündigung des Paulus: Eine biblisch-theologische Untersuchung* (Halle: Numeyer, 1888), 241.

[80] On this connection, cf. 1 Thess. 2:9–12; 1 Cor. 9:27; et al.; cf. M. Barram, *Mission and Moral Reflection in Paul*; SBL 75 (New York: Lang, 2006), *passim*.

[81] *Pace* Stalder, *Heiligung*, 66.

[82] Heitmüller, *Paulus*, 19. However, see also his more ambivalent definition of πνεῦμα as a 'heavenly, divine substance' (W. Heitmüller, *"Im Namen Jesu": eine sprach- u. religionsgeschichtliche Untersuchung zum Neuen Testament, speziell zur altchristlichen Taufe*; FRLANT 1/2 (Göttingen: Vandenhoeck & Ruprecht, 1903), 321). Nevertheless, not much later he writes that πνεῦμα 'nur denkbar [ist] als göttliche, physisch-hyperphysische Substanz, die natürlich am besten durch ein naturhaftes Medium vermittelt wird' (Heitmüller, *Namen*, 326).

[83] It is methodologically unsafe, *per contra*, to try to determine the concept of 'substance' that was held by this strand of scholarship by turning to modern dictionaries because views of the relation of spirit and matter have developed over time. See, e.g., J.H. Wright, SJ, 'Spirit and Matter: An Essay in Theology, Philosophy and the Natural Science', in M.J. Himes and S.J. Pope (eds.), *Finding God in all Things: Essays in Honor of Michael J. Buckley, S.J.* (New York: Crossroad, 1996), 127–39.

[84] T. Steinmann, 'Substanz', *RGG*[2], II, 869.

[85] See, e.g., K. Lehmkühler, *Kultus und Theologie: Dogmatik und Exegese in der religionsgeschichtlichen Schule*; FSÖT 76 (Göttingen: Vandenhoeck & Ruprecht, 1996), 245 n.74.

osophic usage, 'substance' is free from the notion of 'matter or mass'. Here 'substance' is something basic and independent in existence, standing amongst other realities, and a source of activity.[86] Among the Pauline pneumatologists, Horn needs to be commended for showing awareness of this distinctive usage of 'substance' in his enlisting of six different concepts of the Spirit in Paul. He explains that, for one thing, the Spirit is understood as a *substance* when the Spirit takes up residence within the believer as 'forma substantialis' (1 Cor. 3:16; 6:19; Rom. 8:9; 1 Thess. 4:8). However, he continues that a *material* ('stofflich') concept of the Spirit is presupposed where 'the Spirit, through the above mentioned qualification as substance ["substanzhafte Bestimmung"], enters into such close junction with matter that the Spirit becomes bound to it', as in the sacraments (1 Cor. 10:4; 12:13; etc.), amalgamation with light (1 Cor. 15:43; 2 Cor. 3:8) or connection with water (Rom. 5:5; 2 Cor. 1:21–22).[87]

However, even Horn is not completely consistent with his usage of the term 'substance' for the Spirit.[88] Because of the vagueness with which modern scholarship employs the term 'substance' in their discussions of Pauline pneumatology, and because of the variety of meanings that substance/οὐσία already had at the time of (late) antiquity (e.g. existence; nature; immaterial essence; matter or 'stuff'),[89] it is doubtful whether this term should any longer be used in the study of New Testament pneumatology for describing a particular concept of the Spirit. Therefore, the present study will employ the term 'immaterial substance' for that concept of the Spirit that Horn has named 'substance'/'forma substantialis' (it will be used only in ch. 3, Excursus 1, though). And the terms 'material substance', 'physical substance' or 'matter'[90] (together with the pronoun 'it' for the Spirit) will be used for what Horn has singled out as *Stoff*. This second, material concept of 'substance' is held by most scholars who propose that Paul thought of the Spirit as a substance. It will receive close attention in Part I of the monograph.

Infusion-transformation: This term describes the concept of transformation held by scholars who think that for Paul ethical life is enabled through

---

[86] Steinmann, 'Substanz', 869; cf. R.E. McCall, 'Substance', *NCE*, XIII, 766. However, it should be noted that not all philosophers define 'substance' as exclusively incorporeal (see, e.g., H.W. Arndt, 'Substanz; Substanz/Akzidens', *HWPh*, X, 526).

[87] Horn, *Angeld*, 60. Cf. the brief differentiation in T. Tielemann and J. Büchli, 'Pneuma', *DNP*, IX, 1182: 'Paulus… eliminiert das Naturhafte am griech. Begriff, behält aber das Substanzhafte bei'.

[88] See the parallelism of substance and *Stoff* in his introductory questions in Horn, *Angeld*, 49; cf. Rabens, 'Development', 176.

[89] See C. Stead, *Divine Substance* (Oxford: Clarendon, 1977), 131–56, for a full discussion.

[90] On the potential distinction between 'light' and 'heavy' matter, see 2.1.1.

the transformation of the inner nature of a person by the infusion with a material πνεῦμα.[91] German scholars have often used the adjective 'natur-haft' (sometimes rendered as 'quasi-physical' in the English translations)[92] for this kind of transformation, but it is usually not explained how this notion should be understood.[93] As this approach focuses on the 'interior' or 'substance' of a person (to the depreciation of the person's relationships), it seems justified to classify this approach as *substance-ontological*. How-ever, this designation will be used only rarely in this study, because it would introduce a rather complex philosophical issue into our discussion,[94] and by employing it critically we could give the impression that in our own approach (in Part II) we would want to say that a person 'has' no 'sub-stance' (but only relations).[95] Moreover, we try to avoid confusing the reader by refraining from employing the term 'substance' in this connec-tion as this word has already been used throughout the history of Pauline scholarship for the concept of the Spirit as matter.

We have thus designed the term 'infusion-transformation' for this par-ticular concept of Spirit-transformation. The word 'infusion' originally denotes the pouring in of a liquid. This has some parallels with the ideas of the *religionsgeschichtliche Schule* and its followers who suggest that Paul comprehends the Spirit as a 'fluidum' that is poured into the believer. However, when 'infusion' is used figuratively it refers to the 'action of infusing or introducing a modifying element or new characteristic',[96] as, for example, the infusion of grace into the soul in the Catholic concept *gratia infusa*. Also the concept of 'infusion-transformation' refers to a modifying element, namely, to the physical Spirit that is infused into a person's being and in this way transforms the person's soul. (It appears that the scholars of this approach presuppose that Paul believed the soul to be physical too, otherwise one wonders why such supreme power is ascribed by them specifically to the infusion with a *physical* Spirit). According to the infusion-transformation approach, it is from this new nature ('Natur-

---

[91] See, e.g., Heitmüller, *Namen*, 326, for a succinct formulation of this approach.

[92] Cf. my interaction with Ashton who prefers the translation 'real' (Ashton, *Religion*, 146 n.9).

[93] Stuhlmacher is a positive exception. He defines his notion of 'ontic transformation' as 'Wiedereinsetzung in den schöpfungsmäßigen Urstand der Gottebenbildlichkeit' (Stuhlmacher, 'Erwägungen', 2).

[94] On the complexity of the definition of 'substance' and 'substance(-ontological) transformation', particularly in relation to the sacraments, see N. Slenczka, *Realpräsenz und Ontologie: Untersuchung der ontologischen Grundlagen der Transsignifikationsleh-re*; FSÖT 66 (Göttingen: Vandenhoeck & Ruprecht, 1993), 141–57.

[95] On this see 4.4.1. Cf. now also K. Lehmkühler, *Inhabitatio: Die Einwohnung Gottes im Menschen*; FSÖT 104 (Göttingen: Vandenhoeck & Ruprecht, 2004), 36–37.

[96] *OED*[2], VII, 953.

grundlage')[97] that ethical life flows. See 4.1., especially Diagram 1, for further illustration.

4. The Thesis

In this study we look at the way in which, according to Paul, the Spirit transforms and empowers believers for religious-ethical living. Schweitzer had maintained that Paul remains silent about the psychological processes by which ethical change comes about.[98] Similarly, Fee argues that Paul does not unravel for the recipients of his letters how to walk by the Spirit because he presupposes that they already have a dynamic experience of life in the Spirit (Gal. 3:1–5; 5:25).[99] However, the intention of the present study is to reach a more profound understanding of the ways in which the Spirit enables ethical conduct. We are interested in the theological and 'practical' aspects of transformation and empowering by the Spirit for religious-ethical life in a broad sense (cf. our definitions above). That is, we do not focus on the more specific areas of spiritual guidance and discernment.[100] It is also not our aim to solve the larger controversies of Pauline theology such as: does Paul comprehend the καινὴ κτίσις as an 'ontological entity'?,[101] and: is justification-sanctification for Paul 'forensic-imputed' or 'effective-real'?[102] Nonetheless, the framework of our model of the Spirit's religious-ethical work has implications for these broader discussions. We will elucidate these implications particularly in section 4.4.

Our study will investigate the seven so-called 'undisputed Pauline epistles'. However, sometimes other epistles of the Pauline tradition too will be engaged with (e.g. Eph.), but no argument rests on their evidence alone. The reasoning behind this is that, as Dunn rightly maintains, the disputed Paulines 'should not be wholly disregarded when the attempt is made to

---

[97] Horn, *Angeld*, 388.

[98] A. Schweitzer, *The Mysticism of Paul the Apostle* (London: Black, 1953[2] [1931[1]]), 296–97.

[99] Fee, *Presence*, 433; cf. Appendix 3.2.

[100] On the latter, see esp. A. Munzinger, *Discerning the Spirits: Theological and Ethical Hermeneutics in Paul*; SNTSMS 140 (Cambridge: Cambridge University Press, 2007), *passim*.

[101] So most explicitly Stuhlmacher, 'Erwägungen', 1–35.

[102] For a brief summary of the debate, see U. Mell, *Neue Schöpfung: Eine traditionsgeschichtliche und exegetische Studie zu einem soteriologischen Grundsatz*; BZNW 56 (Berlin/New York: W. de Gruyter, 1989), 4–5.

describe the theology of the apostle whose name they bear'.[103] In the individual Pauline texts that we will study we want to bring to the surface the rationale and moral reasoning that undergirds Paul's Spirit-ethic, even when that rationale is at times not apparent on the surface of the text.[104]

The criteria for choosing the texts which will be investigated are determined by the bipartite structure of our study. In the first part of our study we will cross-examine the infusion-transformation approach to the ethical work of the Spirit. The first of the two chapters of Part I critically examines every passage from Hellenism, the Hebrew Bible and early Judaism that has been used by the proponents of the infusion-transformation approach in support of their theory (ch. 2). The second chapter applies the same scrutiny to the Pauline corpus (ch. 3).

In the second part of our study we will develop an alternative approach to the ethical work of the Spirit in Paul. Our model is relational in that it suggests that it is primarily through deeper knowledge of, and an intimate relationship with, God, Jesus Christ and with the community of faith that people are transformed and empowered by the Spirit for religious-ethical life. The framework of this novel approach is elucidated in chapter 4. Through an in-depth study of a number of writings of Paul's contemporaries, chapter 5 determines that Paul lived in a context in which this dynamic of ethical empowerment was part of the religious framework of various Jewish groups. In chapter 6 we demonstrate exegetically from the Pauline epistles that Paul's view of the Spirit's empowering for religious-ethical life is well comprehended by our relational model epitomized above. The book closes with chapter 7 which summarizes our findings and draws attention to their significance for other aspects of Pauline theology.

---

[103] J.D.G. Dunn, *The Theology of Paul the Apostle* (Edinburgh: T. & T. Clark, 1998), 13.

[104] We are here following the methodology of L.E. Keck, 'Rethinking "New Testament Ethics"', *JBL* 115 (1996), 7–8; cf. Lewis, *Life*, 32. Furthermore, methodological caution is necessary because Paul's letters were written over a span of up to twenty-three years, and his teaching on the Spirit is often incidental to his treatment of other questions (cf. M. Turner, *The Holy Spirit and Spiritual Gifts – Then and Now* (Carlisle: Paternoster, 1999²), 101). We will therefore not attempt to produce a developmental model of Paul's view of the ethically enabling work of the Spirit. Cf. Rabens, 'Development', 174–79.

Religious-Ethical Empowerment through Infusion-Transformation

An Examination of an Established Approach

In the introductory review of scholarship, the infusion-transformation approach[1] to the empowering work of the Spirit in Paul's ethics has attracted our attention. It entered modern studies of Paul through the publications of the *religionsgeschichtliche Schule*, who argued that Paul appears to understand the Spirit 'as a heavenly substance that transforms the human being substantially', and that such an ontic transformation of humanity produces ethical life as its result (Wrede).[2] Also more recent scholars adhere to this view of Pauline pneumatology and ethics, as the work of Horn demonstrates. According to Horn, Paul is suggesting with his statement that 'we were all made to drink of one Spirit' (1 Cor. 12:13), that the Spirit has become 'the substance of the new being'. This means that 'Paul... presupposes that the church is familiar with the fact that the Spirit is comparable to a substance or fluid which has been incorporated sacramentally into the believer; it has thus become the new substance of his existence'.[3] Holiness is effectively passed on through the Spirit to the believer,[4] and 'with the sacramental transferral of the Spirit an ontic basis of the new being is given, from which conduct in harmony with the Spirit is to be expected'.[5]

In Part I of our study the infusion-transformation approach to the ethical work of the Spirit will be carefully scrutinized. For the first time in Pauline research every significant textual datum from Paul's context (ch. 2) and from his own writings (ch. 3) that has been put forward in support of this view will be analysed critically.[6] It will be shown that both the assumed

---

[1] See 1.3. for a definition.

[2] Wrede, 'Paulus', 58–59, 61.

[3] Horn, *Angeld*, 175; 400.

[4] Ibid., 124; 387.

[5] Ibid., 388; 298.

[6] Some scholars have questioned the supposed physical nature of the Spirit before (see particularly Bertrams, *Wesen, passim*; P. Bläser, '"Lebendigmachender Geist": Ein Beitrag zur Frage nach den Quellen der paulinischen Theologie', *BEThL* 12/13 (1959), 404–

physical nature of the Spirit as well as the mode of (substance-ontological) transformation[7] of the believer that is derived from this particular concept of the Spirit rest predominantly on a misinterpretation of metaphoric and symbolic language. In this context it will be necessary to give some space to a methodological discussion of how metaphors can be identified and interpreted. We will do this by examining the prominent example of 1QH^a 15.6–7 in section 2.2.2.1. By utilizing the results of our discussions of figurative language for the remainder of chapters 2–3 we will offer fresh insights into the pneumatology of early Judaism and Paul.

---

13). However, it seems that the studies of these scholars have not convinced the proponents of a *stofflich* view of the Spirit as they were based on logical/philosophical reasoning and not on exegesis of the actual texts which are believed to portray a physical concept of the Spirit.

[7] See 1.3. for the definition of these terms. We do not intend to provide a discussion of the question whether Paul had the notion of substance-ontological transformation at all (on this see 4.4.1.). Rather, Part I will focus on the *infusion-transformation* theory which has the concept of infusion with a material Spirit as its basis.

Chapter 2

Infusion-Transformation through a Material Spirit? An Investigation of Paul's Context

Pauline scholarship has rightly tried to understand Paul from within his own context. While past research has at times overemphasized either Paul's Hellenistic or his Jewish background, modern studies come to see Paul more and more as 'a man of two worlds' who was influenced by both Hellenism and Judaism.[1] One reason for this welcome development is the fact that, since the impact of M. Hengel's magisterial work *Judaism and Hellenism*, it is generally accepted among scholars that from the middle of the third century BCE onwards Judaism came under the influence of Hellenism and thus became Hellenized to various degrees.[2] The present study is also conducted on the basis of this significant insight. Nevertheless, it is still helpful to distinguish between the (non-Jewish) world of Hellen*ism* and Hellen*ization* (of Judaism, etc.). Levine points out that 'Hellenism… refers to the cultural milieu (largely Greek) of the Hellenistic, Roman, and – to a somewhat more limited extent – Byzantine periods, while Hellenization describes the process of adoption and adaptation of this culture on a local level'.[3] It is to the former of these two that we will turn first in our examination of the claim that the concept of infusion-transformation was part of the ethics of Paul's context.

1. Graeco-Roman Literature

As we have seen in the history of research,[4] many New Testament scholars who argue that for Paul ethical life is enabled by an infusion-transformation claim that this is due to Paul's background in Hellenism.

---

[1] See particularly T. Engberg-Pedersen (ed.), *Paul Beyond the Judaism/Hellenism Divide* (Louisville: Westminster John Knox Press, 2001), *passim*.

[2] M. Hengel, *Judaism and Hellenism: Studies in their Encounter in Palestine during the Early Hellenistic Period* (London: SCM Press, 1974), *passim*.

[3] L.I. Levine, *Judaism and Hellenism in Antiquity: Conflict or Confluence?* (Seattle: UWP, 1998), 16–17. We thus use the term 'Hellenistic' more or less interchangeably with 'Graeco-Roman'. Accordingly, some of the texts that will be engaged with in the following section(s) do not officially belong to the 'Hellenistic period' (which ended 30 BCE).

[4] See 1.2.2. and the Appendix.

However, when it comes to supporting this claim, only a few of them explain what these Hellenistic sources were and how they actually came to influence Paul.[5] Nevertheless, it is undebated among classicists that a number of Hellenists understood πνεῦμα as a material substance, and we will look in the following at some important sources that give evidence of such a pneumatology.[6] After that we will ask the question how (and whether at all) this pneumatology was related to ethical transformation.

1.1. The Physical Spirit

Stoicism is the ancient philosophic school that is best known for its (materialistic) pneumatology. Its hylozoistic metaphysics is well reflected in statements like 'God is mixed with matter and pervades the whole of it'. It is obvious that such immanentism also concerns the πνεῦμα, when the description continues:

for if God is on their [i.e. the Stoics'] view body – an intelligent and eternal pneuma – and matter is body, first there will again be body going through body; then this pneuma will certainly be either one of the four uncompounded bodies which they say are also elements, or a compound of them (as, of course they themselves say; for they certainly

---

[5] E.g. Käsemann just declares that '*pneuma* is seen in Hellenistic thought as heavenly matter... which has the capacity of penetrating man's being and, in so doing, to endow with a new nature'. The only 'evidence' that he provides (without any reference) in support of this thesis is Hellenistic Gnosis (Käsemann, 'Doctrine', 115; cf. R. Bultmann, 'ζάω κτλ', *TDNT*, II, 867). However, as recent scholarship has dated Gnosticism later than was assumed at the time of Käsemann, Gnosticism will not be discussed in the present work. Cf., e.g., E.M. Yamauchi, 'Gnosis, Gnosticism', *DPL*, 352–53.

However, scholars who provide some evidence for a material concept of the spirit in Hellenism include Horn, *Angeld*, 55–57; D.B. Martin, *The Corinthian Body* (New Haven/London: Yale University Press, 1995), 21–25; T.W. Martin, 'Paul's Pneumatological Statements and Ancient Medical Texts', in J. Fotopoulos (ed.), *The New Testament and Early Christian Literature in Greco-Roman Context: Studies in Honor of David E. Aune*; SNT 122 (Leiden: Brill, 2006), *passim*; most recently also Engberg-Pedersen, *Cosmology*, esp. 19–22. It should be noted that these scholars frequently do not differentiate between occurrences of πνεῦμα that refer to either the divine or the atmospheric, cosmological or anthropological spirit. This may lead to inexactness in their results, as this distinction was of significance at least for some ancient writers of the Jewish-Christian tradition (see, e.g., Philo, *Gig.* 26–27; Rom. 8:16).

[6] For a broader overview on πνεῦμα in Graeco-Roman literature, see G. Verbeke, *L'Évolution de la Doctrine du Pneuma: du Stoïcisme à S. Augustin*; BISPUL (Paris: Desclée de Brouwer, 1945), *passim*; H. Kleinknecht, 'πνεῦμα, πνευματικός', *TDNT*, VI, 334–43, 354–57; W. Wili, 'Die Geschichte des Geistes in der Antike', *EvJ* 13 (1945), 49–93; T. Paige, 'Who Believes in "Spirit"? Πνεῦμα in Pagan Usage and Implications for the Gentile Christian Mission', *HTR* 95 (2002), 417–36; V. Rabens, 'Geistes-Geschichte: Die Rede vom Geist im Horizont der griechisch-römischen und jüdisch-hellenistischen Literatur', *ZNT* 25 (2010), 46–55.

suppose that pneuma has the substance of air and fire), or, if it is something else, the divine body will be a fifth substance (Alex. Aphr., *Mixt.* 225.1–10).

Therefore, πνεῦμα 'pervades all bodies by being mixed with all of them' (ibid., 224.14–16). Furthermore, Galen says that the Stoics have learnt from Hippocrates about 'the so-called material pneuma [πνεῦμα... ὑλικόν], which is analogous to dry and moist nutriment' (Galen, *Plac. Hipp. Plat.* 2.8.39).[7]

While it may be an overstatement to say that the pneumatology of the Stoics has influenced the majority of the succeeding philosophical schools,[8] one certainly finds a number of individual treatments of pneumatology that give evidence of Stoic influence. For example, in Plutarch's *De Defectu Oraculorum*, Lamprias shares the Stoic view of the spirit in his explanation of Delphic inspiration:

the μαντικὸν ῥεῦμα καὶ πνεῦμα is most divine and holy, whether it issue by itself through the air or come in the company of running waters; for when it is instilled into the body [or: mixed into (καταμειγνύμενον... εἰς τὸ σῶμα)], it creates in souls an unaccustomed and unusual temperament... [i.e.] it opens up certain passages through which impressions of the future are transmitted (432D–E).[9]

---

[7] Other passages that may show that the Stoics thought of the spirit as a substance include Chrysippus, *Frag.* 715; 1009; 1027; Galen, *Plac. Hipp. Plat.* 2.8.48; Sextus Empiricus, *Pyr.* 3.218; Plotinus, *Enn.* 4.7.4. On πνεῦμα in Stoicism see further S. Sambursky, *Physics of the Stoics* (London: Routledge, 1959), esp. 21–48; J.M. Rist, 'On Greek Biology, Greek Cosmology and Some Sources of Theological Pneuma', in J.M. Rist, *Man, Soul and Body: Essays in Ancient Thought from Plato to Dionysius*; CS 549 (Aldershot/Brookfield: Variorum, 1996), 27–47; M. Klinghardt, 'Unum Corpus: Die genera corporum in der stoischen Physik und ihre Rezeption bis zum Neuplatonismus', in A. von Dobbeler (ed.), *Religionsgeschichte des Neuen Testaments*; FS K. Berger (Tübingen: Francke, 2000), esp. 198–99; M.J. White, 'Stoic Natural Philosophy (Physics and Cosmology)', in B. Inwood (ed.), *The Cambridge Companion to the Stoics*; CCP (Cambridge: Cambridge University Press, 2003), 134–35; M.V. Lee, *Paul, the Stoics, and the Body of Christ*; SNTSMS 137 (Cambridge: Cambridge University Press, 2006), 49–54; J.R. Levison, *Filled with the Spirit* (Grant Rapids/Cambridge: Eerdmans, 2009), 137–42; Engberg-Pedersen, *Cosmology*, esp. 19–22. For the materialistic conception of power in Stoicism, see p. 38 below.

[8] See the discussion below.

[9] This text gives evidence of (physical) infusion. However, it does not parallel the concept of infusion-transformation that will be discussed below as there is no connection with ethics. On this prophetic inspiration, see further Verbeke, *Évolution*, 268–78; on further ancient explanations of the divination at Delphi: S. Price, 'Delphi and Divination', in P.E. Easterling and J. Muir (eds.), *Greek Religion and Society* (Cambridge: Cambridge University Press, 1985), 138–41; Paige, 'Usage', 428–29; C. Tibbs, *Religious Experience of the Pneuma: Communication with the Spirit World in 1 Corinthians 12 and 14*; WUNT II/230 (Tübingen: Mohr Siebeck, 2007), 115–19. On πνεῦμα in Plutarch: F. Büchsel, *Der Geist Gottes im Neuen Testament* (Gütersloh: Bertelsmann, 1926), 49–53.

Likewise, Stoic thinking is also evident in the much later Pseudo-Aristotle when he delineates that πνεῦμα 'means that which is in plants and animals and pervading every substance that brings life and generation' (*Mund.* 4.394ᵇ). Finally, in some writings of the *Corpus Hermeticum* a Stoic pneumatology possibly shines through.[10] For instance, in *Hermetic Excerpt* 23.14–15 God is said to have taken 'of his own πνεῦμα as much as would suffice, and blended it with intelligent fire, and mingled the blend with certain other materials [ὕλαις] unknown to men' in order to create 'soul-stuff'.[11]

It is generally undisputed that the *Stoic* system could be described as 'materialistic monism'.[12] However, Martin goes much further by saying that within *Hellenism in general* there was no distinction at all between the material and the immaterial. According to Martin, all ancients were monistic,[13] and the kind of dualism of which many think as Platonic was really developed only by Descartes. Moreover, Martin claims that Platonism had lost its influence from the first century BCE onwards, where after Stoicism became the dominant philosophy.[14]

However, for one thing, the fact that the Platonic Academy as such no longer existed after 88 BCE does not necessarily imply that Platonism had entirely lost its influence on the philosophy at the turn of the ages. Slezák has even stated recently that '[n]ach der vorübergehenden Abkehr der Akademie von P[laton] in der skeptischen Phase... erhob sich P[laton]s

---

[10] *Corp. Herm.* 3.1b, 2b; 10.13, 17 *perhaps* evidence such a notion. However, to interpret the power(s) mentioned in 13.9 to be a substance and to say that *this substance is the Spirit*, as Stuhlmacher does (Stuhlmacher, *Gerechtigkeit*, 218), seems a bit too far-fetched.

[11] On the somatic nature of the (anthropological) spirit in *Corpus Hermeticum*, see further C.H. Dodd, *The Interpretation of the Fourth Gospel* (Cambridge: Cambridge University Press, 1953), 216–19; W. Bousset, 'J. Kroll, Die Lehren des Hermes Trismegistos', in W. Bousset, *Religionsgeschichtliche Studien: Aufsätze zur Religionsgeschichte des Hellenistischen Zeitalters*; SNT 50 (Leiden: Brill, 1979), 172–80.

[12] See B. Inwood, 'Stoizismus', *DNP*, XI, 1015. However, see also A.A. Long, *Hellenistic Philosophy: Stoics, Epicureans, Sceptics* (London: Duckworth, 1974), 154.

[13] However, see Martin, *Body*, 272 n.10 (cf. p. 115), where he says that *dualism* 'was simply "in the air" in first-century popular philosophy'.

[14] Ibid., 12, 15. Martin partly builds these assertions on Dillon, who writes that 'the disappearance from the philosophic scene, after 88 B.C., of the Platonic Academy as an institution is now, I think, following the researches of John Lynch and John Glucker, an accepted fact' (J.M. Dillon, '"Orthodoxy" and "Eclecticism": Middle Platonists and Neo-Pythagoreans', in J.M. Dillon and A.A. Long (eds.), *The Question of "Eclecticism": Studies in Later Greek Philosophy*; HCS (London: UCP, 1988), 103, referring to J.P. Lynch, *Aristotle's School: A Study of a Greek Educational Institution* (London: UCP, 1972), 177–89, and J. Glucker, *Antiochus and the Late Academy*; H.UAN 56 (Göttingen: Vandenhoeck & Ruprecht, 1978).

Œuvre ab dem 1.Jh.v.Chr. zur dominierenden (Mittelplatonismus), und schließlich zur allein bestimmenden Kraft (Neuplatonismus)'.[15]

More important, however, is the question whether modern scholarship is indeed guilty of projecting Cartesian dualism onto the ancient mind of monism. To answer this question properly would mean to engage in an extensive study;[16] however, it will suffice for our purposes to offer a few suggestions that throw critical light on Martin's sweeping statement.

Martin builds his thesis that Plato was no immaterial/material dualist mainly on what Plato says in the *Timaeus*, 39E–40A. According to Martin, Plato teaches here that 'the divinities are material (in our sense of the word) in so far as they are made of fire and are spherical'.[17] Martin's argument presupposes that Plato understood both fire and what is spherical as material. Unfortunately, however, Martin never provides evidence for this supposition. As it is debatable how Plato and other Hellenists comprehended the nature of these elements,[18] it would be better not to rest an argument for the materiality of the divine on such evidence. What is more, both ancient (see, e.g., Plutarch, *Mor.* 882D) and modern scholars assert that Plato did have a notion of the immaterial and that he differentiated it from the material world.[19] Plato's concept of the immateriality of the di-

---

[15] T.A. Slezák, 'Platon', *DNP*, IX, 1107. Cf. S. Lange, 'The Wisdom of Solomon and Plato', *JBL* 55 (1936), 302. Martin admits that Platonism existed even after the decline of Academic Platonism and mentions Philo as an example. However, he emphasizes that this is a *Stoicized* Platonism (Martin, *Body*, 13). For a balanced overview over the dominant philosophical schools in the Hellenistic period, see A.A. Long and D.N. Sedley, *The Hellenistic Philosophers. Vol. 1: Translation of the Principal Sources, with Philosophical Commentary* (Cambridge: Cambridge University Press, 2001 [1987[1]]), xi, 1–6.

[16] Like, e.g., C. Baeumker, *Das Problem der Materie in der griechischen Philosophie: eine historisch-kritische Untersuchung* (Münster: Aschendorff'sche Buchhandlung, 1890).

[17] Martin, *Body*, 11.

[18] E.g., Leisegang believes that many Greek philosophers conceived aether, light, fire and air as incorporeal and immaterial (H. Leisegang, *Der Heilige Geist: Das Wesen und Werden der mystisch-intuitiven Erkenntnis in der Philosophie und Religion der Griechen, I/1: Die vorchristlichen Anschauungen und Lehren vom ΠΝΕΥΜΑ und der mystisch-intuitiven Erkenntnis* (Leipzig: Teubner, 1919), 29 n.1; followed by L. Dürr, *Die Wertung des göttlichen Wortes im alten Testament und im antiken Orient: Zugleich ein Beitrag zur Vorgeschichte des neutestamentlichen Logosbegriffes*; MVAG 42/1 (Leipzig: Hinrichs, 1938), 146 n.3).

[19] M. Pohlenz, 'Stoa und Semitismus', *JWJ* 2 (1926), 261; F. Rüsche, 'Pneuma, Seele, Geist: Ein Ausschnitt aus der antiken Pneumalehre', *TGl* 23 (1931), 611; F. Rüsche, *Das Seelenpneuma: Seine Entwicklung von der Hauchseele zur Geistseele – Ein Beitrag zur Entwicklung der antiken Pneumalehre*; SGKA 18/3 (Paderborn: Schöningh, 1933), 10, 16; Stead, *Substance*, 146. On (the lack of) πνεῦμα in Plato, see, e.g., H. Siebeck, 'Die Entwicklung der Lehre vom Geist (Pneuma)', *ZVS* 12 (1880), 387–89; Wili, 'Geschichte', 81, 86, followed by Horn, *Angeld*, 57 n.6; Paige, 'Usage', 424; Engberg-Pedersen, *Cosmology*, 210–11 n.21.

vine even influenced the late Stoic writer Poseidonius who comprehended πνεῦμα as being immaterial, as Rüsche and Wili contend.[20]

The statement that the ancient mind could not but conceive everything, including πνεῦμα, as either fine or heavy matter[21] thus seems ill-founded.[22] Apart from this, it needs to be borne in mind that we have discussed in this section only those passages that potentially portray a physical view of πνεῦμα. However, a broader look at Graeco-Roman literature uncovers different and contradictory images of the nature of 'spirit'.[23]

1.2. Infusion-Transformation

It has already been mentioned that the proponents of infusion-transformation regard Hellenism as the breeding ground of this concept of ethical enabling in Paul. For example, Horn explains in the conclusion to his analysis of the background of pneumatic enthusiasm in the church at Corinth that 'Die gemeinantike Wasser-Geist-Metaphorik läßt im Taufritus den Ort erblicken, wo das πνεῦμα substanzhaft übermittelt wird und den Täufling in einem magischen Sinn als πνευματικός verstehen läßt.'[24] However, as Horn does not provide textual evidence for this 'common view of antiquity'[25] we will need to scrutinize the potential evidence ourselves.

Similar questions can be raised concerning Martin's almost identical argument regarding Aristotle (Martin, *Body*, 8). See particularly Stead, who points out that Aristotle had a concept of immaterial being (Stead, *Substance*, 89–97; cf. Rüsche, 'Pneuma', 612–13, 617; Rüsche, *Seelenpneuma*, 10, 16). Also Aristotle's concept of πνεῦμα was most likely that of an immaterial and not of a material substance (see, e.g., M. Heinze, *Die Lehre vom Logos in der griechischen Philosophie* (Oldenburg: Schmidt, 1872), 73; Rüsche, *Seelenpneuma*, 7; Horn, *Angeld*, 57 n.6). However, this aspect of his view of πνεῦμα remains somewhat obscure (see, e.g., *Gen. An.* 2.3, 736[b]; 2.6, 744[a]; and the discussions in F. Solmsen, 'The vital Heat, the inborn Pneuma and the Aether', in F. Solmsen, *Kleine Schriften. Vol. 1*; Collectanea 4/1 (Hildesheim: Georg Olms Verlagsbuchhandlung, 1968), 605–611; M.C. Nussbaum, *Aristotle's De Motu Animalum* (Princeton: Princeton University Press, 1978), 158–64; G. Freudenthal, *Aristotle's Theory of Material Substance: Heat and Pneuma, Form and Soul* (Oxford: Clarendon, 1995), 106–48).

[20] Rüsche, *Seelenpneuma*, 7, 17 [but see 11]; Wili, 'Geschichte', 86; followed by Horn, *Angeld*, 57 n.6; however, see also E.d.W. Burton, *Spirit, Soul, Flesh*; HLSLNT II/3 (Chicago: University of Chicago Press, 1918), 121. This return to the Platonic tradition gives further support to Slezák's assessment above of the influence of Platonism (cf. also Siebeck, 'Lehre', 387; Leisegang, *Geist*, 30 n.1; Brandenburger, *Fleisch*, 159).

[21] On this distinction, see further Martin, *Body*, 10.

[22] This conclusion has recently been confirmed by Engberg-Pedersen, 'Spirit', 182 n.18.

[23] Cf. the works cited in n.6 above.

[24] Horn, *Angeld*, 248.

[25] Horn admits that the *religionsgeschichtlich* comparison shows that in the texts of the mystery cults the spirit is not conferred on the person to be baptized, and that the

One of the two possible sources for the concept of infusion-transfor-mation is the philosophy of *Stoicism*. We have seen above that the litera-ture by and about the Stoics clearly indicates that major strands of Stoi-cism had a materialistic concept of πνεῦμα. Hence, the first constituent of the infusion-transformation approach is given. Another presupposition for this concept to work seems to be present too: in contrast to Plato, Aristotle and other ancient philosophers, the Stoics understood the human soul to be physical,[26] so that the idea of an (in)fusion with the potentially ethically overwhelming material spirit might be thought at least possible.

However, the central question is whether these material concepts of spirit and soul were connected by the Stoics to the sphere of ethics. On the one hand, it is clear that it was an ideal of Stoic ethics to live in accordance with both human nature in general as well as with one's own nature in particular (which is part of common Nature).[27] According to this last as-pect, the constitution of an individual determines his ethical life (cf. Alex. Aphr., *Fat.* 196.24–197.3 [*LS* 61M]; Seneca, *Ep.* 41.9; 94.8). On the other hand, the Stoics ascribed a powerful role to πνεῦμα in causing differences in things by differentiation of itself. Πνεῦμα possesses the power to act and to fashion matter by virtue of the fact that it is a corporeal entity.[28]

Against the background of these various aspects of Stoic ethics and physics one might suppose that the Stoics really did have a concept of infusion-transformation. Indeed, on a closer look one discovers that the fashioning force of πνεῦμα is not limited to cosmology but also includes anthropology. All bodily sensation occurs as the result of the transmission of impulses from the peripheral sense organs through the medium of dif-ferent πνεύματα to the command centre (Iamblichus, *Anima* 1.368 [*LS* 53K]). Chrysippus explains bodily tension by means of an image of the spider in its web: if a small insect lands in the web, the impulse is trans-

---

Mithras liturgy evidences a different pneumatology too (Ibid., 244–45, 245 n.71). Cf. R. Bultmann, *Theology of the New Testament. Vol. 1* (London: SCM Press, 1952), 141.

[26] So, e.g., Cicero, *Tusc.* 1.10.20; Seneca, *Ep.* 106.4–5; Diogenes Laertius 7.156–57. Cf. M. Pohlenz, *Die Stoa: Geschichte einer geistigen Bewegung. Vol. 2* (Göttingen: Vandenhoeck & Ruprecht, 1964³), 73–74; Long, *Philosophy*, 151; Long and Sedley, *Philosophers. I*, 274; D.E. Aune, 'Human Nature and Ethics in Hellenistic Philosophical Traditions and Paul: Some Issues and Problems', in T. Engberg-Pedersen (ed.), *Paul in his Hellenistic Context*; SNTW (Edinburgh: T. & T. Clark, 1994), 292–94; on Aristotle see particularly A. Scott, *Origen and the Life of the Stars: A History of an Idea* (Oxford: Clarendon, 1991), ch. 2, esp. p. 27.

[27] E.g. Cicero, *Off.* 1.110–11 [*LS* 66E]; cf. A.A. Long, *Stoic Studies* (Cambridge: Cambridge University Press, 1996), 140–44, 147; Inwood, 'Stoizismus', 1013–14.

[28] Cf. Cicero, *Acad.* 1.39 [*LS* 45A]; Alex. Aphr., *Mixt.* 225.1–2 [*LS* 45H]; Long, *Phi-losophy*, 160, 150, 148, 161; Long and Sedley, *Philosophers. I*, 273–74; M. Forschner, *Die Stoische Ethik: Über den Zusammenhang von Natur-, Sprach- und Moralphilosophie im altstoischen System* (Stuttgart: Klett-Cotta, 1981), 61.

mitted to the spider at the web's centre as a result of the tension in the web.[29] This physical animation of all biological operations within the human being also extends to one's feelings and character. Even virtues and vices are different physical states, so that one can say that ethical action is derived from a particular physical disposition.[30]

However, despite some claims to the contrary, one only finds very few Stoic texts in which the ethical effect of πνεῦμα is explicitly treated. For example, in his description of Stoic physics, Diogenes Laertius only mentions in passing that the Stoics 'consider that the passions are caused by the variations of the vital breath' (αἰτίας δὲ τῶν παθῶν ἀπολείπουσι τὰς περὶ τὸ πνεῦμα τροπάς, 7.158).[31] Moreover, even what seems to be the only extant text written by one of the (later) Stoics themselves that explicitly connects πνεῦμα and ethics (though not on the grounds of physics) shows differences to infusion-transformation: in *Ad Lucilium Epistulae Morales* 41.1 Seneca says that 'a holy spirit indwells within us, one who marks our good and bad deeds, and is our guardian. As we treat this spirit, so are we treated by it. Indeed, no man can be good without the help of God.' In this passage, Seneca clearly connects ethics to a holy spirit. When he later asks the question what this 'property of the human' is, he answers that the spirit 'is soul, and reason brought to perfection in the soul. For a

---

[29] Calcidius 220 (SVF 2.879; [*LS* 53G part]). Cf. M. Lapidge, 'Stoic Cosmology', in J.M. Rist (ed.), *The Stoics*; MTS 1 (Berkeley: University of California Press, 1978), 172–73.

[30] See, e.g., Sextus Empiricus, *Pyr.* 3.188: the 'goods of the soul are certain arts, namely the virtues... [T]here takes place in the ruling principle [ἡγεμονικόν], which according to them [i.e. the Stoics] is breath [πνεῦμα], a deposit of perceptions, and such an aggregation of them as to produce art...'. Cf. Seneca, *Ep.* 106; Plutarch, *Stoic. rep.* 1034D–E [*LS* 61C]; D. Frede, 'Stoic Determinism', in B. Inwood (ed.), *The Cambridge Companion to the Stoics*; CCP (Cambridge: Cambridge University Press, 2003), 185 (citing Philo, *Leg. All.* 2.22 [SVF 2.458] in support; cf. Philo, *Deus Imm.* 35, where πνεῦμα is described as the ἕξις of wood and stone). For further discussion, see F. Solmsen, 'Cleanthes or Posidonius? The Basis of Stoic Physics', in F. Solmsen, *Kleine Schriften. Vol. 1*; Collectanea 4/1 (Hildesheim: Georg Olms Verlagsbuchhandlung, 1968), 451–52 (who emphasizes that there is no specific evidence amoung the Stoics on how they related πνεῦμα to the θερμόν of the soul); Long, *Philosophy*, 162–63; B. Inwood, *Ethics and Human Action in Early Stoicism* (Oxford: Clarendon, 1985), 31, 39, 144, 166; Rist, 'Biology', 46; C. Gill, *The Structured Self in Hellenistic and Roman Thought* (Oxford: Oxford University Press, 2006), 80.

[31] Engberg-Pedersen mentions an additional passage that may give evidence of the connection of πνεῦμα and ethics in Stoicism. He submits that, according to Cicero, *Nat. d.* 2.167, the following is 'required for human beings to see completely aright: a particularly strong "portion" of the pneuma of the Stars "blown into them" from above, which will generate the proper tension in their *nous*' (Engberg-Pedersen, *Cosmology*, 21). However, Cicero speaks about divine inspiration (*aliquo adflatu divino*), and neither the text nor the context explicitly connects this to a physical 'pneuma of the Stars'.

human is a reasoning animal. Therefore, one's highest good is attained, if he has fulfilled the good for which nature designed him at birth' (41.8–9). Accordingly, while there are similarities with infusion-transformation, the differences cannot be obliterated: for Seneca the holy spirit is part of human nature since birth. It is not infused into people at conversion-initiation, enabling henceforth ethical life. Rather, the holy spirit is identified with the human spirit/soul/reason (cf. 41.5–7), as for Seneca 'living according to reason (the Stoic ideal) and living according to one's own nature are synonymous because one's own nature consists in part of a spirit, the god within'.[32]

Generally speaking, therefore, Büchsel and Keener have rightly pointed out that for the Stoics, the physical concept of πνεῦμα did not explicitly play a central role in their *ethics* but in their *physics*.[33] We can thus conclude that the Stoics had a materialistic pneumatology, but not an ethic of substantive transformation that is built upon it. After birth, a supplementary increase or 'compression' of one's individual πνεῦμα through external intervention by the divine is not intended in Stoic philosophy. Rather, *cognitive* transformation through philosophy and active reasoning played a central role in Stoic ethics.[34] Philosophy's ethical function is understood as that of *toning up* the soul – developing its muscles, assisting its use of its own capabilities more effectively (Seneca, *Ep.* 15).[35]

---

[32] J.R. Levison, *The Spirit in First Century Judaism*; AGJU 29 (Leiden: Brill, 1997), 71, cf. 147; Levison, *Filled with the Spirit*, 141–42. On Seneca, *Ep.* 41, see the detailed discussion in J. Ware, 'Moral Progress and Divine Power in Seneca and Paul', in J.T. Fitzgerald (ed.), *Passions and Moral Progress in Greco-Roman Thought*; RMCS (London: Routledge, 2008), 267–83.

The pantheistic concept of God that shines through in this passage and that is characteristic of Stoicism in general (cf. Cicero, *Leg.* 1.9.27; Galen, *Plac. Hipp. Plat.* 4.5.3–8; Diogenes Laertius 7.158–59; Frede, 'Determinism', 202) constitutes an additional contrast to the alleged concept of infusion-transformation in Paul.

[33] Büchsel, *Geist*, 47; Keener, *Spirit*, 7. However, physics and ethics are interrelated, as we have seen above.

[34] See, e.g., Seneca, *Ep.* 6.1–2; 73.15–16; 110.1, 10; Marcus Aurelius 8.14 [*LS* 61P]. Cf. Long and Sedley, *Philosophers. I*, 346–54, 359–68, 381–86; Forschner, *Ethik*, 151; M. Nussbaum, *The Therapy of Desire: Theory and Practice in Hellenistic Ethics* (Princeton: Princeton University Press, 1994), esp. ch. 9; C. Horn, *Antike Lebenskunst: Glück und Moral von Sokrates bis zu den Neuplatonikern*; BsR 1271 (Munich: C. H. Beck, 1998), chs. 1 and 4; T. Engberg-Pedersen, *Paul and the Stoics* (Edinburgh: T. & T. Clark, 2000), ch. 3; Ware, 'Progress', 267–83; Johnson, *Gentiles*, 70–71.

[35] This is not just a metaphor but a physical idea, as Nussbaum, *Therapy*, 317–18, points out. On Stoic physics of the mind, see Long and Sedley, *Philosophers. I*, 313–23. On the potential change of one's soul, see Plutarch, *Prof.* 75C [*LS* 61S]; *Comm. Not.* 1063B [*LS* 61T] (cf. Long and Sedley, *Philosophers. I*, 368, 385–86; S.K. Stowers, 'Does Pauline Christianity Resemble a Hellenistic Philosophy?', in T. Engberg-Pedersen (ed.), *Paul Beyond the Judaism/Hellenism Divide* (Louisville: Westminster John Knox Press,

The other potential source that might give evidence for the presence of the infusion-transformation approach within Hellenistic pneumatology is the *Corpus Hermeticum*.[36] Stuhlmacher needs to be commended for being, as it seems, the only one who provides a reference for the thesis that, like a Hellenist, Paul thought of the Spirit as a mighty substance which eliminates ἀδικία within a person in a powerful act of ontic change, namely *Corpus Hermeticum* 13.9.[37] Unfortunately, however, 'spirit' is not mentioned at all in 13.9 or its cotext, so that Stuhlmacher's thesis cannot be verified. In a similar manner, Willoughby claims that in Hermeticism the individual was in a

> supreme moment of ecstasy… endowed with spirit, a deific light-substance, and equipped with *gnosis*, a divinely given mental illumination absolutely essential to salvation. As a result of this rebirth, the individual felt himself possessed of such divine power that he could live an upright moral life.[38]

However, Willoughby provides no textual evidence for this thesis; and where he does give references, these are not always translated accurately (e.g., in his rendering of 7.3 he translates νοῦς as 'spirit'). Moreover, while he uses this text to support his statement that 'in the moral life of the regenerate, the spirit was given a notable rôle to play', Willoughby nonetheless has to admit that in Hermeticism the emphasis in (ethical) transformation is on νοῦς and not on πνεῦμα (so, e.g., 4.4–5; cf. 10.6).[39] Indeed, in those places where Hermeticism does mention substance-ontological transformation, this is based on the ecstatic apprehension of the (ἀσώματος)[40] γνῶσις of the Go(o)d (10.6, 9), and not on infusion with πνεῦμα.[41] Besides, unlike in infusion-transformation, the rebirth experience in Hermeticism is a *process* that requires careful preparation.[42]

2001), 91), and Seneca, *Ep.* 6.1–2: 'I am being not only reformed, but transformed'. While this is a sudden change in which 'my spirit [*animi*] is altered into something better', it is nonetheless not yet complete (there are 'elements within me which need to be changed'). Moreover, it is placed within the relational context of friendship (6.2–7), not physics. Seneca is clear that 'the living voice and the intimacy of a common life will help more than the written word' of books (6.5).

[36] On the Hellenistic mystery cults as a third option, see n.25 above and Paige, 'Usage', 431–33.

[37] Stuhlmacher, *Gerechtigkeit*, 218. Cf. pp. 221, 230, where he does not give textual evidence for this 'Hellenistic view'.

[38] H.R. Willoughby, *Pagan Regeneration: A Study of Initiations in the Graeco-Roman World* (Chicago: University of Chicago Press, 1929), 221; cf. 260.

[39] Ibid., 219.

[40] 10.9, cf. 4.5. Matter, *per contra*, is frequently perceived as evil (see, e.g., 10.10, 15).

[41] Cf. J. Dey, *ΠΑΛΙΓΓΕΝΕΣΙΑ: Ein Beitrag zur Klärung der religionsgeschichtlichen Bedeutung von Tit 3,5*; NTA 17.5 (Münster: Aschendorff, 1937), 119–23.

[42] On the latter, cf. Willoughby, *Regeneration*, 220–21.

We have thus observed that, although it has been repeatedly attempted to portray Hellenism as the breeding ground of infusion-transformation, we can merely confirm that Stoicism provided a number of rudimental presuppositions for this theory. However, the chain of argument 'infusion by a material πνεῦμα results in a substance-ontological transformation which results in ethical life' as such could not be found in Graeco-Roman literature (at least up to 100 CE).[43]

2. Judaism

After having established that a number of Hellenists were well-acquainted with a physical conception of πνεῦμα but not with the idea of infusion-transformation as such, we now seek to find out whether Judaism provides better support for this approach. As the aim of this section is to investigate those passages that have been put forward by the proponents of the infusion-transformation approach, it should be noted that the results of this analysis will therefore not provide evidence as to what was the *dominant* view regarding the Spirit's nature or the Spirit's ethical work in the different strands of Judaism (on this matter, see 5.1.).

The Jewish sources which are said to give confirmation to the infusion-transformation approach and its presupposed concept of the Spirit will now be explored in the order of their probable chronology and degree of Hellenization.[44] The chief texts, namely the Hebrew Bible, Qumran, *Joseph and Aseneth* and Philo will be analysed in the main body, whereas the Apocrypha, Pseudepigrapha and Rabbinical texts will receive briefer treatment in the footnotes.

2.1. The Hebrew Bible

As far as the Hebrew Bible is concerned, it appears that no-one has argued that the Spirit transforms people substance-ontologically because of the physical nature of the Spirit. Nevertheless, scholars *have* argued that רוּחַ was conceived as a physical substance in the Old Testament.

Although it was Gunkel who put forward that 'the real definition of the Spirit' and the chief factor of the concept of the Spirit in the Old Testament

---

[43] With regard to the potential reception of Stoic pneumatology in Paul's churches, see 3.3. below.

[44] On the classification of different 'degrees of Hellenization', see art. 'Hellenization', *DJBP*, I, 286; J.M.G. Barclay, *Jews in the Mediterranean Diaspora: From Alexander to Trajan (323 BCE – 117 CE)* (Edinburgh: T. & T. Clark, 1996), 82–124.

and in early Judaism 'is always that he is a supernatural *power*',[45] it was the same scholar who provided the most sophisticated argumentation for the view that ancient Judaism understood the Spirit also as a 'supernatural substance'. We will briefly look at Gunkel's argumentation and subsequently offer an evaluation of it.

Gunkel believes that the Spirit is conceived of as a physical substance because it is compared to wind in the Old Testament. In fact, the same term is used for Spirit and wind, which leads to the conclusion that 'the Hebrew conceived of the Spirit as a kind of wind, more mysterious, more supersensual, perhaps, but nonetheless as a delicate, airy substance'. Why is the wind believed to be a material substance? For Gunkel the reason is the presence of formulations like 'the "weight" of the wind' (Job 28:25) and 'the "storehouses" of the wind' (Ps. 135:7; Jer. 10:13; Job 37:9). He argues that the underlying reason for the analogy of the Spirit with the wind is that 'both are mighty in their effects, mysterious..., imperceptible to the human eye, not weighable by human measure, and not to be restrained by human strength'.[46] And, besides that,

the notion of a force without any material substrate requires a highly developed capacity for abstraction which we may not assume the ancient Hebrews had. Indeed, we can say that the more vividly the Spirit's activities are experienced, and the more lively and graphically he is conceived, the more certainly the Spirit will be taken as a supersensous substance.[47]

Gunkel thus establishes his view of the Old Testament conception of the nature of the Spirit from his comparison with what he believes was the Old Testament concept of 'wind'.[48] He may indeed be right when he says that the reason why the term רוּחַ came to be used not only for wind but also for (God's) Spirit is to be seen in the fact that *both* are mighty in their effects and indifferent to human measurements. It is questionable, however,

---

[45] H. Gunkel, *The Influence of the Holy Spirit: The Popular View of the Apostolic Age and the Teaching of the Apostle Paul* (Philadelphia: Fortress Press, 1979), 64, italics added.

[46] Ibid., 60.

[47] Ibid., 59, cf. 61.

[48] Gunkel was followed in his reasoning by P. Volz, *Der Geist Gottes und die verwandten Erscheinungen im Alten Testament und im anschließenden Judentum* (Tübingen: J.C.B. Mohr (Paul Siebeck), 1910), 57–59, and others. Burton follows Gunkel too, but he rightly remarks that the possibility that spirit was an immaterial substance was ignored by Gunkel and his conversation partners, 'probably with reason in view of the lack of evidence that the Hebrews ever thought of immaterial substance'. Burton thinks that it is neither possible to go with certainty beyond Gunkel's results nor beyond the observation that the Hebrews denied to spirit the *ordinary* attributes of matter (Burton, *Spirit*, 58). However, we will demonstrate below that even Gunkel went beyond the boundaries of sound interpretation.

whether one should necessarily conclude that if *one* of them (i.e. the wind) might be of physical nature, this needs to be true for the *other* of them (i.e. the Spirit) too.

Apart from that, it is doubtful whether the Hebrew Bible conceives of the wind as a (material) substance at all. The proof texts which Gunkel provides for this view are taken exclusively from poetic genre. However, we will see below (2.2.2.1.) that it is illegitimate to establish a scientific definition of the ontology of the Spirit on the basis of what appears to be strongly metaphorical language. For now it should suffice to illustrate this point from a different piece of Old Testament poetry that also contains 'cosmological' imagery:

LORD my God, you are very great.
　　You are clothed with honour and majesty, wrapped in light as with a garment.
You stretch out the heavens like a tent,
　　you set the beams of your chambers on the waters,
you make the clouds your chariot, you ride on the wings of the wind,
　　you make the winds your messengers, fire and flame your ministers (Ps. 104:1–4).

Does the Psalmist believe that God, honour, majesty and light are material objects?[49] And, could the same indeed be said of the wind as it has 'wings' on which God can ride? According to such a method of interpretation, however, the wind would at the same time be a personal subject who can act as a messenger. For this reason, Gunkel would have been much more persuasive had he been able to provide philosophical/scientific discourses in the Hebrew Bible that would pertain to the matter under question. That, however, would have proved a challenging task since such discourses are not evident in the Hebrew Bible.[50]

Leading on from that, the second pillar of Gunkel's argument is also founded on shaky grounds, namely on the claim that ancient Hebrews did not have 'a highly developed capacity for abstraction' and therefore could

---

[49] For a discussion of the incorporeity of God in the OT, see A. Schart, 'Die "Gestalt" YHWHs: Ein Beitrag zur Körpermetaphorik alttestamentlicher Rede von Gott', *TZ* 55 (1999), 26–41.

[50] Regarding the OT concept of רוח, see also Gese's interesting comment that 'das Riechen ebenso wie das Luftförmige für alttestamentliches Verständnis als immateriell gilt. Es gibt als Materielles nur Flüssiges und Festes, denn das hat beides feste Ausdehnung. Der Ausdehnungsbegriff setzt den Materiebegriff. Was keine feste Ausdehnung hat, ist nicht Materie. Die Magdeburger Kugeln sind noch nicht erfunden, und die einfache sinnliche Wahrnehmung ist ja die, daß Ausdehnung Materie bestimmt, nicht Gewicht, wie wir das haben' (P. Stuhlmacher, 'Hartmut Gese about "Das Alte Testament in der Johannesoffenbarung"' (University of Tübingen: Unpublished Minutes of an *Oberseminar/Sozietät* Session, 04.07.2000), 3). This criticism would also apply to Gunkel's interpretation of the passages of the OT Pseudepigrapha mentioned in Gunkel, *Influence*, 60. See further Appendix 1.3., esp. n.53.

not but have the concept of the Spirit that is suggested by Gunkel. However, it is *Gunkel's idea* of רוּחַ as a 'supersensous substance' (*über-
sinnlicher Stoff*) that is a 'highly developed abstraction'! According to
Gunkel, the Jews of the Old Testament must have attributed to the Spirit
something like 'supersensual weight'.[51] The reason for this is that, on the
one hand, on the basis of Job 28:25 the Spirit is supposed to have weight
(and therefore is *Stoff*). On the other hand, Gunkel says that the Spirit is
'not weighable by human measure' (and therefore is *übersinnlich*). However, even a tremendously vivid experience of the Spirit would not necessarily lead one to such altitudes of abstraction. In fact, it needs to be asked
more generally how Gunkel can claim that the more lively one's experience of the Spirit, the more certainly will one take the Spirit to be a supersensous substance. Would it not be equally conceivable (and possibly even
more natural) to comprehend the Spirit as a (personal?) power and not as
übersinnlichen Stoff on the basis of such an experience?

As we have seen above, Gunkel would reply to the latter question that
these two are anyway identical in the ancient mind. And, at least in a certain strand of Hellenism, this is indeed true. For instance, Diogenes Laertius records that the Stoics think that πᾶν τὸ ποιοῦν σῶμά ἐστιν (7.56),
and Nemesius, likewise referring to Stoicism, conveys that 'power
(δύναμις) is matter (ὕλη τις)' (*Nat. Hom.* 30 [MPG 540b]).[52] While it is
thus a matter of fact that the Stoics thought about power in material terms,
it is nonetheless unfounded to conclude that 'ancients' could not think
differently about power or spirit. One only needs to recall the dualistic
cosmology of Platonism.[53] However, as we are discussing Old Testament/
Hebraic and not Greek thought, Gunkel would have needed to give evidence for parallel conceptions of matter and force from the Hebrew Bible.
But this he fails to do.

Finally, to return to the debated nature of Hebraic thinking, the proposal
made in the present study is that what Gunkel calls the Old Testament
'naiveté not yet troubled by reflection'[54] did not lead the writers to comprehend the Spirit as a supersensous substance; rather, contrary to Gunkel
and the scholars of similar opinion before and after him, it is exactly *this
lack of 'highly developed abstraction' that has kept the Old Testament
writers from engaging at all in philosophical/scientific discourse about the*

---

[51] This is our own coinage by which we try to capture Gunkel's thought about the
weight of רוּחַ.

[52] Cf. the slightly different statement in *Nat. Hom.* 40 (MPG 561a; referring to Aristotle): 'matter is power'. On the Stoic concept of power, see further M.P. Nilsson, *Geschichte der Griechischen Religion, II: Die Hellenistische und Römische Zeit* (Munich:
Beck'sche Verlagsbuchhandlung, 1961²), 266.

[53] See the discussion in 2.1.1.

[54] Gunkel, *Influence*, 61.

ontology of the Spirit (as one can find it in Hellenism, *per contra*).[55] This proposal is confirmed by Tengström:

The OT does not concern itself with questions about the "nature" of things. Observations of the physical world are registered, but they are always associated intimately with human experience and put in the service of analogical thought and metaphorical imagery.[56]

On a similar note, Gese argues in his essay 'The Question of a World View' that the given framework of the prescientific world view of the ancients did not progress beyond human sense-perception, that is, their world view was constituted by how they perceived nature and the world through the human senses of vision, hearing, etc.[57] Gese explains that 'so

---

[55] This is not to set up the kind of antithesis between Hebrew and Greek thought as Köhler and Boman have done (L. Köhler, *Hebrew Man: Lectures Delivered at the Invitation of the University of Tübingen, December 1–16, 1952* (London: SCM Press, 1956), *passim*; T. Boman, *Hebrew Thought Compared with Greek*; LHD (London: SCM Press, 1960), *passim*). Rather, the differences referred to above are highlighted on the basis of a comparison of the nature and content of the literature on pneumatology that was analysed in 2.1. on the one hand, and that in the current section and 2.2.2. on the other. For a thorough critique of the methodology of the works cited above, see J. Barr, *The Semantics of Biblical Language* (Oxford: Oxford University Press, 1961).

[56] S. Tengström, 'רוּחַ', *TDOT*, XIII, 381, mentioning Isa. 7:2; Prov. 25:23 and Hos. 8:7 as examples. Cf. D. Hill, *Greek Words with Hebrew Meanings: Studies in the Semantics of Soteriological Terms*; SNTSMS 5 (Cambridge: Cambridge University Press, 1967), 212 n.1.

Also Snaith criticizes the kind of hermeneutic put forward by Gunkel when he charges Volz (who followed Gunkel's reasoning) of 'the old error of trying to force undeveloped ideas into modern categories' (N.H. Snaith, *Distinctive Ideas of the Old Testament* (Philadelphia: Westminster, 1946), 200). He applies this judgement also to Volz's interpretation of Num. 11:25 (Volz, *Geist*, 23–24; cf. Gunkel, *Influence*, 61; A.H.J. Gunneweg, 'Aspekte des alttestamentlichen Geistverständnisses', in A.H.J. Gunneweg, *Sola Scriptura. Vol. I: Beiträge zu Exegese und Hermeneutik des Alten Testaments* (Göttingen: Vandenhoeck & Ruprecht, 1983), 102). Contrary to Volz, Snaith takes רוּחַ here as a supra-human power which 'is not conceived as being material, because the idea belongs to a time when the... distinctions between "personal" and "impersonal", or between "material" and "spiritual", were not made' (N.H. Snaith, *Leviticus and Numbers*; NCB (London: Nelson, 1967), 230). The passage may hence be best interpreted by a different metaphor: Yahweh took some of the *endowment* of the Spirit that was on Moses and gave it to the elders (perhaps in order that the seventy might work with Moses 'in one spirit and purpose' [so E.J. Young, *My Servants the Prophets* (Grand Rapids: Eerdmans, 1953), 69]). The elders thus came 'under the influence of Yahweh's Spirit, which had been on Moses. More specific than this we cannot be' (T.R. Ashley, *The Book of Numbers*; NICOT 16 (Grand Rapids: Eerdmans, 1993), 214).

[57] In modern natural science, *per contra*, the limits of sense-perception are constantly violated: in fact, scientific instruments for measurement have taken the place of sensual perception (H. Gese, *Essays on Biblical Theology* (Minneapolis: Augsburg Publishing House, 1981), 228).

many of the biblical texts are poetic, because it was only in this form that the truth could be expressed. Poetic language brings a statement closer to what our senses can perceive, while at the same time intensifying it metaphorically.'[58]

Against this background we are now in a position to give an answer to the question that we have raised above regarding the validity of Gunkel's claim that the more lively one's experience of the Spirit, the more certainly will one take רוּחַ to be a supersensous substance. Our discussion above leads us to the conclusion that the more lively one's experience of the Spirit (i.e. the more sense-perception is involved), the more difficult it is to formulate this Spirit-experience in a literal statement and the more likely it is that one will talk about it in figurative language.[59]

However, modern interpreters often find themselves challenged how to understand such metaphorical and symbolic language. Gese observes that one either allegorizes such language or interprets it 'realistically in a literal manner, which is as foolish as trying to discover the zoological species of the fish that swallowed Jonah'.[60] To apply this insight to the interpretation of the Spirit-language of the Hebrew Bible means that interpreters have to beware of both materialization as well as spiritualization of phrases like 'the Spirit is poured upon us from on high' (Isa. 32:15, RSV).[61]

We can thus conclude that it is a modern misconception to assume that when the writers of the Hebrew Bible describe religious experiences in sensory language they were making statements relating to science. This conclusion should prevent us from trying to conceptualize the Spirit in the Hebrew Bible in such highly developed notions like 'substance', 'super-sensous substance' or even 'immaterial substance'.

2.2. Qumran

Some scholars believe that they find support for the idea of an infusion-transformation of the believer in the Qumran documents. However, the evidence that has been put forward mainly regards the concept of the nature of the Spirit. It has been argued, too, that the physical Spirit of God fuses with the human spirit, although this has not been linked to transfor-

---

[58] Ibid., 235.

[59] Cf. J.M. Soskice, *Metaphor and Religious Language* (Oxford: Clarendon, 1985), 96; G. Lakoff, 'The Contemporary Theory of Metaphor', in A. Ortony (ed.), *Metaphor and Thought* (Cambridge: Cambridge University Press, 1993[2]), 239–41.

[60] Gese, *Essays*, 243.

[61] On the interpretation of this metaphor, see M. Dreytza, *Der theologische Gebrauch von Ruah im Alten Testament: Eine wort- und satzsemantische Studie* (Giessen/Basel: Brunnen, 1990), 224–25; Rabens, 'Development', 169–71; and section 2.2.2.1. below.

mation and ethics.[62] Before the first assumption, namely the material nature of the Spirit, will be analysed, we will briefly look at this second part of the argument.

Betz contends that in 1QH[a] 8.22 the Spirit of God fuses with the spirit of the believer and becomes one with it. Betz builds this reasoning on his translation of לפניך [ולעו]לם [...]...[...]אל[התערב ברוח עבדך as 'before you [...] to mix with the spirit of your servant...'. However, both at the time of arguing this case as well as more recently Betz was aware of the fact that this translation is very speculative because of the immense fragmentation of the manuscript in this place.[63] It is hence not surprising that the modern translation of García Martínez and Tigchelaar offers a very different rendering of 8.22: 'in your presence [forev]er. [May... not] associate with the spirit of your servant...', supplying '[לעו]' in the first and '[אל...]' in the last gap. One can conclude from these disagreements that it will be better not to rest any case concerning the precise nature of the influence of the divine Spirit on Qumran members on this passage.

Contra Betz, the supposed (physical) fusion of the divine and the human S/spirits likewise cannot be supported by alluding to Josephus, who says that the Essenes believe the soul to emanate from the finest ether (λεπτότατος αἰθήρ [*J.W.* 2.154]).[64] First of all, the soul is not identified with λεπτότατος αἰθήρ (which is not necessarily material anyway) but is said to *emanate from* it. Moreover, Beall points out that Josephus' description of the Essenes' views is in this place particularly coloured by Greek thought, due to his apologetic intention.[65]

---

[62] The passages quoted by Stuhlmacher in this context explicitly mention spirits – not the Spirit of God (Stuhlmacher, 'Erwägungen', 13). His thesis has come under attack by J. Baumgarten, *Paulus und die Apokalyptik: Die Auslegung apokalyptischer Überlieferungen in den echten Paulusbriefen*; WMANT 44 (Neukirchen-Vluyn: Neukirchener Verlag, 1975), 164–65.

As 1QH[a] 15.6–7 relates an ethical effect of the Spirit, the passage could be interpreted as potentially referring to infusion-transformation if one were to understand רוח as a physical substance. However, this understanding will be challenged below.

[63] Betz, *Offenbarung*, 130. Betz mentioned in a private conversation on 04.06.2002 that he would now prefer the translation '[may not come an evil spirit] to mix with the spirit of your servant'.

[64] Ibid., 131. Also the passages mentioned in Betz, *Offenbarung*, 134, do not support the claim that the Spirit is understood as a (physical) substance, because 1QS 3.4–9 speaks about *cleansing* by the Spirit (and not glorification), and 1.11–13 does not mention רוח at all.

[65] T.S. Beall, *Josephus' Description of the Essenes Illustrated by the Dead Sea Scrolls*; SNTSMS 58 (Cambridge: Cambridge University Press, 1988), 105. Interestingly, Betz does not offer support for this view from the DSS themselves. For a similar critique, see A.R.C. Leaney, *The Rule of Qumran and Its Meaning* (London: SCM Press, 1966), 36–37.

While it was relatively easy to see that the line of thought depicted above is problematic, it is more complex to evaluate the arguments that have been submitted in support for the supposed material nature of the Spirit, to which we now turn.

The main proponents for a physical concept of the Spirit in the Qumran documents are Betz and Horn. The clearest example of Horn's proof texts is 1QH[a] 15.6–7.[66] This passage is particularly interesting for our purpose, because should the author here operate with a physical concept of the Spirit, one could conclude that he may also be inclined to think of the work of the Spirit in infusion-transformation categories, for he ascribes ethical effects to the inception of the Spirit. With regard to the text, Horn seems to go along with the standard translation since he argues that one can deduce a substantial view of the Spirit from the Spirit-water-imagery ('Wasser-Geist-Metaphorik') in these lines: 'you have upheld me with your strength, your Holy Spirit you have poured over me so that I will not stumble' (15.6–7; cf. 4.26).[67] Betz' model of the Spirit in Qumran is founded on these two passages from the *Hodayot* too (and further: 23.9). However, Betz renders the verb הניף, that is here used of the Spirit, as 'swung into', on the basis of its cultic use for wave offerings in the Hebrew Bible. 'The ether-like substance of the Spirit can be moved, "swung" as the wind moves the air, a view that is caused by the term רוח.'[68] We will briefly look at this and other options for translating הניף.

The decisive advantage of Betz' rendering of הניפותה בי is its utilization of the literal meaning of the word. Although he was not followed by many scholars,[69] his rendering nevertheless appears to be right. However, while his translation may be the correct one, the inference that we are therefore dealing with a concept of the divine Spirit as an ethereal substance is an unsubstantiated claim which does not hold ground upon close scrutiny (cf. 2.2.1. above).

A similar translation of the line is chosen by Holm-Nielsen, García Martínez and Tigchelaar and others, who translate 'you have spread your

---

[66] On Horn's other textual data, see further Rabens, 'Development', 170, 163 n.5. For a critique of a sacramental interpretation of 1QS 3.4–9 as held by Horn, see J. Schreiner, 'Geistbegabung in der Gemeinde von Qumran', *BZ* 9 (1965), 177, and Betz, *Offenbarung*, 134.

[67] Horn, *Angeld*, 59. Translation by E. Lohse (ed.), *Die Texte aus Qumran: hebräisch und deutsch, mit masoretischer Punktation, Übersetzung, Einführung und Anmerkungen* (Munich: Kösel, 1981²), 139.

[68] Betz, *Offenbarung*, 130–31.

[69] Stuhlmacher appears to be the only one (Stuhlmacher, 'Erwägungen', 13).

holy spirit over me'.[70] This idea of 'spreading' may be due to YHWH's 'waving' of his רוח. Like Betz' rendering, the wording of this rendering does not suggest that the Qumran-psalmist had a material concept of the Spirit of YHWH.

Finally, also the translations of Lohse, Horn and others ('poured/shed/ sprinkled over'; 'distilled into'[71]) have strong evidence in their favour. Namely, הניף is used in Psalm 68:10 for rain. Moreover, cognate evidence in 1QS 4.21 and in the Hebrew Bible[72] indicates that verbs of 'pouring' are frequently used in connection with רוח. Although the translation of Holm-Nielsen, García Martínez and Tigchelaar may still be preferable,[73] we will concentrate in the following on Horn's translation and interpretation because the wind and air imagery has already been discussed in 2.2.1. above.

While the most accurate translation of 1QH[a] 15.6–7 is difficult to determine, it seems to be less difficult to ascertain that one is here dealing with a metaphor. Even Horn is positive about this, as we have seen. What is not clear, however, is how such a metaphor should be interpreted. Therefore, some light shall be shed on this complex issue in the following section where 1QH[a] 15.6–7 will be analysed as a primary example in the context of some more general considerations about metaphors.[74] Since some observations about metaphors have already been made in passing in section 2.2.1., it is important to ask now more systematically

1) what a metaphor is,

2) how one can recognize a metaphor, and

3) how one can interpret a metaphor, because metaphors will be repeatedly encountered throughout Part I.

2.2.1. Strategies for Interpreting Metaphors (Demonstrated in the Example of 1QH[a] 15.6–7)

1) Metaphors are a hotly debated field of study among linguists and phi-

---

[70] Holm-Nielsen sees support for this translation in the combination of Isa. 11:15 and 30:28 (S. Holm-Nielsen, *Hodayot: Psalms from Qumran*; AThD 2 (Aarhus: Universitetsforlaget, 1960), 131 n.2).

[71] M. Mansoor, *The Thanksgiving Hymns*; STDJ 3 (Leiden: Brill, 1961), 149.

[72] E.g. Isa. 19:14; 29:10; 32:15; 44:3; Ezek. 39:29; Joel 2:28–29; Zech. 12:10 (cf. A.E. Sekki, *The Meaning of Ruaḥ at Qumran*; SBLDS 110 (Atlanta: Scholars Press, 1989), 79). Cf. Acts 2:17–18, 33; 10:45; Tit. 3:6.

[73] For a similar discussion with the same conclusion, see now also S.T. Um, *The Theme of Temple Christology in John's Gospel*; LNTS 312 (London: T. & T. Clark, 2006), 96 n.145.

[74] 1QH[a] 15.6–7 has been selected because it is textually the best preserved of the passages mentioned above. Moreover, it has strong potential for supporting the infusion-transformation approach because the result of the Spirit-infusion is religious-ethical life (see esp. 15.7c).

losophers, so it is not surprising that one finds different views even when it comes to the theory of what metaphor is. Buntfuß distinguishes between weak and strong metaphor theories,[75] a classification that is shared by Soskice and Harré, though they speak of substitution and Gestalt theories. Basic to the former is the idea that metaphor is another way of saying what could also be said literally.[76] However, this traditional view is no longer accepted by modern scholars. Gestalt theorists emphasize that what is expressed by metaphor cannot be expressed in the same way by other means. The combination of primary subject (tenor) and modifying term (vehicle) results in a new and unique agent of meaning – which means that the designation of a word or phrase as '*merely* metaphorical' is absurd.[77] In the broad line of this strand of scholarship we will henceforth employ the definition of metaphor of Soskice: 'metaphor is that figure of speech whereby we speak about one thing in terms which are seen to be sugges- tive of another'.[78]

On the basis of this definition we may infer that in 1QH[a] 15.7 God's *giving* of the *Spirit* (tenor) is spoken of in terms which are suggestive of the *pouring* of a fluid, most likely of *water* (vehicle),[79] thus resulting in a new meaning.

2) How can one recognize that one is dealing with a metaphor in a given text? Various criteria for discerning the presence of a metaphor could be mentioned and discussed at this point,[80] but for the sake of brevity we will focus here on the most important one, namely, a 'jarring deviation from the previous topic of discussion that would result from taking the sentence literally'.[81] With Dawes one might describe this 'metaphorical warrant'

---

[75] M. Buntfuß, *Tradition und Innovation: die Funktion der Metapher in der theologi- schen Theoriesprache*; TBT 84 (Berlin/New York: W. de Gruyter, 1997), 3.

[76] J.M. Soskice and R. Harré, 'Metaphor in Science', in Z. Radman (ed.), *From a Metaphorical Point of View: A Multidisciplinary Approach to the Cognitive Content of Metaphor*; PW.TS 7 (Berlin/New York: W. de Gruyter, 1995), 290–91.

[77] Cf. Ibid., 290–91. See also H. Weinrich, *Sprache in Texten* (Stuttgart: Klett, 1976), 276–341, who speaks about an 'image-receptor' and an 'image-contributor'.

[78] Soskice, *Metaphor*, 15 (italics removed). Cf., e.g., M. Black, *Models and Meta- phors: Studies in Language and Philosophy* (Ithaca: Cornell University Press, 1962), 236–37; A.P. Martinich, 'Metaphor', *REPh*, VI, 335.

[79] Cf. 1QS 4.21: 'He will sprinkle over him the Spirit of truth like lustral *waters*.' Cf. Isa. 32:15; 44:3.

[80] See the helpful analysis in G.W. Dawes, *The Body in Question: Metaphor and Meaning in the Interpretation of Ephesians 5:21–33*; BIS 30 (Leiden/Boston/Cologne: Brill, 1998), 48–55. Further criteria can be drawn from our exposition of the notion of 'contexts' in 3a).

[81] M.C. Beardsley, 'Metaphor and Falsity', *JAAC* 35 (1976), 219–20. Black further explains that the decisive criterion is often 'the patent falsity or incoherence of the literal reading – but it might equally be the banality of that reading's truth, its pointlessness, or

as 'a certain semantic tension between an expression and its context'.[82]

This point is well illustrated by an example from Paul, who writes to the Philippians: 'I am fully satisfied, now that I have received from Epaphroditus the gifts you sent, a fragrant offering, a sacrifice acceptable and pleasing to God' (4:18b–c). It is entirely surprising that Paul, as he talks about a material gift, suddenly says that this is an ὀσμὴν εὐωδίας (lit. 'an odour of a sweet smell'). Taken literally, this designation would mean that Paul thinks that one/God can smell the gift. But as Paul is writing here in the context of his friendship with the Philippians about a (possibly financial) gift, even with imagery of accounting in 4:18a, we are confronted with a semantic tension when interpreting a fragrant offering literally (as it is to be understood in Gen. 8:21; Exod. 29:18, 25, 41; Lev. 1:9–17, *per contra*, where animals are being burnt). This indicates that we are dealing with a metaphor.

A similar tension can be observed in 1QH[a] 15.6–7 where the writer thanks God for his *spiritual strengthening* (cf. vv.8, 10, 14), using in 15.7a

---

its lack of congruence with the surrounding text and nonverbal setting. The situation in cases of doubt as to how a statement is best taken is basically the same as in other cases of ambiguity. And just as there is no infallible test for resolving ambiguity, so there is none to be expected in discriminating the metaphorical from the literal' (M. Black, 'More about Metaphor', in A. Ortony (ed.), *Metaphor and Thought* (Cambridge: Cambridge University Press, 1993[2]), 34). Cf. J.J.A. Mooij, *A Study of Metaphor: On the Nature of Metaphorical Expressions, with Special Reference to Their Reference*; N-HLS 27 (Oxford: North-Holland, 1976), ch. 2, esp. p. 26; J.R. Searle, 'Metaphor', in A. Ortony (ed.), *Metaphor and Thought* (Cambridge: Cambridge University Press, 1993[2]), 103. For further scholars, see the overview in J.G. van der Watt, *Family of the King: Dynamics of Metaphor in the Gospel according to John*; BJS 47 (Leiden: Brill, 2000), 7–8.

[82] Dawes, *Body*, 50; cf. 51–52; M. Brändl, *Der Agon bei Paulus: Herkunft und Profil paulinischer Agonmetaphorik*; WUNT II/222 (Tübingen: Mohr Siebeck, 2006), 233–35. One way to recognize such a 'semantic impertinence' (P. Ricœur, *The Rule of Metaphor: Multi-disciplinary Studies of the Creation of Meaning in Language* (London/Henley: Routledge & Kegan Paul, 1978), 132) is to review the 'typicality conditions' (R. Jackendoff, *Semantics and Cognition*; CSLS 8 (London: MIT Press, 1995 [1983[1]]), 121–22) of the tenor and the vehicle. In other words, it is helpful to investigate the defining characteristics of both tenor (here: 'Holy Spirit') and vehicle (here: [something] 'poured') and consider whether or not they can be linked on a literal level (for more details and examples, see D.H. Aaron, *Biblical Ambiguities: Metaphor, Semantics and Divine Imagery*; BRLAJ 4 (Leiden: Brill, 2001), 40–41, 77–79).

In order to identify metaphors it may be of further help to know what metaphors can look like. Of the various classifications of metaphors that have been offered, Baldauf provides one of the most nuanced ones. She specifies attribute, ontological, picture-schematic and constellation metaphors (C. Baldauf, *Metapher und Kognition: Grundlagen einer neuen Theorie der Alltagsmetapher*; SGBS 24 (Frankfurt: Lang, 1997), 83–84). See particularly her analysis of ontological and picture-schematic metaphors, as the OT/NT Spirit-metaphors fit mainly into these two categories (Baldauf, *Metapher*, 119–38).

for the strengthening by the Spirit a phrase that is associated with *literal liquid* (cf. the physical imagery in vv.7b–9). The judgment that one is dealing in this (and similar) Qumran text(s) about the Spirit with meta-phor(s) is thus confirmed.

Apart from that, in the case of the Spirit-language of the DSS the inter-textuality with Old Testament Spirit-metaphors raises the expectation that one is here dealing with metaphors too. The Old Testament evidences such a huge variety of examples of Spirit-language that, when interpreting them literally, it would be difficult to assign a particular concept of the Spirit to each different phrase. For example, what ontology of the Spirit would be implied by the assertion that the Spirit 'clothed himself with Gideon' (Jdg. 6:34), and how would such an ontology line up with the Spirit being 'on' (Num. 11:25–26; Isa. 32:15; Joel 2:28–29; etc.), 'rushing on' (Jdg. 14:6; etc.), 'with' (Exod. 31:3; Dan. 4:9; Mic. 3:8; etc.) or 'in' (Gen. 6:3; Num. 27:18; Dan. 5:14; etc.) people? As both individual writers as well as the Old Testament in general freely vary the kinds of (mutually inconsistent) usage of Spirit-locutions, it seems that they do not consider them literal forms of language,[83] particularly as they often appear in literary genres where non-literal language abounds (prayers, prophecies, psalms, etc.).[84]

This point is clearly apparent when looking at the expression that God 'pours out' his Spirit. While the meaning of 'pour out' may be literal (where the object is plainly so, as in the case of water), non-literal usage abounds in the Old Testament, having objects such as anger (Isa. 42:25; Jer. 44:6), wrath (Jer. 10:25; Ezek. 7:8; etc.), indignation (Ezek. 21:31), heart (Ps. 62:8; Lam. 2:19), soul (Isa. 53:12), life (Lam. 2:11), lust (Ezek. 23:8), folly (Prov. 15:2), wickedness (Prov. 15:28; Jer. 14:16), words (Ps. 94:4; Sir. 39.6), thoughts (Prov. 1:23), proverbs (Sir. 18.9), teaching (Sir. 24.33), blessing (Isa. 44:3; Mal. 3:10), grace (Ps. 45:2), praise (Ps. 119:171), wisdom (Sir. 50.27), etc. Against this background it would be erroneous to presuppose that the collocation of 'pour out' with 'Spirit' is literal and that Spirit thus must be a fluid substance. This is particularly obvious when other tropes used in connection with רוח suggest a different meaning.[85]

---

[83] Cf. G.B. Caird, *The Language and Imagery of the Bible* (London: Duckworth, 1980), 190, who makes clear that the juxtaposition of a number of different images in a text is a mark of the linguistic awareness of the writer that she is using metaphors.

[84] Cf. M.M.B. Turner, 'Spirit Endowment in Luke-Acts: Some Linguistic Considera-tions', *VoxEv* 12 (1981), 56–58. Searl rightly remarks that one cue for spotting meta-phorical utterances is the knowledge that certain literary genres, like poetry, are more prone to metaphorical language than others (Searle, 'Metaphor', 103).

[85] On this see M. Turner, '"Trinitarian" Pneumatology in the New Testament? – To-wards an Explanation of the Worship of Jesus', *ATJ* 57 (2003), 178–79.

On the point of method it should be noted further that an *a priori* decision to interpret every utterance literally unless one is forced to do otherwise does not do justice to the process of interpretation. This becomes clear when one looks at the negation of the metaphorical statement 'Man is a wolf': 'Man is not a wolf' could be either metaphorical or literal! Only by enquiring the context is it possible to decide for one of the two options.[86]

3) Finally, some principles for interpreting metaphors should be singled out. In section a) the importance of analysing the contexts of metaphors will be elucidated and under b) we will discuss whether and how one can gain closer access to the meaning of a metaphor by paraphrasing it.

a) 'Contexts' of metaphors. Fowler has provided a helpful interpretative matrix for understanding texts. He emphasizes that any unit of communication has to be understood within three contexts: context of utterance, of culture and of reference.[87] We will briefly look at each of these and apply them to the Qumran text under discussion.

Firstly, one needs to identify the *context of utterance*, the situation within which discourse is conducted. This context comprises the (physical) surroundings in which the communication takes place, the relation of the participants of the discourse to each other, and the channel of communication employed. In the case of a letter, for example, the context of utterance is split; that is to say, the text is written and received at different times and in different places.[88] Most likely this is also true for the *Hodayot*. The writer of 1QH[a] 15.6–25, possibly a/the t/Teacher, composed and recorded a prayer of thanksgiving for God's help to him, which was probably re-used at a later stage on special communal occasions, like being chanted at a banquet celebrated by the community or recited by newly initiated members at the Feast of the Renewal of the Covenant.[89] However, as no first-hand data about the context of utterance of 1QH[a] 15.6–25 is available, one should refrain from drawing firm conclusions from this parameter for the interpretation of the metaphor concerned.

---

[86] Cf. J.M. Soskice, 'Metaphor und Offenbarung', in J.-P. van Noppen (ed.), *Erinnern, um Neues zu sagen: Die Bedeutung der Metapher für die religiöse Sprache* (Frankfurt: Athenäum, 1988), 80; Black, 'Metaphor', 34; S. Glucksberg, 'How Metaphors Create Categories – Quickly', in R.W. Gibbs, Jr. (ed.), *The Cambridge Handbook of Metaphor and Thought* (Cambridge: Cambridge University Press, 2008), 68, 70.

[87] R. Fowler, *Linguistic Criticism*; Opus (Oxford: Oxford University Press, 1996[2]), 110–16. Cf. P. Cotterell and M. Turner, *Linguistics and Biblical Interpretation* (Downers Grove: IVP, 1989), 301.

[88] Fowler, *Criticism*, 112–13.

[89] Cf. Philo, *Vit. Cont.* 80. Cf. G. Vermes, *The Complete Dead Sea Scrolls in English* (London: Penguin, 1995[4]), 244.

Secondly, in order to interpret a metaphor properly, one needs to take into consideration the *context of culture*. This, according to Fowler, is 'the whole network of social and economic conventions, all the institutions and familiar settings and relationships, constituting the culture at large, especially insofar as these bear on particular utterance contexts'.[90] Against this background we can agree with Machamer's statement that 'we should *ask not about the meaning of metaphors but about how people understand metaphors*',[91] because 'to comprehend is to give structure to the mind by forming a model, and this structure takes its form from our perceptions and prior knowledge of the world, including the social world (which itself includes language)'.[92]

Applied to the interpretation of 1QH[a] 15.7, this means that the comprehension of the phrase 'your Holy Spirit you have poured over me' depends on *a priori* conceptions of the Spirit. If the Qumran sectarians who used this phrase were accustomed to the idea that the Holy Spirit is a material substance (although the grounds for this assumption would need first to be established) they might very well apply this spectrum of meaning to the idiom (as scholars like Betz and Horn do).[93] However, if the Qumran believers did not have such a view of the Spirit, a metaphorical interpretation of the phrase would suggest itself, as 'by their tensions and collisions certain metaphors continue to call us beyond the literal meaning of words and let their figurative meaning become active'.[94] In this case the Qumran members might have interpreted the phrase on the basis of its intertextuality with similar Old Testament phraseology encapsulating Spirit-experiences,[95] or against the background of their own experience.[96]

---

[90] Fowler, *Criticism*, 114.

[91] P. Machamer, 'The Meaning of Metaphor: A Plea for Understanding', in T. Borsche, et al. (eds.), *Blick und Bild im Spannungsfeld von Sehen, Metaphern und Verstehen*; SAM III (Munich: Fink, 1998), 255. Cf. S.R. Levin, 'Language, Concepts, and Worlds: Three Domains of Metaphor', in A. Ortony (ed.), *Metaphor and Thought* (Cambridge: Cambridge University Press, 1993[2]), 122–23. Soskice remarks with regard to the recipient of the metaphor: 'It is one's metaphysics, not metaphor which is at issue' (Soskice, *Metaphor*, 90).

[92] Machamer, 'Meaning', 257. This point can be illustrated by Machamer's example 'e-mail is ruining thought'. One will only understand (though perhaps not agree with the truth-claim of) this metaphor if one can construct a model for what 'ruining thought' could mean, and if one knows what e-mail is (Machamer, 'Meaning', 260).

[93] On the pre-scientific metaphysics of the ancient Hebrew world, cf. 2.2.1. above.

[94] K. Harries, 'The Many Uses of Metaphor', in S. Sacks (ed.), *On Metaphor* (Chicago: University of Chicago Press, 1981), 169.

[95] These locutions may have become 'dead metaphors' by the time the *Hodayot* was written. (See Baldauf, *Metapher*, 86, for a critical discussion of the concept of 'dead metaphors'.)

Thirdly, one needs to look at the *context of reference*, which is 'the topic or subject-matter of a text', in order to receive a metaphor adequately.[97] On a similar note, Cotterell and Turner explicate that one's comprehension of a metaphor is enhanced by the availability of a cotext from which the purpose of the metaphor might be deduced.[98]

1QH[a] 15.7 is placed within the cotext of 15.6–25, which is – particularly in the immediate cotext (vv.6, 8) – concerned with God's strengthening of the writer. It is not an academic discourse on the nature of the Spirit but an emotive hymn of thanksgiving. Therefore, it is highly unlikely that the metaphor was intended to convey insights about a topic (i.e. the ontology of the Spirit) that is *not* the subject-matter.[99] As has been pointed out in section 2.2.1., one would rather need a philosophical dis-

---

[96] It is important that both creator and recipient of a metaphor share a range of experiences because these form part of one's presupposition pool. See Machamer, 'Meaning', 261; Cotterell and Turner, *Linguistics*, 300–301.

[97] Fowler, *Criticism*, 114.

[98] Cotterell and Turner, *Linguistics*, 301; on 'cotext' (or literary context): 16; cf. U. Eco, *Semiotics and the Philosophy of Language*; Advances in Semiotics (Bloomington: Indiana University Press, 1984), 123.

[99] Both author(s) and recipients of metaphorical speech may nevertheless hold certain views about the Spirit as part of their presupposition pool. However, these presuppositions need to be reconctructed on the basis of less ambiguous evidence (on this see above).

The same methodological criticism needs to be applied to the way in which Davies quotes Rabbinic sources in support of a similar hypothesis (W.D. Davies, *Paul and Rabbinic Judaism: Some Rabbinic Elements in Pauline Theology* (Philadelphia: Fortress, 1980[4] [1948[1]]), 184–85, building on J. Abelson, *The Immanence of God in Rabbinical Literature* (London/New York: Hermon, 1969 [1912[1]]), 212–221; however, Abelson can also be read differently: see Hill, *Words*, 233, 274). For one thing, Davies fails to give textual evidence for the assumption that Hebrews conceived of light, fire and sound as matter. Moreover, also his only case that is indeed suggestive of a physical concept of the Spirit, i.e. *Lev. Rab.* 15.2, seems to crumble when one looks at the cotext. Particularly the parallel thought of

weight of the wind (Job 28:25) ~ weight of the Spirit on a prophet (R. Aha)
    (1.A.–C.), and

measuring of the waters (Job 28:25) ~ measures of the Torah (R. Yudan b. R. Samuel)
    (1.F.–H.)

indicates that to arrive at conclusions about the nature of the substance of the Spirit/ Torah on the basis of the physicalities of the vehicles 'weight'/'measures of' would mean to appeal to aspects of the literal referents that have no relation to the context of reference, because to comprehend the instalments of the Torah (Scripture, Mishnah, Talmud, etc.) as having the same physical substance as water would be absurd. Similarly, one cannot infer that the Spirit of prophecy has the same material essence as the 'weight of the wind', simply because the two are brought together in this allegorical construction. Rather, the main point of R. Aha seems to be that the work of the Spirit is not of same intensity with every individual prophet.

course with mainly literal language to establish the conception of the Spirit that is held by a given group of people. Such a systematic reflection about the nature of the Spirit is provided by the theologian Pannenberg, to give an illustration for what we do *not* find at Qumran. He uses the modern Spirit-metaphor 'force field' not only as a model for how the Spirit works but also for what it is. In the case of Pannenberg we have a writer (as well as readers) whose context of culture clearly comprises the knowledge of ancient and modern physics and philosophy, so that he is able (and willing) to unfold the various aspects of the model of force fields, and in this course he explicitly discusses the materiality/immateriality of the Spirit.[100]

b) Paraphrasing metaphors. We have finally reached the significant question, whether and how one can express without the metaphor concerned at least part of the spectrum of meaning that the metaphor maybe designed to convey. On the first part of the question, it has already been indicated under 1) that this study is conducted in line with the consensus of modern metaphor theorists, who emphasize that 'no metaphor is completely reducible to a literal equivalent without consequent loss of content'.[101] Some scholars take this position so far as declaring that a metaphor cannot be explained or paraphrased at all.[102]

However, there is a more balanced view. For example, Eco argues that 'if a metaphor has epistemological value, then it ought to be possible to paraphrase it'.[103] Consequently, while interpreting a metaphor does not mean searching for one unique paraphrase, it nevertheless means searching

---

[100] W. Pannenberg, *Systematische Theologie. Vol. 1* (Göttingen: Vandenhoeck & Ruprecht, 1988), 414–16. Alternatively, see Welker's detailed application to pneumatology of the force field model which refrains from going as far as philosophizing about the physical/non-physical nature of the Spirit (M. Welker, *God the Spirit* (Minneapolis: Fortress, 1994), 239–48).

For an exposition of what Hengel thinks are Essenic tendencies of trying to systematically comprehend the mysterious, see M. Hengel, 'Qumrân und der Hellenismus', in M. Delcor (ed.), *Qumrân: Sa piété, sa théologie et son milieu*; BETL 46 (Paris/Gembloux/Leuven: LUP, 1978), esp. 371–72.

On the conception of theory-constitutive metaphors (in science) as opposed to literary metaphors, see R. Boyd, 'Metaphor and Theory Change: What is "Metaphor" a Metaphor for?', in A. Ortony (ed.), *Metaphor and Thought* (Cambridge: Cambridge University Press, 1993²), 488–90, 521.

[101] Soskice, *Metaphor*, 94.

[102] So, e.g., Black, *Models*, 237; M. Hesse, 'Die kognitiven Ansprüche der Metaphern', in J.-P. van Noppen (ed.), *Erinnern, um Neues zu sagen: Die Bedeutung der Metapher für die religiöse Sprache* (Frankfurt: Athenäum, 1988), 133–34.

[103] U. Eco, *Die Grenzen der Interpretation* (Munich: Carl Hauser, 1992), 212. The exceptions are dead metaphors.

for principles that will narrow down the choice of possible paraphrases to a plausible set of alternatives.[104]

With regard to 1QH[a] 15.6–7, some principles for narrowing down the choice of possible paraphrases of line 7a have been identified in the above discussion of the contexts of the metaphor. We have seen that a writer (and later perhaps a community) expresses in a pre-scientific, Hebrew setting his gratefulness to God in a hymn of thanksgiving (possibly alluding to the metaphorical promise of the 'out-poured' Spirit in Isa. 44:3–4). When it comes to finding a plausible set of alternative paraphrases for what the speaker may have wanted to convey with the metaphor 'your Holy Spirit you have poured over me', the cotext proves in this case to be of particular help:

a 'you have upheld me with your strength' (v.6b)
a' 'your Holy Spirit you have poured over me so that I will not stumble' (v.7a).

The parallelism of line 6b and line 7a suggests a similar meaning of the two sentences (cf. the intertextuality with the parallelism of Isa. 44:3a and v.3b, followed up by 44:4–5).[105] One possible paraphrase for line 7a could therefore be 'you have strengthened me by your Holy Spirit so that I will not stumble'.[106] However, one might argue that this paraphrase reduces to nothing the emotive character of refreshing waters being poured upon the writer. As an alternative one could therefore propound: 'you have caused me to experience the power of your Holy Spirit', or 'you have refreshed me by your Holy Spirit so that I will not stumble'.[107]

---

[104] Cf. G.A. Miller, 'Images and Models, Similes and Metaphors', in A. Ortony (ed.), *Metaphor and Thought* (Cambridge: Cambridge University Press, 1993[2]), 392; Searle, 'Metaphor', 103–104. Halliday therefore prefers to speak of the 'congruent', rather than the 'literal' expression that somewhat corresponds to the metaphorical expression (M.A.K. Halliday, *Introduction to Functional Grammar* (London: Arnold, 1985), 321).

[105] Cf. M. Fatehi, *The Spirit's Relation to the Risen Lord in Paul: An Examination of Its Christological Implications*; WUNT II/128 (Tübingen: Mohr Siebeck, 2000), 70. Cf. 1QH[a] 15.7–8: 'you have fortified me against the wars of wickedness' and 'you placed me like a sturdy tower'. For a detailed structural analysis of 15:6–25, see Um, *Temple*, 95–97.

[106] It should be noted that the phraseology of being 'upheld' and 'not stumbling' is also metaphorical. *Per contra*, see the non-figurative language of 1QH[a] 8.15: I look 'to be strengthened by [your] ho[ly] spirit... to serve you in truth...'.

On the justification of the method of paraphrasing that has been applied, see further M. Leezenberg, *Contexts of Metaphor: Semantic and Conceptual Aspects of Figurative Language Interpretation*; ILLCDS 1995–17 (Amsterdam: Elsevier, 1995), 186.

[107] Baumgarten suggests that a combination of רוח and יצק ('to pour'; our text uses הניף, as discussed above), may indicate a purifying activity of the Spirit (J.M. Baumgarten, 'The Law and Spirit of Purity at Qumran', in J.H. Charlesworth (ed.), *The Bible and the Dead Sea Scrolls: The Second Princeton Symposium on Judaism and Christian Origins. Vol. 2* (Waco: Baylor University Press, 2006), 101). While this meaning cannot

Once again, some may still ask whether one should not try to carry over the material denotation of the literal referent of the modifying term (a fluid being poured) to the primary subject (Spirit). However, to do so would be a methodologically questionable undertaking, both on the grounds of the contexts of the metaphor which indicate that this aspect does not appear to have been an option in the original setting, as well as from the point of view of semantics. For metaphors in a given co(n)text do not have two meanings, one literal and one metaphorical, but one meaning.[108] This meaning is constituted by the interplay of tenor and vehicle because, as we have already observed, 'by their tensions and collisions... metaphors... call us beyond the literal meaning of words and let their figurative meaning become active'.[109] It needs to be decided on the basis of the context, which of the defining characteristics of the (literal) vehicle are intended to give new definition to the tenor in order to convey (figurative) meaning.[110]

How strongly figurative each metaphor is, however, needs to be decided in each individual case. Some non-literal language may be what Aaron calls 'ascriptive' or 'weakly figurative', whereas other statements are 'strongly figurative'. The actual placing of a particular statement on the continuum between 'literal meaning' on one side and 'nonsense' on the other depends on how one judges the degree of convergence of the defining characteristics of the tenor and the vehicle. In the case of major convergence, a phrase is 'less metaphorical' than in the case of minor convergence. Aaron has helpfully illustrated this 'gradient model of the meaning continuum' with the following diagram:[111]

---

be excluded in our passage, there is also no indication that it is intended (e.g. by cultic language – unless one comprehends הניף against the background of a wave offering).

[108] Soskice, *Metaphor*, 85; cf. Eco, *Grenzen*, 215; Beardsley, 'Metaphor', 220. See esp. the nuanced discussion in Glucksberg, 'Metaphors', 73, 78.

[109] Harries, 'Uses', 169. See also the broader discussion in Glucksberg, 'Metaphors', 68, 70, 74; R. Giora, 'Is Metaphor Unique?', in R.W. Gibbs, Jr. (ed.), *The Cambridge Handbook of Metaphor and Thought* (Cambridge: Cambridge University Press, 2008), 150, 156.

[110] Cf. M.C. Beardsley, *Aesthetics from Classical Greece to the Present: A Short History* (New York: Macmillan, 1966), 144; cf. further Ricœur, *Rule*, 96–99; R. Zimmermann, 'Einführung: Bildersprache verstehen oder Die offene Sinndynamik der Sprachbilder', in R. Zimmermann, *Bildersprache verstehen: Zur Hermeneutik der Metapher und anderer bildlicher Sprachformen*; Übergänge 38 (Munich: Fink, 2000), 30–33.

[111] Aaron, *Ambiguities*, 112; cf. 28–29, 59–67, 122–24.

The Meaning Continuum and the Relative Role of Ambiguity

As ambiguity increases, so do the resonances of non-literal meaning,
until one reaches levels of obscurity that result in nonsense.

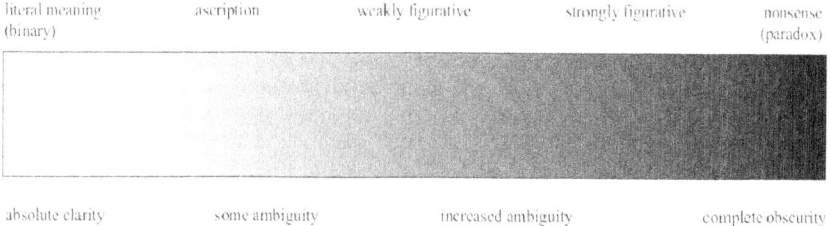

literal meaning (binary)	ascription	weakly figurative	strongly figurative	nonsense (paradox)

absolute clarity	some ambiguity	increased ambiguity	complete obscurity

Again, we can use Philippians 4:18 to illustrate this insight. It can be attested that the semantic tension that has been observed in the sentence 'I have received... the gifts you sent, a fragrant offering, a sacrifice acceptable and pleasing to God' calls beyond the literal meaning of 'fragrance'. A semantically absurd carrying over of all aspects of the vehicle would be, for instance, to declare that the gifts of the Philippians have the same physical nature as that of a fragrance (unless it was a bottle of perfume, of course). However, nothing in the contexts of the metaphor indicates that this aspect of 'fragrance' could be triggered in verse 18. Rather, it is much more likely that 'in speaking of the Philippians' gifts as a "fragrant odour" Paul is asserting that they are of the highest worth since they are pleasing to God'.[112]

Also in 1QH[a] 15.7 one needs to untie the vehicle 'poured out' from those denotations and connotations which are not activated by the context and seek those which *are* invoked by it (i.e. 'to ask for the similar within the dissimilar'[113]). The new meaning that results from speaking of the Spirit in terms which are appropriate for the pouring of water in the contexts of 15.7 is constituted by the new insight that is conveyed into how the Qumran-believer was strengthened by God: it was through the life-giving and refreshing power of God's Holy Spirit. The material denotation of water is not invoked in this context. Nor is a material denotation of wind or air (in the case of the rendering of הניף as 'wave/spread') invoked in this context.[114]

---

[112] P.T. O'Brien, *The Epistle to the Philippians: A Commentary on the Greek Text*; NIGTC (Grand Rapids: Eerdmans, 1991), 541. Cf. the parallels that 1QH[a] 15.7 would have with this interpretation of Phil. 4:18 should הניף be comprehended against the background of a wave offering.

[113] Schart, 'Gestalt', 35.

[114] On this see further 2.2.1.

For this study of the nature and work of the Spirit in the DSS (as well as for other literature, including that of Paul) it can be *concluded*, therefore, that it is methodologically illegitimate to base one's theory of how a community thought about the materiality/immateriality of the Spirit solely on metaphorical language in contexts that do not indicate that this question could be under consideration.[115] No scholar has provided instances of non-metaphorical language (as the philosophic discourses of Hellenism) in the DSS that would bear upon the question whether the Spirit is to be understood as a substance, which leads to the conclusion that there is no reason for believing that this concept and concern played a role in Qumran pneumatology. Accordingly, there is also no basis for assuming that the work of the Spirit was conceptualized as infusion-transformation in the Qumran community.

2.3. *Joseph and Aseneth*

The Jewish-Hellenistic romance *Joseph and Aseneth* (probably written in the second half of the first century CE)[116] has been taken as evidence for

---

[115] Cf. the statements in C.H. Pinnock, 'The Concept of the Spirit in the Epistles of Paul' (Manchester University: Unpublished PhD Thesis, 1963), 26–27; R. Lauha, *Psychophysischer Sprachgebrauch im Alten Testament: Eine Strukturalsemantische Analyse von לב, נפש und רוח*; AASF.DHL 35 (Helsinki: Tiedeakatemia, 1983), 240–41; Rabens, 'Development', 170–71 (followed by W. Schenk, 'Wortforschung: II. Neues Testament', *TRE*, XXXVI, 336). See more generally on the pneumatological language of OT and DSS: Fatehi, *Relation*, 80; Wenk, *Power*, 110.

[116] See the discussion in R.D. Chesnutt, *From Death to Life: Conversion in Joseph and Aseneth*; JSPSup 16 (Sheffield: Sheffield Academic Press, 1995), 80–85; M. Vogel, 'Einführung', in E. Reinmuth (ed.), *Joseph und Aseneth*; SAPERE 15 (Tübingen: Mohr Siebeck, 2009), 12–15. This majority view has been challenged by R.S. Kraemer, *When Aseneth Met Joseph: A Late Antique Tale of the Biblical Patriarch and His Egyptian Wife, Reconsidered* (Oxford: Oxford University Press, 1998), *passim* (cf. Bauckham's agreement in R. Bauckham, 'Review of R.S. Kraemer, *When Aseneth Met Joseph: A Late Antique Tale of the Biblical Patriarch and His Egyptian Wife, Reconsidered*', *JTS* 51 (2000), 226–28). She thinks that the book may have been written in the third or fourth century CE. She also raises doubts about the novel's supposed Jewish origin; and she argues that the shorter text used by Philonenko is earlier than the longer version employed by C. Burchard (M. Philonenko, *Joseph et Aséneth: Introduction, Texte Critique, Traduction et Notes*; SPB 13 (Leiden: Brill, 1968); C. Burchard, 'Ein vorläufiger griechischer Text von Joseph und Aseneth', in C. Burchard, *Gesammelte Studien zu Joseph und Aseneth. Berichtigt und ergänzt herausgegeben mit Unterstützung von Carsten Burfeind*; SVTP 13 (Leiden: Brill, 1996), 161–209; translated by C. Burchard, 'Joseph and Aseneth: A New Translation and Introduction', *OTP*, II, 177–247). However, Humphrey has cogently challenged Kraemer's case (E.M. Humphrey, *Joseph and Aseneth*; GAP (Sheffield: Sheffield Academic Press, 2000), 19–21, 35–37; cf. R.D. Chesnutt, 'Review of R.S. Kraemer, *When Aseneth Met Joseph: A Late Antique Tale of the Biblical Patriarch and His Egyptian Wife, Reconsidered*', *JBL* 119 (2000), 760–62; Vogel, 'Einführung', 12–13).

the presence of the idea of Spirit-worked infusion-transformation of the believer in Hellenistic Judaism. We will discuss the two aspects of this concept in two separate subsections.

2.3.1. The Physical Spirit

Joseph and Aseneth is believed chiefly by Sänger and Horn to contain a physical conception of the Spirit. Sänger claims that the book draws on Jewish wisdom theology which is heavily influenced by Stoicism. Focusing on the heavenly gift of a honeycomb which is said to be πνεῦμα ζωῆς in 16.14, Sänger argues that *Joseph and Aseneth* gives evidence of the Stoic principle that everything that exists is 'körperlich-substanzhaft'. In the case of *Joseph and Aseneth* this principle is applied to the abstract, theological-philosophical entity wisdom/*Weisheitspneuma* which is understood to be transmitted substantially through the honeycomb.[117] Horn builds on Sänger's view and adds that 'ein substanzhaftes Pneumaverständnis... sakramental vermittelt war' through bread and drink (8.9) and through Joseph's kiss (19.11).[118] He concludes that it is obvious that one can only comprehend this conception on the basis of the Hellenistic presupposition that πνεῦμα is a substance.[119]

However, is all of this really so obvious? While it is *possible* that such a conception of πνεῦμα is in the background of *Joseph and Aseneth*, it will be argued here that this conclusion is not at all pressing. For one thing, the 'difficulties of genre,... proper text, original language, date and provenance, function, and... "message"'[120] of the work should prevent us from drawing firm conclusions concerning the philosophical concepts that may or may not have been in its background. What is more, those who have in the past tried to determine the precise characteristics of πνεῦμα in *Joseph and Aseneth* have failed to base their theories on a method of interpretation that is adequate to the actual genre of this piece of literature. The following analysis will therefore try to treat 8.9, 16.14 and 19.11 in accordance with

---

Our study is hence conducted in line with the majority view regarding text, date and background of *Jos. Asen.*.

[117] D. Sänger, *Antikes Judentum und die Mysterien: Religionsgeschichtliche Untersuchungen zu Joseph und Aseneth*; WUNT II/5 (Tübingen: J.C.B. Mohr (Paul Siebeck), 1980), 196–97.

[118] Horn, *Angeld*, 59. Cf. E. Brandenburger, 'Die Auferstehung der Glaubenden als historisches und theologisches Problem', *WD* 9 (1967), 25.

[119] Horn, *Angeld*, 44–45 n.11.

[120] E.M. Humphrey, *The Ladies and the Cities: Transformation and Apocalyptic Identity in Joseph and Aseneth, 4 Ezra, the Apocalypse and the Shepherd of Hermas*; JSPSup 17 (Sheffield: Sheffield Academic Press, 1995), 31.

the genre (which will be discussed first) and linguistic structure within which they occur.[121]

As far as the genre (and authorship) of *Joseph and Aseneth* is concerned, Philonenko summarizes his research thus: '*Joseph et Aséneth* est un roman mystique, écrit en grec, à l'époque romaine, par un Juif d'origine égyptienne.'[122] While most scholars agree that *Joseph and Aseneth* should be classified as a novel or 'romance in the wider sense of the word',[123] some lay stronger emphasis on the *Jewish* character of the book than Philonenko. For example, Ruppert highlights *Joseph and Aseneth*'s midrashic nature and Pervo puts forward that it should be understood as a Jewish Sapiential Novel.[124] However, it is difficult (and for our purposes not crucial) to give a clear-cut definition of the very specifics of the genre of *Joseph and Aseneth*.[125] Nevertheless, it should be clear from these preliminary considerations that reading and interpreting a work of which 'the first two thirds... are occupied with symbolic and allegorical narrative'[126] and which contains apocalyptic material,[127] will require particular sensitivity towards this very imagery and literary structure on which the novel is built.

We will therefore begin by carefully analysing the linguistic structure of Joseph's prayer for Aseneth in 8.9. Although Horn's claim is based primarily on the appeal to God in C_{1a} and $C_{2a\ b}$, it is important to understand the position of these lines within the entire linguistic unit because the appeal is thematically foreshadowed in the address (*A–B*):

---

[121] The evidence on which Sänger and Horn rest their arguments concerning the latter two verses (namely, the phrase τοῦτο τὸ κηρίον ἐστὶ πνεῦμα ζωῆς in 16.14 and the Spirit-transferral through Joseph's kiss in 19.11) do not occur in the shorter text of Philonenko.

[122] Philonenko, *Joseph*, 109.

[123] Burchard, 'Joseph', 186; Vogel, 'Einführung', 6–11.

[124] L. Ruppert, 'Liebe und Bekehrung: Zur Typologie des Romans Josef und Asenat', in F. Link (ed.), *Paradeigmata: Literarische Typologie des Alten Testaments. Vol. 1*; SL 5/1 (Berlin: Duncker & Humbolt, 1989), 35; R.I. Pervo, 'Joseph and Aseneth and the Greek Novel', *SBLSP* 112 (1976), 171.

[125] Cf. Chesnutt, *Death*, 90.

[126] Pervo, 'Aseneth', 175.

[127] Cf. Humphrey, *Ladies*, 35.

A	κύριε ὁ θεὸς τοῦ πατρός μου Ἰσραὴλ
	ὁ ὕψιστος ὁ δυνατὸς τοῦ Ἰακὼβ

B	ὁ ζωοποιήσας τὰ πάντα
B₁ₐ	καὶ καλέσας ἀπὸ τοῦ σκότους εἰς τὸ φῶς
b	καὶ ἀπὸ τῆς πλάνης εἰς τὴν ἀλήθειαν
c	καὶ ἀπὸ τοῦ θανάτου εἰς τὴν ζωὴν

C	σὺ κύριε εὐλόγησον τὴν παρθένον ταύτην
C₁ₐ	καὶ ἀνακαίνισον αὐτὴν τῷ πνεύματί σου
b	καὶ ἀνάπλασον αὐτὴν τῇ χειρί σου τῇ [κρυφαίᾳ]
c	καὶ ἀναζωοποίησον αὐτὴν τῇ ζωῇ σου
C₂ₐ	καὶ φαγέτω ἄρτον ζωῆς σου
b	καὶ πιέτω ποτήριον εὐλογίας σου
C₃	καὶ συγκαταρίθμησον αὐτὴν τῷ λαῷ σου
	ὃ ἐξελέξω πρὶν γενέσθαι τὰ πάντα
C₄	καὶ εἰσελθέτω εἰς τὴν κατάπαυσίν σου
	ἣν ἡτοίμασας τοῖς ἐκλεκτοῖς σου
C₅	καὶ ζησάτω ἐν τῇ αἰωνίῳ ζωῇ σου εἰς τὸν αἰῶνα χρόνον.

The structure of the prayer can be delineated in the following way:

A Address: invocation (directed to God)

B Address: introductory description (of God) with unparalleled syntax
- which is spelled out by a thematic unit of three syntactically identical subordinate clauses ($B_{1a\,c}$).

C Appeal: introductory imperative clause (directed to God) with unparalleled syntax
- which is spelled out by a thematic unit of three syntactically identical subordinate clauses ($C_{1a\,c}$):
- καί + verb imper. aor. act. 2nd sing. with prefix ἀνα- + αὐτήν + def. art. + dat. obj. + σου
- which is spelled out further by a thematic unit of two syntactically identical subordinate clauses, differing from the preceding triad with regard to syntax (and content) ($C_{2a\,b}$):
- καί + verb imper. aor. act. 3rd sing. + acc. obj. + gen. attrib. + σου
- which is spelled out further by three subordinate clauses with independent syntax and content ($C_{3\,5}$).

Within the appeal, lines $C_{1a\,c}$ form a parallelism with identical syntax, and so do $C_{2a\,b}$. However, the relation of C_1 and C_2 cannot truly be seen as a parallelism because a similar (or even identical) syntactical structure is missing. In the same way, lines $C_{3\,5}$ too do not form a parallelism with C_1 or C_2. It is therefore precarious to argue that bread and cup ($C_{2a\,b}$) should be understood as the *means* by which the renewal by the Spirit (C_{1a}) is established. This is even more so as $C_{2a\ b}$ do not form the immediate cotext of C_{1a} because $C_{1b\ c}$ are placed between them.

However, even if ἄρτος and ποτήριον were instrumentally related to πνεῦμα in Joseph's prayer, it does not follow that the Spirit was therefore thought to be transferred *materially* through a physical piece of bread or a drink from the cup. The cardinal reason why it is not at all necessary to hold this view of the pneumatology of *Joseph and Aseneth* lies in the fact that this thesis rests on an unproven assumption, namely, that bread and cup are to be understood as a ritual or sacrament. While a number of scholars hold this position, another group of interpreters has convincingly argued that bread and cup rather function as a symbol for the entire Jewish way of life.[128] So, should there indeed be a connection between C_{1a} and $C_{2a\ b}$, it nevertheless remains precarious to infer from this that the Spirit was believed to be a material substance as it is the life *more judaico* (and here perhaps particularly the relational aspect of table-fellowship) that bread and cup symbolize, rather than connoting physical substance(s) which transmit transformation (cf. 21.21 with 21.13–14; cf. further: 8.5).

However, even if bread and cup did refer to a cultic meal, it does not need to follow that the Spirit was therefore perceived to be transferred (materially) through these elements, at least as far as the remainder of the book is concerned. The reason for this objection is simple: nowhere in the conversion narrative does Aseneth actually eat bread or drink from a cup! Instead, Aseneth is given a honeycomb to eat (16.15–16). It is this honeycomb to which we now turn.

Charlesworth aptly summarizes the state of research when he says that 'the sacred meal and the honeycomb... have utterly defied our attempts to explain them'.[129] Even Sänger admits that the giving of a heavenly honeycomb to Aseneth belongs to the scenes most difficult to interpret.[130] While it is generally recognized that the honeycomb alludes to manna (Exod. 16:31), different suggestions have been made with regard to its theological

---

[128] So, e.g., C. Burchard, 'The Importance of Joseph and Aseneth for the Study of the New Testament: A General Survey and a Fresh Look at the Lord's Supper', *NTS* 33 (1987), 109–117; R. Schnackenburg, *Das Johannesevangelium. Vol. 4: Ergänzende Auslegungen und Exkurse*; HTKNT 4 (Freiburg: Herder, 1994³ [1984¹]), 128; Chesnutt, *Death*, 130–31; Vogel, 'Einführung', 20. For an overview of both positions, see Chesnutt, *Death*, 128, ch.1.

[129] J.H. Charlesworth, *The Old Testament Pseudepigrapha and the New Testament: Prolegomena for the Study of Christian Origins*; SNTSMS/OTPNT 54 (Cambridge: Cambridge University Press, 1985), 25.

[130] Sänger, *Judentum*, 191. Humphrey goes yet further by suggesting that the resistance to interpretation may be inherent in the text, because the passage might well be 'for mystification, not for interpretation' (Humphrey, *Ladies*, 54 n.52).

significance. As these have been discussed by previous scholarship,[131] it will suffice here to highlight a few difficulties that one is confronted with when emphasizing the *physical* nature of the Spirit on the basis of a *physical* honeycomb.

Is the honeycomb a physical object? At face value this truly seems to be the case because in the story Aseneth literally eats a part of it (16.15).[132] However, the question is whether the author is really concerned with this aspect of the narrative event. It appears that he or she is not,[133] for otherwise the dew of the roses of life that was collected by the bees of the paradise of delight (16.14) would need to be interpreted as being physical too since the comb is made from it. But is this view in the back of the author's mind? It is unlikely, in the same way as also the bees were most likely not perceived in the same way as earthly bees: the ones that produce a honeycomb of this kind are white and their wings are purple/violet/scarlet and like gold-woven linen cloaks, and they have golden diadems on their head (16.18). Many authors have therefore concluded that the significance of these creatures lies in the realm of the allegorical.[134] These bees are related to the honeycomb in a somewhat similar way as is πνεῦμα ζωῆς in 16.14: ten thousand times ten thousand of them rise out of the comb when the angel speaks to the comb (16.17y). Nevertheless, despite the fact that the comb 'is' πνεῦμα ζωῆς and 'contains' bees (and, likewise, 'is' bread of life, cup of immortality and ointment of incorruptibility [16.16]), the honeycomb is destroyed by fire in 17.3. All of this shows that the author does not work with a systematic reflection of the (physical) nature of the honeycomb or of the Spirit; nor does she give evidence for the assumption that

---

[131] See the helpful synopsis in C. Burchard, *Joseph und Aseneth*; JSHRZ II/4 (Gütersloh: Mohn, 1983), 605–606. A more recent suggestion is that of Hubbard, who thinks that the eating of honey indicates that the author of *Jos. Asen.* portrays Aseneth's conversion as a new birth since eating honey is often associated with infancy (see esp. *Barn.* 6.11–17; Isa. 7.15) (M.V. Hubbard, 'Honey for Aseneth: Interpreting a Religious Symbol', *JSP* 16 (1997), 105).

[132] It is a 'literal' eating rather than a metaphorical eating as one finds it in 16.16 (the latter one being the metaphorical eating of the bread of life and metaphorical drinking of the cup of immortality that is symbolized by the eating of the honeycomb) and 16.14 (on which see below).

[133] The author may have been a woman. See the discussion in Humphrey, *Joseph*, 77–78.

[134] See, e.g., G. Bohak, 'Asenath's Honeycomb and Onias' Temple', in D. Assaf (ed.), *Proceedings of the Eleventh World Congress of Jewish Studies: Jerusalem, June 22–29, 1993 – Division A: The Bible and Its World* (Jerusalem: Magnes, 1994), 166; but cf. E.M. Humphrey, 'On Bees and Best Guesses: The Problem of *Sitz im Leben* from Internal Evidence as Illustrated by *Joseph and Aseneth*', *CR.BS* 7 (1999), 231. More convincing: Burchard, 'Importance', 115–16.

πνεῦμα ζωῆς had materially fused with the comb (as the comb is portrayed as being consumed by fire).[135]

This observation is further confirmed by the role that is ascribed to the honeycomb in the process of conversion in general. The angel proclaims: 'happy (are) all who attach themselves to the Lord God in repentance, because they will eat from this comb' (16.14). One can assume that these words that the author has put into the angel's mouth are not meant to say that everyone who converts to Judaism will eat of this very honeycomb that is given to Aseneth (otherwise there would be extensive evidence in Judaism of a 'honey communion'). The subsequent statement of the angel (τοῦτο τὸ κηρίον ἐστὶ πνεῦμα ζωῆς) may therefore, and this is the main point, be paraphrased as 'For this comb represents the spirit of life' (cf. 16.8: ἡ πνοὴ αὐτοῦ [i.e. of the comb] ὡς πνοὴ ζωῆς). That is, the giving of the honeycomb *symbolizes* the giving of the spirit of life both to Aseneth (as prototype) and subsequently to all other converts to Judaism.[136] As the Spirit is thus *not* (physically) *identical* with the comb, it would need further evidence to uphold the view that the author nevertheless understood the Spirit to be a material entity.[137]

One might object at this point that a symbolic interpretation of the honeycomb is unjustifiable. For example, Chesnutt concludes that 'if we cannot discern a special ritual meal in *Joseph and Aseneth*, neither should we conclude that the language is merely literary and symbolic'.[138] However, the narrow definition of symbolism that is presupposed in Chesnutt's lines is not employed in this study. Rather, more broadly speaking, 'a symbol is an image, an action, or a person that is understood to have transcendent significance',[139] that means, it 'points toward something other than itself

---

[135] Cf. the stones in 12.2 which are called λίθοι ζῶντες. A similar conclusion can be drawn with regard to *T. Levi* 18.11 (mentioned by Horn, *Angeld*, 170). It should be clear from the apocalyptic paradise-imagery in the cotext of the verse that the author is here not concerned with a physical fruit of the tree of life that would impart the Spirit (cf. *1 En.* 24–25, mentioned by Horn, *Angeld*, 170).

[136] For a critical evaluation of the supposed parallels in *Jos. Asen.* with the Eucharist, see Burchard, 'Importance', 118–28. It should be clear, in any case, that our suggestion above does not touch upon the debate between Zwingli and Luther, etc., as we are dealing with an entirely different genre in the case of *Jos. Asen.*.

[137] On the method of interpreting symbols that has been employed here, see P. Ricœur, *Interpretation Theory: Discourse and Surplus of Meaning* (Forth Worth: Texas Christian University Press, 1976), 55–57; D.A. Lee, *The Symbolic Narratives of the Fourth Gospel: The Interplay of Form and Meaning*; JSNTSup 95 (Sheffield: Sheffield Academic Press, 1994), 33.

[138] Chesnutt, *Death*, 135; but see 139.

[139] C.R. Koester, *Symbolism in the Fourth Gospel: Meaning, Mystery, Community* (Minneapolis: Fortress, 1995), 4.

and in some way presents and represents that to which it points'.[140] This conception of (symbolic) *representation* utilized above does not imply that a symbol could not refer to something concrete (as opposed to an idea), so that there are no problems in agreeing with Chesnutt when he concludes that the meal (here: bread and cup) 'represents something very concrete in the Jewish community – the effort to maintain a distinctively Jewish way of life'.[141]

What needs to be understood, however, is the fact that a narrative text like *Joseph and Aseneth* that contains symbolism presents a powerful (and, *contra* Chesnutt, not 'merely') symbolic or alternative world which the reader enters through a suspension of the ordinary world. McFague explains that '[t]here are, of course, connections with ordinary reality in poetic fictions, but in order to appreciate the power of its alternative world, one must suppress ordinary reality for the time being, allowing the new world of the text to control one's perception'.[142] This means for our investigation that in the same way as other poetic texts demand both a moment of intense concentration on the world presented and a moment of assimilation to one's already constituted world, so also in *Joseph and Aseneth* attention must be focused on the text so that the novelty of the world it offers can be assimilated appropriately and powerfully.[143] The pneumatology of the community of the author of *Joseph and Aseneth* can hence not be reconstructed by inserting the physics of the ordinary world (or that of the Stoic world view) into the symbolic/alternative world of the narrative. This holds true for the passages in *Joseph and Aseneth* which were employed by Sänger and Horn, but it also applies to the Jewish wisdom tradi-

---

[140] L.P. Jones, *The Symbol of Water in the Gospel of John*; JSNTSup 145 (Sheffield: Sheffield Academic Press, 1997), 14; cf. 15–19.

The relation between metaphor and symbol is often described as difference between a literary and a non-literary phenomenon. More precisely, metaphors are figures of speech and are not events or things, as symbols can be, although symbols can also be words (D.R. Stiver, *The Philosophy of Religious Language: Sign, Symbol, and Story* (Oxford: Blackwell, 1996), 124, 122). Likewise, Ricœur points out that 'the bound character makes all the difference between a symbol and a metaphor. The latter is a free invention of discourse; the former is bound to the cosmos' (Ricœur, *Interpretation*, 61; cf. 69). Cf. the discussion in J.D.G. Dunn, '"Baptized" as Metaphor', in S.E. Porter and A.R. Cross (eds.), *Baptism, the New Testament and the Church: Historical and Contemporary Studies in Honour of R.E.O. White*; JSNTSup 171 (Sheffield: Sheffield Academic Press, 2000), 297–298.

[141] Chesnutt, *Death*, 135.

[142] S. McFague, *Metaphorical Theology: Models of God in Religious Language* (Philadelphia: Fortress, 1982), 59.

[143] Cf. Ibid., 60; P. Ricœur, 'The Narrative Function', *Semeia* 13 (1978), 194.

tion which Sänger rightly sees in the background of *Joseph and Aseneth*.[144] One passage from Proverbs 9 (vv.1–6, 13–14) is worth quoting in full, as it further elucidates the two texts from *Joseph and Aseneth* that have been discussed above.

> Wisdom has built her house, she has hewn her seven pillars.
> She has slaughtered her animals, she has mixed her wine, she has also set her table.
> She has sent out her servant-girls, she calls from the highest places in the town,
> "You that are simple, turn in here!" To those without sense she says,
> "Come, eat of my bread and drink of the wine I have mixed.
> Lay aside immaturity, and live, and walk in the way of insight." […]
> My child, eat honey, for it is good, and the drippings of the honeycomb are sweet to your taste. Know that wisdom is such to your soul; if you find it, you will find a future, and your hope will not be cut off.

Here one finds a similar cluster of motifs as in the passages mentioning bread, cup and honey in *Joseph and Aseneth*. In Proverbs, the metaphorical eating and drinking of these victuals refers to the virtuous life in and reception of wisdom (for the imagery of eating and drinking representing wickedness, on the other hand, see 4:17). In *Joseph and Aseneth*, the announcement of Aseneth's eating and drinking of bread and cup most likely refers to the virtuous life of those who follow the Jewish customs (for the imagery of eating and drinking representing idolatry, on the other hand, see 8.5; 21.13–14), and her actual eating of a honeycomb (in the narrative world of the text) symbolizes the reception of the spirit of life (that is closely related to wisdom, as Sänger has rightly recognised[145]). While more parallels could be listed, the most important one for this study should finally be mentioned: both texts are of a similar genre – a genre that presents a symbolic world that, as we have above clarified methodologically, cannot be transferred one-to-one into the hylozoistic world view of the Stoics. Hence, it can be said of neither of the books that it gives unambiguous evidence of a Stoic conception of the Spirit (or of wisdom).[146]

This conclusion also applies to 19.10. Horn's (and Brandenburger's) reasoning seems to be built upon a shaky hypothesis, namely, that in the kiss the Spirit fuses with the saliva and thus is/becomes a physical substance.[147] It is much more at hand, however, that it is *the process of kissing*

---

[144] Cf. A. Standhartinger, 'Weisheit in Joseph und Aseneth und den paulinischen Briefen', *NTS* 47 (2001), 482–92.

[145] Sänger, *Judentum*, 193–97.

[146] In the case of Proverbs this can be stated without providing an analysis of its other passages that deal with wisdom/spirit, because it was written before the rise of Stoicism.

[147] This has been partly inferred on the basis of Horn's description of Hellenistic pneumatology that he sees in the background of *Jos. Asen.* (Horn, *Angeld*, 57): 'Die Übertragung des Geistes bedarf verschiedener Hilfsstoffe, an die sich das πνεῦμα stofflich bindet (Wasser, Öl, Speisen etc)', drawing on F. Preisigke, *Die Gotteskraft in der früh-*

overall that symbolizes the reception of a/the S/spirit of truth,[148] as this is much more in accordance with the silence in the narrative regarding the specific details of the transferral. In *Joseph and Aseneth* there is no focus on the saliva, in the same way as no-one so far has seriously tried to argue that the Spirit could only be conveyed on the occasion of the laying on of hands (e.g. Deut. 34:9; Acts 8:18–19) when the person bestowing the Spirit has sweaty hands. (Likewise, no-one has tried to establish that sin was conceived as a physical substance on the basis that it is transferred through laying on of hands [see, e.g., Lev. 16:21–22]).[149]

In summary, none of the three texts in *Joseph and Aseneth* in which the Spirit is mentioned plainly suggests the presence of a materialistic pneumatology. As there is no evidence of Stoic (or any other Hellenistic philosophical) language or discourse in these texts, it can be concluded that it is highly speculative to claim that the author holds a physical concept of the Spirit.

2.3.2. Infusion-Transformation

Does the conclusion above also hold true more generally with regard to the potential presence of the concept of infusion-transformation in *Joseph and Aseneth*? As it seems, Stuhlmacher, Horn, Brandenburger and Sänger would doubt this. Stuhlmacher says about the Spirit in *Joseph and Aseneth* that he is the 'ontic concretion' of the recreating word of God (12.2).[150] In the same way as at Qumran, where he thinks the Spirit was comprehended as a physical substance,[151] *Joseph and Aseneth* presents the Spirit as a 'seinshafte, seinsstürzende und zugleich auf den Weg der Erneuerung...

---

christlichen Zeit; PH 6 (Berlin: W. de Gruyter, 1922), 30; on p. 18 Preisigke specifies saliva.

[148] Since Aseneth's sin is particularly associated with her lips (see 6.3–7; 8.5; 12.4–5; 21.13–14), it is not insignificant that it is through Joseph's kiss that he imparts to her a/the 'S/spirit of truth' (cf. Hubbard, 'Honey', 102).

[149] Furthermore, Chesnutt points out that 'to ascribe ritual status to Joseph's kissing Aseneth is to assign to Joseph a priestly or mystagogical function not consonant with his role elsewhere in the text'. When Joseph returns to Aseneth her conversion is already a *fait accompli* (Chesnutt, *Death*, 138). On a similar note, Sänger rightly emphasizes that 'etwas qualitativ und substantiell Neues können die drei Josephs Küsse auszeichnenden Gaben von ζωή, σοφία und ἀλήθεια nicht sein. Durch das Essen des Stückchens Honigwabe, die ἄρτος ζωῆς, ποτήριον ἀθανασίας (vgl. auch 21,21: ποτήριον σοφίας) und χρίσμα ἀφθαρσίας zugleich ist,... besitzt Aseneth ja bereits alle die Eigenschaften, die den von Joseph stammenden Küssen innewohnen' (Sänger, *Judentum*, 165–66; cf. 206–208). Burchard therefore concludes that the author perhaps 'just makes use of a different tradition to express the same general idea that adherence to Judaism means life' (Burchard, 'Joseph', 234).

[150] Stuhlmacher, 'Erwägungen', 18.

[151] Ibid., 13.

stellende Segensmacht'.[152] This is evident, for example, from Aseneth's beauty, which is an expression of the Spirit's ontic recreation (*geistlich-ontische Neuerschaffung*).[153] Horn adopts a similar line when he sees a present 'substanzhafte[s] Verwandlungsgeschehen' in *Joseph and Aseneth* 16.16, 17.6, 18.9 and 20.7, where recreation and Spirit-reception are understood as the transferral of attributes of the heavenly δόξα onto the convert.[154] Brandenburger expresses the same view slightly differently: Aseneth 'is filled up with heavenly-pneumatic substance [*Wesen*], so that she visibly radiates it'.[155] Finally, in connection with his case for a materialistic pneumatology in *Joseph and Aseneth*, Sänger explains that the book gives evidence of a wisdom-theological interpretation of *Stoic* traditions concerning (ethico-anthropological) transformation.[156]

The first and the last of these arguments are easy to evaluate. It has already been demonstrated above that *Joseph and Aseneth* does not supply any appropriate evidence upon which one could build the case that the author held a material conception of the Spirit. This also applies to Stuhlmacher's assertion that the Spirit is the 'ontic concretion' of the recreating word of God (12.2). For one thing, the Spirit is not mentioned at all in chapter 12.[157] Besides that, even the fact that the honeycomb comes from the angel's mouth (because its πνοή is like that of the angel's mouth [16.10]) cannot be counted as plain evidence for the claim that word and Spirit are in this way linked.[158] However, even if *Joseph and Aseneth* would presuppose or build a link between word and Spirit, this connection does not establish the view that the Spirit is the (physical?) concretion of the word. Sänger's argument likewise loses its strength on closer inspection: he does not provide any evidence for infusion-transformation in Stoicism in his elaboration of the supposed fusion of wisdom theology with Stoic traditions. However, we have demonstrated in 2.1.2. that there is no clear evidence of infusion-transformation in Stoicism.

---

[152] Ibid., 19.

[153] Ibid., 18 n.72; cf. J.S. Vos, *Traditionsgeschichtliche Untersuchungen zur Paulinischen Pneumatologie* (Assen: van Gorcum & Comp. B.V., 1973), 69.

[154] Horn, *Angeld*, 44–45.

[155] Brandenburger, 'Auferstehung', 25.

[156] Sänger, *Judentum*, 197.

[157] The same critique applies to Bertone's judgement of 21.10–21 which he interprets as a 'reference to the Spirit's transformative power in Aseneth's religious and ethical life' (J.A. Bertone, *'The Law of the Spirit': Experience of the Spirit and Displacement of the Law in Romans 8:1–16*; SBL 86 (New York: Lang, 2005), 71). While the majority of the section is a prayer of repentance, the only verse that does mention the cause of her change (v.21) specifies *Joseph* as the agent.

[158] *Pace* Humphrey, *Ladies*, 52 n.49. Humphrey does not speak about 'ontic concretion', though.

In order to assess the other arguments of Stuhlmacher, Horn and Brandenburger for the thesis that the Spirit's work is comprehended by the
author of *Joseph and Aseneth* as having substance-ontological (and thus
ethical) effects, it will be necessary to look first at the time-frame of Aseneth's transformation and then at the nature of the transformation itself.

Horn's contention that recreation and Spirit-reception portray a present
'substanzhafte[s] Verwandlungsgeschehen' comes close to suggesting that
Joseph and Aseneth has a realized eschatology.[159] However, it is important
to see, first of all, that the reception of the Spirit (through the symbolic
eating of the honeycomb [16.14–16]) is only one of many factors that play
a role in Aseneth's transformation. Wedderburn highlights the decisive fact
that 'the moment of Aseneth's reception into the Jewish faith and the Jewish community is not linked with any of the various symbolic rites described in the work, fasting, eating a honeycomb or a cultic meal, the
putting on of festal garments, but takes place between them, in response to
Joseph's petition and Aseneth's confession'[160] (see especially 15.7). It
should be noted, secondly, that wherever the Spirit is explicitly linked to
the transformation of Aseneth, this is done with a verb in the imperative
form (8.9) or the *future tense* (16.16).[161] This is also recognized by
Stuhlmacher (though he focuses on 15.4–5 where the Spirit is not mentioned),[162] and his description of the Spirit as a power that puts people *onto*
the way of renewal can thus be endorsed.

Nevertheless, how does this analysis fit Stuhlmacher's remaining definition of the work of the Spirit as 'seinsstürzend'? Like Horn's (and Brandenburger's) definition, it has two aspects. The time-factor has just been
dealt with. However, second, we will now look at the nature of the transformation itself.

Both Stuhlmacher and Horn base their thesis that the Spirit works a substance-ontological transformation in Aseneth explicitly on the gift of
beauty that is given to Aseneth. While none of them states overtly that this
substance-ontological transformation into 'divine' beauty implies ethical
change, this aspect is clearly implied in their claims. However, this assumption could be challenged from within the story line of *Joseph and*

---

[159] However, Horn is aware of Burchard, *Joseph [1983]*, 609 n.119, who warns of interpreting the eschatology of *Jos. Asen.* as realized (Horn, *Angeld*, 45 n.11).

[160] A.J.M. Wedderburn, *Baptism and Resurrection: Studies in Pauline Theology
against its Graeco-Roman Background*; WUNT 44 (Tübingen: J.C.B. Mohr (Paul Siebeck), 1987), 157–58. The various symbols, which need to be considered within their
mutual relationship, are rather used at the literary level to reiterate the principal that
immortality is attained by adherence to Jewish faith (Chesnutt, *Death*, 138–39).

[161] On 19.10, see n.149 above. Horn's other reference, 17.6, is also future tense but it
does not mention the Spirit.

[162] Stuhlmacher, 'Erwägungen', 19.

Aseneth. Chesnutt draws attention to the fact that the contrast of Aseneth's arrogance at the beginning of the story with her meekness and magnanimity later is not dwelt upon as though it represents the essence of her conversion or constitutes a recreation.[163] In a similar vein, Burchard observes that 'ethics is an important concern of the author, although it is not preparatory to, instrumental in, or a consequence of salvation'.[164] Against this background it is justified to conclude with Chesnutt that there is 'no hint of a psychological transformation by which Aseneth becomes disinclined to evil and predisposed to good. Neither do we find any suggestion of a fallen state of sinfulness out of which Aseneth is unable to rise except by divine rejuvenation.'[165]

However, how can we express positively how the language of renewal and restoration in *Joseph and Aseneth* should be understood? Chesnutt thinks that this language

simply denotes advancement from the nothingness of heathen existence to the glorious existence of one who worships God... The change is of status, not of essential nature. The emphasis is on the contrast between Aseneth's former status and her present status, and the contrast is so radical that it is best expressed in the language of re-creation.[166]

However, one may not want to endorse all aspects of Chesnutt's formulation. Particularly his contrast between 'change of status' and 'change of essential nature' appears to be a false antithesis when one comprehends Aseneth's conversion-transformation as a change of relationships (on this, see further 4.4.1.).[167] Moreover, certainly Aseneth's future role as 'city of refuge' (16.16), and possibly the idea of ἀνακαινόω (8.9), have ethical aspects. Nevertheless, it should be clear that Aseneth's beauty cannot be interpreted *unambiguously* as ethical refashioning, not least because of the figurative/symbolic nature of the language which prohibits a clear-cut definition of the transformation.

---

[163] Chesnutt, *Death*, 148.

[164] Burchard, 'Joseph', 193.

[165] Chesnutt, *Death*, 148.

[166] Ibid., 148–49; cf. 175–76. Cf. Burchard, 'Importance', 108.

[167] The concept of relational change is supported by Mell, who points out that 'Das Ziel des in JosAs geschilderten Initiationsritus als Inkorporation in die Synagoge ist es... nicht, nach Art der Mysterien den Initianten über die Teilhabe am Schicksal der Gottheit in eine höhere ontologische Lebensqualität einzuführen, sondern eine schöpfungsgemäße Lebensweise coram deo zu begründen' (Mell, *Schöpfung*, 247). This relational transformation has parallels on the horizontal level: the change of Aseneth's garments is part of the transformation, and it signifies a new relation: from mourning into marriage (15.10; 18.5–6; that marriage is part of the renewal is clear from 15.5–6). On the role of the Spirit in this relational change, see Mell, *Schöpfung*, 246, 248, 235–37; J. Buchegger, *Erneuerung des Menschen: Exegetische Studien zu Paulus*; TANZ 40 (Tübingen: Francke, 2003), 75–76 n.73.

However, even if Aseneth's transformation was meant as an ontic change with ethical effects based on this new nature (which cannot be ruled out), the special role that Aseneth plays in the narrative should caution against believing that the nature of this transformation gives a full representation of the concept that the author had of the ethical work of the Spirit. Chesnutt rightly says that it is 'extremely doubtful that we should extrapolate from the very special and prototypical case of Aseneth a pattern of Jewish conversion in which an epiphanic or revelatory experience results in a visible physical transformation'.[168]

It can be concluded that *Joseph and Aseneth* neither gives evidence of a physical notion of the Spirit, nor of the idea that this physical Spirit would perform a substance-ontological transformation of believers that would have ethical life as its (automatic) outflow. Rather, Stuhlmacher's description of the Spirit as a power that puts people onto the way of renewal seems to be most fitting for the pneumatology of *Joseph and Aseneth*.

2.4. Philo

Finally, also the writings of the Jewish-Hellenistic philosopher Philo of Alexandria (ca. 15 BCE–45 CE) have been understood by some scholars to give indication of the existence in Hellenistic Judaism of a conception of πνεῦμα as a material substance and of the idea of infusion-transformation. At least the first part of this contention is not necessarily surprising, because Philo attempts to 'express ideas of Hebrew origin in forms derived from and congenial to Greek philosophic thought, a process which modified both their form and substance'.[169] Philo's writings represent a philosophical defence and presentation of Judaism, in the course of which he employs concepts from various religious and philosophical strands. Some writers believe that Philo was predominantly influenced by Stoicism.[170]

---

[168] Chesnutt, *Death*, 137. Cf. G.W.E. Nickelsburg, *Jewish Literature Between the Bible and the Mishnah: A Historical and Literary Introduction* (Philadelphia: Fortress, 1981), 263. For further reasons why Aseneth's conversion and transformation cannot be understood as representative, see C. Burchard, 'Der jüdische Asenethroman und seine Nachwirkung: Von Egeria zu Anna Katharina Emmerick oder von Moses aus Aggel zu Karl Kerényi', in C. Burchard, *Gesammelte Studien zu Joseph und Aseneth. Berichtigt und ergänzt herausgegeben mit Unterstützung von Carsten Burfeind*; SVTP 13 (Leiden: Brill, 1996), 434.

[169] Burton, *Spirit*, 157. Cf. V. Rabens, 'Philo's Attractive Ethics on the "Religious Market" of Ancient Alexandria', in P. Wick and V. Rabens (eds.), *Religions and Trade: Religious Formation, Transformation and Cross-Cultural Exchange between East and West;* DHR 5 (Leiden: Brill, 2013), forthcoming.

[170] So, e.g., E. Turowski, *Die Widerspiegelung des stoischen Systems bei Philon von Alexandreia* (Borna/Leipzig: Universitätsverlag Robert Noske, 1927), *passim*. This influence may be observed, e.g., in *Gig.* 27 and *Deus Imm.* 35 where the idea of an all-

Other scholars (particularly Levison), while not denying that Philo was influenced by Stoicism (and by other popular Graeco-Roman conceptions),[171] demonstrate that Philo is reluctant to adopt Stoicism uncritically and that he sometimes actually distances his pneumatology from Stoic ideas.[172] Levison and others rather give more weight to the influence of Platonism on Philo's pneumatology[173] and argue that ultimately Philo is loyal to Judaism.[174]

Partly as a result of this mixture of at least these three different *Weltanschauungen* in Philo, 'the details of his doctrine of Spirit are complicated, difficult, and not always clearly consistent'.[175] This is particularly obvious with respect to Philo's views on the (im/material) nature of πνεῦμα which seem to be wavering between Platonism and Stoicism (so Siebeck, Rüsche, Pulver and Engberg-Pedersen),[176] so that Goodenough calls this aspect of Philo's pneumatology 'one of the most baffling problems of late Greek and

---

permeating πνεῦμα is expressed (Burton, *Spirit*, 160; W. Bieder, 'πνεῦμα, πνευματικός', *TDNT*, VI, 372; cf. J.M.G. Barclay, 'Πνευματικός in the Social Context of Pauline Christianity', in G. Stanton, et al. (eds.), *The Holy Spirit and Christian Origins: Essays in Honor of James D. G. Dunn* (Grand Rapids/Cambridge: Eerdmans, 2004), 164). However, see also Isaacs and Fatehi, who rightly stress that Philo maintains and asserts both the immanence *and* the transcendence of God('s Spirit) (M.E. Isaacs, *The Concept of the Spirit: A Study of Pneuma in Hellenistic Judaism and its Bearing on the New Testament* (London: Heythrop Monographs, 1976), 29; Fatehi, *Relation*, 119).

[171] Levison, *Spirit in First Century Judaism*, 20, supporting Leisegang, *Geist*, 34; cf. H. Lewy, *Sobria Ebrietas: Untersuchungen zur Geschichte der antiken Mystik*; BZNW 9 (Gießen: Toepelmann, 1929), 66.

[172] Levison, *Spirit in First Century Judaism*, 137, 148–51, 159.

[173] Ibid., 151, 159; Verbeke, *Évolution*, 259; R. Radice, 'Observations on the Theory of the Ideas as Thoughts of God in Philo', *SPA* 3 (1991), 133–34; G. Sellin, 'Die religionsgeschichtlichen Hintergründe der paulinischen "Christusmystik"', *TQ* 176 (1996), 20, 27; D. Winston, 'Judaism and Hellenism: Hidden Tensions in Philo's Thought', in G.E. Sterling (ed.), *The Ancestral Philosophy: Hellenistic Philosophy in Second Temple Judaism. Essays of David Winston*; BJS 331/SPM 4 (Providence: Brown Judaic Studies, 2001), 198; Engberg-Pedersen, 'Understanding', 106–108.

[174] Levison, *Spirit in First Century Judaism*, 160; Burton, *Spirit*, 157; Bieder, 'πνεῦμα', 373–75; Isaacs, *Spirit*, 50–51; Winston, 'Judaism', 198; cf. Verbeke, *Évolution*, 255, 238; Büchsel, *Geist*, 85–86; F. Philip, *The Origins of Pauline Pneumatology: The Eschatological Bestowal of the Spirit upon Gentiles in Judaism and in the Early Development of Paul's Theology*; WUNT II/194 (Tübingen: Mohr Siebeck, 2005), 101 n.106; *pace* Leisegang, *Geist*, 30, 143.

[175] K. Lake, 'The Holy Spirit', in F.J.F. Jackson and H.J. Cadbury (eds.), *The Beginnings of Christianity. Part I: The Acts of the Apostles. Vol. 5* (Grand Rapids: Baker, 1979 [1933¹]), 101; cf. Burton, *Spirit*, 160; Wedderburn, *Baptism*, 273.

[176] Siebeck, 'Lehre', 392; Rüsche, *Seelenpneuma*, 31–32; M. Pulver, 'Das Erlebnis des Pneuma bei Philon', *ErJb* 13 (1945), 123, 126–27; Engberg-Pedersen, *Cosmology*, 25.

early Christian terminology'.[177] As our understanding of his pneumatology is further complicated by the fact that Philo – although he *does* formulate abstract statements about the Spirit – is not attempting to give a systematic treatment of πνεῦμα,[178] one may wonder whether it is at all wise to use Philo as support in a case that is being made for a certain view of the nature (and resulting work) of the Spirit to be present in Hellenistic Judaism. Nevertheless, as a number of scholars have employed Philo's writings for such a proposal, it will be necessary to examine their arguments, first those for the material nature of the Spirit and then those for infusion-transformation by the Spirit.

2.4.1. The Physical Spirit

To date no-one has written more extensively and more influentially on Philo's pneumatology than Leisegang in 1919. As the question of the (im/material) nature of πνεῦμα receives a fair amount of attention throughout his monograph, it is important to look at his work in some depth. After that we will single out some further arguments from individual scholars who reason that Philo had a materialistic pneumatology.

Leisegang divides Philo's usage of πνεῦμα into two categories each with two subcategories: 1) πνεῦμα as a *cosmological principle*: 1a) as air, 1b) as knowledge and wisdom; 2) πνεῦμα as a *psychological principle*: 2a) as power of life that resides continually within humankind, 2b) as a heavenly power that is suddenly infused by God into the human soul.[179] Leisegang sets out his treatment of the first category by explaining that when Philo uses πνεῦμα θεοῦ in the sense of 'air' as the third of the four created ele-

---

[177] E.R. Goodenough, *By Light, Light: The Mystic Gospel of Hellenistic Judaism* (Oxford/New Haven: Oxford University Press/Yale University Press, 1935), 271.

[178] Cf. Verbeke, *Évolution*, 247; Dodd, *Interpretation*, 219; Isaacs, *Spirit*, 55; Levison, *Spirit in First Century Judaism*, 151. Pulver even thinks that Philo's pneumatology is full of contradictions (Pulver, 'Erlebnis', 123), and with regard to Philo's teaching on matter, Baeumker remarks that it is 'a muddled picture' (Baeumker, *Problem*, 388).

[179] Leisegang, *Geist*, 19–136. Similar classifications have been made by Verbeke, *Évolution*, 236–60; A. Laurentin, 'Le Pneuma dans la Doctrine de Philon', *ETL* 27 (1951), 391–424; R.P. Menzies, *The Development of Early Christian Pneumatology – With Special Reference to Luke-Acts*; JSNTSup 54 (Sheffield: JSOT Press, 1991), 63–67; Fatehi, *Relation*, 108–109; C. Bennema, *The Power of Saving Wisdom: An Investigation of Spirit and Wisdom in Relation to the Soteriology of the Fourth Gospel*; WUNT II/148 (Tübingen: Mohr Siebeck, 2002), 71–74.
It is important to keep these distinctions in mind when trying to fathom Philo's concept of πνεῦμα θεοῦ. However, it is likewise necessary to be aware of the fact that Philo is not always consistent in distinguishing the different lexemes of πνεῦμα (our discussion of *Gig.* 22 below serves as an example *par excellence*). Cf. the discussion in Philip, *Origins*, 102–103.

ments in *De Gigantibus* 22, it is to be understood as matter.[180] Leisegang *may* be right with this judgement, because ἀήρ in this passage is praised as being 'light' (κοῦφος).[181] However, Leisegang is certainly right when he continues that Philo briefly mentions this meaning of πνεῦμα θεοῦ only in order to then elaborate its other meaning, namely, 'pure knowledge'.[182] Furthermore, Leisegang maintains that this short mention of πνεῦμα as air at the creation of the world (*Gig.* 22a) is certainly not an exhaustive explanation, but that it is rather intended to show that he is not contradicting what he has elsewhere developed more fully, particularly in *De Opificio Mundi* 29. Here Philo tries to harmonize the Mosaic creation account with Plato's *Timaeus*. Everything that happened on the first day of creation (including the creation of πνεῦμα) refers to the creation of an incorporeal ideal world which serves as an archetype for the corporal, 'real' world which is created on the five consecutive days. Πνεῦμα is hence an 'immaterial substance' which belongs to the seven incorporeal ideas of the κόσμος νοητός.[183]

However, it seems that Leisegang undermines his own case for the materiality of πνεῦμα θεοῦ in *Gigantibus* 22 when he claims that *De Opificio Mundi* 29 can serve as an elucidation of the meaning of πνεῦμα in the former passage. For if Leisegang is right,[184] this means that his (unsupported) claim regarding *Gigantibus* 22 is ruled out by the explicit definition of πνεῦμα (in *Op. Mund.* 29) as ἀσώματος οὐσία. Moreover, Leisegang

---

[180] Leisegang, *Geist*, 23; cf. H. Saake, 'Pneuma', in G. Wissowa (ed.), *Paulys Real-Encyclopädie der classischen Altertumswissenschaft. Suppl. XIV* (Stuttgart: Metzler, 1973), 396. Unfortunately, Leisegang does not mention how he arrives at the qualification of πνεῦμα as *created*. Probably he is drawing on the parallel that he sees in *Op. Mund.* 29.

[181] Büchsel notes, however, that Philo usually distinguishes expressly between πνεῦμα as air and πνεῦμα as God's Spirit (e.g. *Det. Pot. Ins.* 83), *Gig.* 22 being an exception to this rule (Büchsel, *Geist*, 86). In *Quaest. in Gen.* 1.90 Philo even seems to contradict *Gig.* 22a by stating 'the divine spirit is not a movement of air but intelligence and wisdom'. Wedderburn suggests that 'presumably what Philo means here is that the sense of "spirit" in question is not air in motion but the other' (Wedderburn, *Baptism*, 273 n.18). – On πνεῦμα as the ἕξις of lifeless things as wood and stone, see *Deus Imm.* 35.

[182] Leisegang maintains that even in this spiritualized meaning of πνεῦμα one can sense the Stoic overtones of the 'Attribute der materialistisch aufgefaßten Weltvernunft', namely ἄτμητος and ἀδιαίρετος (Leisegang, *Geist*, 23). However, it is doubtful whether one can establish the materiality of an object on the basis of the adjectives 'undivided' and 'indivisible' (cf. Verbeke, *Évolution*, 259).

[183] Leisegang, *Geist*, 23–25.

[184] Leisegang is aware of the different nuances of Philo's employment of πνεῦμα in *Gig.* 22 (where Philo says that the Spirit of God is used in the sense of *air*) and *Op. Mund.* 29 (where the emphasis appears to be on the πνεῦμα as *life-breath* or power of life) (Ibid., 25). However, he explains that Philo rarely upholds this distinction because air is *Lebenssubstanz per se* (Leisegang, *Geist*, 26; 24).

subsequently argues that for Philo air belongs no longer to the 'irdische Körperwelt', but that he understands it as an incorporeal, spiritual substance. 'In this way also πνεῦμα in the sense of air, and particularly πνεῦμα as πνεῦμα θεοῦ, is removed from the physical world. It is to be understood as an "immaterial substance".'[185] Consequently, it appears that Leisegang has clearly contradicted his initial judgement that Philo understands the Spirit of God to be material (especially in *Gig.* 22).

Nevertheless, Leisegang continues – without giving further explanation[186] – that one can see that even the Jewish philosopher Philo, who is deeply convinced of the immateriality of YHWH, finds it difficult to distance himself completely from the hylozoistic Greek philosophy of his time. 'The Spirit needs to have a body to which it is bound, yes it has to be body itself, even though the lightest and finest and unearthly one.'[187] Either Leisegang is here overtly contradicting himself[188] or he is possibly working with the same presuppositions that were discussed in 2.1.1, namely that the ancient mind necessarily perceived an ἀσώματος οὐσία to be somewhat material.[189] However, we have demonstrated in 2.1.1. that such a hypothesis is unsubstantiated. We can thus wind up our discussion

---

[185] Leisegang, *Geist*, 29.

[186] Leisegang writes a few paragraphs later that πνεῦμα 'mit dem Äther fast zusammenfällt und auch seinerseits im höchsten Grade der Verfeinerung stofflos als Idee gefaßt werden kann. Daß... πνεῦμα doch... unbewußt als stofflicher empfunden wird als der reine Lichtäther, kann man wohl daraus entnehmen, daß Philon Gott selbst sowie auch den Logos metaphorisch häufig dem Lichte gleichstellt, niemals aber dem πνεῦμα' (Ibid., 31–32; cf. 33). However, while it seems that Leisegang's second sentence is contradicted by the first one, his second claim would in any case need more evidence in order to be removed from the realm of mere speculation about Philo's unconscious impressions, particularly as Philo is not a systematic writer (as Leisegang himself admits [Leisegang, *Geist*, 58–59]) and as he in places equates God with πνεῦμα (on this see further below).

[187] Leisegang, *Geist*, 30; 58.

[188] This seems to be true at least for Pulver's work on this matter (Pulver, 'Erlebnis', 111–32).

Leisegang himself explains that Philo is forced to use Greek language as that is the only one available for him. Nevertheless, he is not interested in the natural sciences as such or in presenting a consistent system of physics. Rather, he eclectically employs different theories that serve his purpose which is beyond the world of physics. Only against this background is it possible to comprehend the inconsistencies and contradictions within Philo's pneumatology (Leisegang, *Geist*, 58–59). For a critique of Leisegang's general method, see Paige, 'Usage', 418–20.

[189] See Leisegang's own explanations on this matter (Leisegang, *Geist*, 29 n.1, 30 n.1). See further the discussions by Verbeke, *Évolution*, 246–47; H.A. Wolfson, *Philo: Foundations of Religious Philosophy in Judaism, Christianity and Islam. Vol. 2: Structure and Growth of Philosophic Systems from Plato to Spinoza* (London: Harvard University Press, 1982 [1947¹]), 106–107; R.M. Berchman, *From Philo to Origen: Middle Platonism in Transition*; BJS 69 (Chico: Scholars Press, 1984), 32, 38.

of Leisegang's treatment of πνεῦμα θεοῦ by concluding that no reliable evidence of the *Stofflichkeit* of πνεῦμα in Philo's thought has been provided.

However, other scholars have pointed to further passages in Philo that might be interpreted as evidence for a materialistic pneumatology. For example, Dodd says that Philo gives πνεῦμα 'its usual place among the material elements (e.g. *Ebr.* 106 οὐρανός, γῆ, ὕδωρ, πνεῦμα...)'.[190] However, it is doubtful whether the possible materiality is the intended *tertium comparationis* of these four elements. It rather seems that Philo's words preceding this list give a clue to their common denominator: they are all part of the creation (τό γεγονὸς πᾶν).[191] And, in any case, πνεῦμα here is used in the sense of air and not as a reference to the Spirit of God.[192]

A similar argument has recently been put forward by Engberg-Pedersen. While he is generally of the opinion that Philo's pneumatology is Platonic,[193] he submits that Philo displays a Stoic concept of πνεῦμα when he attributes the Stoic terms 'strength', 'vigour' and 'power' to the Spirit (πνεῦμα νενόηται κατὰ τὴν ἰσχὺν καὶ εὐτονίαν καὶ δύναμιν; *Leg. All.* 1.42).[194] However, while Engberg-Pedersen is right that these characteristics are Stoic virtues, one needs clearer evidence in order to ascertain that Philo implied that the object described is therefore material. For one thing, we have already seen that when Philo defines the substance of πνεῦμα, he explicitly says that it is an ἀσώματος οὐσία. Moreover, in a Platonic manner Philo compares the ἰδέαν νοῦς (rendered as 'immaterial' by Engberg-Pedersen)[195] and the material mind (ὁ δὲ ἐκ τῆς ὕλης) in this passage. Whereas the former partakes of πνεῦμα, the latter partakes of a πνοή that is like 'a gentle and moderate kind of breeze and exhalation' or 'a thin and very light air, being as it were a sort of exhalation'.[196] It seems rather unlikely that Philo intends to convey that in contrast to the light material of πνοή, which the material mind takes part of, the immaterial mind would partake of heavier matter (i.e. πνεῦμα). Rather, the point of contrast is the lack of strength (ῥώμη) of reasoning in the material mind due to its share in πνοή and lack of πνεῦμα (cf. 1.41).

Other passages that have been appealed to as evidence for Philo's supposed material concept of the Spirit either concern his view of the anthro-

---

[190] Dodd, *Interpretation*, 219.

[191] This fact *may* imply that they are physical, because the second creation is corporeal (*Op. Mund.* 16, 36, et al.). However, *Op. Mund.* does not mention πνεῦμα as being created as part of the corporeal world.

[192] Cf. the translation of Colson and Whitaker (LCL): 'the air we breathe'.

[193] Engberg-Pedersen, *Cosmology*, 24–25.

[194] Engberg-Pedersen, 'Spirit', 186 n.32.

[195] Ibid., 186 n.32.

[196] *Leg. All.* 1.42, translation by Yonge.

pological spirit[197] or do not contain references to πνεῦμα at all[198] and hence do not deserve close attention in this study. We will rather conclude this section by giving a voice to those scholars who provide arguments in favour of the view that Philo did *not* think of πνεῦμα θεοῦ as being physical (or at least that if he did, that this was not central to his pneumatology, as Büchsel contends).[199]

The most convincing arguments for the *immateriality* of πνεῦμα in Philo are presented by Isaacs. She points out that in contrast to Stoic materialism, Philo's Jewish belief in the gulf between humans and God meant his insistence upon the immaterial nature of the divine.[200] For Philo, πνεῦμα is that which is of God – both in that God is its author (*Leg. All.* 1.37), and in that πνεῦμα is the essence of the divinity. Hence, God and πνεῦμα can be described in the same terms (e.g. invisibility: *Plant.* 18; simple nature: *Leg. All.* 2.2; *Mut. Nom.* 184; *Deus Imm.* 56; *Gig.* 26–27).[201] This argument finds support in Verbeke's detailed comparison of Philo's conception of the divine Spirit and the οὐράνιος ἄνθρωπος, which leads him to the conclusion that both are of the same (immaterial) nature. Verbeke therefore argues that Philo thought of God's Spirit as being divine.[202] Additionally, Isaacs highlights the fact that Philo asserts that it is because of the incorporeal and moral nature of πνεῦμα that it cannot remain a permanent possession of human beings who are corporeal and sinful (*Gig.* 19, 28, 53; *Deus Imm.* 2; *Quaest. in Gen.* 1.90).[203]

We can conclude that Philo defines πνεῦμα as ἀσώματος οὐσία (*Op. Mund.* 29 et al.). Through employing such abstract language, and through the fact that he defines the Spirit at all, Philo differentiates himself from

---

[197] So, e.g., the references by Martin, *Body*, 13; see also the discussion in Burton, *Spirit*, 158–60.

[198] So, e.g., *Fug.* 202 and *Migr.* 39, mentioned by Horn, *Angeld*, 44–45 n.11, building on Sänger, *Judentum*, 193–96.

[199] Büchsel rather argues that for Philo πνεῦμα 'is the power of wisdom and prophecy that comes from God as a spiritual power' (Büchsel, *Geist*, 86). Cf. Rüsche, who explains that it is Philo's aim to view πνεῦμα as immaterial, but he does not always succeed doing so (Rüsche, *Seelenpneuma*, 20–23, 28, 33–35).

Scholars who put forward that for Philo the Spirit was immaterial but who do not provide textual evidence for this claim include Bieder, 'πνεῦμα', 372; P. Schäfer, 'Geist/Heiliger Geist/Geistesgaben II: Judentum', *TRE*, XII, 174; Wolfson, *Philo. II*, 31–32. Those who deny that Philo's pneumatology was influenced by Stoic materialism include Verbeke, *Évolution*, 247; Pinnock, 'Spirit', 76; Bieder, 'πνεῦμα', 373–75 (allowing for the language of Stoicism but not for its concepts); Isaacs, *Spirit*, 56.

[200] On the immateriality of God, see further Wolfson, *Philo. II*, 110–26.

[201] Isaacs, *Spirit*, 19, 30, 44; cf. Fatehi, *Relation*, 116–17, 120; Bennema, *Power*, 83.

[202] Verbeke, *Évolution*, 245–47; cf. his additional arguments for the immateriality of πνεῦμα θεοῦ in Philo on pp. 256–59.

[203] Isaacs, *Spirit*, 19.

the rest of the Jewish sources that have been called upon in support for the thesis that ancient Judaism comprehended the Spirit as a material substance. It needs to be conceded that when Philo describes ἀήρ, which is set into relation with πνεῦμα, as 'light' in *Gigantibus* 22, that this *may* imply that Philo's exegesis of Genesis 1:2 allows for a concept of the Spirit as 'light matter'. Nevertheless, the explicit evidence in Philo's writings clearly points in a different direction, and it is methodologically much more sound to explain the ambiguous instances with the clearer ones (or else allow for some contradiction within Philo).[204] This explicit evidence, however, indicates that Philo comprehended πνεῦμα θεοῦ as being immaterial.

2.4.2. Infusion-Transformation

The only scholar whose views on Philo reflect the concept of infusion-transformation is Brandenburger. In the context of his exegesis of *Quod Deus immutabilis sit* 122–83, particularly of §§123 and 138, he writes that Philo thinks of conversion

auf substanzhafter Grundlage... Auch nimmt nicht mehr der transzendente Gott im Menschen Wohnung, sondern der göttliche Logos, der als lichtgestaltige, pneumatisch-unsterbliche Wesenheit in die Seele einzieht und das sterbliche Wesen vernichtet. Die Wandlung des Verhaltens basiert auf einem Austausch zugrundeliegenden Wesens. Unsterblich-pneumatisches Wesen schließt das sterblich-irdische grundsätzlich aus.[205]

However, it seems that Brandenburger has overstated his case. As far as §123 is concerned, it appears at first sight as if Philo were indeed thinking in substance-ontological categories when he says that 'when the incorruptible element takes its rise in the soul, the mortal is forthwith corrupted'. However, when Philo elucidates this in the next sentence by saying that 'for [γάρ] the birth of noble practices is the death of the base', it seems that what causes the change is the noble *practices* (ἐπιτηδευμάτων) rather than a new substance.[206] This judgement is confirmed in §§125–26

---

[204] Cf. Siebeck, 'Lehre', 396: 'Allein was als das echte und wahre Pneuma für Philo in Betracht kommt ist doch nichts anderes als ein Ausfluss göttlichen Wesens, immateriell in Bezug auf seine Substanz gedacht und nur hinsichtlich seiner Wirkungsweise zum Zwecke der Begrifflichkeit derselben noch in Anlehnung an Sinnliches wie Luft und Wärme gehalten.'

[205] Brandenburger, *Fleisch*, 182; 185. However, see pp. 227, 233 where Brandenburger allows for relational categories next to the substance-ontological concepts in Philo.

[206] This interpretation rests on rendering the 'birth' (γένεσις) metaphorically as the point when a person starts acting nobly. A more literal interpretation may allow understanding 'birth' in the sense of an infusion. However, as Philo continues with metaphorical speech (about light and darkness), a metaphorical interpretation of 'birth' is more suggestive.

where Philo explains that it is a *cognitive process* that is responsible for the change, because it is in the light of 'the healthy and the living' that a conviction of the soul's transgressions is being produced (cf. §§128–30). The same holds true for §138. More important, however, is the fact that Philo avoids πνεῦμα in this passage (and instead speaks about λογός), as Brandenburger himself admits.[207] Hence, *Quod Deus immutabilis sit* 122–83 cannot function as support for the infusion-transformation view.

A different argument could be brought forward to demonstrate the existence of the infusion-transformation approach in Philo, namely Philo's view of Abraham's experiences with the divine Spirit:

> Whenever he [Abraham] was possessed, everything in him changed to something better, eyes, complexion, stature, carriage, movements, voice. For the divine spirit which was breathed upon him from on high made its lodging in his soul, and invested his body with singular beauty, his voice with persuasiveness, and his hearers with understanding (*Virt.* 217).

This passage could be interpreted as portraying a (physical) πνεῦμα that has lasting ethico-physical effects on Abraham's soul (and body) and thus 'automatizes' ethical life – although it seems that no-one has opted for this reading. We will nevertheless suggest difficulties for this view.

We concede that Philo ascribes physical effects to the divine Spirit. But this is not infusion-transformation. For one thing, Philo does not say that the Spirit transformed Abraham's *interior*. He merely states that the Spirit sometimes made its lodging in Abraham's soul. Nor does Philo express that *ethical life* was the (inevitable) consequence of this temporal inhabitation of the soul. Rather, Philo makes explicit that the state of physical transformation of Abraham occurred only at certain times (ὁπότε γοῦν, *Virt.* 217),[208] so that one cannot say that according to Philo the divine

---

[207] Brandenburger, *Fleisch*, 186.

[208] On this see further (and more generally) Leisegang, *Geist*, 114–15; Wolfson, *Philo. II*, 32–33; Wedderburn, *Baptism*, 273; S. Vollenweider, 'Der Geist Gottes als Selbst der Glaubenden: Überlegungen zu einem ontologischen Problem in der paulinischen Anthropologie', *ZTK* 93 (1996), 171–72; F. Back, *Verwandlung durch Offenbarung bei Paulus: Eine religionsgeschichtlich-exegetische Untersuchung zu 2 Kor 2,14–4,6*; WUNT II/153 (Tübingen: Mohr Siebeck, 2002), 37; see particularly Fatehi, *Relation*, 113.

Philo's portrayal of Moses is an exception to this in that the Spirit remains at his side permanently and guides him on the path to perfection (e.g. *Gig.* 54–55; see further Levison, *Spirit in First Century Judaism*, 92; Fatehi, *Relation*, 117; Wenk, *Power*, 93; Back, *Verwandlung*, 38). However, Back points out that Moses' transformation was not a singular event but that *Vit. Mos.* 1.57–59 and 2.250ff., particularly 272 and 280, give evidence of further (prophetic) transformations throughout his life (Back, *Verwandlung*, 33–34, drawing on D. Zeller, 'La Métamorphose de Jésus comme Épiphanie (Mc 9,2–8)', in A. Marchadour (ed.), *L'Évangile exploré: Mélanges offerts à Simon Légasse à l'occasion de ses soixante-dix ans*; LD 166 (Paris: Les Éditions du Cerf, 1996), 177).

Spirit creates a new, ethical nature within Abraham (or other believers)[209] that would be based on a physical transformation.

What is it, then, that changes when the Spirit is breathed upon Abraham? The answer is found in the realm of rhetoric. Philo spells out that it is Abraham's *body* that is being changed, namely his eyes, complexion, stature, carriage, movements and voice, in order to further his persuasiveness. Levison has convincingly elucidated the parallels that exist between the values of Graeco-Roman rhetoricians and Philo's description of Abraham in *De Virtutibus* 216–17 as an ideal ruler *cum rhetor* (e.g. *Rhet. Her.* 1.3; Cicero, *De Orat.* 1.18; *Rep.* 2.4).[210]

However, Philip criticizes Levison for ignoring the larger cotext of §217 where, according to Philip, ethics and morals are clearly in focus ('a virtuous life is the basis for εὐγενία').[211] Nevertheless, while Philip is right in highlighting the role of ethics in the cotext of §217, he seems to have overlooked that §217 neither mentions virtues in the sense of a 'basis' for the inception of the Spirit, nor as its consequence.[212] The only explicit point of reference of the effects of the Spirit regards the enhancement of communication. This is confirmed by Noack, who adds that the listeners are included in the work of the Spirit: they receive the gift of understanding.[213] Moreover, Noack points out that the (missiological) connection of physical beauty and rhetorical persuasiveness in Philo is supported by *De Specialibus Legibus* 1.321; *De Vita Mosis* 1.57–59; 2.69 (cf. Porphyry, *Vit. Pyth.* 18).[214] We can conclude, then, that the transformation that is de-

---

[209] Cf. W. Schweitzer, 'Gotteskindschaft, Wiedergeburt und Erneuerung im Neuen Testament und in seiner Umwelt' (Eberhard-Karls-Universität Tübingen: Unpublished PhD Thesis, 1944), 105, 107; G. Schneider, 'Die Idee der Neuschöpfung beim Apostel Paulus und ihr religionsgeschichtlicher Hintergrund', *TTZ* 68 (1959), 46; Buchegger, *Erneuerung*, 75.

[210] Levison, *Spirit in First Century Judaism*, 90–97 (cf. 146).

[211] Philip, *Origins*, 113–114 n.180.

[212] Philip's contention does not apply to the crucial Spirit-passage *Virt.* 217, but to §218 ('God... rewards the lovers of piety with imperial powers'; cf. *Gig.* 47, et al.; cf. Leisegang, *Geist*, 115, 157, 160; Schweitzer, 'Gotteskindschaft', 109–110; Verbeke, *Évolution*, 251; Levison, *Spirit in First Century Judaism*, 97; Wenk, *Power*, 92–93). Abraham's nobility and striving for intimacy with God in §218 are *possibly* understood by Philo as effects of the inception of the Spirit in §217. See further 5.1.1.

[213] C. Noack, *Gottesbewußtsein: Exegetische Studien zur Soteriologie und Mystik bei Philo von Alexandria*; WUNT II/116 (Tübingen: Mohr Siebeck, 2000), 78: the Spirit 'schafft ein geisterfülltes *Feld*, das Lehrer und Zuhörer heilvoll umfaßt' (cf. his p. 80).

[214] Cf. Ibid., 89–92. While *Vit. Mos.* 2.69 mentions both the Spirit and inward (religious-ethical) transformation, this is not infusion-transformation because it is not clear whether the inspiration or the contemplation or both are the cause of the transformation. *Vit. Mos.* 2.272 also mentions inward change, but the ethical dimension is not drawn out and the Spirit not named. See further 5.1.1.

scribed in *De Virtutibus* 217 clearly focuses on the furtherance of Abraham's powers of persuasion.[215] While this characteristic of the Spirit's work is an empowering for religious-ethical life in the broad sense, it has become evident that this is not based on a physical transformation of Abraham's interior (which would be due to the potentially physical nature of the πνεῦμα) and hence does not support the concept of infusion-transformation.

In conclusion, Philo's writings neither give evidence for a material concept of the divine Spirit (possibly with the exception of one small trace), nor for the infusion-transformation approach to ethics.

The same conclusion also applies to *Wisdom of Solomon, contra* Horn. Horn argues that in Wisdom of Solomon 7.22 the Spirit is thought of in categories of fine substance, and that 'it is because of this that the indwelling of the spirit in the soul changes people that open up to it'.[216] Of the 21 adjectives by which πνεῦμα is described in 7.22–23, Horn has probably taken the adjective 'fine' (λεπτός) in v.22 to refer to a substance. However, it is methodologically questionable to arrive at such a conclusion on the basis of a single adjective which is part of a catena of various personifying adjectives, and which can be rendered as 'zart' (*Einheitsübersetzung*), 'pure' (based on *Anax.* B 12)[217] and (metaphorically) as 'refined' (LSJ, 'λεπτός', §II). While various scholars see Stoic and Platonic philosophy in the background of the pneumatology of Wisdom of Solomon,[218] many are aware that it is precarious to establish on the basis of this terminology that Pseudo-Solomon had a materialist pneumatology.[219] In fact, a great number of scholars affirm that despite some Greek philosophic language, Wisdom of Solomon remains faithful to OT theology.[220] Isaacs is even convinced that Wisdom of Solomon affirms the immaterial

---

[215] Cf. M. Turner, *Power from on High: The Spirit in Israel's Restoration and Witness in Luke-Acts*; JPTSup 9 (Sheffield: Sheffield Academic Press, 1996), 103; Back, *Verwandlung*, 37–38.

[216] Horn, 'Wandel', 155, drawing on Georgi (who, however, is referring to 7.23; D. Georgi, *Weisheit Salomos*; JSHRZ III/4 (Gütersloh: Mohn, 1980), 428); cf. Burton, *Spirit*, 156; Pinnock, 'Spirit', 79; M. Christoph, *Pneuma und das neue Sein der Glaubenden: Studien zur Semantik und Pragmatik der Rede von Pneuma in Röm 8*; EUS 23/813 (Frankfurt: Lang, 2005), 158; with parallels from Stoicism: Sänger, *Judentum*, 197 n.27; regarding wisdom: B.E. Gärtner, 'The Pauline and Johannine Idea of "To Know God" Against the Hellenistic Background', *NTS* 14 (1967), 230.

[217] See H. Hübner, *Die Weisheit Salomons: Liber Sapientiae Salomonis*; ATD Apokr. 4 (Göttingen: Vandenhoeck & Ruprecht, 1999), 104–105.

[218] E.g. J. Fichtner, *Weisheit Salomos* (Tübingen: J.C.B. Mohr (Paul Siebeck), 1938), 31; Isaacs, *Spirit*, 20–23; cf. D. Winston, *The Wisdom of Solomon: A New Translation with Introduction and Commentary*; AB 43 (Garden City/New York: Doubleday, 1981), 178–81.

[219] So, e.g., Verbeke, *Évolution*, 232; Bieder, 'πνεῦμα', 371–72; Lake, 'Spirit', 100; M. Neher, *Wesen und Wirken der Weisheit in der Sapientia Salomonis*; BZAW 333 (Berlin/New York: W. de Gruyter, 2004), 111. See also the nuanced discussion in Engberg-Pedersen, *Cosmology*, 22–24.

[220] So, e.g., J. Fichtner, 'Die Stellung der Sapientia Salomonis in der Literatur- und Geistesgeschichte ihrer Zeit', *ZNW* 36 (1937), 129–31; G. Ziener, *Das Buch der Weisheit*;

nature of πνεῦμα against Stoicism.[221] It seems, then, that Horn would have needed to give more and clearer evidence from other parts of Wisdom of Solomon's pneumatology for his case for the presence of a physical concept of the Spirit to be convincing. However, even if Wisdom of Solomon did have a materialist pneumatology, the book nevertheless provides no explicit or implicit evidence that it would be due to this feature of πνεῦμα that it transforms people ethically. Rather, the cotext of 7.22 reveals a relational concept of the Spirit's/Wisdom's ethical work (see 22a, 28).[222]

However, what we do find in Philo is the (abstract) type of language, as well as the (philosophical) genre from which it is hermeneutically legitimate to single out the writer's (or community's) concept of the nature of the Spirit, particularly as this is one explicit topic of Philo's discourses. This is mainly due to the intention with which Philo writes, namely, to give a philosophical defence of Judaism. He is not representative of the rest of Judaism in respect to his pneumatological language and concerns as one can see when one compares Philo with the other strands of Judaism that have been analysed above. However, he still remains faithful to (his understanding of) his ancestral religion in that he argues that the Spirit is an incorporeal entity.[223]

3. Conclusion

We have explored the different Hellenistic and Jewish sources which various scholars believe to contain both the concept of the divine Spirit as a material substance and the idea of infusion-transformation by this Spirit. With regard to the first concept, a clear difference in genre and focus could be observed between certain strands of Hellenistic pneumatology and the Jewish writings that talk about the Spirit. Many Hellenistic philosophers are interested in the ontology of πνεῦμα, and they discuss its im/material nature in their discourses. Some of them, particularly the Stoics, are con-

---

WB-KK 12 (Düsseldorf: Patmos-Verlag, 1970), 55; H. Hübner, 'Zur Ethik der Sapienta Salomonis', in W. Schrage (ed.), *Studien zum Text und zur Ethik des Neuen Testaments*; BZNW 47; *FS* H. Greeven (Berlin/New York: W. de Gruyter, 1986), 175, 186; H. Hübner, 'Die Sapientia Salomonis und die antike Philosophie', in H. Hübner (ed.), *Die Weisheit Salomos im Horizont biblischer Theologie*; BThSt 22 (Neukirchen-Vluyn: Neukirchener Verlag, 1993), 67, cf. 72–77.

[221] Isaacs, *Spirit*, 23; cf. Stead, *Substance*, 177.

[222] Cf. ch. 5 n.29.

[223] On Philo's place within Judaism and his (lack of) relationship with Paul, see the literature cited in Rabens, 'Development', 170–71 n.20; cf. Barclay, *Jews*, 390–91; L.W. Hurtado, 'Does Philo Help Explain Christianity?', in R. Deines and K.-W. Niebuhr (eds.), *Philo und das Neue Testament: Wechselseitige Wahrnehmungen. I. Internationales Symposium zum Corpus Judaeo-Hellenisticum, 1.–4. Mai 2003, Eisenach/Jena*; WUNT 172 (Tübingen: Mohr Siebeck, 2004), 76–77.

vinced that the spirit has a physical substance. Within Judaism, however, this interest could not be traced. The Jewish writings give evidence of statements regarding the Spirit's work but not regarding its im/material nature (with the exception of Philo, who explicates that the Spirit is an ἀσώματος οὐσία).[224] As far as the concept of infusion-transformation is concerned, however, neither Hellenism nor Judaism give any proof for its existence in Biblical times.

Consequently, claims like those of Horn, who thinks that Paul presupposes that the Corinthian church is familiar with the fact that the Spirit is comparable to a substance or fluid which 'become[s] the new substance of his [i.e. the believer's] existence',[225] need to be dismissed – at least as far as the New Testament-church's Hellenistic-Jewish background is concerned. Whether the church could be familiar with the infusion-transformation approach to religious-ethical life from Paul's teaching and letters themselves will need to be explored in the next chapter.

---

[224] Nonetheless, according to Turner it is possible to deduce from different passages of ancient Jewish writings that 'God's Spirit is always... the extension of God's *own* personality, vitality and power, the very "breath of his mouth" (Job 33:4; 34:14; Ps. 33:6; Wis. 11.20, etc.)... The "Spirit of the LORD" is, in other words, a way of speaking of God himself, present and active' (Turner, *Spirit*, 168).

[225] Horn, *Angeld*, 175.

Chapter 3

Infusion-Transformation through a Material Spirit?
An Investigation of Paul

At the beginning of the last century Heitmüller argued that for Paul ethical life is only possible by means of a new, ontological basis (*'naturhafte* Grundlage'*) which is founded upon the reception of the Spirit. For Heit-müller, this Spirit is 'only conceivable as a divine, physical-hyperphysical substance which is at best transferred via a physical medium ["*naturhaftes* Medium"]'.[1] This view of πνεῦμα and its work has had a strong impact on subsequent scholarship. While not all strands of scholarship accept this thesis,[2] it still plays an important role in some pneumatologies today.[3] The significance of this theory for modern studies is well illustrated by Horn's monograph on Pauline pneumatology. Taking up the suggestion of his supervisor, Georg Strecker, he puts forward that the answer to the question whether the Spirit is to be understood as function/power or as a physical substance provides the key to understanding early Christian pneumatology in general as well as Pauline theology and pneumatology in particular.[4]

It is important, therefore, to analyse carefully the passages Heitmüller, Horn and others use to support their case for the existence of a physical concept of πνεῦμα and its substance-ontological work in Paul. Interest-ingly, almost all of those passages are taken from 1 Corinthians. Conse-quently, one may ask whether it was the specific situation and problems of the Corinthians (e.g. their misconceptions regarding the sacraments[5] and the [material] πνεῦμα and its gifts, which are part of what has been termed 'pneumatic enthusiasm',[6] the latter being a component of their so-called

---

[1] Heitmüller, *Namen*, 326, italics added; cf. 319.

[2] See 1.2.1. and the Appendix.

[3] E.g., see T. Engberg-Pedersen, 'Body Language in Paul' (19th British New Testament Conference, Manchester: Unpublished Paper, 2001), *passim*, and Martin, 'Statements', 105–26, as cited below.

[4] Horn, *Angeld*, 5, 49. Horn's affirmative answer with regard to all three of these op-tions has been delineated in 1.2.2.3.

[5] See U. Schnelle, *Einleitung ins Neue Testament*; UTB 1830 (Göttingen: Vanden-hoeck & Ruprecht, 2007⁶), 85–86. Cf. 3.2.

[6] Horn, 'Spirit', 272–73; Horn, *Angeld*, 219, 221; for further aspects of 'pneumatic enthusiasm', see Horn, *Angeld*, 251, 262.

overrealized eschatology;[7] etc.)[8] that has made Paul use this very language (or even made him employ a new concept of πνεῦμα, as Horn believes[9]). This question should be borne in mind as we investigate these proof texts of 1 Corinthians and their possible backgrounds.[10]

It should be noted at the outset of our analysis that the infusion-transformation approach to the ethical work of the Spirit in Paul appears to rest on an anthropological presupposition that is unfortunately never made explicit or even discussed by its proponents. Namely, if it is mainly due to a *physical* Spirit that a substance-ontological change takes place within the believer, it seems to follow that the proponents of this approach presuppose that Paul must have understood the human interior (ψυχή/καρδία/νοῦς/πνεῦμα etc.) to be a *physical entity* too. It should suffice here to highlight this weakness as it would go beyond the scope of the present study to scrutinize this presupposition in detail. However, we will discuss every significant verse that has been called upon in support of the view that Paul believed the Spirit to be *Stoff*, even if a particular passage is not directly linked to ethical transformation (like 1 Cor. 15:44) because it is nevertheless a presupposition of and part of the infusion-transformation approach.

---

[7] G.D. Fee, *The First Epistle to the Corinthians*; NICNT (Grand Rapids: Eerdmans, 1987), 12; cf. A.C. Thiselton, 'Realized Eschatology at Corinth', *NTS* 24 (1978), 510–26. In his commentary, Thiselton shows how the cultural milieu of the city Corinth 'encouraged concerns about "high status" as "people of the Spirit who were gifted" within a Christian subculture with its own autonomous value system' (A.C. Thiselton, *The First Epistle to the Corinthians: A Commentary on the Greek Text*; NIGTC (Cambridge/Carlisle: Eerdmans/Paternoster, 2000), 40). For a critique of the 'overrealized eschatology'-view, see Martin, *Body*, 105–106; H. Tronier, 'The Corinthian Correspondence between Philosophical Idealism and Apocalypticism', in T. Engberg-Pedersen (ed.), *Paul Beyond the Judaism/Hellenism Divide* (Louisville: Westminster John Knox Press, 2001), 189.

[8] For an overview of scholarship on this issue, see W. Schrage, *Der erste Brief an die Korinther (1Kor 1,1–6,11)*; EKKNT VII/1 (Zürich/Braunschweig: Benziger/Neukirchener Verlag, 1991), 47–63. See Horn, *Angeld*, 263 n.1, for a list of those scholars who think that the experience of the Corinthians and the resulting pneumatology mark a 'decisive point' in the history of the early church.

[9] Horn, *Angeld*, 399–400, 430.

[10] One should allow for the option that there was no common denominator among the various problems of the Corinthians, so that it is 'methodologically safer not to construct a systematic picture which would in turn govern our reading of the text', as Hays cautions (R.B. Hays, *First Corinthians*; Int (Louisville: John Knox Press, 1997), 8). Rather, one should first investigate the text and then possible backgrounds. For this reason we will not engage in a detailed discussion of the background of 1 Cor. at this stage.

Excursus 1: The Alleged Concept of the Spirit as Immaterial Substance
(Rom. 8:9; 1 Cor. 3:16; 6:19; etc.)

The infusion-transformation approach to Paul's ethics builds on a concept of the Spirit as a *physical* substance. However, as at least one scholar, namely Horn, has suggested that Paul operates in certain passages with a concept of the Spirit as an *immaterial* substance, we will briefly deal with some of the proof texts for this hypothesis.

In the context of his differentiation of what he thinks are various concepts of the Spirit in Paul, Horn states that the Spirit is understood as an immaterial substance 'when the Spirit takes up residence within the believer as "forma substantialis" (1 Cor. 3:16; 6:19; Rom. 8:9; 1 Thess. 4:8).'[11] Unfortunately, however, Horn never explains how he reaches this conclusion. He gives no justification for introducing the scholastic concept *forma substantialis* into Paul.[12] What is more, when, at a later stage in his monograph,

---

[11] Horn, *Angeld*, 60, 429–30.

Lehmkühler raises a similar question: 'Es wäre exegetisch zu untersuchen, ob die paulinische Beschreibung... der Einwohnung... des Geistes... zwar einen "substantiellen", nicht aber einen "physischen" Vorgang beschreiben wollen. Das Adjektiv "substantiell" bezeichnet dann lediglich die Tatsache, daß hier etwas beschrieben wird, was in sich selbst Bestand hat und aller Reflektion vorausgeht. ... [n.110:] Der Begriff "Substanz" wäre dann fundamentalontologisch gebraucht (subsistere = in sich selbst Bestand haben), nicht... zur Bezeichnung lediglich eines bestimmten Gebietes des Seins (Substanz als Materie)' (Lehmkühler, *Kultus*, 251). However, Lehmkühler does not provide any exegesis, nor does he spell out how such an exegetical enterprise should be undertaken. Additionally, the plausibility of the outcome as well as the benefit of such an endeavour can be questioned. For one thing, it seems unrealistic that Paul thought about the reception of the Spirit consciously or subconsciously in the 'fundamental-ontological' way that Lehmkühler suggests, as 'something that exists in itself'. And, secondly, even if one could ascertain that in Paul Spirit-reception means 'something that exists in itself and precedes all reflection' one wonders what this may add to our understanding of Paul's pneumatology in general and to his statements of indwelling in particular.

[12] Aquinas, e.g., referring to 'forma substantialis' (as distinguished from 'forma accentalis', see, e.g., *S. Th.* I.77.6), defines that 'it is, however, proper to the substantial form that it gives matter being as such; for it is by means of this form that a thing is the thing it is' (*Anima*, 9; cf. *S. Th.* I.77.1, 6; 115.3–5). Aquinas thus differentiates *forma substantialis* from matter. On *forma substantialis* in early scholasticism, see B. Wald, 'Substanz; Substanz/Akzidens: II.-A. Frühscholastik', *HWPh*, X, 509.

The idea of *forma substantialis* was later to be criticized, beginning with J. Locke. (For philosophers who were critical of the idea of 'substance' in general, see Arndt, 'Substanz', 526–28.) Locke maintains that substantial forms are unintelligible and unclear (J. Locke, *An Essay Concerning Human Understanding*; Edited with an Introduction, Critical Apparatus and Glossary by P.H. Nidditch (Oxford: Clarendon, 1975), II, 31 §6; III, 6 §§10, 24, 33). Nevertheless, Locke too distinguishes corporeal and incorporeal substances, with the Spirit belonging to the latter category (Locke, *Essay*, II, 23 §§3–5, 15).

In personal correspondence, Horn acknowledged that introducing such a medieval philosophical diction into the antique history of religions runs the danger of taking theological preliminary decisions on a linguistic level which may strain early Christian views. He also admitted that today he would want to take into account to a greater extent

Horn provides a detailed exegesis of the passages mentioned above, the idea of the Spirit as an immaterial substance has become immaterial – it is not mentioned a single time. This may be partly due to the fact that Horn would otherwise have to assign the concept of *forma substantialis* also to various Tanakhic and Jewish-Hellenistic authors, as the Pauline indwelling- and temple-motifs have their roots in this tradition.[13]

An attempt to prove or disprove that Paul held a particular scholastic concept of the Spirit does not appear to promise a greater understanding of Paul's pneumatology. Therefore, this excursus will be limited to identifying some of the complexities of the interpretation of Paul's indwelling statements and to suggesting some possible solutions, focussing on Romans 8:9.[14] Moo's analysis of this verse will serve as a starting-point for our discussion. He writes that

…from the moment of conversion on, the Holy Spirit is a settled resident within. That Paul in the same verse can speak of the believer as "in the Spirit" and the Spirit as being "in" the believer reveals the metaphorical nature of this language. In the one case, the Spirit is pictured as entering into and taking control of the person's life; in the other, the believer is pictured as living in that realm in which the Spirit rules, guides, and determines one's destiny.[15]

In these lines, Moo has helpfully expressed that Paul, by means of his indwelling-language, conveys that the convert has come under the control of the Holy Spirit. However, against the background of the dominant linguistic theories of metaphor, it seems as if Moo is wavering between a literal and a metaphorical interpretation of Romans 8:9. On the one hand, Moo appears to say that the Spirit has literally become 'a settled resident within'.[16] On the other hand, he emphasizes that one is here dealing with metaphorical

---

the metaphorical nature of, e.g. the 'indwelling statements' that Paul applies to the Spirit (letter from 18.10.2001). Nonetheless, in an article published 2003 Horn upholds the substantial aspect although he acknowledges that the indwelling statements are metaphorical. See ch. 1 n.65 (Horn, 'Redaktionsgeschichte', 210).

[13] See Horn, *Angeld*, 65–76. On the parallels in the OT and (Hellenistic) Judaism, see Brandenburger, *Fleisch*, 137; D. Zeller, *Der Brief an die Römer*; RNT 6 (Regensburg: Pustet, 1985), 158; Fee, *Presence*, 114–15; Hays, *Corinthians*, 57; R.F. Collins, *First Corinthians*; SP 7 (Collegeville: Liturgical Press, 1999), 249; on the parallels to the notion of the Spirit's indwelling in the *body*, see H.-C. Meier, *Mystik bei Paulus: Zur Phänomenologie religiöser Erfahrung im Neuen Testament*; TANZ 26 (Tübingen: Francke, 1998), 253–55; *pace* Horn, *Angeld*, 72; W. Schrage, *Der erste Brief an die Korinther (1Kor 6,12–11,16)*; EKKNT VII/2 (Zürich/Braunschweig: Benziger/Neukirchener Verlag, 1995), 33.

[14] Further texts that could be discussed in this context in addition to those mentioned by Horn are Gal. 4:6; 1 Cor. 2:11; 12:13 (on this see 3.2. below).

[15] D. Moo, *The Epistle to the Romans*; NICNT (Grand Rapids/Cambridge: Eerdmans, 1996), 490.

[16] Such a 'local' rendering goes back to A. Deissmann, *Die neutestamentliche Formel 'in Christo Jesu'* (Marburg: Elwert'sche Verlagsbuchhandlung, 1892), 91–92. While Moo does not explicate that he holds a 'local' rendering of ἐν, this is nevertheless suggested by assertions like: 'having the Spirit of God dwelling in the person' is the condition for being 'in the Spirit'; 'Paul believes that every Christian is indwelt by the Spirit of God'; 'possession of the Spirit goes hand-in-hand with being a Christian' (Moo, *Romans*, 490).

language and that 'the Spirit is *pictured as* entering into... the person's life'.[17] This raises the question whether the Spirit has indeed taken *residence within* the believer, or whether Paul 'only' wants to communicate that the Spirit has commenced a new set of activities or experiences in the person.[18] This differentiation needs to be made because a literal rendering of the indwelling statements may mean both, firstly, that the person is locally indwelt by God/Christ/the Spirit[19] and, secondly, that she has come under the influence of the divine and belongs to God. A figurative interpretation, however, covers the second meaning of the literal rendering (a new influence and belonging) but not the first one (literal indwelling).

While Moo does not give reasons why he thinks of the phrase πνεῦμα θεοῦ οἰκεῖ ἐν ὑμῖν as a (literal) residence of the Spirit within the Romans, he does give reasons why he opts for a metaphorical interpretation: ἐν is metaphorical because Paul uses it synonymously when he explains earlier on in the same verse ὑμεῖς... ἐστε... ἐν πνεύματι.[20] Fitzmyer holds the same view. He says that 'both modes express the same reality'.[21] Fitzmyer's formulation is helpful, because Paul employs many metaphors by which he can describe the reality of coming under the influence of the Spirit (e.g. having been 'given' the Spirit [Rom. 5:5]; 'receiving' [e.g. Gal. 3:2, 14] and 'having' [e.g. Rom. 8:9, 23; 1 Cor. 6:19][22] the Spirit).[23]

However, one may wonder whether these modes of the Spirit's influence over the convert nonetheless describe *different aspects* of the same reality. While all of these

---

Engberg-Pedersen thinks that such a notion of local indwelling shows that Paul believed the Spirit to be a material substance (Engberg-Pedersen, *Cosmology*, 174).

[17] Moo, *Romans*, 490, italics added.

[18] For the latter view, cf. Turner, 'Spirit Endowment', 58, focussing on Lukan pneumatology; however, see also his more recent interpretation of Rom. 8:9–10: 'the description of the Spirit as "the Spirit of Christ" draws attention to the Spirit as bringing *the presence* and activity of the risen Lord into the life of the believer' (Turner, *Spirit*, 121, italics added). See also M. Theobald, *Der Römerbrief*; EdF 294 (Darmstadt: Wissenschaftliche Buchgesellschaft, 2000), 244–45.

[19] Cf. the change of subjects in 1 Cor. 6:19–20 from πνεῦμα to θεός. Likewise, in Rom. 8:9–10 πνεῦμα θεοῦ and πνεῦμα Χριστοῦ are co-referential for the Holy Spirit, and the subject changes from πνεῦμα to Χριστός (cf. N.Q. Hamilton, *The Holy Spirit and Eschatology in Paul*; SJTOP 6 (London: Oliver & Boyd, 1957), 6; Turner, *Spirit*, 121; Fatehi, *Relation*, 210, 213). On the differentiation of Χριστός and πνεῦμα being in the believer, see Fatehi, *Relation*, 269, *pace* C. Kourie, 'Christ-Mysticism in Paul', *The Way Supplement* 102 (2001), 78.

[20] Cf. Schrage, *Korinther. II*, 34.

[21] J.A. Fitzmyer, S.J., *Romans: A New Translation with Introduction and Commentary*; AB 33 (New York/London/Sydney: Geoffrey Chapman/Doubleday, 1993), 490; *pace* Fee, *Presence*, 547 n.210.

[22] Fee comments with regard to πνεῦμα ἔχειν that Rom. 8:9, 23 'and the clear language of 1 Cor 6:19 demonstrate [that] one "has" the Spirit only in the loosest sense of this verb. That is, this is a form of popular speech to reflect the reality of the indwelling Spirit' (Fee, *Presence*, 548).

[23] One could ask Horn how he distinguishes these passages from the ones that he has singled out as portraying the Spirit as an immaterial substance. It is likely that his criterion for deciding where the Spirit is a 'forma substantialis' and where not is Paul's usage of the prepositions εἰς and ἐν of the *indwelling*-statements.

phrases emphasize the believer's belonging to (the sphere of influence of) the Spirit,[24] it nevertheless seems that Paul's formulation that the Spirit 'dwells within' the believers refers to a more intimate reality of the Spirit than that conveyed by the other tropes. By expressing that the Spirit has been 'given' or 'received', no clear statement has been made about the precise location of the Spirit, whether these phrases are taken literally or not.[25] However, if one takes some of the more literal/local aspects of οἰκεῖν ἐν ὑμῖν and comprehends them as being part of the intended force of Paul's Spirit-language in Romans 8:9, one has to conclude that for Paul the Spirit was not only a new and dominant influence in a person's life but that Paul also wanted to convey that a new and intimate relationship to God/Christ/the Spirit has commenced through God/Christ/the Spirit's (')living in(') the believer. We deliberately placed the inverted commas within brackets in the last sentence. In this way we try to indicate that a binary interpretation of this verse in the sense of *either* literal *or* metaphorical will not suffice. By adopting this strategy of interpretation we apply Aaron's gradient model of meaning as a continuum, according to which the indwelling statement could be designated with the term 'ascriptive'.[26] In other words, one could place Paul's indwelling statements into category 'two' on a scale on which 'one' would stand for 'literal' and 'ten' for 'strongly metaphorical'.[27] It is a 'quasi-local' indwelling by the Spirit.

We can summarize our interpretation of Paul's concept of the indwelling Spirit by employing a different statement from Moo. In the context of his explanation of the indwelling language regarding Christ in v.10 (and its relation to the believer's being in Christ), Moo formulates very aptly that what is stressed is 'the believer's *intimate union with*, and domination by, Christ'.[28] The advantage of this formulation, which should not be confused with fusion, is its potential ambiguity that comes close to Paul's usage of ἐν in the indwelling statements. The concept of intimate union allows for a more or less *local* indwelling (which, on that matter, would concur with the anthropologies of Paul's time)[29] as well as for an interpretation which emphasizes the concept of being strongly

---

[24] Cf. the explanation of 'not having the Spirit of Christ' as 'not belonging to him' in v.9b.

[25] The same holds true with regard to the believer's being in the Spirit. Kourie writes concerning the concept of 'being in Christ': 'The person in Christ has not lost his or her personality in another, nor does he or she feel merged into the ground of the universe, but lives uniquely in another, namely the risen and glorified Lord. Such a union is not spatial, but personal: to be in Christ indicates that the adherent is under the power and influence of the spiritual and personal Lord, who is identified with the crucified Jesus' (Kourie, 'Christ-Mysticism', 75). In the case of πνεῦμα θεοῦ οἰκεῖ ἐν ὑμῖν, however, the spatial aspect of ἐν has a lot more weight because ancient anthropology often comprehended the human being as a vessel, temple, room, body, sanctuary, etc., that is to be filled or inhabited (cf. n.29 below; see also our Appendix n.158.). God's Spirit, *per contra*, is nowhere explicitly portrayed as a unit that contains other entities.

[26] Aaron, *Ambiguities*, 112, see 2.2.2.1. above.

[27] Whiteley has proposed the term 'secondary literal sense' to indicate that being a 'member of Christ' is not precisely literal (as the hand is a member of one's body), nor simply metaphorical (as one is a member of a college) (D.E.H. Whiteley, *The Theology of St Paul* (Oxford: Blackwell, 1974[2]), 133).

[28] Moo, *Romans*, 491 n.101, italics added.

[29] Cf. Meier's summary of his study of the conceptual background of 1 Cor. 3:16 and 6:19: 'Die Charakterisierung des Einzelnen als Tempel... geht direkt aus dem Menschen-

influenced by and belonging to the subject that is said to 'indwell' the person.[30] It has to remain uncertain whether Paul ever understood God's Spirit as an immaterial substance, but it is certain that for Paul this new reality and new self-understanding as people who are indwelled by God's Holy Spirit has by necessity an impact on the realm of ethics.

1. The Alleged Material Nature of the Spirit (1 Cor. 15:44)

Paul's treatment of the resurrection body in 1 Corinthians 15, particularly his locution σῶμα πνευματικόν, has a long-standing tradition of being employed as a major argument for the thesis that Paul understood πνεῦμα to be a material entity. As early as 1872, Lüdemann proposed that Paul's notion of the σῶμα πνευματικόν and hence of πνεῦμα is one of a 'heavenly

---

bild hervor. Wie mit der Bezeichnung als Gefäß der Mensch als offene Struktur beschrieben wird, so steht hinter der Benennung als "Heiligtum" die Vorstellung eines zugänglichen bzw. bewohnbaren Raumes. Die Grundlage dieses Denkens ist auch in 2Kor 5,1–4 greifbar, wo der Leib des Menschen als "irdisches Zelthaus" bezeichnet ist, das der Mensch bewohnt. Wo aber der Geist Gottes in diese Behausung einzieht, wandelt sich der Leib zum göttlichen Heiligtum' (Meier, *Mystik*, 257–58). See further K. Berger, *Identity and Experience in the New Testament* (Minneapolis: Fortress, 2003), 68–69; and M. Vahrenhorst, *Kultische Sprache in den Paulusbriefen*; WUNT 230 (Tübingen: Mohr Siebeck, 2008), esp. 154 n.78 on the methodology of employing parallels from contemporary cults in Paul's context.

[30] In this sense one can speak of the indwelling of the Spirit as 'mystical'. 'Mysticism' is here broadly defined as 'a form of religiosity which has the immediate experience of divine reality as its centre. This experience, which transcends everyday consciousness and cognition based on reason, is at the same time the *experience of an intimate closeness to the divine reality*. The concrete manifestations of mysticism are part of the historical and cultural context of a religion' (Meier, *Mystik*, 20, italics added). See Meier's insightful application of the various elements of this definition to Paul's indwelling statements in Meier, *Mystik*, 268–71. For further definitions and discussions of Pauline mysticism, see A. Deissmann, *Paul: A Study in Social and Religious History* (London: Hodder & Stoughton, 1926), 149, 152 (cf. the critique in S.J. Hafemann, *Paul, Moses, and the History of Israel: The Letter/Spirit Contrast and the Argument from Scripture in 2 Corinthians 3*; WUNT 81 (Tübingen: J.C.B. Mohr (Paul Siebeck), 1995), 419); K. Deißner, *Paulus und die Mystik seiner Zeit* (Leipzig/Erlangen: Deichert'sche Verlagsbuchhandlung, 1921²), 122–23, 127, 136–38; Kourie, 'Christ-Mysticism', 71–72; R.N. Longenecker, *Galatians*; WBC 41 (Dallas: Word, 1990), 153–54; U. Luz, 'Paul as Mystic', in G. Stanton, et al. (eds.), *The Holy Spirit and Christian Origins: Essays in Honor of James D. G. Dunn* (Grand Rapids/Cambridge: Eerdmans, 2004), 131–43. Sanders thinks that '"mysticism" has generated so much misunderstanding... that perhaps it is better to drop it than to hedge it by repeated definitions' (E.P. Sanders, *Paul and Palestinian Judaism* (London: SCM Press, 1977), 435 n.19; cf. Käsemann, *Romans*, 220–21). He prefers to speak of Paul's 'pattern of religion' as 'participationist eschatology' (Sanders, *Palestinian Judaism*, 548–49).

light substance'.[31] Pfleiderer developed this idea further and spoke of 'heavenly, supersensuous matter'.[32] They have been followed by many scholars since then.[33] However, this view has met not only with approval but also with criticism (e.g., right from the beginning from Wendt).[34] Nevertheless, in recent times, Dale Martin (followed by Padgett, Sumney, as well as the more elaborate Engberg-Pedersen)[35] has come back to this tradition and has given it a proper grounding by investigating 1 Corinthians 15 as well as the popular philosophies of the time. The following analysis is designed to engage with Martin's arguments for the material nature of the σῶμα πνευματικόν and πνεῦμα itself.

As we have seen in section 2.1.1., Martin is convinced that antiquity knew no distinction between matter and non-matter. Consequently, he argues that one cannot find any evidence that either Paul or the Corinthians were bothered by the prospect of an eternally existing materiality. Rather, the problem for the Corinthians lies in the resurrection of the *body*, not in the existence, in the present or the future, of matter.[36] The Corinthians question the idea that human *bodies* can survive after death and be raised to immortality. This would be a natural response if, as Martin assumes, popular philosophy and its deprecating ideology of the body had influenced them.[37] Martin believes that it was particularly the group of 'the

---

[31] H. Lüdemann, *Die Anthropologie des Apostels Paulus und ihre Stellung innerhalb seiner Heilslehre. Nach den vier Hauptbriefen* (Kiel: Universitäts-Buchhandlung, 1872), 149.

[32] O. Pfleiderer, *Paulinism: A Contribution to the History of Primitive Christian Theology. Vol. 1: Exposition of Paul's Doctrine* (London: Williams and Norgate, 1877), 201.

[33] E.g., Gunkel, *Influence*, 124–26; E. Sokolowski, *Die Begriffe Geist und Leben bei Paulus in ihrer Beziehung zueinander: Eine exegetisch-religionsgeschichtliche Untersuchung* (Göttingen: Vandenhoeck & Ruprecht, 1903), 63–64; M. Dibelius, *Die Geisterwelt im Glauben des Paulus* (Göttingen: Vandenhoeck & Ruprecht, 1909), 85–88; J. Weiss, *Der erste Korintherbrief*, KEK 5 (Göttingen: Vandenhoeck & Ruprecht, 1970⁹ [1910⁹]), 371–73; Bultmann, *Theology. I*, 198, 334; Käsemann, *Leib*, 135; cf. Käsemann, *Romans*, 212; Davies, *Paul*, 182–85; E. Brandenburger, 'Alter und neuer Mensch, erster und letzter Adam-Anthropos', in W. Strolz (ed.), *Vom alten zum neuen Adam: Urzeitmythos und Heilsgeschichte*; VSOD 13 (Freiburg: Herder, 1986), 207–208; E.E. Ellis, *Pauline Theology: Ministry and Society* (Exeter/Grand Rapids: Paternoster Press/Eerdmans, 1989), 33; Horn, *Angeld*, 60, 394; G. Strecker, *Theologie des Neuen Testaments (Bearbeitet, ergänzt und herausgegeben von Friedrich Wilhelm Horn)* (Berlin/New York: W. de Gruyter, 1996), 172–73; E. Kamlah and W. Klaiber, 'πνεῦμα', *ThBNT²*, 706.

[34] Wendt, *Fleisch*, 144. For further authors, see below.

[35] A.G. Padgett, 'The Body in Resurrection: Science and Scripture on the "Spiritual Body" (1 Cor 15:35–58)', *WW* 22 (2002), 155–163; J.L. Sumney, 'Post-Mortem Existence and Resurrection of the Body in Paul', *HBT* 31 (2009), 14–19; Engberg-Pedersen, 'Transformation', 124–29; Engberg-Pedersen, *Cosmology*, ch. 1.

[36] Martin, *Body*, 107.

[37] Ibid., 122.

Strong' at Corinth that was influenced by (this) contemporary philosophy and who thus claimed the status of being wise. Hence, early-Christian preaching about the resurrection of the dead had divided the Corinthian church along social status lines as 'the Strong' opposed the idea of a resurrection body.[38] 'The Strong' heard Paul's language about 'resurrection of the dead' (νεκροί) as referring to the resuscitation of a 'corpse', the normal meaning of the term νεκρός, and they found such a view philosophically ridiculous.

For Martin, this analysis is confirmed by the fact that both the questions of the Corinthians ('How are the dead raised? With what kind of body do they come?', v.35) as well as Paul's response show that the objection to the resurrection of the body centred on the issue of the *nature* of that body. The Corinthians assumed that no body could be so constructed that it could be raised and made immortal.[39]

In his answer to the Corinthians, Paul declares that the resurrected body will be a 'heavenly body' as opposed to an 'earthly body'. It will have its own substance and 'glory', on analogy with the heavenly bodies of the sun, moon, and stars (vv.39–49).[40] Like the 'earthly bodies' (v.39), the 'heavenly bodies' have their own hierarchy (v.41); however, the latter are not made out of σάρξ like the former.[41] Martin draws on Plato's *Timaeus* (32B-C2) in order to support his contention that the stars (the 'body of heaven') are made up of the four elements (and are thus material).[42]

How do humans relate to these 'heavenly bodies'? Martin explains that

> Paul, like the philosophers, assumes a physiological hierarchy of the cosmos, a scale of stuff along which the stuff (or more precisely, the various stuffs) of the human self can be placed. Unlike most Greek philosophers, Paul does not speak of the *psychē* ("soul"), but rather of the pneuma as the entity held in common by human beings and stars.[43]

Martin argues that also Jewish circles believed in this parallelism. For example, in Daniel 12:3, at the resurrection the wise 'shall shine like the brightness of the sky, and those who lead many into righteousness, like the stars forever and ever'.[44] According to Paul's system, then, Martin propounds that 'the resurrected body is stripped of flesh, blood, and soul (*psychē*); it has nothing of the earth in it at all, being composed entirely of

---

[38] Ibid., 105–108.

[39] Ibid., 125. Padgett is even more explicit when he says that the passage is about the 'physics' (φύσις) of the resurrection body (Padgett, 'Resurrection', 159).

[40] Martin, *Body*, 117, 126.

[41] Ibid., 125. Nevertheless, also the elements of the 'heavenly hierarchy' are material: 'all the "stuff" here talked about is indeed stuff' (128).

[42] Ibid., 118.

[43] Ibid., 126. Cf. Engberg-Pedersen, 'Spirit', 28, 32.

[44] Martin, *Body*, 118; see his p. 274 n.57 for further references.

the celestial substance of pneuma'.[45] Martin thus thinks that Paul does not reject the physiological and cosmological hierarchy of his disputants but rather 'assumes it and redefines the term "body" in order to allow it a place higher in the hierarchy and hence the possibility of immortality'.[46]

Like the older history-of-religions interpretation of the resurrection body, Martin's fresh analysis of 1 Corinthians 15 has had both affirming[47] and critical[48] reactions. As Martin's thesis has provoked a new discussion, it is necessary to investigate his arguments for the material nature of the σῶμα πνευματικόν and test their validity on contextual, rhetorical, logical and linguistic grounds.

The most important contextual presupposition of Martin's thesis has already been dealt with in section 2.1.1. There, it was concluded that, upon a careful reading of Plato, Martin's claim that the ancient mind could not but conceive everything, including πνεῦμα, as either fine or heavy matter, cannot be upheld. Likewise, Martin's support for his assertion that after death human souls will become (physical) heavenly bodies, which he sees *inter alia* in Plato's *Timaeus* 32C, is questionable. Contrary to Martin's interpretation of this passage, Plato does not speak of a 'body of heaven' as opposed to the body of the earth. Rather, he simply says that the body of the cosmos (κόσμου σῶμα) is made up of the four elements. He does not mention the stars in particular, nor does he suggest that the fire which they are made of (40A) is material, or that human souls will become like them. Apart from that, there is no clear evidence in Stoicism that the heavenly bodies, including the stars, were made up of πνεῦμα, as Martin and Engberg-Pedersen claim. Even Engberg-Pedersen has to admit this in a footnote.[49] Moreover, also Daniel 12:3 does not provide grounds for Martin's central claim. One is dealing here with a simile and not with an equation, which is indicated by the preposition כ/ὡς – the wise will shine as brightly *as* or *like* stars. The 'shining' is the point of comparison, and there is no mention that the discerning will be located among the stars, or will even become stars themselves.[50] Star imagery was deployed to indicate royal

---

[45] Ibid., 129.

[46] Ibid., 129.

[47] E.g. Engberg-Pedersen, 'Body', 16.

[48] E.g., Thiselton, *Corinthians*, 1269, 1276–77.

[49] Engberg-Pedersen, 'Spirit', 217 n.76.

[50] Cf. J.E. Goldingay, *Daniel*; WBC 30 (Dallas: Word, 1989), 308 (see also W.F. Smelik, 'On Mystical Transformation of the Righteous into Light in Judaism', *JSJ* 26 (1995), 124, who, however, only knows of the two options of metaphorical or mystical interpretation). The same holds true for *2 Bar.* 51.10 and the other texts cited by Martin (Martin, *Body*, 118).

position, so that one should hardly imagine that Daniel's expectation centres on an actual celestial transformation.[51]

Thus far we have seen that Martin's view of Paul's context is scarcely convincing. When we now look at Martin's interpretation of Pauline and Corinthian metaphysics, it appears that he is right that neither the apostle nor the Corinthians were bothered by 'the prospect of an eternally existing materiality'. It is doubtful, nevertheless, that when Paul, in his answer to the Corinthian queries, points his readers to a σῶμα πνευματικόν, he is deliberately building on a Stoic pneumatology with its explicit material concept of the Spirit. We will show that Paul's discussion of the resurrection body rather seems to focus on the inadequacy of what is 'merely human' or natural as opposed to what is of the Spirit and 'supernatural', the latter being the result of a transformation of the body at the resurrection.

The absence of any obvious concern for the materiality of the resurrection body is clearly apparent from a rhetorical analysis of the text. To begin with, Martin and Padgett partly rest their claim that Paul discusses the φύσις of the resurrection body on the formulation of the Corinthian questions in verse 35. However, they both may have underestimated Paul's immediate answer to this question: 'You fool!' (v.36). Wright points out that this sharp reaction makes best sense if one assumes that Paul takes these questions to be posed, like the Sadducees' question in the Gospels, not as a genuine enquiry but as a dismissive put-down.

"How are the dead raised?", in other words, probably implies "We all know it's impossible!";[52] "In what sort of body will they come back?" implies "I can't imagine any sort of body that would do that!" The word "how" itself can carry this overtone: "How can you say that the dead are raised?"[53]

Accordingly, the most natural way of reading the first question is not 'How, that is, in what appearance or type of body, are the dead raised?', but 'By what agency or power can this extraordinary thing happen?'[54] The second question ('what sort of thing is it') shows that the Corinthians wanted to know what kind of embodiment believers would have at the resurrection, but it does not specify an interest in the very physics of it.

---

[51] J.B. Green, *Body, Soul, and Human Life: The Nature of Humanity in the Bible*; STI (Milton Keynes: Paternoster, 2008), 174.

[52] Cf. Thiselton, *Corinthians*, 1261, drawing on Weiss, *Korintherbrief*, 367, and F. Lang, *Die Briefe an die Korinther*; NTD 7 (Göttingen: Vandenhoeck & Ruprecht, 1994[17] [1986[1]]), 232.

[53] N.T. Wright, *The Resurrection of the Son of God. Christian Origins and the Questions of God* (London: SPCK, 2003), 342; for support see his n.89. It could be added that 'corpse' is not the 'normal meaning' of νεκρός; according to BDAG, the predominant meaning is 'dead'.

[54] Ibid., 343.

It thus appears that the questions that were raised by the Corinthians did not focus on the issue of matter. Next, we need to analyse the rhetoric and logic of Paul's answer in order to find out whether the text implies such an interest on Paul's part. Paul starts his answer with two analogies, one from the plant-world (vv.36–38) and one from the animated and the celestial worlds (vv.39–41). It should be noted, contrary to Martin, that Paul does not set up a hierarchy of bodies in these verses; rather his list of the different bodies is determined by the (reverse) order of the first creation account (Gen. 1:16, 20–26).[55] Then, in verses 42–50, Paul explicitly addresses the Corinthian questions regarding the resurrection *body* (in vv.51–57 he continues more generally about the time and significance of the resurrection). His discussion consists of a series of contrasts as displayed in the chart below.

A vv.42–44   ἡ ἀνάστασις τῶν νεκρῶν: general statements about the resurrection

vv.42–44	σπείρεται (it is sown)	ἐγείρεται (it is reaped)
v.42	ἐν φθορᾷ (in corruption)	ἐν ἀφθαρσίᾳ (in incorruption)
v.43	ἐν ἀτιμίᾳ (in dishonour)	ἐν δόξῃ (in glory)
v.43	ἐν ἀσθενείᾳ (in weakness)	ἐν δυνάμει (in power)
v.44	σῶμα ψυχικόν (a natural body)	σῶμα πνευματικόν (a spiritual body)

B vv.45–47   οὕτως καὶ γέγραπται...: application to first and last Adam

v.45	ψυχὴν ζῶσαν (living being)	πνεῦμα ζῳοποιοῦν (life-giving spirit)
v.46	ψυχικόν (natural)	πνευματικόν (spiritual)
v.47	ἐκ γῆς χοϊκός (from the earth)	ἐξ οὐρανοῦ (from heaven)

B' vv.48–49   οἷος... τοιοῦτοι...: application to the Christian community

v.48	ὁ χοϊκός/οἱ χοϊκοί (the one/those of dust)	ὁ ἐπουράνιος/οἱ ἐπουράνιοι (the one/those of heaven)
v.49	φορεῖν τὴν εἰκόνα τοῦ χοϊκοῦ (bearing the image of the one of dust)	φορεῖν τὴν εἰκόνα τοῦ ἐπουρανίου (bearing the image of the one of heaven)

A' v.50   Τοῦτο δέ φημι...: general statements about the resurrection

v.50	σὰρξ καὶ αἷμα (flesh and blood)	βασιλεία θεοῦ (kingdom of God)
v.50	ἡ φθορά (the perishable)	ἡ ἀφθαρσία (the imperishable)

The discourse is structured by an ABBA-chiasm. The pair φθορά–ἀφθαρσία is mentioned at the beginning of verse 42 and at the end of verse 50 (and again in vv.52–54). Verses 42–44 (A) are general statements about the natural body (which is sown) and the spiritual body (which is reaped). In verses 45–47 (B) this is then specifically applied to the first natural

---

[55] Cf. Collins, *Corinthians*, 566–67; C. Burchard, '1 Korinther 15,39–41', in C. Burchard, *Studien zur Theologie, Sprache und Umwelt des Neuen Testaments*; WUNT 107 (Tübingen: Mohr Siebeck, 1998), 207–208; M. Hauger, 'Die Deutung der Auferweckung Jesu Christi bei Paulus', in H.-J. Eckstein and M. Welker (eds.), *Die Wirklichkeit der Auferstehung* (Neukirchen-Vluyn: Neukirchener Verlag, 2002), 46 n.70.

body in time (Adam) and the first spiritual body in time (Christ). What is said here is applied to the Christian community in verses 48–49 (B'). Verse 50 (A') comes back to the initial contrast and concludes the section.

Martin also charts the contrasts in Paul's discourse. However, he starts his table with the opposition of σώματα ἐπίγεια and σώματα ἐπουράνια in verse 40.[56] This is significant because it supports his thesis that for Paul the σῶμα πνευματικόν is analogous to the substance of the σώματα ἐπουράνια. However, at least on discourse analytical grounds, this parallelism appears forced. As is clear from the chart above, Paul's mentioning of σῶμα πνευματικόν in verse 44 is part of a textual unit (vv.42–44) which works on the contrast between what is sown and what is reaped.[57] Verse 40, however, is part of the previous section and works on the differentiation of earthly and heavenly bodies, introduced by verse 39 ('Not all flesh is alike, but there is one kind for...'). Verses 39–41 (cf. vv.36–38) describe different bodies within the present creation. Verses 42–44 (cf. vv.45–50), *per contra*, discuss not only a present, created body, but also a transformed (future) body that will be available only after death.[58] Moreover, it is problematic to apply the meaning of the descriptive dative-constructions in verses 42–44 to the σώματα ἐπουράνια of verse 40, as this application would mean, for example, that Paul views the *created* stars as incorruptible. Such a cosmology, however, seems foreign to Paul (see, e.g., Rom. 8:19–23, esp. v.22: πᾶσα ἡ κτίσις συστενάζει).

Two additional claims of parallelism between the heavenly bodies and the resurrection body need to be questioned. Firstly, when Martin states that the resurrection body will have its own substance and glory analogous to the heavenly bodies, he ignores the fact that Paul says of the resurrection only that 'it' is *raised* (ἐγείρεται) *in glory* (ἐν δόξῃ) (v.43). He neither

---

[56] Martin, *Body*, 127.

[57] It is hard to pigeonhole these contrasts into one (mode, not substance [so Thiselton, *Corinthians*, 1276]) or two categories (nature and mode [so Wright, *Resurrection*, 437]). Dunn responds to Thiselton that 'the terms "dishonor" and "power" (15:43)... denote mode rather than substance of being. At the same time it is difficult to escape the impression that an antithesis is being pressed at this point (mode, not substance) which does not reflect the range of contrasts envisaged. The dominant term, *phthora, phtharton* ("corruption," "corruptible") says something about the nature of present existence/life; it can hardly be separated from the thought that the substance of this body corrupts and decays.' Thus, a 'distinction between the what and the how of heavenly being is hard to discern' (J.D.G. Dunn, 'How are the Dead Raised? With What Body do They Come? Reflections on 1 Corinthians 15', *SwJT* 45 (2002), 14).

[58] One might add that Paul uses two different words for the oppositions: in vv.39–41 the opposition is between ἐπίγειος and ἐπουράνιος, whereas in verses 42–50 (vv.48–49) the opposition is between χοϊκός and ἐπουράνιος (with the exception of v.47: ἐκ γῆς χοϊκός; nevertheless, the difference may be in this particular case that Paul is talking about origin [ἐκ/ἐξ] and that he does not use an adjectival description).

speaks about substance nor does he name 'glory' as an attribute of the resurrection body.[59] Moreover, when Paul uses 'glory' as an attribute in verses 40–41, it is in reference to *both* earthly *and* heavenly bodies. This shows, once again, that it is not possible to place verses 39–41 in parallel with verses 42–44 (where 'in glory' refers to the raising of the σῶμα πνευματικόν, but not to the sowing of the σῶμα ψυχικόν).

Secondly, Martin explains that Paul speaks of 'the pneuma as the entity held in common by human beings and stars'.[60] However, when Paul speaks about the stars (v.41) he does not mention πνεῦμα at all (and, in fact, πνεῦμα is not mentioned in the context of the σῶμα ψυχικόν [v.44] either). It rather seems that Paul is using πνεῦμα here in a theological and not an anthropological way, as we will see below.

The fact that Paul employs πνεῦμα in the present passage only in connection with the resurrection body is a significant drawback for Martin's 'anthropological' interpretation of the text. Martin believes that 'for Paul, the current human body is made up of sarx, psyche, and pneuma. The resurrected body will shed the first two of these entities – like so much detritus – and retain the third, a stuff of a thinner, higher nature.'[61] However, Paul does not indulge in anthropological speculation like Martin. Otherwise Paul would have had to arrange his various terms, understood according to Martin as individual anthropological components, by placing σῶμα, σάρξ, ψυχή *and* πνεῦμα on the left ('merely human') side of the chart above, and σῶμα and πνεῦμα on the right ('resurrected') side. However, Paul uses his terms here mainly in a *pars pro toto* and broader theological fashion. This is obvious when he says that 'flesh and blood' cannot inherit 'the kingdom of God' (v.50) or employs πνεῦμα ζῳοποιοῦν for Christ (v.45). Therefore, when Martin claims that 'the resurrected body is

---

[59] Neither here nor in 2 Cor. 3:8, 18 does Paul give any hint that would justify a materialistic interpretation of δόξα as 'light-substance' (with Wendt, *Fleisch*, 144–45; Bertrams, *Wesen*, 115–18; et al. against Pfleiderer, *Paulinism*, 201; Lüdemann, *Anthropologie*, 21; Dibelius, *Geisterwelt*, 86–87; J. Koenig, 'The Knowing of Glory and its Consequences (2 Corinthians 3–5)', in R.T. Fortna and B.R. Gaventa (eds.), *The Conversation Continues: Studies in Paul and John in Honor of J. Louis Martyn* (Nashville: Abingdon, 1990), 160–62; Horn, *Angeld*, 60; Burchard, 'Korinther', 208–209; Engberg-Pedersen, 'Body', 19; et al.). Otherwise the contrast to ἐν δόξῃ in 1 Cor. 15:43, namely ἐν ἀτιμίᾳ, and the parallel to ἐν δόξῃ, namely ἐν δυνάμει, would need to be comprehended as substances too. The same problem arises for 'the ministry of the Spirit': its glory is set in correlation with the glory of 'the ministry of death' (2 Cor. 3:8), which renders its interpretation as heavenly '"light-substance"… which was considered to be more real, more lasting, and more solid than what we would customarily think of as matter' (Koenig, 'Glory', 160–61) as extremely unlikely. On the interpretation of 2 Cor. 3:18, see further 6.2. esp. n.62.

[60] Martin, *Body*, 126.

[61] Ibid., 128.

stripped of flesh, blood, and soul (*psyche*); it has nothing of the earth in it at all, being composed entirely of the celestial substance of pneuma', it seems that he is mistaking Paul for Plato.[62] According to Paul's discourse, however, it is σῶμα that stands for the continuity of the believer before and after the resurrection, and not πνεῦμα (which is not mentioned on the left side).[63]

What then, positively speaking, does Paul affirm about the resurrection body? It has already been mentioned that a central point in Paul's answer to the first question of the Corinthians is that it is only by means of a *transformation* that a (bodily) resurrection is possible (vv. 42–44 [building on vv.36–38], further elaborated in vv.51–53). By affirming that this resurrection embodiment is πνευματικός, Paul then provides further insight into the 'how' and the 'what' of the resurrection body.

At the outset of an investigation of the term πνευματικός in 1 Corinthians 15, one needs to note the rhetorical effect that Paul's use of the word must have had when used in association with σῶμα. Fee believes that 'it is hard to imagine the shock these words must have registered when first read aloud to the church in Corinth. A "spiritual body"... would surely offend those whose view of the material world is such that "spirituality" at least minimally has to do with being done with the physical body.'[64] When Paul uses σῶμα, however, it does not connote '(despised) physical body'. Otherwise Paul would have employed σῶμα only in the left column of the contrasts. The fact that he uses this term also in the right column demonstrates that Paul holds a holistic concept of σῶμα according to which the body is intended for the continuity of personal identity between this world and the next.[65]

---

[62] In fact, Martin's view seems to come close to that of the Corinthians. Cf. the description of the Corinthian position in B.A. Pearson, *The Pneumatikos-Psychikos Terminology in 1 Corinthians: A Study in the Theology of the Corinthian Opponents of Paul and its Relation to Gnosticism*; SBLDS 12 (Missoula: Scholars Press, 1973), 25.

[63] Contrary to Martin, Paul does not say that the immortal and incorruptible part of the human body will be resurrected, but he envisaged the transformation of the whole person in his or her embodiment (Dunn, *Theology*, 60 n.44).

[64] Fee, *Presence*, 263.

[65] Cf. A. Strobel, *Der erste Brief an die Korinther*; ZBK.NT 6/1 (Zürich: TVZ, 1989), 259. Further, W. Reinhard, *Das Wirken des heiligen Geistes im Menschen nach den Briefen des Apostels Paulus: Eine biblisch-theologische Untersuchung*; FTS 22 (Freiburg: Herder, 1918), 91; I. Hermann, *Kyrios und Pneuma: Studien zur Christologie der paulinischen Hauptbriefe*; StANT 2 (Munich: Kösel, 1961), 117; Dunn, 'Dead', 15–16. Thiselton is more systematic: 'it would be appropriate to conceive of the raised body as a form or mode of existence of the whole person including every level of intersubjective communicative experience that guarantees both the continuity of personal identity and an enhanced experience of community which facilitates intimate union with God in Christ

Paul uses σῶμα πνευματικόν in close connection with σῶμα ψυχικόν. This is particularly obvious in verse 44b where it forms the apodosis of a first class conditional sentence.[66] The logical conclusion from this linguistic observation has been brought to the attention of scholarship for many years. Already Deißner had pointed out that in the same way as σῶμα ψυχικόν does not designate a body that consists of ψυχή, soul-substance, so also σῶμα πνευματικόν cannot mean a body that is formed out of πνεῦμα, Spirit-stuff.[67] Rather, as Fee explains,

The present body is ψυχικός, "natural," in the sense that it is fitted for life in the present age. Belonging to the present, it is thereby subject to decay, humiliation, and weakness. The new body will be πνευματικόν, "spiritual," in the sense that it belongs to the final world, the world of the Spirit,... Thus, in keeping with the possessive form of the adjective, the "spiritual body" is a body that belongs to the Spirit in its final "glorified, imperishable" expression.[68]

This interpretation of ψυχικός and πνευματικός is supported by lexicographical research. Wright highlights the fact that, although it is precarious to generalize in so widespread and pluriform a language as Koine Greek, it is generally true that adjectives formed with the ending -ικός have ethical or functional meanings (cf. 1 Cor. 2; 3:1; Rom. 7:14; etc.)[69] rather than referring to the material or substance of which something is composed (for which the ending -ινός is characteristically used).[70]

---

and with differentiated "others" who also share this union' (Thiselton, *Corinthians*, 1279).

[66] Cf. S. Brodeur, *The Holy Spirit's Agency in the Resurrection of the Dead: An Exegetico-Theological Study of 1 Corinthians 15,44b–49 and Romans 8,9–13*; TGSG 14 (Rome: Editrice Pontificia Università Gregoriana, 1996), 90.

[67] K. Deißner, *Auferstehungshoffnung und Pneumagedanke bei Paulus* (Leipzig: Deichert, 1912), 34. Cf. R.H. Gundry, *Sôma in Biblical Theology: With Emphasis on Pauline Anthropology*; SNTSMS 29 (Cambridge: Cambridge University Press, 1976), 165–66; C. Wolff, *Der erste Brief des Paulus an die Korinther*; THKNT 7 (Berlin: Evangelische Verlagsanstalt, 2000²), 407; Turner, *Spirit*, 122; Tronier, 'Correspondence', 190; Hauger, 'Auferweckung', 48; et al. *Pace*, most recently, Engberg-Pedersen, *Cosmology*, 32, who draws in support on J.A. Asher, *Polarity and Change in 1 Corinthians 15: A Study of Metaphysics, Rhetoric, and Resurrection*; HUTh 42 (Tübingen: Mohr Siebeck, 2000).

[68] Fee, *Presence*, 263.

[69] This ethical aspect of πνευματικός can be seen in the present passage by the fact that Paul makes clear that to be truly πνευματικός is to bear the likeness of Christ (v.49) in a transformed body that is under the ultimate domination of the Spirit and fitted for the new age (Deißner, *Auferstehungshoffnung*, 34–35; Fee, *Corinthians*, 786; Wolff, *Erste Brief*, 407; Thiselton, *Corinthians*, 1278–79). Cf. Phil. 3:21.

[70] Wright, *Resurrection*, 351–52; cf. M.J. Harris, *Raised Immortal: Resurrection and Immortality in the New Testament* (Grand Rapids: Eerdmans, 1985), 120; Brodeur, *Agency*, 99, 102; Kamlah and Klaiber, 'πνεῦμα', 699; Thiselton, *Corinthians*, 1276–77; et al. Cf. n.179 below.

We can conclude, then, that for Paul the resurrection body is 'spiritual' – *not in Martin's sense of 'material'*, or of 'immaterial', but 'supernatural' (as Paul explains with the help of Scripture in v.45), because it will have been recreated by Christ, who himself through his resurrection came to be 'a life-giving Spirit'.[71] By calling the resurrection body πνευματικός, Paul conveys that the natural body will be transformed, animated and enlivened by God's Spirit (cf. Rom. 8:11 and parallels).[72] It is the most elegant way Paul can find of saying both that the new body is the *result* of the Spirit's work (answering 'how does it come to be?') and that it is the appropriate *vessel for* the Spirit's life (answering 'what sort of a thing is it?').[73] Moreover, we have seen that it is the *resurrection body* that is the focus of our text and not the nature of πνεῦμα. It is thus methodologically misleading to make the phrase σῶμα πνευματικόν the basis of one's understanding of πνεῦμα in Paul as well as his theology in general, as Engberg-Pedersen has recently done.[74]

2. The Alleged Infusion by the Material Spirit through the Sacraments (1 Cor. 12:13; 6:11; 10:3–4)

The so-called 'sacramental passages' in Paul are the *locus classicus* for establishing an infusion-transformation approach to Paul's view of the Spirit's enabling of ethical life. Particularly with regard to baptism, the infusion-transformation view draws upon what has almost become the

---

[71] Cf. Fee, *Corinthians*, 786 (in a later publication he specifies that Christ did not become *the* life-giving Spirit, but *a* life-giving spirit [Fee, *Presence*, 267]). We do not intend to contest that σῶμα could not be physical in this context. Rather, our point is that the resurrection body is a σῶμα renovated by the Spirit of Christ and therefore suited to heavenly immortality (cf. the discussion in Gundry, *Sôma*, 165–66). This does not imply, however, that when Paul said 'that the last "Adam" (Christ) became "life-producing pneuma", what he meant is that Christ became the kind of heavenly "stuff" called pneuma' (Engberg-Pedersen, 'Spirit', 30), because it is precarious to force the (potential) characteristics of the heavenly σῶμα onto πνεῦμα. Moreover, the logic of Christ being a 'life-producing pneuma' (v.45) is *explicitly* built on Gen. 2:7, not on Stoic cosmology.

[72] Cf. Bertrams, *Wesen*, 121–43, esp. 132; A.T. Lincoln, *Paradise Now and Not Yet: Studies in the Role of the Heavenly Dimension in Paul's Thought with Special Reference to his Eschatology*; SNTSMS 43 (Cambridge: Cambridge University Press, 1981), 42; Lang, *Korinther*, 234–35; Brodeur, *Agency*, 103, 263; R.B. Gaffin, '"Life-Giving Spirit": Probing the Centre of Paul's Pneumatology', *JETS* 41 (1998), 577; Dunn, 'Dead', 17–18; Wright, *Resurrection*, 351, 353.

[73] Wright, *Resurrection*, 353.

[74] Engberg-Pedersen, *Cosmology*, 14: 'Our guiding question will be how we should understand the *sôma pneumatikon*, and hence the pneuma. The answer to this question will turn out to have huge consequences for everything else we should say about Paul.'

communis opinio of critical scholarship, namely that Paul understands the Spirit to be imparted to believers by means of water-baptism.[75] A number of scholars, like Strecker, believe that this connection of Spirit and water 'most likely derives from the fact that the Spirit enters into a substantial union with the water'.[76] Berger explains that – due to the material concept of the Spirit that was predominant in antiquity and the Bible – the 'problems of transmission ["Transmissionsprobleme (Übergang, Vermittlung zwischen Geist und Körper)"], which were to become characteristic of western philosophy', did not arise.[77] On the basis of this line of thinking, Horn draws the following conclusion in relation to Paul's ethics: 'The holiness of the church is settled by the gift of the spirit (1 Thess. 4:8; 1 Cor. 3:16; 6:19) because it is sacramentally transferred (1 Cor. 6:11).'[78]

---

[75] See, e.g. H.-J. Klauck: The Spirit 'is infused by means of the *pneuma*-containing sacramental signs, through baptism and through the gifts of the Eucharist' (H.-J. Klauck, *Herrenmahl und hellenistischer Kult: Eine religionsgeschichtliche Untersuchung zum ersten Korintherbrief*; NTA NS 15 (Münster: Aschendorff, 1986²), 334). See further C.K. Barrett, *A Commentary on the First Epistle to the Corinthians*; BNTC (London: Black, 1971²), 289; U. Schnelle, *Gerechtigkeit und Christusgegenwart: Vorpaulinische und nachpaulinische Tauftheologie*; GTA 24 (Göttingen: Vandenhoeck & Ruprecht, 1983), 125–26, 133, 164; G. Haufe, 'Taufe und Heiliger Geist im Urchristentum', *TLZ* 101 (1976), 169, 419; M.-A. Chevallier, *Souffle de Dieu: Le Saint-Esprit dans le Nouveau Testament. Vol. 2: L'apôtre Paul etc.*; Le Point Théologique 26 (Paris: Beauchesne, 1990), 381; S. Chester, *Conversion at Corinth*; SNTW (London: T. & T. Clark, 2003), 281; A.J.M. Wedderburn, 'Pauline Pneumatology and Pauline Theology', in G. Stanton, et al. (eds.), *The Holy Spirit and Christian Origins: Essays in Honor of James D. G. Dunn* (Grand Rapids/Cambridge: Eerdmans, 2004), 151; D. Zeller, *Der erste Brief an die Korinther*; KEK 5 (Göttingen: Vandenhoeck & Ruprecht, 2010), 397; Engberg-Pedersen, *Cosmology*, 69. For a list of further scholars who hold this view, see J.D.G. Dunn, *Baptism in the Holy Spirit: A Re-examination of the New Testament Teaching on the Gift of the Spirit in Relation to Pentecostalism Today* (Philadelphia: Westminster Press, 1970), 98 n.11, and, with specific reference to 1 Cor. 12:13, A.R. Cross, 'Spirit- and Water-Baptism in 1 Corinthians 12.13', in S.E. Porter and A.R. Cross (eds.), *Dimensions of Baptism: Biblical and Theological Studies*; JSNTSup 234 (London: Sheffield Academic Press, 2002), 121 n.2.

[76] Strecker, *Theologie*, 173 n.79.

[77] K. Berger, *Theologiegeschichte des Urchristentums: Theologie des Urchristentums*; UTBW (Tübingen/Basel: Francke, 1995²), 53. Cf. Horn, *Angeld*, 57. Levison even thinks that πνεῦμα is released through the penis during sexual intercourse (J.R. Levison, 'The Spirit and the Temple in Paul's Letters to the Corinthians', in S.E. Porter (ed.), *Paul and His Theology*; PS 3 (Leiden: Brill, 2006), 206). More generally, Engberg-Pedersen puts forward that 'When people become Christians, according to Paul, they are infused... with a distinct, divine, wholly physical entity, the *pneuma*' (Engberg-Pedersen, 'Body', 17). Cf. Martin, 'Statements', 125–26.

[78] Horn, *Angeld*, 387, 298. For further references, see the summaries of Käsemann, Stuhlmacher and Horn in 1.2.2.

The verdict that the Spirit is transferred through baptism is opposed by a number of scholars,[79] and various authors propose a more differentiated view of the matter.[80] However, this section will not focus on this rather broad question which has already received considerable scholarly treatment. Instead, we will analyse the theory outlined above, namely, that it is the *material* Spirit of God that is transferred through the sacraments, and that in this way believers are substance-ontologically transformed and enabled for ethical life. In the context of this discussion we will utilize Dunn's widely accepted concept of 'conversion-initiation'.[81] Dunn argues that the event of becoming a Christian comprises both water-baptism and

the more inward, subjective (even mystical) aspects… like repentance, forgiveness, union with Christ. I shall therefore use "initiation" to describe the ritual, external acts as distinct from these latter, and "conversion" when we are thinking of that inner transformation as distinct from, or rather without including the ritual acts. The total event of becoming a Christian embraces both "conversion" and "initiation", and so we shall call it "conversion-initiation".[82]

It will become clear in the course of our analysis of the central proof-texts used in support of the infusion-transformation approach (1 Cor. 6:11; 10:3–4; 12:13) that Paul does not offer in these verses a separate treatment of conversion on one side and initiation on the other. Rather, as Hofius and others have argued, the Spirit is received *in the process of* (or as part and parcel of) conversion-initiation.[83]

2.1. Infusion by the Material Spirit at Baptism? (1 Cor. 12:13a; 6:11)

The focus of our investigation will be on 1 Corinthians 12:13 as this text plays a pivotal role in the argumentation of those who adhere to an infusion-transformation approach to Paul's pneumatology. It should be noted at the outset of the discussion that it is generally accepted among scholars

---

[79] E.g. Büchsel, *Geist*, 426–27; Stalder, *Heiligung*, 79, 201–202, 447; M. Barth, *Die Taufe – Ein Sakrament? Ein exegetischer Beitrag zum Gespräch über die kirchliche Taufe* (Zollikon-Zürich: Evangelischer Verlag, 1951), *passim*; W.F. Orr and J.A. Walther, *1 Corinthians*; AB 32 (Garden City: Doubleday, 1976), 284; Meier, *Mystik*, 271; Fatehi, *Relation*, 169.

[80] E.g. Dunn, *Theology*, 450–55; see also Horn's developmental model of the connection of baptism and Spirit-transferral (Horn, *Angeld*, 142–43).

[81] See Cross, 'Corinthians', 126 n.18, for an extensive list of scholars who have adopted Dunn's concept.

[82] Dunn, *Baptism*, 7.

[83] O. Hofius, 'Wort Gottes und Glaube bei Paulus', in M. Hengel and U. Heckel (eds.), *Paulus und das antike Judentum: Tübingen-Durham-Symposium im Gedenken an den 50. Todestag Adolf Schlatters (19. Mai 1938)*; WUNT 58 (Tübingen: J.C.B. Mohr (Paul Siebeck), 1991), 400–401; Hauger, 'Auferweckung', 54, esp. n.109; Cross, 'Corinthians', 132.

that this verse, as well as 1 Corinthians 6:11 and 10:3–4, belongs to those passages in Paul that present the interpreter with numerous exegetical riddles.[84] This fact in itself makes the infusion-transformation view less persuasive, because it is precarious to rest a case on tenuous evidence.

Throughout the first part of this monograph we have quoted Horn as one of the major proponents of the infusion-transformation approach. As we have seen in the introduction to Part I, Horn places a lot of weight particularly on 12:13c ('we were all made to drink of one Spirit'). However, we will begin our analysis of this verse with 12:13a ('For by the one Spirit we were all baptized into one body'). Agreeing with those scholars who think that Paul here speaks about water-baptism, Horn further develops this view by claiming that 'ἐν ἑνὶ πνεύματι not only signifies an instrumental aspect but surely also has the task of naming the common substance that enables the transferral of the πάντες εἰς ἓν σῶμα.'[85] It is not clear here whether Horn intends to characterize the Spirit as a physical substance, or whether he is suggesting a soteriological and perhaps even ethical 'ontology' and effect of the Spirit as 'gemeinsame Substanz'. However, it appears that Horn implies all these aspects of 'substance' when he later summarizes his interpretation of the entire verse: 'Paul... presupposes that the church is familiar with the fact that the Spirit is comparable to a substance or fluid which has been incorporated sacramentally into the believer; it has thus become the new substance of his existence.'[86]

Recently, Troy W. Martin has provided new arguments in support of this position. Martin writes

Paul's association of the reception of the Spirit with water baptism in 1 Cor 12:13a implicates the pores of the moistened skin as the ports of the Spirit's entry into the human body. The author of *Nutriment* writes that moisture is the vehicle of nutriment and without moisture the body cannot assimilate nutriment. Thus, water baptism is necessary for receiving the nutriment of Spirit.[87]

Martin thus attempts to explain 12:13a with parallels from ancient literature and even finds support within the biblical tradition itself. He believes that Mark's account of Jesus' baptism implicates the moistened pores as the entrance of the Spirit. Mark 1:10 narrates that as Jesus stepped out

---

[84] E.g. Wedderburn, *Baptism*, 241; Fee, *Presence*, 142; D.E. Garland, *2 Corinthians*; NAC 29 (Nashville: Broadman & Holman, 1999), 591.

[85] 'Hierbei kommt ἐν ἑνὶ πνεύματι neben einem instrumentalen Aspekt gewiß auch die Aufgabe zu, die gemeinsame Substanz zu benennen, die solche Überführung der πάντες εἰς ἓν σῶμα möglich macht' (Horn, *Angeld*, 173). Cf. the scholars mentioned by Barth, *Taufe*, 324.

[86] Horn, *Angeld*, 175; cf. 388, 400.

[87] Martin, 'Statements', 116–17, referring to Hippocrates, *Alim.* 55.1.

(ἀναβαίνων ἐκ) of the water, the Spirit stepped into (καταβαῖνον εἰς αὐτόν) him. Martin concludes:

> Since baptism does not involve drinking the holy water until later among the Gnostics and Mandaeans but rather involves immersing the body in water, the baptismal reception of the Spirit in 1 Cor 12:13a does not reflect an understanding of the Spirit's entry through the digestive system or through the oro-nasal passages but rather through the pores of the moistened skin.[88]

The foundations on which Martin rests his case are shaky. For one thing, in Mark 1:10 the Spirit came *from above* (like the voice from heaven), not 'from below' out of the water that Jesus is leaving behind.[89] More importantly, while Martin is right that the ancient medics understood πνεῦμα to be a physical element that is physically transferred, he has over-looked that all of these sources deal with πνεῦμα in the sense of *air* (or sometimes with the anthropological spirit) and thus need to be differentiated from texts concerned with the Spirit of God.[90] The following quotation of Erasistratus, who is frequently cited by Martin, gives ample evidence that there are no parallels between Paul's writings and those of the medics. Erasistratus maintains that 'when an artery was severed, the *pneuma* it contained escaped unperceived and created a vacuum whose pull drew blood from the adjacent veins *(paremptôsis)* through fine capillaries *(sunanastomôses)* which were normally closed. This blood then spurted out of the artery after the escaping *pneuma* [VII.19 & 20].'[91] Paul's language and purpose differ considerably from this medical account. In 12:13 Paul is concerned with the basis of the Corinthians' unity and not with the mode of the reception of the S/spirit and of spiritual nutriment.

Martin takes issue with Fatehi's and my criticism of Horn's position. He maintains that the ancient medical context of Paul's Spirit-texts permits them to be interpreted either literally or metaphorically, for even if the statements were completely metaphorical, the ancient physiology of πνεῦμα would have provided the perceived reality from which the metaphors arose.[92] He is, of course, right that the context of a passage is an

---

[88] Ibid., 117.

[89] Had there been anything physical involved in the reception of the Spirit, it would have been transferred via the dove and not via the water. However, it is important to note that the author explicitly says '*like* a dove'. Moreover, εἰς needs to be rendered as 'upon' (so all major translations) in the sense of empowering and not 'into' in Martin's sense of 'entry'.

[90] Cf. 2.1.1.

[91] Galen, *Plac. Hipp. Plat.* 6.6 (548–50K = *CMG* V.4,1,2 p. 396 De Lacy = *Erasistratus* Fr. 201 Garofalo), quoted according to J. Longrigg, *Greek Medicine From the Heroic to the Hellenistic Age – A Source Book* (London: Duckworth, 1998), 95.

[92] Martin, 'Statements', 117 n.57, referring to Rabens, 'Development', 169–72, and Fatehi, *Relation*, 168–69.

important exegetical clue. However, as we have seen in the previous chapter, various aspects need to be taken into account in the process of interpreting a metaphor. We will look at these aspects below when our own interpretation of 12:13 is presented.

In any case, it seems obvious that Martin has overstated his case because his claim that 'water baptism is necessary for receiving the nutriment of Spirit' is contradicted both by the ancient medics and by himself. All of them know other entry points of the Spirit apart from the pores of the skin. More generally, one wonders why the Spirit would first need to move into the water and then into the believer. In the case of baptism in the running waters of a river this would mean that for Paul the river would need to be indwelled or fused with πνεῦμα so that πνεῦμα could be received by the person to be baptized. It thus seems that it is the proponents of the infusion-transformation approach who have created 'problems of transmission'[93] and not those who are sceptical that Paul had such a view of water and of the Spirit of God. (These supposed 'problems of transmission' cannot either be solved by attributing both an instrumental and a locative/distributional sense to ἐν ἑνὶ πνεύματι, as Horn does, because even if a locative or distributional usage of ἐν were in view, this does not mean that the Spirit is therefore the 'gemeinsame Substanz'.[94])

In order to gain a deeper understanding of 1 Corinthians 12:13a, we will now investigate the reading of βαπτίζειν as a metaphor for conversion (in the context of which we will arrive at a more nuanced interpretation of the verse than that offered in our 1999 article).[95] Although Schrage is of the opinion that such a reading of βαπτίζειν 'is nothing but a postulate',[96] it will become evident that this judgement of the scholarly debate is inadequate. Dunn and Fee in particular have offered substantial arguments in favour of this understanding of 12:13.[97]

In his 1970 monograph *Baptism in the Spirit*, Dunn championed the view that 1 Corinthians 12:13a speaks about Spirit-baptism which effects incorporation into the Body and union with Christ. Paul does not speak about water at all.[98] Dunn builds this view on tradition-historical, linguistic and other exegetical grounds.

---

[93] Berger, *Theologiegeschichte*, 53, as quoted above.

[94] *Pace* Horn, *Angeld*, 173.

[95] See n.92 above.

[96] W. Schrage, *Der erste Brief an die Korinther (1Kor 11,17–14,40)*; EKKNT VII/3 (Zürich/Braunschweig: Benziger/Neukirchener Verlag, 1999), 216 n.607.

[97] Cf. Barth, *Taufe*, 318–38; Hays, *Corinthians*, 214; E.J. Schnabel, *Der erste Brief des Paulus an die Korinther*; HTA (Wuppertal/Giessen: Brockhaus/Brunnen, 2006), 729–30.

[98] Dunn, *Baptism*, 129. Cf. Barth, *Taufe*, 321.

First, Dunn maintains that Paul was familiar 'with the most striking utterance' of John the Baptist: 'I baptize you with water, but he [the Coming
One] will baptize you with the Holy Spirit (and fire).' This prediction is
recalled in all four Gospels, and it plays a crucial role in Acts (1:5; 11:16).
Dunn concludes that it is most natural that Paul is thus drawing on this
very tradition when he uses the phrase ἐν ἑνὶ πνεύματι… ἐβαπτίσθημεν.[99]
Fee agrees and adds that in contrast to a locative interpretation of ἐν,
which he prefers, one cannot find anywhere in the New Testament an instrumental use of this dative with 'baptize' (i.e. the Spirit doing the baptizing). Rather, it always refers to the element 'in which' one is baptized.[100]

Second, Dunn believes that 12:13a is metaphorical. He argues that 'for
Paul βαπτίζειν has only two meanings, one literal and the other metaphorical: it describes either the water-rite pure and simple (I Cor. 1.13–17) or
the spiritual transformation which puts the believer "in Christ", and which
is the effect of receiving the gift of the Spirit (hence "baptism in the
Spirit").'[101] Thus, the imagery of 'baptized in Spirit' is both coined as a
metaphor from the rite of baptism and set in some distinction from or even
antithesis to the rite of baptism.[102] Dunn contends that when Paul used the
metaphor, he was never concerned with the relation between water-baptism
and the gift of the Spirit. He does not say how close or how distinct they
are. However, Dunn points to two exceptions. Namely, in Romans 6:4 and
Colossians 2:12 the rite is explicitly related to the reality.[103] With regard to
the present passage, nevertheless, Dunn is certain that the force of the
metaphor is dependent on the metaphor being distinguished from, even
liberated from the rite from which it was drawn. 'Here again… we are
cautioned against relating the metaphor to particular actions in such a way
as to prevent the metaphor from triggering off the full range of associations.'[104]

Fee also believes that 12:13a is metaphorical. However, his assertions
are more moderate than Dunn's. He too argues that baptism and the reception of the Spirit, while both are assumed to be at the beginning of Christian experience, are not specifically tied together in such a way that the
Spirit must be received at baptism. Nevertheless, he thinks that for the
Corinthians the point of reference for the metaphor would be their own
baptism in water. This does not mean, however, that Paul intended the rite

---

[99] Dunn, *Theology*, 450–51.
[100] Fee, *Corinthians*, 605–606.
[101] Dunn, *Baptism*, 130.
[102] Dunn, *Theology*, 451.
[103] Dunn, *Baptism*, 130; cf. 227.
[104] Dunn, 'Baptized', 302. Cf. Hays, *Corinthians*, 214.

here or that the Corinthians would have thought him to be referring to it.[105] Apart from that, Fee provides an additional argument for the metaphorical nature of βαπτίζειν. He contends that 13a and 13c are most likely a piece of Semitic parallelism, where both clauses make essentially the same point. It is the clearly metaphorical sense of 13c that argues most strongly for a metaphorical, rather than literal, meaning for ἐβαπτίσθημεν in the parallel clause 13a.[106]

Third, Dunn and Fee derive further support for their non-sacramental interpretation of 12:13a from the cotext of the locution. It is not only the fact that 13c contains a metaphor that speaks against water-baptism as the reference of 13a, as mentioned above. It is also because 13c focuses on a common, unifying experience of the Spirit, making clear that Paul does not have a literal meaning in view. Building on verse 11 ('one and the same Spirit'), verse 12 ('one body') and verse 13 ('one Spirit... one body... one Spirit'), Dunn and Fee suggest that the *unity* that is brought about by the Spirit is the central point of the passage (cf. vv.1–4). It is the Corinthians' common experience of the new life through the Spirit that unifies them, and not the sacrament of baptism. 'Paul does not say "one baptism, therefore one body", but "one *Spirit,* therefore one body".'[107] It is not Paul's concern to outline how an individual becomes a believer, but rather to explain how they, though many, are one body. The emphasis lies on the 'one Spirit' (twice repeated), rather than the verb: it was by being baptized in *one Spirit* that they had been made into *one body*.[108]

Dunn and Fee have performed an important service in disengaging assumptions in New Testament scholarship which had tied the Spirit invariably to water-baptism in Paul's epistles in general and in 1 Corinthians 12:13 in particular.[109] Dunn and Fee have provided an insightful investigation of 12:13 which needs to be taken into account by every serious interpreter of this intricate passage. However, some aspects of their view can be refined. Building on Dunn's and Fee's work, we will try to offer a fresh interpretation of 12:13a while analysing their individual arguments.

First, Dunn's and Fee's contextualization of 12:13a within the tradition of John the Baptist's prophesied baptism in the Spirit appears to be the most obvious reading of the verse. However, a detailed comparison of the word order of the legomena unveils significant differences:

---

[105] Fee, *Corinthians*, 604 n.24.

[106] Fee, *Presence*, 180. Cf. Barth, *Taufe*, 323; Hays, *Corinthians*, 214.

[107] J.D.G. Dunn, *Jesus and the Spirit: A Study of the Religious and Charismatic Experience of Jesus and the First Christians as Reflected in the New Testament* (London: SCM Press, 1975), 261.

[108] Dunn, *Theology*, 450–51; Fee, *Corinthians*, 603–604; Fee, *Presence*, 178, 182.

[109] However, see already Barth, *Taufe*, *passim*.

Matt. 3:11 αὐτὸς ὑμᾶς βαπτίσει ἐν πνεύματι ἁγίῳ καὶ πυρί
Mk. 1:8 αὐτὸς δὲ βαπτίσει ὑμᾶς ἐν πνεύματι ἁγίῳ
Lk. 3:16 αὐτὸς ὑμᾶς βαπτίσει ἐν πνεύματι ἁγίῳ καὶ πυρί
Jn. 1:33 οὗτός ἐστιν ὁ βαπτίζων ἐν πνεύματι ἁγίῳ
Acts 1:5 ὑμεῖς δὲ ἐν πνεύματι βαπτισθήσεσθε ἁγίῳ[110]
Acts 11:16 ὑμεῖς δὲ βαπτισθήσεσθε ἐν πνεύματι ἁγίῳ
1 Cor. 12:13 καὶ γὰρ ἐν ἑνὶ πνεύματι ἡμεῖς πάντες εἰς ἓν σῶμα ἐβαπτίσθημεν

In all of these verses except two the verb comes before the preposition. In Acts 1:5 the verb interrupts the prepositional phrase. In 1 Cor. 12:13 both prepositional phrases come before the verb (and ἁγίῳ is omitted).[111] The question arises whether these differences in wording have any significance (because Greek word order may usually follow a certain pattern). Does Paul refer to the same event as the Gospels and Acts (i.e. baptism in/with the Spirit), merely employing a different style of writing? Or does Paul wish to convey a different idea, while following a standard pattern of Greek word order?

Porter suggests that fixed and flexible word order languages should be seen as arranged on a continuum. Thus, English and Greek, for example, differ in degrees of flexibility (rather than in kind) with regard to which particular elements of each language can be moved.[112] An itemized survey of New Testament-Greek has led Porter to the conclusion that the normal or non-descript word pattern centres on the verb (and its modifiers). The second-most-basic element of structure is the complement, occurring most commonly after the predicate.[113] With regard to our text this would mean that βαπτίζω ἐν πνεύματι should be slightly more common than ἐν πνεύματι βαπτίζω.[114] Porter continues that 'when the subject is expressed, the most common pattern for the Greek of the New Testament is for the subject to occur first.'[115]

Before Porter's findings can be directly transferred to 12:13a, further research would need to be done concerning the position the agent of a passive verb would usually take. Nevertheless, it is not difficult to see that

---

[110] On the textual variant, see B.M. Metzger, *A Textual Commentary on the Greek New Testament* (Stuttgart: Deutsche Bibelgesellschaft, 1994²), 242–43.

[111] These observations derive from my own research, but they have more recently been confirmed and expanded by M.B. O'Donnel, 'Two Opposing Views on Baptism with/by the Holy Spirit and of 1 Corinthians 12.13: Can Grammatical Investigation Bring Clarity?', in S.E. Porter and A.R. Cross (eds.), *Baptism, the New Testament and the Church: Historical and Contemporary Studies in Honour of R.E.O. White*; JSNTSup 171 (Sheffield: Sheffield Academic Press, 2000), 335–36.

[112] S.E. Porter, *Idioms of the Greek New Testament*; Biblical Languages: Greek 2 (Sheffield: JSOT Press, 1994²), 287.

[113] Ibid., 293 n.2, 295.

[114] Cf. O'Donnel, 'Baptism', 335.

[115] Porter, *Idioms*, 295.

if a writer was wishing to indicate the agent, she might place the word in the position that the subject of an (active) verb would usually occupy – that is before the verb.[116] If one assumes that 13a follows the normal Greek word order, it would therefore seem reasonable to conclude that ἐν ἑνὶ πνεύματι is the agent or instrument of ἐβαπτίσθημεν and not the element into which the Corinthians were baptized.

In addition to this line of argument from the field of syntactics, Turner draws on semantics in order to arrive at the same result: the verb 'we were all baptized/immersed' is semantically far more tightly related to the phrase 'into/for the one body', which immediately precedes it, than to the loose 'in one Spirit', which commences the sentence.[117] Dunn and Fee may thus be faced with a syntactical and semantic problem in that 'baptized/immersed' would have a double (local) reference in their interpretation (namely, both in the one Spirit and in[to] the one body).

Our reasoning thus far indicates a number of linguistic probabilities on which alone one cannot rest a case. Therefore, we will provide further arguments for our proposal that ἐν ἑνὶ πνεύματι should be interpreted as a dative of means or instrument.[118] One such piece of support is the way in which ἐν πνεύματι is used in the cotext of 12:13a. In 12:8–9 Paul uses ἐν interchangeably with διά when he stresses that it is *by* or *through* the same Spirit that people are given words of wisdom, faith and other gifts (cf. twice in 12:3).[119] Nevertheless, one could hold against this rendering that when Paul refers to baptism elsewhere, he never names the Spirit as an instrument (or any other agent preceded by ἐν, unless one reads 1 Cor. 6:11 as a primary reference to baptism).[120] While this fact indeed does not function as a support for the interpretation that we have adopted, it does not pose a threat either. In fact, the present interpretation is fully in line with Paul's soteriology in general: people are not being baptized/plunged *into the body of Christ* by a human individual, but by God (cf. the *passivum*

---

[116] O'Donnel, 'Baptism', 335.

[117] M. Turner, 'Receiving Christ and Receiving the Spirit: In Dialogue with David Pawson', *JPT* 15 (1999), 14.

[118] On this grammatical decision, cf. D.B. Wallace, *Greek Grammar Beyond the Basics: An Exegetical Syntax of the New Testament* (Grand Rapids: Zondervan, 1996), 374, cf. 165–66; F. Hahn, *Theologie des Neuen Testaments. Band 1: Die Vielfalt des Neuen Testaments – Theologiegeschichte des Urchristentums* (Tübingen: Mohr Siebeck, 2003), 277; et al.

[119] Cf. G.R. Beasley-Murray, *Baptism in the New Testament* (London: Macmillan, 1962), 167; K. McDonnel and G.T. Montague, *Christian Initiation and Baptism in the Holy Spirit: Evidence from the First Eight Centuries* (Collegeville: Liturgical Press, 1991), 43.

[120] So Barth, *Taufe*, 322; Beasley-Murray, *Baptism*, 167; Fee, *Presence*, 181. On 1 Cor. 6:11 see below.

divinum in Rom. 6:3–4; cf. Col. 2:12). As will be shown below, 12:13 is concerned with the common experience of the Spirit in both conversion-and-initiation, and 13a expresses the Spirit as an agent in this process. Nonetheless, the fact that Paul most likely does not refer to the 'baptism in the Spirit'-tradition in 13a does not prove that water-baptism must have been the reference point of ἐβαπτίσθημεν. It is also possible that Paul used the verb metaphorically as being 'plunged' (i.e. incorporated) into the one body by the agency of the Spirit. However, as we will see next, this may well have been connected to water-baptism.[121]

Second, Dunn's metaphorical reading of 12:13a rests on a number of linguistic judgments regarding the nature of metaphors. Dunn's insights agree with our findings in 2.2.2.1. when he affirms that a proper interpretation of a metaphor needs to beware of triggering off the full range of possible associations of the locution. However, Dunn appears to go too far in claiming that 'for Paul βαπτίζειν has only two meanings, one literal and the other metaphorical: it describes either the water-rite pure and simple... or the spiritual transformation which puts the believer "in Christ"...'.[122] Dunn seems to forget that for Paul there is *always* a spiritual reality connected with the rite of baptism (and not only in Romans 6:4 and Colossians 2:12 which Dunn explicitly acknowledges). *Contra* Dunn, there is no evidence in Paul's epistles that would place Spirit-baptism/reception in antithesis to water-baptism in the way in which John the Baptist differentiates *his* baptizing from that of the Coming One. Galatians 3:27–28, for instance, relates baptism to putting on Christ and to converts from diverse backgrounds becoming one. 12:13a also refers to baptism, though here the emphasis is put on the unifying work of the Spirit (cf. Joel 2:28–29). This is clearly apparent from the emphasized position of ἐνὶ πνεύματι/ἐν πνεῦμα in 12:13 and in the whole of 12:4–13.[123] Spirit and baptism are thus brought into connection in 12:13a, although Dunn and Fee are right that Paul neither here nor anywhere else explicates the exact details of the relationship of baptism and the reception of the Spirit.[124]

How then are Spirit and baptism linked in 12:13a? As we have indicated above, verse 13 reminds the Corinthians of their common experience of the

---

[121] Cf. Dunn's more nuanced treatment in J.D.G. Dunn, *The Epistle to the Galatians*; BNTC (London: Black, 1993), 203–204.

[122] Dunn, *Baptism*, 130. For a linguistic critique of such a binary conceptualization of meaning, see Aaron, *Ambiguities*, esp. ch. 3; cf. 2.2.2.1. above.

[123] That 13a puts the emphasis on the activity of Spirit is confirmed by Porter's analysis of the linear structure of NT Greek: normally the first position is reserved for the most important element (Porter, *Idioms*, 296, drawing on BDF, §472[2]). Stress is further put in v.13 on the *one* Spirit that was experienced by *all* Corinthians.

[124] Cf. C.F.D. Moule, *The Holy Spirit* (London: Mowbrays, 1978), 77–78; Thiselton, *Corinthians*, 1000.

Spirit at conversion-initiation. That the emphasis is placed on the Spirit has already been demonstrated. That Paul talks about conversion-initiation, however, is evident because he names *different elements* of the Corinthians' past (aorist) conversion-initiation (having been baptized [13a], united by the one Spirit into one body [13a/b], having received the Spirit [13c]).[125] It is most likely, therefore, that Paul uses baptism in 12:13a as *pars pro toto* for conversion-*initiation* (in 12:13c the emphasis seems to shift to *conversion*-initiation). The linguistic term for this usage is thus not metaphor but synecdoche.[126] A synecdoche designates one object by the name of another; a part is being used as a reference to the whole (or the other way round).[127] By means of this rhetorical device Paul is able to dispense with naming all the elements of the process of conversion-initiation (for other elements see, e.g., 1 Cor. 6:11; Gal. 3:2; etc.). He can remind the Corinthians of their common experience of (water-)baptism by which the Spirit has united them in the body of Christ and in this way calls attention to their experience of the one Spirit at the outset of their new life (cf. Rom. 7:6).[128] Against the backdrop of this interpretation, 13a and 13c

---

[125] It needs to be noted that the aorist tense does not inevitably indicate past action. See the discussions by Porter, *Idioms*, 20–26, 35–39; Wallace, *Greek*, 504–12, 554–65. However, the fact that Paul refers to baptism and to the Corinthians' diversity before their uniting in one body is a clear indicator that he refers to an event in the past.

[126] We are indebted to Cross for this linguistic insight. His thorough critique of Dunn's work has confirmed and deepened our own research. However, in his interpretation of 12:13a Cross understands Spirit-baptism as the primary reference (Cross, 'Corinthians', 142) and puts forward that both Spirit-baptism and water-baptism are in view (thus coming close to J.A. Brown, 'Metaphorical Language in Relation to Baptism in Pauline Literature' (University of Edinburgh: Unpublished PhD Thesis, 1982), 313, who thinks that 'baptism' functions here both literally and metaphorically). The position suggested in our study differs in that we think that Paul mentions water-baptism as a synecdoche for conversion-*initiation*. Whether conversion-initiation included for Paul the notion of Spirit-baptism needs to remain uncertain (*contra* Gloël, *Geist*, 142, who says the character of water-baptism is [here] Spirit-baptism) as there is no clear evidence in Paul's epistles for this language/concept.

[127] P. Schofer and D. Rice, 'Metaphor, Metonymy, and Synecdoche Revis(it)ed', *Semiotica* 21 (1977), 121–49; see particularly pp. 141–42 on the difference between metaphor and synecdoche. Cf. Caird, *Language*, 137: in synecdoche the link between the two referents is contiguous while in metaphor it is comparative.

[128] Cf. F.F. Bruce: 'If it is remembered that repentance and faith, with baptism in water and reception of the Spirit, followed by first communion, constituted one complex experience of Christian initiation, then what is true of the experience as a whole can in practice be predicated of any element in it. The creative agent, however, is the Spirit' (F.F. Bruce, *The Epistle to the Galatians: A Commentary on the Greek Text*; NIGTC (Exeter/Grand Rapids: Paternoster/Eerdmans, 1982), 186). However, if the focus were exclusively on *water*-baptism as such, this would be a novum in Paul because nowhere else is the Spirit conceptualized as being instrumental in water-baptism.

can be seen as a parallelism, as Fee has pointed out. However, to understand this parallelism too tightly and to claim that since 13c is metaphorical, 13a has to be too (or, because 13c speaks about Spirit-reception and
13a about baptism, therefore the Spirit is received at baptism), seems to
stretch the evidence too far. Rather, (water-)baptism by means of the Spirit
is the experiential focus of 13a and Spirit-reception that of 13c.[129]

Third, it should be clear from what has been said above that Dunn's and
Fee's argument that the focus in 12:13 is on the Spirit (and not on baptism)
cannot work as a proof for a metaphorical interpretation of βαπτίζειν.
While the (experience of the) one Spirit is indeed the focus of the verse
and the entire section, this does not disprove that baptism too was a powerful part of conversion-initiation (cf. Rom. 6:3–4; Gal. 3:27–28).[130] Hence
we can agree with Dunn, if we apply his interpretation of Galatians 3:27 to
1 Corinthians 12:13a: 'Evidently Paul could assume that that experiential
reality [of conversion-initiation] was so vivid in his own and his converts'
memory that he could refer to it directly (see... [Gal.] iii.2); whether
through a reference to baptism as metaphor or ritual act is a matter of less
moment; it was their experience of the Spirit as such to which his primary
appeal was addressed.'[131]

We can conclude that 1 Corinthians 12:13a does not lend any support to
the infusion-transformation approach to Paul's ethics. The Spirit is not
portrayed as *Stoff* that is transferred through the water of baptism in order
to re-organize the interior of believers in such a way that holy living would
be a natural result. Nor is it likely that the half-line has the Synoptic tradition of 'baptism in the Spirit' in view (*pace* Barth, Dunn, Fee, Fatehi et
al.), although it is possible that Paul uses βαπτίζειν as a metaphor for being
'plunged' (i.e. incorporated) into the one body by the one Spirit. More
likely, however, Paul reminds the Corinthians of their common experience
of the one Spirit at their baptism.

The same conclusion holds true for 1 Corinthians 6:11.[132] In this verse,
however, the reference to water-baptism is even less definite. Paul uses
ἀπελούσασθε along with two other verbs (ἡγιάσθητε, ἐδικαιώθητε), and he

---

[129] The parallelism works because conversion-initiation is the reference point of both.
In 13a via synecdoche, in 13c via metaphor (however, even on a literal rendering of 13c,
drinking could be a synecdoche for conversion-initiation).

[130] Cf. L. Hartman, *'Into the Name of the Lord Jesus': Baptism in the Early Church*;
SNTW (Edinburgh: T. & T. Clark, 1997), 66; Cross, 'Corinthians', 135, 145; Chester,
Conversion, 282–83.

[131] Dunn, *Galatians*, 203–204.

[132] However, to press one's interpretation of 6:11 by reference to 12:13 (so Fee, *Corinthians*, 247; et al.) would mean explaining one exegetical riddle with another.

does not name or single out baptism.[133] Again, Paul refers the Corinthians back to their conversion-initiation,[134] and the Spirit, though not the single focus of the verse, is portrayed as an instrument of sanctification (cf. Ezek. 36:25–26).[135] Nevertheless, this connection provides no clues that Paul would in this way introduce the concept of infusion-transformation (at the Corinthian's conversion-initiation) as an answer to the ethical problems[136] of the Corinthian Christians.[137]

2.2. Infusion by the Material Spirit at the Lord's Supper?
(1 Cor. 12:13c; 10:3–4)

As we turn to the remaining 'sacramental passages' used in support of the infusion-transformation approach, one has to notice that 1 Corinthians 12:13c and 10:3–4 are often considered as mutually interpretative keys. For instance, Horn explains that 12:13c reads like an allusion to 10:4 and verifies that Paul 'im Sakramentsgeschehen eine substanzhafte Übereignung des πνεῦμα gegeben sieht'.[138] How is this understanding of 12:13c (which is the main focus of our investigation) reached by its proponents?

Within scholarship in general, and among the advocates of the infusion-transformation view in particular, two major lines of interpretation of 13c are followed. One strand of scholarship understands the phrase πάντες ἓν πνεῦμα ἐποτίσθημεν to refer to baptism. The reasons for this interpretative choice are threefold. First, the fact that Paul employs the aorist tense suggests that he refers to a single event in the past. Baptism falls into this

---

[133] Cf. D. Schneider, *Der Geist des Gekreuzigten: Zur Paulinischen Theologie des Heiligen Geistes* (Neukirchen-Vluyn: Aussaat, 1987), 30. *Pace* Schnelle, *Christusgegenwart*, 39; et al.

Dunn and Fee interpret ἀπολούω as a metaphor but allow baptism to be a secondary reference (Dunn, *Baptism*, 121; Dunn, 'Baptized', 300–301; Fee, *Corinthians*, 246; Fee, *Presence*, 131). However, the presence of 'in the name of the Lord Jesus' increases the likelihood that baptism is primarily in mind. In any case, as we have pointed out above, in Paul the ritual is not divorced from the spiritual reality.

[134] Cf. Barrett, *First Epistle*, 141; Chester, *Conversion*, 141.

[135] Cf. Fee, *Presence*, 130.

[136] The prevailing moral problems of the Corinthians are evident from the letter as a whole as well as from the immediate cotext of 6:11.

[137] Horn writes that it was the Corinthians who misinterpreted this verse with a magical understanding of the sacraments (Horn, *Angeld*, 257). Elsewhere, however, he states that in (early) Pauline theology 'the holiness of the church is settled by the gift of the spirit... because it is sacramentally transferred (1 Cor. 6:11)' (387; cf. 388).

[138] Ibid., 170. Cf. M. Preß, *Jesus und der Geist: Grundlagen einer Geist-Christologie* (Neukirchen-Vluyn: Neukirchener Verlag, 2001), 145.

category and the Lord's Supper does not.[139] Second, Paul seems to relate
13c closely to 13a, both with regard to style (two aorists) and content
(Spirit-activity at baptism).[140] Weiss comments that the 'miracle is worked
through the Spirit who is effectively present in baptism and fills the water
with His powers... The believer is washed around and wholly penetrated
by the powers of the Spirit operative in the water.'[141] Third, this conclusion
is believed to be supported by Old Testament-prophecies about the coming
outpouring of the Spirit (e.g. LXX Ezek. 36:25–27; Joel 3:1–2; Zech.
12:10).[142]

However, a second strand of scholarship understands πνεῦμα ἐποτίσθημεν as a reference to the drinking that takes place in the Lord's Supper
(so already Luther and Calvin).[143] Klauck, for example, is unconvinced by
the arguments for a baptismal reading of 13c. He points out, first of all,
that the fact that Paul uses the aorist tense in reference to the drinking does
not preclude the Eucharist as an interpretative option of the locution.
Rather, it is only for reasons of style that Paul uses an aorist, thus intending a wordplay with the aorist of 13a (ἐβαπτίσθημεν... ἐποτίσθημεν). And,
with regard to content, Paul seems to intend the ingressive *Aktionsart* in
order to indicate that the 'initial incorporation of the individual into the
Spirit-penetrated Christ-body' through Communion is in view. In this way
Klauck also challenges the second pillar of the interpretation of 13c as
referring to baptism. Additionally, he suggests that 13a and 13c would be
so closely paralleled on the baptismal reading of 13c, that 13c would be
reduced to a redundant repetition of 13a. Apart from that, Klauck highlights the fact that 'drinking the Spirit' is not a suitable image for baptism.[144] Finally, with respect to the third pillar of the baptismal interpreta-

---

[139] Büchsel, *Geist*, 430 n.2; H. Halter, *Taufe und Ethos: Paulinische Kriterien für das
Proprium christlicher Moral* (Freiburg: Herder, 1977), 173; Barrett, *First Epistle*, 289;
Wolff, *Erste Brief*, 299; Schrage, *Korinther. III*, 217; et al.

[140] Schrage, *Korinther. III*, 217.

[141] J. Weiss and O. Baumgarten, *Die Schriften des Neuen Testaments* (Göttingen: Vandenhoeck & Ruprecht, 1907²), 134, quoted according to Beasley-Murray, *Baptism*, 170.

[142] E.g. Wolff, *Erste Brief*, 299. He explains that the imagery of 'being watered' means
'taking up the Spirit, being penetrated by it'.

[143] So recently H.-U. Weidemann, 'Zur Einführung', in E. Peterson, *Der erste Brief an
die Korinther und Paulus-Studien*; ed. by H.-U. Weidemann; AS 7 (Würzburg: Echter,
2006), LXVI–LXVIII.

[144] Klauck, *Herrenmahl*, 335; in support of his last point he quotes W. Bousset, *Der
erste Brief an die Korinther*; SNTG 2 (Göttingen: Vandenhoeck & Ruprecht, 1917³), 138:
'The picture would totally fit the issue if the holy water was being drunk.' Cf. Horn,
Angeld, 174; Horn adds that it is nonetheless 'denkbar, daß ποτίζω bereits als Taufmeta-
pher Verwendung findet. 1. Kor 3,5 beschreibt die Wirksamkeit des Apollos, der ja in
Nähe zur Täuferbewegung steht, mit diesem Verb. Doch gilt sogleich zu beachten, daß Pl
ab 3,1ff. eine Bildmetaphorik anschlägt, die nicht zwingend zum Sakrament führt (3,2:

tion, Schrage argues that the verses of the Old Testament on which scholars build this interpretation show no verbal parallels to 13c – ποτίζειν is missing.[145]

Positively speaking, Klauck and those following him[146] build their interpretation of 12:13c as a reference to the Lord's Supper mainly on its parallels in chapter 10. In 10:2 Paul mentions baptism (ἐβαπτίσθησαν; cf. 12:13a) and in 10:4 he talks about the Lord's Supper (πνευματικὸν ἔπιον πόμα; cf. 12:13c). Klauck thinks that the omission of the bread in 13c is no threat to his line of interpretation because in 10:17 the drink is likewise omitted.[147]

Horn supplies further support for this line of reasoning by bringing the Hebrew Scriptures into play. He explains that 13c presupposes the assurance of the 'outpouring of the Spirit' and is closely related to the language of the Septuagint (Isa. 29:10: πεπότικεν ὑμᾶς κύριος πνεύματι κατανύξεως). The verb is then translated as 'we were watered'. However, he continues that when ποτίζειν is applied to human beings it is usually best translated as 'to give somebody something to drink' (Sir. 15.3: ὕδωρ σοφίας ποτίσει αὐτόν; Jer. 16:7). According to Horn, this insight adds further weight to the interpretation of 13c as a reference to the Lord's Supper.[148]

Martin elucidates the nature of the disagreement between these two lines of interpretation. In physiological terms, this disagreement centres on whether one accepts that the Spirit is received through the pores of the skin in baptism on the one hand, or through the digestive system in the Eucharist on the other hand. Martin sides with Klauck and Horn, because 'the Eucharistic reception of the three necessary nutrients of solid food, liquid beverage, and Spirit through the digestive system correlates well with the understanding of nutrition in the ancient medical texts'.[149] For Martin, this reception of the material Spirit involves what one could name a 'conditional infusion-transformation'. In the context of his interpretation of 1 Corinthians 11:27–34, Martin explains that 'the spiritual food and the spiritual drink consumed in the Eucharist replenish the Spirit through the digestive system[,] and the Spirit cannot nourish a person whose constitu-

---

γάλα ὑμᾶς ἐπότισα).' Stuhlmacher thinks that both sacraments present interpretative options (Stuhlmacher, *Theologie. I*, 353, cf. 376). Cf. Blischke, *Begründung*, 226.

[145] Schrage, *Korinther. III*, 218 n.616. Nevertheless, Schrage acknowledges that Sir. 15.3 and Jer. 29:10 can illuminate the imagery of 12:13c.

[146] Particularly, Horn, *Angeld*, 174–75; Martin, 'Statements', 118. See already E. Peterson, *Der erste Brief an die Korinther und Paulus-Studien*; ed. by H.-U. Weidemann; AS 7 (Würzburg: Echter, 2006), 293.

[147] Klauck, *Herrenmahl*, 335; cf. Horn, *Angeld*, 174.

[148] Horn, *Angeld*, 174; cf. Klauck, *Herrenmahl*, 335.

[149] Martin, 'Statements', 118.

tion or condition prohibits the assimilation of these spiritual foods.'[150] Martin is thus aware that the religious-ethical effects[151] of infusion with the πνεῦμα are partly dependent on the condition of the recipient of bread and wine. In this regard, Horn is less nuanced in his conclusions regarding 13c. He does not discuss 11:27–34 in this context or elsewhere, but argues that 'Paul... presupposes that the church is familiar with the fact that the Spirit is comparable to a substance or fluid which is sacramentally incorporated into the believer and has thus become the new substance of his existence.'[152]

However, next to baptism and the Lord's Supper there is also a third line of interpretation of 13c. Barth, Thiselton and others believe that Paul has a metaphorical drinking of the Spirit in mind.[153] In accordance with this view, we will propose that πάντες ἓν πνεῦμα ἐποτίσθημεν is a metaphor for the Corinthians' reception of the Spirit, functioning as a *pars pro toto* reference to the Spirit's activity at conversion-initiation. We will test this hypothesis against the strategies for interpreting metaphors that were developed in 2.2.2.1., and, while doing this, the infusion-transformation interpretation of 13c, as outlined above, will be evaluated.

If one applies the definition of metaphor that was adopted in 2.2.2.1. to 12:13c, one arrives at the view that the giving of πνεῦμα (tenor) is spoken of in terms which are suggestive of the *drinking* of a fluid (vehicle), thus resulting in a new meaning.[154] A literal interpretation of the locution, *per contra*, expresses that the Spirit itself is a fluid (or fuses with the wine in the Eucharist or the waters of baptism) and enters the person via the skin at baptism or via the mouth and digestive system at the Eucharist.

In order to find out whether 13c should be interpreted literally or metaphorically, we draw on the main criterion for discerning the presence of a metaphor that was singled out in the previous chapter. This criterion was described as 'a certain semantic tension between an expression and its context'.[155] On a first reading, a literal understanding of 13c may not appear as a 'jarring deviation from the previous topic of discussion'[156] (another way of describing this criterion). However, if one looks more closely at the context of the expression πνεῦμα ἐποτίσθημεν, one will find that a

---

[150] Ibid., 124–25.

[151] Cf. Martin's list of the life-giving and life-transforming effects of the Spirit in Ibid., 124–25.

[152] Horn, *Angeld*, 175.

[153] Barth, *Taufe*, 322–26; Thiselton, *Corinthians*, 1000–1001. Cf. Dunn, *Theology*, 418.

[154] Our argument works in the same way on the alternative rendering of ἐποτίσθημεν against an agricultural background as 'we were watered'.

[155] Dawes, *Body*, 50.

[156] Beardsley, 'Metaphor', 219–20.

metaphorical interpretation strongly suggests itself. This will become clear as we look at the context(s) of the locution.

Context of Culture. Of the list of contexts that has been established by Fowler for the interpretation of texts, two seem to be particularly relevant for our endeavour: the context of culture and the context of reference.[157] With regard to the context of culture one has to recognize that the comprehension of the phrase 'we were all made to drink of one Spirit' depends on the *a priori* conceptions that Paul and the Corinthians had of the Spirit of God. A non-metaphorical interpretation of this phrase was, for them, only an option if they had been acquainted with the concept that the Spirit of God is or can be fluid or can fuse with a fluid and that it can be drunk in this form. In our discussion of Hellenistic pneumatology (2.1.) we saw that πνεῦμα was comprehended as a fine substance by the Stoics. Against this backdrop, Weiss' claim that the Spirit fills the baptismal water with its powers so that the believer is fully penetrated by it is indeed a logical possibility. Πνεῦμα would penetrate the water and would be received by the believer through the pores of the skin. Likewise, on the rendering of ποτίζω as drinking, the physical πνεῦμα would first fuse with the drink and then with the believers in order to transform them.

However, it is a significant drawback that none of the proponents of the infusion-transformation approach provide evidence from Paul's context that πνεῦμα was understood to fuse with a drink – not even in the case of πνεῦμα being understood as air, which seems to be Martin's main reference point. Nor do they provide examples for the concept of πνεῦμα as a fluid that would be drunk.[158] According to Stoic physics, πνεῦμα permeates everything, and it is not injected into certain entities (i.e. human beings) by virtue of a transmitter (i.e. fluid) that first needs to be injected with it. On top of this, the question concerning the existence of facilities for taking in *divine* πνεῦμα through the human skin or digestive system does not receive satisfactory treatment. The medical texts specified by Martin allow for the reception of air (πνεῦμα) through the stomach. They also discuss the constitution of the human body as a prerequisite for the consumption of certain beverages.[159] However, it seems that Martin has overlooked that his model for understanding 12:13c needs to be applicable to the Spirit *of God*, whose nature may permit different 'entry points' than air, and whose life-giving activity is in Paul usually not focussed on the physical aspect of

---

[157] Fowler, *Criticism*, 110–16. See 2.2.2.1. above.

[158] On the contrary, in some contexts πνεῦμα and fluid are even put in opposition to each other. Martin states that one ancient author 'describes the body as having many hollow parts that in health are filled with *pneuma* but in disease with fluid' (Martin, 'Statements', 114, citing Hippocrates, *De arte* 10.9–12).

[159] Ibid., 122–23.

life, but more explicitly on the 'spiritual' which may include or have consequences for the physical (cf. Rom. 7:6; 8:2, 10–11; 2 Cor. 3:6; Gal.
6:8).[160] Moreover, 11:27–34 does not talk about physical, but about *religious-ethical* prerequisites for receiving the Lord's Supper.[161]

However, the cultural context of 12:13c not only encompasses Hellenistic philosophy and medicine but also the Hebrew Bible and early Judaism.
In fact, although these lines were dynamically interrelated, one result of
our study is that Paul's pneumatology was particularly dependant on Jewish sources (see esp. ch. 5). Therefore, the question arises whether this
context suggests that the readers of Paul's epistles would understand
πνεῦμα ποτίζειν as a literal concept. Those who interpret 13c as a reference to Spirit-reception at baptism frequently draw on the tradition of the
promised outpouring of the Spirit (Joel 2:28–29, etc.), although the verb as
such is missing in those prophecies. In connection with the translation of
ἐποτίσθημεν as 'we have been watered' this is indeed a possible background – but it is not possible to take this as a support for the infusion-
transformation view. As has been argued in detail in section 2.2.2.1., non-
literal usage of 'pouring out' abounds in the Hebrew Bible and subsequent
Judaism, and there is no evidence that it was ever used (literally) with a
clear implication of a material concept of the Spirit.

Nevertheless, could references from the Septuagint that *do* contain
ποτίζειν serve as a more suitable backdrop for a literal interpretation of
13c? The literal meaning of ποτίζειν in the Septuagint is either 'to water'
(e.g., Gen. 13:10; Ps. 103:13) or 'to drink' (e.g., Prov. 25:21; Jer. 16:7).
The problem that arises for the baptismal reading of 12:13c is the fact that
when the verb is applied to a human being (as opposed to a plant or animal), the meaning is usually 'to drink'.[162] Literal drinking, however, has no
correspondence at Christian baptism.

This is, of course, different for the Lord's Supper where literal drinking
takes place. However, one does not find any reference to a literal drinking
of the Spirit in Paul's Jewish context.[163] Whenever ποτίζειν is used in the
Septuagint for an object other than water or beverage, it has an overt meta-

---

[160] Cf. 1 Cor. 15:44 on the future work of the Spirit (see 3.1.).

[161] If Martin's focus on the physical aspect of the food and drink and on the physical
conditions of the recipients in the Holy Communion were right, this would have strong
implications for our understanding of any food and drink in a religious context in the
Bible (e.g. the Jewish Temple cult; food in the context of idol-worship [1 Cor. 8; 10:14–
30]; etc.).

[162] BDAG, s.v., §1; Klauck, *Herrenmahl*, 334–35; Horn, *Angeld*, 174; et al. However,
see also the usage of ποτίζειν as an agricultural metaphor in 1 Cor. 3:6–8.

[163] Cf. 2.2.3.1.

phorical meaning (e.g., LXX Pss. 35:9; 59:5; Isaiah 29:10;[164] Sir. 15.3; 24:21: 'those who drink me [i.e. wisdom] will thirst for more'; *Pss. Sol.* 8.14; etc.; cf. Jn. 7:37–39). None of these verses lend support to the idea that the writer is suggesting that splendour, wisdom, a spirit of deep sleep, *et alia*, have a material nature and are received via the mouth, stomach and intestines. Therefore, from the perspective of the 'context of culture' of 1 Corinthians 12:13c, it is highly improbable that Paul's locution 'we were all made to drink of one Spirit' refers to physical drinking.

As there is, on the one hand, no evidence in the context of culture that would suggest that Paul and his readers understood ἐν πνεῦμα ἐποτίσθημεν literally, but, on the other hand, plenty of evidence for a metaphorical usage of ποτίζειν, we can conclude that most probably this meaning is also intended in 12:13c.[165] Whether Paul has primarily a metaphorical drinking[166] or a metaphorical watering[167] in mind, is of secondary importance. In both cases the Spirit is pictured as being given to the converts to take in new life and sustenance.[168]

Context of Reference. The context of reference (especially the topic or subject-matter of a text)[169] provides further reasons for preferring a metaphorical reading of 12:13c over a literal one. The subject of Paul's exposition in 1 Corinthians 12 is the unity of the many members in the one body of Christ that is based on the work of the one Spirit. While the beginning and end of the chapter deal with the present work of the Spirit through the gifts, verse 13 (like an *inclusio* or centrepiece) places specific emphasis on the work of the Spirit in Paul's and the Corinthians' past. With the two aorists (13a and 13c) Paul refers back to their conversion-initiation. 12:13a clearly marks an unrepeated event in the past, namely baptism. If Paul intends some kind of parallelism between ἐβαπτίσθημεν and ἐποτίσθημεν, it is likely that, in 13c, Paul does not refer to the (repetitive) Eucharist. How-

---

[164] Isa. 29:10 has 'spirit [of deep sleep]' in the dative, not accusative as in 1 Cor. 12:13c and the other examples from the LXX above (cf. Fee, *Corinthians*, 605 n.28; Garland, *2 Corinthians*, 591).

[165] Cf. P. Feine, *Theologie des Neuen Testaments* (Berlin: Evangelische Verlagsanstalt, 1953[8] [1911[2]]), 260–61.

[166] So, e.g., Fee, *Presence*, 179–80.

[167] So, e.g., Dunn, *Baptism*, 131; F. Lang, 'Das Verständnis der Taufe bei Paulus', in J. Ådna, et al. (eds.), *Evangelium – Schriftauslegung – Kirche: Festschrift für Peter Stuhlmacher zum 65. Geburtstag* (Göttingen: Vandenhoeck & Ruprecht, 1997), 263. Cf. the German 'übergossen werden', which is preferred by Schnabel, *Korinther*, 731, and N. Baumert, *Die Sorgen des Seelsorgers: Übersetzung und Auslegung des ersten Korintherbriefes*; Paulus neu gelesen (Würzburg: Echter, 2007), 202–203. Baumert points out that this rendering strengthens the communal aspect of the verse (as opposed to a more 'individual' drinking).

[168] Cf. Str–B II, 433–36; L. Goppelt, 'πίνω κτλ', *TDNT*, VI, 135–60.

[169] See Fowler, *Criticism*, 114; cf. 2.2.2.1.

ever, as we have seen, this does not leave baptism as an alternative interpretation for 13c. This is because, in addition to our critique of this option
in our treatment of the 'context of culture' above, Klauck and others have
demonstrated that this view is implausible from the 'context of reference'
of 12:13c. In this context of reference there is no indication that the unity
of the body is based on the infusion of a material Spirit. Neither is Paul
concerned with the mode of reception or the ethical effect of the Spirit (in
the sense of transferral of a [new] substance).[170] He does not provide a
(philosophical) discourse on any of these specific topics but rather has the
soteriological (conversion-initiation) and ecclesiological (unity of the body
of Christ) work of the Spirit in general in view. While this does not rule
out that Paul had a literal drinking of the Spirit in the Lord's Supper in
mind, it does not work in favour of this interpretation either.

What speaks clearly against the interpretation of 13c as a reference to
the Eucharist, however, is the fact that in the wider (literary) context of
reference, namely 1 Corinthians, Paul always connects the Lord's Supper
with (the blood of) Christ and not with the Spirit (e.g. 10:16; 11:25, 27).[171]
The presupposition for a literal drinking of the (physical) Spirit at the
Eucharist would be a transubstantiation of wine into πνεῦμα. This line of
thought, however, does not appear to be Pauline at all. Had he wanted to
point to the Lord's Supper in 13c, the natural way of doing so would have
been to write 'we were all made to drink of the blood of Christ' or 'we
were all made to drink Christ'.[172]

On top of this, the argument that is deemed by the proponents of the
Eucharistic interpretation to be the strongest one, namely the supposed
parallel to 1 Corinthians 10:3–4, is hardly convincing. The judgement of
Horn and others that 'it can hardly be disputed that Paul here displays a
realistic understanding of the sacraments, that is, the Spirit is transferred

---

[170] The same conclusion also applies to Horn's interpretation of Spirit as *Stoff* in 2
Cor. 1:22; 5:5 (Horn, *Angeld*, 393–94). See Rabens, 'Development', 171, for a discussion
of Horn's exegesis. Cf. Hofius, 'Wort', 400–401, and S. Kim, *Paul and the New Perspective: Second Thoughts on the Origin of Paul's Gospel* (Cambridge/Grand Rapids: Eerdmans, 2002), 117–21, for a critical evaluation of a baptismal reading of these verses.

[171] On the potential exception in 10:3–4, see below.
What is more, Paul usually mentions both bread and cup together when he talks about
the Lord's Supper. Klauck has overlooked that this is true also in 1 Cor. 10:16 and 10:21,
so that the single reference to the bread in 10:17 is not at all a parallel to 12:13c where
one cannot find any other Eucharistic language apart from ἐποτίσθημεν (and this, as it has
become evident, is not an unambiguous reference either).

[172] An additional question arises in respect to the view that the (material) Spirit has
been/is infused into believers in order to transform their substance: If the believer has
already received a new substance through the (physical) Spirit at baptism (13a), one may
wonder what exactly is being gained additionally at the Eucharist (13c). However, this
matter is not discussed by those who opt for an infusion-transformation interpretation.

substantially with the food',[173] is indeed disputable.[174] Horn, following Käsemann,[175] builds this view on the interpretation of πνευματικός in πνευματικὸν βρῶμα and πόμα. However, we have already seen in our discussion of 1 Corinthians 15:44–45 that adjectives with the ending -ικός do not normally refer to the material or substance of which something is composed. Rather, it is much more likely[176] that πνευματικός points here to food that is 'miraculously provided by the Spirit of God, not food with a heavenly taste or texture. Nor indeed was the water spiritual in character. It was, rather, spiritually provided, just as the rock was spiritually enabled to give water.'[177]

This interpretation is supported by Exodus 16:15: Upon the Israelites' asking what the manna was, Moses answered them, 'It is the bread that the Lord has given you to eat' (cf. Ps. 78:25; Wis. 16.20; Jn. 6:32). Also the drink was spiritual or supernatural *because* it was provided by a spiritual rock (ἔπινον γὰρ ἐκ πνευματικῆς... πέτρας, 10:4).[178] The fact that the (physical) rock too is described as πνευματικός, therefore, does not supply further reasons for the alleged material nature of the Spirit (otherwise, what implications would this have for the make-up of ὁ Χριστός in the same verse?).[179] Rather, an attributive adjective (like πνευματικός in 10:3–4) functions to describe the noun it modifies, and not the other way round.[180] Hence, 'food' and 'drink' do not give definition to πνεῦμα in that the latter would be affected in its substance by the material nature of the manna and the water. The same conclusion applies to the Eucharist which

---

[173] Horn, *Angeld*, 169 ('ein realistisches Sakramentsverständnis'); cf. 171, 200–201, 257. Cf. Brandenburger, *Fleisch*, 188; Klauck, *Herrenmahl*, 255; Schrage, *Korinther. I*, 392–93; Martin, 'Statements', 118.

[174] See Wedderburn, *Baptism*, 241–48, for a list of alternative explanations.

[175] See the detailed discussion of Käsemann's theology of the sacraments in 1.2.2.1.

[176] Many scholars think that the exact meaning of Paul's locution has to remain in doubt (so, e.g., Wedderburn, *Baptism*, 247–48; Dunn, *Theology*, 615).

[177] B. Witherington III, *Conflict and Community in Corinth: A Socio-Rhetorical Commentary on 1 and 2 Corinthians* (Grand Rapids/Carlisle: Eerdmans/Paternoster, 1995), 219; cf. Fee, *Corinthians*, 447; Fee, *Presence*, 143–44; Thiselton, *Corinthians*, 726; Schnabel, *Korinther*, 529. Cf. the methodological caution of Sandelin, who warns of pushing the analogy between the spiritual gifts in the desert (10:3–4) and the Lord's Supper (10:16–17, 21) too far (K.-G. Sandelin, 'Does Paul Argue Against Sacramentalism and Over-Confidence in 1 Cor 10.1–14?', in P. Borgen and S. Giversen (eds.), *The New Testament and Hellenistic Judaism* (Aarhus: AUP, 1995), 171–73).

[178] Cf. D.E. Garland, *1 Corinthians*; BECNT (Grand Rapids: Baker Academic, 2003), 454–55.

[179] Similar questions could be raised concerning the nature of πνευματικός in relation to χάρισμα (Rom. 1:11), νόμος (Rom. 7:11), εὐλογία (Eph. 1:3) and ᾠδή (Eph. 5:19). Cf. Barclay, 'Πνευματικός', 162–63.

[180] Cf. Brodeur, *Agency*, 103.

is touched upon by Paul in 10:14–22 as he continues to speak out against idolatry.[181] Thus, 10:3–4 neither supports an infusion-transformation interpretation of the sacraments in 10:1–22 nor in 12:13.

Paraphrase. Returning to our analysis of 12:13c, all evidence points to the conclusion that the drinking of the Spirit is best understood metaphorically. This is true not only because all attempts of a literal reading have proven to be a cul-de-sac. It is also supported by the fact that in 1 Corinthians and in his other letters, Paul uses many different expressions for the reception and experience of the Spirit, all of them metaphorical to a greater or lesser degree (see Excursus 1). Drawing on this variety of Pauline Spirit-language, it may be possible to paraphrase 13c as: 'we were all granted to receive the one Spirit' or, to include more of the refreshing and life-giving character of drinking water, 'we were all granted to take in the one Spirit of life'. However, as we have noted in 2.2.2.1., no paraphrase can embody all that is conveyed by the metaphor itself. In the case of 12:13c it could be added, for instance, that πνεῦμα ποτίζειν implies the effect of the Spirit *within* the believer (whereas 13a implies that the Spirit acts *upon* the believer). The metaphor 'drinking' stresses this internality more than a simple 'you have received the Spirit' would have done. It may also hint more clearly at the experiential dimension of Spirit-reception than do the classical metaphors of Spirit-indwelling (οἰκεῖ ἐν, Rom. 8:9; etc., cf. Excursus 1).

Apart from that, it is noteworthy that this locution is more strongly metaphorical than the other metaphors which were discussed throughout Part I. 1QH^a 15.7 is clearly figurative, but a metaphorical interpretation of the language of pouring with regard to the Spirit does not completely rule out that a material understanding of רוח is in the background (however, it has been demonstrated that there are no good reasons for assuming this literal aspect of 'pouring' to be in the author's mind).[182] Romans 8:9 has been described as 'ascriptive' in Excursus 1 because 'the Spirit of God dwells within you' may encompass both the aspect of more or less local indwelling and the aspect of being under the influence of the Spirit. In 1 Corinthians 12:13c, however, a literal reading of 'we were all made to drink of one Spirit' as a reference to either baptism or the Eucharist conjures a different semantic field than that of a metaphorical drinking of the

---

[181] Paul's concern in 10:1–22 is with the Corinthians' idolatry and not with their misconceptions regarding the sacraments (Fee, *Presence*, 143; Garland, *2 Corinthians*, 454). Cf. Baumert, *Sorgen*, 141.

[182] Cf. 2.2.2.1.

Spirit in the sense of receiving the Spirit. While these two concepts may not be far removed from each other theologically, semantically they are.[183]

In conclusion to 3.2. it can be determined that none of the 'sacramental passages' lend support to the concept of infusion-transformation. We have seen that 1 Corinthians 12:13, which has been the focus of our investigation, reminds the Corinthians of their common experience of the Spirit at conversion-initiation. In 13a πνεῦμα is the subject of divine action in that the Spirit is portrayed as the instrument of baptism. In 13c πνεῦμα is the object of divine action in that the Spirit is granted to be taken in by the converts. However, we have not seen any evidence that the Spirit was assumed by Paul to be a (physical) substance that would be incorporated into believers through the baptismal waters or the Eucharistic drink in order to become the new substance of their existence.

3. Conclusion

Part I of this study has investigated the question whether the concept of substance-ontological transformation through a material Spirit could be traced in Paul and his context. While the idea of a physical πνεῦμα was found in some Hellenistic sources, it could not be found in Judaism or Paul.[184] The concept of infusion-transformation, however, could not be

---

[183] For this reason we cannot agree with Martin, who writes with respect to Horn's and my different interpretations of 12:13: 'The basis of this disagreement over the nature of the Spirit lies in the metaphorical degree of Paul's statements. Fatehi and Rabens assess the statements as being more metaphorical than in Horn's assessment. The ancient medical context of these statements permits these statements to be interpreted either literally or metaphorically, for even if the statements are completely metaphorical, the ancient physiology of *pneuma* provides the perceived reality from which the metaphors arise' (Martin, 'Statements', 117 n.57). However, a metaphorical interpretation of 13c differs too much from a literal reading for this view to be correct; the latter refers to and interprets the sacraments, whereas the former has no semantic link to the Eucharist. What is more, there is no evidence for 'drinking the Spirit' in the ancient medical texts. Thus it is more than doubtful that this is the 'perceived reality from which the metaphors arise'. Apart from that, even if literal drinking was in view, this would not mean that the Spirit was considered to be drunk as a material substance and that this would lead to an ethical reconstitution of the person drinking it.

[184] With regard to the OT and Paul, so recently also E. Lohse, *Der Brief an die Römer*; KeK (Göttingen: Vandenhoeck & Ruprecht, 2003), 233.

However, even if one would find evidence of a material concept of the Spirit in Judaism and in Paul (which is implausible), this would not mean that Paul was not able to think differently of the ethical transformation by the Spirit than in the terms provided by an infusion-transformation framework. While this insight is not denied by scholars like Horn, neither is it integrated in their treatment of Paul's ethics.

traced in any of these strands of theology and philosophy. Particularly with regard to Paul we have seen that the verses on which this view has been built belong to those most controversially debated. On the basis of our exegesis we have reached the conclusion that the evidence that has been provided by the *religionsgeschichtliche Schule* and the modern proponents of the infusion-transformation approach is not satisfactory. We could not determine an explicit inclusion, transformation or even densification of (nor a demarcation from) Stoic pneumatology in Paul's writings.

However, from the perspective of the *reception* of Paul's letters it cannot be ruled out that Paul's Spirit-language, as for instance the image of being made to drink of the Spirit (1 Cor. 12:13c), evoked associations of Stoic pneumatology in Paul's audience. Nonetheless, as we have seen, the philosophic language of Stoicism fundamentally differs from that of Paul. Furthermore, the proponents of the infusion-transformation view would need to provide evidence that Stoic pneumatology was part of the general education of the members of Paul's churches (and not just of the educated elite), and that they would, over and above that, be able to fill the logical gaps between the role of πνεῦμα in Stoic physics and the infusion-transformation concept of ethical enabling.

Apart from that, a methodological weakness of the infusion-transformation approach has come to the fore. When Horn says that 'with the sacramental transferral of the [physical] Spirit an ontic basis of the new being is given, from which conduct in harmony with the Spirit is to be expected,'[185] it is clear that a lot of weight is being placed on the (physical) nature of the Spirit and the precise mode of its reception.[186] However, our investigation has shown that Paul does not attribute such an importance to these factors; rather, he leaves these matters open. Therefore, it seems wise not to establish our own approach to the relationship of Spirit and ethics in Paul on the basis of a particular interpretation of such ambiguous data. Rather, in Part II we will try to develop a model of the work of Spirit in Paul's ethics that is based on the actual *effects* which are attributed to the Spirit in Judaism and in Paul.

---

[185] Horn, *Angeld*, 388. Cf. Engberg-Pedersen, 'Understanding', 121–22.

[186] Cf. the underlying reasoning in the following statement from Wedderburn: '... from an impersonal view of the spirit, be it conceived of materially or immaterially, there could easily arise the idea that its benefits and effects were automatically conferred, automatically received; its presence could be detached from the grace of the God who gave it and whose presence it was' (Wedderburn, *Baptism*, 267).

Part II

Religious-Ethical Empowerment by the Relational Work of the Spirit

A New Approach

Chapter 4

Prolegomena to a Relational Approach to the Ethical Work of the Spirit in Paul

In Part I of this study we have analysed a long-established approach to the relationship of pneumatology and ethics in Paul. This view, which we have termed the 'infusion-transformation' approach, did not bear close examination. In Part II of our investigation we will propose a new approach to the ethical work of the Spirit in Paul. It will be argued that *it is primarily through deeper knowledge of, and an intimate relationship with, God, Jesus Christ and with the community of faith that people are transformed and empowered by the Spirit for religious-ethical life.*[1] We will develop this view on the basis of an exegetical study of Paul's context (ch. 5) and Paul's epistles themselves (ch. 6). However, we will start off in the present chapter by explaining our model in more detail and elucidating its presuppositions.

1. Definition of Terms

We have provided definitions of the central terms that have been employed in this study so far in 1.3. Before we can unfold our new model of the work of the Spirit in Paul's ethics in more detail, we also need to define its key concepts.

Relationship: Fundamentally, a relationship is about 'the state of being related; a condition or character based upon this' (*OED*[2], XIII, 551). However, a definition that is based on empirical observations of human relationships provides further insight. According to Hinde, a 'relationship implies first some sort of intermittent interaction between two people, involving interchanges over an extended period of time. [...] In addition, "relationship"... carries the... implication that there is some degree of continuity between the successive interactions.'[2] Human relationships are thus

---

[1] For further factors linked to the empowering by the Spirit for virtuous living, see 6.1.

[2] R.A. Hinde, *Towards Understanding Relationships*; EMSP 18 (London: Academic Press, 1979), 14. Cf. W.W. Hartup, 'Relationships and their Significance in Cognitive

based on contact and communication, and as both vary in intensity and in character they give shape to the relationship.[3]

In this study we will frequently refer to *close* or *intimate relationships*. We adopt the definition of Laurenceau and Kleinman who describe *intimacy* as 'a personal, subjective... sense of connectedness that is the outcome of an interpersonal, transactional process consisting of self-disclosure and... responsiveness'.[4] It is further characterized by a 'warm, close and communicative exchange with others – an interpersonal interaction perceived as an end in itself rather than a means to another end'.[5] Accordingly, *close* or *loving relationships* are exemplified by intimacy, care, sensitivity, and mutual support.[6]

'Relationship' is not a Pauline word. However, there are sufficient grounds for employing this term for our focal theory because, as we will demonstrate in 4.3. below, the notion of relationships, particularly that of fictive family relationships, is evidently present both in Paul and in his context.

Transformation: The Greek verb μεταμορφόω means 'to change in form' or 'to change inwardly in fundamental character or condition' (BDAG, s.v., §2). In the same way as the English equivalent ('transformation'), it thus

---

Development', in A.-N. Perret-Clermont, et al. (eds.), *Social Relationships and Cognitive Development* (Oxford: Clarendon, 1985), 74, who distinguishes between social *interactions* (meaningful encounters between individuals) and social *relationships* (aggregations of interactions between individuals that persist over time and that involve distinctive expectations, affects, and configurations).

[3] Cf. art. 'Beziehung', in G. Wenninger (ed.), *Lexikon der Psychologie. Vol. 1* (Heidelberg: Spektrum Akademischer Verlag, 2000), 225. 'Relation' may be differentiated from 'relationship' in that the former is broader and does not primarily concern human relationships but also that of objects, data, ideas and events (and additionally holds other meanings like 'narration').

[4] J.-P. Laurenceau and B.M. Kleinman, 'Intimacy in Personal Relationships', in A.L. Vangelisti and D. Perlman (eds.), *The Cambridge Handbook of Personal Relationships* (Cambridge: Cambridge University Press, 2006), 638.

[5] D.P. McAdams, 'Motivation and Friendship', in S. Duck and D. Perlman (eds.), *Understanding Personal Relationships: An Interdisciplinary Approach* (London: SAGE, 1985), 87, italics removed. Cf. H.T. Reis and P. Shaver, 'Intimacy as an Interpersonal Process', in S.W. Duck (ed.), *Handbook of Personal Relationships: Theory, Research and Interventions* (Chichester: Wiley & Sons, 1988), 367–68. For further differentiations, see K.J. Prager, *The Psychology of Intimacy*; GSPR (London: Guilford, 1995), 18–27.

[6] H. LaFollette, *Personal Relationships: Love, Identity, and Morality* (Oxford: Blackwell, 1996), 18. Davis and Todd explain that intimacy includes sharing experiences by virtue of doing things together and, in many cases, by virtue of confiding in each other. Intimacy may extend to physical intimacy, but it need not take such forms to count as intimacy (K. Davis and M. Todd, 'Assessing Friendship: Prototypes, Paradigm Cases and Relationship Description', in S. Duck and D. Perlman (eds.), *Understanding Personal Relationships: An Interdisciplinary Approach* (London: SAGE, 1985), 19).

leaves open the precise nature of the change (e.g. how 'substantial' or complete it is, whether it refers to 'inward' or 'outward' change, etc.). This is also true for the way in which Paul employs μεταμορφόω in his letters. The fact that he uses the present passive and the formulation ἀπὸ δόξης εἰς δόξαν in 2 Corinthians 3:18, and the present imperative passive in Romans 12:2, suggests, for one thing, that the change is not yet complete (cf. 6.2.2.1.).

'Transformation' can be distinguished from 'empowering' in so far as 'empowering' has a more functional and temporary aspect (see further below), whereas 'transformation' has a more lasting effect on the person.[7] Nevertheless, one should use adjectives like 'substance-ontological' (*substanzhaft* or *naturhaft*) with care precisely because Paul does not specify the exact nature of the transformation. Our use of the term 'transformation' can thus be differentiated from the concept of 'infusion-transformation'[8] which utilizes exactly these adjectives and which specifies a particular mode of transformation (i.e. by means of a material πνεῦμα).

Empowerment/Empowering: The English 'to empower' means 'to impart or bestow power to an end or for a purpose; to enable' (*OED*[2], V, 192). It is equivalent to the Pauline terms for 'strengthening': κραταιόω (1 Cor. 16:13; cf. Eph. 3:16: 'that you may be strengthened in your inner being with power through his Spirit');[9] στηρίζω (Rom. 1:11: 'that I may share with you some spiritual gift to strengthen you'; 16:25; 1 Thess. 3:2, 13; cf. 2 Thess. 2:17; 3:3);[10] οἰκοδομέω (1 Cor. 8:1; 14:4: 'those who prophesy

---

[7] Transformation could thus be described in the words of Brümmer as '*a process* of remodelling in which the believer's life is on the one hand purified from false ways of feeling, thinking, and acting which are contrary to the Will of God, and on the other hand regains the likeness of the Divine love which was lost through sin' (V. Brümmer, *The Model of Love: A Study in Philosophical Theology* (Cambridge: Cambridge University Press, 1993), 221, italics added; on the notion of the *process* of maturation, cf. J.G. Samra, *Being Conformed to Christ in Community: A Study of Maturity, Maturation and the Local Church in the Undisputed Pauline Epistles*; LNTS 320 (London/New York: T. & T. Clark, 2006), 3–4). The 'fruit of the Spirit' (Gal. 5:22) should probably be seen in this context (cf. Berger, *Identity*, 206), although it clearly has aspects of empowering too.

[8] Cf. the definition in 1.3.

[9] BDAG translates the verbs in this list predominantly with 'to strengthen'. However, Louw and Nida are more detailed. They understand κραταιόω as 'to become strong psychologically... The implication is that the believer is to be sufficiently strong as to be able to dominate any evil influence' (L&N §76.10). BDAG translates ἱκανόω (2 Cor. 3:6), which we have not cited in our list, as '*make sufficient, qualify* (perh. shading into the sense *empower, authorize...*)' (BDAG, s.v.).

[10] 'To cause someone to become stronger in the sense of more firm and unchanging in attitude or belief' (L&N §74.19)

build up the church' [cf. 14:3, 26]; 1 Thess. 5:11; etc.);[11] ἐνδυναμόω (Phil. 4:13; Rom. 4:20; cf. Eph. 6:10; 1 Tim. 1:12; 2 Tim. 2:1; 4:17);[12] βεβαιόω (1 Cor. 1:8; 2 Cor. 1:21; etc.);[13] etc.

'Empowering' includes the aspect of 'receiving motivation' for moral life. However, its stereotypical meaning is broader in that it refers to the reception of power and enabling for a particular task in a more encompassing way. While there is some overlap with the idea of 'transformation', we nonetheless do not use 'empowering' where Paul appears to employ concepts which are better captured by 'transformation' (as, e.g., in 2 Cor. 3:18 where a lasting change in character seems to be in view and Paul uses μεταμορφόω).

2. The Relational Model

Pauline scholars agree that Paul believes the Spirit to be a fundamental factor in the divine enabling for ethical living. In line with this consensus, the present study seeks to further our understanding of the relationship of Spirit and ethics in Paul by seeking to find out what indications Paul's epistles offer in order to answer the question *how* the Spirit enables religious-ethical life. According to the infusion-transformation approach, the Spirit brings about ethical life predominantly by means of the ontologically transforming effect of its *physical nature*. In our relational approach, however, we suggest that the Spirit effects ethical life predominantly by means of *intimate relationships* created by the Spirit *with God ('Αββα), Jesus and fellow believers*. (The reason why we have emphasized both 'intimate relationships' and those with whom this relationship has been created is that it is not the relationships themselves that are the enabling factor as if they could be separated from those to whom the believers are related; rather 'Αββα, Χριστός and the ἀδελφοί give shape to these Spirit-created relationships.)[14]

The difference between these two models can be illustrated with the following two diagrams.

---

[11] 'To increase the potential of someone or something, with focus upon the process involved' (L&N §74.15)

[12] 'To cause someone to have the ability to do or to experience something – "to make someone able, to give capability to, to enable, to strengthen, to empower."' (L&N §74.6)

[13] 'To cause someone to be firm or established in belief' (L&N §31.91)

[14] Cf. 4.4.1. below.

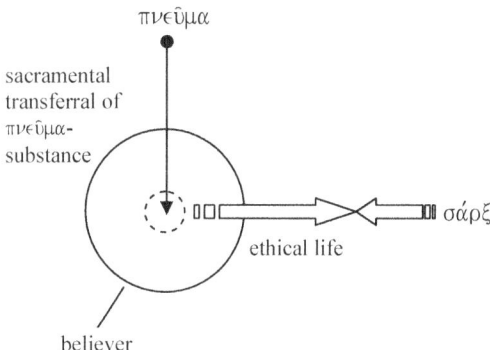

sacramental
transferral of
πνεῦμα-
substance

πνεῦμα

ethical life

σάρξ

believer

Diagram 1: The 'infusion-transformation model': 'static' transformation

Diagram 1 is a sketch of the infusion-transformation view of the work of the Spirit in Paul's ethics. The (material) πνεῦμα is infused into the person, namely into her interior or 'inner being' (ψυχή/καρδία/νοῦς/πνεῦμα/ἔσω ἄνθρωπος etc.), symbolized by the inner circle (the line is broken because we understand the person in her totality as a psychosomatic unity [symbolized by the outer circle, the somatic boundary][15]). Ethical life is the outflow of this transformation, and it shows itself (also) in the face of the opposing σάρξ (although this is not explicitly discussed by the proponents of infusion-transformation).[16]

While diagrams like this are in danger of over-simplifying the matter, it nevertheless has to be acknowledged that the proponents of the infusion-transformation approach are not very clear whether, and if so how further change or empowering is to be applied after the person has been changed through the πνεῦμα-substance at baptism.[17] The (ethical) significance of further impartation of πνεῦμα-substance at the Eucharist is not explicitly spelled out. Furthermore, other activities like the guidance of the Spirit are scarcely seen in relation to the transformation of the human interior as the

---

[15] On this aspect of Paul's anthropology, see, e.g., C.D. Müller, *Die Erfahrung der Wirklichkeit: Hermeneutisch-Exegetische Versuche mit besonderer Berücksichtigung alttestamentlicher und paulinischer Theologie* (Gütersloh: Mohn, 1978), 179–82; C.K. Chamblin, *Paul and the Self: Apostolic Teaching for Personal Wholeness* (Grand Rapids: Baker, 1993), 42–46; Dunn, *Theology*, §3, esp. 54–59; Berger, *Identity*, 61–62.

[16] Horn discusses the tension between Spirit and flesh in the context of his exegesis of Gal. 5–6 (Horn, *Angeld*, 356–64), but he does not draw the link to his concept of infusion-transformation.

[17] However, see the relational aspect of Käsemann's and Stuhlmacher's pneumatologies as presented in 1.2.2.

foundation of ethics.[18] It therefore seems justified to call this model 'static'.

The relational model that is suggested by this study is a dynamic one, and hence more complex:

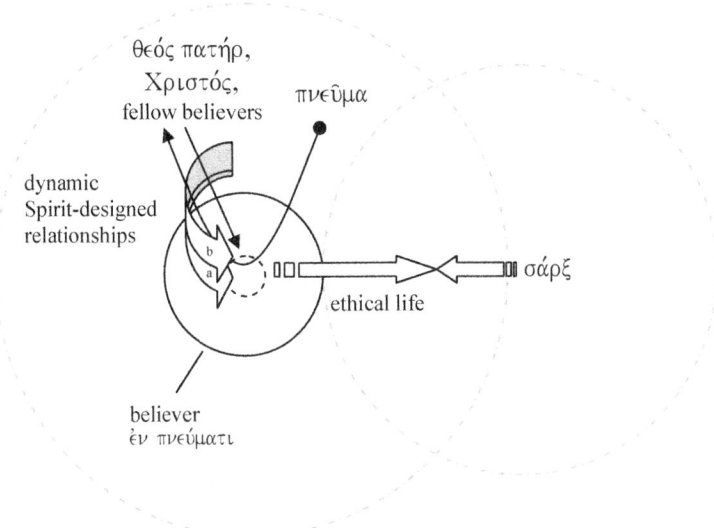

θεός πατήρ,
Χριστός,
fellow believers

πνεῦμα

dynamic
Spirit-designed
relationships

ethical life

σάρξ

believer
ἐν πνεύματι

Diagram 2: The 'relational model': dynamic transformation (a) and empowering (b)

In accordance with the relational approach to the work of the Spirit in Paul's ethics, Diagram 2 depicts the believer as influenced by relationships. At the outset, this is marked by the transferral of the believer into the sphere of influence of the Spirit (ἐν πνεύματι, indicated by the large hatched circle). The consequence is a different (i.e. more remote) relation to σάρξ[19] and a new relationship to πνεῦμα.[20] The first part ('a') of the

---

[18] However, different aspects of Paul's Spirit-ethics are at least listed together in Horn, *Angeld*, 388.

[19] This transferral is explicitly expressed in Rom. 8:9 (cf. Gal. 5:24). Σάρξ is therefore depicted as a force external and not internal (anthropological) to the believer. However, it still impinges on the believer in the context of the eschatological struggle (cf. Gal. 6:8 where Paul uses F/flesh in a double entendre [see J.L. Martyn, *Galatians: A New Translation with Introduction and Commentary*; AB 33A (New York: Doubleday, 1997), 553]). For further discussion, see 6.1. and 6.3.2. Cf. Appendix 2.3. and 3.2.

[20] In contrast to Vang (P. Vang, 'God's Empowering Presence and the Issue of Holiness: A Relational Interpretation of Paul's Pneumatology' (Southwestern Baptist Seminary: Unpublished PhD Thesis, 1994), 235, 243), this view is not centred on a relationship to the Spirit as a person. See our discussions in 4.4.2. and ch. 3 Excursus 1.

model covers the aspect of transformation. In 2 Corinthians 3:18 Paul describes (ethical) transformation as the result of the Spirit's relational work (creating deeper understanding of, encounter with and beholding of [the glory of] the Lord). In the diagram this is symbolized by the big round arrow 'a': the transforming power is drawn from the believer's Spirit-created relationships to θεός (ἀββα ὁ πατήρ), Χριστός, and fellow believers. These intimate relationships are signified by the two converse arrows which are initiated by πνεῦμα. As 2 Corinthians 3:18 speaks about *transformation*, round arrow 'a' is targeted at the inner being of the believer. However, the force of Paul's phrase ἀπὸ δόξης εἰς δόξαν is taken into account, so that our model differs from the infusion-transformation approach not only with regard to the understanding of the mechanics of the Spirit's work, but also in respect of its effect. The transformation is hence comprehended as 'gradual' or 'dynamic' rather than 'instant' or 'static'.[21] Furthermore, this aspect can be integrated effectively with the empowering work of the Spirit.

The second big round arrow ('b') represents those passages in Paul (e.g. Rom. 8:12–17; Rom. 1:11–12) which do not specify that the Spirit's relational work transforms believers but which imply *empowering* for religious-ethical life.[22] Round arrow 'b' is hence not aimed at the core of the person. However, the core of the person does not remain unaffected in the process of empowering because the change of the believer's relationship to God, Christ, and fellow believers has transforming effects on the person (identity etc.).[23] This is indicated by the fact that the arrow that leads from πνεῦμα to God *et alii* takes its route through the core of the believer.[24] The result of these intimate relationships is that the believer is strengthened and empowered.

While we have developed this model on the basis of the exegesis that will be presented in chapter 6, it is worth noting that modern psychological research is nevertheless in agreement with the results of our exegesis. For example, the broad influence that relationships have on people is expressed

---

[21] By choosing the term 'dynamic' we do not intend to suggest that the Spirit does not take permanent residence in the believer. Believers are hence also related to Christ/the Spirit when they are unconscious of the relationship, e.g., when they sleep. See ch. 3 Excursus 1.

[22] However, there is a conceptual overlap in a number of passages. See the reflections at the end of 6.1.

[23] Cf. V. Rabens, 'Coming Out: "Bible-Based" Identity Formation in 2 Corinthians 6:14–7:1', in U. Rembold and R.G. Czapla (eds.), *Gotteswort und Menschenrede: Die Bibel im Dialog mit Wissenschaften, Künsten und Medien*; JIG 73 (Bern/Oxford/New York: Lang, 2006), 64–66. See also 4.4.1. below.

[24] This further symbolizes the intimacy of the relationship that is caused by the fact that the Spirit *indwells* the believer. See ch. 3 Excursus 1.

by the psychologist Hinde: '[I]t is… clear that what we are is determined at least in part by the relationships we have had. Early family relationships have special importance here, but relationships all through life continue not only to affect us in the short term but also influence our subsequent behaviour and relationships.'[25] In particular, 'definitions of self, our view of reality, our attitudes and personality are continuously influenced by our interactions and relationships with others.'[26]

Apart from this recognition of the general effects of relationships, numerous researchers have also observed the *positive* impact of relationships on a person in the sense of personal growth, transformation or empowering.[27] Interestingly, this includes not only mental and emotional energy but

---

[25] Hinde, *Understanding*, 4; 14, 273. Cf. L. Stecher, *Die Wirkung sozialer Beziehungen: Empirische Ergebnisse zur Bedeutung sozialen Kapitals für die Entwicklung von Kindern und Jugendlichen* (Munich: Juventa, 2001), 249–50; P.R. Shaver and M. Mikulincer, 'Attachment Theory, Individual Psychodynamics, and Relationship Functioning', in A.L. Vangelisti and D. Perlman (eds.), *The Cambridge Handbook of Personal Relationships* (Cambridge: Cambridge University Press, 2006), 251–71; B.R. Sarason and I.G. Sarason, 'Close Relationships and Social Support: Implications for the Measurement of Social Support', in A.L. Vangelisti and D. Perlman (eds.), *The Cambridge Handbook of Personal Relationships* (Cambridge: Cambridge University Press, 2006), 435–40.

[26] Hinde, *Understanding*, 326.

[27] See, e.g., Hartup, 'Relationships', 66, 75–80; Davis and Todd, 'Friendship', 88; V. von Weizsäcker, *Der Gestaltkreis: Theorie der Einheit von Wahrnehmen und Bewegen* (Stuttgart: Thieme, 1986[5] [1940[1]]), 187, cited and discussed in S. Emondts, *Menschwerden in Beziehung: Eine religionsphilosophische Untersuchung der medizinischen Anthropologie Viktor von Weizsäckers*; Problemata 131 (Stuttgart-Bad Cannstatt: Frommann-Holzboog, 1993), 401, cf. 404; C.R. Rogers, *On Becoming a Person: A Therapist's View of Psychotherapy* (Boston: Houghton Mifflin, 1961), 35–40; J. Bowlby, *A Secure Base: Parent-Child Attachment and Healthy Human Development* (New York: Basic Books, 1988), 119–36; Prager, *Psychology*, 293; LaFollette, *Relationships*, 89–90, 197–199, 207–209; D. Sattler, *Beziehungsdenken in der Erlösungslehre: Bedeutung und Grenzen* (Freiburg: Herder, 1997), 173, 199–254; D. Cramer, *Close Relationships: The Study of Love and Friendship* (London: Arnold, 1998), 49–52.

In addition, Christian psychologists have sought to study the effects on people's lives of their relationship to the divine. For instance, Dodds' case study finds that people experience empowering for religious-ethical life by means of the communication of God's love through the Holy Spirit (L.A. Dodds, 'The Role of the Holy Spirit in Personality Growth and Change', *JPsyChr* 18 (1999), 134. The question that could be raised here, however, is how the subjects were able to identify their experiences as specifically 'pneumatic' rather than more generally as 'divine'.).

Kirkpatrick and Shaver observe that it is not only one's relationship with God that influences one's relationship to others, but that one's experiences of one's (primary) relationships have a profound influence on the kind of relationship one has with the God of Christianity (L.A. Kirkpatrick and P.R. Shaver, 'An Attachment-Theoretical Approach to Romantic Love and Religious Belief', *PSPB* 18 (1992), 270–71). Cf. M. St. Clair, *Human Relationships and the Experience of God: Object Relations and Religion* (New York: Paulist Press, 1994), 31–49; more generally: B. Fletcher Brokaw and K.J. Edwards, 'The

also resistance to physical stress and disease.[28] The spectrum of effects that relates to our study is well expressed by Williams:

The discovery that we are loved does have a causally efficacious power which creates through that experience the transformation of the self. This is one of the most important themes in the psychoanalytic doctrine of love.... The attitudes and responses which the self finds in others are powerful factors in moving the self. Being loved creates a new person. We can make the general statement that inter-personal relations constitute a field of force in which action in any part of the field alters the structure of the field and all the elements within it.[29]

While it is difficult for both psychological as well as Pauline studies to fathom the very 'mechanics' by which intimate relationships transform and empower people, we will provide sufficient exegetical evidence from Paul's letters to demonstrate *that* a primary mode of the Spirit's enabling for religious-ethical life occurs in the context of such Spirit-designed intimate relationships. Moreover, we will be able to fill in a number of details of this relational enabling. Our exegesis will show that in Paul's letters a major aspect of transformation and empowering for religious-ethical life is the experience[30] of the intimate presence, love and immediacy of the di-

---

Relationship of God Image to Level of Object Relations Development', *JPsyTh* 22 (1994), 367.

[28] R. Buck, 'Emotional Communication in Personal Relationships: A Developmental-Interactionist View', in C. Hendrick (ed.), *Close Relationships*; RPSP 10 (London: Sage, 1989), 157, 161; see the discussion of von Weizsäcker's work in Emondts, *Menschwerden*, 406, 421–23. Further: Cramer, *Relationships*, ch. 3; Sattler, *Beziehungsdenken*, 195–96, and the works cited there.

[29] D.D. Williams, *The Spirit and the Forms of Love*; LCT (Digswell Place: Nisbet, 1968), 120. Cf. T.E. Wartenberg, *The Forms of Power: From Domination to Transformation* (Philadelphia: Temple University Press, 1990), 211; M. Volf, *After Our Likeness: The Church as the Image of the Trinity*; SD (Grand Rapids/Cambridge: Eerdmans, 1998), 182–86; S. Motyer, '"Not Apart from Us" (Hebrews 11:40): Physical Community in the Letter to the Hebrews', *EQ* 77 (2005), 237; Samra, *Christ*, 31–32.

[30] The notion of *experience* has often been overlooked in previous studies of Paul's pneumatology (and ethics), particularly in the last century. However, see Gunkel, *Influence*, 17–18, 77–78, 92; Dunn, *Jesus and the Spirit*, e.g. 223–25; Fee, *Presence*, 433, 880; Rabens, 'Development', 172–73; followed by Christoph, *Pneuma*, 81–83, 203–204; Fatehi, *Relation*, 7–22; J.D.G. Dunn, 'Towards the Spirit of Christ: The Emergence of the Distinctive Features of Christian Pneumatology', in M. Welker (ed.), *The Work of the Spirit: Pneumatology and Pentecostalism* (Grand Rapids: Eerdmans, 2006), 21–25; Tibbs, *Experience*, chs. 2 and 4; V. Rabens, 'Die Geisterfahrung in den paulinischen Gemeinden', *GlLern* 26 (2011), forthcoming. More generally: L.T. Johnson, *Religious Experience in Earliest Christianity: A Missing Dimension in New Testament Studies* (Minneapolis: Fortress, 1998), *passim*; Ashton, *Religion*, 26–28; chs. 7–8; S.J. Kraftchick, 'Death's Parsing: Experience as a Mode of Theology in Paul', in J.C. Anderson, et al. (eds.), *Pauline Conversations in Context: Essays in Honor of Calvin J. Roet-*

vine by the Spirit (2 Cor. 3:18; Gal. 4:4–9; Rom. 5:5; 8:12–17; etc.).[31] A further 'mechanism' of ethical transformation and empowering of believers is their receiving true knowledge of the Lord and his message through the Spirit (see esp. our exegesis of 2 Cor. 3:18).[32] Finally, one cannot overlook the 'ecclesiological factor' in Paul's writing regarding the empowering for religious-ethical life, namely, the 'building up' of people as they relate to one another in the power of the Spirit (e.g. 1 Cor. 12:7; Rom. 1:11–12).[33] In the course of Part II we will shed more light on these factors.

---

zel; JSNTSup 221 (Sheffield: Sheffield Academic Press, 2002), 144–66; Berger, *Identity*, e.g. 203, 206.

[31] This exegetical result (particularly the motif of the Spirit-created sonship of believers in Rom. 8 and Gal. 4) is to some extent mirrored in studies that elucidate the positive, identity-creating impact of intimate parent-child relationships (see, e.g., Hinde, *Understanding*, 320–22). Further, in her study on soteriology Sattler points out that various psychotherapeutic schools have discovered the transforming effects of the therapist-client relationship and have made it an integral part of the process of emotional healing and growth (Sattler, *Beziehungsdenken*, 190–97). Cf. Wartenberg, *Forms*, 220, cf. 190–93; P.A. DeYoung, *Relational Psychotherapy: A Primer* (New York/Hove: Brunner-Routledge, 2003), 32–33, 152, 184–85, 208–209. More recent research draws special attention to the healing effect of the 'common factors' of the therapeutic alliance like empathy, warmth, caring, unconditionality, respect and congruency. See, e.g., A.O. Horvath and L. Luborsky, 'The Role of the Therapeutic Alliance in Psychotherapy', *JCCP* 61 (1993), 561–73; M.J. Lambert and D.E. Barley, 'Research Summary on the Therapeutic Relationship and Psychotherapy Outcome', *Psychotherapy* 38 (2001), 357, 359.

[32] The ethical impact of this insight may be partly explained by the observation that revealing oneself to another person increases liking for oneself in that person. If one likes someone, however, one is more willing to do things for that person (Hinde, *Understanding*, 282; cf. 30). Moreover, in his challenge of Gunkel's denial of the ethical impact of teaching, Turner argues convincingly that 'Many kinds of teaching or writing... have the power to grip us and transform us. They exercise such power when they subvert our self-understanding and give us a different view of our universe, challenging our ideals and fundamentally reshaping our motivations – for to a large extent we are shaped by the "stories" we believe. In addition, it is also undoubtedly the case that some personal encounters can themselves have similar transforming effects (most commonly at the level of falling in love)....' In applying this insight to pneumatology, Turner submits that one might 'expect that the Spirit who discloses God's presence and activity, reveals his nature and will, enlightens with God's wisdom and convicts of the truth of God's claim on us, would – precisely in doing these things – profoundly transform the outlook and motivations which fuel our lives' (Turner, *Power*, 122). On the notion of cognitive transformation, see further Hartup, 'Relationships', 75–76; DeYoung, *Psychotherapy*, 184.

[33] The rendering of συμφέρω in 1 Cor. 12:7 as 'building up' has been chosen on the basis of 1 Cor. 10:23 where it is parallel to οἰκοδομέω (cf. Thiselton, *Corinthians*, 936).

In addition to the psychological insights on interpersonal relationships that have been referred to above, a number of Christian studies give support for the significance of this aspect of the relational work of the Spirit. See, e.g., V.H. Hine, 'Pentecostal Glossolalia: Toward a Functional Interpretation', in W.E. Mills (ed.), *Speaking in Tongues: A Guide to*

3. The Centrality and the Empowering Character of Relationships in Paul and His Context

We have outlined above that our focal theory submits that it is through *intimate* relationships that believers are transformed and empowered by the Spirit for religious-ethical life. In the present section we will provide evidence that relationships in general were highly significant for Paul and his context. Towards the end of our portrayal we will further show that intimate relationships were understood by Paul to be transforming and empowering.

It is not difficult to demonstrate the centrality of relationships in the writings of Paul and in the tradition on which he draws. For one thing, it is clear that biblical ethics itself concerns relationships – how one lives in relation to God, others and self. Moreover, even though the term 'relationship' as such does not exist in the biblical tradition, the following themes nevertheless give evidence of its prominence:[34]

– all of creation is understood as being created in relationship to YHWH (Gen. 1–2; Pss. 42; 63; 95:6–7; etc.)

Research on Glossolalia (Grand Rapids: Eerdmans, 1986), 456–58 (however, cf. the more critical analysis by H.N. Maloney and A.A. Lovekin, *Glossolalia: Behavioural Science Perspectives on Speaking in Tongues* (Oxford: Oxford University Press, 1985), esp. 185–87).

[34] The majority of the data in the list below is discussed more fully in R. Boschki, *"Beziehung" als Leitbegriff der Religionspädagogik: Grundlegung einer dialogisch-kreativen Religionsdidaktik*; Zeitzeichen 13 (Ostfildern: Schwabenverlag, 2003), 239–60.

It would be worth inquiring into Paul's Hellenistic and early Jewish context too, but for reasons of space we will limit ourselves to the OT and NT in this introduction (see ch. 5 for further details). Nevertheless, one theme that stands out among many others which give evidence for the presence of the concept of relationships in Hellenism (as well as in Jewish writings [e.g. 1 Sam. 18–20, etc.; LXX Prov. 10:12; 15:17; 25:10; Wis. 7.14; Sir. 6.17; 22.20; 25.1; 1 Macc. 10.20–26; 12; 2 Macc. 6.22; 4 Macc. 8.5]) is that of φιλία. Konstan shows that φιλία was used in all periods of ancient Greek history to indicate 'an intimate relationship predicated on mutual affection and commitment' (D. Konstan, *Friendship in the Classical World*; KTAH (Cambridge: Cambridge University Press, 1997), 19). See also the insightful essay by Fitzgerald, who singles out partnership (κοινωνία), intimacy (συνήθεια), concord (ὁμόνοια), equality (ἰσότης) and confident trust in one another as vital components of the Greek concept of affectionate relationships (J.T. Fitzgerald, 'Paul and Friendship', in J.P. Sampley (ed.), *Paul in the Greco-Roman World: A Handbook* (Harrisburg/London: Trinity Press International, 2003), 325–27). Cf. Seneca, *Ep.* 2.2–7; 48.2–3; Winston, *Wisdom*, 188–89; Nussbaum, *Therapy*, 341–45; P.A. Harland, 'Familial Dimensions of Group Identity: "Brothers" (Ἀδελφοί) in Associations of the Greek East', *JBL* 124 (2005), 491–513; R.R. Cox, *By the Same Word: Creation and Salvation in Hellenistic Judaism and early Christianity*; BZNW 145 (Berlin/New York: W. de Gruyter, 2007), 84–87.

- God is portrayed as the initiator of a close relationship with his people (e.g. Gen. 18; Exod. 3:14–15; YHWH as shepherd [Ps. 23; Ezek. 34; etc.],[35] liberator [Exod. *passim*; etc.], husband [Isa. 54:5–8; Hos. *passim*; etc.], etc.)

- human beings are viewed as *relational beings* (e.g. as children of their parents, as brothers and sisters, as ancestors, etc.)

- God's relating to people becomes tangible within time and space (Gen. 1:1; Exod. 20:2; cf. Mk. 1:15//s; Lk. 22:19;[36] etc.)[37]

- the covenant gives structure to the relationship with God (Gen. 12; Sinai pericope; Jer. 31:31–34; Hebr. 9; etc.)[38]

- sin is rendered as a violation of the relationships with God and others (Gen. 4; Lk. 5:17–26; etc.)

- the relationships of people to God and to fellow humans are portrayed as interdependent (e.g. in the Decalogue; Lev. 19:18; Matt. 22:36–40//s; 25:31–46, cf. the sermon on the mount; etc.)

- God is a dialogue partner as people communicate and argue with him even and especially in the face of suffering (Gen. 18:22b–33; 32:23–33; 2 Chron. 20; Pss. 3–5; 7; 11; 17; 38; 41; 88; cf. Mk. 5:21–24, 35–43; etc.)[39]

- the motif (and reality) of God's seclusion (as well as his presence) plays an important role in the biblical tradition: 'The interpenetration of both of these essential characteristics (intimacy and withdrawal), are at the heart of the biblical understanding of God and his relating' (e.g. Job 28:20–21; 36:26; Pss. 10:1; 13:2; 27:9; 42:10; 69:18; 74:19; 102:3; 143:7; Isa. 8:17; 40:28; 45:15)[40]

- Jesus' life and fate are characterized by relationships: Jesus' ministry and preaching created relationships and in this way fundamentally transformed people (e.g. Lk. 19:1–10; Matt. 28:20; his relationships to his family, to his disciples, to his people, to women and children; his table fellowship; his healing action towards the sick and wounded; his relationship-transforming message of the in-breaking kingdom of God; etc.).

---

[35] Cf. the analysis of this and other biblical relationship metaphors provided by Sattler, *Beziehungsdenken*, 365–82.

[36] Although the NT writings which are referenced in this list postdate Paul's epistles, we have nevertheless included them as they give some evidence of the Jesus-tradition which predates Paul.

[37] Cf. Sattler, *Beziehungsdenken*, 384–404.

[38] Cf. Ibid., 343–61; D. Sheriffs, 'The Human Need for Continuity: Some ANE and OT Perspectives', *TynBul* 55 (2004), 15.

[39] Sheriffs points out that one 'strand of Hebrew meditation, related to worship and an intimate relationship with God, deals with an enjoyment of the Presence of God. There is a quiet waiting before God for him to act and a processing of traumatic or disturbing experience, such as we find in Lamentations or in Psa 37's perspectives on the wicked' (D. Sheriffs, *The Friendship of the Lord: An Old Testament Spirituality* (Carlisle: Paternoster, 1996), 147).

[40] Boschki, *Beziehung*, 258, italics removed. On the relational emphasis of the OT see further B. Janowski, 'Der Mensch im alten Israel: Grundfragen alttestamentlicher Anthropologie', *ZTK* 102 (2005), 17–19.

While this list is not intended to be exhaustive, it nevertheless paints a larger picture of the relational thinking in the biblical tradition of which our focal theory of the relational work of the Spirit's ethical enabling in Paul is a part. More importantly, the centrality of relationships can be seen in Paul's theology as a whole. This is evident from

- Paul's emphasis on love (Gal. 5:6; Rom. 5:5; 13:10; 15:30; 1 Cor. 13; 2 Cor. 5:14; cf. Eph. 3:17; etc.) – of God (Rom. 8:28; 1 Cor. 2:9; 16:22 [Christ]; etc.) and of one another (e.g. Rom. 12:9–10; 13:8; 15:7; 1 Thess. 3:12; 4:9; cf. Eph. 1:15; 4:23–5:2)[41]

- Paul's emphasis on close fellowship and partnership (κοινωνία with Christ: 1 Cor. 1:9; 10:6; Phil. 3:10, etc.; κοινωνία πνεύματος: Phil. 2:1; 2 Cor. 13:13; κοινωνία with fellow believers: 2 Cor. 1:7, etc., extending also to the sharing of possessions [e.g. 2 Cor. 8; Phil. 4:14–18])

- Paul's powerful usage of prepositions gives evidence of relational thinking:[42] e.g. σύν (e.g. Rom. 6:4–6, 8; 1 Thess. 4:17)[43] and ἐν (e.g. ἐν θεῷ in Rom. 2:17 NRSV; particularly the notion of being in Christ or in the Spirit is of importance [e.g. Rom. 8:1, 9; 12:5],[44] as well as that of Christ or the Spirit being in believers [e.g. 2 Cor. 13:5 'Do you not realize that Christ is in you'; Gal. 2:20; cf. Eph. 3:17; Rom. 8:9; 1 Cor. 3:16; 6:19; 1 Thess. 4:8])[45]

---

[41] Cf. e.g. M. Wolter, *Theologie und Ethos im frühen Christentum: Studien zu Jesus, Paulus und Lukas Michael Wolter*; Wissenschaftliche Untersuchungen zum Neuen Testament (Tübingen: Mohr Siebeck, 2009), 146–53.

[42] For a justification of this approach of using prepositions for establishing relationships, see Berchman, *Philo*, 38; cf. G. Ebeling, *Dogmatik des Glaubens. Vol. 1* (Tübingen: J.C.B. Mohr (Paul Siebeck), 1987³), 348–49.

[43] See U. Schnelle, 'Transformation und Partizipation als Grundgedanken paulinischer Theologie', *NTS* 47 (2001), 65; S. Sabou, *Between Horror and Hope: Paul's Metaphysical Language of Death in Romans 6:1–11*; PBM (Milton Keynes: Paternoster, 2005), 109–116.

[44] Cf. Müller, *Erfahrung*, 179; F. Neugebauer, 'Das paulinische "In Christo"', *NTS* 4 (1957/58), 129; Stuhlmacher, *Theologie. I*, 362; Hays, *Vision*, 38–39; Longenecker, *Galatians*, 154; W. Elliger, 'ἐν', *EWNT²*, I, 1094; E. Schweizer, *Jesus* (London: SCM Press, 1971), 107; W.B. Barcley, *Christ in You: A Study in Paul's Theology and Ethics* (Lanham: University Press of America, 1999), ch. 3; U. Schnelle, *Apostle Paul: His Life and Theology* (Grand Rapids: Baker Academic, 2005), 481–82, 489; Bertone, *Law*, 184. See further ch. 3 Excursus 1; 6.1.

[45] See further πρός (e.g. 2 Cor. 1:12, translated by the NIV as 'our relations with you'); ὑπό (e.g. Rom. 6:14); διά (e.g. Rom. 5:17); ὑπέρ (ὑμῶν) (e.g. 1 Cor. 11:24); ἀπό (e.g. Rom. 8:21) and most other presuppositions of Paul's language. If one were to extend this characteristic into a full-blown linguistic study, one could identify many more elements of Paul's language that specify relationships, like, e.g., the different cases (on this see J. Becker, *Paulus: Der Apostel der Völker*; UTB 2014 (Tübingen: Mohr Siebeck, 1998 [1989¹]), 444; Wallace, *Greek*, 81–84; etc.).

- faith (e.g. Gal. 2:20) and justification-reconciliation (e.g. 2 Cor. 5:18–21; Gal. 3:11) are relational concepts[46]
- intimate 'sharing in' and becoming 'part of' Christ through the sacraments (e.g. Rom. 6:1–11; 1 Cor. 10:16)[47]
- Paul's emphasis on prayer (Rom. 10:1; 12:12; 15:30; 1 Cor. 14:13–15; 2 Cor. 1:11; 13:7, 9; Phil. 1:4, 9, 19; 4:6; 1 Thess. 3:10; 5:17; etc.)
- Paul's ecclesiology
  - the church as the body of Christ (Rom. 12:4–5; 1 Cor. 6:15; 12:12–27; cf. Eph. 1:22–23; 4:15–16; Col. 1:18, 24; 3:15)
  - the church's relationship to Christ as that of a marriage-relationship (1 Cor. 6:16–17; 2 Cor. 11:2; etc.)
  - Paul's concern for the unity of and mutuality within his churches, across ethnic, social and sexual borders (Gal. 3:28; 1 Cor. 12:13; 1:10, 13; 3:3; 6:1, 4–9; 8:9, 13; 11:33–34; 12–14; Rom. 15:5–6; Phil. 1:27; 2:2; 4:2–3; etc.; cf. Eph. 2:11–22; 4:3–6; etc.)[48]
  - holy kissing as one expression of close relationships (Rom. 16:16; 1 Cor. 16:20; 2 Cor. 13:12; 1 Thess. 5:26)
- Paul's emphasis on the family (e.g. household codes: Eph. 5:21–6:9; Col. 3:18–4:1; the church as a household: Gal. 6:10; cf. Eph. 2:19; etc.) and fictive family relations: fatherhood as an image for God's relationship to believers, individually and corporately (e.g. Rom. 1:7; 8:14–17; 1 Cor. 1:3; 8:6; 2 Cor. 2:1; Gal. 1:3–4; 4:5–7; Phil. 1:2; 4:20; 1 Thess. 1:3; 3:11–13; Phlm. 3; etc.); fatherhood (and motherhood: Gal. 4:19; 1 Thess. 2:7) as an image for Paul's relationship to his churches (1 Cor. 4:14–15; 1 Thess. 2:11);[49] brother and sisterhood of believers (1 Cor. 8:11–13; 1 Thess. 1:4; 2:1, 9, 14, 17; etc.)

---

[46] See Dunn, *Theology*, 341–44; Furnish, *Theology*, 146, 152–53; E. Jüngel, *Paulus und Jesus: Eine Untersuchung zur Präzisierung der Frage nach dem Ursprung der Christologie*; HUT 2 (Tübingen: J.C.B. Mohr (Paul Siebeck), 1986⁶), 34–38, 43; J.B. Green and M.D. Baker, *Recovering the Scandal of the Cross: Atonement in the New Testament and Contemporary Contexts* (Downers Grove: IVP, 2000; Carlisle: Paternoster, 2003), 56, 95–96; G.W. Burnett, *Paul and the Salvation of the Individual*; BIS 57 (Leiden: Brill, 2001), 118–20, 127; D.M. Hay, 'Paul's Understanding of Faith as Participation', in S.E. Porter (ed.), *Paul and His Theology*; PS 3 (Leiden: Brill, 2006), 52–53.

[47] On this aspect of baptism, see, e.g., Schnelle, *Paul*, 479–81; on the Lord's Supper, see Käsemann, 'Doctrine', 118; P. Lampe, 'Identification with Christ: A Psychological View of Pauline Theology', in T. Fornberg and D. Hellholm (eds.), *Texts and Contexts: Biblical Texts in Their Textual and Situational Contexts. Essays in Honor of Lars Hartman* (Oslo: Scandinavian University Press, 1995), 938; et al.

[48] Cf. J.M.G. Barclay, 'Manna and the Circulation of Grace: A Study of 2 Corinthians 8:1–15 ', in J.R. Wagner, et al. (eds.), *The Word Leaps the Gap: Essays on Scripture and Theology in Honor of Richard B. Hays* (Grand Rapids/Cambridge: Eerdmans, 2008), 423–26.

[49] Cf. T.J. Burke, 'Paul's Role as "Father" to his Corinthian "Children" in Socio-Historical Context (1 Corinthians 4:14–21)', in T.J. Burke and J.K. Elliott (eds.), *Paul and the Corinthians: Studies on a Community in Conflict. Essays in Honour of Margaret Thrall*; NovTSup 109 (Leiden: Brill, 2003), 95–113.

- Paul's ethical commands regarding interrelational matters (e.g. his lists of vices and virtues [Gal. 5:19–23; Rom. 12; cf. Eph. 4:25–32; Col. 3:12–13], his writing on reconciliation [2 Cor. 5:18; Phil. 4:2–3; cf. Col. 3:13; etc.]; etc.)
- the importance that Paul gives to open and intimate relationships in his own life (with his friends and fellow workers: Rom. 16:1–2, 13; 1 Cor. 4:17; Phil. 2:22; 1 Thess. 3:2; Phlm. 2, 10; etc.; with his churches: Rom. 1:11–12; 1 Cor. 10:14; 16:24; 2 Cor. 7:2; Phil. 1:8; 2:12; 1 Thess. 3:12; 1:4; 2:8, 17; etc.)
- the centre of Paul's life and theology is a relationship – what he values most in his life is 'the surpassing value of knowing Christ Jesus my Lord... that I may gain Christ and be found in him' (Phil. 3:7–14; cf. Gal. 2:20; etc.)[50]

Also this list is by no means complete, but it can function as an eye-opener to a much larger perspective on Paul's life and theology. This perception is well summarized in Dunn's words: 'Paul's theology is *relational*'.[51]

Moreover, Paul's epistles amply evidence that the apostle comprehended *intimate and loving relationships* to be *empowering*. This is true, firstly, for Paul's concept of love in general. For example, in Philippians 2:1 Paul lists a number of factors that empower believers for ethics (2:2): 'If then there is any encouragement in Christ, *any consolation from love*, any sharing in the Spirit, any compassion and sympathy...'. The fact that he describes love as providing incentive encouragement and comfort (παραμύθιον) shows that Paul feels strengthened by the love he experiences in the relationships to Christ and fellow believers (cf. 1 Cor. 8:1–3: 'Knowledge puffs up, *but love builds up*.... But anyone who loves God is

---

[50] Cf. M. Bockmuehl, *The Epistle to the Philippians*; BNTC (London: Black, 1997), 206; V. Koperski, *The Knowledge of Christ Jesus my Lord: The High Christology of Philippians 3:7–11*; CBET 16 (Kampen: Pharos, 1996), *passim*; Dunn, *Theology*, 47; Engberg-Pedersen, *Stoics*, 94–95. On the aspect of 'knowing', see further 2 Cor. 4:6; 5:16; and 6.2.1.

[51] Dunn, *Theology*, 53. Cf. E. Schweizer, 'σάρξ κτλ', *TDNT*, VII, 135; B.J. Malina and J.H. Neyrey, *Portraits of Paul: An Archaeology of Ancient Personality* (Louisville: Westminster John Knox Press, 1996), 196–97; Campbell, *Quest*, 61. Cf., with further information on ANE societies: C. Osiek, 'Relatedness', in J.J. Pilch and B.J. Malina (eds.), *Handbook of Biblical Social Values* (Peabody: Hendrickson, 1998), 176–78.
Further insights into the relational dimension of Paul's theology can be gained by studying Paul from the perspective of patron-client relationships (so, e.g., J.H. Neyrey, SJ, *Render to God: New Testament Understandings of the Divine* (Minneapolis: Fortress Press, 2004), 150–54, 195–202). On this perspective, the Spirit would function as broker between the believer-client and God/Jesus-patron, communicating divine benefits to the client, including intimacy with God, etc. Nonetheless, should one have to choose a single model for the relationship between believer and God, the parent-child relationship, expressed, e.g., in Gal. 4:6–7 and Rom. 8:15–16, seems to be more characteristic for this medium of transformation and empowering. This is so because it is a Pauline image, one that implies the concept of intimacy (cf. 6.3.3.1.).

known by him'; 2 Cor. 1:3–5: we can console because we have been consoled by God; 1 Thess. 3:12–13).

Further, more specifically Paul understands believers to be empowered by divine love. For instance, in Romans 8:35, 38–39 Paul praises the intimacy of Christ's love – no one and nothing can separate 'us' from it. Paul says this in the face of persecution. However, on the basis of this love the church is able to persevere in adverse situations: 'in all these things we are more than conquerors *through him who loved us*' (8:37;[52] cf. 5:5; 15:30: 'I appeal to you... by the love of the Spirit, to join me in earnest prayer to God...'; 2 Cor. 2:14; 4:6–8; 5:14).[53]

Finally, Paul also knows the empowering impact of loving relationships on an interpersonal level. For example, Paul says in Romans 1:12 that he longs to meet up with the Romans 'so that we may be mutually encouraged by each other's faith, both yours and mine'. Paul thus trusts that he and his fellow believers are strengthened through meaningful encounters with others in the faith community (cf. 2 Cor. 2:2–4; 3:2–3; Philem. 1:20).[54]

4. The Framework of the Relational Model

4.1. Philosophical, Theological and Anthropological Presuppositions

In the summary of our theory in 4.2. above we have highlighted a number of dissimilarities between our relational model of the Spirit's work in Paul's ethics and the concept of infusion-transformation. Does this mean, philosophically speaking, that we try to read Paul through the lenses of a relational ontology as opposed to an ontology of substance?

According to Ebeling, a substance-ontological approach to being and relating focuses on separate entities whose states of Being (*Sein*) exist independently of another. In the (substance) ontologies of scholasticism, relations were perceived as the weakest factor determining the nature of an essence. This is due to the primacy of substance in these ontologies. Ebeling thinks that the same holds true for modern scientific thought with

---

[52] Christ is here presented as *the loving one*. There is hence no need to discuss whether it is Christ or love that transforms. Cf. J.D.G. Dunn, *Romans 1–8*; WBC 38A (Texas: Word, 1988), 512.

[53] Negatively speaking, the influence of relationships on people's lives can also be seen, for instance, from the adverse effects of the dislocated relationship to God (and others) in Rom. 1–3.

[54] The impact of interpersonal relationships can be observed further from the way in which Paul suggests that religious-ethical life can be shaped, namely, by looking at the apostle's example and imitating him. See 1 Cor. 4:16; 11:1; Phil. 3:17; 1 Thess. 1:6; 2:14; etc.

its objectivizing rational view of reality. Ebeling himself, *per contra*, decides for a theology in which primacy is given to 'being' as *relational*, as 'being together', because relations have a constitutive character.[55] Such a move is echoed in Schulthess' assessment of the history of philosophy in general: 'In post-Kantian philosophy... a fundamental change in the nature of relation occurs: things, the objects, are defined by relations, not by an οὐσία (substance), and Nature as a whole is thought of as a system of relations. This change could be characterized as a change from an ontology of substance to an ontology of functions or relations.'[56]

While it is not our concern here to solve philosophical questions that have vexed generations of philosophers, it is nevertheless of great interest to see how these philosophies find expression in exegetical studies of Paul. For example, Brandenburger reflects an ontology of substance when he submits that for Paul, the transferral of a person from the sphere of the flesh into the sphere of the Spirit must be comprehended as a substance-ontological transformation.[57] Brandenburger also shows how this framework can be applied to our understanding of Paul's ethics: 'What is proposed... is the idea of the original rootedness of righteous or... sinful behaviour before God in a substance which exercises power. A change of behaviour in the broadest sense (thinking, wanting, acting) is based on an exchange of the underlying being ["zugrundeliegenden Wesens"].'[58]

---

[55] Ebeling, *Dogmatik*, 221–22, 348. See Sattler, *Beziehungsdenken*, 254–325, for a historical overview of substance and relation ontologies, and Lehmkühler, *Inhabitatio*, 257–86, who discusses substance-ontological and relation-ontological tendencies in the continental interpretation of Luther, and in this context also offers a critique of Ebeling. See Boschki, *Beziehung*, 312, on relational ontology and Martin Buber's philosophy of encounter. On the evaluation of substance and relational ontologies, see further J. Turner, 'Ontology', in J. Hastings (ed.), *Encyclopædia of Religion and Ethics. Vol. IX* (Edinburgh: T. & T. Clark, 1917), 498. Cf. Slenczka, *Realpräsenz*, *passim*, with Sattler, *Beziehungsdenken*, 436.

[56] P. Schulthess, 'Relation I: History', in H. Burkhardt and B. Smith (eds.), *Handbook of Metaphysics and Ontology. Vol. 2*; Analytica (Munich: Philosophica, 1991), 778. For suggestions of *a via media*, see Volf, *Likeness*, 182–86; Motyer, 'Not Apart', 237. Interestingly, a similar paradigm-shift is evident in psychotherapy, where Freud's emphasis on the change of the drives of a person has to give way to the 'common factors' approach which suggests that it is the therapeutic relationship that plays the greatest part in healing.

[57] Brandenburger, *Fleisch*, 44: '...muß eine substanzhaft gedachte "Verwandlung" stattfinden'; cf. 105; Horn, *Angeld*, 388. On the translation 'substance-ontological', see 1.3.

[58] Brandenburger, *Fleisch*, 227. However, Brandenburger himself calls this a 'combination of substance and relation categories' (Brandenburger, *Fleisch*, 227, cf. 82, 232). On p. 233 he is more specific about this combination: 'Freilich denkt die dualistische Weisheit die Antithese von Fleisch und Geist, den Einwohnungs- und Raumaspekt und Verwandtes substanzhaft; doch ist das der Intention nach immer noch Grundlage eines

Whereas Brandenburger allows also for relational thinking in Paul, other scholars tend to choose one of these two systems of thought over the other. For instance, Dockery, writes with regard to the above-mentioned renewal of the person that '"old person" and "new person" are not... ontological but relational in orientation. They speak not of a change in nature, but of a change in relationship.'[59]

Of itself it is to be welcomed that these exegetes reflect on philosophical aspects of the theology of Paul's writings,[60] because every text has dimensions that lie beneath its surface. However, one needs to be careful not to project one's own philosophical tradition into Paul's letters and in this way ignore or even contradict the text itself. Sanders is aware of this difficulty regarding the above-mentioned terminological and conceptual opposites (which relate to similar pairings that have been created in the history of scholarship, e.g., justification-sanctification as either 'forensic-imputed' or 'effective-real').[61] He therefore comments with respect to Paul's language of 'real participation':

> But what does this mean? How are we to understand it? We seem to lack a concept of 'reality' – real participation in Christ, real possession of the Spirit – which lies between naïve cosmological speculation and belief in magical transference on the one hand and a revised self-understanding on the other. I must confess that I do not have a new category of perception to propose here.[62]

The stalemate that is so honestly described in Sanders' lines also extends to the attempts that have been made to fathom Paul's thought on the sanctifying work of the Spirit, as we have demonstrated in our review of scholarship (1.2. and Appendix). In order to break this deadlock we would like to

---

sündig-verfehlten oder gerechten Standes vor Gott, also einer bestimmten theologisch qualifizierten Relation.' However, generally speaking, Brandenburger's monograph seems to reflect more of the substance-ontological approach (cf. 2.2.3.–2.2.4. above).

[59] D.S. Dockery, 'New Nature and Old Nature', *DPL*, 628; followed by J.M. Howard, *Paul, the Community, and Progressive Sanctification: An Exploration into Community-Based Transformation within Pauline Theology*; SBL 90 (New York: Lang, 2007), 81 n.61. Cf. Buchegger, *Erneuerung*, 295; Schweizer, 'σάρξ', 135; cf. also Dunn's comment on Rom. 8:9: 'What is in view is not ontological transformation but a change in orientation and motive centers' (Dunn, *Romans 1–8*, 428). However, see the more recent statements by Dunn below.

[60] For further scholars, see the research review in Lehmkühler, *Inhabitatio*, 30–37; see particularly Vollenweider, 'Geist', 163–92, and our summary and critique of his contribution in the Appendix n.158.

[61] For further pairs, see Lehmkühler, *Inhabitatio*, 30–43; M.F. Bird, *The Saving Righteousness of God: Studies on Paul, Justification, and the New Perspective*; PBM (Milton Keynes/Eugene, OR: Paternoster/Wipf & Stock, 2007), 7–18.

[62] Sanders, *Palestinian Judaism*, 522–23. However, see his *Paul*, where Sanders clearly speaks of participation as real change (E.P. Sanders, *Paul*; Past Masters (Oxford/New York: Oxford University Press, 1991), 74–76).

suggest that Dunn's answer to the questions regarding justification-sanctification which are raised in the quotation of Sanders, also shows the way ahead with respect to the (supposed) opposition of a substance onto-logical *or* a relational concept of the work of the Spirit in Paul's ethics. Dunn explains that

...the basic idea assumed by Paul was of a relationship in which God acts on behalf of his human partner, first in calling Israel into and then in sustaining Israel in its covenant with him. So once again the answer is not one or the other but both. The covenant God counts the covenant partner as still in partnership, despite the latter's continued failure. But the covenant partner could hardly fail to be transformed by a living relationship with the life-giving God.[63]

Applying Dunn's position on justification-sanctification to our question regarding ontological frameworks means to appreciate that the dominance of the (covenant) relationship of God with his people in Paul's thinking rules out the 'relational-as-opposed-to-ontological' approach to Paul's theology and anthropology that is evidenced by Dockery and others. Paul's thinking rather encompasses both these aspects, and they are well captured by the concept of *transforming relationships*.[64]

---

[63] Dunn, *Theology*, 344. Cf. Furnish, *Theology*, 152–54; Berger, *Identity*, 206. Less explicitly: Käsemann, 'Doctrine', 117; Käsemann, *Romans*, 223; Stuhlmacher, *Gerechtigkeit*, 225; C.K. Barrett, *Paul: An Introduction to his Thought*; OCT (London: Chapman, 1994), 99; Strecker, *Theologie*, 164–66; A. Schlatter, *The Theology of the Apostles: The Development of New Testament Theology* (Grand Rapids: Baker, 1998), 270; J.D.G. Dunn, 'Philippians 3.2–14 and the New Perspective on Paul', in J.D.G. Dunn, *The New Perspective on Paul: Collected Essays*; WUNT 185 (Tübingen: Mohr Siebeck, 2005), 479–81; more abstract: 'Der Heilsindikativ des neuen Seins [ist] eine ontologische Wirklichkeit in einem *personal-dynamischen* Sinn' (Halter, *Taufe*, 419).

[64] Cf. V. Rabens, 'Transforming Relationships: The Spirit's Empowering for Reli-gious-Ethical Life According to the Apostle Paul' (18th British New Testament Confer-ence, London: Unpublished Paper, 2000), 16. As an example of this balance, see 2 Cor. 5:17, where the protasis (εἴ τις ἐν Χριστῷ) seems to place weight on the new relation-ship and the apodosis (καινὴ κτίσις) weight on the new being. Cf. M.E. Thrall, *A Critical and Exegetical Commentary on the Second Epistle to the Corinthians. Vol. 1: Introduc-tion and Commentary on II Corinthians I–VII*; ICC (Edinburgh: T. & T. Clark, 1994), 420–29; C. Hoegen-Rohls, 'Κτίσις and καινὴ κτίσις in Paul's Letters', in A. Chris-tophersen, et al. (eds.), *Paul, Luke and the Graeco-Roman world: Essays in Honour of Alexander J. M. Wedderburn*; JSNTSup 217 (London: Sheffield Academic Press, 2002), 117–18; on the correlation of 2 Cor. 5:17 and Paul's pneumatology, see M.V. Hubbard, *New Creation in Paul's Letters and Thought*; SNTSMS 119 (Cambridge: Cambridge University Press, 2002), 183–85 (however, Baumgarten and Mell think that Paul does not [explicitly] connect the Spirit with the new creation motif [Baumgarten, *Apokalyptik*, 170; Mell, *Schöpfung*, 305]). Cf. on Gal. 2:20, J.M.G. Barclay, 'Paul's Story: Theology as Testimony', in B.W. Longenecker (ed.), *Narrative Dynamics in Paul: A Critical Assessment* (Louisville: Westminster John Knox, 2002), 143, 155–56.

With regard to Paul's anthropology, this means that Paul understood people as being in and being influenced by relationships,[65] but without giving up the notion of the individual (and hence, e.g., conceiving the indwelling of the Spirit as a fusion[66]).[67] Also the ethical work of the Spirit evidences two sides of one coin. On one side we have Paul's portrayal of the Spirit as empowering believers for religious-ethical life (see the passages discussed in 6.3.–6.4.). The other side of the coin can be seen when Paul is talking about the transformation of the 'heart' by the Spirit (1 Thess. 4:7–8 and 2 Cor. 3:3 [cf. v.18], with Ezek. 36–37 and Jer. 31 in its background).[68]

Moreover, our relational model also offers the capacity of providing a conceptual unity for the two elements of Paul's theology-and-ethics singled out by Engberg-Pedersen (following the legacy of Bultmann[69]): Engberg-Pedersen sees Paul operating predominantly within a cognitive framework of understanding and self-identification, but he does not want to exclude the possibility that Paul's more 'substantive language' was a

---

[65] Cf. Bultmann, *Theology. I*, 191; Malina and Neyrey, *Paul*, 190; B.W. Longenecker, *The Triumph of Abraham's God: The Transformation of Identity in Galatians* (Edinburgh: T. & T. Clark, 1998), 186; Dunn, *Theology*, 53; Campbell, *Quest*, 41.

[66] Rom. 8:16, 26; Gal. 4:6; etc. clearly speak against fusion. *Pace* Pfleiderer, *Paulinism*, 213–16. See further ch. 3 Excursus 1; Appendix 1.2. and n.73. On 1 Cor. 6:17, see Fee, *Presence*, 133–34. Cf. H.-D. Wendland, *Vom Leben und Handeln der Christen: Eine Betrachtung zu Römer 6* (Stuttgart: Calwer Verlag, 1972), 35–36. Barclay, 'Story', 143, comments on Gal. 2:20: 'Both statements of subjectivity – both that "Christ lives in me" and that "I live" – can be taken as true, in a dialectical fashion.' On Paul's anthropology, see further ch. 3 (Introduction and Excursus 1).

[67] Cf. Müller, *Erfahrung*, 179, 181–82; Vollenweider, 'Geist', 184–85; Engberg-Pedersen, *Stoics*, 294; Schnelle, 'Transformation', 69, 72; Burnett, *Salvation*, *passim*; Hubbard, *Creation*, 129, 233; Berger, *Identity*, 26–43; Munzinger, *Spirits*, 185; Lewis, *Life*, 29–30.

[68] For an (substance-)ontological interpretation of 1 Thess. 4:7–8, see W. Pfister, OP, *Das Leben im Geist nach Paulus: Der Geist als Anfang und Vollendung des christlichen Lebens*; SF II/34 (Freiburg: Universitätsverlag, 1963), 16; Becker, 'Erwählung', 88; Horn, *Angeld*, 127; cf. T.J. Deidun, *New Covenant Morality in Paul*; AnBib 89 (Rome: Biblical Institute Press, 1981), 53–62. However, see also Fee, *Presence*, 53, for a more relational interpretation of the passage. Moreover, a 3–stage interpretation of Ezek. 36:25–27, which somewhat distances the divine Spirit from the renewal of heart and spirit, has been proposed by P. van Imschoot, 'L'Esprit de Jahvé, Principe de Vie Morale dans l'A. T.', *ETL* 16 (1939), 463; W. Zimmerli, *Ezechiel*; HAT I/13 (Tübingen: J.C.B. Mohr (Paul Siebeck), 1955²), 879; P. Joyce, *Divine Initiative and Human Response in Ezekiel*; JSOTSup 51 (Sheffield: Sheffield Academic Press, 1989), 110–11; R. Koch, *Der Geist Gottes im Alten Testament* (Frankfurt: Lang, 1991), 132–33. See further 5.1.3. On 2 Cor. 3, see further 6.2.1.

In Rom. 8:5 perhaps both an 'ontological' and a 'functional' aspect shines through (κατὰ σάρκα/κατὰ πνεῦμα ὄντες; τὰ τῆς σαρκός/τὰ τοῦ πνεύματος φρονοῦσιν).

[69] On Bultmann, cf. Appendix 2.1.

realistic building block of Paul's paraenesis too.[70] Both these aspects come together in our relational concept of the work of the Spirit in Paul's ethics in that, for one thing, deeper understanding of God and oneself as well as a new (sense of) identity is part of the intimate relationships created by the Spirit with both God and the fellowship of believers. Likewise, we have seen above that believers can 'hardly fail to be transformed by a living relationship with the life-giving God'[71] which implies that Paul's more 'substantive language' has a place in our concept of the relational work of the Spirit in Paul's ethics too.

The adjacent pairs which are often conceived as opposites (i.e. relational versus substance-ontological transformation; [functional] empowering versus [ontological] transformation; new self-understanding versus a completely new self) thus converge in our concept of *transforming relationships*. We will demonstrate in chapter 6 that particularly 2 Corinthians 3:18 displays lucidly how these various perspectives of the two different sides are part of the same coin (a growing relationship, a deepening of knowledge of God and self, and a 'substantive' transformation). What is more, this verse also provides an answer to a tantalizing question that might be addressed to our relational model of the Spirit's work in Paul's ethics: Is it the *Spirit* that transforms and empowers, or is it the *relationships*, or is it those (i.e. Ἀββα, Χριστός, ἀδελφοί) with whom believers are brought into relation?[72] The solution is that for Paul, these aspects cannot be set against one another. It is the *Spirit* (καθάπερ ἀπὸ κυρίου πνεύματος), the *relationships* (expressed by intimacy that is created by the unveiling of faces, as well as the beholding) and the one that 'we all' are being related to (i.e. τὴν δόξαν κυρίου) who effect the transformation (μεταμορφούμεθα).

We seek to demonstrate with this study that the relational aspect of the ethical work of the Spirit has thus far been underestimated. We will argue

---

[70] Engberg-Pedersen, *Stoics*, 224–25, 252–54, 302; followed tentatively by Munzinger, *Spirits*, 178–84; cf. Lewis, *Life*, 13. The 'substantive' element of Engberg-Pedersen's model of Paul's ethics is fully elaborated in his recent book, *Cosmology and the Self in the Apostle Paul*. It builds on the presupposition that Paul operates with a Stoic concept of the Spirit which we have dismissed in Part I of this study.

[71] Dunn, *Theology*, 344. Cf. F. Young and D.F. Ford, *Meaning and Truth in 2 Corinthians* (Grand Rapids: Eerdmans, 1988), 243.

[72] Cf. 4.2. above. On the interplay of relations and *relata* (i.e. the entities that are being related) in relation ontologies, see the philosophical discussions in J.J. Schaaf, 'Beziehung und Beziehungsloses (Absolutes)', in D. Heinrich and H. Wagner (eds.), *Subjektivität und Metaphysik: Festschrift für Wolfgang Cramer* (Frankfurt: Klostermann, 1966), 277–89; Schulthess, 'Relation', 778; T.L.S. Sprigge, 'Relation III: Internal Relations', in H. Burkhardt and B. Smith (eds.), *Handbook of Metaphysics and Ontology*; Analytica (Munich: Philosophica, 1991), 782; H.A. Harris, 'Should We Say that Personhood is Relational?', *SJT* 51 (1998), 224–26, 234.

that our relational model is the key to understanding how the Spirit enables believers for religious-ethical life according to Paul.

4.2. Pneumatological Presuppositions

Chapters 1–3 have clearly demonstrated (and critically reviewed) that the infusion-transformation approach to Spirit and ethics in Paul builds on the concept of the Spirit as a material substance. The question that arises for our own approach is whether we too want to apply such a methodology, though perhaps with a different concept of the Spirit. A scholar who walks this path is Vang. He puts forward that for Paul 'spiritual fruit depends upon the relationship between the *person of the Spirit* and the person of the believer'.[73] However, while Vang's relational approach to Paul's pneumatology needs to be appreciated, it is unfortunate that Vang fails to provide support for the concept of the Spirit as a person which is an integral part of his proposal.[74] This is particularly regrettable as it is a matter of variegated scholarly debate whether Paul indeed evidences the concept of the Spirit as a person.[75]

We have argued elsewhere at greater length that a good way of conceptualizing the notion of the Spirit with which Paul appears to operate in his

---

[73] Vang, 'Presence', 244, italics added; cf. 235.

[74] Cf. Vang's conclusion to his exegesis of 2 Corinthians 13:13: 'To the church that was marred with problems from a host of would-be πευματικοί, he [Paul] pronounces the intimate fellowship with the Spirit as the solution for every (πάντων ὑμῶν) Corinthian Christian' (Ibid., 118). However, it seems doubtful whether Paul indeed emphasizes fellowship with the Spirit in the way in which Vang's model assumes. For one thing, Paul does not operate with a fully developed concept of the Spirit as a 'person' (on this see further below). Apart from that, Paul does not appear to place so much weight on the fellowship with the Spirit as 'the solution' to ethical fatigue. 2 Corinthians 13:13 and Philippians 2:1 are the only two places where Paul employs the ambiguous phrase κοινωνία [τοῦ ἁγίου] πνεύματος. See our discussion of these verses in 6.4.2.

[75] Recently Tibbs and Williams sought to shift scholarly opinion on the nature of πνεῦμα in Paul into the opposite direction. They argue that πνεῦμα in Paul refers to a 'spirit world' (Tibbs, *Experience*, *passim*; C. Tibbs, 'The Spirit (World) and the (Holy) Spirits among the Earliest Christians: 1 Corinthians 12 and 14 as a Test Case', *CBQ* 70 (2008), 321–30; G. Williams, *The Spirit World in the Letters of Paul the Apostle: A Critical Examination of the Role of Spiritual Beings in the Authentic Pauline Epistles*; FRLANT 231 (Göttingen: Vandenhoeck & Ruprecht, 2009), *passim*). However, πνεῦμα is in Paul regularly qualified as πνεῦμα Ἰησοῦ, πνεῦμα Χριστοῦ, τὸ πνεῦμα τοῦ υἱοῦ (Rom. 8:9, 11; Gal. 4:6; Phil. 1:19), τὸ πνεῦμα τοῦ θεου (e.g. Rom. 15:19; 1 Cor. 2:11; 6:11; 7:40; 12:3; Phil. 3:3; cf. 1 Thess. 4:8), ἓν πνεῦμα, τὸ... αὐτὸ πνεῦμα (e.g. 1 Cor. 12:4, 8–9, 11, 13), etc. These unambiguous passages, which contradict a plural rendering of πνεῦμα as 'spirit world', suggest that Paul may also refer to this *one* Spirit when he uses πνεῦμα without qualification (unless he employs πνεῦμα with an anthropological reference etc., as e.g. in Rom. 8:16) or as πνεῦμα ἅγιον (e.g. 1 Cor. 12:3).

letters is to view the Spirit as having 'personal traits'.[76] Due to the methodological complexities of establishing the nature of the Spirit in the
Pauline corpus, this language is to be preferred to speaking of the Spirit
explicitly as a person.[77] Nevertheless, we have indicated in our conclusion
to Part I that it is methodologically unwise to build one's model of the
Spirit's enabling of religious-ethical life in Paul on a particular concept of
the ontology of the Spirit. We therefore reaffirm that our model will rather
be based on the actual *effects* which are attributed to the Spirit in Hellenism, Judaism and in Paul.[78] To this we will now turn in the remaining two
chapters.[79]

---

[76] Rabens, 'Development', 177. Apart from the literature discussed there, see more
recently the similar positions of Turner, '"Trinitarian" Pneumatology', 167–86; U.
Schnelle, *Paulus: Leben und Denken* (Berlin/New York: W. de Gruyter, 2003), 563;
Berger, *Identity*, 34; I.H. Marshall, *New Testament Theology: Many Witnesses, One
Gospel* (Downers Grove: IVP, 2004), 430; Campbell, *Quest*, 41, 61; R.C. Fay, 'Was Paul
a Trinitarian? A Look at Romans 8', in S.E. Porter (ed.), *Paul and His Theology*; PS 3
(Leiden: Brill, 2006), 341–45.

[77] Cf. K. Berger, *Ist Gott Person? Ein Weg zum Verstehen des christlichen Gottesbildes* (Gütersloh: Gütersloher Verlagshaus, 2004), 86–87. Nonetheless, against the background of our determination that the Spirit evidences 'personal traits' in Paul, it seems
justified to occasionally use the relative pronoun 'he' for the divine Spirit. We have
indicated that this could run the danger of projecting a fully developed personalism onto
Paul's pneumatology. However, it seems closer to Paul's presentation of the Spirit of God
or of Christ than a reference to 'it'. Secondly, we are also aware of the usefulness of a
thorough discussion of whether 'she' would be a better rendering of τό πνεῦμα (רוּחַ is
usually feminine). However, as this discussion transcends the space and purpose of our
study, we will adopt the present scholarly convention and occasionally apply the male
pronoun. Cf. the discussion in C.H. Pinnock, *Flame of Love: A Theology of the Holy
Spirit* (Downers Grove: IVP, 1996), 15–17.

[78] Saarinen calls such an approach 'Wirkungsdenken' (as opposed to 'Wesensdenken')
(R. Saarinen, 'Gottes Sein – Gottes Wirken: Die Grunddifferenz von Substanzdenken und
Wirkungsdenken in der evangelischen Lutherdeutung', in S. Peura and A. Raunio (eds.),
Luther und Theosis: Vergöttlichung als Thema der abendländischen Theologie; VLAR
15; SLAG 25 (Erlangen/Helsinki: Martin-Luther-Verlag/Luther-Agricola-Gesellschaft,
1990), 118 n.52). Cf. B.J. Hilberath, *Pneumatologie*; LTh 23 (Düsseldorf: Patmos, 1994),
78–79; A.K. Gabriel, 'Pauline Pneumatology and the Question of Trinitarian Presuppositions', in S.E. Porter (ed.), *Paul and His Theology*; PS 3 (Leiden: Brill, 2006), 361.

[79] Our study thus fills a gap in Pauline studies recently lamented by D.A. Campbell,
The Deliverance of God: An Apocalyptic Rereading of Justification in Paul (Grand
Rapids/Cambridge: Eerdmans, 2009), 211 n.83.

Chapter 5

Religious-Ethical Empowerment by the Relational Work of the Spirit:
A Selective Discussion of Paul's Context

The proponents of the infusion-transformation approach discussed in Part I of our study have painted one particular picture of the ethical work of the Spirit in Paul's context. We have analysed the passages that have been put forward by these scholars in chapter 2. In the present chapter we will show that there is a significant number of further passages relevant to the question how the Spirit enables religious-ethical life in Paul's context. The purpose of the chapter is to demonstrate that *there is adequate material in Paul's religious and philosophical context against which our relational model of the ethically empowering work of the Spirit can be read*. Accordingly, we will not try to unravel every possible factor of (the Spirit's) ethical empowering in the various strands of Graeco-Roman and early Jewish literature.[1] Rather, we endeavour to uncover traces in Paul's Jewish-Hellenistic matrix of our focal theory which submits that it is typically through facilitating deeper knowledge of God and an intimate relationship with him and with the community of faith that the Spirit empowers people for religious-ethical living. Should this investigation evidence positive results and reveal parallels between the relevant literature and Paul, we will be able to conclude that Paul was not the first to discover the transforming and empowering ethical effects of Spirit-created intimate relationships. It will increase the likelihood that our relational model is accurate, although it will not inevitably follow that Paul was dependent on the very sources discussed in this chapter.[2]

---

[1] E.g., we will engage only in passing with Wenk's emphasis on the role of Spirit-endowed leaders of the community as facilitating ethics (Wenk, *Power*, 117–18; however, see 2.2.4.2. above). Likewise, an analysis of how relationships in the Jesus tradition empower ethical living and whether, and if so how, this is related in the Gospels to the Spirit would go beyond the scope of this the present study. However, see the brief notes on the general emphasis on relationships in Paul's tradition (including the Jesus-tradition) in 4.3.

[2] For similar methodological considerations, see Charlesworth, *Pseudepigrapha*, 78.

1. Early Jewish Literature

Contrary to the belief of some scholars, many ancient Jewish writers related God's Spirit to ethical living (see the passages discussed below, and, e.g., *T. Sim.* 4.4; *T. Levi* 18.7; *T. Benj.* 8.2; *1 En.* 49:3; *4 Ezra* 6.26–27; *Jos. Asen.* 8.9; cf. *Odes* 3.10).[3] However, the question of our inquiry is whether early Jewish literature gives any indication *how* this work of enabling is achieved by the Spirit. While it would go too far to claim that Second Temple Judaism explicitly asked this question, it is nevertheless clear that this topic was much more on the minds of the Jews of the Second Temple Period than of the authors of the Hebrew Bible. As it seems that Second Temple Judaism is trying to fill in some of the gaps left open in the Hebrew Bible, this section will devote more attention to the former than to the latter.[4]

Generally speaking, there is ample evidence in the Hebrew Bible and early Judaism that an intimate relationship with God (including deeper understanding of him and his deeds) and with the community of faith was comprehended as transforming and empowering for religious-ethical living:

a) Empowering through an intimate relationship with *God* is evident in Pss. 18:1–2 (the relationship to God strengthens the Psalmist); 23; 27; 40:1–4, 11, 16 (trusting in YHWH saves from going astray, his love is salvation); 42:1–2 (being with God produces strength/refreshment); 63:1–8; 84 (strength [v.7] and happiness [vv.4, 12] are the result of an intimate relationship with YHWH); 1 Sam. 10:6–7 (the Spirit of YHWH and the presence of God is with Saul and transforms him); Isa. 6; Ezek. 37:27–28 (God's presence sanctifies); *1 En.* 39.14; 71.10–11; *2 En.* 22; *3 En.* 12 (transformation in the presence of the divine);[5] *Deut. R.* 6.14 (as the Spirit/the Divine Presence rests on the people they will receive understanding of the Torah and dwell in peace [drawing on Joel 3:1 and Isa. 54:13]); etc.[6]

---

[3] For an overview of the discussion between those denying and those defending the presence of a pneumatological ethics in Judaism, see Appendix 3.1. and Turner, *Power*, ch. 5. On *Jos. Asen.* 8:9, see 2.2.3.; on *Odes*, see n.72 below.

[4] On this methodology, see more generally: J.C. VanderKam, 'Biblical Interpretation in *1 Enoch* and *Jubilees*', in J.H. Charlesworth and C.A. Evans (eds.), *The Pseudepigrapha and Early Biblical Interpretation*; JSPSup 14/SSEJC 2 (Sheffield: JSOT Press, 1993), 118.

[5] On these and further texts from early Judaism, see C.R.A. Morray-Jones, 'Transformational Mysticism in the Apocalyptic-Merkabah Tradition', *JJS* 43 (1992), 1–31; M. Himmelfarb, *Ascent to Heaven in Jewish and Christian Apocalypses* (Oxford: Oxford University Press, 1993), 47–71.

[6] On the negative effects of the absence of God's presence, see, e.g., Isa. 6:9–10; Jer. 2:5. Cf. Samra, *Christ*, 119 n.47: 'Whereas those who draw close to God are positively transformed, in Jer. 2:5 those who have strayed from God after worthless idols have themselves become worthless.'

b) Empowering through intimate relationships within the *community of faith* is evident in Pss. 42:4–5 (the Psalmist is uplifted by the memory of worshipping God in the community); 133:1, 3 (well-being ['blessing'] is the consequence of intimate relationships ['unity']);[7] 1 Sam. 20 (David and Jonathan draw strength from their intimate friendship in times of trouble); etc.[8]

Such intimate relationships, particularly closeness to God and deeper understanding of him, are typically portrayed by the Jewish writers as the work of the Spirit (see, e.g., Isa. 11:2–4; Ezek. 39:29; *T. Levi* 18.7; *1 En.* 49.3; *Deut. R.* 6.14; cf. Ps. 51:11: the Spirit and God's presence are identified, and ethical ministry is the result of this transforming interaction with the divine [v.13]).[9]

One can observe that the three themes mentioned above (i.e. the Spirit, closeness to God/the community of faith, and ethics) were comprehended in early Judaism as being dependent on one another. For example, in Sirach 39.5–8 people who devote themselves to the study of the law of the Most High are described as seeking an intimate relationship with him. God gives them the S/spirit of understanding (πνεύματι συνέσεως ἐμπλησθήσεται) that facilitates further closeness to God (e.g. giving thanks to the Lord in prayer). The consequence is that they 'will glory in the law of the Lord's covenant'.

In the ensuing search for the presence of the idea in Paul's context that the relational work of the Spirit empowers virtuous living, it will become clear that there are numerous further passages in early Judaism that testify to this interconnection of Spirit, intimate relationships and ethics. We will concentrate on the Qumran documents as a case for the more Palestinian branch of Judaism and on the more Hellenized Philo as a second avenue into early Jewish literature. These two perspectives will be complemented by a look at the traditions developed on the basis of Ezekiel 36–37. In the course of this investigation we will come across a number of passages where a soteriological and an ethical reference point overlap (see, e.g., our exegesis of 1QH[a] 8.19–20). However, the angle chosen by our study is ethical and does not pay explicit attention to questions regarding the entrance into the salvific community.

---

[7] Cf. L.C. Allen, *Psalms 101–150*; WBC 21 (Waco: Word, 1983), 215.

[8] If one reads 'love' in Song 8:6–7 in a more general (i.e. not specifically erotic) manner, love (expressed in relationships) is presented as an all-transforming power. Further examples from early Judaism will be discussed below; cf. 4.3.; Samra, *Christ*, 120 n.51.

[9] On the Spirit as bringing knowledge in early Judaism, see further C.S. Keener, *The Spirit in the Gospels and Acts: Divine Purity and Power* (Peabody: Hendrickson, 1997), 10–12.

1.1. Philo

Philo of Alexandria lends strong support both to a central pillar of our focal theory as well as to our model as a whole.[10] We will first give evidence of Philonic texts that demonstrate the ethically empowering impact of an intimate relationship with God, and then of the instrumental role of the divine Spirit in this process.

a) Life-changing encounters with God. Philo is at heart a theologian for whom the intimate experience of 'the One who Is' is of paramount importance. Noack rightly remarks that Philo 'betreibt als Exeget *Erfahrungstheologie*, in der er Wege zur verwandelnden Erfahrung göttlicher Gegenwart sucht'.[11] For example, when he interprets Deuteronomy 30:20, Philo emphasizes the love of God and the effects of what we may call a mystical union[12] with God in the following way:

Moses... bids them [i.e. the Israelites] "cleave to Him," bringing out by the use of this word how constant and continuous and unbroken is the concord and union that comes through making God our own. [...] But so unceasingly does he [i.e. Moses] himself yearn to see God and to be seen by Him, that he implores Him to reveal clearly His own nature (Exod. xxxiii. 13), which is so hard to divine, hoping thus to obtain at length a view free from all falsehood, and to exchange doubt and uncertainty for a most assured confidence (*Poster. C.* 12–13).[13]

Philo explains here that Moses wants to truly 'partake in the glory' (δόξης μεταλαβών), and that a firm faith (βεβαιοτάτην πίστιν) will be the result of this intimate encounter of 'seeing God and being seen by Him'.

The religious-ethical effect of this mystical relationship comes more clearly to the fore in *De Legatione ad Gaium* 4–5. Philo expresses that seeing God

---

[10] On the introductory matters regarding Philo and his pneumatology, see 2.2.4.

[11] Noack, *Gottesbewußtsein*, 247. Cf. Bousset, *Kyrios*, 226; D. Winston, 'Philo's Ethical Theory', in W. Haase (ed.), *Principat*; ANRW II.21.1 (Berlin/New York: W. de Gruyter, 1984), 372–77; J.R. Levison, 'Philo's Personal Experience and the Persistence of Prophecy', in M.H. Floyd and R.D. Haak (eds.), *Prophets, Prophecy, and Prophetic Texts in Second Temple Judaism*; LHB/OTS 427 (New York/London: T. & T. Clark, 2006), 196–209. Cf. D.M. Hay, 'Philo of Alexandria', in D.A. Carson, et al. (eds.), *Justification and Variegated Nomism. Vol. 1: The Complexities of Second Temple Judaism*; WUNT II/140 (Tübingen: Mohr Siebeck, 2001), 366: 'The "psychology" that matters to Philo is an understanding of the soul of the individual in relation to God.'

[12] Cf. the definition of mysticism in ch. 3 Excursus 1; on Philo's mysticism, see more specifically D. Winston, 'Philo's Mysticism', *SPA* 8 (1996), 74–82. This notion of mysticism should not be confused with that of the mystery cults which Pascher anachronistically ascribes to Philo (J. Pascher, *Η ΒΑΣΙΛΙΚΗ ΟΔΟΣ: Der Königsweg zu Wiedergeburt und Vergottung bei Philon von Alexandreia*; SGKA 17–3/4 (Paderborn: Schöningh, 1931), 164–67, 177, 183). See also the differentiation in the body text at n.38 below.

[13] On the human longing for an intimate relationship with God, see further *Op. Mund.* 70–71; *Ebr.* 152; et al.

seems to me of all possessions, public or private, the most precious. For if the sight of seniors or instructors or rulers or parents stirs the beholders to respect for them and decent behaviour and the desire to live a life of self-control, how firmly based is the virtue and nobility of conduct which we may expect to find in souls whose vision has soared above all created things and schooled itself to behold the uncreated and divine, the primal good, the excellent, the happy, the blessed, which may truly be called better than the good, more excellent than the excellent, more blessed than blessedness, more happy than happiness itself (*Leg. Gai.* 4–5).

The impact of an intimate encounter with God is thus attested as 'firmly based... virtue and nobility of conduct'. Philo does not unravel whether the ethical life of those who have 'beheld the uncreated and divine' results from a feeling of duty (as, e.g., in *Gig.* 47) or a sense of empowering, although the latter seems more likely. Perhaps the best way of categorizing the effect is that it furthers the *motivation* for ethical life. More specifically, however, in *Quaestiones et Solutiones in Exodum* 2.7 Philo finds a way to describe figuratively how such a religious-ethical transformation happens: 'just as one who comes near the light is straightaway illumined, so also is filled the entire soul of him to whom God has appeared' (cf. *Gig.* 49; *Quaest. in Gen.* 4.25). Philo here speaks of God's empowering presence as the motor of change in a person and not so much of moral obligation. Knowledge and wisdom are central agents in this process,[14] aiming at the person's being 'full of every good' (*Quaest. in Exod.* 2.7).

This transforming and empowering effect of an intimate encounter and relationship with God is still more clearly expressed by Philo in *De Migratione Abrahami* 34–36. When speaking about his state of divine inspiration during which he is 'filled with amazement at the might of Him that IS', he explains that 'Now the thing shewn is the thing worthy to be seen, contemplated, loved, the perfect good, *whose nature it is to change all that is bitter in the soul and make it sweet*, fairest seasoning of all spices, turning into salutary nourishment even foods that do not nourish... (Ex. xv. 25)' (*Migr.* 36; cf. 37 on the explicitly ethical aspect of the transformation).

Numerous further passages could be discussed as evidence of the often overlooked fact that for Philo, an intimate relationship with the divine empowers religious-ethical life (see, e.g., *Gig.* 49; *Quaest. in Gen.* 4.4, 29, 140; *Vit. Cont.* 90; *Migr.* 132; *Plant.* 64–66; *Deus. Imm.* 3–4; *Rer. Div. Her.* 70–71; *Praem. Poen.* 41–48; *Abr.* 58–59; *Leg. All.* 3.71; *Cher.* 24, 50; *Somn.* 1.149; 2.232; *Fug.* 82; *Virt.* 163–64, 181, 215–16, 218; cf. *Vit. Mos.*

---

[14] Cf. Bennema, *Power*, 75, 81–83; Munzinger, *Spirits*, 109–110, cf. more generally, 111–21. Hellemann points out that the change that results from the close relationship to God is conceptualized by Philo as a *process* (W.E. Hellemann, 'Philo of Alexandria on Deification and Assimilation to God', *SPA* 2 (1990), 62–63, 70–71). Accordingly, Schweitzer believes that one better speaks of the product of this transformation as a new relationship and not of a new creation (Schweitzer, 'Gotteskindschaft', 108).

1.156).[15] However, we will now turn to the question whether the Spirit has a place in this scenario.

b) Religious-ethical empowering by the Spirit in the context of relationships. The place of the Spirit in the context of relational empowering for ethics comes to the fore, first of all, in that the Spirit relates humans to God. Bennema points out that 'the mind or divine πνεῦμα constitutes a union between man and God (*Leg. All.* 1.37) and provides the basis of knowing God, the means of a relationship with God (*Plant.* 18; *Leg. All.* 1.33–34, 37–38).'[16] Likewise, Philo clearly relates the Spirit to the furtherance of virtuous life (e.g. *Vit. Mos.* 2.265; *Gig.* 23, 28, 47; *Mut. Nom.* 123–24; *Leg. All.* 1.33–34; *Quaest. in Gen.* 4.140).[17] More specifically, however, Philo provides evidence that these two aspects of the Spirit's work – the creation of intimacy with God and the empowering for ethics – are interconnected in his thinking. In order to demonstrate this, we will first look at two passages in which Philo mentions the divine πνεῦμα as the rational aspect of the human soul breathed into humankind at creation, and then at Moses' endowment with the prophetic Spirit.[18]

---

[15] Noack comments on *Vit. Mos.* 1.156 that 'Angelpunkt des gesamten Lebensstils ist... die Gottesbeziehung. Wer mit Gott als Quelle der Tugend verbunden ist, erhält folglich Anteil an allen anderen Tugenden' (Noack, *Gottesbewußtsein*, 71, cf. 73).

Empowering via an intimate relationship with God modelled in the relationship of a father and his children is also present in Philo: 'But those who are free from self-love and hasten to God obtain from above His visitations and care as from a father, and as from a husband (they obtain) the sowing of good thoughts and intentions and words and deeds' (*Quaest. in Exod.* 2.3; cf. *Conf.* 145). *Vit. Cont.* 2 describes worship as healing (cf. the overview of empowering relationships and further aspects of maturation among the Therapeutae in J.G. Samra, 'Being Conformed to Christ in Community: A Study of Maturity, Maturation and the Local Church in the Undisputed Pauline Epistles' (University of Oxford: Unpublished DPhil Thesis, 2004), 79–85).

It should be noted that some of the passages in the list above imply that ethical life can also be a presupposition for seeing God. However, Philo generally portrays God as the initiator of moral life. Cf. W. Völker, *Fortschritt und Vollendung bei Philo von Alexandrien: Eine Studie zur Geschichte der Frömmigkeit*; TU IV/4//1 (Leipzig, 1938), 302–303; J.M.G. Barclay, '"By the Grace of God I am what I am": Grace and Agency in Philo and Paul', in J.M.G. Barclay and S.J. Gathercole (eds.), *Divine and Human Agency in Paul and his Cultural Environment*; ECC/LNTS 335 (London: Continuum, 2006), 141–48.

[16] Bennema, *Power*, 73, cf. 74–77, 82; followed verbatim by Philip, *Origins*, 105. Cf. Isaacs, *Spirit*, 57; F. Siegert, *Philon von Alexandrien: Über die Gottesbezeichnung "wohltätig verzehrendes Feuer" (De Deo)*; WUNT 46 (Tübingen: J.C.B. Mohr (Paul Siebeck), 1988), 88.

[17] Cf., e.g., Turner, *Power*, 124–25; Bennema, *Power*, 74–83. On the Spirit as originator and consequence of virtue, see Wenk, *Power*, 92–93, and the critique by Bennema, *Power*, 79 n.151.

[18] On (the difficulty of) distinguishing between these two notions of the divine πνεῦμα, see Turner, *Power*, 124; Bennema, *Power*, 72–74. For the justification of em-

In his exegesis of Genesis 2:7, Philo explains that God breathes his Spirit into the mind of man. He says that a union of God, πνεῦμα and mind comes about as 'God projects the power that proceeds from Himself through the mediant breath till it reaches the subject' (*Leg. All.* 1.37). The reason for this endowment with πνεῦμα is so that 'we may obtain a conception of Him', for this is possible only by the Spirit.

For the mind of man would never have ventured to soar so high as to grasp the nature of God, had not God Himself drawn it up to Himself, so far as it was possible that the mind of man should be drawn up, and stamped it with the impress of the powers that are within the scope of its understanding. The breathing "into the face" is to be understood both physically and ethically (ἠθικῶς) (*Leg. All.* 1.38–39).

Philo continues that this divine inbreathing is 'ethical' because the Spirit-transformed mind is the master of all other parts of the body (§§39–41). We can see from this text that the divine Spirit creates a close relationship with God and that it is related to ethics. The reason why this close encounter with God is comprehended by Philo as ethically empowering comes clearer to the fore when one looks at the paragraphs preceding our quotation. In 1.34–35 Philo answers his first question regarding Genesis 2:7, namely, why God considered the human mind worthy of receiving the divine Spirit at all (1.33). The first reason that he gives is that the inbreathing of πνεῦμα demonstrates God's exceeding greatness of his own wealth and goodness. The second, related reason is that the human soul needs to experience this divine goodness and virtue in order to live a virtuous life. This experience of the overflowing goodness of God is conveyed through the reception of πνεῦμα. In this way the Spirit empowers virtuous life through providing an encounter with and profound comprehension of God in his overflowing goodness. This is also evidenced in the next passage.

In *De Opificio Mundi* 144, Philo reasons that after his creation, as he was conversing and consorting with 'spiritual and divine natures', man could not but live in unalloyed bliss.

And being akin and nearly related to the ruler of all, inasmuch as a great deal of the divine spirit had flowed into him, he was eager both to say and to do everything which might please his father and his king, following him step by step in the paths which the virtues prepare and make plain (*Op. Mund.* 144).[19]

Turner uses this text as a prime example for his view on the ethical influence of the Spirit in Philo, namely that 'both gifts [i.e. the divine inbreathing into man at creation and the prophetic Spirit] share the important characteristic that they enable the (ethically and spiritually orientated) wisdom

---

ploying both impartations of the Spirit in a study of Spirit and ethics in Philo, see further Horn, 'Wandel', 158–59.

[19] Translation by C.D. Yonge, *The Works of Philo* (Peabody: Hendrickson, 1995³), 20.

which facilitates knowledge of – and fellowship with – God.'[20] This conclusion needs to be endorsed. However, it is possible to go further than this
if one takes an additional aspect of the connection of Spirit, ethics and
fellowship with God into consideration. Namely, *De Opificio Mundi* 144
(and the passages that will be discussed below) seems to suggest that a
causal relationship between the three elements under consideration in Philo
is not limited to the order proposed by Turner (i.e. 1. gift of the Spirit → 2.
virtue → 3. fellowship with God), but that the Spirit is also seen directly as
the cause of closeness to God which leads to ethical life (i.e. 1. gift of the
Spirit → 2. closeness to God → 3. virtue [→ 4. enhancement of virtue and
fellowship with God]). This may be in mind when Philo says that man was
'akin and nearly related' (συγγενής τε καὶ ἀγχίσπορος) to God (2.), '*inasmuch as* (ἅτε) a great deal of the divine spirit had flowed into him' (1.).[21]
Hence, man's desire to 'please his father and king' (3.) appears to be the
consequence of the Spirit-created closeness to God. The result is true religious-ethical life in which following both the father and the 'highways cut
out by virtue' (LCL) play a guiding and empowering role (4.). (Generally
speaking, however, we will see that the three aspects of our relational
model of the Spirit's ethical empowering [i.e. in Paul: 1: the Spirit facilitates 2: an intimate relationship with God and fellow believers, both of
which facilitate 3: ethical life] are not always as clearly related by Philo in
this sequential order as here.[22])

We turn to the ethical influence of the prophetic Spirit on Moses.[23]
When Philo interprets Exodus 24:2 in *Quaestiones et Solutiones in Exodum* 2.29, he writes

For when the prophetic mind becomes divinely inspired and filled with God, it becomes
like the monad, not being at all mixed with any of those things associated with duality.
But he who is resolved into the nature of unity, is said to come near God in a kind of

---

[20] Turner, *Power*, 125, italics removed; followed by Bennema, *Power*, 79.

[21] This interpretation of 'being akin and nearly related' to God draws on *Virt.* 218,
where similar language is used unambiguously for Abraham's search for closeness to
God (πρὸς θεὸν συγγενείας ὀρεχθέντα), and on *Leg. All.* 1.38, where Philo explains the
purpose of the inbreathing with πνεῦμα to be that 'we may obtain a conception of Him'
(cf. *Quaest. in Exod.* 2.29 and *Gig.* 53–54, as discussed below). However, the cotext of
Op. Mund. 144 may suggest that closeness to God is here not primarily a proximity of
relationship (i.e. intimacy) but one of kind (i.e. being created in the likeness of God) (see
Op. Mund. 139, 145–46; cf. *Rer. Div. Her.* 56). Nonetheless, both interpretations can be
found in concert in *Det. Pot. Ins.* 84–86, 89–90 and *Plant.* 18–19 and 23, so that it seems
difficult to exclude the aspect of interrelational closeness in *Op. Mund.* 144. See further,
Gärtner, 'Idea', 213–15; Munzinger, *Spirits*, 118–19.

[22] On Philo's 'resistance to systematisation', see more generally, Völker, *Fortschritt*,
288, 293. Cf. 2.2.4.

[23] On the inspiration of Abraham, see 2.2.4.2. More generally, cf. J.R. Levison, 'Inspiration and the Divine Spirit in the Writings of Philo Judaeus', *JSJ* 26 (1995), 280–308.

family relation, "for having given up and left behind all mortal kinds," he is changed into the divine, so that such men become kin to God and truly divine (*Quaest. in Exod.* 2.29).

That 'divine inspiration and filling with God' (ἐνθουσιᾷ καὶ θεοφορεῖται) implies the presence and work of the Spirit is suggested by Philo's interpretation of the same experience of Moses in *De Vita Mosis* 1.175: Moses 'became possessed (ἔνθους)... and... filled with the spirit which was wont to visit him' (cf. *Virt.* 217; et al.). Philo elucidates in *Quaestiones et Solutiones in Exodum* 2.29 how such a possession leads to ethical life (becoming like the monad),[24] intimacy and closeness to God (coming near God in a kind of family relation),[25] and how this results in the person's further (religious-ethical) transformation (becoming kin to God and truly divine).

A similar effect of inspiration and contemplation is portrayed in *De Vita Mosis* 2.69. To begin with, the inspiration is not explicitly connected with πνεῦμα (cf. Yonge's more literal translation 'he began to prophesy and to feel a divine inspiration', whereas Colson [LCL] translates 'possessed by the spirit, he entered his work as a prophet'). However, it is certain that the Spirit is implied by Philo, because later on in the same paragraph he uses the term καταπνεόμενος for the inspiration. How closely the inspiration by the Spirit (καταπνεόμενος) and the beholding of God (θεωρία) are connected is evident from the fact that it is difficult to decide whether they have a (sequential) relationship of cause and effect and whether only one or both of them are responsible for the change in Moses.[26] It is clear, however, that the three elements of our relational model of the religious-ethical work of the Spirit are present: inspiration by the Spirit, an intimate encounter with God, and advancement of strength and well-being of the mind or soul (and body). The latter is not explicitly related to virtues in this passage, but it is clearly part of the broader perspective of Moses' transformation.[27]

A final text of Philo's interpretation of Moses' endowment with the ethical Spirit, namely *De Gigantibus* 54–55, provides further evidence for the above-mentioned triad. When Moses begins to worship God (by the aid of the Spirit, cf. §53), he enters the darkness, the invisible region, and he abides there

while he learns the secrets of the most holy mysteries. There he becomes not only one of the congregation of the initiated, but also the hierophant and teacher of divine rites,

---

[24] On the term 'monad' in Philo, see Noack, *Gottesbewußtsein*, 132–41.

[25] Cf. Wedderburn, *Baptism*, 283; Noack, *Gottesbewußtsein*, 147.

[26] Cf. Back, *Verwandlung*, 32 n.34.

[27] On 'growing in grace' of the *body*, as well as the question whether Moses' transformation was temporal or permanent, see 2.2.4.2. On Moses' special place in Philo, see further W.A. Meeks, *The Prophet-King: Moses Traditions and the Johannine Christology*; NovTSup 14 (Leiden: Brill, 1967), 100–131; see also ch. 2 n.208 above.

which he will impart to those whose ears are purified. He then has ever the divine spirit at his side, taking the lead in every journey of righteousness (*Gig.* 54–55).

This passage suggests that it is in the close proximity to God that the divine Spirit is active and experienced as a guide 'in every journey of righteousness'. In this connection, it appears that the intimacy of worship not only leads (by means of the Spirit) to ethics in a narrow sense, but also encompasses an empowering for ministry (teaching divine truths).[28]

We can conclude that the writings of Philo of Alexandria give strong confirmation that the connection of the divine Spirit with an intimate relationship to God and with ethical life had a clear place in Paul's context.[29] While it remains to a certain extent open whether Philo had a defined concept of how these three aspects of our model were related sequentially, the Philonic material nevertheless evidences unequivocal parallels to the ideas that we find in Paul, particularly in 2 Corinthians 3:18.[30]

---

[28] Regarding the Spirit's religious-ethical influence through the communication of deeper understanding of God, see *Somn.* 2.252–53: Philo hears 'the voice of the invisible spirit, the familiar secret tenant', saying '[…] Know then, good friend, that God alone is the real veritable peace, free from all illusion, but the whole substance of things created only to perish is one constant war.' The Spirit continues to give further insight into the nature of God, and then implies that this should lead people to forsake war and cross over to the camp of those whose character echoes that of God. We can see in this passage that the Spirit (of God: see Levison, 'Inspiration', 299–300) enables a deeper understanding of God and his designs (i.e. peace). Although the passage is not very explicit in ascribing 'the strength to forsake war and Fatality' to this deepening of the cognitive aspect of people's relationship to the divine, it is most likely that this is exactly what Philo wants to say here (cf. *Quaest. in Exod.* 2.7 and *Leg. All.* 1.37–38, as above).

On the communal experience of the empowering work of the Spirit, see esp. *Gig.* 26–28.

[29] For a similar role of Wisdom and the divine Spirit in *Wisdom of Solomon*, see, e.g., 7.27–28: Wisdom 'renews all things; in every generation she passes into holy souls and makes them friends of God, and prophets; for God loves nothing so much as the person who lives with wisdom'. (The Spirit of) Wisdom thus relates people intimately to God, and living by W/wisdom means living a virtuous life (6.18–19; 7.14; 8.7; 9.10–12, 18; 15.2; cf. Wedderburn, *Baptism*, 287; Turner, *Power*, 125–26; Wenk, *Power*, 86–88; C. Bennema, 'The Strands of Wisdom Tradition in Intertestamental Judaism: Origins, Developments and Characteristics', *TynBul* 52 (2001), 71–72; Bennema, *Power*, 62–63, 66; Philip, *Origins*, 93–95). This judgement is also confirmed by Winston: 'the desire for Wisdom leads… to immortality and nearness to God, and it is the intimacy with the divine that is the ultimate source of all human sovereignty (Wis. 6.17–21)' (D. Winston, 'The Sage as Mystic in the Wisdom of Solomon', in J.G. Gammie and L.G. Perdue (eds.), *The Sage in Israel and the Ancient Near East* (Winona Lake: Eisenbrauns, 1990), 394–95, cf. 396). On the close association of Wisdom and the divine Spirit, see Wis. 1.4–6; 7.22; 9.17 (cf. Horn, 'Wandel', 154–56; Bennema, *Power*, 65, esp. n.101). Cf. our conclusion to section 2.2.4.2.

[30] See 6.2., esp. 6.2.1.2.3.

1.2. Qumran

The term רוח is very common in the Dead Sea Scrolls (more than 500 occurrences).[31] Many of these references – which of course do not all regard the divine Spirit[32] – can be found in the *Hodayot* and the *Community Rule*. There has been some debate whether the passages on רוח in these two books need to be treated separately as there may be considerable development and dissimilarities between both. However, recent scholarship has tended to place at least equal weight on the similarities of the 'pneumatologies' of the two scrolls.[33] For this reason, and, more significantly, as our purpose is not to show trajectories of development within Qumran

---

At the same time, Philo's mysticism also differs from Pauline pneumatology. E.g., Philo generally seems to place more emphasis on mystical and even ecstatic experiences than Paul (see, e.g., *Rer. Div. Her.* 70–71; 264–65: 'the mind is evicted at the arrival of the divine Spirit, but when that departs the mind returns to its tenancy'; cf. *Spec. Leg.* 4.49; *Quaest. in Gen.* 3.9) (cf. Levison, 'Inspiration', 281–88; Noack, *Gottesbewußtsein*, 132, 183–91; Philip, *Origins*, 108–109). Luz points out that 'in contrast to the Hellenistic mysticism of Philo..., which emigrates out of the lower spheres of earthly existence, [in Paul] the power and the life of God are effective in the depths of bodily existence' (mentioning *Op. Mund.* 69; *Rer. Div. Her.* 69; *Cher.* 13.3, 10) (Luz, 'Paul', 141). On the relation of Philo and Paul see further 2.2.4.2.

[31] See M.G. Abegg, et al., *The Dead Sea Scrolls Concordance. Vol. 1,2* (Leiden/ Boston: Brill, 2003), 673–77, 922–23.

[32] On the distinction between the anthropological and the divine S/spirits, see, e.g., J. Pryke, '"Spirit" and "Flesh" in the Qumran Documents and Some New Testament Texts', *RevQ* 19 (1965), 345–46; Vos, *Untersuchungen*, 58, 61; Sekki, *Meaning*, 72–85; Keener, *Spirit*, 10; R.W. Kvalvaag, 'The Spirit in Human Beings in Some Qumran Non-Biblical Texts', in F.H. Cryer and T.L. Thompson (eds.), *Qumran between the Old and New Testaments*; JSOTSup 290 (Sheffield: Sheffield Academic Press, 1998), esp. 171 n.39. For a discussion of the impact of the reception of the divine Spirit on the anthropological spirit in 1QS and 1QHᵃ, see Kvalvaag, 'Spirit', 170–180. Cf. Betz, *Offenbarung*, 127–28, 141; M.A. Elliott, *The Survivors of Israel: A Reconsideration of the Theology of Pre-Christian Judaism* (Grand Rapids: Eerdmans, 2000), 403–404, 409, 418–19; Bennema, *Power*, 87–92.

More generally on the difficulties and (possibly intentional) ambiguities of differentiation between the various meanings of רוח, see J.E. Robson, 'Word and Spirit in Ezekiel' (Middlesex University: Unpublished PhD Thesis, 2004), 18–21, cf. 219. See also Bennema's model of the relational work of the Spirit on an anthropological and soteriological level that calls a hard and fast distinction between the anthropological and the divine S/spirit into question (Bennema, *Power*, 95–97, cf. 90 n.193; more generally: Levison, *Filled with the Spirit*, chs. I.2. and II.1.).

[33] So, e.g., Turner, *Power*, 129; Wenk, *Power*, 99–100; Fatehi, *Relation*, 73–78; Bennema, *Power*, 85–92 (for less recent scholarship, see, e.g., W. Foerster, 'Der Heilige Geist im Spätjudentum', *NTS* 8 (1961), 128–31; cf. the accordant approach of Sekki, *Meaning*, passim [however, see his pp. 193–94]); *pace* Menzies, *Development*, 78–87. However, see also the more nuanced Kvalvaag, 'Spirit', 159–80.

theology,[34] we will treat the two scrolls in concert with the other Qumran texts that will be examined.

It is unquestionable that the divine Spirit was understood by the writers of the DSS to empower ethical living (see, e.g., 1QH^a 4.25–26; 15.6–7: see 2.2.2. above; 1QS 3.7–9; 4.20–21;[35] 4Q521 *frag.* 2 *col.* 2.6; and the texts discussed below).[36] However, the question is whether the DSS give any indication *how* this work of enabling is achieved by the Spirit. In our investigation of this question, we will argue that the DSS demonstrate that our model of the relational empowering by the Spirit in Paul is not foreign to the Qumran community. It will become clear that it is predominantly through facilitating cognitive and experiential knowledge of God that the Spirit enables righteous living.[37]

We have already seen in Philo that knowing God has a cognitive-noetic and an existential-mystical aspect (e.g. in *Leg. All.* 1.38; *Praem. Poen.* 43–46). As a person draws near to God, she will know God better *cognitively*, in that she will gain a deeper insight into who God is and what he wants, and *existentially*, in that she experiences a kind of 'I-Thou'-encounter with the divine ('knowing and being known', cf. *Poster. C.* 12–13).[38] While in Philo both aspects of knowing God appear to receive equal weight (perhaps with a slight leaning towards the mystical), we will see that the cognitive side comes more to the fore in Qumran.

---

[34] For such an approach, see M. Bockmuehl, '1QS and Salvation at Qumran', in D.A. Carson, et al. (eds.), *Justification and Variegated Nomism. Vol. 1: The Complexities of Second Temple Judaism*; WUNT II/140 (Tübingen: Mohr Siebeck, 2001), 382–86.

[35] The majority of scholars interpret רוח קודש here as the divine Spirit (see Sekki, *Meaning*, 207–208). Cf. the general comments in n.51 below.

[36] Cf. G. Johnston, '"Spirit" and "Holy Spirit" in the Qumran Literature', in H.K. McArthur (ed.), *New Testament Sidelights: Essays in Honor of Alexander Converse Purdy* (Hartford: HSFP, 1960), 40–41: 'This material teaches... that the Holy Spirit is a power or influence from God that makes for holiness and righteousness, and enables the elect to weather the storms of life' (cf. E. Puech, 'L'Esprit Saint à Qumrân', *SBFLA* 49 (1999), 288–89). Schulz argues that the concept of the Spirit is transformed and ethicized in the Qumran community (Schulz, *Ethik*, 350). However, Horn somewhat disagrees with this: he believes the Spirit is not connected to observance of the law (Horn, 'Wandel', 160–62). Nonetheless, it is clear from the passages discussed below that the ethical work of the divine Spirit was a significant part of the Qumran teaching on the Spirit even if it is not always explicitly linked to observance of the Torah. In this regard, see also 1Q34 *frag.* 3.2, and the exegesis in Wenk, *Power*, 104.

[37] See Turner, *Power*, 127–28, for similar observations but with less emphasis on the relational aspect of the empowering. Cf. more generally, A. Dietzel, 'Beten im Geist', *TZ* 13 (1957), 23–24; Betz, *Offenbarung*, 135–40; Bennema, *Power*, 88–89, 95.

[38] Cf. the existential meaning of יָדַע (e.g. Hos. 2:20; incl. sexual knowing, e.g. Gen. 4:1). Cf. R. Bultmann, 'γινώσκω κτλ', *TDNT*, I, 709–710. See also the parallel to *Poster. C.* 12–13 in Gal. 4:8–9; cf. 1 Cor. 8:3; 13:12.

In the ensuing analysis we will locate the individual elements of our focal theory in the writings of the Qumran community: *a)* the Spirit's relating believers closer to God through wisdom and understanding; and the ethical empowering that results from intimate knowledge of God; and *b)* the transforming aspects of Spirit-prompted encounters and existential interaction with God and with fellow members of the community. *c)* Subsequently, we will demonstrate that these elements are conceptually linked in a number of Qumran psalms.

a) The DSS give ample evidence how the Spirit relates the believer more closely to God by providing revelation and wisdom: the Spirit delights the psalmist with divine truth (1QH[a] 17.32); the community knows God and his favourable deeds and plans through the gift of the Spirit (1QH[a] 5.24–27; 21 *bottom* 12–15; 4Q504 *frag.* 4.4–5 ['a holy spirit']=4Q506 *frags.* 131–32.9–11 ['the holy Spirit']); the spirit of truth is instrumental in receiving knowledge of the Most High (1QS 4.20–23);[39] and the 'spirit of the true counsel of God' engenders proximity to God, enlightening and cleansing (1QS 3.6–9).[40]

That intimate knowledge of God is related by the writers of the DSS to virtuous living is evinced by many passages. For example, in 1QS 11.3–7 the author declares that the truth of God is the rock of his steps, and YHWH'S might is the support of his right hand. 'From the spring of his justice is my judgement and from the wonderful mystery is the light in my heart. My eyes have observed what always is, wisdom…, knowledge and prudent understanding…, [which is the] fount of justice and well of strength…' (11.6–7). In lines 16–18 he goes on to ask God to open his

---

[39] The interpretation of 1QS 4.20–23 depends on taking the 'knowledge of the most high' (עליון בדעת, 4.22) as an objective genitive (cf. 1QS28b 5.25–26: 'spirit of knowledge and fear of the Lord'). However, Knibb understands it as a subjective genitive (M.A. Knibb, *The Qumran Community*; CCWJCW 2 (Cambridge: Cambridge University Press, 1987), 103; cf. the LXX of Num. 24:16: ἐπιστήμην παρὰ ὑψίστου). In any case, the reference point of 1QS 4.20–23 is the eschatological future (cf. H. Lichtenberger, *Studien zum Menschenbild in Texten der Qumrangemeinde*; SUNT 15 (Göttingen: Vandenhoeck & Ruprecht, 1980), 137–42; Um, *Temple*, 90 n.122). On the meaning of 'spirit of truth' in the context of the teaching on the two spirits, see Sekki, *Meaning*, 89, ch. 8; Turner, *Power*, 128–29; cf. n.35 above on 'holy spirit' in 4.21.

[40] Closeness to God is expressed if one takes 'light of life' (החיים באור; cf. Job 33:30; Ps. 56:14; cf. Jn. 8:12) in 1QS 3.7 to be a reference to (the face of) God, as Hossfeld and Zenger read the phrase in Ps. 56:14 (F.-L. Hossfeld and E. Zenger, *Psalmen 51–100*; HThKAT (Freiburg: Herder, 2000), 116). Knibb, however, interprets it in 3.7 as 'the enlightenment which the member receives in the community' (Knibb, *Qumran*, 93). On the references to the S/spirit in these lines, cf. Kvalvaag, 'Spirit', 171–72.

On the role of the anthropological and the divine S/spirit in the process of acquiring knowledge, see Kvalvaag, 'Spirit', 176–79 (cf. p. 166, where he maintains that the Hebrew for 'understanding' means 'spirit' in several 1QH[a] contexts).

heart to knowledge and establish all his deeds in justice. He wishes to be close to God (being 'everlastingly in your presence'), because he knows that only with God can behaviour be perfect (cf. 1Q28b 4.25–28; 1QH[a] 19.12–13; 22 *bottom* 12; 4Q418 *frag.* 2.6–7; *frags.* 43–45 *col.* 1.4–6).[41] Elsewhere, the connection of knowledge and religious-ethical life comes to the fore as healing and liberation are mentioned together with teaching regarding the deeds of God (CD-A 13.7–10). The maturation and building up of other members is an additional ethical effect of submitting to God's truth and sharing one's knowledge within the community (1QS 1.11–15).[42]

b) Many of the passages that we have mentioned so far focus on the cognitive aspects of an empowering relationship with God. However, the Qumran sect is also aware of the transforming effects of existential en-counters with God (in fact, one of the aims of teaching is 'existential knowing' of God: 4Q381 *frag.* 1.2) and with fellow members of the com-munity. Regarding the 'vertical' relationship, we can see that closeness to God leads to living according to the law (4Q504 *frag.* 6.6–17).[43] In concert with many biblical Psalms, the DSS celebrate the strengthening effect of intimacy with God (1QH[a] 17.29–34;[44] cf. 1Q28b 2.24; the Spirit plays a role in both passages). Like the cognitive aspects of knowing God, so is also this intimacy-aspect of the empowering relationship with God pro-moted by the Spirit. Accordingly, in 4Q504 *frags.* 1–2 *col.* 5.15–16 the psalmist thanks God for pouring his Holy Spirit (and his blessing) upon the community 'so that we would look for you in our anguish'. Such intimacy with God is also desired by the writer of 1QH[a] 8.14–15, who seeks God's spirit of knowledge, because he knows that as he cleaves to God's spirit of holiness, he is empowered to hold fast to the truth of YHWH's covenant, so 'that [I may serve] Thee in truth and wholeness of heart, and that I may

---

[41] Cf. Vos, *Untersuchungen*, 59; A.R. Brown, *The Cross and Human Transformation: Paul's Apocalyptic Word in 1 Corinthians* (Minneapolis: Fortress, 1995), 57–58; Ben-nema, *Power*, 85; Samra, 'Christ', 76.

[42] Cf. C.A. Newsom, 'The Sage in the Literature of Qumran: The Functions of the *Maśkîl*', in J.G. Gammie and L.G. Perdue (eds.), *The Sage in Israel and the Ancient Near East* (Winona Lake: Eisenbrauns, 1990), 377, who points out that instruction provides members with knowledge of their own identity in the context of the divine plan for the world. 'Even at its most esoteric such knowledge is functional and serves the formation of character and identity for the member and for the community as a whole' (Newsom, 'Sage', 381).

[43] However, this passage is merely suggestive because of its fragmentation.

[44] Cf. J.H. Hellerman, *The Ancient Church as Family* (Minneapolis: Fortress Press, 2001), 74, 77–80. See also Betz, 'Geburt', 320–21, who interprets the intimacy as that of the community with its teachers.

love [Thy Name].'[45] Both intimacy with God ('that I may love [Thy Name]') and religious-ethical life (serving God and holding fast to the covenant)[46] are hence evidently ascribed to the work of the Spirit.

Next to the closeness to God, 'horizontal' relationships also further ethical living. For instance, the individual receives encouragement and correction within the community (CD-B 20.17–18; cf. 1QS 2.24–3.1; 9.3).[47] Again, the Spirit plays a decisive role in this process (see, e.g., 1QH[a] 23 *bottom* 9–15, where ['your holy'] 'spirit' creates spiritual communion and causes 'walking in the light'). Wenk highlights the fact that in the DSS the Spirit is the foundation of the community's self-understanding that shaped its ethos. 'The words and the wisdom of the Holy Spirit created a new reality – the renewed community as the heirs of the promise.'[48] However, this interpersonal empowering by the work of the Spirit in the community is not divorced from the cognitive aspects unfolded above. In CD-A 2.12–13, the writer expounds that God 'made known His Holy Spirit to them [i.e. Israel] by the hand of His anointed ones, and He proclaimed the truth (to them). But those whom He hated He led astray.'[49] The Holy Spirit, (the leaders of) the Spirit-inspired community and truth are thus clearly related to religious-ethical living.[50]

---

[45] Translation by Vermes, *Scrolls*, 251. Cf. 1QH[a] 8.2–3, as reconstructed by J. Licht (see Betz, *Offenbarung*, 119); cf. Vermes, *Scrolls*, 251; Kvalvaag, 'Spirit', 173; Philip, *Origins*, 138.

[46] Closeness to God is further expressed in the Qumranic understanding of the covenant; see E.J. Christiansen, 'The Consciousness of Belonging to God's Covenant and What it Entails According to the Damascus Document and the Community Rule', in F.H. Cryer and T.L. Thompson (eds.), *Qumran between the Old and New Testaments*; JSOTSup 290 (Sheffield: Sheffield Academic Press, 1998), 69–97.

[47] Cf. Brown, *Cross*, 57–58. On 1QS 9.3, see esp. Wenk, *Power*, 105. On the Qumran community's encountering God and on the maturing effect of being part of the community, see further Samra, 'Christ', 71–77.

[48] Wenk, *Power*, 108. Cf. Vos, *Untersuchungen*, 57–58; Elliott, *Survivors*, 411–13.

[49] Translation by Vermes, *Scrolls*, 128.

[50] Whether one takes this passage to relate to ethics depends on how one interprets the phrase ובפרוש שמו שמותיהם (v.13) which is left out in the translation of Vermes utilized above. García Martínez and Tigchelaar translate 'and their names were established with precision' (cf. Lohse (ed.), *Qumran*, 69; Knibb, *Qumran*, 27; J.H. Charlesworth (ed.), *The Dead Sea Scrolls: Hebrew, Aramaic, and Greek Texts with English Translations. Vol. 2: Damascus Document, War Scroll, and Related Documents*; PTSDSSP (Tübingen/Louisville: Mohr Siebeck/Westminster John Knox Press, 1995), 15). Knibb and Charlesworth suggest that it may foreshadow the 'exact list of names' promised in 4.4–6. However, while the precise meaning may remain equivocal, the contrast of the phrase with 'But those whom He hated He led astray', points toward a soteriological or ethical reference point. The ethical interpretation is further supported by the way in which the text continues (2.14–16): The teacher proclaims that as his addressees will listen to him, he 'shall open your [i.e. the addressees'] eyes so that you can see and understand the deeds of

c) After this overview of the interplay of the Holy Spirit, relational knowledge and religious-ethical life in the DSS, we will now illustrate our discoveries by devoting closer attention to three passages from the *Hodayot*. We begin with a prayer from column 6, which clearly evidences the conceptual connection of the three elements named above in accordance with our relational model (i.e. people are empowered by the Spirit for religious-ethical life through deeper knowledge of and an intimate relationship with God and fellow believers).

And I know through the understanding which comes from Thee, that in Thy goodwill towards m[a]n [Thou hast] increa[sed his inheritance] in Thy Holy Spirit [רוח קודשך][51] and thus Thou hast drawn me near to the understanding of Thee [לבינתך][52]. And the closer I approach, the more I am filled with zeal against all the workers of iniquity and the men of deceit (1QHᵃ 6.12–14).[53]

In these lines we see how the gift of the Holy Spirit leads to a deeper understanding of who God is. That this deeper understanding of God equals an intimate relationship with God is suggested by the way in which the prayer continues: the believer approaches (God) more closely. However, Kvalvaag argues that the verb נָגַשׁ in 'Thou hast drawn me near to the understanding' is a *terminus technicus* for entrance into the Qumran community.[54] If this is indeed implied by the author, a further relational dimension is added: not only is the relationship to God intensified by the Spirit, but also that to the believers around him. In any case, the consequence of the Spirit-created intimacy is ethical. The closer the believer comes to God (and the community), the more he is filled with zeal against (the men of) deceit.[55]

God, so that you can choose what he [God] is pleased with and repudiate what he hates, so that you can walk perfectly on all his paths...' Here we see again how a deeper understanding of God's character and deeds by means of receiving Spirit-empowered teaching in the community enables virtuous living.

[51] Cf. Ps. 51:11. Most scholars take רוח קודש to refer to the divine Spirit (so, e.g., Sekki, *Meaning*, 79; Um, *Temple*, 91 n.126 and the scholars cited there; cf. Lohse (ed.), *Qumran*, 169). However, García Martínez and Tigchelaar translate 'the spirit of your holiness' (cf. the general discussions in Mansoor, *Hymns*, 76–77, cf. 181; Leaney, *Qumran*, 35, 158–59; Tibbs, *Experience*, 185–87).

[52] Lit. 'to understanding', translated by García Martínez and Tigchelaar as '[approach] your intelligence' (cf. Mansoor, *Hymns*, 181; however, Mansoor translates the next line 'the nearer I draw *to Thee*' [italics added]).

[53] Translation by Vermes, *Scrolls*, 248. Cf. 1QHᵃ 19.16–20.

[54] Kvalvaag, 'Spirit', 173, cf. 166–67 n.26; cf. Holm-Nielsen, *Hodayot*, 221 n.9; Mansoor, *Hymns*, 181 n.8. See further Wenk, *Power*, 102–105.

[55] Cf. the way in which the prayer continues: 'Thou hast favoured me, Thy servant, with a spirit of knowledge, [that I may choose] truth [and goodness] and loathe all the ways of iniquity. And I have loved Thee freely and with all my heart; [contemplating the

A different aspect of the connection of Spirit and ethics comes to the fore when the psalmist a little later seems to continue reflecting upon his entry into the community:

> I have appeased your face by the spirit which you have placed [in me,] to lavish your [kind]nesses on [your] serv[ant] for [ever,] to purify me with your holy spirit, to bring me near by your will according to the extent of your kindnesses (1QHᵃ 8.19–20).

Here the Holy Spirit effects the ethical transformation that is necessary for 'getting in and staying in' the salvific community, namely, purification. Again, the two sides of 'drawing near' as a consequence of the work of the Spirit seem to be in mind: intimacy with God (Vermes translates 'drawing me near to Thee by Thy grace')[56] and the fellowship within the community. A further ethical impact of this cleansing and intimacy-creating activity of the Spirit may be indicated when the (unfortunately fragmented) text seems to say that the consequence of this is being in God's will (i.e. in the place of those who keep God's precepts) (8.21).[57]

A final passage will demonstrate how both cognitive and existential knowledge of God provided by the Spirit empowers ethical action.

> And I, the Instructor, have known you, my God, through the spirit which you gave in me, and I have listened loyally to your wonderful secret through your holy spirit. You have [op]ened within me knowledge of the mystery of your wisdom, and the source of [your] power, ... according to the abundance of kindness, and zeal for annihilation... (1QHᵃ 20.11–14=4Q427 *frags.* 2–3 *col.* 2.12–14).

The teacher describes the work of the S/spirit in two clauses that form a parallelism. It is therefore likely that 'the spirit which you gave in me' means the same as 'your holy spirit'.[58] The first activity that is ascribed to the Spirit is drawing the teacher close to God. 'I have known you, my God' implies a personal encounter with YHWH. The next clause draws attention to the cognitive aspect of this Spirit-inspired knowing, namely, the writer's listening 'loyally to your wonderful secret through your holy spirit'. It seems that here the focus is not so much on the Spirit-imbued teaching of knowledge (as, e.g., in CD-A 2.12–13), but on the Spirit-enabled perception of its content.[59] The existential encounter with God and the compre-

---

mysteries of] Thy wisdom [I have sought Thee]. For this is from Thy hand and [nothing is done] without [Thy will]' (6.25–26; Vermes, *Scrolls*, 249).

[56] Ibid., 252. Cf. Um, *Temple*, 90, 93.

[57] The text may thus be drawing on Ezek. 36–37. Cf. Wenk, *Power*, 103; Philip, *Origins*, 86; more generally, Sekki, *Meaning*, 87–89; Turner, *Power*, 127–29; Bennema, *Power*, 88, 91 n.197; *pace* Hubbard, *Creation*, 118–19.

[58] Cf. Sekki, *Meaning*, 85.

[59] The content of the 'knowledge of God' would typically relate to the Torah (cf. Gärtner, 'Idea', 228; Johnston, 'Spirit', 41). See also Brown's categorisation of knowledge in the DSS: Brown, *Cross*, 55–56, 58–59.

hension of 'the source of [God's] power' finally seems to provoke an ethical reaction (i.e. 'zeal for annihilation') that is similar to that of 6.12–14 (i.e. 'zeal against all the workers of iniquity').[60]

We can conclude that the DSS provide strong support for our relational model of the ethical work of the Spirit. We have seen that by relating believers intimately to God (by providing cognitive and existential knowledge) and the community, the Spirit transforms and empowers them to live according to God's precepts.

1.3. Traditions Based on Ezekiel 36:25–28

A number of further passages from early Judaism give evidence of the connection of the relational and the ethical work of the Spirit. However, it seems that in most of these passages the causal connection between the intimacy-creating work of the Spirit and ethical life is not as explicit as in Philo and the DSS. Nonetheless, they offer further support for our relational model of the Spirit's empowering of ethical life in Paul's context.

The texts that we will briefly examine tend to be influenced by the prophecies transmitted in Ezekiel 36. Ezekiel 36:25–26, one of the most central passages on the S/spirit in the Hebrew Bible, speaks about God's cleansing of Israel and her (anthropological) renewal. In 36:27–28 the divine oracle continues by promising the giving of God's Spirit, which (together with the renewal mentioned in vv.25–26)[61] will result in both obedience to God's commands, and in a renewal and intensification of relationships (to the land [v.28a], and to God [v.28b]: 'and you shall be my people and I shall be your God') (cf. 37:14; Isa. 44:3–6; for the opposite effect, cf. Isa. 63:10).[62]

---

[60] Cf. K. Berthelot, 'Zeal for God and Divine Law in Philo and the Dead Sea Scrolls', *SPA* 19 (2007), 122–23.

[61] It is debatable whether the divine Spirit is linked to the anthropological renewal mentioned in v.26 or not. E.g., Schneider thinks that the 'new spirit' of v.26 is the divine Spirit of v.27 (Schneider, *Wiederkehr*, 29). However, the majority of scholars interpret 'heart' and 'spirit' in v.26 together and treat it separately from the theological Spirit in v.27. See our discussion in ch. 4 n.68. Cf. the overview of scholarship in Philip, *Origins*, 38–42, and the detailed treatment in J.E. Robson, *Word and Spirit in Ezekiel*; LHB/OTS 447 (London/New York: T. & T. Clark, 2006), 241–52.

[62] Cf. Wenk, *Power*, 60: 'When God will put his Spirit in them, they will have a more intimate relationship with their God; they will follow his laws' (cf. Schneider, *Wiederkehr*, 31).

Grammatically speaking, however, not the Spirit but God is the subject causing Israel to follow his statutes (...וְעָשִׂיתִי אֵת אֲשֶׁר־בְּחֻקַּי). Nevertheless, Bennema downplays the significance of this by arguing that Ezek. 37 ascribes the same activities to the Spirit that are mentioned in Ezek. 36 as those of God (Bennema, *Power*, 171–72 n.39). However, while this holds true for the creation of intimacy, the ethical work of the Spirit is not explicitly named in Ezek. 37 (unless one interprets the promise 'and you shall live' [vv.6,

Lapsley explains that the way in which the Spirit enables this ethical renewal is through providing intimate knowledge of God, as this is suggested
elsewhere in Ezekiel when the Spirit falls on the prophet.[63] 'Thus the declaration in 36:27, "I will put my רוח within them," resounds with echoes
from other passages, evoking the knowledge of God which fills and transforms Ezekiel, and promising to the people a similar transformation of
identity.'[64] The traditions based on Ezekiel 36 (e.g. 1QS 4.20–21; 1QH[a]
8.19–20;[65] Ezek[Tg] 36.25–27; *Midr. Ps.* 14.6; 73.4; *Num. R.* 9.49; *Deut.
R.* 6.14; *Cant. R.* 1.1 §9; *Sot.* 9.15; *Ber.* 32; *Pesiq. Rab.* 1.6)[66] evidence a
similar combination of the notions of Spirit, intensification of relationship
to God and ethical life.[67] We will quote two texts in full.

The first passage with strong potential for supporting our theory is *Jubilees* 1.23–25 (written in the middle of the second century BCE).[68]

(23) And I shall cut off the foreskin of their heart and the foreskin of the heart of their
descendants. And I shall create for them a holy spirit, and I shall purify them so that they
will not turn away from following me from that day and forever. (24) And their souls will
cleave to me and to all my commandments. And they will do my commandments. And I
shall be a father to them, and they will be sons to me. (25) And they will all be called

---

14] ethically). In any case, YHWH and רוח appear conceptually linked in 36:27–28, so
that the grammatical differentiation plays no major role.

[63] See 2:2 (cf. 3:24); 11:5, setting up a contrast to the false prophets in 13:3 who 'follow their own spirit, and have seen nothing!'.

[64] J.E. Lapsley, *Can these Bones Live? The Problem of the Moral Self in the Book of
Ezekiel*; BZAW 301 (Berlin/New York: W. de Gruyter, 2000), 167. See also the detailed
discussion of these texts in Robson, *Word*, 114–22.

[65] Cf. n.57 above. On the influence of Ezek. 36–37 on 1QH[a] in general, see Bertone,
Law, 100–107.

[66] For some of these as well as further connections between the Spirit and ethics in the
targumic and rabbinical material, see Turner, *Power*, 123–24, 130–31.

[67] The combination in Ezek. 36 is not clearly sequential as there are no conjunctions
between the different elements of the renewal apart from the (untranslated) ו. Should one
feel pressed to identify a conceptual link between the three components of our theory in
36:27–28, it would be 1. giving of the Spirit → 2. obedience to the law → 3. change of
relationships. This sequence agrees with Turner's model of ethical empowering by the
Spirit in Judaism (M. Turner, 'The Spirit of Prophecy and the Ethical/Religious Life of
the Christian Community', in M.W. Wilson (ed.), *Spirit and Renewal: Essays in Honour
of J. Rodman Williams*; JPTSup 5 (Sheffield: Sheffield Academic Press, 1994), 186).
Alternatively, one could interpret the giving of the Spirit בְּקִרְבְּכֶם in v.27 in the sense of
an interpersonal 'among you' (cf. C. Bennema, *Excavating John's Gospel: A Commentary
for Today* (Delhi: ISPCK, 2005), 46). This might suggest that it is the *relational* work of
the Spirit among the people of Israel that leads to ethical living. Apart from that, some of
the traditions cited above clearly evidence a causal connection of the Spirit to either
deeper knowledge of God or ethical living.

[68] J.C. VanderKam, *The Book of Jubilees*; GAP (Sheffield: Sheffield Academic Press,
2001), 21; G.S. Oegema, 'Das Buch der Jubiläen', in G.S. Oegema (ed.), *Unterweisung
in erzählender Form*; JSHRZ IV 1,2 (Gütersloh: Gütersloher Verlagshaus, 2005), 82.

"sons of the living God." And every angel and spirit will know and acknowledge that they are my sons and I am their father in uprightness and righteousness. And I shall love them (*Jub.* 1.23–25).

The relational effect of the renewal is here portrayed with still greater intensity than in Ezekiel ('their souls will cleave to me', 'I shall be a father to them, and they will be sons to me', 'I shall love them', etc.).[69] Next to verse 24, where doing God's commandments is presented as parallel to being close to God (cleaving to him with one's soul), the ethical impact of this intimate relationship comes most clearly to the fore in verse 28: 'And the Lord will appear to the eyes of all, and all shall know that I am the God of Israel and the Father of all the children of Jacob... And Zion and Jerusalem shall be holy'.[70] The passage thus supports our thesis. However, as it is uncertain whether the 'holy spirit' in verse 23 is indeed the divine Spirit,[71] we will now turn to a yet clearer passage.[72]

---

[69] Relational intimacy and ethical life seem to be the consequence of all three aspects of God's action: circumcision of the heart, giving of a holy spirit, and purification (v.23). It is possible that instead of or in addition to Ezek. 36:25–27, the tradition implied here is 11:19–20 in combination with Ps. 51:10–11 (cf. Levison, *Spirit in First Century Judaism*, 252; Hubbard, *Creation*, 46; *pace* Wenk, *Power*, 79 n.34).

[70] Like with Ezek. 36:25–27, one of the difficulties of interpreting *Jub.* 1.23–28 is that the conjunction linking the individual elements of the process(?) of renewal is merely 'and'.

[71] Those who interpret 'holy spirit' here as the divine Spirit include Horn, 'Wandel', 162; J.M. Scott, *Adoption as Sons of God: An Exegetical Investigation into the Background of ΥΙΟΘΕΣΙΑ in the Pauline Corpus*; WUNT II/48 (Tübingen: J.C.B. Mohr (Paul Siebeck), 1992), 114 (cf. 115, 179, 185); Munzinger, *Spirits*, 105–106; a theological reading is further implied in C.E.B. Cranfield, *A Critical and Exegetical Commentary on the Epistle to the Romans. Vol. 1: Introduction and Commentary on Romans I–VIII*; ICC (Edinburgh: T. & T. Clark, 1975), 157 n.3; J.M.G. Barclay, *Obeying the Truth: A Study of Paul's Ethics in Galatians*; SNTW (Edinburgh: T. & T. Clark, 1988), 84; W.L. Kynes, 'New Birth', *DJG*, 574–75; Martyn, *Galatians*, 286 n.17; 392 n.17; Bertone, *Law*, 88; et al. The following scholars have argued against a theological interpretation: Johnston, 'Spirit', 33; Menzies, *Development*, 74 n.6 (cf. R.P. Menzies, 'A Fitting Tribute: A Review Essay of *The Holy Spirit and Christian Origins: Essays in Honor of James D. G. Dunn*', *Pneuma* 28 (2006), 139); Wenk, *Power*, 79 n.34; Hubbard, *Creation*, 45; Bennema, *Power*, 92; Christoph, *Pneuma*, 156; et al. However, see how closely the 'upright' (πνεῦμα εὐθές) and the 'divine' (πνεῦμα τὸ ἅγιόν σου) S/spirit are linked in Ps. 50:10–11 LXX (cf. R.J. Morales, 'The Spirit and the Restoration of Israel: New Exodus and New Creation Motifs in Galatians' (Duke University: Unpublished PhD Thesis, 2007), 67 n.13, who further points out that 'Ezekiel 11 and 18 speak of God creating a new spirit for the Israelites, but Ezekiel 36, 37 and 39 refer to God putting his own Spirit within them'). This suggests that the two may not be as strongly differentiated as is often assumed. For an alternative approach, see further Turner, *Power*, 128 n.32: 'The "holy spirit" to be "created" (cf. Ps. 51.10–11) for Israel by God in *Jub.* 1.20–24 should probably be understood in a similar way as a sphere of God's power for righteousness set antithetically over against the "spirit of Beliar".' Cf. G.C. Kenney, *Translating H/holy*

Our second passage is taken from the *Testament of Judah*, namely 24.2–3. Scholars are in two minds whether this text, which has its origins in the second century BCE,[73] has gone through the process of Christian redaction[74] or not.[75] However, the point that we intend to draw out seems not to depend on a specifically Christian tradition but on Ezekiel 36–37 (and possibly 2 Sam. 7:14 and Zech. 12:10).[76]

And the heavens will be opened upon him to pour out the spirit as a blessing of the Holy Father. And he will pour the spirit of grace on you. And you shall be sons in truth, and you will walk in his first and final decrees (*T. Jud.* 24.2–3).

In this text we can see that the pouring out of the Spirit (by the Messiah), an intimate relationship to God (sonship as status and content of the relationship) and ethical living[77] are sequentially linked (the conjunction,

---

S/spirit: 4 Models: Unitarian, Binitarian, Trinitarian, and Non-Sectarian (Lanham: University Press of America, 2007), 7–8.

[72] Further evidence of the Spirit's ethical empowering through intimate relationships is provided by the *Odes of Solomon*, esp. 3, 11 (vv.2–3 building on Ezek. 36:25–27) and 13. However, as the *Odes* are post-Pauline and partly mixed with Christian ideas they cannot be treated as strong support for the presence of our focal theory in Paul's context (cf. J.H. Charlesworth, 'The Odes of Solomon', *OTP*, II, 725–32; J.H. Charlesworth, *Critical Reflections on the Odes of Solomon. Vol. 1: Literary Setting, Textual Studies, Gnosticism, the Dead Sea Scrolls and the Gospel of John*; JSPSup 22 (Sheffield: Sheffield Academic Press, 1998), 24–25; M. Lattke, 'Die Oden Salomos: Einleitungsfragen und Forschungsgeschichte', *ZNW* 98 (2007), 296; J.H. Charlesworth, *The First Christian Hymnbook: The Odes of Solomon. Translated by James H. Charlesworth* (Eugene: Cascade Books, 2009), xviii–xix).

[73] So, e.g., H.C. Kee, 'Testaments of the Twelve Patriarchs: A New Translation and Introduction', *OTP*, I, 777–78.

[74] So generally and with regard to the passage under study: H.W. Hollander and M. de Jonge, *The Testaments of the Twelve Patriarchs: A Commentary*; SVTP 8 (Leiden: Brill, 1985), 83–85, 227–28; J.H. Ulrichsen, *Die Grundschrift der Testamente der zwölf Patriarchen: Eine Untersuchung zu Umfang, Inhalt und Eigenart der ursprünglichen Schrift*; AUU.HR 10 (Stockholm: Almqvist & Wiksell International, 1991), 232; A. Strotmann, *"Mein Vater bist du!" (Sir 51,10): Zur Bedeutung der Vaterschaft Gottes in kanonischen und nichtkanonischen frühjüdischen Schriften*; FTS 39 (Frankfurt: Knecht, 1991), 161–64; Horn, *Angeld*, 39–40; Turner, *Power*, 84–85 n.7.

[75] So with great erudition: A. Hultgård, *L'eschatologie des Testaments des Douze Patriarches. Vol. 1: Interprétation des textes*; AUU.HR 6 (Uppsala: Almqvist & Wiksell, 1977), 204–213, and Scott, *Adoption*, 109–112; followed tentatively by Fatehi, *Relation*, 138–39. Cf. E.R. Stuckenbruck, 'The Spirit at Pentecost', in C.R. Wetzel (ed.), *Essays on New Testament Christianity: A Festschrift in Honor of Dean E. Walker* (Cincinnati: Standard Publishing, 1978), 96. It is also not marked as an interpolation in the critical edition by R.H. Charles, *The Apocrypha and Pseudepigrapha of the Old Testament* (Oxford: Clarendon Press, 1913), II, 324.

[76] So Scott, *Adoption*, 113–14.

[77] *Pace* Horn, 'Wandel', 162, who neither sees a connection to ethics here nor in *Jub.* 1.23.

though, is the ambiguous καί). *Testament of Judah* 24.2–3 thus lends further support for our relational model of ethical empowering by the Spirit.[78]

We conclude that Ezekiel 36–37 was not only an important witness to the ethical work of the Spirit in the Hebrew Bible, but that it also had a broad influence on early Jewish texts on the Spirit. These early Jewish texts interpret and develop Ezekiel 36–37 in a way that supplies further evidence for the strong presence of the notion of ethical empowering by means of Spirit-created relationships in Paul's context.

Next to Paul's roots in early Judaism, Graeco-Roman Literature also forms part of Paul's context (cf. ch. 2 above). To this we finally turn.

2. Graeco-Roman Literature

Trying to find support for our relational model of the Spirit's ethical empowering in Graeco-Roman literature is a complex endeavour. The reason for this is simple: the divine spirit is hardly ever connected to ethics in these writings at all.[79] This, however, is to some extent due to the fact that πνεῦμα only seldom refers to the divine Spirit in the Graeco-Roman writings.[80]

In Hellenistic philosophy, moral transformation is achieved through various means (e.g. in Stoicism, by living according to one's nature, according to νοῦς, etc.).[81] One of these ways is human dependence on divine care and goodwill (e.g. Cicero, *Nat. d.* 2.164–67; Seneca, *Ep.* 41.2, 5; Arrian, *Epict. diss.* 1.14.69; 1.19.9–12; 3.24.2–3; cf. 1.15.5).[82] While πνεῦμα does not play a role in this way of empowering for ethical living, we will nonetheless demonstrate at the example of Cleanthes' *Hymn to*

---

[78] Cf. *4 Ezra* 6.26–28; *Pss. Sol.* 17.37; *T. Levi* 18.7–8 (where the phrase 'in the water' seems to be a Christian addition), 11–13. For further connections between the Spirit and ethics in *T. 12 Patr.*, see Turner, *Power*, 126–27; Wenk, *Power*, 75–79.

[79] However, potential exceptions are Pseudo-Plato, *Virtue* 379C–D (although it refers to inspiration and does not mention πνεῦμα), and Seneca, *Ep.* 41.1–2 (although the divine πνεῦμα here refers to the human soul). Cf. G.T. Cage, *The Holy Spirit: A Source Book with Commentary* (Reno: Charlotte House, 1995), 327, 337. See the fuller discussion at 2.1.2. above.

[80] On this see the more nuanced treatment in Rabens, 'Geistes-Geschichte', 47, 52–53; cf. 2.1. above.

[81] See the literature mentioned in 2.1.2., esp. n.34.

For a discussion of how *human* relationships can transform a person according to Socrates, see Wartenberg, *Forms*, esp. 206–211. On the relational concept of φιλία in Hellenism, see ch. 4 n.34.

[82] See the detailed treatment in Johnson, *Gentiles*, ch. 5, esp. 72–73.

Zeus [*LS* 54I] that the concept of ethical enabling in an intimate relationship with the divine was not totally foreign to Hellenistic religiosity.[83]

Cleanthes (ca. 330–230 BCE) has the reputation of being the most religious of the Stoics.[84] His *Hymn to Zeus* is widely recognized as an excep-
tional document combining serious philosophical thought with 'the warm-
est tones of Hellenistic piety'.[85] In lines 18–19, Cleanthes praises Zeus for
knowing 'how to make the uneven even and to put into order the disorderly; even the unloved is dear to you'.[86] Cleanthes thus 'holds out the
hope that Zeus is able to change the disorder resulting from the actions of
the κακοί into order and to restore the harmony of his rule.'[87] Cleanthes'
lines may even suggest that it is Zeus' very love that makes 'the uneven
even'. More confidently, it is by means of deeper knowledge of Zeus (who
is addressed as 'father') and trust in his judgement that change is brought
about (vv.34–39). Along the same lines, Thom expounds that the way in
which Zeus is able to integrate the κακοί into the order manifested by
nature in general 'is suggested by the prayer at the end: Zeus is requested
to save men from their ignorance and to grant them insight, in order that
they may be able to praise his order. "Praising the universal law" (v.39) is
a metaphor for assenting to, obeying, Zeus' rule.'[88]

---

[83] The notion of an 'intimate relationship' presupposes that Zeus was comprehended
as having personal traits. See J.C. Thom, *Cleanthes' Hymn to Zeus: Text, Translation, and
Commentary*; STAC 33 (Tübingen: Mohr Siebeck, 2005), 20–21, 25–26, for a discussion
of the relationship of theism and pantheism in Cleanthes' Stoic thought.

[84] Long and Sedley, *Philosophers. I*, 332.

[85] U. von Wilamowitz-Moellendorff, *Der Glaube der Hellenen. Vol. 2* (Berlin: Weidmannsche Buchhandlung, 1932), 291. Cf. E.V. Arnold, *Roman Stoicism: Being Lectures
on the History of the Stoic Philosophy with Special Reference to its Development within
the Roman Empire* (Cambridge: Cambridge University Press, 1911), 221; Pohlenz,
'Semitismus', 262–63; J.C. Thom, 'Cleanthes' *Hymn to Zeus* and Early Christian Literature', in A.Y. Collins and M.M. Mitchell (eds.), *Antiquity and Humanity: Essays on
Ancient Religion and Philosophy Presented to Hans Dieter Betz on his 70th Birthday*
(Tübingen: Mohr Siebeck, 2001), 480.

[86] This translation follows Thom, 'Literature', 482–83. However, Long and Sedley's
translation [*LS* 54I] is more literal and renders the neuter plurals (τὰ περισσά, etc.) as
referring to 'things crooked', 'things disorderly' and 'things unloved'. Nonetheless,
Thom's translation seems to accord better with the immediate cotext of vv.18–19, namely
the (deeds of) 'bad people' (κακοί, v.17) (J.C. Thom, 'The Problem of Evil in Cleanthes'
Hymn to Zeus', *AC* 41 (1998), 45–57).

[87] Thom, 'Problem', 56, cf. 55.

[88] Ibid., 51.
On friendship with the gods and the resulting εὐδαιμονία, see already Plato, *Leg.*
716C–D. Cf. E. Peterson, 'Der Gottesfreund: Beiträge zur Geschichte eines religiösen
Terminus', *ZKG* 42 (1923), 161–72, who also discusses further Stoic philosophers (e.g.
Epictetus, *Diss.* 2.17.29).

Cleanthes' *Hymn* thus demonstrates that deeper knowledge of the divine in the context of an intimate relationship to the deity was part of some traditions of Hellenistic ethics.[89] Nonetheless, while this shows that this aspect of ethical empowering played a role in Paul's (Graeco-Roman) context, the value of this finding is to some extent limited in that πνεῦμα does not have a part in this model and is hardly ever connected to ethics at all.

3. Conclusion

Our investigation of Graeco-Roman and early Jewish literature has clearly shown that intimate relationships were comprehended as ethically empowering in Paul's religious and philosophical context. While this is not linked to the divine Spirit in Hellenism, the Jewish sources that were examined demonstrate that this intensification of people's relationship to God is a central means by which the Spirit empowers religious-ethical life. In Philo, the Spirit's work in the context of empowering for ethics regards predominantly mystical encounters with God. The resulting knowledge of God has both cognitive and existential aspects. In Qumran, the cognitive side of knowing God comes more strongly into play. Through deeper knowledge of God and a closer relationship to the community the individual is enabled to live according to God's statutes. Philo and Qumran thus provide strong support for our focal theory. In the traditions based on Ezekiel 36:25–28, however, the Spirit, intimate relationships and ethical living are interconnected, though not unequivocally in the sequence of our relational model of the Spirit's ethical work. Nevertheless, these passages offer general affirmation that these three elements were often seen together in early Judaism.

While Paul may not have expressly used Philo, the DSS or some of the traditions based on Ezekiel 36 as sources for his epistles, they nonetheless function as intertexts, forming part of the horizon of interpretation of Paul and his readers.[90] The analysis of the different strands of Judaism provided

---

[89] In many strands of Graeco-Roman philosophies and religions, deeper knowledge played a role in regeneration and transformation (see, e.g., Gärtner, 'Idea', 211–12; G. Filoramo, 'The Transformation of the Inner Self in Gnostic and Hermetic Texts', in J. Assmann and G.G. Stroumsa (eds.), *Transformations of the Inner Self in Ancient Religions*; SHR 83 (Leiden: Brill, 1999), 143–45; cf. Leisegang, *Geist*, 222, 225; Bousset, *Kyrios*, 226–27; Arnold, *Stoicism*, 85). Seneca even relates this to the divine spirit that has 'come down in order that we may have nearer knowledge of the divinity' (*Ep.* 41.5, cf. vv.1–2 which identify the holy spirit with the human soul; see 2.1.2. above).

[90] On intertextuality, see further J.H. Charlesworth, 'The Odes of Solomon and the Jewish Wisdom Texts', in C. Hempel, et al. (eds.), *The Wisdom Texts from Qumran and*

in this chapter thus significantly strengthens the probability of our focal theory, in that we were able to show that Paul was part of a milieu in which the ethical work of the Spirit was often implicitly or explicitly linked to deeper knowledge of and an intimate relationship with God and with the community of faith.

---

the Development of Sapiential Thought; BETL 159 (Leuven: Leuven University Press/ Peeters, 2002), 328–29; Bennema, *Power*, 39.

Chapter 6

Religious-Ethical Empowerment by the Relational Work of the Spirit in Paul

1. Introduction: The Fundamentals of Spirit and Ethics in Paul

It is uncontested that for the apostle Paul the Spirit was actively related to ethical living.[1] Numerous Pauline passages testify to this conceptual link (see, *inter alia*, Rom. 2:29; 8:2–14; 12:11; 14:17; 15:13; 1 Cor. 3:16; 6:11, 19; 2 Cor. 3:3; 3:18; Gal. 5:5, 16–26; Phil. 3:3; 1 Thess. 4:7–8; cf. Eph. 3:16; 2 Thess. 2:13). The aim of this chapter, however, is not to provide further support for the fact *that* the Spirit is related to ethics but to ask *how*, according to Paul, the Spirit empowers people for religious-ethical life.

In the most fundamental way, the Spirit enables ethical life in that in conversion-initiation human beings are transferred from the existence 'in the flesh' to being 'in the Spirit' (Rom. 8:9).[2] The different aspects of this transferral are aptly summarized by Backhaus:

Einziger objektiver Grund des Übergangs von jenem in diesen Existenzbereich ist der Sühnetod Jesu am Kreuz (2Kor 5,14–21; Gal 2,19–21), subjektiver Grund die vertrau-ende Annahme der göttlichen Heilstat (Röm 3,21–31), tragende Macht das Pneuma (1Kor 6,11), wirksames Zeichen die Taufe (Röm 6,1–11). So verwandelt die Begegnung mit dem Gekreuzigten die Identität des Glaubenden radikal… (2Kor 5,17; vgl. 4,6; Gal 6,15). Die Neuheit erweist sich insofern als "Neuheit des Geistes" (Röm 7,6), als der Versöhnte das tödlich-bindende Magnetfeld der auf sich selbst geworfenen Sarx verlassen und Zugang gewonnen hat zum pneumatischen Freiheitsraum der Sohnschaft (Gal 3,26–29; 4,5–7; Röm 8.12–17).[3]

The existence-transforming result ('existenzverändernde Konsequenz')[4] of this transferral is thus well comprehended in relational terms:[5] it is *freedom*

---

[1] However, see Horn, 'Wandel', 149–70, as discussed in Appendix 3.1. Excursus 2.

[2] On the nature of these two modes of existence, see 6.3.2.

[3] K. Backhaus, 'Evangelium als Lebensraum: Christologie und Ethik bei Paulus', in U. Schnelle and T. Söding (eds.), *Paulinische Christologie: Exegetische Beiträge; FS* H. Hübner (Göttingen: Vandenhoeck & Ruprecht, 2000), 15. Cf. Wendland, *Leben*, 35–36.

[4] C. Landmesser, 'Der Geist und die christliche Existenz: Anmerkungen zur paulini-schen Pneumatologie im Anschluß an Röm 8.1–11', in U.H.J. Körtner and A. Klein (eds.), *Die Wirklichkeit des Geistes: Konzeptionen und Phänomene des Geistes in Philo-*

from sin, the flesh, the law, the enslaving powers, etc., and *a new, intimate relationship with* God, Christ, the Spirit[6] and the Christian community (Rom. 7:5–6; 8:2–11; Gal. 4:3–7; 1 Cor. 12:13; etc.). A change of allegiance has happened, with the consequence of a new belonging (see, e.g., Rom. 8:9: ἔστιν αὐτοῦ; Gal. 5:24): the converts are now united with Christ by the Spirit – they are in 'in Christ' (Rom. 8:1; 1 Cor. 1:30; 2 Cor. 5:17; Gal. 3:26; etc.), 'in the Spirit' (Rom. 8:9; etc.), and Christ by his Spirit indwells them (Rom. 8:9–10; etc.; see ch. 3 Excursus 1).

The language of mutual indwelling has many facets.[7] The clearest and most relevant aspect for the present question is the notion that converts have entered the *realm of influence* of Christ and the Spirit.[8] They have been taken out of the sphere where they were fixed on the things of the flesh and have been transferred into the realm where the Spirit is the primary influence and power in their lives,[9] so that their minds are now set on the things of the Spirit (Rom. 8:5).

---

sophie und Theologie der Gegenwart (Neukirchen-Vluyn: Neukirchener Verlag, 2006), 141. Cf. Schnelle, 'Transformation', 68–72; Blischke, *Begründung*, 458–59. *Pace* Engberg-Pedersen, *Stoics*, e.g. 251, this change cannot be reduced to a mainly cognitive endeavour (cf. Engberg-Pedersen, 'Logic', 248).

[5] See the full discussion in ch. 4, esp. 4.4.1.

[6] 'Relationship with the Spirit' is not meant to imply that the Spirit is conceived as a person to whom Paul would suggest one should actively relate (cf. 4.4.2.). However, as the Spirit 'indwells' believers (cf. ch. 3 Excursus 1) it is possible to speak of a new relationship.

[7] Fatehi singles out three meanings of ἐν Χριστῷ in Paul: 'The three notions of representation, sphere of influence, and union through the Spirit, when combined seem to be sufficient for explaining Paul's language' (Fatehi, *Relation*, 254). Cf. W. Thüsing, *Per Christum in Deum: Studien zum Verhältnis von Christozentrik und Theozentrik in den paulinischen Hauptbriefen*; NTA NS 1 (Münster: Aschendorff, 1965), 15, 65; and Strecker who particularly emphasizes the horizontal dimension of the *Christuscommunitas*, i.e. 'in Christ' as a shorthand indicating the identity of the community of the saved and the affiliation to it (C. Strecker, *Die liminale Theologie des Paulus: Zugänge zur paulinischen Theologie aus kulturanthropologischer Perspektive*; FRLANT 185 (Göttingen: Vandenhoeck & Ruprecht, 1999), 191–92, 205–206).

[8] Cf. A. Wikenhauser, *Pauline Mysticism: Christ in the Mystical Teaching of St. Paul* (Freiburg/Edinburgh-London: Herder/Nelson, 1960), 57; E. Schweizer, 'πνεῦμα, πνευματικός', *TDNT*, VI, 425; Brandenburger, *Fleisch*, 45–46, 55–56; Käsemann, *Romans*, 221; R. Jewett, *Paul's Anthropological Terms: A Study of their Use in Conflict Settings*; AGJU 10 (Leiden: Brill, 1971), 54, 94; et al.; see also ch. 3 Excursus 1; ch. 4 n.44. Horn speaks of ἐν Χριστῷ/ἐν πνεύματι as *Heilsraum* (Horn, *Angeld*, 333), and Schweizer comprehends being ἐν Χριστῷ as living 'in an atmosphere informed by love' (Schweizer, *Jesus*, 107). For parallels in Paul's *religionsgeschichtlich* context, see Elliott, *Survivors*, 409; Sellin, 'Hintergründe', 20–21; et al.

[9] On the Spirit as power, see Rom. 15:13 (cf. Eph. 3:16), and the discussion of Wendt, *Fleisch*, 142–47; Gloël, *Geist*, 373–74; Stalder, *Heiligung*, 29–35 (cf. the Appendix).

However, in contrast to the contentions of the infusion-transformation approach to the ethical work of the Spirit discussed in Part I (cf. 4.2. and 4.4.1.), there is no automatism of ethical living involved in the transferral into the realm of the Spirit. The prime aspect of this change is that, in contrast to life *remoto Christo* (cf. Rom. 7:18; 8:7–8), one is now *able* to live according to God's precepts.[10] Nonetheless, the fact that Paul entreats his churches to live in accordance with this new reality[11] shows that there is *need for continual empowering* for religious-ethical life. As the possibility of living 'according to the flesh' still exists (Rom. 8:12–13, see 6.3.2.), believers need to 'keep in step with the Spirit' (Gal. 5:16, 25) so that their lives will become more and more 'christomorphic' (cf. Gal. 4:19: μορφωθῇ Χριστὸς ἐν ὑμῖν; 2 Cor. 3:18; Rom. 8:29; etc.; cf. 6.2.2.2.).[12]

In this chapter we will argue that the above described transferral by the Spirit into a new relationship with God, Christ and the Christian community is not merely a transforming event in the converts' lives at the occasion of their entry into the salvific realm. Rather, while scholarship has often focussed on this initial transferral as the prime aspect of the Spirit's enabling of religious-ethical life according to Paul (cf. the infusion-transformation approach), it is our contention that the Spirit *continually* transforms and empowers believers for ethical conduct by enlivening and even intensifying these intimate relationships. Accordingly, the two following sections (6.2.–6.3.) will demonstrate how people are transformed and empowered for religious-ethical living by the Spirit's provision of a deeper knowledge of *God* (and Christ) and an intimate relationship with him. The final section (6.4.) will then elucidate the *communal nature* of the empowering work of the Spirit by delineating how believers draw strength for ethical living from Spirit-shaped intimate relationships with fellow believers.

---

[10] Cf. the structure of Rom. 7–8 as summarized in Rom. 7:5–6 (cf. Stuhlmacher, *Römer*, 96–97; H. Lichtenberger, *Das Ich Adams und das Ich der Menschheit: Studien zum Menschenbild in Römer 7*; WUNT 164 (Tübingen: Mohr Siebeck, 2004), 119–20, 187; et al.).

[11] So, e.g., Gal. 5:25. This tension is commonly expressed in the phrase 'become what you are' (see, e.g., Bultmann, *Theology. I*, 332). However, as this may suggest that one has to establish the reality of the new creation by one's own actions, a number of preferable alternatives have been formulated: 'You are; therefore be!' (M.J. Harris, *The Second Epistle to the Corinthians: A Commentary on the Greek Text*; NIGTC (Grand Rapids/Milton Keynes: Eerdmans/Paternoster, 2005), 514; '*remain* what you are – and show it in practice' (Engberg-Pedersen, *Stoics*, 367 n.12); etc. On the so-called 'indicative-imperative' dialectic in Paul, see further Appendix 2.1. Excursus 1.

[12] The term 'christomorphic life' is to be preferred to 'cruciform conduct' as Paul does not reduce Christ to 'the cross' (cf. Munzinger, *Spirits*, 182–83; *pace* M.J. Gorman, *Cruciformity: Paul's Narrative Spirituality of the Cross* (Grand Rapids/Cambridge: Eerdmans, 2001), *passim*; Lewis, *Life*, e.g. 18).

While structuring the chapter in this way is helpful for highlighting the different aspects of our focal theory, it nevertheless needs to be noted at the outset that the (ethical) work of the Spirit discussed in the respective sections cannot be limited to the aspects under which they are subsumed. For example, adoption into God's family, which is considered in section 6.3., has both a *communal* aspect (although the communal work of the Spirit is specifically in focus only in 6.4.) and it can also be viewed as a *transformation* of the believer (although, following Paul, the term 'transformation' is used with reference to the work of the Spirit only in our exegesis of 2 Cor. 3:18 in 6.2.).[13]

The passages that will be discussed are chosen in accordance with our question, namely, how the Spirit empowers religious-ethical living not only at the time of conversion-initiation but also in the course of Christian life. We have seen above that these two aspects belong together. This will be further illustrated in the subsequent exegesis. However, some of the passages in the list provided at the outset of this section only relate the initial action of the Spirit in the process of sanctification (as, e.g., 1 Cor. 6:11: 'you were sanctified... in the Spirit of our God') or simply do not move beyond the statement *that* the Spirit works ethically (e.g. Gal. 5:22: the 'fruit of the Spirit'). Such passages will not receive in-depth treatment in this chapter, as we will rather bring a number of new passages into the discussion of *how* the Spirit empowers ethical conduct in Paul. These texts evidence that the Spirit primarily enables religious-ethical living through creating and nourishing intimate relationships.

2. Ethical Transformation through Spirit-Enabled Contemplation of the Divine (2 Cor. 3:18)

In 2 Corinthians 3, Paul defends his ministry by contrasting it with that of Moses. Towards the end of the chapter (vv.14–18) he shifts the focus away from the *ministers* of the old and new covenants to the *recipients* and the *effects* of the respective ministries.[14] In verses 14–15 Paul describes the recipients of the old covenant ministry, the Israelites, as hardened and veiled. The 'Mosaic ministry' is not able to effect any change of this condition 'up to this day', because only through Christ is the veil taken away. Those who have turned to the Lord, *per contra*, have been unveiled and experience the freedom of the Spirit (vv.16–17). Then, in verse 18, Paul reaches the heights of his exposition. Including all Christian believers

---

[13] On the minor differences between the concepts of transformation and empowering, see 4.1.–4.2.

[14] Cf. Fee, *Presence*, 315–16; Hafemann, *Paul*, 409–410.

(ἡμεῖς... πάντες)[15] as the recipients of the effects of this new covenant ministry, Paul proclaims 'And we all, with unveiled face, beholding the glory of the Lord as in a mirror, are being transformed into the same image from one glory to another; for this comes from the Lord, the Spirit'.

Paul's climactic statement in verse 18 provides fundamental support for our relational model of the Spirit's enabling of religious-ethical life in Paul's thought. In our ensuing exegesis of the passage it will be argued that the Spirit causes people to come to know God in Christ more intimately through a deeper understanding as well as personal encounter with him. As a result believers are being transformed into the image of the Lord, which means that their lives will portray more of the characteristics of Christ. This, however, clearly involves enabling for religious-ethical conduct.

2 Corinthians 3, and verse 18 in particular, has been called 'the Mount Everest of Pauline texts as far as difficulty is concerned...'[16]. Many who have tried to grasp the nuances of Paul's argument have at times felt that they have a veil over their minds. Cataloguing the exegetical perplexities of the passage would, therefore, go beyond the scope of the present study.[17] In our analysis below we will rather limit ourselves to the issues relevant to our argument. Our investigation will focus on two questions regarding the religious-ethical transformation in 2 Corinthians 3:18: 1) How is the transformation achieved? and 2) What is the result of the transformation?

2.1. How is the Transformation Achieved?

The leading question of this monograph is how religious-ethical living is enabled by the Spirit. It follows from this that it is important to look in some detail at how Paul understands the transformation mentioned in 2 Corinthians 3:18 to be achieved. We will do so by first of all analysing the two elements central to the process of transformation: the unveiling of the

---

[15] Cf. K. Prümm, *Diakonia Pneumatos: Theologische Auslegung des zweiten Korintherbriefes. Vol. I* (Freiburg: Herder, 1967), 166; R. Bultmann, *Der zweite Brief an die Korinther*; KEK (Göttingen: Vandenhoeck & Ruprecht, 1976), 93; Fee, *Presence*, 314; S. Hulmi, *Paulus und Mose: Argumentation und Polemik in 2 Kor 3*; SFEG 77 (Göttingen/Helsinki: Vandenhoeck & Ruprecht/Finnische Exegetische Gesellschaft, 1999), 91; Back, *Verwandlung*, 127, 148; Harris, *Corinthians*, 313; et al. *Pace* L.L. Belleville, *Reflections of Glory: Paul's Polemical Use of the Moses-Doxa Tradition in 2 Corinthians 3,1–18*; JSNTSup 52 (Sheffield: JSOT Press, 1991), 275–76, 296.

[16] A.T. Hanson, 'The Midrash in II Corinthians 3: A Reconsideration', *JSNT* 9 (1980), 19, cited with consent by D.E. Garland, 'The Sufficiency of Paul, Minister of the New Covenant', *CTR* 4 (1989), 21.

[17] For a brief overview of the central difficulties, see, e.g., W.C. van Unnik, '"With Unveiled Face": An Exegesis of 2 Corinthians iii 12–18', in W.C. van Unnik, *Sparsa Collecta. Vol. 1: Evangelia, Paulina, Acta*; NovTSup 29 (Leiden: Brill, 1973), 195–97.

face and the beholding of the glory of the Lord. After that we will ask what role Paul attributes to the Spirit in this process.

2.1.1. The Unveiled Face

Paul specifies that the beholding of the glory of the Lord is 'with unveiled face' (ἀνακεκαλυμμένῳ προσώπῳ). This adverbial phrase is a dative of manner or means in relation to the beholding (κατοπτριζόμενοι) and can be translated as 'by means of an unveiled face' or simply 'with unveiled face'.[18] Harris explains that προσώπῳ is a distributive singular and 'refers figuratively (by metonymy) to recognition and understanding so that the whole phrase... refers to the unimpeded vision of Christians in contrast to the impeded vision of Jews (vv. 14–15).'[19]

However, the question arises whether Paul gives any indication what the object or content of the 'unimpeded vision' is. Perhaps the most straightforward answer is that 'the glory of the Lord' is the object, as it is by means of the unveiling that it can be beheld.[20] However, a closer look at Paul's employment of the notion of '(un)veiling' in 2 Corinthians 3:7–4:6 shows that it is not only connected to the concepts of 'glory' and 'face', but also to the 'minds', and (the message of) the 'gospel' and 'Moses'/'the old covenant'. In order to discover the conceptual link between these individual words we have structured the occurrences of these concepts in the text as follows:

A- the Israelites could not look at Moses' face because of its glory, fading as it was (3:7)
  - Moses put a veil over his face because the glory was fading away (3:13)

B - a veil lies over the minds of Israel whenever Moses/the old covenant is read
  (3:14–15)

C - turning to the Lord removes the veil (3:16); we all behold the glory of the Lord with
  unveiled face (3:18)

B' - the gospel is veiled to those perishing (4:3),
  - their minds are blinded, keeping them from seeing the light of the gospel of the glory
  of Christ, who is the likeness of God (4:4)

A' - God has shone in our hearts to give the light of the knowledge of the glory of God in
  the face of Christ (4:6)

We do not intend to suggest that Paul consciously organized the text according to this chiastic structure (which does not display every verse of the entire passage anyway). However, the analysis above can function as a

---

[18] See Harris, *Corinthians*, 313, for scholars opting for a dative of manner. Hafemann adopts the translation 'by means of' (Hafemann, *Paul*, 408, 427).
[19] Harris, *Corinthians*, 313.
[20] So J. Behm, 'μεταμορφόω', *TDNT*, IV, 758; Hafemann, *Paul*, 408–409.

heuristic model for understanding how Paul connected '(un)veiling' to the surrounding concepts. While further points could be drawn out from the model, we have highlighted above that in sections A, A' and the centre-piece C, '(un)veiling' is connected with the 'face', which in turn is linked to 'glory'.[21] In B and B', however, '(un)veiling' is connected with the 'minds' of Israel and unbelievers (3:14; 4:4), which in turn are linked to (the message of) the 'gospel' and 'Moses'/'the old covenant'.[22]

This suggests that 'unveiling' in 3:18 has two aspects. On the one hand there is a cognitive aspect: by means of unveiling the minds of people, the Spirit provides proper understanding of the gospel.[23] The gospel is speci-fied as that 'of the glory of Christ, who is the likeness of God' (4:4), which indicates that the deeper understanding is of a relational nature – it regards the person of Christ. On the other hand, Paul associates 'unveiling' with personal closeness and immediacy. This is obvious from his notion of '(un)veiling' the *face*.[24] A veiled face prevents direct contact and a personal encounter with the 'glory' of the respective person (Moses in 3:7, 13; contrasted by Christ in 4:6). However, the Spirit has unveiled the faces of 'us all', so that an unprecedented freedom (3:17) and immediacy of access to and intimacy with God is possible (knowing 'in our hearts... the glory of God on the face of Christ' [4:6]).

Paul connects the cognitive and the immediacy-creating character of 'unveiling' in 3:18 through a dative with the 'beholding of the glory of the Lord', which suggests that the 'beholding' is achieved by way or means of 'unveiling'. The relational work of 'unveiling' is thus causally linked to

---

[21] In 4:6 'unveiling' is not explicitly mentioned, but it is implied by the contrast with 4:3–4 and by the immediacy worked by God's shining 'in our hearts... the light of the knowledge of the glory of God'.

[22] A structural element not discussed in our rough sketch above is a parallel between 4:4 and 4:6: 4:4 mentions 'minds' in connection with 'the light of the gospel...'; 4:6 mentions 'hearts' in connection with 'the light of the knowledge...'. In the model above we assume that (blinded) 'minds' and 'gospel' here have a slightly stronger cognitive emphasis than 'hearts' and 'knowledge' (on 'knowing', cf. chapter 5 n.38, and our con-clusion to 6.2.1.2.1.). Apart from that, like 4:6, 4:4 also mentions 'glory' (of Christ), but the focus is here on the gospel (cf. 4:3).

[23] Cf. Turner, *Spirit*, 116: the Spirit 'removes "the veil" of misunderstanding that blinds Judaism – and the most natural explanation of this is that the Spirit achieves such an end... by enabling the kind of wisdom or revelation that yields authentic understand-ing of the kerygma.'

[24] On the notion of closeness as expressed by πρόσωπον in the LXX (e.g. Num. 6:25–26), in early Judaism (e.g. Josephus, *J.W.* 1.263) and in the NT (e.g. 1 Cor. 13:12 [πρόσωπον πρὸς πρόσωπον]; 1 Thess. 2:17), see E. Lohse, 'πρόσωπον', *TDNT*, VI, 771–78. Van Unnik rightly points out that the notion of the 'unveiled face' is further eluci-dated by the concept of παρρησία (3:12) that is placed in contrast to Moses veiling his face (3:13) (van Unnik, 'Face', 200–201).

the (religious-ethical) transformation which is a consequence of the beholding.

2.1.2. Beholding as in a Mirror

What does Paul mean when he says that we all are 'beholding the glory of
the Lord as in a mirror'? Three options can be differentiated.

2.1.2.1. Beholding as Receiving (Cognitive) Revelation

Whether one interprets 'beholding the glory of the Lord as in a mirror' as
the reception of (cognitive) *revelation*, or a (personal) *encounter*, depends
to some extent on how one identifies the object of the beholding.[25] The
first interpretation usually emphasizes the role of the *gospel* in the process
of beholding, whereas the second interpretation focuses on *Christ* as the
object that is beheld.

The interpretation of 'beholding' as the reception of cognitive revelation
has most recently been supported by Back.[26] Back argues that when Chris-

---

[25] A communal interpretation of κατοπτριζόμενοι as 'reflecting' rather than 'beholding' has been championed by Wright, Belleville and Gruber (based on suggestions by van
Unnik (van Unnik, 'Face', 208–209). They believe that 'the "mirror" in which Christians
see reflected the glory of the Lord is... *one another.* [...] [W]hen they [the Christians]
come face to face with one another they are beholding, as in a mirror, the glory itself'
(N.T. Wright, *The Climax of the Covenant: Christ and the Law in Pauline Theology*
(Edinburgh: T. & T. Clark, 1991), 185; cf. Belleville, *Reflections*, 279–83; M.M. Gruber,
*Herrlichkeit in Schwachheit: Eine Auslegung der Apologie des Zweiten Korintherbriefs 2
Kor 2,14–6,13*; FB 89 (Würzburg: Echter, 1998), 267, 281–82; for further scholars
preferring 'reflecting' to 'beholding', see Back, *Verwandlung*, 133 n.22; Howard, *Paul*,
68–69, claims that Paul intends both meanings, 'beholding' and 'reflecting'). However,
while it is theologically correct to emphasize the communal nature of religious-ethical
transformation in Paul (on this see 6.4.), the present passage provides no explicit evidence for this characteristic. For one thing, προσώπῳ as a distributive singular renders an
interpretation as believers 'coming face to face with one another' unlikely. Moreover, the
logically correct inference of Gruber, that ἀπὸ δόξης εἰς δόξαν needs to be understood as
'Steigerung..., weil die Doxa des je einzelnen im empfangenden Sehen der Doxa des
anderen wächst' (Gruber, *Herrlichkeit*, 282), seems to stress the anthropological dimension of the transformation in a way otherwise untypical of Paul. Therefore, we can conclude with Thrall that 'it remains more probable that the transformation is effected
through vision... than that it is the result of "reflecting". If believers already reflect the
glory, what is the point of the following μεταμορφούμεθα? The transformation, in that
case, has already occurred. For "reflection" is the *consequence* of transformation' (Thrall,
Corinthians. I, 291, along with the majority of commentators).

[26] Prior to Back, a number of other scholars argued for a cognitive interpretation.
Jervell notes that 'beholding' comes very close to 'hearing the gospel', particularly when
read against the background of Sir. 17.13: 'Their eyes saw his glorious majesty, and their
ears heard the glory of his voice' (J. Jervell, *Imago Dei: Gen 1,26f. im Spätjudentum, in
der Gnosis und in den paulinischen Briefen*; FRLANT 76/NF 58 (Göttingen: Vanden-

tians behold 'the glory of the Lord', they do not behold Christ but they prophetically see in the gospel as in a mirror that Christ has been made alive.[27] This interpretation of 'beholding' as reception of revelation (*Offenbarungsempfang*; 'prophetisches "Sehen" der Christusbotschaft')[28] is based on how she conceptualizes the aspect 'as in a mirror' of κατοπτριζόμενοι[29] as well as her understanding of this New Testament *hapax legomenon* as *prophetic* inspiration. She derives her interpretation of both elements mainly from the perceived parallel of 3:18 with 1 Corinthians 13:12.

Back believes that the cotext of 1 Corinthians 13:12 (i.e. 13:8–12) indicates that Paul understands 'seeing with a mirror' (βλέπομεν... δι' ἐσόπτρου, 13:12) as a reference to the prophetic reception of revelation. 'With the "looking in the mirror" and the knowing in 1 Cor 13,12 Paul picks up on the γινώσκειν and the προφητεύειν of 1 Cor 13,9f. in reverse order.'[30] Back thus counts 'looking into a mirror' among the prophetic gifts.[31] However, while 'knowledge' is mentioned both in 13:9 and 13:12, there is no syntactic or semantic indication that 13:12 takes up 'prophecy' from 13:9. Besides, the 'knowledge' mentioned in 13:9 is a gift of the Spirit of which Paul says that it is not available to everyone (12:8). The 'knowledge' mentioned in 13:12, *per contra*, is not a special insight but a personal 'face to face' knowing of God that is available to all Christians (πρόσωπον πρὸς πρόσωπον... ἐπιγνώσομαι καθὼς καὶ ἐπεγνώσθην).

Back's usage of 'prophecy' in 2 Corinthians 3:18 evidences the same deficiency. Even if Back were right that in 1 Corinthians 13:12 the mirror motif is a clear reference to the gift of prophecy, her designation of κατοπτριζόμενοι in 2 Corinthians 3:18 as a prophetic charisma that has been given to all who have received the Spirit[32] appears to introduce a

---

hoeck & Ruprecht, 1960), 186; followed by V.P. Furnish, *II Corinthians*; AB 32A (New York: Doubleday, 1984), 242). Belleville thinks that by 'glory' Paul has in mind the knowledge of the salvific work of God in the gospel. She finds reason for this in the notion of 'knowledge' in 4:6 and in the usage of μεταμορφόω (3:18) in Rom. 12:2 for the renewal of the *mind* (Belleville, *Reflections*, 285, 293; see also L.E. Di Fortunato, *The Gramma – Pneuma Antithesis: An Exegetical Study of Three Pauline Texts and the Hermeneutical Value of the Antithesis Examined on the Apostle's Exposition of the Scriptures* (Zürich: Stiftung Zentralstelle der Studenterschaft der Universität Zürich, 1993), 125–26). See further n.68 below.

[27] Back, *Verwandlung*, 146, cf. 141, 144.

[28] Ibid., 145.

[29] Linguistically, the reading 'beholding *as in a mirror*' as opposed to 'beholding' is suggested by a number of ancient sources, most prominently Philo, *Leg. All.* 3.101 (see, e.g., H. Lietzmann, *An die Korinther I/II*; HNT 9 (Tübingen: J.C.B. Mohr (Paul Siebeck), 1969⁵), 113).

[30] Back, *Verwandlung*, 137.

[31] Ibid., 140.

[32] Ibid., 140–41.

different (non-Pauline) concept of the gift of prophecy. For Paul, by contrast, emphasizes that the gift of prophecy is not given to all.[33] Along these lines it is also not easy to agree with Back when she further suggests that it is because of Paul's attribution of the look into the mirror to *the work of the Spirit* that κατοπτριζόμενοι needs to be understood as reception of revelation (*Offenbarungsempfang*).[34]

While Back's support for her interpretation of the look into the mirror as a prophetic charisma gives reason for doubt, she may nevertheless be right in proposing that the similarities between 3:18 and 4:3–4 (both passages mention '[un]veiling' and 'glory') suggest that the mirror of 3:18 is the gospel of 4:3–4 because in it one can see the glory of Christ. This reading of the mirror is usually linked with the interpretation of the 'Lord' in τὴν δόξαν κυρίου (3:18) as Christ. It is based on the parallel with 4:4 where Paul talks about τῆς δόξης τοῦ Χριστοῦ, as well as on Paul's calling Jesus explicitly 'Lord' in 4:5 (whereas he uses θεός when he speaks of God [4:2, 4, 6]).[35]

Alternatively, however, Christ himself could be interpreted as the mirror (which would suggest that κατοπτριζόμενοι is at least as much about a personal encounter as about cognitive revelation [cf. 6.2.1.2.2. below]). This would fit 4:6, where Paul declares that God's glory is revealed in the face of Christ.[36] It is further supported by the use of the mirror metaphor in Wisdom of Solomon 7.26, where Wisdom herself is the mirror. Paul describes Christ as God's wisdom (1 Cor. 1:30), and this may suggest that in Christ believers see the reflection of the very nature of God as in a mirror.[37] On this more probable reading of 'beholding the glory of the Lord as

---

[33] 1 Cor. 12:10, 29; Rom. 12:6; however, see also 1 Cor. 14:5. Turner argues that the pneumatology of 2 Cor. 3 does not represent a move away from the Jewish concept of the 'Spirit of prophecy' because the Spirit functions as revealer and illuminator of the Christ-event, bringing Ezek. 36 to increasing fulfilment (Turner, *Spirit*, 116). However, in contrast to Back, Turner does not use 'prophecy' here in the specific sense as one of the charisms (cf. his definition on pp. 7–9). Back's treatment would have likewise benefited from a clear definition of how she uses 'prophecy'.

[34] Back, *Verwandlung*, 136.

[35] Ibid., 135–36, and the scholars mentioned there; cf. Fatehi, *Relation*, 290–302; T. Stegman, *The Character of Jesus: The Linchpin to Paul's Argument in 2 Corinthians*; AB 158 (Rome: Editrice Pontificio Instituto Biblico, 2005), 234–35. It may be further supported by the occurrence of κυρίου δόξαν in 2 Cor. 8:19 which is possibly explained by δόξα Χριστοῦ in v.23. Grindheim even seems to suggest that κυρίου here is the gospel when he writes that 'those who look at the glory of the gospel are transformed to the same glory (3.18; 4.4)' (S. Grindheim, 'The Law Kills but the Gospel Gives Life: The Letter–Spirit Dualism in 2. Corinthians 3.5–18', *JSNT* 84 (2001), 107).

[36] Cf. *1 Clem.* 36:2 (see the discussion in Thrall, *Corinthians. I*, 284 n.663).

[37] So e.g. Ibid., 284, 293; C.S. Keener, *1–2 Corinthians*; NCBC (Cambridge: Cambridge University Press, 2005), 170; see the detailed discussion in Meier, *Mystik*, 87–92,

in a mirror' (3:18), then, κυρίου refers to God, not to Christ. The 'glory of Christ' in 4:4 is thus described more precisely as the 'glory of God on the face of Christ' in 4:6. This reading finds support in the usage of δόξα κυρίου in the Septuagint for the glory of YHWH, including, significantly, passages that refer to Sinai (Exod. 24:17; cf. 33:19, discussed in section 6.2.1.2.2. below) and the 'tent of meeting' (Exod. 40:34–35; Lev. 9:6, 23; Num. 14:10).[38] Moreover, as Thrall notes, 'since for Paul δόξα and εἰκών are similar concepts, and in 4.4 the εἰκών of God is Christ, we should expect that τὴν δόξαν here likewise refers to Christ, who is thus the glory of the Lord as he is the image of God.'[39]

Nonetheless, the mirror motif may not (only) be intended to signify Christ (or the gospel),[40] but Paul may have brought it into play simply in order to indicate the indirectness of the beholding.[41] This notion is clearly present in 1 Corinthians 13:12, indicated by the adverbial qualification ἐν αἰνίγματι. However, this phrase is missing in 2 Corinthians 3:18,[42] and, what is more, recent research has shown that mirrors in antiquity were not so much associated with fuzziness and ambiguity but with participation and transformation.[43] This result, however, lends itself to the interpretation

---

who further draws on the usage of the mirror-motif in Philo, *Leg. All.* 3.101. On the interplay of the concepts of mirror, δόξα and εἰκών, see Jervell, *Imago*, 185–86.

[38] Cf. J.F. Collange, *Énigmes de la deuxième épître de Paul aux Corinthiens: Étude exégétique de 2 Cor. 2:14–7:4*; SNTSMS 18 (Cambridge: Cambridge University Press, 1972), 118–19; J.D.G. Dunn, '2 Corinthians III. 17 – "The Lord is the Spirit"', *JTS* 21 (1970), 318; Thrall, *Corinthians. I*, 283; Fee, *Presence*, 317; Turner, *Spirit*, 114–16; Harris, *Corinthians*, 314–15. – Wright brings a third option into play: the 'Lord' in τὴν δόξαν κυρίου refers to the Spirit. However, while this may fit 3:17a and an interpretation of κυρίου πνεύματος in 3:18 as 'the Lord who is the Spirit' (RSV; Harris, *Corinthians*, 317; see 6.2.1.3. below), Paul might have given clearer evidence in 3:18 that he is using this phrase differently from the Jewish tradition. Furthermore, the rendering 'glory of the Spirit' appears to attribute a character to the Spirit that is otherwise foreign to Paul (however, see 3:8).

[39] Thrall, *Corinthians. I*, 283.

[40] On the idea that fellow believers are the mirror, see n.25 above. Philip suggests that the mirror signifies the Spirit because the Spirit is the agent of the transformation (Philip, *Origins*, 189–90). However, he fails to demonstrate how the function of the mirror is interrelated with that of the Spirit in vv.17–18.

[41] The eschatological reserve is stressed, e.g., by Keener, *Corinthians*, 170. Cf. Ashton, *Religion*, 137; Harris, *Corinthians*, 315.

[42] Cf. Furnish, *Corinthians*, 239; Thrall, *Corinthians. I*, 293.

[43] A. Weissenrieder, 'Der Blick in den Spiegel: II Kor 3,18 vor dem Hintergrund antiker Spiegeltheorien und ikonographischer Abbildungen', in A. Weissenrieder, et al. (eds.), *Picturing the New Testament: Studies in Ancient Visual Images*; WUNT II/193 (Tübingen: Mohr Siebeck, 2005), 315; 321: 'Die antiken Spiegel... erreichten... die *Magie der Verwandlung*, Verzerrung, der Verkleinerung oder Vergrößerung und der Lichtbrechung. Dies ist in dem unterschiedlichen Material begründet – dort Metalle,

of 3:18a as 'transformation through contemplation' which we will discuss in section 6.2.2.3. below.

While it remains difficult to decide which aspect of the possible interpretations of the mirror was most prominently on the mind of Paul (the most probable candidates are beholding the glory of God on the face of Jesus as in a mirror as well as the notion of participation and transformation), it is clear that deeper understanding of the gospel (whether as an aspect of 'beholding' or, as established at 6.2.1.1. above, as an aspect of unveiling) should not be reduced to the reception of *cognitive* knowledge. Understanding the gospel more deeply is for Paul not divorced from knowing Christ more intimately.[44] This is obvious, for example, from Paul's personal testimony in Philippians 3:8, where he speaks about 'the surpassing value of *knowing Christ Jesus my Lord*' that is closely tied to his appreciation of the gospel message as one of participation in Christ (and his righteousness) in the following verse (3:9).

Also 2 Corinthians gives evidence that for Paul knowledge is not merely propositional but knowledge by direct acquaintance. In 2:14 Paul describes his ministry of preaching the gospel as a means by which God 'spreads in every place the fragrance that comes from *knowing him*'. In the immediate cotext of 3:18 this is expressed as 'the light of the *knowledge* of the glory of God *in the face of Jesus Christ*' (4:6, cf. 4:4; 5:16; on the role of the Spirit in this context, cf. 1 Cor. 2:10–12). It is of no doubt that such knowledge transforms a person (see esp. the parallel in Rom. 12:2 where μεταμορφόω is linked to the renewal of the mind).[45] We will return to this interpretation of 'beholding' as *receiving relational knowledge* in the context of our discussion of the third interpretative option, namely 'beholding' as contemplation.

---

heute Glas – aber auch in ihrer Intention: Nicht die Vorstellung der Repräsentation, sondern die der *Strahlen...* [und] die der *(verzerrten) Gestaltung* steht hinter der Produktion von Spiegeln in der Antike.' However, see Jam. 1:23–24 where the motif is used for looking at oneself and forgetting the representation of oneself in the mirror.

[44] Cf. Dunn, *Theology*, 47; Stegman, *Character*, 246–47; I.W. Scott, *Implicit Epistemology in the Letters of Paul: Story, Experience and the Spirit*; WUNT II/205 (Tübingen: Mohr Siebeck, 2006), 150–54; T. Engberg-Pedersen, 'Self-Sufficiency and Power: Divine and Human Agency in Epictetus and Paul', in J.M.G. Barclay and S.J. Gathercole (eds.), *Divine and Human Agency in Paul and his Cultural Environment*; ECC/LNTS 335 (London: Continuum, 2006), 128, 134, 138; Munzinger, *Spirits*, 156–57.

[45] Cf. A. de Oliveira, *Die Diakonie der Gerechtigkeit und der Versöhnung in der Apologie des 2. Korintherbriefes: Analyse und Auslegung von 2 Kor 2,14–4,6; 5,11–6,10*; NA 21 (Münster: Aschendorff, 1990), 223; Turner, 'Spirit of Prophecy and the Ethical/Religious Life', 188–89. Cf. 6.2.2.2. below.

2.1.2.2. Beholding as Encounter

We have indicated above that interpreting τὴν δόξαν κυρίου κατοπτριζόμενοι as beholding the glory of God on the face of Jesus is a likely reading of 3:18. More pointedly formulated, 'it is by beholding Christ that believers behold God's glory.'[46] This may suggest that 'beholding' has a visionary experience as reference point.[47] Accordingly, Segal states that 'for Paul, as for the earliest Jewish mystics, to be privileged to see the *Kavod* or Glory *(doxa)* of God is a prologue to transformation into his image *(eikōn).* Paul does not say that all Christians have made the journey literally but compares the experience of knowing Christ to being allowed into the intimate presence of the Lord.'[48]

This interpretation of 'beholding' is supported by a closer look at the Moses-narrative in the Old Testament on which 2 Corinthians 3:7–18 is built. Exodus 34:29 says that the appearance of Moses' face was glorified because God had *spoken with him.* This aspect of the narrative encourages an interpretation of the beholding in 2 Corinthians 3:18 as the reception of (relational) knowledge (as at 6.2.1.2.1. above). However, if Paul had conflated the beginning of Exodus 34 with the end of Exodus 33 he could have concluded that Moses did *see* God.[49] God replies to Moses' request to see the Lord's glory (33:18) that he will allow Moses to see his back after his

---

[46] Thrall, *Corinthians. I,* 283, italics removed. Cf. C.K. Barrett, *A Commentary on the Second Epistle to the Corinthians;* BNTC (London: Black, 1982), 125; Furnish, *Corinthians,* 239; Samra, *Christ,* 102.

[47] So e.g. Philip, *Origins,* 184. Cf. our interpretation of the 'unveiled face' in 6.2.1.1. above. *Pace* J. Lambrecht, 'Transformation in 2 Cor 3,18', *Bib* 64 (1983), 250; cf. Back who appears to deny the visionary dimension of the encounter (she interprets 'seeing' as a metaphor for *Offenbarungsempfang:* Back, *Verwandlung,* 136, 141, 145, 148, etc. [on this, cf. n.56 below]; she plays off the Spirit against transformation by vision: 134, 146, cf. 20; however, see also 13, 133, 148, and her critique of Lambrecht, 141–42).

[48] A.F. Segal, *Paul the Convert: The Apostolate and Apostasy of Saul the Pharisee* (New Haven: Yale University Press, 1990), 60–61, implying an almost literal rendering of 'beholding/seeing as in a mirror'. For an interpretation of 3:18 as a reference to Paul's Damascus road experience, see more specifically Kim, *Perspective,* 167–68, 173, 191; Philip, *Origins,* 182–93. Dunn rightly points out that μεταμορφούμεθα may here include experiences of ecstasy (influenced by Jewish apocalyptic [esp. *2 Bar.* 51.3, 10] and his own special brand of mysticism) (Dunn, *Jesus and the Spirit,* 216; cf. Hafemann, *Paul,* 419). For a critical discussion of the value of *2 Bar.* 51 in this context, see Thrall, *Corinthians. I,* 294. For more on Pauline mysticism, see ch. 3 n.30.

[49] Cf. the formulations of God's presence in Exod. 34: 'The LORD descended in the cloud and stood with him there' (v.5), and 'He was there with the LORD forty days and forty nights' (v.28). – On 2 Cor. 3:12–18 as a 'midrash' on Exod. 34:29–35, see J.D.G. Dunn, *Beginning from Jerusalem;* Christianity in the Making 2 (Grand Rapids/Cambridge: Eerdmans, 2009), 847–48 and the literature cited there.

glory has passed Moses by (33:19, 20–23; cf. 34:6–8).[50] More explicitly, in Numbers 12:8 LXX God says with regard to Moses that 'I speak to him mouth to mouth apparently, and not in dark speeches; and he has seen the glory of the Lord' (cf. Philo, *Leg. All.* 3.101–103). This indicates that Moses' experience of God on Mount Sinai can be comprehended both as reception of (oral) revelation as well as a visionary encounter.[51]

In the same way in which 'the familiarity with God transforms Moses',[52] so also Christians are transformed in the new era through encountering God. Hafemann explains that 2 Corinthians 3:18 is an expression of real participation in the presence of God in Christ mediated through the Spirit.[53] Beholding the revelation of God's presence, that is, the glory of God, effects transformation into his likeness.[54] We will discuss this means of transformation in more detail as we now look at the interpretation of 'beholding' as contemplation.

2.1.2.3. Beholding as Contemplation

The *Oxford English Dictionary* defines 'to contemplate' as '1. to look at with continued attention, gaze upon, view, observe… (Now usually with mixture of sense 2: To observe or look at thoughtfully)'.[55] Accordingly, the word 'contemplation' encompasses both visual as well as mental beholding. For this reason we suggest that conceptualizing 'beholding as in a mirror' in 3:18 as 'contemplating' is a welcome *via media* between those interpretations that render the word mainly metaphorically as referring to a deeper understanding of Christ via the gospel and those that emphasize the visionary aspect of an encounter with Christ as mirror and glory of God.[56] An additional reason for comprehending beholding as contemplation is the fact that a number of scholars have shown that the 'mechanism' of transformation in 3:18 may be well explained by the ancient notion of 'transformation through contemplation' (as e.g. in Plato, *Tim.* 90c–d; etc.).[57]

---

[50] Thrall observes that in the LXX, παρέρχομαι is used in 33:22 of the passing by of the δόξα and in 34:6 of the passing of the κύριος (Thrall, *Corinthians. I*, 295).

[51] Cf. Ibid., 295.

[52] Zeller, 'Métamorphose', 170.

[53] Hafemann, *Paul*, 419.

[54] Cf. J.M. Scott, *2 Corinthians*; NIBCNT 8 (Carlisle: Paternoster, 1998), 82; Garland, *2 Corinthians*, 199–200.

[55] *OED²*, III, 811.

[56] On these two aspects, cf. Meier, *Mystik*, 92–94, and, less explicitly, Barrett, *Second Epistle*, 125; Gruber, *Herrlichkeit*, 280; Stegman, *Character*, 234–35, 241–42, 315 (with a stronger leaning towards the cognitive aspect).

[57] On the parallels in antiquity, see D. Sedley, '"Becoming like God" in the *Timaeus* and Aristotle', in T. Calvo and L. Brisson (eds.), *Interpreting the Timaeus – Critias: Proceedings of the IV Symposium Platonicum*; IPS 9 (Sankt Augustin: Academia, 1997),

According to this concept, transformation is 'von dem Bilde aus angeregt und bewirkt',[58] that is, its power is inherent within the object which is being observed.[59]

The motif of 'transformation through contemplation' has often been seen to have its origin in Hellenism.[60] Particularly the mystery cults were believed to have influenced Paul at this point;[61] but in current scholarship this theory does not meet with much support.[62] However, a more potent

---

332, 335–36; R. Reitzenstein, *Hellenistic Mystery-Religions: Their Basic Ideas and Significance*; PTMS 15 (Pittsburgh: Pickwick, 1978), 455–56; Behm, 'μεταμορφόω', 758; Keener, *Corinthians*, 170. In addition, Horn mentions the following (post-Pauline) references: Porphyry, *Marc.* 13; Apuleius, *Met.* 11.23–24; *Odes* 13.1–4; *Acts John* 95, 111–13; *1 Clem.* 36.2; *Corp. Herm.* 4.11 (Horn, *Angeld*, 425; cf. the references to *Corp. Herm.* in Furnish, *Corinthians*, 240).

[58] H. Windisch, *Der zweite Korintherbrief*; KEK NT 6 (Göttingen: Vandenhoeck & Ruprecht, 1924[9]), 128.

[59] Cf. Horn, *Angeld*, 428; Sokolowski, *Geist*, 63; Bultmann, *Korinther*, 98; K. Prümm, *Diakonia Pneumatos: Der Zweite Korintherbrief als Zugang zur apostolischen Botschaft. Vol. II/1: Apostolat und christliche Wirklichkeit: Theologie des ersten Briefteils, Kap. 1–7* (Freiburg: Herder, 1960), 276.

[60] See some of the sources cited in n.57 above, and the summary in van Unnik, 'Face', 195, which is read by Fitzmyer as an agreement by van Unnik with this view (J.A. Fitzmyer, S.J., 'Glory Reflected on the Face of Christ (2 Cor 3:7–4:6) and a Palestinian Jewish Motif', *TS* 42 (1981), 643). However, Fitzmyer overlooks that in contrast to the scholars that van Unnik had described, van Unnik himself believes in the same way as Fitzmyer that Paul's mysticism is Jewish-Christian and not Hellenistic (van Unnik, 'Face', 209). Garland highlights the fact that the moral axiom of becoming like the gods we serve is also found elsewhere in Paul himself, e.g. Rom. 1:18–32 (Garland, *2 Corinthians*, 200).

[61] So, e.g., Reitzenstein who argued against this background that 3:18 suggests the believer's ἀποθέωσις (or substantial μεταμόρφωσις) through the reception of the Spirit. Reitzenstein deduced this from the connection of the words δόξα and πνεῦμα which, for him, evidenced the thought of complete transformation of the nature of the believer through γνῶσις θεοῦ (Reitzenstein, *Mystery-Religions*, 454–59; cf. Heitmüller, *Paulus*, 20–21; Sokolowski, *Geist*, 63–64; Bousset, *Kyrios*, 227 n.68). For a more recent materialistic interpretation of δόξα as 'light-substance', see Koenig, 'Glory', 160–61. See also Prümm, *Diakonia. I*, 192–93 (however, see his criticism of Reitzenstein: Prümm, *Diakonia. I*, 176); Hulmi, *Paulus*, 92. Cf. ch. 3 n.59.

[62] While there clearly is some affinity between Paul's language and that of Hellenistic mysticism, a closer look uncovers that the common ground hardly reaches beyond verbal parallels. For one thing, the transformation in 3:18 is by *Spirit-wrought* beholding of the glory of the Lord, not by means of ritual exercises of the believers (cf. 4:7). Secondly, Paul is talking of a process (μεταμορφούμεθα [present tense] ἀπὸ δόξης εἰς δόξαν, cf. 6.2.2.1. below) rather than of instantaneous, magical transformation (cf. Bultmann, *Korinther*, 98; Horn, *Angeld*, 426). Thirdly, in this present age the vision of the glory of the Lord has provisional character (2 Cor. 5:7; 1 Cor. 13:12; Rom. 8:24). And finally, within the cotext of our passage, Paul characterizes Christian existence as 'carrying-around the death of Jesus', and contrasts with the 'present slight affliction' the promised

way of explaining the logic behind this mode of transformation against a Hellenistic background has been presented by Weissenrieder's recent research on ancient conceptions of 'looking into a mirror'. She expounds that in antiquity seeing was comprehended as the radiation of rays by both the eye as well as by the object that is viewed. Seeing is thus a kind of 'feedback' that works via the compression of the air between object and eye. Weissenrieder continues that the expected result of looking into a mirror was not the representation but the transformation of reality (mainly due to the making of mirrors out of metal rather than glass).[63] The examples that she analyses lead her to conclude that the beholders participate in the mirror image and are transformed by what they see.[64]

It is indeed possible that Paul's readers were familiar with this somewhat scientific explanation of 'transformation through contemplation' from their acquaintance with popular philosophy and literature. However, the most obvious background of the motif is the pentateuchal narrative of Moses' encounter with God on Mount Sinai itself. It follows from our discussion of Exodus 33–34 and Numbers 12:5–8 above that the narrative contains all the necessary elements for the elucidation of 'transformation through contemplation': Moses is transformed upon speaking with God and encountering his glory.[65] The pentateuchal tradition of Moses' transformation was broadly received in early Judaism,[66] particularly in Philo (esp. *Vit. Mos.* 2.69 [where inspiration by the Spirit and beholding of God are causally linked with Moses' transformation] and *Poster. C.* 12–13

'eternal weight of glory' (4:10, 17) (cf. W.G. Kümmel, *The Theology of the New Testament: According to Its Major Witnesses, Jesus – Paul – John* (London: SCM Press, 1974), 223; Behm, 'μεταμορφόω', 758–59). All of this leads to the conclusion that Paul is not talking about the present substantial deification of Christians. Rather, the transformation into the *image* or *likeness* (αὐτὴν εἰκόνα) of the glory of the Lord (and not into δόξα itself) maintains a certain distance between the divine and the human. Cf. A. Schlatter, *Paulus, der Bote Jesu Christi: Eine Deutung seiner Briefe an die Korinther* (Stuttgart: Calwer Verlag, 1962³ [1931¹]), 520–21; Furnish, *Corinthians*, 240–41; T.C. Smith, 'Influences That Shaped the Theology of Paul', *PRSt* 25 (1998), 151–62; Back, *Verwandlung*, 47–48, 156; Harris, *Corinthians*, 317.

[63] Cf. n.43 above.

[64] Weissenrieder, 'Blick', 315, 339, 342–43. Cf. Ashworth, who formulates on the basis of ἀνακεκαλυμμένῳ that 'people see and simultaneously come to participate in the glory that is seen; they become what they see' (T. Ashworth, *Paul's Necessary Sin: The Experience of Liberation* (Aldershot: Ashgate, 2006), 211).

[65] Cf. Thrall, *Corinthians. I*, 295 (however, see the critique by Back, *Verwandlung*, 147–49); Lambrecht, 'Transformation', 251.

[66] However, Back rightly points out that Moses' transformation was not always explicitly connected with the Sinai-narrative. Nonetheless, it was often seen as an authentication of Moses as recipient as well as mediator of divine revelation (Back, *Verwandlung*, 75). Cf. our discussion in 2.2.4.2.

[Moses wants to truly 'partake in the glory']; see the discussion in 5.1.1.)[67] and *Pseudo-Philo*.[68]

However, it seems that the pentateuchal narrative of Moses' transforming encounter with God is part of a broader Jewish tradition that is reflected in the Hebrew Scriptures and early Judaism. We have surveyed this tradition in 5.1. One strand of it employs very similar motifs to 2 Corinthians 3:18. For example, the Psalmist prays in Psalm 16:15 LXX: 'But I shall behold your face (τῷ προσώπῳ σου) in righteousness [and] I shall be satisfied [or: fed] upon beholding your glory (τὴν δόξαν σου).' The Psalmist thus expresses that beholding the glory of the Lord makes a difference in his life (cf. Ps. 63:1–8). That this difference may be understood as a kind of transformation comes more clearly to the fore in Psalm 33:6 LXX: 'Draw near to him, and be enlightened: and your faces shall not be ashamed.'[69]

---

[67] Back further mentions *Vit. Mos.* 1.57, where Moses is described as being transformed (μεταμορφούμενος) as a consequence of prophetic inspiration (Ibid., 148 n.82). However, in contrast to the tradition of Exod. 34, *Vit. Mos.* 2.66–70 and 2 Cor. 3, the narrative of *Vit. Mos.* 1.57 relates no encounter with God in the context of this inspiration. Nonetheless, Back suggests that 1.57 should be read in this light (Back, *Verwandlung*, 34).

[68] Back believes that her reading of 2 Cor. 3:18 as the reception of (cognitive) revelation (see 6.2.1.2.1. above and n.47) is particularly supported by the reception of Exod. 34 in *L.A.B.* 12.1 and 19.16 (Back, *Verwandlung*, 24–30). 19.16 indeed lends itself to this view because Pseudo-Philo comments that when Moses heard what God revealed to him, 'he was filled with understanding and his appearance became glorious'. However, it is a draw-back that 19.16 is the narration of Moses' *death* (on Mount Abarim) and not of his 'glorification' on Mount Sinai (related in Exod. 34 and 2 Cor. 3). Moreover, it is unfortunate that Back starts her reading of Pseudo-Philo's account of Moses' transformation on Mount Sinai only at 12.1 when Moses descends from the mountain. A closer look at the description of Moses' time *on the mountain*, however, demonstrates that limiting this experience to the reception of (cognitive) revelation does not do justice to the account. Rather, Moses is consciously aware that he will *meet* with God who was right there ('sciens quoniam ibi erat Deus', 11.15). This is also reflected in the response of the Israelites to the event: 'Behold, today we know that God speaks to a man *face to face* and that man may live' (11.14). Hence, the Sinai event is about meeting with God, and (cognitive) revelation is one part of this personal encounter. This is further confirmed by the parallel that is drawn by Pseudo-Philo with Joseph's meeting with his brothers. In Pseudo-Philo's synopsis of that encounter, the writer seems to place special emphasis on the (experiential) recognition of the brothers rather than on the revelation of cognitive insights (*L.A.B.* 12.1).

[69] *Pace* Bousset, *Kyrios*, 222, who denies any OT background to 'transformation through contemplation'. On the desire for 'beholding God' (and its positive effects on the Psalmist), see more generally, Pss. 27:4; 42:1–5; 63:2; et al. On the OT background to the transforming work of the Spirit in 2 Cor. 3:18, see further Ezek. 36–37 (and the parallel in Jer. 31; cf. 5.1.3), as examined by C.K. Stockhausen, *Moses' Veil and the Glory of the New Covenant: The Exegetical Substructure of II Cor. 3,1–4,6*; AB 116 (Rome: Editrice

The Qumran Psalmist relates a similar experience: 'I praise you, Lord, for you have illumined my face with your covenant [...] I will seek you; like the true dawn of morning, you have appeared to me for enlightenment' (1QH^a 12.5–6; cf. 27–29; 11.3; 1QS 2.3).[70] Moreover, God has put Israel on new grounds (i.e. his covenant) by granting her both (cognitive) revelation by the Spirit as well as an encounter with his glory: 'You have renewed your covenant with them in the vision of glory, and in the words of your holy [spirit]' (1Q34 *frag. 3 col.* 2.6–7). That contemplation of God and his revelation leads to a transformation of the heart is further expressed by the author of 1QS 11.3–7: 'From the spring of his justice is my judgement and from the wonderful mystery is *the light in my heart. My eyes have observed what always is*, wisdom…, knowledge and prudent understanding…, [which is the] fount of justice and well of strength….'

Also Philo is part of this tradition when he explains that 'just as one who comes near the light is straightaway illumined, so also is filled the entire soul of him to whom God has appeared' (*Quaest. in Exod.* 2.7).[71] One of the clearest parallels to 2 Corinthians 3:18 in Philo, however, is *De Migratione Abrahami* 34–36. There Philo speaks about his state of divine inspiration during which he is 'filled with amazement at the might of Him that IS to Whom is due the opening and closing of the soul-wombs'. He says that

Now the thing shewn is the thing *worthy to be seen* [Yonge: *beheld*], *contemplated, loved* (ἀξιόρατον καὶ ἀξιοθέατον καὶ ἀξιέραστόν), the perfect good, *whose nature it is to change all that is bitter in the soul and make it sweet*, fairest seasoning of all spices, turning into salutary nourishment even foods that do not nourish… (Ex. xv. 25) (*Migr.* 36).

Pontificio Instituto Biblico, 1989), 42–86; H. Hübner, 'Der Heilige Geist in der Heiligen Schrift', *KD* 36 (1990), 203; S.J. Hafemann, 'The "Temple of the Spirit" as the Inaugural Fulfilment of the New Covenant within the Corinthian Correspondence', *ExAud* 12 (1996), 36–42; Turner, *Spirit*, 114–16; J.-C. Maschmeier, *Rechtfertigung bei Paulus: Eine Kritik alter und neuer Paulusperspektiven*; BWANT 189 (Stuttgart: Kohlhammer, 2010), 110–13. However, see the hesitance of O. Hofius, 'Gesetz und Evangelium nach 2. Korinther 3', in O. Hofius, *Paulusstudien. Vol. 1*; WUNT 51 (Tübingen: Mohr Siebeck, 1994²), 120, and the critical discussion of Hafemann's methodology of applying these texts to 2 Cor. 3 (Hafemann, *Paul*, e.g. 156–73) by J. Schröter, 'Schriftauslegung und Hermeneutik in 2 Korinther 3: Ein Beitrag zur Frage der Schriftbenutzung des Paulus', *NovT* 40 (1998), esp. 245, 249, 253. Scott further sees Ezek. 1 in the background (J.M. Scott, 'The Triumph of God in 2 Cor. 2.14: Additional Evidence of Merkabah Mysticism in Paul', *NTS* 42 (1996), 277; Scott, *Corinthians*, 82–83, 100).

[70] Translation by Fitzmyer, 'Glory', 640. On the distribution of this illumination to others, see 1QH^a 12.27–28.

[71] See 5.1.1. Cf. *2 Bar.* 51.3, 10.

Here we see the concept of beholding and contemplating God in a loving relationship which leads to a (religious-ethical [cf. *Migr.* 37]) transformation ('change') and empowering ('nourishment') of the soul. This is further expressed in *De Legatione ad Gaium* 4–5: 'how firmly based is *the virtue and nobility of conduct* which we may expect to find in souls whose vision has soared above all created things and schooled itself to *behold the uncreated and divine*'.

What is more, both Philo and Qumran see the divine Spirit as playing a central role in stimulating a transforming relationship with God. As we have demonstrated in detail in chapter 5, the Spirit provides both cognitive-noetic as well as existential-mystical knowledge of God that transforms and empowers the recipient for religious-ethical life (e.g. in Philo's *Quaest. in Exod.* 2.29, Moses is enabled by the Spirit to 'come near God in a kind of family relation' and is consequently 'changed into the divine'; cf. *Gig.* 54–55; etc. as at 5.1.1.; for Qumran, see, e.g., 1QH^a 8.19–20; 20.11–14; etc. as at 5.1.2.).[72] It is this tradition – next to the pentateuchal narrative of Moses' transformation – that is most prominently in the background of the concept of 'transformation through contemplation' in 2 Corinthians 3:18 because it not only relates transformation as a consequence of encountering God and receiving divine revelation, but it also accommodates the important role of the Spirit in this process that is attributed to κυρίου πνεύματος in 3:18. We will turn to this agency of the Spirit in the next section.

We can *conclude* that there is ample evidence that both 'unveiling' as well as 'beholding' in 3:18 are relational activities which are seen to be instrumental in the process of transformation. This can be explained through the notion of 'transformation through contemplation' which has a broad basis in early Judaism, particularly in the Qumran-community and Philo, who see the Spirit as an important agent in this process. In this tradition, however, the power of transformation is not only inherent in the object of contemplation (as suggested by some Hellenistic sources), but also in the dynamics of the very relationship to the object (i.e. transformation through an intimate relationship with God). We have seen in chapter 4 that the transforming effects of such a dynamic are also attested by Paul's

---

[72] This tradition is further reflected in non-Pauline strands of the NT; see esp. 1 Jn. 3:2: 'when he is revealed, we will be like him, for we will see him as he is' (cf. R. Schnackenburg, *Die Johannesbriefe*; HTKNT (Freiburg: Herder, 2002^7 [1984^7]), 171–74). Of the references mentioned by Horn in n.57 above, esp. *Odes* 13 fits the evidence of 2 Cor. 3:18 because the Spirit appears to play a role similar to that of the Jewish sources cited above ('Behold, the Lord is our mirror. Open [your] eyes and see them in him. And learn the manner of your face, then declare praises to his Spirit... Then you will be unblemished at all times with him.'). However, on the somewhat limited value of this text see ch. 5 n.72.

anthropology and theology more generally as well as by modern psychological research.

We may finally ask for the *Sitz im Leben* of 'beholding as in a mirror' – when and where does it happen? Philip appears to be slightly too narrow-minded when he identifies κατοπτριζόμενοι almost exclusively with Paul's conversion on the road to Damascus, employed by Paul to defend his authority as an apostle.[73] While 'beholding' may include conversion (cf. 'turning to the Lord' in 3:16), it is clearly not limited to it, and particularly not limited to Paul's conversion. As we have argued above, Paul includes all believers as the recipients of the effects of the new covenant ministry. Furthermore, κατοπτριζόμενοι is not only a plural but also a present tense (like μεταμορφούμεθα), which suggests a continuous activity. We may thus submit with Hafemann and others that 'beholding the glory of the Lord' takes place, for one thing, through the existential confrontation that is brought about by the preaching of the gospel of Jesus Christ (cf. 6.2.1.2.1. above). However, 'inasmuch as the Gospel unleashes the power of the Spirit, the glory of God is also revealed through the renewed lives of those who now possess the Spirit as his "temple" (cf. esp. 1 Cor. 6:19f.)'.[74] Further, this proclamation of the gospel is inextricably bound up with Paul's ministry of suffering (cf. 2 Cor. 2:14–17; 4:7–18).[75] It is therefore possible to say that the glory of the Lord is beheld in the 'richness of authentic Christian life',[76] particularly when the presence of the Lord is experienced individually and corporately in the worship of the gathered community (in the Lord's Supper, in songs, Scriptures, teachings and revelations, etc.; see, e.g., 1 Cor. 14:26; Rom. 8:15–16; Gal. 4:6; cf. 6.3. and 6.4.).[77]

2.1.3. The Role of the Spirit

We have argued above that believers are transformed by means of deeper knowledge of and an intimate encounter with the (glory of the) Lord. However, Paul not only ascribes the transformation to the unveiling of the faces and to the (resulting) beholding of the glory of the Lord, but he also specifies that this is achieved *by the Spirit*. When Paul at the end of 3:18

---

[73] Philip, *Origins*, 189–90; cf. 182–93. Cf. C.C. Newman, *Paul's Glory-Christology: Tradition and Rhetoric*; NovTSup 69 (Leiden: Brill, 1992), 233–35; Kim, *Perspective*, 167–74.

[74] Hafemann, *Paul*, 425.

[75] Cf. Ibid., 425.

[76] Lambrecht, 'Transformation', 250–51. Cf. the still broader formulation of Preß: the place of this transformation is 'der ganze Geist-Raum "en Christo"' (Preß, *Jesus*, 142).

[77] Cf. Bousset, *Kyrios*, 159; Hafemann, *Paul*, 426; Gruber, *Herrlichkeit*, 283–84; Garland, *2 Corinthians*, 200. See esp. the very nuanced Thrall, *Corinthians. I*, 284–85; Meier, *Mystik*, 92–94.

says that καθάπερ ἀπὸ κυρίου πνεύματος, he puts forward that the origin or agency (ἀπό) of the relational work of unveiling and beholding that causes the transformation is to be expected (καθάπερ, 'just as') from the Spirit. A paraphrase of the verse could therefore be formulated like this:

As a result of the work of the Spirit, we are all transformed into the same image, from one glory to another.
The transformation takes place by means of an unveiled face
and by means of beholding the glory of the Lord as in a mirror,
just as this is accomplished from the Lord, the Spirit.[78]

There has been a great deal of debate whether to render κυρίου πνεύματος as 'the Lord, who is the Spirit' (RSV, NIV, etc.), 'the Spirit of the Lord' (KJV, Thrall, etc.), or still differently,[79] and whether the 'Lord' here refers to YHWH (as in Exodus 34) or to Christ.[80] However, for our purposes it is not necessary to recapitulate the discussion here or argue for one of the options because there is no debate with regard to what is significant for our argument, namely, that the forgone activities and the resulting transformation are ascribed to the work of *the Spirit*.[81]

The means of the transforming work of the Spirit in 3:18 are thus *relational*: the believer is brought into the presence of the Lord (cf. 3:17a)[82] and an intimate relationship is established through the unveiling of the faces and the contemplation of the (glory of the) Lord. Stated concisely in

---

[78] Cf. Hafemann, *Paul*, 427.

[79] Thrall and Harris provide helpful discussions of the various interpretative options (Thrall, *Corinthians. I*, 287–88; Harris, *Corinthians*, 317–18).

[80] The interpretation of κύριος in 3:18 usually depends on how one identifies κύριος in 3:17a. However, Prümm thinks that in 3:17a 'the Lord' is YHWH, whereas in 3:18 it is Christ (Prümm, *Diakonia. I*, 170). Those who take κύριος to refer to YHWH include Dunn, '2 Corinthians III. 17', 318; Fitzmyer, 'Glory', 631–32; Furnish, *Corinthians*, 242; N. Richardson, *Paul's Language about God*; JSNTSup 99 (Sheffield: Sheffield Academic Press, 1994), 156; Turner, *Spirit*, 116; L.L. Belleville, 'Paul's Polemic and the Theology of the Spirit in Second Corinthians', *CBQ* 58 (1996), 300–302; Gruber, *Herrlichkeit*, 283; Marshall, *Theology*, 430; Harris, *Corinthians*, 317–18. Those who prefer a Christological interpretation include Hermann, *Kyrios*, 54–58; Hill, *Words*, 278; Di Fortunato, *Gramma*, 129; Hofius, 'Gesetz', 119; Schröter, 'Schriftauslegung', 271–72; Fatehi, *Relation*, 289–302; Luz, 'Paul', 136.

[81] Cf. Barrett, *Second Epistle*, 126. On the pneumatological emphasis of the transformation, cf. Thrall, *Corinthians. I*, 288; Fee, *Presence*, 319; Back, *Verwandlung*, 146 (although she is unclear how this relates to the unveiling and beholding: see n.47 above); Philip, *Origins*, 190; Harris, *Corinthians*, 318. The only interpretation of κυρίου πνεύματος that could diminish this accentuation is 'the Lord of the Spirit'. However, Thrall rightly rules out this option as it has no NT parallels. Moreover, she draws attention to a parallel text where both κύριος and πνεῦμα are mentioned (Rom. 8:11, 13–15). Also there 'it is the Spirit, not "the Lord", that is the transformative agent' (Thrall, *Corinthians. I*, 287, cf. 288).

[82] On 3:17a, cf. Hill, *Words*, 278; Fee, *Presence*, 319; et al.

Dunn's words: 'the distinctive mark of the eschatological Spirit is an immediacy of relationship with God which makes the believer more like Jesus (if we may use such simple, pietistic language).'[83] Dunn builds this conclusion on 3:18, but he does not unfold how the Spirit creates this intimate relationship[84] and how this transforms the believer. However, we have provided a detailed analysis of exactly that in the first part of our discussion of 3:18. In the second part we will now look more closely at the ethical dimension of the transformation.

2.2. What is the Result of the Transformation?

We have established in 6.2.1. that the transformation in 2 Corinthians 3:18 is achieved by the relational work of the Spirit. The aim of 6.2.2. is to demonstrate that this transformation has an ethical aspect. Before we will do so below, we will briefly take a more general look at the concept of transformation in 3:18.

2.2.1. The Meaning of 'Being Transformed from Glory to Glory'

In the delineation of our usage of the term 'transformation' in the Prolegomena to Part II (4.1.) we have indicated that the dictionary definitions of μεταμορφόω ('to change in form' or 'to change inwardly in fundamental character or condition') leave open the precise nature of the change (e.g. how 'substantial' or complete it is, whether it refers to 'inward' or 'outward' change, etc.). In order to get closer to the meaning of μεταμορφούμεθα as well as the adverbial qualification ἀπὸ δόξης εἰς δόξαν in 3:18, we will ask whether the transformation is physically visible and whether it refers to a progressive development.

Moses was *physically* transformed upon his encounter with God on Mount Sinai (2 Cor. 3:7, 13). Some scholars assume on this basis (and other sources like the apocryphal *Acts of Paul* 2.3) that this characteristic also applies to the transformation described in 3:18.[85] However, 3:8 indi-

---

[83] Dunn, *Jesus and the Spirit*, 320.

[84] Dunn seems to derive this creation of intimacy with God by the Spirit from the notion of transformation τὴν αὐτὴν εἰκόνα. He thinks that as Jesus is the image of God, transformation 'into Christ' means having the same intimate relationship to God as Christ has (Ibid., 320; cf. de Oliveira, *Diakonie*, 222–23). However, while Dunn is certainly correct with his contention in view of Paul's overall pneumatology, it does not appear that this is Paul's concern in the present text.

[85] E.g. Thüsing, *Christum*, 127; van Unnik, 'Face', 208; C. Wolff, *Der zweite Brief des Paulus an die Korinther*; THKNT 8 (Berlin: Evangelische Verlagsanstalt, 1989), 79; N. Baumert, *Mit dem Rücken zur Wand: Übersetzung und Auslegung des zweiten Korintherbriefes*; Paulus neu gelesen (Würzburg: Echter, 2008), 71; Engberg-Pedersen, 'Transformation', 137–40 (building on a material concept of πνεῦμα). Cf. Scott, *Corinthians*,

cates that the 'glory' of the 'ministry of the Spirit' will transcend that of Moses. This might suggest that the 'glory' of 3:18c, superseding the glory of Moses, is not focussed on outward appearance (although it may include it; cf. 4:10–11). Moreover, when Paul *does* address physical transformation, he speaks of the resurrection body which is conferred instantly and in the future, not gradually in the present (1 Cor. 15:52–53, cf. section 3.1.; 2 Cor. 4:14; Rom. 8:11; Phil. 3:21).[86] Apart from this, it is questionable whether Paul wants to say that the aim or outcome of the transformation is 'glory' (as a state of the believer), because believers are not described in 3:18 to be transformed εἰς δόξαν but τὴν αὐτὴν εἰκόνα (which precedes μεταμορφούμεθα in a parallel fashion as τὴν δόξαν κυρίου precedes κατοπτριζόμενοι).[87] In the light of all this it seems most likely that the transformation of believers means that the 'life and death' of Christ becomes manifest in them (4:7–15). This may include their bodies (4:10–11),[88] but it is focussed on the 'inner being' (4:6, 16; cf. 3:15–16)[89] and is particularly visible in their Christ-like behaviour,[90] so that they represent Christ to the world.[91]

It has been mentioned above that the history-of-religions approach to the transformation in 3:18 is not convincing because, among other reasons, the transformation is portrayed by Paul not as an instant deification but as *gradual* or continuous.[92] This is evinced by Paul's use of the present

---

82–83, who, however, sees the physical aspect of the transformation as proleptic. See also the Synoptic tradition of the transfiguration of Jesus (Mk. 9:2–3//s), and the potential parallels in extra-biblical literature mentioned in Belleville, *Reflections*, 282.

[86] Cf. Prümm, *Diakonia. I*, 185; J.W. Yates, *The Spirit and Creation in Paul*; WUNT II/251 (Tübingen: Mohr Siebeck, 2008), 147–51.

[87] Cf. Garland, *2 Corinthians*, 200. See n.62 above, and the discussion below of ἀπὸ δόξης εἰς δόξαν and τὴν αὐτὴν εἰκόνα.

[88] V.H.T. Nguyen, *Christian Identity in Corinth: A Comparative Study of 2 Corinthians, Epictetus and Valerius Maximus*; WUNT II/243 (Tübingen: Mohr Siebeck, 2008), 193–94. However, see, e.g., Thrall, *Corinthians. I*, 337, who explains that Paul is 'thinking of the constant occasions of deliverance from mortal peril he has experienced, and in general of the power by which he is enabled to suffer without being totally overcome by suffering'.

[89] Cf. Jervell, *Imago*, 193–94; Furnish, *Corinthians*, 242; Lang, *Korinther*, 276; Horn, *Angeld*, 427–28; Garland, *2 Corinthians*, 200; C. Tilling, 'Paul's Divine-Christology: The Relation Between the Risen Lord and Believers in Paul, and the Divine-Christology Debate' (Brunel University: Unpublished PhD Thesis, 2010), 105. See esp. the syntactical and theological parallels between 3:18 and 4:16 drawn out by Buchegger, *Erneuerung*, 135–36.

[90] Cf. Harris, *Corinthians*, 316.

[91] Cf. Back, *Verwandlung*, 152–54, although she denies that there is an ethical dimension to this.

[92] See esp. n.62 above.

tense.[93] However, is this also the idea of the phrase 'from glory to glory'? Those who take εἰς δόξαν to be the aim of the transformation usually see ἀπὸ δόξης as its basis or source and hence do not believe that the phrase indicates gradual transformation. Rather, they think that the first δόξα refers to the glory of God that causes the transformation of believers into δόξα.[94] This agrees with our view of the relational transformation through beholding 'the glory of the Lord' presented in 6.2.1.2. above. The main argument that speaks for this interpretation is the fact that in the succeeding phrase, καθάπερ ἀπὸ κυρίου πνεύματος, ἀπό is causative too.[95]

However, other scholars insist that both occurrences of δόξα have the same referent (i.e. the glory of believers).[96] Therefore, the phrase 'from glory to glory' emphasizes – in contrast to Moses' glory that faded away (3:11, 13) – 'the non-fading reality and ever-increasing dimension of the glory that is now ours through the ministry of the Spirit – as we continually behold Christ and are being constantly renewed into his likeness.'[97]

Both of these interpretations of ἀπὸ δόξης εἰς δόξαν are attractive. However, we can agree with Horn that it does not really matter which of

---

[93] That Paul is using the present tense with a present continuous aspect is indicated by the fact that κατοπτριζόμενοι is in the present tense too (cf. the present tense in vv.14b–15, intensified by 'to this very day'), both standing in contrast to the past tense of the old covenant (vv.7–14a), and both relating non-punctiliar action (cf. Wallace, *Greek*, 517–18, on verbs prone to the punctiliar present).

[94] So e.g. Sokolowski, *Geist*, 62–66; Wolff, *Zweite Brief*, 79; de Oliveira, *Diakonie*, 227; Wright, *Climax*, 188; Newman, *Glory-Christology*, 227; Hafemann, *Paul*, 414; Gruber, *Herrlichkeit*, 270.

[95] Cf. e.g. Schlatter, *Paulus*, 521; Meier, *Mystik*, 84.

[96] So e.g. Thrall, *Corinthians. I*, 286. This rendering may be further supported by the potential parallel in *2 Bar.* 51.3, 7, 10.

[97] Fee, *Presence*, 318. Cf. Behm, 'μεταμορφόω', 758; Hill, *Words*, 278; van Unnik, 'Face', 209; Bultmann, *Korinther*, 98; Barrett, *Second Epistle*, 125; R.P. Martin, *2 Corinthians*; WBC 40 (Dallas: Word, 1986), 72; Di Fortunato, *Gramma*, 127; Scott, *Corinthians*, 82; Kim, *Perspective*, 174; W. Schrage, 'Schöpfung und Neuschöpfung bei Paulus in Kontinuität und Diskontinuität', *EvT* 65 (2005), 256. This notion of development is not one of idealism (although Prümm, *Diakonia. I*, 185, 193, 200, may come close to this philosophy); rather, the culmination of the transformation will take place in the eschaton. Cf. G. Kittel, 'δόξα', *TDNT*, II, 251; Lang, *Korinther*, 276; Samra, *Christ*, 101–102. An alternative interpretation along the lines of the contrast between the ministry of Moses and Paul has recently been suggested by Duff. He paraphrases this part of v.18 thus: 'Like Christ, we are being transformed *from* (the ministry of) *death to* (the ministry of) *life* (i.e., "from glory to glory") because Moses' glorious ministry brought condemnation and the sentence of death upon us but my ministry (i.e., the ministry of the Spirit and righteousness) brings reconciliation with God which is tantamount to life' (P.B. Duff, 'Transformed "from Glory to Glory": Paul's Appeal to the Experience of His Readers in 2 Corinthians 3:18', *JBL* 127 (2008), 774, italics added).

the two one chooses.[98] The idea of gradual or continual transformation is also indicated by the present tense of μεταμορφούμεθα, and the notion of transformation through divine glory is prominent in the phrase 'beholding the glory of the Lord' (with its slightly stronger emphasis on the instrumental function of the *relationship* to [the glory of] the 'Lord' than the short ἀπὸ δόξης).

However, it *does* matter for our thesis that the transformation in 3:18 has an ethical dimension. To this we finally turn.

2.2.2. The Ethical Dimension of the Transformation ('Being Transformed... into the Same Image')

Most scholars believe that the transformation described in 2 Corinthians 3:18 has an ethical dimension. However, this view has recently been challenged by Back. Arguing against Schlatter, Hafemann and many others,[99] she contends that 'der Kontext von 2 Kor 3,18 spricht... dagegen, daß Paulus mit dem Verwandlungsgedanken ein ethisches Interesse verbindet. Er enthält für eine paränetische Deutung von 2 Kor 3,18 keine Hinweise.'[100] Back sees support for this claim in an article by Hofius.[101] However, while Hofius is hesitant to comprehend the transformation described in 3:18 as a fulfilment of Ezekiel 36:26–27,[102] he is nonetheless very explicit that 'transformation into the same image' in 3:18 means that believers 'become "in Christ" a καινὴ κτίσις – people who are set free from their

---

[98] Horn, *Angeld*, 426 (although, the grammatical basis on which Horn's point rests may be questioned: see Samra, *Christ*, 102 n.50). Cf. Stockhausen, *Veil*, 90 n.12. Gunkel thinks that it is not possible to interpret the phrase ἀπὸ δόξης εἰς δόξαν beyond any question (Gunkel, *Influence*, 125).

[99] See Back, *Verwandlung*, 153 nn.100–102, for a number of scholars who take 3:18 as relating to ethics. Here is a slightly more comprehensive list: Schlatter, *Paulus*, 521; E.E. Ellis, 'II Cor. 5:1–10 in Pauline Eschatology', *NTS* 6 (1959/60), 215; Thüsing, *Christum*, 128–29; Collange, *Énigmes*, 120–21; Dunn, *Jesus and the Spirit*, 320; M.D. Hooker, *From Adam to Christ: Essays on Paul* (Cambridge: Cambridge University Press, 1990), 63; Belleville, *Reflections*, 288; Thrall, *Corinthians. I*, 285; Hafemann, *Paul*, 421–24; Scott, *Corinthians*, 83; Garland, *2 Corinthians*, 201; Kim, *Perspective*, 174; Buchegger, *Erneuerung*, 132; Stegman, *Character*, 243; Harris, *Corinthians*, 315–16; less explicitly: Jervell, *Imago*, 191–94; Prümm, *Diakonia. I*, 180; K.H. Schelkle, *The Second Epistle to the Corinthians*; NTSR 14 (New York: Herder, 1969), 58; Vos, *Untersuchungen*, 142; Segal, *Convert*, 59–60; R.W. Scholla, S.I., 'Into the Image of God: Pauline Eschatology and the Transformation of Believers', *Greg* 78 (1997), 50–51; BDAG, 'μεταμορφόω', §2; J.D.G. Dunn, 'The New Perspective on Paul: Whence, What and Whither?', in J.D.G. Dunn, *The New Perspective on Paul: Collected Essays*; WUNT 185 (Tübingen: Mohr Siebeck, 2005), 76.

[100] Back, *Verwandlung*, 154.

[101] Ibid., 154 n.150, citing Hofius, 'Gesetz', 120.

[102] Hofius, 'Gesetz', 120. See further n.69 above.

old existence enslaved to sin and are endowed with a new, consecrated ["heilvoll"] existence.'[103] This definition, however, surely involves ethical enabling.

Nevertheless, Back intends to support her thesis further by pointing out that there is no connection between Romans 12:2 (where μεταμορφόω is used in a paraenetic context) and 2 Corinthians 3:18.[104] We will look at this potential correlation further below. However, we can already say that at least in her quotation above, Back appears to unduly limit the meaning of 'ethics' to 'paraenesis', which introduces a certain opacity into the discussion.[105] Additionally, it is even more difficult to fathom how Back's own definition of transformation could work as a contrast to the ethical interpretations that she dismisses. She writes that transformation means that believers 'become like Christ' – they are 'von Christus geprägt',[106] 'in das "Christusbild" verwandelt, das heißt, an die Christusgestalt angeglichen'.[107] According to Back, this transformation is overtly visible and should not be 'spiritualized', although it is not physically perceptible (as in Philo, *Vit. Mos.* 2.69–70; *Virt.* 217).[108] Rather, it means that believers make the glorified Christ present and visible, representing him to the world as a 'letter of Christ' (2 Cor. 3:3).[109] It seems, then, that Back's own definition of transformation hardly differs from an 'ethical interpretation' as that of Hafemann which she explicitly rejects. Hafemann believes that being transformed is 'to take on those attitudes and actions which correspond to the way in which Christ himself lived as the "second Adam"'.[110]

Apart from that, Back may be right that the focus of 2 Corinthians 3 is not on the individual. However, she appears to create a false antithesis when she contrasts the sanctification of the individual with the Christian witness of the larger group: 'Nicht die Verbesserung des Einzelnen steht in

---

[103] Ibid., 116.

[104] Back, *Verwandlung*, 151–52. *Pace* Horn and others (see n.89) she also disclaims a connection between 3:18 and 4:16.

[105] 'Paraenesis' is customarily defined as '(moral) exhortation'. However, it is plain from her categorization of the scholarly voices which she dismisses that she also uses the term 'ethical' in its usual, broader sense which corresponds to our own definition in 1.3.

[106] Back, *Verwandlung*, 152.

[107] Ibid., 149, cf. 151.

[108] Ibid., 152–53.

[109] Ibid., 151–52, 156.

[110] Hafemann, *Paul*, 422, quoted by Back, *Verwandlung*, 154. Perhaps one could argue that Back appears to place slightly more weight on the missiological aspect of the religious-ethical transformation than Hafemann does. However, the context of 3:18 as outlined below shows the interconnectedness of Christian witness and ethical living; see further 1 Thess. 2:9–12; 1 Cor. 9:27; et al. Cf. E.J. Schnabel, *Early Christian Mission. Vol. II: Paul & the Early Church* (Downers Grove/Leicester: IVP/Apollos, 2004), 1362–64.

2 Kor 3 zur Diskussion, sondern die Sichtbarkeit der christlichen Botschaft an der Gruppe der verwandelten Christen.'[111] However, if a group gets transformed in order to reflect the message of the gospel, how is it possible that this would not affect the individual members of the group? Moreover, what constitutes this making visible of the Christian message if it is reflected neither in outward appearance nor in ethical living? Back does not provide an answer to this fundamental question.[112]

As Back's critique of an ethical interpretation of the transformation in 3:18 raises more questions than it solves, we will use the remainder of this section to demonstrate that *there is compelling evidence to comprehend the transformation in 3:18 as having an ethical dimension.*

Some scholars who argue that the transformation described in 3:18 relates to ethics see the reason for this in the idea that believers are said to be changed 'into glory' (ϵἰς δόξαν).[113] However, while it is indeed possible to maintain that 'glory' may have an ethical connotation in a number of places in Paul (e.g. Rom. 1:23; 2:7; 3:23;[114] 8:30;[115] 1 Cor. 2:7;[116] cf. Eph. 3:16; 2 Thess. 2:14),[117] we have already indicated above that for grammatical reasons it seems more plausible that the aim of transformation in 3:18 is focussed on 'the same image'. For this reason, an investigation into the potential ethical nature of the transformation in 3:18 will have to focus on τὴν αὐτὴν εἰκόνα.

The best way to fathom the reference point of 'the same image' is by looking at 4:4.[118] There, Paul speaks about 'the light of the gospel of the glory of *Christ, who is the likeness of God.*' As Christ is described as the εἰκὼν τοῦ θεοῦ in 4:4, it is most likely that τὴν αὐτὴν εἰκόνα in 3:18 likewise refers to Christ.[119]

---

[111] Back, *Verwandlung*, 155.

[112] Perhaps Back could answer that the transformation is solely visible through preaching the gospel. However, her own more holistic formulations regarding the transformation speak against such a limited view. See n.110 above.

[113] So, e.g., Prümm, *Diakonia. I*, 192–93; *pace* Stalder, *Heiligung*, 164–65.

[114] Cf., e.g., Dunn, *Romans 1–8*, 168.

[115] Cf., e.g., Cranfield, *Romans. I*, 433.

[116] Cf., e.g., Barrett, *First Epistle*, 71.

[117] Cf. R.B. Gaffin, 'Glory, Glorification', *DPL*, 349. In the case of this interpretation, Paul's use of 'glory' in 2 Cor. 3:18 would be more influenced by the succeeding verses in chapter 4 rather than by the previous verses in chapter 3.

[118] Moreover, the above suggested background of Paul's mirror-metaphor in Wis. 7.26 also provides a parallel with regard to the concept of εἰκών. For Wisdom is not only 'a spotless mirror of the working of God' but also 'an image of his goodness' (εἰκὼν τῆς ἀγαθότητος αὐτοῦ). This, however, ascertains a clearly ethical character to the notion of εἰκών which is probably also in the background of Paul's employment of the term here.

[119] Cf. Col. 1:15. See, e.g., Prümm, *Diakonia. I*, 192, along with the majority of scholars. See also our discussion of δόξα κυρίου above. *Pace* Belleville, *Reflections*,

However, what is the significance of being transformed into the image of God, that is, Christ? To begin with, the creation account of Genesis 1:26–27 suggests itself as a potential theological background, as there humankind is said to be made in the image of God (κατ᾽ εἰκόνα θεοῦ ἐποίησεν, LXX).[120] However, it is clear from 2 Corinthians 3 that a transformation of humanity is nonetheless necessary,[121] because there is need for a new creation (5:17) in which the Christ-like character (being a 'letter of Christ') is 'written... with the Spirit of the living God... on tablets of human hearts' (3:3). This description of the contrast between the old covenant ('written... with ink... on tablets of stone', 3:3; 'their minds were hardened... to this very day', 3:14) and the new is reminiscent of Ezekiel 36:26–27, where the transformation is explicitly related to ethics (cf. 5.1.3.).[122]

Likewise, the concept of being a 'letter of Christ', or 'representing Christ to the world', as Back puts it,[123] has an ethical aspect because ethical living is part of the testimony in the world: 'Indeed, this is our boast, the testimony of our conscience: we have behaved in the world with frankness and godly sincerity, not by earthly wisdom but by the grace of God' (1:12; cf. 4:10–11; 10:3–6). This ethical dimension of the ministry in the world has its grounding in the change described in 3:3 and 3:18. It is further evident from the immediate cotext of 3:18, because in 4:1–2 Paul

---

290–91; cf. nn.25, 38 above. Yates draws on 1 Cor. 15:49 as a further parallel (Yates, *Spirit*, 115).

[120] Cf. Jervell, *Imago*, 173–77; Hafemann, *Paul*, 424; Buchegger, *Erneuerung*, 103–108. *Pace* Back, *Verwandlung*, 150.

[121] 2 Cor. 3, 6, 14; cf. Gen. 3; 2 Cor. 4:4, 6; 5:19, 21; Rom. 1:18–32; 3:23; *Apoc. Mos.* 20–21; etc. See further R. Scroggs, *The Last Adam: A Study in Pauline Anthropology* (London: Blackwell, 1966), 33–38.

[122] Cf. Ezek. 11:19–20; Jer. 38:33. Cf. Hafemann, *Paul*, 424; Schröter, 'Schriftauslegung', 272; Harris, *Corinthians*, 265; Stockhausen, *Veil*, 42–86, and n.69 above. Even Back herself emphasizes this background. She says that instead of the Torah, now Christ is written on the hearts of believers. 'Die Metapher vom „Brief Christi" signalisiert zum einen die... *reale Veränderung ihrer Person durch den Geistempfang*, zum anderen aber auch ihre Außenwirkung: Als „Brief" werden die Korinther von allen Menschen gelesen, das heißt, „Christus" wird an ihnen sichtbar' (Back, *Verwandlung*, 132, italics added). See further Rom. 2:29 and Phil. 3:3 which give additional evidence of relational transformation by the Spirit in Paul (on the covenant as a relational concept, see 4.3. above).

[123] See n.122 above, and Back, *Verwandlung*, 131 n.12; 156. In contrast to most commentators, Back takes Χριστοῦ not as subjective or authorial genitive but as genitive of content. The author of the letter is the Spirit and the content is Christ (cf. B. Kuschnerus, *Die Gemeinde als Brief Christi: Die kommunikative Funktion der Metapher bei Paulus am Beispiel von 2 Kor 2–5*; FRLANT 197 (Göttingen: Vandenhoeck & Ruprecht, 2002), 162–63; likewise Schröter, 'Schriftauslegung', 249 n.56, who, however, takes Paul to be the author). This agrees with ἐγγεγραμμένη... πνεύματι θεοῦ ζῶντος (3:3) and would parallel the concept of transformation 'into Christ' in 3:18.

causally connects the transformation of 3:18 both to the empowerment of his ministry ('*For this reason* [i.e. because of the transformation just described]... we do not lose heart.') as well as to its ethical standard ('We have renounced the shameful things that one hides; we refuse to practise cunning or to falsify God's word; but by the open statement of the truth we commend ourselves to the conscience of everyone in the sight of God.').

Still further clarity can be brought into the discussion of the ethical notion of transformation 'into the same image', that is Christ, when one looks at how Paul uses this idea elsewhere.[124] The most frequently cited parallel is found in Colossians 3:10. Although this verse is not part of the so-called 'undisputed Pauline epistles',[125] the concept of transformation in this text is nonetheless one of the clearest parallels to 2 Corinthians 3:18. Buchegger comments that 'die gesamte Erneuerungsaussage in Kol 3,10 (ἀνακαινούμενον... κατ᾽ εἰκόνα) gibt im Grunde das in 2 Kor 3,18 (und 4,16) beschriebene wieder'.[126] The concept of 'being transformed', or as Colossians puts it, of 'being renewed in knowledge after the image of its [i.e. that of the νέον ἄνθρωπον] creator' is overtly related to ethics in Colossians 3:10.[127] This is obvious from the fact that the renewal after God's image[128] is closely intertwined with 'putting on the new self' which is

---

[124] See Kim, *Perspective*, 166, for an extensive list of possible parallels. See also Samra's definition of 'being conformed to Christ': it refers to the 'actualization in the lives of believers of the attitudes and actions exemplified by Christ in his incarnation, life and death/resurrection so that the character of believers is aligned with or conformed to the character of Christ' (Samra, *Christ*, 3).

[125] On the methodology of using epistles which are part of the Pauline tradition but not necessarily written by Paul himself, see 1.4.

[126] Buchegger, *Erneuerung*, 247. Cf. T.B. Savage, *Power through Weakness: Paul's Understanding of the Christian Ministry in 2 Corinthians*; SNTSMS 86 (Cambridge: Cambridge University Press, 1996), 148, 151–52; et al.

[127] As in 2 Cor. 3:18, knowledge is a relational concept in Col. 3:10 as it is linked to God (cf. Col. 1:10; cf. the instrumental role of the mind in Rom. 12:2).

[128] Back seems to think that Col. 3:10–11 is not important for the discussion of 2 Cor. 3:18 because the former speaks about transformation into the image of God whereas the latter is about transformation into the image of the Lord, i.e. Christ (Back, *Verwandlung*, 150). However, she does not unfold in what way this difference is significant to the discussion. In any case, Dunn highlights that the concept of renewal into the divine image in Col. 3:10 'merges into Adam christology, where Christ as the divine image... is the middle term between the creator and his first creation and his re-creation (cf. Rom. 8:29; 1 Cor. 15:49; 2 Cor. 3:18; 4:4; cf. Ign. *Eph.* 20:1...). In this way Paul and Timothy in true Pauline style manage to hold together creation and salvation in the thought of Christ as both the creative power of God (1:15) and as the archetype for both creation and redeemed, renewed humanity' (J.D.G. Dunn, *The Epistles to the Colossians and to Philemon: A Commentary on the Greek Text*; NIGTC (Carlisle/Grand Rapids: Paternoster/Eerdmans, 1996), 222). Cf. the relation of putting on the 'new self' and 'putting on Christ' as elucidated below.

brought into ethical focus in the preceding verses (the practices of the *old self* are lying, etc., see esp. 3:9). Dunn explains that 'the thought is equivalent to "putting on Christ" in Rom. 13:14, as Col. 3:3–4 also implies. At its simplest, this means that the manner of Christ's living, as attested in the Jesus tradition, provided the pattern for this new self life (2:6–7)'.[129] Such an interlocking of being 'created according to the likeness of God', putting on the new self, and paraenesis can also be observed in the parallel text, Ephesians 4:24.[130] Here the transformation is described as happening in the ethical qualities of righteousness and holiness.[131]

However, also the 'undisputed epistles' show evidence of an ethical usage of the concept of transformation 'into Christ'. In Romans 8:29 Paul says that believers are 'predestined to be conformed to the image of his Son' (προώρισεν συμμόρφους τῆς εἰκόνος τοῦ υἱοῦ αὐτοῦ).[132] This passage is particularly interesting, as Dunn notes, because 'it draws together the thought of Rom. 8.14ff. and of II Cor. 3.18: to experience the Spirit's working is not only to experience sonship but also to become more like the Son, to take on increasingly the family likeness'.[133] The ethical significance of becoming more like the Son is more specifically drawn out by Cranfield. He explains that

the believers' final glorification is their full conformity to the εἰκών of Christ glorified; but it is probable… that Paul is here thinking not only of their final glorification but also of their growing conformity to Christ here and now in suffering and in obedience – that is, that συμμόρφους, κ.τ.λ. is meant to embrace sanctification as well as final glory, the former being thought of as a progressive conformity to Christ, who is the εἰκών of God,

---

[129] Dunn, *Colossians*, 221. Cf. G. Kittel, 'εἰκών', *TDNT*, II, 397; M.M. Thompson, *A Commentary on Colossians and Philemon*; THNTC (Grand Rapids: Eerdmans, 2005), 78. On the ethical aspect, see esp. J.H. Kim, *The Significance of Clothing Imagery in the Pauline Corpus*; JSNTSup 268 (London: T. & T. Clark, 2004), 174–75. On the notion of identification with Christ, see Lampe, 'Identification', 937.

[130] On the similarities and differences between Col. 3:9–11 and Eph. 4:22–24, see Buchegger, *Erneuerung*, 233–34.

[131] Righteousness and holiness are specified as characteristics of God in LXX Ps. 144:17 and Deut. 32:4. Cf. A.T. Lincoln, *Ephesians*; WBC 42 (Dallas: Word, 1990), 288; Kim, *Significance*, 187–91.

[132] Lambrecht notes that Paul uses the concept of *trans*formation in 3:18 (and Rom. 12:2) whereas he uses that of *con*formation in Rom. 8:29 and Phil. 3:10, 21. He explains that both terms refer to the same reality. Nonetheless, he concludes that 'a deeper unity, i.e., identity (be it without consequent loss of distinct being), is indicated more by transformation than by conformation' (Lambrecht, 'Transformation', 253–54, 251). See further the more detailed analysis of the semantic overlap of the verbs central to the parallel passages discussed in the present section, in Buchegger, *Erneuerung*, 156–62. For further parallel passages, see Samra, *Christ*, 74–75; Dunn, *Jesus and the Spirit*, 321.

[133] Dunn, *Jesus and the Spirit*, 321.

and so as a progressive renewal of the believer into that likeness of God which is God's original purpose for man (cf. Col. 3.9f).[134]

This thought is also expressed in Galatians 4:19, where Paul is concerned that 'Christ is formed' in the Galatians (μορφωθῇ Χριστὸς ἐν ὑμῖν).[135] In the situation of the Galatians' developing enmity towards Paul through turning away from him (and from the truth, 4:16) and returning into bondage to the beggarly elemental spirits (4:9; cf. 6.3.3.2.), that is, to the law (4:21), Paul is in (labour) pains that Christ within them (2:20) will shape the character of the community to such an extent that they will be able to 'share in the fullness and freedom of life "in the flesh" (2:20) which Christ himself had enjoyed – not least in regard to the law.'[136] This religious-ethical transformation also implies that the Galatians will be viable for life apart from Paul's presence among them (4:18, 20).[137]

It is surprising that none of the parallel texts outlined above are discussed by Back in her rebuttal of the ethical interpretations of 3:18. However, we have seen that they clearly give an (affirmative) answer to the question whether the phrase 'being transformed into the same image' has an ethical dimension. Nonetheless, in contrast to the above passages which evidence overt verbal *and conceptual* parallels with 3:18, Back is right that such correspondence cannot be established on the basis of a single verbal parallel alone, as in the case of Romans 12:2 which also employs μεταμορφόω. Back contends that the word has 'totally different meanings' in the two places, because in one case it is an indicative present passive (2 Cor. 3:18) whereas in the other it is an imperative present passive (Rom. 12:2).[138]

However, a closer look at Romans 12:2 reveals that Paul here uses a *passivum divinum* which indicates that God (the Spirit) is the one who achieves the transformation. The verb can be translated as 'continue to let yourselves be transformed'.[139] Romans 12:2 thus upholds the typical Pau-

---

[134] Cranfield, *Romans. I*, 432; cf. Kittel, 'εἰκών', 396–97.

[135] The best way to render ἐν ὑμῖν is 'among you' rather than 'in (each of) you' (Martyn, *Galatians*, 425 n.103; D.F. Tolmie, 'Liberty – Love – the Spirit: Ethics and Ethos according to the Letter to the Galatians', in J.G. van der Watt (ed.), *Identity, Ethics, and Ethos in the New Testament*; BZNW 141 (Berlin/New York: W. de Gruyter, 2006), 250 n.246). However, the former rendering implicitly includes the latter.

[136] Dunn, *Galatians*, 241. Cf. Longenecker, *Triumph*, 72, 158; Martyn, *Galatians*, 429–30. Cf. the ethical notion of 'having the mind of Christ' in 1 Cor. 2:16, which is linked to discernment in 2:15. See further Rom. 15:5 (κατὰ Χριστὸν Ἰησοῦν).

[137] Martyn, *Galatians*, 424.

[138] Back, *Verwandlung*, 154.

[139] C.E.B. Cranfield, *A Critical and Exegetical Commentary on the Epistle to the Romans. Vol. 2: Commentary on Romans IX–XVI and Essays*; ICC (Edinburgh: T. & T. Clark, 1979), 607. Cf. Buchegger, *Erneuerung*, 168–69; et al.

line tension of both indicative and imperative, whereas 2 Corinthians 3:18 just relates the indicative. Accordingly, the two verses do not display 'totally different meanings' of μεταμορφόω but use the same concept of (religious-ethical) transformation with slightly different nuances with regard to how much human involvement is indicated.[140] Therefore, as both verses use μεταμορφόω with an ethical connotation,[141] the way in which μεταμορφόω is employed in Romans 12:2 can be seen as an additional support that the Spirit-worked transformation in 2 Corinthians 3:18 has an ethical dimension.[142]

2.3. Conclusion

2 Corinthians 3:18 expounds a 'pivotal Pauline theme'.[143] While the language of the verse is very condensed and at times perplexing, the results of our unfolding of the passage show that its content is anything but 'nonsense'.[144] Rather, we were able to demonstrate that the verse evidences a relational concept of how the Spirit transforms people in order to facilitate religious-ethical life. Through the cognitive and the immediacy-creating character of 'unveiling', the Spirit enables people to be transformed through 'beholding the glory of the Lord as in a mirror'. We have argued that this activity is best comprehended through the concept of 'transformation through contemplation', which entails both deeper knowledge of as well as a personal encounter with the divine. On the basis of this Spirit-created intimate relationship to God in Christ, believers are transformed 'into the same image', that is, their lives portray more of the characteristics

---

[140] Cf. Buchegger, *Erneuerung*, 169; Behm, 'μεταμορφόω', 759; Lambrecht, 'Transformation', 251; Horn, *Angeld*, 427; Savage, *Power*, 147. Those who think that human involvement is nonetheless implied in 2 Cor. 3:18 include Stalder, *Heiligung*, 56; Garland, *2 Corinthians*, 201; Buchegger, *Erneuerung*, 295; Keener, *Corinthians*, 171; and, seeing the human involvement explicitly in κατοπτριζόμενοι: Stegman, *Character*, 241–42.

[141] This is indicated in Romans 12:2 through its usage in an ethico-paraenetical context (Buchegger, *Erneuerung*, 187), and indicated in 2 Corinthians 3:18 through its usage in a religious-ethical context (2 Cor. 3:3; 4:1–2) as well as through the notion of a Christ-like character as the expressed aim of the transformation (cf. the parallel passages above). On the basis of Rom. 8:29 Samra sees the image of Christ to be also the object of μεταμορφοῦσθε in Rom. 12:2 (Samra, *Christ*, 99).

[142] Cf. Stegman, *Character*, 243. Further, Belleville, *Reflections*, 287–88, points out that μεταμορφόω is used in Plutarch, *Mor.* 52E and Philo, *Spec. Leg.* 4.147 with regard to attitude and moral character.

[143] Jervell, *Imago*, 190. Cf. Lambrecht, 'Transformation', 254, who concludes that the verse explains 'the essence of Christian life.'

[144] *Pace* Ashton, *Religion*, 138, who surmises regarding Paul's theology of transformation in general and 2 Cor. 3:18 in particular: 'Most of this is, strictly speaking, nonsense.'

of Christ. We have seen from the way how Paul uses this concept in its context in 2 Corinthians 3:18 and elsewhere that 'becoming more like Christ' (cf. Rom. 8:29; Gal. 4:19) evidently encompasses enabling for religious-ethical life.

3. Ethical Empowering through a Spirit-Shaped Filial Relationship with God (Rom. 8:12–17; et al.)

Pauline scholarship has frequently failed to pay adequate attention to the connection between Spirit-worked sonship of God and ethics. This is the (justified) observation of Burke in his recent monograph *Adopted into God's Family*. He writes that the 'ethical perspective of *huiothesia* is an important one for the apostle and has often been overlooked by commentators and scholars in the past. Burke (1995: 64) says, "the *ethical* responsibility for God's sons to live circumspectly pervades Paul's thesis of adoption"....'[145]

However, in this section we will go beyond Burke's judgment and maintain that previous scholarship has not so much missed the fact that Paul employs the motif of sonship with a sense of moral obligation[146] but that scholars (including Burke himself) have rather failed to see that Paul comprehends this Spirit-created filial relationship with God as an *empowerment* for ethical living.[147] In order to demonstrate that believers draw strength and motivation for religious-ethical life from their adoption into God's family and the loving relationship thus initiated by the Spirit, we will focus in this section on how Paul connects these two themes in Romans 8:12–17. In this context we will also look at the parallel passage Galatians 4:1–9 as well as further texts on sonship and empowering love imparted by the Spirit (6.3.3.2.).

---

[145] T.J. Burke, *Adopted into God's Family: Exploring a Pauline Metaphor*; NSBT 22 (Downers Grove: IVP, 2006), 42, citing T.J. Burke, 'The Characteristics of Paul's Adoptive-Sonship (HUIOTHESIA) Motif', *IBS* 17 (1995), 64.

[146] Next to Burke, see Pfister, *Paulus*, 70–71; H. Giesen, 'Söhne und Töchter Gottes kraft des Geistes: Zur ekklesialen Dimension des Christseins', in J. Eckert, et al. (eds.), *Pneuma und Gemeinde: Christsein in der Tradition des Paulus und Johannes*; FS J. Hainz (Düsseldorf: Patmos, 2001), 95; P. Balla, *The Child-Parent Relationship in the New Testament and its Environment*; WUNT 155 (Tübingen: Mohr Siebeck, 2003), 190; et al. Cf. T.R. Schreiner, *Romans*; BECNT (Grand Rapids: Baker, 1998), 424–26, who seems to recognize both the notion of the work of the Spirit and that of the believer in this context.

[147] An exception is the brief note in Dunn, *Jesus and the Spirit*, 320.

*3.1. Relationships Individual and Corporate: Romans 8:12–17
and Its Cotext*

Except for 1 Corinthians, Paul's epistle to the Romans contains the largest amount of Spirit material in the Pauline corpus. The Spirit is mentioned at least 30 times, 20 of which occur in chapter 8.[148] In chapter 8, verse 13 has the most explicit ethical admonition, relating the Spirit instrumentally to an implicit imperative of a protasis: *'if by the Spirit you put to death the deeds of the body* you will live'. However, the question arises whether Paul gives any indication *how* the Spirit can function as an instrument for this ethical action. The preceding verse appears to convey one part of the answer: since the Spirit dwells within the Romans they are no longer debtors to the flesh. We have discussed this new reality in 6.1. above. Most tellingly, however, Paul connects the two succeeding verses via 'because' (γάρ) to the implicit imperative of verse 13. The significance of this causal link is often overlooked.[149] However, we will argue below that it is the very experience described in verses 14–17 that provides the second part of the answer to the question raised above. Namely, it is *the Spirit-shaped*[150] *experience of being adopted by God as a loving Father* that *empowers the Roman Christians to put to death the works of the body*.

Before we can demonstrate this thesis in detail, we will need to look at the broader cotext of verses 12–17. This is crucial, particularly because Thompson argues that the cotext of our section conveys that Paul is here *not* concerned with the Spirit-created experience of familial intimacy with God. Thompson criticizes the line of interpretation that

— has taken the verb 'to cry' (κράζειν, v.15) to refer to emotional, enthusiastic or spontaneous prayer;

---

[148] Cf. Fee, *Presence*, 472. Dunn rightly calls the passage the 'high point of Paul's theology of the Spirit' (Dunn, *Theology*, 423).

[149] Burke and Bertone are major exceptions (T.J. Burke, 'Adoption and the Spirit in Romans 8', *EQ* 70 (1998), 319–20; Burke, *Adopted*, 143–44; Bertone, *Law*, 192–93, 304–305). Cf. Cranfield, *Romans. I*, 393, 401. However, the linguistic link is also observed by P. von der Osten-Sacken, *Römer 8 als Beispiel der paulinischen Soteriologie* (Göttingen: Vandenhoeck & Ruprecht, 1975), 134; B. Byrne, S.J., *'Sons of God' – 'Seed of Abraham': A Study of the Idea of the Sonship of God of All Christians in Paul Against the Jewish Background*; AB 83 (Rome: Biblical Institute, 1979), 98 (however, he thinks that 'Paul's ethical excursus' of 6:1–8:13 concludes with v.13: B. Byrne, S.J., 'Living Out the Righteousness of God: The Contribution of Rom 6:1–8:13 to an Understanding of Paul's Ethical Presuppositions', *CBQ* 43 (1981), 580); Deidun, *Morality*, 78–79; Scott, *Adoption*, 260; Fee, *Presence*, 562; Moo, *Romans*, 498–99; Schreiner, *Romans*, 422; Christoph, *Pneuma*, 224; R. Jewett, *Romans: A Commentary*; Hermeneia (Philadelphia/Edinburgh: Fortress/Alban, 2006), 496.

[150] 'Spirit-shaped' is used with the meaning 'modelled *by* the Spirit', not 'modelled *on* the Spirit'.

- reads the address of God as *Abba* (v.15) as pointing to the believers' sense of intimacy in relationship with God, and
- interprets the 'Spirit bearing witness with our spirit' (v.16) as the reality of this intimate relationship within the realm of the individual's experience or faith.[151]

Thompson believes that this misconstruction of Paul's meaning in these verses is due to an unfortunate isolation of Romans 5–8 from chapters 1–4 as well as 9–11. It leads to 'reading Romans 8 primarily in *individualistic, subjective*, and *experiential* terms. But this misses the heart of Paul's argument, which should be read first in *cosmic, corporate, eschatological*, and *theocentric* terms.'[152] Neglecting the cotext that precedes chapters 5–8 means losing sight of the fact that Paul is concerned in chapters 1–4 with God's righteousness as revealed in adopting Jew and Gentile together into one family in fulfilment of the promise to Abraham. Thompson thinks that in this way the narrative thread from Abraham, to Christ, to the Spirit is cut. Furthermore, she continues that

if the affirmations about calling on God as Father refer entirely to individual experience, then the eschatological aspect of Paul's theology is diluted. No longer is Paul's argument a statement of the eschatological work of God in Christ. It is rather a declaration of the affective results of that work of God in Christ.[153]

Likewise, Thompson states that those who interpret Romans 8 as referring to religious experience usually treat chapters 9–11 as an excursus or afterthought. In contrast, she argues that in this section Paul continues on the theme of adoption because it is to Israel that it rightly belongs (9:4). Moreover, Jew and Gentile *together* are adopted into one family who, as descendants of Abraham, inherit together in Jesus Christ (15:8–9).[154] Thus, Thompson thinks that Paul is best paraphrased in this way: 'God has done what the law could not do: by sending his own Son he created a family of Jew and Gentile together, adopting them as his own, not through the law, which could not effect unity, but through the Spirit'.[155] Accordingly, she concludes that in Paul's argument, 'the use of Father for God is not simply expressive of the knowing subject's experience but of the activity of the

---

[151] M.M. Thompson, *The Promise of the Father: Jesus and God in the New Testament* (Louisville: Westminster John Knox Press, 2000), 126. Cf. M.M. Thompson, '"Mercy upon All": God as Father in the Epistle to the Romans', in S. Soderlund and N.T. Wright (eds.), *Romans and the People of God: Essays in Honor of Gordon D. Fee on the Occasion of His 65th Birthday* (Grand Rapids/Cambridge: Eerdmans, 1999), 211–15.

[152] Thompson, *Promise*, 126.

[153] Ibid., 127. Thompson admits that Paul has concerns with the individual and with the individual's response to God in Christ; but she wants to argue that these are not the focus of material dealing with God as Father.

[154] Ibid., 129.

[155] Ibid., 130.

God who is experienced. Paul's statements have more to do with what God has done than how God is experienced.'[156]

With her criticism of an experience-focused reading of Romans 8:12–17 Thompson has put her finger on an important aspect of interpretation. Namely, it is indispensable to take the overall argument of a letter into consideration when dealing with an individual section. A recent study that demonstrates how this can be done in detail is that of Christoph. Her monograph investigates the pneumatology of Romans 8 with special attention to the occasion and the communicative situation of Romans. However, she reaches the opposite conclusion from Thompson with regard to the role that is played by the experience of the Spirit and of God as Father. The fact that she comprehends Paul's appeal to these experiences to be of primary importance in the course of his argumentative strategy[157] shows that a closer interaction with the overall purpose of the letter will not necessarily lead to the interpretation favoured by Thompson. This is partly due to the fact that Thompson appears to see mainly one particular cause for Paul's writing (namely, to expound the eschatological unification of Jews and Gentiles through adoption into one family)[158] whereas Christoph knows at least two broader motivations (namely, to strengthen the church [1:11–12] and to present his gospel of which no one needs to be ashamed [1:16]).[159]

Against this background it is worth noting that monocausal explanations of the occasion of Romans have generally been called into question in the more recent history of extensive research on this topic.[160] Scholarship has increasingly accepted that there are multiple reasons that have lead to the writing of the epistle.[161] This fact should caution against an overconfident interpretation of Romans against one particular background.[162] Nonetheless, there are good reasons to see the likely conflict between Jews and Gentiles as *one* of Paul's reasons for writing Romans (see Rom. 1:16; 2:9–

---

[156] Ibid., 130.

[157] Christoph, *Pneuma*, esp. chs. 1–2. See the discussion in V. Rabens, 'Review of M. Christoph, *Pneuma und das neue Sein der Glaubenden: Studien zur Semantik und Pragmatik der Rede von Pneuma in Röm 8*', *RBL* [http://www.bookreviews.org] (2007), 1–5.

[158] Cf. Thompson, *Promise*, 131–32.

[159] Christoph, *Pneuma*, 56–62.

[160] See, e.g., A.J.M. Wedderburn, *The Reasons for Romans* (Edinburgh: T. & T. Clark, 1988), 140; V. Gäckle, *Die Starken und die Schwachen in Korinth und in Rom: Zu Herkunft und Funktion der Antithese in 1Kor 8,1–11,1 und in Röm 14,1–15,13*; WUNT II/200 (Tübingen: Mohr Siebeck, 2005), 323; Christoph, *Pneuma*, ch. 1.

[161] So, e.g., Dunn, *Romans 1–8*, lviii; Theobald, *Römerbrief*, 40–41; Gäckle, *Starken*, 323–24.

[162] Moreover, a number of scholars argue that Romans was not directed to a mixed congregation but to a Gentile church (so, e.g., A.A. Das, *Solving the Romans Debate* (Minneapolis: Fortress, 2007), *passim*). If this were correct, Thompson's thesis would be significantly flawed.

10; 3:9, 29; 9–11; 10:12; 14:1–15:13; 16:17).[163] However, even against this background, chapters 5–8 should not be seen as a digression, as Gäckle rightly highlights. Rather, the passage is

in ihrer Darstellung christlicher Existenz im Licht der Heilstat Christi ein essentieller Bestandteil der Paulus gestellten Aufgabe. Der Apostel muss erklären, *wie das Sein des Christen* (und zwar sowohl des Juden- wie des Heidenchristen) *und sein Leben vor Gott bestimmt werden kann*, wenn die Tora als die das jüdische Leben bestimmende und definierende Instanz in Christus ein heilsgeschichtliches Ende gefunden hat (Röm 10,4) und die Gabe des heiligen Geistes als Kraft des neuen Lebens den Christen geschenkt wurde.[164]

Therefore, one needs to agree with Thompson that this broader perspective on Romans should be kept in mind when studying chapter 8. Nonetheless, it appears that Thompson has overdrawn her point. While her paraphrase of Paul reflects an important aspect of Paul's message to the Romans, it is telling that Romans 8:3–4, which she follows in her rewording, precisely does *not* say that God sent his Son in order to unify Jew and Gentile. Rather, Paul explains the purpose of Christ's coming as condemning sin in the flesh, 'so that the just requirement of the law might be fulfilled in us, who walk not according to the flesh but according to the Spirit'. It seems that Thompson finds it hard to integrate this theme of ethical life before God into her model.[165] This may be partly due to a polarized thinking regarding Paul's theology that becomes evident when she builds on Martyn's declaration that 'the gospel is about the divine invasion of the cosmos (theology), not about human movement into blessedness (religion)'.[166]

However, a closer look at 8:12–17 uncovers that this model creates a false antithesis. The Spirit-shaped relationship to God set out in 8:14–17 is,

---

[163] Cf., e.g., F. Watson, 'The Two Roman Congregations: Romans 14:1–15:13', in K.P. Donfried (ed.), *The Romans Debate* (Edinburgh: T. & T. Clark, 1991²), 206; T.L. Carter, *Paul and the Power of Sin: Redefining 'Beyond the Pale'*; SNTSMS 115 (Cambridge: Cambridge University Press, 2002), 143; D.A. DeSilva, *An Introduction to the New Testament: Contexts, Methods and Ministry Formation* (Downers Grove/Leicester: IVP/Apollos, 2004), 606; D.A. Carson and D.J. Moo, *An Introduction to the New Testament* (Leicester: Apollos, 2005²), 406; Burke, *Adopted*, 160–69; J.C. Miller, 'The Jewish Context of Paul's Gentile Mission', *TynBul* 58 (2007), 108–111. *Contra* O. Michel, *Der Brief an die Römer*; KEK IV (Göttingen: Vandenhoeck & Ruprecht, 1978⁵), 259, who perceives Paul's definition of sonship as having anti-Judaistic force.

[164] Gäckle, *Starken*, 334, italics added.

[165] Cf. Carter, who explicitly says that in Rom. 8:12–13 'Paul is not exhorting his readers to adopt a moral rather than an immoral lifestyle'. Rather, living κατὰ σάρκα 'refers to life lived in the present aeon' (Carter, *Paul*, 200). However, the connection of σάρξ and sin appears to be obvious in 7:5, 18; 8:3, 7 et al.

[166] Thompson, *Promise*, 131, citing J.L. Martyn, 'The Abrahamic Covenant, Christ, and the Church', in J.L. Martyn, *Theological Issues in the Letters of Paul*; SNTW (Edinburgh: T&T Clark, 1997), 170.

on the one hand, described as 'invading', namely, it liberates from slavery (v.15). On the other hand, however, it also describes an emotional experience, namely the removal of fear and the address of God as loving Father (v.15). Contrary to Thompson, admitting this experiential aspect or even emphasis of verse 15 does not mean diluting the eschatological aspect of Paul's theology. Paul has no problems keeping together the two accents of verse 15 just mentioned. The eschatological perspective comes further to the fore in the concepts of 'inheritance' and suffering in verse 17 (which is part of the present section[167]) and in the opposition of 'flesh' and 'death' versus 'killing' the works of the body and 'life' in verse 13 (which is linked to v.15 via the argumentative chain elucidated at the beginning of this section).[168] The experiential aspect of verse 15 will be enlarged upon below in 6.3.3.

It is to be welcomed that after her bold criticism of the individual aspects of an experience-focused reading of 8:14–16, what Thompson appears to propose in the end is a matter of discovering the right nuances in the section. As cited above, she says that 'Paul's statements have more to do with what God has done than how God is experienced.' Nonetheless, it is generally not easy to verify such a distinction from a text like 8:14–16.[169] This is particularly the case when one compares the text with the parallel in Galatians 4:1–7. For in contrast to Galatians 4:6, where it is the *Spirit* who cries 'Abba! Father!', Romans 8:15 specifies that it is *we* who

---

[167] *Pace* Bertone, who uses word statistics in support of his decision to make Romans 8:1–16 the focal passage of his monograph to the exclusion of v.17 (which is for good reasons regarded by most scholars as part of Paul's treatment of sonship of God in vv.14–17). Apart from the statistical appearances of πνεῦμα and νόμος in the text, Bertone gives as a second reason for the break between v.16 and v.17 that v.17 has little bearing on Paul's understanding of the law (Bertone, *Law*, 20). However, next to the grammatical link between the two verses (cf. the elliptical ἐσμέν in v.17 which is carried forward from v.16), the concept of 'inheritance' in v.17 is intimately related to the law and the covenant. It hence has a bearing on how Spirit-worked sonship of God relates to the promises that were bound up with law observance in the old covenant (cf. Gal. 4:1, 7). Apart from that, it has been pointed out by a number of scholars that in this passage the Spirit is much more characterized by *life* than by its opposition to the law (see 8:2, 6, 10–11, 13; cf. Fay, 'Paul', 340; Yates, *Spirit*, 125–26, 130–32, and the authors listed there). On Bertone's work, see further V. Rabens, 'Review of J.A. Bertone, *'The Law of the Spirit'*: *Experience of the Spirit and Displacement of the Law in Romans 8:1–16'*, RBL [http://www.bookreviews.org] (2007), 1–6.

[168] Cf. M. Theobald, 'Angstfreie Religiosität: Röm 8,15 und 1Joh 4,17f. im Licht der Schrift Plutarchs über den Aberglauben', in M. Theobald, *Studien zum Römerbrief*, WUNT 136 (Tübingen: Mohr Siebeck, 2001), 446.

[169] Cf. the broader hermeneutical considerations in Rabens, 'Development', 172–73; followed by Christoph, *Pneuma*, 81–82.

do the crying (κράζομεν). It should be clear that it is more than doubtful that this activity can be separated from personal experience.

Also Romans 7, which belongs to the immediate cotext of chapter 8, suggests that human experience is part of Paul's focus when he writes this part of the epistle (see esp. 7:15–24). In chapter 7 one listens to the 'I' of the unredeemed human being, whereas in chapter 8 the ecclesial 'we' is dominant.[170] Thompson is therefore right to emphasize that chapter 8 has an ecclesiological perspective.[171] However, Paul does not play off the collective against the individual. Contrary to Thompson, liberation clearly has a 'cosmic' *and* a 'personal' dimension in Romans 8. The global perspective has already been outlined above. However, Paul applies this expressly to the individual, as is clear from verse 2: 'the law of the Spirit of life in Christ Jesus has set *you* [σε, *singular*] free from the law of sin and of death' (the same is true for the textual variant με).[172] Likewise, being indwelt by the Spirit is an individual event: 'Anyone who does not have the Spirit of Christ does not belong to him' (8:9b). And, as already mentioned, the ethical action outlined in verse 13 has an eschatological-cosmic aspect, but this eschatological aspect is in no way divorced from a view to the individual, as is evident from the formulation 'killing the works of the *body*' (singular, as opposed to v.11: σώματα ὑμῶν).

Returning to the title of this subsection, we can conclude that Romans 8:12–17 deals with relationships individual and corporate. In the course of the succeeding exegesis it will be important not to lose sight of the corporate relationships as established through the reconciliation between Jews and Gentiles. However, in the following it will become evident that what Paul says likewise applies to the individual, focussing in verses 12–17 on the relationships of the believers to ἀββα ὁ πατήρ and to fellow ἀδελφοί.

3.2. Establishing Religious-Ethical Life (Rom. 8:12–14)

Byrne and Engberg-Pedersen have suggested that Romans 8:13 forms the conclusion to the paraenetic section 6:1–8:13. '8:14 introduces a quite new idea of sonship, which is central in 8:14–17 and continues into 8:18–39'.[173] However, apart from the fact that the concept of sonship has a bearing

---

[170] Cf. Giesen, 'Söhne', 69.

[171] Thompson, *Promise*, 129.

[172] Cf. Gal. 4:7: 'So you are [εἶ, *singular*] no longer a slave but a child, and if a child then also an heir, through God.'

[173] Engberg-Pedersen, *Stoics*, 187; Byrne, 'Righteousness', 580. Cf. Bertone, *Law*, 194: 'The concern with ethics ceases after v. 13'. For a more plausible analysis of the structure of Rom. 8, see Theobald, 'Religiosität', 446.

upon the broader theme of unity between Jews and Gentiles in Romans,[174] a closer look at verse 14 shows that the verse functions as the chain link of the interlocking of the themes of ethics (ὅσοι… πνεύματι θεοῦ ἄγονται) and sonship (υἱοὶ θεοῦ εἰσιν) in verses 12–17. It therefore seems to be ill-founded to drive a wedge between verses 13 and 14 (or between vv.14 and 15). This will become even more obvious in the course of the following study of Romans 8 which is aimed at demonstrating how ethical living (vv.12–14) is causally connected to sonship (vv.14–17). In accordance with this aim, we will not discuss every exegetical issue arising from the text. Rather, we will first take a brief look at how religious-ethical life is to be established according to verses 12–14 and then develop in more detail how the Spirit of sonship empowers such ethical action in the following section (6.3.3.).

In 8:12 Paul draws a conclusion for ethical living from his preceding argument. He writes, 'So then, brothers and sisters, we are debtors, not to the flesh, to live according to the flesh'. He thus reiterates the reality described in verse 9, namely, that the Romans are no longer in the flesh but in the Spirit since the Spirit of God indwells them. However, he now makes explicit that this new reality has a consequence for religious-ethical living. As established in 6.1., the transferral from the realm of the flesh into the realm of the Spirit has established new relational realities. In the words of verse 12, this means that believers are no longer debtors to the flesh. In the Roman legal context, 'obligation' is defined as 'bind[ing] another person to give, do, or perform something for us' (*Digest of Justinian* 44.7.3). Hence the Roman Christians are no longer bound by their former patron, the flesh, and have escaped its regulative principle.[175]

The rhetoric of verse 12 raises the expectation that Paul will go on to explain further what the termination of the allegiance to the flesh means for present religious-ethical living. And this is indeed what Paul is doing in verse 13. Verse 13 sets two alternatives before the audience: living according to the flesh and consequent death on the one hand, and killing the works of the body by the Spirit and consequent life on the other.[176] This

---

[174] Cf. our discussion above; see esp. 9:4; cf. 4:11–13 on Jews and Gentiles being children of Abraham.

[175] Cf. Jewett, *Romans*, 493–94.

[176] More precisely, life and death are presented in a chiastic structure:

  A life (κατὰ σάρκα ζῆτε) (present)
  B death (μέλλετε ἀποθνῄσκειν) (future/eschatological)
  B death (πράξεις τοῦ σώματος θανατοῦτε) (present)
  A life (ζήσεσθε) (future/eschatological).

For a similar observation, see Giesen, 'Söhne', 79. The parallel in Gal. 6:8 indicates that the focus is on eschatological life (ζωὴν αἰώνιον) rather than on a better life in the present (although these two aspects should not be seen as contrasts).

opposition recalls verse 6, where Paul expounds that the mind (or aspiration, φρόνημα) of the flesh is death, and the mind (or aspiration) of the Spirit is life and peace.[177] As the φρόνημα τῆς σαρκός is further described in verse 7 as being 'hostile to God', it seems that the φρόνημα τοῦ πνεύματος too has a relational aspect in that it means by implication 'closeness to God', or, explicitly, 'peace' (εἰρήνη, v.6). The truth that the Spirit desires closeness to God may hint at the way in which the Spirit enables (πνεύματι, v.13) believers to put to death the works of the body, namely, by creating the intimacy with God that is described in verses 15–16 and causally linked to verse 13 (via γάρ).

Before we investigate this mode of empowering further, we need to look briefly at what it is that Paul asks from the Romans. While Paul made clear in verse 12 that believers are no longer debtors to the flesh, he nonetheless stresses in verse 13 by means of an implicit imperative[178] that they need to 'kill the works of the body' by the Spirit. As one can see from the variant readings, one question that has already vexed the copyists of Paul's letters arises from Paul's usage of σῶμα instead of σάρξ in this verse. One would have expected Paul to employ 'flesh' instead of 'body', as the former more obviously has a negative connotation in Paul (see, e.g., 1 Cor. 15:50: 'flesh and blood cannot inherit the kingdom of God', whereas the body can; in contrast to the flesh, the body is being transformed [15:44]). However, both terms also overlap in Paul's usage,[179] and he can even use them interchangeably in 1 Corinthians 6:16 (cf. 1 Cor. 7:34 ['body and spirit'] with 2 Cor. 7:1 ['flesh and spirit'][180] and 2 Cor. 4:10 with 4:11). For this reason a number of scholars have suggested that this is also the case in Romans 8:13.[181]

---

[177] The genitives are most likely subjective genitives (Cranfield, *Romans. I*, 386).

[178] Bornkamm rightly observes that – grammatically speaking – Rom. 8 does not contain a single imperative (G. Bornkamm, *Paulus* (Stuttgart: Kohlhammer, 1993[7] [1969[1]]), 165). The genre is therefore that of a theological argument, not paraenesis (Fee, *Presence*, 559). Burke comments that in contrast to Rom. 7, 'now in chapter 8 where the Spirit is in view the believer has a new freedom and energy to live as God intended. This is due to the fact that life in the Spirit is controlled and lived out not by an external regulatory code (Rom. 7:7) but through the indwelling power of the *pneuma* (Rom. 8:4, 9)' (Burke, *Adopted*, 136).

[179] Cf. Dunn's helpful illustration (Dunn, *Theology*, 72):

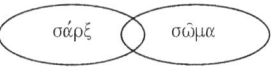

negativ   *neutral*

[180] On the charge that this latter formulation is un-Pauline, see Rabens, 'Coming Out', 46–47.

[181] So, e.g., Michel, *Römer*, 258–59; Dunn, *Theology*, 71; Lohse, *Römer*, 238–39; Giesen, 'Söhne', 79; Christoph, *Pneuma*, 218; Landmesser, 'Geist', 145 n.43.

However, Paul usually attaches a qualifying phrase or adjective to σῶμα when he uses it negatively (as, e.g., 'body *of sin*', 6:6; '*mortal* body', 8:11).[182] Against this background one might assume that Paul has a reason for using σῶμα instead of σάρξ in verse 13. Indeed, Fee argues that, since Paul has in the previous verses expounded that believers are no longer in the flesh, it follows that he asks the Romans to kill the works of the body, not of the flesh.[183] This interpretation seems quite plausible.[184]

However, perhaps it is possible to discover a more nuanced relation between Paul's concepts of σῶμα and σάρξ in this context. For one thing, there appears to be a greater overlap between the two terms than, for example, Keck allows. Keck thinks that the reason for the employment of 'body' is that 'only the body does deeds; as a domain, "flesh" does not act'.[185] However, one wonders whether Paul saw a significant difference between the πράξεις τοῦ σώματος and the ἔργα τῆς σαρκός mentioned in Galatians 5:19. A potential explanation could be that the 'works of the flesh', as concrete as they are (fornication, impurity, licentiousness, etc.), refer more broadly to the desires of the (external) 'domain' of the flesh, whereas the 'deeds of the body' refer to the desires[186] of (the bodies of) the individual believers.[187] As σῶμα can be dedicated to God *or* to evil[188] it

---

[182] Cf. Dunn, *Theology*, 71.

[183] Fee, *Presence*, 558, cf. 822; Schreiner, *Romans*, 421.

[184] On Paul's Spirit–flesh contrast, see more generally Turner, *Spirit*, 125; Barclay, *Truth*, ch. 6. There is some debate concerning the origin and exact nature of the Spirit–flesh contrast in Paul (see, e.g., the overview in Christoph, *Pneuma*, 131–32, 142–43). However, it suffices here to agree with Kuss that in this regard 'Paul does not work with a system of sharply honed terminology' (O. Kuss, *Der Römerbrief. Vol. 2 (Röm 6,11 bis 8,19)* (Regensburg: Pustet, 1963²), 506).

[185] Keck, *Romans*, 206.

[186] Theobald explains that in the light of Rom. 6:12 it is clear that the 'deeds of the body' refer to its ἐπιθυμίαι (M. Theobald, '*Concupiscentia* im Römerbrief: Exegetische Beobachtungen anläßlich der lutherischen Formel "simul justus et peccator"', in M. Theobald, *Studien zum Römerbrief*; WUNT 136 (Tübingen: Mohr Siebeck, 2001), 273; cf. H. Schlier, *Der Römerbrief*; HTKNT VI (Freiburg/Basel/Wien: Herder, 2002 [1977¹]), 202; Giesen, 'Söhne', 81). Cf. Gal. 5:17.

Jewett thinks that the 'deeds of the body' are more likely social than sensual (Jewett, *Romans*, 495). However, sensual activities usually have social implications, so that it may be better to formulate that the issue is 'dependence on a physical and social indulgence which distances from God' (Dunn, *Romans 1–8*, 458), or even broader: 'getötet werden soll all das, was der intimen Beziehung zwischen den Christen und Gott und damit dem wahren Leben entgegensteht' (Giesen, 'Söhne', 78).

[187] While it is possible that σῶμα should not be individualized in 8:10 (so Dunn, *Romans 1–8*, 431), it is clear that in 8:13 the individual is part of Paul's horizon as the 'deeds of the body' cannot be other than the deeds of persons themselves (cf. Gundry, *Sôma*, 50, cf. 188).

thus seems likely that σάρξ uses σῶμα as a vehicle for its attacks (cf. perhaps 1 Cor. 9:27).[189] This conclusion is supported by Schnelle who writes that

> in Rom. 8:9 the apostle explicitly emphasizes the change of existence that transpires in baptism from the realm of σάρξ into the realm of the πνεῦμα (Spirit). Thus Rom. 8:10–11. 13 can no longer speak of being determined by σάρξ but only of being confronted by σάρξ. Σῶμα as such has not become a slave to the alien powers of σάρξ and ἁμαρτία and thus deprived of its own will, yet it finds itself in the constant danger of being taken over by them again.[190]

This potential of σάρξ exercising influence via σῶμα raises the question whether Paul regards the Christian life to be a constant struggle.[191] However, as we have indicated in 6.1., the contrast that Paul sets up between Romans 7 and 8 conveys that people who have been transferred 'into' (ἐν) Christ and the Spirit are now *able* to resist the temptations of the body and the flesh (cf. Gal. 5:24), and they are in a relationship that provides further empowering for such action (cf. πνεύματι θανατοῦτε [v.13], πνεύματι ἄγονται [v.14] and vv.15–16). Nonetheless, this seems to be taken too far by Fee when he claims that, according to Paul, 'God's people... *are not even to engage with sin in battle*; rather, by the Spirit's help they are to put it to death'.[192] Fee appears to overlook that 'putting to death' and 'battle' belong to the same semantic field. Paul himself is clearly of the opinion that he lives in a warfare context: 'Let us then cast off the works of darkness and put on the armour of light' (Rom. 13:12). And 'putting to death the deeds of the body' may indeed sometimes involve some kind of struggle, for putting something to is not always a matter of an instant.[193] This

---

[188] Gundry highlights the fact that in Rom. 12:1 σῶμα 'is not merely capable of redemption, but is Paul's precise term for a human life dedicated to God. But elsewhere Paul uses *soma* for a human life enslaved to sin (Rom 1:24; 6:6; 7:24; 8:10, 13; cf. Col 3:5)' (Gundry, *Sôma*, 36).

[189] Cf. Ibid., 39; Käsemann, *Romans*, 226; E. Mauerhofer, *Der Kampf zwischen Fleisch und Geist bei Paulus: Ein Beitrag zur Klärung der Frage nach der Stellung des Gläubigen zur Sünde im paulinischen Heiligungs- und Vollkommenheitsverständnis* (Frutingen: Trachsel, 1980), 173; G.E. Ladd, *A Theology of the New Testament* (Grand Rapids: Eerdmans, 1993²), 517; Vollenweider, 'Geist', 188; Moo, *Romans*, 495; Schreiner, *Romans*, 421. *Pace* Giesen, 'Söhne', 79.

[190] Schnelle, *Paul*, 496; cf. U. Schnelle, *Neutestamentliche Anthropologie: Jesus – Paulus – Johannes*; Biblisch-theologische Studien 18 (Neukirchen-Vluyn: Neukirchener Verlag, 1991), 67.

[191] Cf. the position of Dunn, summarized in Appendix 2.3.

[192] Fee, *Presence*, 559, italics added. However, see also his more nuanced description of Christian life later on the same page: 'If there is no internal struggle with sin evident in Paul's theologizing, nor is there triumphalism.' On Fee's position, see more fully Appendix 3.2.

[193] Cf. Fee himself who admits that 'old habits die hard' (Ibid., 559).

seems to be supported by Paul's use of the present indicative (θανατοῦτε) which can indicate continuous activity.[194]

Fee thinks that for the practically minded, such an imperative causes great frustration because neither here nor elsewhere in his epistles does Paul explain how one can by the Spirit put to death the works of the body.[195] However, it seems that the way in which Paul has structured the present section gives significant clues for finding an answer to this question. We have already pointed out above that verse 14 is linked to verse 13 via γάρ, which suggests that verse 14 provides a foundation or further explanation of verse 13. This observation finds additional support in the fact that verses 13b and 14 are written in a synthetic parallelism:[196]

εἰ   πνεύματι   τὰς πράξεις τοῦ σώματος θανατοῦτε,   ζήσεσθε
ὅσοι   πνεύματι θεοῦ   ἄγονται,   οὗτοι υἱοὶ θεοῦ εἰσιν

It is particularly noteworthy that the active τὰς πράξεις τοῦ σώματος θανατοῦτε is set in parallel with the passive ἄγονται. This reiterates the fact that the 'killing' is to be done 'by the Spirit' (v.13b). Verses 13b and 14 thus paint a picture of an interplay between divine and human activity, with the precedence falling on the activity of the Spirit, as is indicated by the instrumental πνεύματι in 13b and the passive πνεύματι θεοῦ ἄγονται in the explanatory verse 14.[197] The putting to death of the works of the body by the Spirit (v.13b) is thus a matter of being led, directed, impelled and controlled by the Spirit (v.14). Contrary to Marshall and Burke, the emphasis in verse 14 is not on the action of the believers, as if 'only as men behave like God can they really prove themselves to be the sons of

---

[194] Giesen, 'Söhne', 79, even suggests that the present tense here indicates a 'life-long task'. Cf. Burke's metaphorical description that believers must 'starve it [i.e. sin in their lives] of its oxygen supply and not allow it any room to breathe' (Burke, *Adopted*, 144).

[195] Fee, *Presence*, 559, n.254. The only thing that Fee submits is that 'in light of the basic thrust of v.6 and 12:1–2, it at least means that one must put the "renewed mind" to it; that is, it must be focused and intentional'.

[196] The parallelism is also recognized by Bertone, *Law*, 192. However, Bertone surprisingly states that v.14 has nothing to do with ethics (p. 194, esp. n.122). Nevertheless, he rightly recognizes that ἄγειν is 'directly associated and occasioned by Paul's previous descriptions of the Spirit', and he mentions 'walking by the Spirit' (v. 4) as the first one (p. 194; cf. Giesen, 'Söhne', 84). 'Walking by the Spirit', however, is evidently ethical in that it is explained by Paul as being equivalent to the just requirement of the law being fulfilled in believers (v.4; cf. Gal. 5:16). Cf. Bertone's (self-contradictory) claim on pp. 301–302 that the notion of being led by the Spirit (v.14) suggests that the Spirit is the primary agent in Christian ethics.

[197] On the element of human decision and involvement, see further the discussions in Christoph, *Pneuma*, 216–17, and ch. 7 below.

God'.[198] Rather, the stress is on the activity of the Spirit – the believers *are* led by the Spirit (passive), and the definition is, no doubt deliberately, framed in open and not restrictive terms: 'as many as', not just 'only those who' are led by the Spirit of God are his children.[199]

As argued above, verse 14 interconnects the topics of religious-ethical living (vv.12–13) and being children of God (vv.15–17). This connection of ethics and sonship extends into verses 15–17 because they are linked to verses 13–14 via 'because'. Therefore, verses 15–17 provide further details in answer to Fee's question mentioned above. The connection of verses 15–17 with verses 12–14 has also been discovered by Cranfield, who explains that

> This then is what it means to live after the Spirit, to mortify by the Spirit the deeds of the body, and to be led by the Spirit of God – simply to be enabled by that same Spirit to cry, "Abba, Father". And it is here expressed not as an imperative but as an indicative: Christians do as a matter of fact do this. The implicit imperative is that they should continue to do just this, and do it more and more consistently, more and more sincerely, soberly and responsibly. This is all that is required of them. [...] That this necessarily includes seeking with all our heart to be and think and say and do what is well-pleasing to Him... should go without saying.[200]

Cranfield's reasoning supports the argument that we have developed above. However, a more comprehensive understanding of the text can be gained by paying closer attention to the aspect of *empowering* for the action that the Roman believers are asked to perform by means of the Spirit. Cranfield states that believers are implicitly asked (to continue) to cry 'Abba, Father' by the Spirit and that this also includes living in a way that is pleasing to God. However, we will argue below that – in accordance with the syntactical structure of verses 13–15 (esp. the connection via γάρ) – these are not merely two parallel activities,[201] but that *by means of* the Spirit-created intimate relationship to God expressed in verses 15–17 the Spirit provides the empowering for the ethical action required in verse 13.

---

[198] L.H. Marshall, *The Ethics of the New Testament* (London: Macmillan, 1960), 259, cited with consent by Burke, *Adopted*, 146. Cf. Burke, 'Spirit', 319–20.

[199] Cf. Dunn, *Romans 1–8*, 459. See also n.261 below.

[200] Cranfield, *Romans. 1*, 401. Cf. Bertone, *Law*, 193, 304.

[201] In fact, Cranfield almost appears to collapse Paul's ethical imperative into κράζομεν· αββα ὁ πατήρ when he says that 'God's holy law is established and its "righteous requirement" (v. 4) fulfilled, and... the whole of Christian obedience is included' in this prayer which he believes to be 'everything that there is to say in the way of Christian ethics' (Cranfield, *Romans. 1*, 393). Besides, when he says regarding this address of God that 'nothing more [is] *required* of us than that we *should* do... this' (Cranfield, *Romans. 1*, 393, italics added), Cranfield seems to overstress what possibly is an *implicit* recommendation in v.15.

3.3. Empowered by the Spirit of Adoption as Sons (Rom. 8:15–16)

In verses 15–16 Paul continues the thought from verses 12–14. He explains to the Romans that they have not received the spirit of slavery (to the law of sin and death, 8:2) and consequent fear[202] but they have received the Spirit of 'adoption as sons'.[203] In a similar manner as slavery is contrasted with sonship, 'fear' has a counterpart in the loving relationship (cf. 8:35, 37, 39) expressed in the cry 'Abba, Father' that is the consequence of the presence of the Spirit.[204] The 'Spirit of adoption' thus brings about adoption as sons ('you *received* the Spirit of adoption', referring back to conversion-initiation)[205] as well as affirms it (in the continuous ἐν ᾧ κράζομεν· αββα ὁ πατήρ).[206] The aspect of affirmation is given further weight in verse 16 where Paul says that the Spirit testifies with our spirit that 'we' (now explicitly including women)[207] are children of God.[208] Such dual witness vividly establishes the reality of the new relationship with

---

[202] On the interplay of slavery and fear under the rule of desire, see Philo, *Rer. Div. Her.* 270–71. Cf. the dark scenario described in Rom. 7.

[203] On the rendering of υἱοθεσία as 'adoption as sons', see further below.

[204] Cf. Theobald, 'Religiosität', 446; Christoph, *Pneuma*, 231.

[205] Cf. Betz, 'Geburt', 326; Fee, *Presence*, 566; etc. Πνεῦμα λαμβάνειν had become a *terminus technicus* for the initial reception of the Spirit in Paul (cf. Gal. 3:2, 14; 2 Cor. 11:4) as well as in early Christianity more generally (cf. Jn. 7:39; 14:17; 20:22; Acts 2:38; 8:15, 17, 19; etc.) (cf. Bertone, *Law*, 197; et al.). *Pace* B. Weiß, *Lehrbuch der biblischen Theologie des Neuen Testaments* (Berlin/Stuttgart: Hertz/Cotta'sche Buchhandlung, 1903[7] [1868[1]]), 323, who sees Spirit-reception as consecutive to adoption. However, the fact that ἐλάβετε is an aorist is not enough evidence to argue that the Spirit was received *in baptism* (*pace* Michel, *Römer*, 260; Giesen, 'Söhne', 87). See further 3.2.1.

[206] Cf. Bertone, *Law*, 200. Burke argues against the first of these two agencies on grammatical grounds. However, his own reading of πνεῦμα υἱοθεσίας as a descriptive genitive does not appear to be significantly different to the two options outlined above. For Burke the phrase expresses that Spirit and adoption are 'inseparable; stated in another way, they are reciprocally related' (Burke, *Adopted*, 142–43).

[207] This is indicated by the replacement of υἱοί (v.14) by τέκνα (cf. Lohse, *Römer*, 241; Jewett, *Romans*, 500; etc.).

[208] Cf. Burke, *Adopted*, 149, who observes that most scholars interpret συμμαρτυρεῖ as the human spirit joining with the divine Spirit in witnessing to the adoption. Regarding the intricate notion of αὐτὸ τὸ πνεῦμα, Jewett argues that 'It is preferable to accept Paul's idea that both the apportioned Spirit granted to believers and the "Spirit itself" confirm that believers are "children of God," despite the "logical difficulties in conceptualizing this in modern terms." Paul's goal is not to produce a doctrine of the Spirit or a consistent anthropology but to convince the Roman believers that their charismatic experience bears witness that they are τέκνα θεοῦ' (Jewett, *Romans*, 500, drawing on Jewett, *Terms*, 199). Cf. R. Jewett, 'The Question of the "Apportioned Spirit" in Paul's Letters: Romans as a Case Study', in G. Stanton, et al. (eds.), *The Holy Spirit and Christian Origins: Essays in Honor of James D. G. Dunn* (Grand Rapids/Cambridge: Eerdmans, 2004), 198–200; Levison, *Filled with the Spirit*, 238–39.

God, because a case is settled by two or more witnesses (Deut. 17:6; 19:15; 2 Cor. 13:1; cf. Matt. 18:16), this being particularly true for the practice of adoption in the ancient Roman world.[209]

Burke has recently argued that υἱοθεσία functions as an organizing soteriological metaphor[210] for Paul. It covers three aspects: 1. it is focussed on the person and work of God's Son, Jesus Christ; 2. it demands an appropriate ethical response; 3. it expresses the eschatological tension between the 'now' and the 'not yet'.[211] We will briefly look at aspects 3 and 1 as well as 2.

In his outline of the eschatological aspect of adoption (3.), Burke underlines the truth that adoption has 'a retrospective and a prospective dimension' (i.e. an alpha and an omega point).[212] The retrospective dimension looks back to what has been accomplished by Jesus at the cross (thus covering aspect 1) and its taking effect in individual lives through coming to faith, whereas the prospective dimension looks ahead to the future consummation (8:23).[213] However, while these two aspects are surely part of Paul's concept of υἱοθεσία, it seems that the eschatological 'now' of υἱοθεσία has a stronger force in Paul than Burke's presentation suggests.[214] For one thing, the translation of υἱοθεσία as 'adoption' could give the

---

[209] Cf. Dunn, *Galatians*, 219; Burke, *Adopted*, 150–51.

[210] It is generally accepted that 'adoption' and 'sonship' are used *metaphorically* by Paul. Accordingly, in his discussion of 'adoption' as a metaphor Burke never even raises the question whether or not Paul understands 'adoption' as metaphorical (Burke, *Adopted*, ch. 1; cf. his methodology on p. 63: 'What did adoption mean in law and practice, and hence metaphorically?'). However, Thompson rightly points out that 'There is a sense in which the predication that God is "father" of Israel is a literal statement. God is the Father of Israel as its founder, the ancestor of the "clan" of the Israelite nation insofar as he brought it into being (Jer. 31:9; Deut. 32:4–6; cf. Deut. 32:18)' (Thompson, *Promise*, 41). Moreover, on the basis of passages like Eph. 3:14–15 some authors suggest that God is the archetype of all fatherhood, that human fatherhood is more or less an imperfect reflection of his perfect fatherhood, and that to call God 'Father' is therefore not to project human language onto God but simply to acknowledge what he ultimately is in himself (cf. Athanasius, *C. Ar.* 1.23). For a rebuttal of this view, see Lincoln, *Ephesians*, 203; cf. D.G. Chen, *God as Father in Luke-Acts*; SBL 92 (New York: Lang, 2006), 80–86. On criteria for identifying metaphorical language, see 2.2.2.1.

[211] Burke, *Adopted*, 41–45, drawing on S.B. Ferguson, 'The Reformed Doctrine of Sonship', in N. de S. Cameron and S.B. Ferguson (eds.), *Pulpit and People: Essays in Honour of William Still on His 75th Birthday* (Edinburgh: Rutherford, 1986), 86–87.

[212] Burke, *Adopted*, 44, quoting Ferguson, 'Doctrine', 87.

[213] Burke, *Adopted*, 43–45.

[214] However, Burke mentions that the 'alpha point' is the present reality of the Spirit of υἱοθεσία (8:15) (Ibid., 44; cf. his discussion of the relevance for today of Paul's concept of adoption, p. 196). Nonetheless, this aspect appears to be underemphasized in his treatment, particularly as one would naturally associate the concept of an 'alpha point' with the *retrospective* dimension of adoption (cf. his analogy with justification on p. 44).

impression that the concept may indeed be subsumed under the heading of 'soteriology' in the sense of 'entering salvation'.[215] However, υἱοθεσία, which is best translated as 'adoption as sons',[216] is fully equivalent to 'sonship' in Paul.[217] This is indicated, for example, by the way in which in Galatians 4 the consequence of ἵνα τὴν υἱοθεσίαν ἀπολάβωμεν (v.5b) is expressed as "Ὅτι δέ ἐστε υἱοί... (v.6a), and from the interplay in Romans 8 of υἱοὶ θεοῦ (v.14), υἱοθεσίας (v.15) and τέκνα θεοῦ (vv.16–17).[218] Below we will see in more detail that 'adoption as sons' is therefore not only a metaphor relating to the beginning (and end) of Christian life, but that it characterizes the very essence of Christian existence. This new identity as children of God and the loving relationship to ἀββα ὁ πατήρ determines the self-understanding, being and acting of the community of believers in Rome.

It is evident from the discussion in the preceding section that Burke's second aspect of adoption as sons is also correct in that Paul indeed relates sonship to ethics. However, it seems too narrow to limit this to what Burke calls 'the ethics of the eschaton – the duty of all God's adopted sons to live circumspectly in the last days'.[219] While it is true that 'in the ancient world all sons, including those who had been adopted, were expected to behave in a manner that would not discredit their father or besmirch the family name', Burke's conclusion that 'it is the responsibility for spiritually adopted sons belonging to the divine household to live scrupulously and blamelessly by bringing glory to their holy, heavenly Father'[220] does not appear to be Paul's major concern, at least not in Romans 8. Rather, the theological 'indicatives' in verses 14–17, which are causally related to the ethical (implicit) 'imperative' in verse 13, are true grammatical indicatives in that they constitute verbs of activity. That is, verses 14–17 not only describe a new *status* or *being* from which the Romans would need to derive moral conduct (vv.12–13); rather, verses 14–17 convey the *activity of the Spirit* that is already taking place in the lives of the Romans.[221] And

---

[215] However, in his introduction Burke had set out to challenge such narrow notions of υἱοθεσία (Ibid., 25–26).

[216] Cf. P. Wülfing von Martitz, 'υἱοθεσία', *TDNT*, VIII, 397; Scott, *Adoption*, 55. On the rendering of υἱοθεσία as 'adoption', see BDAG, s.v.; Dunn, *Romans 1–8*, 452; Theobald, *Römerbrief*, 245.

[217] Cf. Dunn, *Romans 1–8*, 460; Dunn, *Galatians*, 217.

[218] See also the application of the term to Israel in 9:4.

[219] Burke, *Adopted*, 147; cf. 175.

[220] Ibid., 43.

[221] This is further supported by the fact that Paulus is drawing in these verses on the exodus tradition of the Hebrew Scriptures which focuses on *God's* salvific action in Israel's history. On the intertextual echoes with this tradition in Rom. 8, see R.B. Hays,

these activities empower ethical living, as is clear from the syntactical structure of the passage as outlined above and from the concept of being guided by the Spirit (v.14).

This notion of Spirit-empowering will come to the fore still more clearly in the ensuing investigation of the characteristics of adoption and sonship in Paul and his context. It will thus be shown that Paul's usage of 'adoption as sons' is not exhausted by looking at its inauguration (Burke's aspects 1. & 3.) and its goal (2. & 3.), but that it gives shape to the *present* life of believers as a loving as well as empowering relationship to ἀββα ὁ πατήρ.

3.3.1. Characteristics of Adoption and Sonship in Paul (esp. Rom. 8) and His Context

A number of scholars think that Paul derived his concept of 'adoption as sons' exclusively from the Hellenistic world. For example, Esler writes that 'Paul has drawn this convenient image of adoption from Greco-Roman legal systems, since first century CE Judeans did not use adoption.'[222] However, while the term υἱοθεσία is not used in Jewish literature, the concept of 'adoption as sons' is nonetheless not foreign to Jewish thought.[223] Most explicitly, Philo employs the concept metaphorically in *De Sobrietate* 56 where he says that Abraham 'has registered God as his father and become by adoption His only son' (γεγονὼς εἰσποιητὸς αὐτῷ μόνος υἱός) (see our discussion below). Moreover, the Jewish Scriptures and literature evidence a rich tradition that employs and develops the motif of divine sonship, and, as most scholars recognize, Paul is firmly rooted in this tradition.[224]

a) Adoption and Sonship in Paul's Context. The imagery of human sonship and divine fatherhood has numerous nuances. This is true for the Hebrew Bible, early Judaism as well as the Graeco-Roman world. The aim

---

'Intertextuelle Pneumatologie: Die paulinische Rede vom Heiligen Geist', *ZNT* 25 (2010), 34–35.

[222] P.F. Esler, *Conflict and Identity in Romans: The Social Setting of Paul's Letter* (Minneapolis: Fortress, 2003), 247. Cf. Lohse, *Römer*, 241; B.J. Malina and J.J. Pilch, *Social-Science Commentary on the Letters of Paul* (Minneapolis: Fortress Press, 2006), 259.

[223] See esp. Scott, *Adoption*, 61–117. Scott even sees evidence for the practice of adoption in the OT (Gen. 48:5; Exod. 2:10; Esth. 2:7, 15) (Scott, *Adoption*, 74–75); however, see the critique in Burke, *Adopted*, 199–201.

[224] In addition to Scott, see, e.g., O.L. Yarbrough, 'Parents and Children in the Letters of Paul', in L.M. White and O.L. Yarbrough (eds.), *The Social World of the First Christians: Essays in Honor of Wayne A. Meeks* (Minneapolis: Fortress Press, 1995), 140; Moo, *Romans*, 501; T.H. Tobin, *Paul's Rhetoric in Its Contexts: The Argument of Romans* (Peabody: Hendrickson, 2004), 287; Christoph, *Pneuma*, 229.

of this section is not to paint a comprehensive picture of these motifs in Paul's context. Such analyses have already been provided by previous scholarship.[225] We will, for instance, not investigate the moral obligations of children towards their parents as this topic has received much emphasis in the recent studies by Burke and others.[226] Rather, in this section we intend to demonstrate that *intimacy and closeness* were crucial aspects of the father-son relationship in Paul's context, and that these aspects are clearly present in the Pauline text under discussion. This is particularly important as these aspects are downplayed by Thompson and receive little emphasis in the treatment by Burke.[227]

To begin with, when one looks at the characteristics of *literal* family relationships in the Graeco-Roman and Jewish worlds, there is ample evidence that love and affection played a significant role in how parents related to their children. To give just one example each from Hellenism and Judaism, Plutarch says of the parent-child relationship that 'the end aim of bearing and rearing a child is not utility, but affection' (*Am. Prol.* 496C; cf. *Frat. Amor.* 480G).[228] This view is also reflected in the writings of the

---

[225] Regarding the OT, see A. Böckler, *Gott als Vater im Alten Testament: Traditions-geschichtliche Untersuchungen zu Entstehung und Entwicklung eines Gottesbildes* (Gütersloh: Kaiser/Gütersloher Verlagshaus, 2000), esp. 377–94; Thompson, *Promise*, 40–48; Chen, *God*, 73–111; regarding early Judaism, see J. Jeremias, *The Prayers of Jesus* (London: SCM Press, 1967), 15–29; Strotmann, *Vater*, *passim*; B. Chilton, 'God as "Father" in the Targumim, in Non-Canonical Literatures of Early Judaism and Primitive Christianity, and in Matthew', in J.H. Charlesworth and C.A. Evans (eds.), *The Pseudepigrapha and Early Biblical Interpretation*; JSPSup 14/SSEJC 2 (Sheffield: Sheffield Academic Press, 1993), esp. 166; T.J. Burke, *Family Matters: A Socio-Historical Study of Kinship Metaphors in 1 Thessalonians*; JSNTSup 247 (London: Sheffield Academic Press, 2003), 36–59; Christoph, *Pneuma*, 233–38; Chen, *God*, 113–43; regarding the Graeco-Roman world, see Scott, *Adoption*, 3–13; Burke, *Family*, 60–96; J.C. Walters, 'Paul, Adoption, and Inheritance', in J.P. Sampley (ed.), *Paul in the Greco-Roman World: A Handbook* (Harrisburg/London: Trinity Press, 2003), 42–55; Chen, *God*, 17–72; C. Zimmermann, *Die Namen des Vaters: Studien zu ausgewählten neutestamentlichen Gottesbezeichnungen vor ihrem frühjüdischen und paganen Sprachhorizont*; AJEC 69 (Leiden: Brill, 2007), 64–70.

[226] See Burke, *Adopted*, ch. 3; 144–48 (however, see his p. 65 n.34). Cf. O.L. Yarbrough, 'Parents and Children in the Jewish Family of Antiquity', in S.J.D. Cohen (ed.), *The Jewish Family in Antiquity*; BJS 289 (Atlanta: Scholars Press, 1993), 48–53; Thompson, *Promise*, 45: 'Fathers require obedience and honor, and a father was also accorded the task of discipline and correcting his children (Prov. 1:8; 4:1; 6:20; 15:5; 30:17).' Cf. the overview of the father's duties of correction and discipline in the OT, early Judaism and Paul in A.A. Myrick, '"Father" Imagery in 2 Corinthians 1–9 and Jewish Paternal Tradition', *TynBul* 47 (1996), 164–71.

[227] See the discussion above and at b) below.

[228] Cf. Seneca, *Clem.* 1.14.1–3 (on Préchac's counting: 3.12.1–3). For further examples, see C.S. Keener, 'Family and Household', *DNTB*, 357–58; Yarbrough, 'Letters', 132; Chen, *God*, 28–29.

Jewish philosopher Philo. Upon reading his treatment of the parent-child relationship, one may initially get the impression that Philo is only concerned with duties. However, he provides his readers with a hermeneutical key when he explains that this is mainly due to the fact that he is most of the time exegeting legal texts (see his reflections in *Spec. Leg.* 2.239–40). There is, nonetheless, sufficient proof that affections played a pivotal role in Philo's understanding of the parent-child relationship (e.g. *Spec. Leg.* 2.240: parents 'are fast bound to them [i.e. their children] by the magnetic forces of affection'; cf. 1.137; 2.236, 239; *Abr.* 168–70; *Ios.* 4).[229] Hence, Reinhartz can summarize her findings that 'it is clear that love and affection, particularly of parents towards children, was considered by Philo to be… a very powerful aspect of parenthood'.[230]

However, in accordance with the Pauline passage that we are investigating, the focus of the present section is on *metaphorical* family relations.[231] While there are a number of instances of divine adoption as well as the concept of God as a loving and gracious father in Greek and Roman religion (see, e.g., Seneca, *Ep.* 110),[232] the theme is most dominant in the Jewish tradition. The filial relationship between YHWH and the people of Israel (both corporately and individually)[233] is a seam that runs deep in the Hebrew Bible as well as early Jewish literature (see, e.g., Exod. 4:22; Isa. 43:6; Sir. 51.10; Tob. 13.5; Philo, *Conf.* 145; *Jub.* 2.20; 19.29; *L.A.B.* 16.5; *T. Job* 40.2; see esp. the connection with the giving of the spirit of holiness in *T. Levi* 18.6, 11–13).[234] It is a relationship characterized by the love of

---

[229] Cf. A. Reinhartz, 'Parents and Children: A Philonic Perspective', in S.J.D. Cohen (ed.), *The Jewish Family in Antiquity*; BJS 289 (Atlanta: Scholars Press, 1993), 81; Burke, *Family*, 47–48.

[230] Reinhartz, 'Parents', 81.

[231] Strictly speaking, Paul does not explicitly speak about the 'family' but about father-son language when he speaks about the relationship between God and believers (with the possible exception of Eph. 3:15 [πατριά], cf. n.210 above). However, as Paul does not appear to differentiate strictly between metaphorical fatherhood and motherhood (cf. 1 Thess. 2:11; 1 Cor. 4:15; Phil. 2:22; with Gal. 4:19; 1 Cor. 3:1–2; 1 Thess. 2:7; cf. the Jewish texts discussed below), it seems feasible to use the term 'family' loosely in this context.

[232] See Scott, *Adoption*, 56; A.J. Malherbe, 'God's New Family in Thessalonica', in L.M. White and O.L. Yarbrough (eds.), *The Social World of the First Christians: Essays in Honor of Wayne A. Meeks* (Minneapolis: Fortress Press, 1995), 119; Christoph, *Pneuma*, 232.

[233] God is presented as the Father of the nation (e.g. 4Q504 *frags.* 1–2 *col.* 3.5–7; see further Byrne, *Sons*, 23–63) and of patriarchs and kings, etc. (e.g. Ps. 2:7; see further Chen, *God*, 131–35). Cf. Thompson, *Promise*, 48 n.22.

[234] Burke observes that in the postexilic era we see YHWH desiring a new father-son relationship between himself and Israel, restated and again based upon the principle of reciprocity (e.g. Jer. 3:19) (Burke, *Adopted*, 53).

YHWH for his children (see, e.g., Deut. 32:6, 8–14; Isa. 63:8–10, 16; Sir. 4.10; *4 Ezra* 6.58; *Pss. Sol.* 18.3–4; Wis. 16.26). In order to get an impression of this love and intimacy we will look at some sample texts from various Jewish sources.

The emotive content of divine sonship in the Hebrew Bible is well illustrated by YHWH's proclamation 'When Israel was a child, I loved him, and out of Egypt I called my son... [I]t was I who taught Ephraim to walk, I took them up in my arms; but they did not know that I healed them. I led them with cords of human kindness, with bands of love. I was to them like those who lift infants to their cheeks. I bent down to them and fed them' (Hos. 11:1, 3–4;[235] cf. Deut. 1:31). The female aspects of YHWH's parenthood come (further)[236] to the fore in Isaiah 49:15–16: 'Can a woman forget her nursing child, or show no compassion for the child of her womb? Even these may forget, yet I will not forget you. See, I have inscribed you on the palms of my hands; your walls are continually before me' (cf. 66:13). Passages like these show that God's love is marked by emotional intimacy as well as practical education, even if this love stays unilateral as Israel has the freedom to reject it (see esp. Hos. 11). The filial relationship established by YHWH is characterized by the permanence and dependability of God's parental love (cf. Deut. 7:7–8), and it bestows on Israel a corporate identity as his children.

This biblical tradition is received and internalized by the Qumran community. The author of 1QH[a] 17.35–36 thus describes his relationship to YHWH: 'My father did not know me, and my mother abandoned me to you. Because you are father to all the [son]s of your truth. You rejoice in them, like her who loves her child, and like a wet-nurse you take care of all your creatures on (your) lap.' In this prayer the loving care of YHWH for the faith-community at Qumran is applied to the individual. The believer's relationship to the divine Father bears the marks of love, care, protection, nurture and education (cf. Jer. 31:9; Isa. 64:8–9).[237]

In a similar vein, Aseneth prays in *Joseph and Aseneth* 12.8, 15:

[8] For (just) as a little child who is afraid flees to his father, and the father, stretching out his hands, snatches him off the ground, and puts his arms around him by his breast, and the child clasps his hands around his father's neck,... and rests at his father's breast,... likewise you too, Lord, stretch out your hands upon me as a child-loving father, and snatch me off the earth. [...] [15] What father is as sweet as you, Lord, and who (is) as quick in mercy as you, Lord...?

---

[235] On the textual variants of this passage, see Chen, *God*, 88.

[236] It is possible to argue that the characteristics of God described in Hos. 11 are predominantly female (see the discussion in J.P. Kakkanattu, *God's Enduring Love in the Book of Hosea: A Synchronic and Diachronic Analysis of Hosea 11,1–11*; FAT II/14 (Tübingen: Mohr Siebeck, 2006), 127–30).

[237] Cf. Strotmann, *Vater*, 357–59.

This prayer, which contains a number of echoes of the Hebrew Scriptures (e.g. LXX Pss. 26:10; 67:6), portrays God as a loving father who is both strong and tender, who gives time and attention to his child. He knows what his child needs and acts upon it. Both father (God) and child (Aseneth) relish the intimacy of the relationship, and the child is able to put her trust in her Father. She experiences God as her 'home' where she is safe and valued.

We have already mentioned that in early Judaism the theme of divine sonship could be explicitly linked to the motif of adoption. This is evinced in Philo's depiction of Abraham's relationship with God in *De Sobrietate* 55–56.[238] Philo praises the closeness to God that is able to call God 'saviour and benefactor' rather than only 'master or lord'.

[55] For wisdom is rather God's friend than His servant.[239] And therefore He says plainly of Abraham, "shall I hide anything from Abraham My friend"? (Gen. xviii. 17). [56] But he who has this portion has passed beyond the bounds of human happiness. He alone is nobly born, for he has registered God as his father and become by adoption His only son, the possessor not of riches, but of all riches…

Being adopted (εἰσποιητός) is here seen as an equivalent to being a friend of God in whom he confides his thoughts and (secret) plans. God has become a father to Abraham, and Abraham enjoys the privileges of being his only son who shares in all God's riches and goods that 'ever renew their youth' (56). This state of being adopted as a son is presented as one of extreme happiness, and the human reaction is praise and worship of the heavenly Father (58). On a different occasion Philo even explicitly describes the effects of Spirit-worked 'coming near God in a kind of family relation' as a religious-ethical transformation ('being changed into the divine') that results in further closeness to and likeness of God ('becoming kin to God and truly divine') (*Quaest. in Exod.* 2.29; see 5.1.1.). Philo thus seems causally to connect the elements that we also find in Romans 8:12–17: adoption and sonship of God, an intimate relationship to God, religious-ethical transformation, and the Spirit. However, not all of these elements are present in one and the same passage because Philo does not explicitly relate the Spirit to adoption.

In the *Book of Jubilees*, however, we find all of these elements in 1:23–25 (cf. the full discussion in 5.1.3.). The giving of the S/spirit is connected to an intensification of the eschatological community's relationship to God

---

[238] On the identification of the person adopted, see the discussion in Scott, *Adoption*, 89 esp. n.137. On the religious background of *Sobr.* 55–56, see Scott, *Adoption*, 89–96. More generally on Philo's concept of relating to God as a father, see, e.g., *Quaest. in Exod.* 2.3; *Conf.* 145.

[239] The alternative translation by Yonge ('for what is wise is dearer to God than what is slavish') is linguistically possible too.

('their souls will cleave to me') and to religious-ethical living (doing God's commandments). A filial relationship is established ('I shall be a father to them, and they will be sons to me') which is characterized by love ('I shall love them'). It seems that this text – together with *Testament of Judah* 24.2–3 which, like *Jubilees* 1.23–25, draws on the tradition of Eze-kiel 36:25–28[240] – is most clearly echoed in the Pauline text under investigation because it not only depicts sonship as a loving, identity-forming relationship to God in the way illustrated by our sample passages above, but it also relates this empowering experience to the Spirit and to ethical living. We will return to the dynamics of how sonship of God can enable religious-ethical life in the next section. In the remainder of this section we will see how the characteristics attributed by the Jewish tradition to meta-phorical sonship are reflected in Paul, especially in Romans 8:15–16.

b) Adoption and Sonship in Paul (esp. Rom. 8:15–16). The frequency and variety of childhood language in Paul is conspicuous when compared with his Graeco-Roman contemporaries.[241] However, Paul employs this language mainly metaphorically.[242] Turning to the family imagery in Romans 8:14–17, we have seen that Thompson has put forward that the '*Abba*'-cry (αββα), the '*Abba*'-*cry* (κράζομεν) and the Spirit's bearing witness with our spirit (συμμαρτυρεῖ; vv.15–16) have wrongly been taken to be concerned with an intimate relationship with God.[243] We will briefly look at each of these three issues in turn.

While one may not agree with all aspects of Jeremias' landmark study on 'Abba',[244] scholars largely concur that the term *Abba*

is clearly enough an intimate way of addressing God using family language, whether by a child or an adult, and as such is less formal than addressing God simply as God or Lord. Jeremias's main point is that Jesus' choice of this term [cf. Mk. 14:36] reveals Jesus'

---

[240] See 5.1.3. On the influence of Ezek. 36–37 on Rom. 8:1–17, see H. Hübner, *Biblische Theologie des Neuen Testaments. Vol. 2: Die Theologie des Paulus und ihre neutestamentliche Wirkungsgeschichte* (Göttingen: Vandenhoeck & Ruprecht, 1993), 301–306; Hays, 'Pneumatologie', 32–33.

[241] See R. Aasgaard, 'Paul as a Child: Children and Childhood in the Letters of the Apostle', *JBL* 126 (2007), 154. Rom. has the highest amount of father-metaphors in the corpus (Hellerman, *Church*, 114).

[242] Cf. P. Müller, *In der Mitte der Gemeinde: Kinder im Neuen Testament* (Neukirchen-Vluyn: Neukirchener Verlag, 1992), 370–73.

[243] See 6.3.1.

[244] Jeremias, *Prayers*, 11–65. See the critical evaluation of J. Barr, 'Abba Isn't "Daddy"', *JTS* NS 39 (1988), 28–47; cf. Thompson, *Promise*, 28–34; Burke, *Adopted*, 92; etc.

awareness of his special relationship with God, and it is fair to say that this point withstands the recent critiques of his argument.[245]

In other words, even if 'Abba' was not unique to Jesus it certainly was his *distinctive* form of address, denoting with this language of the home his intimate relationship as the Son with his Father.[246] It is probably best translated with 'dearest Father' as this conveys both intimacy and respect while avoiding overly sentimental connotations.[247] The characteristics of love and affection of the divine-human father-son relationship that have been unfolded above are thus echoed in the filial address 'Abba'. This is also clear from the fact that the 'Abba'-cry functions as a contrast to 'fear' in 8:15 (parallel to the preceding contrast of sonship and slavery),[248] as well as from Paul's ascription of love to (metaphorical) fatherhood and to the Spirit in general.[249]

---

[245] B. Witherington III and L.M. Ice, *The Shadow of the Almighty: Father, Son, and Spirit in Biblical Perspective* (Grand Rapids: Eerdmans, 2002), 22; cf. 25–26, 29, 32; cf. O. Hofius, 'ἀββα', *ThBNT²*, 1722; K.-H. Ostmeyer, *Kommunikation mit Gott und Christus: Sprache und Theologie des Gebetes im Neuen Testament*; WUNT 197 (Tübingen: Mohr Siebeck, 2006), 65–66.

[246] Cf. G.D. Fee, *Pauline Christology: An Exegetical-Theological Study* (Peabody: Hendrickson, 2007), 219.

[247] Cf. Witherington III and Ice, *Shadow*, 25; Burke, *Adopted*, 94–95. Regarding the *Sitz im Leben* of the 'Abba'-cry Fee aptly comments that *Abba* 'is most likely to be heard in the gathered worship of the community. How this took place cannot now be determined with precision. Some would see it more liturgically, perhaps as referring to the address to God that begins the Lord's Prayer. But the language of "crying out" suggests something more spontaneous' (Fee, *Presence*, 409).

[248] Theobald observes that 'Ist die Perspektive der "Knechtschaft" die "Angst" (εἰς φόβον), so fehlt zwar auf der anderen Seite der oppositionelle Begriff, doch dürfte es die "Liebe" (ἀγάπη: 8,35.37.39; vgl. 5,5.8) sein, die jenes sich im Gebetsruf "Abba, Vater" artikulierende, neue Verhältnis der Glaubenden zu Gott am besten charakterisiert' (Theobald, 'Religiosität', 446). He understands 'fear' here as 'Grundstimmung der Angst' (p. 448).

[249] The 'Abba'-address thus receives its meaning not merely on the basis of semantics but also from how God is presented as a father in Paul and his context (cf. the methodological suggestions in Thompson, *Promise*, 33). Cf. Strotmann's conclusion that 'Nicht die individuelle Anrede Gottes mit "mein Vater" im Vokativ oder gar mit "Abba" ist Maßstab für Intimität und Nähe zwischen Gott als Vater und den Menschen als Sohn oder Tochter, sondern die Art und Weise, in der sich Gott fraglos und selbstverständlich für seine Kinder einsetzt und sich ihren Wünschen und Bedürfnissen aussetzt' (Strotmann, *Vater*, 379).

On Paul as a loving father, see, e.g., 1 Cor. 4:14–15; 1 Thess. 2:11–12. On God's fatherhood, see C. Spicq, *Agape in the New Testament. Vol. 2: Agape in the Epistles of St. Paul, the Acts of the Apostles and the Epistles of St. James, St. Peter, and St. Jude* (London: Herder, 1965), 320; Yarbrough, 'Letters', 132–33; Aasgaard, 'Paul', 146–49. On the Spirit, see esp. Rom. 5:5, as discussed the next section.

Thompson believes that the word κράζειν in the 'Abba'-cry does not re-fer to an experiential expression of an intimate relationship with God be-cause it is used in a prophetic context in Romans 9:27. Apart from Romans 8:15 and its parallel passage in Galatians 4:6, Romans 9:27 is the only usage of κράζειν in Paul. As κράζειν is used in the context of prophecy in 9:27, Thompson concludes that Paul uses it in 8:15 'because the Spirit is the ultimate source of these words, rather than because they signify the interior or emotional state of those who are speaking or a particular setting of prayer or worship.'[250] However, there is no need to see these two aspects as being in tension with one another. Moreover, one wonders why Paul by using the word κράζειν should want to emphasize the aspect of 'the Spirit as the source' over the experience of Spirit-moved prayer to God as Father, because he has already in the same verse explicitly stated that the cry is *by the Spirit* (ἐν ᾧ). 'By the Spirit' would therefore be redundant if it were contained in κράζειν. However, it is much more likely that Paul employs the word here with its standard meaning of (fervent) 'crying'.[251] This not only concurs with the majority of Septuagint and New Testament usage[252] but it also fits its present cotext where it is associated with the release from slavery and fear and with the adoption by a loving Father. (Apart from that, the cry in 8:15 is not a future prediction but refers to the *present* relation-ship to God as Father.)

The fact that the Spirit-inspired 'Abba'-cry thus gives expression to a *relationship* is sometimes used as an argument against its experiential side. For example, Burke, building on Dunn, argues that Paul describes a rela-tionship, not just an experience.[253] However, in contrast to Burke, Dunn continues: 'But Paul's language does not permit us to forget that the rela-tionship in view is one which for Paul was expressed in intensity of feeling as well as intimacy of expression.'[254] It therefore seems right to conclude that the 'Abba'-cry does not designate isolated experiences but a continu-

---

[250] Thompson, *Promise*, 128. Thompson's attempt to refer to Fee in support seems to be a case of misinterpretation (n.25, citing Fee, *Presence*, 567). See Fee, *Presence*, 409, where he is explicit that Paul describes 'spontaneous', 'charismatic', 'Spirit-inspired prayer' (cf. 410).

[251] See Jewett, *Romans*, 498. The experiential impact of κράζειν in 8:15 is affirmed by W. Bieder, 'Gebetswirklichkeit und Gebetsmöglichkeit bei Paulus: Das Beten des Geistes und das Beten im Geiste', *TZ* 4 (1948), 26; Käsemann, *Romans*, 227; Schreiner, *Romans*, 426; Witherington III and Ice, *Shadow*, 30; Bertone, *Law*, 201; etc.

[252] E.g. Exod. 22:23; 32:17; Matt. 15:22; 27:50; Mk. 9:24. Cf. Philo (e.g. *Virt*. 147; *Fug*. 15; *Ebr*. 96) and Josephus (e.g. *Ant*. 6.285; 10.117; *J.W.* 2.280; 5.111).

[253] Burke, *Adopted*, 145, referring to J.D.G. Dunn, 'Spirit Speech: Reflections on Ro-mans 8:12–27', in S. Soderlund and N.T. Wright (eds.), *Romans and the People of God: Essays in Honor of Gordon D. Fee on the Occasion of His 65th Birthday* (Grand Rap-ids/Cambridge: Eerdmans, 1999), 85.

[254] Dunn, 'Spirit Speech', 85. Cf. Giesen, 'Söhne', 92.

ous loving relationship which, like every active relationship, has an experiential side.[255] This comes particularly to the fore through the notion of
'crying'.

Finally, also Paul's point that 'the Spirit testifies with our spirit that we
are children of God' (8:16) conveys that the Spirit confirms the new relationship and the new identity that the Romans have come to experience.
Once again, Thompson sees things differently: '8:16 speaks *explicitly* of
the work of the Spirit, not of the "sense of sonship" which believers have.
In Romans 8, Paul celebrates the work of the Spirit in enabling Gentiles to
acknowledge God as the source of their life and salvation.'[256] However,
one wonders how the Spirit's work of testifying with our spirit that we are
children of God can be separated from what appears to be the very goal of
this testimony, namely confirming the filial relationship and the accompa-
nying 'sense of sonship' that is contrasted in verse 15 with slavery and
fear.[257] Moreover, Thompson seems to ignore that the notion of being
children of ἀββα ὁ πατήρ adds significant aspects to the soteriological
scenario described in the earlier parts of the epistle. We have seen that the
theological father-son imagery developed in the Jewish tradition and
adopted by Paul reaches beyond 'acknowledging God as source of one's
life and salvation'. It refers to an intimate, identity-shaping and empowering relationship in the present (and future).[258] Accordingly, Jewett writes
that

---

[255] Cf. the methodological considerations in Rabens, 'Development', 172–73.

[256] Thompson, *Promise*, 128, criticizing Dunn, *Theology*, 49.

[257] Burke cautions that 'this is no mystical experience, as though the Spirit subjective-
ly whispers to us "You are God's son." This "would amount to a new revelation from
God *over and above* the revelation given to us in Scripture"' (Burke, *Adopted*, 150, citing
S.B. Ferguson, *Children of the Living God* (Edinburgh: Banner of Truth, 1989), 73, italics
by Burke). However, this concern appears to project a post-Pauline biblicism upon the
text. Nonetheless, it is possible that Paul is here not concerned with the 'inner witness' of
the Spirit (Fee, *Presence*, 569; but see Cranfield, *Romans. I*, 402; Schreiner, *Romans*,
427). Yet, even if Paul meant to say that the 'Abba'-cry (v.15) *is* the testimony of the
S/spirit(s) (v.16) (thus RSV and NRSV), the Spirit-inspired prayer functioning as witness is
nonetheless an *experience* of being sons and daughters of ἀββα ὁ πατήρ. Cf. 8:23, 26–27,
and Dunn's comment that 'In the intensity of prayer and abandonment to God in what
would otherwise be total human despair, Spirit speech and heart language become as one'
(Dunn, 'Spirit Speech', 91).

On the principle of 'like is known by like' in this context, see Christoph, *Pneuma*,
246.

[258] Cf. P. Müller, 'Gottes Kinder: Zur Metaphorik der Gotteskindschaft im Neuen Testament', *JBTh* 17 (2002), 160–61: 'Mit Hilfe der Metapher "Kind Gottes" macht das
Neue Testament eine beziehungsreiche, das Vorhandene und das Mögliche verbindende,
auf Gegenwart und Zukunft bezogene, zum Handeln anregende und Gemeinschaft stif-
tende Aussage. Mit diesem Bild bewegen sich die frühen Christen innerhalb eines Erfah-

Since the Spirit impels believers to utter their prayers directly to their Abba, this is a powerful, experiential confirmation of their status as children of God. Since the Spirit confirms that they belong to God, there is no longer any basis for anxiety about their status. Their need for honor has been fully met by their relationship with the heavenly parent who loves them unconditionally according to the earlier argument of Romans (5:8, 15; 6:23).[259]

The result of the work of the Spirit is therefore not only (a sense of) sonship but with that also a 'sense of belonging' (this more comprehensive term also includes the 'need for honour' mentioned by Jewett).[260]

We have thus seen that the aspects of love, nurture and intimacy of the divine-human father-son relationship uncovered in Paul's context also apply to Paul's concept of Spirit-worked sonship of God. It has been established that this Spirit-shaped relationship has an experiential dimension (cf. 6.3.1.). We will finally take a closer look at the role of this relationship in the empowering of ethical life by the Spirit in 8:12–17.

3.3.2. Empowered by a Filial Relationship with God

We have argued above that the concern raised by Fee, namely that Paul fails to provide an explanation of how the 'putting to death the works of the body' (v.13b) can be done, is successfully answered by our relational model of the ethical work of the Spirit. We are now in a position to draw together a number of reasons that speak for our thesis that the Spirit-worked relationship to God unfolded in the verses succeeding verse 13 (esp. vv.15–16) explains how the 'putting to death' is empowered by the Spirit.

a) First of all, it has been demonstrated that the *syntactical structure* of 8:12–17 suggests that the Spirit-shaped relationship with God as Father (vv.14–16) empowers the ethical action described in verse 13. While this argumentative structure at first sight appears to allow for Burke's interpretation outlined above (i.e. that it is the believers' *duty* to kill the works of the body because they are children of God), a closer look favours the new reading put forward in our analysis. For one thing, the verse that most explicitly links sonship and ethics (i.e. v.14) specifies that the religious-ethical action (ἄγονται) which is the mark of sonship is *bestowed* upon believers *by the Spirit* (πνεύματι θεοῦ ἄγονται); the fact that ἄγονται is in

---

rungsraums, der sowohl Sprachtradition aufnimmt als auch selbst sprachprägend wirkt und metaphorisch fokussiert wird.' On filial identity, cf. Epictetus, *Diss.* 1.3.1–3.

[259] Jewett, *Romans*, 500.

[260] This conclusion is further supported by the texts discussed in the next section. On the aspect of honour, see also Esler, *Conflict*, 248–49.

the passive voice indicates that it is primarily a gift rather than a duty.[261] More significantly, this reading is further supported by the fact that Paul regularly associates the motif of human sonship of God with privileges (vv.14–17, 29; Gal. 4:5–7, etc.), not with duties.[262]

b) As far as the *content* of Paul's argumentation is concerned, we have seen that 'adoption as sons' is a transformative experience at conversion-initiation as well as a continual empowering in the course of Christian life. We will briefly focus on the empowering factors of new identity, intimacy and commonality of this relationship.

Firstly, upon the reception of πνεῦμα υἱοθεσίας one's *identity* changes from that of a slave to that of a son. Straub explains that 'identity is gained in *transitions*, that is to say, in the mental processing of transitions and transformations, not in fixed unchanging situations.'[263] The mental aspect of the new identity gained in this transition (i.e. adoption) includes a new self-understanding as a child of God as well as the identification with the family of God. Engberg-Pedersen stresses particularly the aspect of identification with Christ and the Father, which has 'the consequence that they [i.e. the Christ-believers] may now (and *only* now) *want for themselves* to do what is (also) God's will'.[264] The truth that identification leads to the internalization of the new identity and the values connected with it does not only resonate with the Stoic theory of οἰκείωσις (so Engberg-Pedersen)[265] but also with the findings of social psychology.[266] However, while psychology would comprehend the proclamation of Paul and potentially also the testimony of the Spirit (v.16) as 'performative language' that *brings about* sonship,[267] in Paul's presentation both the experience of the new reality (cf., e.g., 1 Thess. 1:5–6; Gal. 3:1–5) and the affirmation of it go hand in hand. It would therefore be one-sided to comprehend the new

---

[261] Accordingly, ὅσοι… οὗτοι is read with an inclusive meaning (cf. Cranfield, *Romans. I*, 395; Fee, *Presence*, 562–63; Moo, *Romans*, 498–99; J. Adam, *Paulus und die Versöhnung aller: Eine Studie zum paulinischen Heilsuniversalismus* (Neukirchen-Vluyn: Neukirchener Verlag, 2009), 352 n.67; etc.), not exclusively in the sense of 'only those who put to death/let themselves be guided… are sons of God'.

[262] Cf. the interpretation of 2 Cor. 6:17–18 in Rabens, 'Coming Out', 48 n.29, 64–66.

1 Thess. 5:5–6, where sonship is related to moral duty, does not employ the motif of being sons of God but of being 'sons of light and sons of the day'.

[263] J. Straub, 'Personale und kollektive Identität: Zur Analyse eines theoretischen Begriffs', in A. Assmann and H. Friese (eds.), *Identitäten*; Erinnerung, Geschichte, Identität 3; S-TW 1404 (Frankfurt: Suhrkamp, 1998), 92.

[264] Engberg-Pedersen, *Stoics*, 238; cf. 239, 252, 254. On identifying with Paul as father, see 1 Cor. 4:14–16.

[265] Ibid., 254.

[266] E.g. H.C. Kelman, 'Compliance, Identification, and Internalization: Three Processes of Attitude Change', *JCR* 2 (1958), 51–60.

[267] See Lampe, 'Identification', 940.

identity as a merely cognitive phenomenon. For Paul ascribes to the reality of sonship the experiences of being guided and of crying (vv.14–15), and he also leaves open whether the Spirit's testifying with our spirit is verbal or a non-verbal experience (v.16).[268] We can conclude, then, that the new identity as sons of God empowers believers for religious-ethical living as they come to know cognitively and existentially that they are no longer slaves but belong to God as loving Father, to Christ as their brother and to fellow believers as brothers and sisters (cf. v.29).[269]

Secondly, closely connected to this mode of empowering is the experience of an *intimate relationship* between son(s) and Father. It has become evident in the foregone exegesis that the new relationship described in 8:14–16 is one of closeness and intimacy. That such a relationship has a transforming and empowering effect on its members (or 'recipients' in the case of the divine-*human* relationship) has been demonstrated in chapters 4–5. Both Paul's context (e.g. Philo, *Op. Mund.* 144; *Quaest. in Exod.* 2.29; 1QH^a 8.19–20; *Jub.* 1.23–25; etc.; see ch. 5) as well as Paul's own writings (e.g. Phil. 2:1–2; 1 Cor. 8:1–3; Rom. 1:12; 8:37; see 4.3.) support this observation. Moreover, we have seen in 4.2. that psychological and sociological research likewise underpins our position. On this basis it is sound to conclude that by meeting the need for belonging and being parented,[270] the experience of adoption described in 8:14–17 strengthens believers at the core of their being.[271] With regard to the latter, it is striking that the direct parallel of 8:15, namely Galatians 4:6, specifies that the

---

[268] Cf. n.257 above.

[269] Cf. J. Webster, 'Christology, Imitability and Ethics', *SJT* 39 (1986), 309: 'How we see ourselves... determines how we conduct ourselves.' Ethical behaviour 'is narratively grounded because we act out of who we are' (B.J. Walsh and S.C. Keesmaat, *Colossians Remixed: Subverting the Empire* (Downers Grove: IVP, 2004), 157–58). Cf. Rabens, 'Coming Out', 64–66.

[270] The Spirit-inspired 'Abba'-cry is to some extent 'open' and associative language (cf. Rom. 8:23, 26–27) which has the capacity to express the human desires (of what psychologists call the 'inner child') for being parented (cf. the approach of *Rezeptions-ästhetik* outlined in Christoph, *Pneuma*, ch. 2). It is a channel for giving a voice to the needs left unmet by the deficiency of human parenting. While Paul does not say this *expressis verbis*, it nonetheless is an implication of what he describes, because being parented is one of the most basic experiences of human beings (also of Paul and his churches). Cf. Burke's reflection on the relevance of 8:15–16 in today's world where 'people "crave connectedness"' (Burke, *Adopted*, 196, citing J. Stevenson-Moessner, *The Spirit of Adoption: At Home in God's Family* (Louisville: Westminster John Knox Press, 2003), 1).

[271] Cf. Christoph, *Pneuma*, 263: Paul relates experiences 'die geeignet sind, das Selbstbewusstsein der Glaubenden zu stärken. Das wiederum erleichtert die Zustimmung zum paulinischen Evangelium. Denn wer sich wahrhaft angenommen fühlt, nimmt eher an, was seinem subjektiven Gefühl objektiv zugrunde liegt.'

Spirit of God's Son is given 'into our hearts'. Against the background of Pauline anthropology, this suggests that 'the reality of God's adoption/ acceptance reaches to the motivating and emotive centre of the person'.[272] This interpretation is strengthened by two parallel passages, namely Romans 5:5 and Ephesians 3:16–19, to which we briefly turn.

According to Romans 5:5, God's very love has been poured *into our hearts* through the Spirit,[273] which means that 'God's love for us had there become fully operative, both in *making us aware of its presence*, and in *transforming us*. Those whom he so loves God will not disappoint in the hope they set upon him.'[274] The virtues of endurance, character and hope (5:4) are thus anchored in the consolidating experience of God's love conveyed by the Spirit.[275] Accordingly, our point can be summarized with Berger's words that 'it is the relationship established by love that sets the condition within which and on the basis of which proper action becomes possible'.[276]

This thought is further developed in Ephesians 3:16–19.[277] There Paul prays that God

may grant that you may be *strengthened in your inner being* with power *through his Spirit*, [17] and that Christ may dwell *in your hearts* through faith, as you are being *rooted and grounded in love*. [18] I pray that you may have the power to comprehend, with all the saints, what is the breadth and length and height and depth, [19] and to *know*

---

[272] Dunn, *Galatians*, 219–20, referencing Rom. 2:29; 5:5; 6:17; 10:8–10; 2 Cor. 1:22; 3:2–3; 4:6; Phil. 4:7; 1 Thess. 3:13.

[273] The parallel of the reception εἰς/ἐν τὰς καρδίας ἡμῶν of the Spirit of adoption as sons and of love by the Spirit reiterates our point that the predominant characteristic of the filial relationship with God enabled by the Spirit is that of *love*. On love and the Spirit, see further Rom. 15:30 (διὰ τῆς ἀγάπης τοῦ πνεύματος). Cf. Spicq, *Agape*, 320.

As most scholars agree, one is here dealing with a subjective genitive (so, e.g., A. Nygren, *Commentary on Romans* (Philadelphia: Fortress Press, 1972 [1949¹]), 197–200; Thüsing, *Christum*, 133; Lohse, *Römer*, 169). However, our thesis is likewise supported if Paul intends to say that the Spirit enables us to love God (thus, e.g., Augustine, and P.D. Gardner, *The Gifts of God and the Authentication of a Christian: An Exegetical Study of 1 Corinthians 8–11:1* (Lanham: University Press of America, 1994), 28).

[274] C.K. Barrett, *A Commentary on the Epistle to the Romans*; BNTC (London: Black, 1957), 105, italics added. Cf. Schlatter, *Theology*, 269; Dunn, *Romans 1–8*, 265–66; Munzinger, *Spirits*, 177.

[275] Cf. Käsemann, *Romans*, 135–36; Keck, *Romans*, 138.

[276] Berger, *Identity*, 206.

[277] For our method of dealing with disputed Pauline epistles, see 1.4. For recent cases for the authenticity of Eph., see, e.g., H.W. Hoehner, *Ephesians: An Exegetical Commentary* (Grand Rapids: Baker, 2002), 2–61; F. Beißer, 'Wann und von wem könnte der Epheserbrief verfasst worden sein?', *KD* 52 (2006), 151–64. See also, more generally, V. Rabens, 'Ephesians', in M.D. Coogan (ed.), *The Oxford Encyclopedia of the Books of the Bible* (New York/Oxford: Oxford University Press, 2011), 1:237–43.

the love of Christ that surpasses knowledge, so that you may be *filled with all the fullness of God.*

The theme of love appears twice in this passage: being rooted and grounded in love (v.17), and knowing the love of Christ (v.19). It is evident that the second occurrence regards 'divine' love, whereas in the first instance, where a defining genitive is missing (like ἀγάπην τοῦ Χριστοῦ [v.19]), a number of scholars suggest that the reference could be human love.[278] However, even in this case the notion of divine love should not be ruled out, particularly as it is the basis of human love.[279] In any case, the fact that being grounded and rooted in love refers to an ethical attitude and action in which the believers become established, evidences that in this passage the empowering by the Spirit in the inner being and the intimate presence of Christ (and love) in the heart[280] lead to a strengthened (ethical) character as the result.[281] Turner likewise sees an ethical notion in this passage when he maintains that the phrase 'filled with the whole fullness of God' means living 'in total unity with God and completely under his reconciling sovereignty, i.e. in the "new humanity" ethics of Ephesians 4–6. The revealing and wisdom-enabling "Spirit of prophecy" is thus also a potent ethically-transforming power.'[282] This is particularly true as Paul here speaks of the revelation and existential knowing of the *love* of Christ which roots and grounds the Ephesians in love. Romans 5:5 and Ephesians 3:16–19 thus provide further evidence for our argument developed in this

---

[278] So Hoehner, *Ephesians*, 483, and the scholars mentioned there.

[279] Cf. E. Best, *A Critical and Exegetical Commentary on Ephesians*; ICC (Edinburgh: T. & T. Clark, 1998), 343; Lincoln, *Ephesians*, 207.

[280] The inner being is equivalent to the heart, i.e. Paul is here concerned with the inner being of the *believers*, not with Christ (thus most scholars, as, e.g., J.P. Heil, *Ephesians: Empowerment to Walk in Love for the Unity of All in Christ*; SBL 13 (Leiden: Brill, 2007), 152–53). That the Spirit relates the intimate presence as well as deeper knowledge of God to believers has been set out in the course of Eph. (1:17; 2:22). Particularly relevant for our present discussion of empowerment through filial intimacy is the affirmation that it is *by the Spirit* that we have access to the *Father* (2:18).

[281] Cf. Rabens, 'Transforming Relationships', 15–16; followed by E.A.G.D. Petrenko, '"Created in Christ Jesus for Good Works": The Integration of Soteriology and Ethics in Ephesians' (University of Durham: Unpublished PhD Thesis, 2005), esp. 17 n.84, 205. Now also M. Turner, 'Approaching "Personhood" in the New Testament, with Special Reference to Ephesians', *EQ* 77 (2005), 227–28.

However, scholars disagree whether 'being rooted and grounded in love' is connected to what precedes (thus our argument; cf. the presentation in Best, *Ephesians*, 343) or to what follows (thus Hoehner, *Ephesians*, 483–84).

[282] Turner, *Spirit*, 110. Foster has recently suggested that the 'fullness of God' may alternatively refer to God's glory (R.L. Foster, '"A Temple in the Lord Filled to the Fullness of God": Context and Intertextuality (Eph. 3:19)', *NovT* 49 (2007), 94).

section that a Spirit-shaped, filial relationship with God characterized by love and intimacy empowers believers ethically.

Returning to Romans 8:15–16 and its direct parallel Galatians 4:4–6, it seems that in Romans 8 the Spirit-shaped intimate relationship with God is more clearly linked to religious-*ethical* living (as is clear from vv.12–14), whereas the emphasis in Galatians 4:1–7 is on *religious*-ethical living.[283] This is particularly evident from the way in which Paul continues his argument in Galatians.[284] In the succeeding section (4:8–11) Paul explains to the Galatians that the filial relationship to God that they have come to experience through the Spirit is in stark contrast both to their former life in bondage (indicated by the opening ἀλλά; see also 3:23–27) and to their present inclination to return to this slavery (indicated by the question in v.9). As Barclay evinces, the issues at stake in the Galatian crisis were the identity of the Galatian Christians and their appropriate patterns of behaviour.[285] Paul reacts to this insecurity by pointing them to their Christ-created and Spirit-sustained filial relationship with God which is the reason why they no longer need the law as their identity marker and moral code, or 'guardians and trustees' (v.2) to look after their religious-ethical life. Since they have entered a relationship of filial intimacy with God (v.6; knowing God and being known by him [v.9]) the Galatians need not submit to the law[286] and thus return to being enslaved to the στοιχεῖα τοῦ κόσμου (vv.3, 9),[287] trying to perfect by the flesh what they had begun by the Spirit (3:3). Rather, they are enabled to live according to the values of

---

[283] For further similarities and differences between the two texts, see Horn, *Angeld*, 329 n.70; Fee, *Presence*, 406; Moo, *Romans*, 497–98; Christoph, *Pneuma*, 254, 257. The differences are exaggerated by Tobin, *Rhetoric*, 286–87, 297.

[284] The ethical relevance of the argument in Gal. 4:1–7 for what follows has also been recognized by C.H. Dodd, *The Epistle of Paul to the Romans*; MNTC (London: Fontana, 1959), 143.

[285] Barclay, *Truth*, 73–74.

[286] Cf. Dunn, *Romans 1–8*, 460: Sonship, including adoptive sonship, 'speaks of freedom and intimate mutual trust, where filial concern can be assumed to provide the motivation and direction for living, and conduct be guided by spontaneous love rather than by law' (cf. Dunn, *Galatians*, 226–27). The Spirit provides all the necessary guidance in the fight against the flesh (Barclay, *Truth*, 116).

[287] Cf. Campbell, *Quest*, 41: 'Christ makes Christians into fully relational beings, that is, into real full persons. "In him" they can relate to God and to each other as they ought to. Outside of him, humanity is enslaved to hostile and evil forces that curve people in on themselves, away from God and from others, corrupting and distorting all their relationships.'

For a recent discussion of the reference point of στοιχεῖα τοῦ κόσμου, see Christoph, *Pneuma*, 250–52.

the Spirit (cf. 5:16–24)[288] and thus demonstrate ongoing loyalty and public honour to their heavenly Father[289] in the face of the agitators.

An additional dimension of the Spirit's enabling for religious-ethical life through filial intimacy with God is the fact that receiving the Spirit of S/sonship implies that one's relationship to God is modelled on that of Jesus with his Father. How is this aspect indicated in the text? For one thing, the only other occurrence of the 'Abba'-cry in the New Testament is recorded to be that of Jesus during his earthly ministry (Mk. 14:36). As one can assume that Paul was aware of this tradition, it seems reasonable to comprehend Romans 8:15 and Galatians 4:6 as a deliberate echo of this expression of Jesus' relationship to his Father.[290] More explicitly, in the context of the believers' 'Abba'-cry Paul identifies the Spirit as the *Spirit of the Son* (Gal. 4:6: 'God has sent the Spirit of his Son into our hearts, crying, "Abba! Father!"'; cf. Rom. 8:9–11). Moreover, in Romans 8 Paul draws at least two parallels between the life of Jesus and that of the believers in Rome. In verse 17 the apostle specifies that believers are fellow heirs with Christ, provided they suffer with him. In verse 29 he even speaks of being 'predestined to be conformed to the image of his Son, in order that he might be the first-born among many brethren' (cf. v.11; see also 6.2.2.2., and 1 Cor. 2:16). On this basis one may agree with Longenecker that believers have 'been brought into the sphere of Jesus' own intimate and obedient relationship to God…'.[291] In the same vein, Thüsing

---

[288] When studying the ethical work of the Spirit in Gal. one usually turns to 5:16–24. There Paul is very clear that the Spirit guides and empowers believers in their struggle with the flesh. However, Paul does not seem to indicate in that passage *how* the Spirit empowers ethical life. It thus appears that Paul presupposes certain truths about the work of the Spirit that one would miss when studying exclusively ch. 5. It is our contention that this clue is revealed in 4:1–7.

[289] Cf. W.B. Russel, III, *The Flesh/Spirit Conflict in Galatians* (Lanham: University of America Press, 1997), 99.

[290] Cf. Witherington III and Ice, *Shadow*, 23, 29; Motyer, 'Not Apart', 244. It is striking that when Jesus needs strengthening in the situation of greatest distress and inward struggle (between 'Spirit and flesh', cf. Mk. 14:38), he draws on his intimate relationship with the Father, addressing him with 'Abba'. (For further parallels between the Gethsemane event and Rom. 8, see D. Wenham, *Paul: Follower of Jesus or Founder of Christianity?* (Grand Rapids: Eerdmans, 1995), 276–80).

[291] Longenecker, *Triumph*, 62. However, Longenecker does not give the textual support provided above. He may thus fall prey to Thompson's general criticism that it is not at all clear that one can 'legitimately transfer Jesus' sense of consciousness to believers' (Thompson, *Promise*, 128 n.25). However, the exegesis provided here does not focus on Jesus' *consciousness*. Further, it needs to be admitted that the aspect of obedience is not explicit in Gal. 4:4–6 and Rom. 8:15–16. Nonetheless, the contexts of both passages seem to imply that a more comprehensive imitation of Jesus is in view rather than merely the prayer "Abba" (cf. Rom. 8:14, where sonship has an obvious ethical dimension).

speaks of the 'Einbeziehung in die Sohnschaft Christi selbst',[292] specifying that

wenn dieses Pneuma des Sohnes in uns "Vater" ruft, dann ruft es der Sohn selbst in uns durch seinen Geist, *genauso wie er nach Gal 2,19f in uns für Gott lebt.* Und wie dem Leben Christi in uns sein eigenes Leben für Gott zugrunde liegt, so ist es auch hier: Der erhöhte Christus selbst lebt in der liebenden Anrede an den Vater...[293]

Hence, we can conclude that the intimacy created by the Spirit between believers and their Father is not limited to the emulation of Jesus' prayer-life but seems to extend more comprehensively to the imitation of the Son's religious-ethical life before God. This supports our general conclusion of this sub-point, namely, that Romans 8:12–17, its parallel in Galatians 4:4–6 as well as further Pauline passages (esp. Rom. 5:5; Eph. 3:16–19) demonstrate that the filial intimacy with God that believers come to experience through the Spirit of adoption as sons has become the fundamental formative force in the believers' lives and empowers them for religious-ethical living.

The third and final aspect of the empowering work of the Spirit in Romans 8:12–17 that we will briefly look at is the *communal nature* of the Spirit-shaped filial relationship with God. This aspect has already caught our attention in the context of our discussion with Thompson (6.3.1.). The collective nature of the experience of the Spirit comes to the fore in our text through the way in which Paul integrates himself in the communal prayer that testifies to the intimacy-creating work of the Spirit. In 8:15–16 Paul says that '*you* have received a spirit of adoption. When *we* cry, "Abba! Father!" it is that very Spirit bearing witness with *our* spirit...'. The same movement from 'you' to 'we' is evident in Galatians 4:6: 'because *you* are children, God has sent the Spirit of his Son into *our* hearts, crying, "Abba! Father!"'. This shared experience reinforces existentially the corporate identity as children of God upon the members of the community. However, it cannot be played off against the notion of the individual.[294] Nonetheless, each member is taken beyond herself and becomes part of a (fictive) kin group of brothers and sisters (ἀδελφοί [Rom. 8:12, 29]; τέκνα

---

[292] Thüsing, *Christum*, 119. Turner speaks of the Spirit *recapitulating Jesus' 'sonship' to God* in the disciple (Turner, *Spirit*, 120). Cf. Dunn, *Jesus and the Spirit*, 320; C. Schwöbel, 'Human Being as Relational Being: Twelve Theses for a Christian Anthropology', in C. Schwöbel and C.E. Gunton (eds.), *Persons, Divine and Human: King's College Essays in Theological Anthropology* (Edinburgh: T. & T. Clark, 1991), 155.

[293] Thüsing, *Christum*, 117, italics added.

[294] Cf. 4.4.1.; 6.3.1. On the corporate dimension, cf. 6.4.; Dunn, *Galatians*, 220; Thompson, *Promise*, 129; Christoph, *Pneuma*, 263–64; Horrell, *Solidarity*, 110. Chamblin notes that Paul habitually speaks of God as 'our Father', never as 'my Father' (Chamblin, *Self*, 206).

θεοῦ [v.16]; cf. κληρονόμοι θεοῦ, συγκληρονόμοι Χριστοῦ [v.17]). The communal experience of the Spirit-inspired 'Abba'-prayer in public worship[295] draws the believers closer to the Father as well as to one another as brothers and sisters. Both aspects enforce the formative and empowering character of the religious-ethical work of the Spirit in Romans 8:12–17.

3.4. View Ahead (Rom. 8:17) and Conclusion

Paul brings his argument from verses 12–16 to a conclusion in verse 17.[296] He draws the Romans' attention to further benefits of their adoption as sons, namely, they are heirs of God and joint heirs with Christ. Paul thus takes up a topic started in 4:13 where he explained that Gentile believers have become co-heirs with Jewish believers. In verse 17 Paul reiterates the corporate dimension of being children of God. However, the relational aspect of being an heir is extended from this sociological to a Christological level. Indicated by the triple συν-, Paul stresses that believers have come to be so closely bound up with Christ that they not only share in his inheritance but also in his suffering love. Christ has suffered for them, now they suffer with him. As Käsemann puts it: 'Where Christ is present in the Spirit, one can in no way escape following the Crucified.'[297]

However, the Spirit is present in the midst of this suffering and once again empowers the Romans by drawing them closer to God. This manifests itself, for one thing, in the 'Abba'-*cry* in verse 15, which gives evidence of the realized dimension of adoption as sons.[298] However, as verse 17 conveys, sonship also has a future dimension because believers await the glorification with Christ (cf. v.23: 'we wait for adoption as sons'). In this eschatological tension, 'the Spirit himself intercedes for us with sighs too deep for words... according to the will of God' (vv.26–27).[299] Hence, both in situations of trial by the flesh (vv.12–13) and trial through suffering (vv.17–27) the Spirit draws people into an intimate relationship with God which empowers them to persevere and overcome.

Our analysis of Romans 8:12–17 (and the parallel passages discussed in this context) thus leads to the conclusion that – contrary to Fee's judgement – Paul clearly indicates how the Spirit empowers people to put to death the works of the body: believers draw strength and motivation from

---

[295] Cf. n.247 above.

[296] On the integration of v.17 with vv.12–16, see n.167 above.

[297] Käsemann, *Romans*, 229.

[298] However, as Burke rightly argues, *Abba* may also be a cry of dependency upon God the Father for support and strength for days ahead (Burke, *Adopted*, 95–96, building on Wenham, *Paul*, 276–80).

[299] Prayer is thus presented by Paul as tuning into something that is already there: the Spirit prays within the believers (vv.26–27; Gal. 4:6).

the new identity, the intimacy and the corporate dimension of the Spirit-shaped filial relationship with God, epitomized in the Spirit-inspired prayer 'Abba, dearest Father'.[300]

4. Ethical Empowering through the Communal Work of the Spirit

Throughout the second part of this monograph we have repeatedly seen that the Spirit not only empowers people through an intimate relationship with God, but also through relating them more deeply to the community of faith. This became evident in our study of early Judaism in chapter 5 as well as from the Pauline texts examined in the present chapter (see esp. the preceding section). In this final section we will focus on this 'sociological' aspect of the Spirit's empowering for religious-ethical life because it has been largely ignored by previous discussions of Spirit and ethics in Paul.[301]

4.1. Being Built Up by the Gifts of the Spirit

In his endeavour to discover what for Paul the giving of the Spirit implies for ethics, Horn starts off by discounting the relevance of the catalogue of *charismata* specified in 1 Corinthians 12. Horn justifies this decision with the observation that no ethical aspects are mentioned in the text.[302] However, by means of a brief survey of a variety of Pauline texts dealing with the gifts of the Spirit we will be able to show that the apostle comprehended these effects of the Spirit as a means of building up the community. In this way believers are individually and corporately empowered for religious-ethical living.

While the main focus of our survey will be on 1 Corinthians, we will start by looking at a more general passage that delineates the empowering

---

[300] Fee's question appears to put slightly stronger emphasis on how *the believer* can – by the Spirit – put to death the works of the body (Fee, *Presence*, 559 n.254). The answer to this lies in the perspective on the Spirit's empowering work outlined above: as the believer knows the mode of empowering, she can consciously draw on these sources of strength. See further ch. 7.

[301] While the ethical significance of the gifts of the Spirit has been recognized by a number of scholars (see W. Schrage, *Die konkreten Einzelgebote in der paulinischen Paränese: Ein Beitrag zur neutestamentlichen Ethik* (Gütersloh: Mohn, 1961), 176, 180–86; U. Brockhaus, *Charisma und Amt: Die paulinische Charismenlehre auf dem Hintergrund der frühchristlichen Gemeindefunktionen* (Wuppertal: Brockhaus, 1975), 220; Turner, 'Spirit of Prophecy and the Ethical/Religious Life', 189; Samra, *Christ*, 136–52; Howard, *Paul*, 151), this is usually not integrated into studies on the ethical work of the Spirit.

[302] Horn, 'Wandel', 164.

work of the Spirit in interpersonal dynamics. In Romans 1:11–12 Paul expresses the longing to see the Romans 'so that I may share with you some spiritual gift to strengthen you – or rather so that we may be mutually encouraged by each other's faith, both yours and mine'. Paul does not specify what he has in mind when he speaks of the 'spiritual gift' (χάρισμα πνευματικόν) that he wants to share. It is possible that he refers more narrowly to the 'gifts of the Spirit' listed in 1 Corinthians 12 etc., or more broadly to a 'spiritual blessing' like his intended visit to the Romans.[303] However, with regard to both meanings it is clear that the 'embodiment of grace' (χάρις) of which Paul speaks is 'some act of ministry which is both of the Spirit and a means of grace'.[304] Its effect is strengthening and empowering.[305] This is even intensified by the fact that Paul longs for *mutual* participation in each other's spiritual life which results in both parties being encouraged (v.12).

In 1 Corinthians Paul overtly relates the spiritual gifts to the centre of his ethics, namely love. This is evident from the place that he gives to his major treatment of love: it is the central piece of 1 Corinthians 12–14. Stettler highlights the fact that in this way Paul emphasizes that love is the purpose of and criterion for spiritual gifts. He concludes that Paul's teaching about spiritual gifts is an integral part of his ethical teaching.[306]

In 12:7, which can be seen as containing the teaching of chapters 12–14 in a nutshell,[307] Paul says that 'to each one is given the manifestation of the Spirit for the common good'. The very general 'common good' (συμφέρω) can be rendered as 'building up' (οἰκοδομέω) because in 10:23 the two terms are parallel.[308] This suggests that the Spirit builds up the individual members as well as the faith-community at large through providing gifts that can be used for and within the community. Such building up, however, also means that people are empowered to become, in Dunn's words, 'more fully the corporate embodiment of Christ'.[309] This latter concept is more comprehensively elaborated in Ephesians 4:11–14: 'The gifts he [Christ]

---

[303] For the latter option, see, e.g., Cranfield, *Romans. I*, 79; Fee, *Presence*, 487–88. More generally on the differentiation of Paul's terminology of spiritual gifts, see Samra, *Christ*, 121 n.59. However, it is not necessary for our purposes to discuss the potential differentiations within the broader semantic field of 'gift' in Paul.

[304] Dunn, *Romans 1–8*, 30.

[305] Στηρίζω belongs to the group of words that conveys the central concept of 'empowering' utilized in our study. See the definition in ch. 4. n.10. Cf. Samra, *Christ*, 86.

[306] C. Stettler, 'The "Command of the Lord" in 1 Cor 14,37 – a Saying of Jesus?', *Bib* 87 (2006), 46. Cf. 1 Cor. 8:1.

[307] Cf. Brockhaus, *Charisma*, 136; Schrage, *Korinther. III*, 111; Stettler, 'Command', 44.

[308] Cf. Thiselton, *Corinthians*, 936; Samra, *Christ*, 150.

[309] Dunn, *Jesus and the Spirit*, 321.

gave were that some would be apostles, some prophets, some evangelists, some pastors and teachers, to *equip* the saints for the work of ministry, for *building up* [εἰς οἰκοδομήν] the body of Christ, until all of us come to the *unity of the faith* and of the *knowledge of the Son of God*, to *maturity*, to the *measure of the full stature of Christ*. We must no longer be children....'
The connection of religious-ethical life modelled on Jesus and the gifts of the Spirit (although it is not explicated but probably assumed that these are of the Spirit)[310] clearly indicates the communal work of the Spirit.

1 Corinthians 14 spells out in more detail how the individual gifts can strengthen and empower the body of Christ. For example, the Spirit builds up individuals through the gift of tongues. However, Paul admonishes the Corinthians that as a church they should rather give more space to prophecy as this builds up others within the community (vv.4–5, 12).[311] Paul is thus aware of the empowerment and building up of people that is the result of the Spirit's work in the dynamics of interpersonal relationships. People are influenced by what others say, so that Spirit-inspired speech can convict a person that enters the church and encourage a reaction that can be characterized as 'religious-ethical' ('that person will bow down before God and worship him, declaring, "God is really among you"', vv.23–25).

In this context it is of particular interest that the Spirit shapes the actual structure of the individual interpersonal interactions within the community. Paul says that 'if there is no one to interpret, let them [i.e. those who speak in tongues] be silent in church and speak to themselves and to God' (v.28). The Spirit is thus able to inspire greater sensitivity to others in the community. People need to listen to one another in order to be built up (cf. vv.29–30).[312] Again, the result of this Spirit-inspired dynamic is that 'all may learn and all be encouraged' (v.31).

We have seen that the Spirit strengthens people through the intra-communal interactions inspired by the gifts of the Spirit. In our second and final subsection we will ask whether Paul's employment of the concept of κοινωνία πνεύματος likewise suggests religious-ethical empowering.

---

[310] Cf. Hoehner, *Ephesians*, 541.

[311] Paul does not discredit the 'upbuilding' character of the 'non-prophetic' gifts. Particularly through the gift of tongues the Spirit can empower some (cf. 12:30) believers by thus drawing them closer to God. However, in 1 Cor. 12–14 the emphasis is on the empowering that results from the Spirit-enhanced *interpersonal* dynamic.

[312] On the 'upbuilding' character of prophecy, see further Dunn, *Jesus and the Spirit*, 229–33. On the communal nature of guidance and decision-making, see Furnish, *Theology*, 233–35; Lewis, *Life*, e.g. 220; Munzinger, *Spirits*, 70–73. On the ethical effects of Spirit-imbued teaching, see, e.g., 1 Thess. 1:4–7; and A.W.D. Hui, 'The Concept of the Holy Spirit in Ephesians and its Relation to the Pneumatologies of Luke and Paul' (Aberdeen: Unpublished PhD Thesis, 1992), 283; Turner, 'Spirit of Prophecy and the Ethical/Religious Life', 189; Turner, *Power*, 122. Cf. ch. 4 n.32.

4.2. Participation in the Spirit

In Philippians 2:1 Paul draws on a number of factors that facilitate the ethical attitudes called for in verse 2: 'If then there is any encouragement in Christ, any consolation from love, any sharing in the Spirit, any compassion and sympathy, [2] make my joy complete: be of the same mind, having the same love, being in full accord and of one mind.' In verse 1 Paul singles out a number of aspects of intimate relationships which give him the confidence that the Philippians will be able to put into practice the ethical imperative of verse 2. As κοινωνία πνεύματος is mentioned as one of these relational factors, the question arises whether this concept lends further support to our relational model of the empowering work of the Spirit in Paul's ethics. The answer appears to depend on whether one renders the genitive πνεύματος as subjective or objective. Is Paul suggesting, in line with the previous section, that the fellowship that is created *by* the Spirit empowers the Philippians? Or does he say that it is the fellowship *with* (the person of) the Spirit that strengthens believers?[313]

Although commentators are in two minds regarding this question, a majority appears to side with the view that we are dealing with an objective genitive. However, it is usually not rendered as 'fellowship with the Spirit' but as 'participation in the Spirit'.[314] The grammatical reasons for this decision do not need to be rehearsed here, apart from the additional point that the concept of 'fellowship with the Spirit' does not exists anywhere (else) in the Pauline corpus (cf. 4.4.2. above). Harris explains with regard to the parallel usage in 2 Corinthians 13:13 ('The grace of the Lord Jesus Christ, the love of God, and the communion of the Holy Spirit be with all of you' [NRSV]) that Paul is expressing the wish 'that the Corinthians

---

[313] Thus Vang, 'Presence', 118; cf. our discussion in 4.4.2.

[314] So, with regard to both Phil. 2:1 and 2 Cor. 13:13, J.K. Campbell, 'KOINΩNIA and its Cognates in the New Testament', in J.K. Campbell, *Three New Testament Studies* (Leiden: Brill, 1965), 25–27; H. Seesemann, *Der Begriff KOINΩNIA im Neuen Testament*; BZNW 14 (Gießen: Töpelmann, 1933), 56–73; H.-D. Wendland, 'Das Wirken des Heiligen Geistes in den Gläubigen nach Paulus', in E. Schlink and H. Volk (eds.), *Pro Veritate: Ein theologischer Dialog*; FS L. Jaeger and W. Stählin (Münster: Aschendorffsche Verlagsbuchhandlung, 1963), 137; Dunn, *Jesus and the Spirit*, 261; O'Brien, *Philippians*, 172–74; Fee, *Presence*, 363–64; Dunn, *Theology*, 561–62; M.E. Thrall, *A Critical and Exegetical Commentary on the Second Epistle to the Corinthians. Vol. 2: Commentary on II Corinthians VIII–XIII*; ICC (Edinburgh: T. & T. Clark, 2000), 914–21; Marshall, *Theology*, 430; et al.

Scholars preferring a subjective genitive include Martin, *Corinthians*, 505; L.L. Belleville, *2 Corinthians*; IVPNTCS (Downers Grove/Leicester: IVP, 1996), 338; W.C. Kaiser, Jr., 'The Holy Spirit's Ministry in Personal Spiritual Development: Ephesians 5.15–21', in W. Ma and R.P. Menzies (eds.), *The Spirit and Spirituality: Essays in Honour of Russell P. Spittler*; JPTSup 24 (London: T. & T. Clark, 2004), 54; S.E. Fowl, *A Commentary on Philippians*; THNTC (Grand Rapids: Eerdmans, 2005), 80.

should continue (cf. 1 Cor. 1:7; 12:13) in their common participation in the Spirit's life, power, and gifts (cf. 1 Cor. 12:7; 14:1). Yet this "participation in the Spirit" inevitably results in an ever-deepening fellowship among believers.'[315]

The objective genitive reading thus does not rule out the central aspect of the subjective genitive meaning. In fact, some scholars have even suggested that Paul has both ideas in view.[316] That is, 'the apostle's final prayer in 13:13 functions as a reminder to the community of the Spirit's presence *and* of the community-building behavior that the Spirit enables'.[317] However, while one may not want to go as far as claiming that both renderings of the genitive were in mind *at the same time*, the comprehension of the two meanings as standing in a relationship of cause and effect (as implied by Harris above) seems to be a plausible reading. In other words, for Paul Christian fellowship grew out of common participation in the Spirit; however, the believers' 'experience of the Spirit was one in which others had also shared [and] which provided the bond of mutual understanding and sympathy'.[318]

Against this background of interpretation we can take Paul's strategy of employing the concept of 'participation in the Spirit' in his argumentation in Philippians 2:1–2 and the significance that he attributes to it in his wish for the Corinthians[319] as further support for our relational model of the Spirit's empowering for ethics.

Therefore, we conclude that Paul not only believed the Spirit to facilitate an intimate relationship with the divine in order to empower religious-ethical life. Rather, also the way in which the Spirit shapes the community through spiritual gifts and through common participation in the Spirit strengthens believers for ethical conduct.

5. Conclusion

In this chapter we have demonstrated that the relational model of Spirit-enabling for ethical life suggested in chapter 4 and explored in Paul's context in chapter 5 has a thorough grounding in Paul's letters. In our

---

[315] Harris, *Corinthians*, 941.

[316] So recently again Stegman, *Character*, 319; Samra, *Christ*, 138.

[317] Stegman, *Character*, 319.

[318] Dunn, *Theology*, 562.

[319] The fact that Paul expresses κοινωνία τοῦ ἁγίου πνεύματος as a wish for the Corinthians as well as the parallelism with the 'grace of the Lord Jesus Christ' and 'the love of God' indicates that the experience of this reality is of ultimate benefit for the recipients.

exegesis of 2 Corinthians 3:18 we have seen how believers are transformed through deeper knowledge of, and a more intimate encounter with, the divine. The goal of this transformation is 'the same image', that is, the likeness of Christ. 'Transformation through contemplation' thus has significant implications for religious-ethical life.

In Part I we criticised the proponents of the infusion-transformation approach for building their model on strongly-debated or even enigmatic Pauline texts without providing sufficient exegetical details for their interpretations of these passages. In the case of 2 Corinthians 3:18 we too have employed a debated text. However, we have devoted adequate space to a discussion of alternative readings so that our argument is built on a firm basis.

While Paul employed the concept of 'transformation' in 2 Corinthians, this is not specified in the case of Romans 8:12–17 and the further passages discussed in 6.3. Nonetheless, in our analysis we have established that Spirit-worked adoption into God's family is a transforming and empowering experience. The intimate relationship to God as Father expressed in the 'Abba'-cry shapes the identity of believers and empowers them both individually and corporately to 'kill the works of the body'.

Finally, we were able to show that the communal work of the Spirit has been underestimated in previous studies on Spirit and ethics in Paul. However, Paul portrays the Spirit as drawing believers closer to one another in the way in which he gives different spiritual gifts to different people within the community of faith. Both in this way, as well as through their common experience of 'participation in the Spirit', believers are 'built up' and encouraged in their religious-ethical life.

Part III

Conclusions

Chapter 7

Conclusion

1. The Results of this Study

This study has investigated the ethical work of the Spirit in Paul's epistles. In order to find an answer to the question how the Spirit transforms and empowers believers for religious-ethical living, we have studied various texts from early Judaism, Hellenism and from Paul. In the first part of our study we have looked at passages which had been put forward to support the view that the Spirit substance-ontologically transforms believers by virtue of its physical nature. With regard to the presupposed material nature of πνεῦμα we saw that certain strands of Hellenism subscribed to this view of the spirit. However, neither the Hebrew Bible and early Judaism nor Paul give evidence of this pneumatological concept. Moreover, none of these sources give any indication that believers were believed to be empowered for ethical life through the transformation with such πνεῦμα-*Stoff*. This is also to a large degree true for Hellenism. For this reason we were able to dismiss this approach, which we named 'infusion-transformation', in chapters 2–3 of our study. While Stoic philosophy could have been a potential breeding ground for the concept of infusion-transformation, our study discovered that the actual concept itself is missing in Stoicism (the divine Spirit is not at some point infused into believers and πνεῦμα is only seldomly connected to ethical living). Nonetheless, from the perspective of the *reception* of Paul's letters it cannot be ruled out that Paul's Spirit-language, as for example the image of being made to drink of the Spirit (1 Cor. 12:13), evoked associations of Stoic pneumatology in Paul's audience. However, the philosophic language of Stoicism fundamentally differs from that of Paul, and it would need to be proven that Stoic pneumatology was part of the general education of the members of Paul's churches (and not only of the educated elite), and that they would, over and above that, be able to fill the logical gaps between the role of πνεῦμα in Stoic physics and the infusion-transformation concept of ethical enabling.

In the second part of the book we suggested a novel approach to the ethical work of the Spirit. In our programmatic chapter 4 we have unfolded how Paul's theology, and his approach to the ethical work of the Spirit in particular, can be understood as *relational*. The concept of relational transformation and empowering put forward in our study overcomes the perceived opposition of 'substantive' and 'relational' change. We have argued that the experience of intimate relationships transforms people both in their being as well as empowering them for moral conduct.

In chapter 5 we returned to Paul's religious context. This time we wanted to see whether our proposed model of the ethical work of the Spirit is echoed in the writings of Paul's contemporaries. The results of this investigation were positive. Particularly Philo (with an emphasis on mystical encounters with God), the DSS (with an emphasis on the cognitive side of knowing God), and a number of Jewish traditions based on Ezekiel 36:25–28 give evidence of the concept that the Spirit enables religious-ethical life through providing deeper knowledge of and an intimate relationship with God. A closer relationship with the faith-community also plays a role in this model of Spirit-empowering.

By means of a detailed exegetical investigation of 2 Corinthians 3:18 we were able to show in chapter 6 how the notion of Spirit-worked contemplation of the divine is comprehended by Paul as a means of (religious-ethical) transformation. Romans 8:12–17, Galatians 4:1–7, Romans 5:5 and Ephesians 3:16–19 lend further support to our relational approach. In our close examination of Romans 8:12–17 we have seen how the intimate relationship of sonship of God that is brought about by the Spirit of adoption is presented by Paul as the reason why believers can 'kill the deeds of the body'. Finally, it became evident that also the communal work of the Spirit (through gifts given by and participation in the Spirit; 1 Cor. 12:7; Phil. 2:1–3; etc.) strengthens and enables believers in their religious-ethical life.

2. The Implications of this Study

We will now look at some of the more specific results of this thesis with an eye to their broader implications for the study of early Judaism and the relevant aspects of Pauline theology.

One of the more far-reaching implications of the results of this monograph derives from our study of Spirit-metaphors. In the context of our discussion of 1QH[a] 15 we have applied the insights of current linguistic studies on metaphors to the figurative language of the Spirit as being 'poured out'. The interpretative model that we designed in this context was utilized throughout our study (esp. in our exegesis of 1 Cor. 12:13). The result of this study of Spirit-metaphors significantly contributes to our thesis that both early Judaism and Paul do not evidence a physical concept of the Spirit. This finding is important for future studies that may look at early Jewish and early Christian pneumatology from different perspectives to our own (e.g. cosmology or theology).

However, not only is the *result* of our linguistic study of relevance for further pneumatological research. Rather, the *methodology itself* set out in this context is valuable for future studies of Spirit-metaphors as well as biblical metaphors in general. Applying the methodological steps outlined in 2.2.2.1. will prevent further biblical metaphors being misinterpreted in a way similar to those that were foundational for the infusion-transformation approach.

Moreover, not only is future research on biblical pneumatology in a position to avoid building on the false assumption that early Jewish and Christian writings understood the Spirit as a physical substance, but also the terminological confusion surrounding the concept of 'substance' itself has been cleared up through our differentiations. We have argued in 1.3. that one should henceforth speak of 'physical substance' or 'material substance' when referring to the concept of (Spirit as) *Stoff*. This prevents further confusion with the philosophical notion of 'substance'.

2.1. Further Implications for the Study of Early Judaism

Our investigation of early Jewish pneumatology has provided further support for the view that there is a wide variety of Jewish literature in which the Spirit is comprehended as a moral agent.[1] Although this is the majority position among scholars, it has been challenged by Horn in his response to Gunkel.[2] In our portrait of the ethical work of the Spirit in early Judaism it was striking that the Spirit was related to a broader concept of ethical empowering that has thus far been overlooked by scholarship from Gunkel to Horn and beyond. Namely, ethical life is comprehended as being empowered by deeper knowledge of God and an intimate relationship with him and with the community of faith.

We have demonstrated that the concept of relational empowering also played a role in texts that did not specified the Spirit as the prime agent in this process. In this regard, future researchers may want to inquire whether this broader model of relational transformation and empowering (set out in 4.4.1.) also applies more generally to early Jewish thought.[3] Such a study would deepen our understanding of the anthropology and soteriology of the various strands of early Judaism.

A further implication of our study of the Spirit in early Jewish literature concerns the nature of Jewish thought in this regard. While it would be too

---

[1] See ch. 5, esp. 5.1.

[2] See Appendix 3.1.

[3] See the positive answer to this question that was formulated on the basis of a number of selected texts in the introduction of 5.1.

far-fetched to conclude from our investigation that Jewish thought was generally less interested in abstract notions (like the inquiry into the nature or ontology of the S/spirit), we were nonetheless able to ascertain with regard to the matter of our examination that this interest was not evinced in the literature that was studied (with the exception of Philo). Rather, both the Hebrew Bible and early Jewish literature focus mainly on the effects of the Spirit and the Spirit's work. The Hellenistic writings that were part of our analysis, however, displayed a stronger interest in the ontology of the Spirit. These insights could be taken into account in further studies that try to fathom the more general characteristics of early Jewish and Hellenistic thought.[4]

2.2. Further Implications for Pauline Theology

2.2.1. Implications for Pauline Theology in General

Our research has proven the infusion-transformation approach to the ethical work of the Spirit in Paul to be ill-founded. For further studies on Pauline theology this implies that it is untenable to argue *on the basis that the Spirit is a physical substance* that the change brought about through baptism or the καινὴ κτίσις *et alii* should be primarily understood as substance-ontological transformation. While we have not ruled out that Paul might operate with aspects of a substance-ontological framework, we have suggested an approach that seems to do more justice to Paul's thought. The second part of our study, particularly the programmatic chapter 4, points towards the direction of a more relational understanding of Paul's theology in general. This perspective is undervalued in most Pauline studies.[5]

We have indicated in chapter 4 that this relational perspective on Paul's theology is able to combine a number of aspects that have thus far often been understood as opposite lines of Paul's theology. We will apply our findings to the issue of Paul's ethical 'indicative and imperative' below. As a suggestion for further research, however, it seems that the discussion between the defenders and the critics of the 'New Perspective on Paul' could benefit from adopting this perspective more comprehensively.[6]

---

[4] Nonetheless, we have indicated in 2.2.1. that attempts at generalization of this matter should be treated with caution.

[5] Exceptions are Dunn and Campbell (see 4.3.–4.4.1.). However, it seems that this insight is not the guiding principle of their respective portrayals of Pauline theology.

[6] See Dunn, *Theology*, 344, as cited in 4.4.1., who expresses this perspective *in nuce*. Cf. the discussion in Bird, *Righteousness*, 39, 86–87.

2.2.2. Implications for Pauline Pneumatology

We have seen that Paul relates the Spirit more broadly to ethical living than evinced by Horn in his article on 'Walking by the Spirit'.[7] In this respect, but also regarding the 'mechanics' of the enabling work of the Spirit, Paul's pneumatology is firmly rooted in early Jewish thought. Hence, the contention that Paul adopted major parts of his pneumatology from the Graeco-Roman world did not hold upon close scrutiny.

We have observed that Paul does not discuss the mode of Spirit-reception. It seems that he does not share the concerns of a number of the proponents of the infusion-transformation approach who think that the Spirit needs physical substances like the sacraments in order to be taken up by the believer. Likewise, it appears that Paul is less concerned with the ontology of S/spiritual matter(s) than his Graeco-Roman contemporaries. These observations need to be taken into account in future studies of Pauline pneumatology. It could also be tested whether this hesitation is characteristic of Paul's thought more generally.

In line with the fundamental point of the book *Paul Beyond the Judaism/Hellenism Divide*, edited by Engberg-Pedersen (2001), it is an over-simplification to try to connect Paul to either a 'Hellenistic-materialistic' or to a 'Jewish-immaterialistic' pneumatology. However, it is likewise a false dichotomy when one forces a division between either a Stoic or a Platonic reading of πνεῦμα in Paul, as Engberg-Pedersen appears to do.[8] Engberg-Pedersen does not reckon with a third option, which is that Paul did not follow the agendas of either of these philosophical schools. Paul does not inquire into the (im/material) nature of πνεῦμα. The closest Paul comes to this interest in ontology is when, *upon the question of the Corinthians*, he discusses the nature of the resurrection body (1 Cor. 15:35–54). However, it is the *resurrection body* that is in focus, not the nature of πνεῦμα. It is therefore misleading to make this the starting point not only of one's conception of Pauline pneumatology but also of Paul's theology in general (but thus Engberg-Pedersen: 'Our guiding question will be how we should understand the *sōma pneumatikon*, and hence the pneuma. The answer to this question will turn out to have huge consequences for everything else we should say about Paul.'[9]).

We have seen that the relational model of the ethical work of the Spirit coheres well with Paul's theology in general (ch. 4). In the final section we will now discuss further implications for Pauline ethics.

---

[7] See the summary and critique in Appendix 3.1.

[8] See Engberg-Pedersen, *Cosmology*, 16–19.

[9] Ibid., 14.

2.2.3. Implications for Pauline Ethics

Our study confirms the trend in Pauline scholarship towards understanding Paul's theology and ethics as interwoven.[10] The relational approach established in the second part of our study presents the divine Spirit as deeply integrated in the religious-ethical life of believers. Through being drawn closer to God, Jesus Christ and the community of faith believers are transformed and empowered by the Spirit for religious-ethical life. Moreover, as we have indicated above and discussed in 4.4.1., this model has the capacity to point beyond some of the conceptual impasses of Pauline studies. Here we want to draw attention to the implications of our relational approach to Spirit and ethics for the disputed relation of 'indicative' and 'imperative' in Paul.[11]

First of all, we need to emphasize that the transferral into the realm of influence of the Spirit has established new realities. The 'indicative' of the Spirit being in the believer[12] and the believer being in the Spirit[13] is not a state of affairs that would need to be 'actualized' through the deeds of the believer.[14] While there is an existential element in the Spirit-inspired Abba-cry of the believer (Rom. 8:15; cf. Gal. 4:6), it needs to be stressed that the existential encounter with God as one's Father that gives rise to this cry is part of a continual filial relationship with God. What matters to Paul is therefore not just a new self-understanding as υἱὸς τοῦ θεοῦ but the ongoing experience of God's relating to the believer as his son through the Spirit. The experience of being part of God's family is part and parcel of this reality.

Therefore, one of the strengths of our thesis over against the line of scholarship that seems to collapse the pneumatological 'indicative' into the ethical 'imperative' is that it reckons with the reality of God's empowering presence – of a transcendent God who becomes immanent in his Spirit but is not lost in the immanence of human relationships. Accordingly, the kind of relationality that is at the heart of Paul's Spirit-ethics is one in which Spirit and believer do not fuse but remain independent subjects. In sum,

---

[10] See, e.g., Engberg-Pedersen, *Stoics*, 137; Petrenko, 'Christ', *passim*.

[11] We do not intend to revert to the traditional indicative-imperative approach to Paul's ethics as this schema is inadequate to capture the full breadth of Paul's moral reasoning (cf., e.g., Zimmermann, 'Indikativ', *passim*). Nonetheless, in the present subsection we try to translate a number of the key features of our dynamic, relational model of Paul's Spirit-ethics into the framework of the indicative-imperative structure which has shaped the contours of the scholarly discussion of Paul's moral reasoning throughout the history of research (see the Appendix, esp. 2.1.).

[12] Cf. ch. 3 Excursus 1.

[13] Cf. Rom. 8:9 et al.; see 6.1.

[14] *Pace* Bultmann, *Theology. I*, 336.

the new relational realities are established *by the Spirit*, not by the believer's ethical actions or feelings of being emotionally close to God.

However, while the precedence of the work of the Spirit in the ethical life of Christians needs to be maintained (cf. 6.3.3.), the role of Paul's ethical imperative should not be undermined. Although our relational approach to the *ethical work of the Spirit* in Paul naturally focuses on the Spirit and not on the work of the believer, the being and doing of the believer has a clear place in our model. The Spirit draws believers closer to God and to the faith-community – both initially at conversion-initiation and continuously in the course of Christian life. However, it is *the believer* who is transformed and empowered in the course of this process. Accordingly, it is not the Spirit who lives ethically within the believer. Paul does not present the believer as needing to 'tune in' to the ethical conduct of the Spirit at the core of the person's being in the sense of a co-operation.[15] Rather, the Spirit enables ethical living by drawing believers into the loving and empowering presence of the divine and of the community of faith. The moral character and the ethical actions are that of the believer, but they are lived within these loving relationships and can to a large extent be regarded as an outflow of the continual experience of love (cf. Rom. 5:5; 15:30; Eph. 3:16–19).

There is no automatism implied in the approach to the ethical work of the Spirit according to Paul proposed in this study. When Paul writes in 2 Corinthians 3:18 that 'we all, with unveiled face, beholding the glory of the Lord as in a mirror, are being transformed into the same image from one glory to another' and ascribes this transformation to the Spirit, he neither raises nor answers the question why some of the members of his churches appear to be less transformed into the image of Christ than others. However, a potential answer to this question could be the recognition that it is possible to resist the relational work of the Spirit. That is, resist-

---

[15] *Pace* Deidun, *Morality*, 79–81, 243 (cf. Appendix n.94).

Cf. Barclay's apt summary that 'It appears that human agency is the *necessary expression* of the life of the Spirit, and certainly not its antithesis; the two are not mutually exclusive as if in some zero-sum calculation. And it is necessary not only because God's grace engages the will and action of the believer, but also because it is always possible to reject the grace of God.' Barclay asks further how this human agency as reconstituted in Christ may be comprehended. He explains that 'although in one sense we may speak properly of a "dual agency", in non-exclusive relation, this would be inadequately expressed as the co-operation or conjunction of two agents, or as the relationship of gift and response, if it is thereby forgotten that the "response" continues to be activated by grace, and the believers' agency *embedded within* that of the Spirit' (Barclay, '"By the Grace of God"', 156). Cf. J. Koenig, *Charismata: God's Gifts for God's People*; BPCI (Philadelphia: Westminster Press, 1978), 78; H. Löhr, 'Paulus und der Wille zur Tat: Beobachtungen zu einer frühchristlichen Theologie als Anweisung zur Lebenskunst', *ZNW* 98 (2007), 187–88.

ing the love of God and of Christ and defying the encouragement that can be experienced in the church (see 1 Cor. 12:7; Phil. 2:1–3; etc.) means missing out on the ethically transforming and empowering work of the Spirit.

We will close by formulating positively what has just been said about the potential resistance of believers to the ethical enabling by the Spirit. In this way we shall also be able to summarize our reply to the contentions of Schweitzer and Fee that Paul does not provide enough details for us to comprehend how one can practically walk by the Spirit. While it needs to be granted to Schweitzer that Paul does not offer a psychological analysis of the conscious or subconscious cognitions of the individual in the process of change, it is nonetheless possible to draw out a number of significant components of ethical transformation and empowering by the Spirit. Most fundamentally, we have seen that our focal theory itself provides sufficient details of how such change and empowering happens. We have demonstrated in 4.2. that psychological studies both cohere with our findings and offer further insights into the 'mechanics' of how relationships transform and empower people. Moreover, we can infer from the model of relational empowering that we have discovered to be characteristic of Paul's pneumatology that in situations when ethical living is at stake believers can deliberately draw on these sources of strength (particularly when they are aware of this mode of spiritual empowering). As believers let themselves be drawn by the Spirit into the transforming and empowering relationships with God and the community of faith and then live according to the values set forth by Paul's gospel, the depth of their relationship to God and others will increase. Believers are thus further empowered as they put Paul's imperatives (which are, in fact, aimed at deepening their relationships to God and others) into practice.

Appendix

140 Years of Research on Spirit and Ethics in Paul: A Critical Overview

While many have written with pertinence to Spirit and ethics in Paul, only K. Stalder has made this area the main focus of a monograph. Stalder puts strong emphasis on the need for a history of research in this field. However, he has to regret that his own study cannot provide such a *Forschungsgeschichte* even though it would be 'doubtlessly of the highest value'. The reason for his omission of this task is his caution in avoiding simplification and schematization of this large history.[1] Indeed, Stalder's caution is justified, for it is impossible to summarize the research into this broad subject in only a few words or even try to review all of the various answers that have been given throughout the course of church history. In order to avoid over-simplification, the present *Forschungsgeschichte* will therefore limit itself to the important task of analysing the last 140 years of 'critical' research on the sanctifying work of the Spirit in Paul. Moreover, we will allocate sufficient space for this project, especially as such a work seems to be missing in the English-speaking world. The only major history of research on Pauline pneumatology was part of a *traditionsgeschichtliche* investigation with focus on soteriology, published 1973 in German.[2] For this reason the present history of scholarship will take a slightly broader focus and touch upon pneumatological and ethical issues that relate to our

---

[1] Stalder, *Heiligung*, 5.

[2] Vos, *Untersuchungen*, 1–25. However, see the very focussed studies on aspects of Pauline pneumatology in Fatehi, *Relation*, 23–45; Philip, *Origins*, 3–25; Christoph, *Pneuma*, 11–24. For a comprehensive *Forschungsgeschichte* of NT pneumatology in general, see the recent C. Strecker, 'Zugänge zum Unzugänglichen: "Geist" als Thema neutestamentlicher Wissenschaft', *ZNT* 25 (2010), 3–20. On Pauline ethics in general, see Furnish, *Theology*, 242–79; W.L. Willis, 'Bibliography: Pauline Ethics, 1964–1994', in E.H. Lovering and J.L. Sumney (eds.), *Theology and Ethics in Paul and His Interpreters: Papers in Honor of Victor Paul Furnish* (Nashville: Abingdon, 1996), 306–19; Zimmermann, 'Indikativ', 260–72; N.K. Gupta, 'The Theo-Logic of Paul's Ethics in Recent Research: Crosscurrents and Future Directions in Scholarship in the Last Forty Years', *CBR* 7 (2009), 336–61.

central question (as, e.g., the debate over the nature of the Spirit with its potential consequences in the way in which the Spirit works).[3]

It is difficult to divide the history of scholarship into different phases. For example, it seems that at the time when the *religionsgeschichtliche Schule* was *en vogue* in Pauline studies, not all of the scholars that we are reviewing were influenced by the agenda of this school of thought. Nonetheless, it is possible to say that scholarship before the 1920s was more interested in Paul's religion, whereas the succeeding scholars had a greater focus on Paul's theology.[4] Our own division of the first 120 years of the history of scholarship into two periods of sixty years each (1868–1930: from Ernesti to Schweitzer; 1930–1990: from Bultmann to Dunn) broadly falls into these two categories. However, thereupon follows a third phase which cannot be subsumed according to theological categories. This includes the more recent scholarship from 1990 onwards.

1. The Interplay of Spirit and Ethics in Paul's Religion: 1868–1930 (From Ernesti to Schweitzer)

1.1. The Interpenetration of Human and Divine Activity (H. Ernesti)

The first critical study of Pauline ethics was published by H. Ernesti in 1868. Ernesti maintains that Paul understands the whole ethical life of the Christian as 'walking in the Spirit'.[5] The divine πνεῦμα is the principle of life by whose power the person for whom this objective principle has become a subjective possession lives truly ethically (6). The Holy Spirit brings freedom from the power of sin (43), so that the Christian will 'spontaneously' live 'das aus bewußter Selbstthätigkeit hervorgehende mit dem Gesetze Gottes übereinstimmende Leben', which is the essence of Pauline morality.[6] However, this ethical *Selbstthätigkeit* (self-acting performance) of the believer needs to be differentiated from mere moral conduct since

der Gläubige seine *Selbstthätigkeit* sich als *Gottesthätigkeit* vollziehen läßt, indem derselbe sich nicht aus selbstgemachtem Vorsatz für das entscheidet, was das Gesetz verlangt, sondern sich durch Gottes Wirkung aus dem Geiste der Kindschaft, den er empfangen hat, für Gottes Willen bestimmen läßt (67; cf. 44).

---

[3] On this see esp. 1.2. where the infusion-transformation approach is presented in detail.

[4] Cf. Way, *Lordship*, 52.

[5] Ernesti, *Ethik*, 70, 13, 43.

[6] Ibid., 105; 5, 3. Ernesti believes that although the law has been fulfilled by Christ, it remains the norm of Christian life as law of the Spirit (Ernesti, *Ethik*, 65).

But how does this determination by the Spirit of sonship to do God's will manifest itself? According to Ernesti, life in the Spirit starts when at re-birth God transforms the person into his image at the centre of her person-ality (22–25). This bestowal of an 'ontic and growing ἁγιωσύνη' (2 Cor. 7:1; Phil. 1:9; Eph. 4:15) (41–42) upon the individual effects a *progressive transformation* of all aspects of the person's life in daily renewal (2 Cor. 4:16) (42, 49–51, 60, 65). Thus, both the initial transferral of holiness as well as the following process of sanctification are *God's work* of creative power (2 Cor. 5:18; 1 Cor. 6:11) (23). Nevertheless, in respect to sanctifi-cation (in which holiness is brought to completion) (49), the *work of the Christian* seems to receive more attention in Paul (e.g. 1 Thess. 4:3, 7; Phil. 2:12) since the divine πνεῦμα has become *immanent* to the human spirit (50).[7] Consequently, Paul exhorts his congregations that they need to fight against their 'sarkische Regungen' which oppose the walk by the Spirit. Paul asks 'daß ihr Wollen adäquat gemacht werden müsse mit dem Sollen, welches die ihnen mit der Gabe des Geistes gestellte Aufgabe... vorhält' (66; cf. 61). In sum, Ernesti concludes regarding the interpenetra-tion of the Spirit's and the believer's activity in sanctification that the

mit der Liebe vorhandene Übereinstimmung des Wollens mit dem Sollen ist insofern kein eigenes Werk des Menschen, als die Liebe nichts durch eigenen Vorsatz Selbstgemachtes, sondern eine Gabe des Gottesgeistes ist, Gal. 5, 22..., aber jenes Wollen ist eben die dem erneuerten Menschen eigenthümliche Selbstthätigkeit, wie sie der Glaube, sobald mittelst desselben das πνεῦμα Gottes dem Menschen immanent wird, von Anfang an in sich enthält und aus sich heraus gestaltet (75–76).[8]

As the first critical scholar to research Paul's ethics, Ernesti had the chance to set the scene for the following generations of Pauline scholars. Ernesti was indeed successful in doing so. However, his own thinking was also shaped by previous scholars, in particular F.C. Baur's *Tübingen School* and the influence of idealism. Ernesti's concept of *Selbstthätigkeit* clearly echoes Baur's emphasis on *Selbstbewußtsein*, and his talk of the Spirit of God as 'objective principle' which becomes subjective possession and indeed 'immanent' to the human spirit sounds like Baur at his best.[9]

---

[7] Concerning the human activity which is 'latent in the passivity of Spirit-reception', see Ernesti, *Ethik*, 24–27.

[8] A view similar to Ernesti's was later put forward by *H. von Soden* who speaks of the *fusion* of the (divine) ethical powers with the human personality (H. von Soden, 'Die Ethik des Paulus', *ZTK* 2 (1892), 109–145, esp. 145). However, von Soden has a slightly stronger emphasis on human responsibility when he says that the step from living in the Spirit to walking by the Spirit (Gal. 5:25) is taken by a *Spirit-empowered free decision* (2 Cor. 3:17; von Soden, 'Ethik', 120–21).

[9] F.C. Baur, *Paulus, der Apostel Jesu Christi: Sein Leben und Wirken, seine Briefe und seine Lehre – Ein Beitrag zu einer kritischen Geschichte des Urchristentums. Vol. 2* (Osnabrück: Zeller, 1867[2] [1845[1]]), 133ff. Cf. C. Holsten, 'Die bedeutung des wortes

His notion of continual moral progression is likewise derived from the philosophy of idealism.[10]

However, one may want to question whether this developmental understanding of the ethical life under the influence of the Spirit is really characteristic of Paul. Ernesti has successfully identified many themes essential to Paul's ethic. But Ernesti seems to give too little emphasis to Paul's own pivotal terms. Perhaps partially due to the fact that he does not look at Paul's religious context, Ernesti uses concepts foreign to Paul in order to understand Paul. For instance, when Ernesti accents the Spirit-worked and thus almost automatic *Selbstthätigkeit* of the renewed, one is left with the question where exactly this notion is present in Paul. Also, does Paul really have the cognition of holiness as 'ontic and growing' at the same time? Does this holiness grow out of the 'centre' of the person toward the 'periphery' (42)? And, how does the Holy Spirit become immanent to the human anyway? The answer to these questions can only be determined by an exegetical investigation into Paul's thought, which Ernesti has unfortunately not provided.

1.2. Two Opposite Principles are at Work in Christian Life at Different Times (O. Pfleiderer)

Otto Pfleiderer was the first scholar to give considerable weight to the role played by the Holy Spirit in Paul's theology. He thinks that it was Paul who inaugurated a decisive change of view by which the primitive church made the transition from an abstract, supernatural, ecstatic, apocalyptic concept of πνεῦμα as a *donum superadditum*, to πνεῦμα as an immanent, religious, moral principle which determines the whole of Christian life.[11] Paul developed this view not just from his Jewish background, but mainly from his first 'pneumatic' experience which he interpreted as a manifestation of the glorified Christ:[12]

σάρξ im lehrbegriff des Paulus (1855)', in C. Holsten, *Zum Evangelium des Paulus und des Petrus: Altes und Neues* (Rostock: Stiller'sche Hofbuchhandlung, 1868), 378–88, which was especially dedicated to 'Ferdinand Christian Baur, dem gestorbenen aber nicht toten' (!).

[10] Cf. Baur, *Paulus*, e.g. 233.

[11] Pfleiderer, *Paulinism*, 200, 21–22; O. Pfleiderer, *Lectures on the Influence of the Apostle Paul on the Development of Christianity. The Hibbert Lectures, Delivered in London and Oxford, 1885* (London: Williams and Norgate, 1897³), 82–83.

[12] O. Pfleiderer, *Primitive Christianity: Its Writings and Teachings in their Historical Connections. Vol. 1* (Clifton: Reference Book Publishers, 1965), 369, 377, 409. Pfleiderer acknowledges that he was made aware of the centrality of Paul's conversion experience by Holsten (Pfleiderer, *Paulinism*, v).

Feeling himself by his faith in the Lord, who is the spirit, made into *one* spirit with him, he saw in the holy spirit the indwelling and constant principle, or "law," of his new life, and a principle which does not manifest itself merely in certain extraordinary impulses and miraculous powers, but as the creative energy of a "new creature," in the renewing of the heart, in the sanctification of the entire life, in the generation of every Christian virtue, in a growing likeness to the image of Christ.[13]

However, although it was predominantly his Christology and his own experience which led Paul to employ the Spirit as the foundation of his ethics,[14] these were not the only forces which shaped his thinking. According to Pfleiderer, Paul's theology and especially his view of life in the Spirit was additionally moulded by the fact that Paul had no other forms at command to express his Christian experience than the animistic conceptions of ancient supernaturalism.[15] Paying tribute to this supernaturalism in Paul means for Pfleiderer avoiding the harmonisation of the two Pauline representations of Spirit-reception, namely, through the *word* (Gal. 3:2, 5; 1 Cor. 2:4) and through *baptism* (1 Cor. 6:11; 12:13; Gal. 3:27; Rom. 6:3ff.).[16] Such harmonization is often done by alleging that, since in baptism the faith which is wrought by the word comes first to maturity and completion, it is in *baptism* that the appropriation of the Spirit as the content and power of faith is first brought to completion. In contrast, Pfleiderer reckons it to be better to let these two methods of Spirit-impartation stand side by side without interconnecting them, because in the Pauline description of life in the Spirit the supernatural-*mystical* and the psychological-*ethical* aspects go side by side but are unconnected.

Pfleiderer sees the juxtaposition of these two lines in Pauline pneumatology with especial lucidity in Paul's understanding of the relation of the communicated divine Spirit with the natural human spirit or ego. On the one hand, Paul implies that the divine and the human πνεῦμα co-exist and work upon one another (e.g. Rom. 8:16, 26; 1 Cor. 2:12–13). On the other hand, in many passages the distinction between the divine and the human πνεῦμα in the Christian cannot be maintained; the divine has entered into the human and has become one with the human πνεῦμα, so that one can speak of their relation as that of content and form. The religious activity as well as the ethical self-estimate of the 'spiritual man' is therefore 'accomplished in the strength and according to the norm of the divine Spirit, who, however, has become his own new or divine-human spirit' (e.g. Rom. 8:6,

---

[13] Pfleiderer, *Lectures*, 81.

[14] Pfleiderer, *Paulinism*, 21, 27, 111; Pfleiderer, *Christianity*, 377–388. See further O. Pfleiderer, 'Das paulinische πνεῦμα: Eine exegetisch-dogmatische Studie', *ZWT* 14 (1871), 168–70, which has been overlooked by past scholarship.

[15] Pfleiderer, *Christianity*, 408, 369–76, 383.

[16] On the significance of baptism, see specifically Pfleiderer, 'πνεῦμα', 171; Pfleiderer, *Paulinism*, 194, 203; Pfleiderer, *Christianity*, 387.

9–11; 1 Cor. 4:21; 14:14–15; Gal. 6:1).[17] It is this particular comprehension of the union and distinction of the divine and human πνεῦμα which demonstrates vividly that Paul shared the animistic world-view of antiquity: A divine spiritual being is sent down from heaven into the heart of a person and should there sometimes stand as an independently acting subject in antithesis to the personal ego and sometimes again fuse itself with the latter and become the content and motive-power of the person's consciousness.[18]

According to Pfleiderer, the consequence of the impartation of the divine πνεῦμα for Christian life is the abatement of the inner struggle of the person,[19] since πνεῦμα guides the ἄνθρωπος πνευματικός in the same way as σάρξ drives the παλαιὸς ἄνθρωπος.[20] In order to do good, Christians only need to give themselves up to the natural desire of this Spirit which indwells them.[21] However, Pfleiderer clarifies that it is only the unconditional dominion of sin in the flesh which has ceased in the believer by virtue of having received the Spirit (Rom. 6:14), 'but the impossibility of allowing himself to be led by the flesh is not thereby established (the *non posse non peccare* has ceased, but he has not arrived at the *non posse peccare*, but only at the *posse non peccare*)'.[22] In other words, Pfleiderer will not let the pneumatological indicative dominate over the ethical imperative.[23] Rather, he stresses that for Paul

Spirit and flesh stand in constant strife with one another, and the victory of the Spirit does not come to pass by itself with the unfailing certainty of the laws of nature, but depends on whether the Christian endeavours to walk according to the standard set up by the Spirit, and mortify the deeds of the body, or allows sin again to have dominion over him; whether he sows to the flesh or to the Spirit.[24]

---

[17] Pfleiderer, *Christianity*, 389.

[18] Ibid., 386–90; Pfleiderer, *Paulinism*, 213–16; Pfleiderer, 'πνεῦμα', 174–79. Following Holsten, 'Bedeutung', 378–88, Pfleiderer understands the nature of this 'divine spiritual being' as 'a transcendent physical essence, a supersensuous kind of matter' (Pfleiderer, *Paulinism*, 201; cf. Pfleiderer, *Christianity*, 370–71).

[19] Pfleiderer, 'πνεῦμα', 176: The nature of the spiritual renewal of νοῦς is 'dass sie... den von Haus aus vorhandenen Zwiespalt zwischen geistiger Form und Potenz und ungeistigem Inhalt und wirklichem Zustand aufhebt und also nur *die uranfängliche geistige Anlage und Bestimmung des Menschen zu der widerspruchslosen vollen Realität erhebt.*' Cf. Pfleiderer, *Christianity*, 397–98.

[20] Pfleiderer, *Paulinism*, 208–211.

[21] Ibid., 22.

[22] Ibid., 226.

[23] Cf. Ibid., 216, 218, 226; Pfleiderer, *Christianity*, 398–400.

[24] Pfleiderer, *Christianity*, 404–405. Pfleiderer defines 'sowing to the Spirit' (Gal. 6:8) as 'the moral action of man, by which the forces latent in the spirit are let loose and put in operation, made powerful to impel and produce fruit' (Pfleiderer, *Paulinism*, 226; cf. 220, 224).

Pfleiderer raises the question whether the apparent discrepancy between this ethical estimate of the empirical Christian life and the religious ideal of the new creation (i.e. the 'indicative') could be explained by employing the modern idea of psychological development. Indeed, Pfleiderer himself appears to argue in a number of places that the new life is really present, but only yet as a *principle*, as a potency which only gradually develops into actuality.[25] However, towards the end of his last publication, Pfleiderer determines that one is not justified in importing modern psychology into Pauline pneumatology, since for Paul 'the Spirit' is not a content of human consciousness, which could only develop by a process of consciousness, but a super-human personified spiritual being, who is sent down from heaven and enters into the person to direct his or her life. Pfleiderer recognises, nevertheless, that the logical consequence of this animistic conception of the Spirit would be the degradation of the person to a passive object which the two competing forces Spirit and flesh try to possess. He is therefore delighted to be able to show that for the ethical value of Paul's teaching, Paul did not consistently carry through this conception of 'the Spirit', but allowed the person's ethical self-determination its own right. However, on the basis of the presuppositions of Pfleiderer's theory described above, Paul can only think of 'the Spirit' by alternating between the mystic and the ethical view of Christian life, applying both side-by-side in closest connection, yet without endeavouring to unite them inwardly.[26] Practically, this means that

Sometimes the Spirit is a power which overmasters the man and coerces his free ego, a supernatural wonder-working power which therefore works with automatic certainty, and which by its sole agency makes all things new; sometimes it is man himself who feels himself urged on by the moral impulse of the Spirit but without feeling compelled to follow it, and who is therefore himself responsible for his spiritual or unspiritual will and action.[27]

Pfleiderer believes that now, as he has identified a conceptual limitation to ancient supernaturalism as the cause of this vacillation between the religious and the ethical line of Paul's soteriology, he is entitled to abstract from this the abiding kernel of Pauline ethics: Die to live! Be what you are! In sum, Paul has illustrated out of his own experience that the 'combination of a faith which is self-sustained, and rejoices in the present and inward salvation, with a hope and effort which unweariedly reach out

---

[25] Pfleiderer, 'πνεῦμα', 177–79; Pfleiderer, *Paulinism*, 194–95, 215–16.
[26] Pfleiderer, *Christianity*, 406–407; cf. 396–97.
[27] Ibid., 407.

beyond themselves towards the high goal of perfection' is the fundamental characteristic of the ethico-religious attitude of the Christian.[28]

Like Ernesti, Pfleiderer is indebted to Baur, who was in fact his teacher. Again, in his work one finds the idea of moral development. However, Pfleiderer is original – although influenced by Baur's dialectical theology – in that he applies the model of two lines in Paul's thinking (previously developed by Lüdemann)[29] to the area of ethical life. The question which will be discussed in later scholarship as the riddle of Paul's 'indicative and imperative' is posed by Pfleiderer as the antithesis of the fusion of the divine Spirit with the human ego on the one hand, and their separateness on the other. These two types of relation between Spirit and believer are associated with two divergent mechanisms of ethical life, that of being overmastered and supernaturally renewed by the πνεῦμα, and that of being oneself responsible for one's ethical actions.[30] While most scholars after Pfleiderer have sought to bring these two *Lebensäußerungen* of the Spirit into a coherent system for understanding Paul, one may ask whether it does not do more justice to Paul to leave the tension unresolved. Only in a second step may one then ask how one can appropriate this model for (systematic) theology. At least Pfleiderer seems to separate these two steps when he says that the *abiding kernel* of Pauline ethics, formulated without animistic language, is 'Be what you are!', by which believers are encouraged to 'reach out beyond themselves towards the high goal of perfection'. Pfleiderer has thus raised the issue of the right interpretation of the tensions in Paul's thought – should one leave them unresolved or should one abstract or even psychologize them in order to appropriate them to a worldview free from ancient supernaturalism?

Nevertheless, some may question the legitimacy of Pfleiderer's particular synthesis as it portrays once again the ideal of human progress towards

---

[28] Ibid., 408–409. Cf. J. Weiss, *Earliest Christianity: A History of the Period A.D. 30–150* (New York: Harper, 1959), 518–20, who was the first to major on the eschatological nature of this ethic ('Be what you may become'). Similar to Pfleiderer, *Weiss* recognises the tension in Paul's ethics: as ἅγιοι and πνευματικοί who have experienced purification in baptism and those who with Christ have crucified their flesh with its passions and desires, Paul's churches should not be in need at all of ethical exhortation. But the realities of the community clashed with the concept of the ideal of the saints. In contrast to Pfleiderer, Weiss understands this tension as a *development* within Paul: The 'transition from the uncontrolled morality of spiritual men to obedience towards statutes can already be observed in its inception, in Paul' (Weiss, *Christianity*, 558).

[29] On Lüdemann's model, see E. Käsemann, 'On Paul's Anthropology', in E. Käsemann, *Perspectives on Paul* (London: SCM Press, 1971), 6, and Way, *Lordship*, 35. Cf. Heitmüller, *Paulus*, 36.

[30] Pfleiderer thus makes us clearly aware that one cannot discuss one (the mode of Spirit impartation) without the other (the nature of the Spirit's ethical work).

perfection.[31] Moreover, one needs to inquire by which method Pfleiderer establishes the existence of the mystical and ethical line in Paul's thought. It is obvious that Pfleiderer's understanding of Pauline pneumatology is strongly influenced by Paul's supposed religious background. Pfleiderer believes Paul's pneumatic experience of conversion (by which Paul felt his whole being completely transformed) to lie at the heart of Paul's doctrine of the impartation of the divine πνεῦμα as facilitating ethical purity. However, Pfleiderer is not able to support this hypothesis by autobiographical remarks from Paul himself or by any other indications from the Pauline epistles. More significantly, Pfleiderer does not give literary evidence of the 'popular animistic theory of spirits which was common to the Jews and heathen of his [Paul's] time',[32] nor does he demonstrate exegetically how Paul would have taken up these *religionsgeschichtlich* concepts. For example, the fusion of the divine and human πνεῦμα to *one spirit* 'den wir ebensowohl den menschlichgewordenen Gottes- als den göttlichgewordenen Menschengeist benennen könnten'[33] is only sustained by too brief a look at a few verses in which, according to Pfleiderer, the union of the theological and the anthropological spirit is presupposed.

Pfleiderer forbids us to interpret by means of the psychological notion of moral development Paul's vacillation between his mystical and his ethical line of thought. Pfleiderer's reason for this is Paul's animistic conception of the Spirit. Nevertheless, Pfleiderer himself psychologizes Paul's animistic forces (i.e. Spirit and flesh) as psychic conditions of the human consciousness.[34] This inconsistency indicates that Pfleiderer did not employ a well thought-out methodology with respect to the use of psychology in the interpretation of Paul. For example, he does not give any methodological justification for his unquestioning reduction of spiritual beings to psychic conditions. Also with regard to his opposition to developmental approaches to ethical life according to Paul, Pfleiderer stands in tension with himself. For he himself applies the idea of ethical development to Paul's writings not just in his earlier publications but also in his last: he talks of the 'progressive carrying out of... morality' which could be summed up in the central imperative of Paul's pneumatological ethics 'Be

---

[31] However, see the issues raised in Samra, *Christ*, 6–7, 168, who challenges scholars writing after the decline of idealism for often being over-concerned with the (Pauline) notion of moral development.

[32] Pfleiderer, *Christianity*, 370.

[33] Pfleiderer, 'πνεῦμα', 177. This thought was later taken up, again in somewhat idealistic fashion, by H. Jacoby, *Neutestamentliche Ethik* (Königsberg: Thomas & Oppermann, 1899), 301–401, and A. Juncker, *Die Ethik des Apostels Paulus. Vol. 1* (Halle: Niemeyer, 1904), 139–63.

[34] Pfleiderer, *Christianity*, 390–91, 408.

what you are.'[35] This certainly implies the notion of development, and thus, according to Pfleiderer, is in disagreement with Paul's (animistic) concept of spiritual life. That Paul is indeed so strongly influenced by animism as Pfleiderer suggests, however, remains in need of exegetical demonstration.

In the history of scholarship, *H. Wendt* and *J. Gloël* were the first to criticize Pfleiderer for not grounding his Paulinism well enough in exegesis of Pauline texts. To begin with, Wendt demonstrates by means of detailed exegesis that the passages listed by Pfleiderer in support of the thought that Paul thought of πνεῦμα as material substance[36] do not require such an animistic understanding at all.[37] Rather, Wendt contends that Paul did not have any other words at his command apart from those that could in a different context also be used of a material essence. Therefore, Wendt argues – in the rationalistic spirit of Ritschl – that nothing can prevent us from applying the Old Testament comprehension (*Begriff*) of the Spirit as divine *Kraftwirkung* to Paul.[38] Indeed, Paul often connects πνεῦμα and δύναμις in his writing (e.g. Rom. 1:4; 15:13, 19; 1 Cor. 2:4; Gal. 3:5) and sometimes even uses both interchangeably (1 Cor. 5:4; 6:14; 2 Cor. 13:4). Furthermore, in many places the effective power of πνεῦμα is contrasted with the ineffective γράμμα (e.g. Rom. 2:29; 7:6; 2 Cor. 3:6); πνεῦμα has life-giving power (e.g. Rom. 8; 1 Cor. 15:45) which determines the supernatural existence in heaven and the ethical life on earth.[39]

Gloël approves of Wendt's criticism of the materialistic interpretation of the Pauline Spirit.[40] He further goes along with Wendt in seeing the Spirit as *wirkende Gotteskraft*. However, he does not want to follow Wendt's conclusion that the Spirit is thus also *göttliche Kraftwirkung*, since, while the Spirit does manifest himself by his effects, he is not to be identified with these effects. According to Paul, the Spirit exercises ἐνεργεῖν, but he is not himself ἐνέργημα (1 Cor. 12:6, 10–11). The Spirit is purely the *medium* of the supernatural *Gotteskraft*. Nevertheless, while the Spirit is not a material substance, Paul does see the Spirit as a 'uniform, living entity of *objective reality...*, the *effective life-power*'.[41]

---

[35] Ibid., 398–400.

[36] See Pfleiderer, *Paulinism*, 201.

[37] For a summary of Wendt's exegesis, see Rabens, 'Development', 169. Pfleiderer operates with an unusual definition of 'animistic'. Commonly, when πνεῦμα is regarded as a substance, e.g. a fluid, filling the person (rather than a personal power invading the person), the term is 'dynamistic' (cf. Bultmann, *Theology. I*, 155).

[38] Wendt, *Fleisch*, 142–45.

[39] Ibid., 146–47.

[40] Gloël, *Geist*, 372.

[41] Ibid., 373–74.

Furthermore, Wendt and Gloël disagree with Pfleiderer's belief that Paul was the first to connect the Spirit with ethics. Wendt declares that 'der traditionelle πνεῦμα-Begriff den Paulus in seine christliche Anschauung übernehmen konnte, viel inhaltreicher und tiefer gewesen zu sein scheint, als Pfleiderer annehmen zu dürfen glaubt'.[42] Wendt continues that 'in Paul we do not find the Old Testament terminology of the Spirit with a broadened *content* but rather with a broadened *application*; but exactly this, namely that the Spirit of God would find a broader application in the expected end-time, was part of the *content* of the Old Testament idea of this Spirit'.[43] In the same vein, Gloël concludes that the Pauline cognition of the Spirit as ethically renewing did not lack positive presuppositions in the Old Testament, nor points of contact with early Christian preaching (e.g. Jn. 3; 8:32ff.; 1 Jn. 3:19, 5:6; 1 Pet. 1:2; Acts 2:28, 42–47; 4:32; 6:5; 11:24).[44]

1.3. The Spirit as Overwhelming Ethical Power (H. Gunkel)

In 1888 a major attack on the idealistic tradition of German Liberal theology was launched by Hermann Gunkel's groundbreaking *Die Wirkungen des heiligen Geistes nach der populären Anschauung der apostolischen Zeit und der Lehre des Apostels Paulus*. Gunkel re-emphasized the originality of Paul's ethical pneumatology, argued for the exclusively experiential origin of this originality and gave further impetus to the discussion of the nature of the Spirit.

a) The originality of Paul's pneumatology over against the popular view of the apostolic age. Gunkel believes that the popular view of the earliest (non-Pauline) Jewish-Christian community (*Urgemeinde*) did not entertain any explicit reflection or doctrinal statement regarding the Spirit.[45] From the main sources, which are the Gospels and Acts, it is evident that only certain supernatural experiences (e.g. glossolalia, miracles, ecstasy) were traced to the Spirit; for the Spirit was not conceived of as author of all Christian religious and ethical life.[46]

Paul is rooted deeply in the soil of this ancient popular faith: for him, too, an activity of the Spirit is that in which an inexplicable power, the mysterious and mighty, is manifest (85). Just as others of his time, Paul thinks in thoroughly supernaturalistic fashion (95). And yet, there is a principal difference between the Pauline and the popular view. The same

---

[42] Wendt, *Fleisch*, 151.
[43] Ibid., 153.
[44] Gloël, *Geist*, 241, 238–240; cf. 354.
[45] Gunkel, *Influence*, 14. Unless stated otherwise, all references are to the ET.
[46] Ibid., 11, 16, 18–19.

judgement which the early apostolic circles give of a few definitely extraordinary appearances, Paul gives of the entire Christian life.

> The community... regards as pneumatic what is extraordinary in Christian existence, but
> Paul what is usual; the community what is individual and unique, but Paul what is com-
> mon to all; the community what abruptly appears, but Paul what is constant; the commu-
> nity what is isolated in Christian existence, but Paul the Christian life as such (96; cf.
> 115–16).

According to Paul, everything in this new life is derived from the Spirit:
the new state of existence, the ethical powers, the charismata (111). Indeed, by the virtue of the Spirit's work upon the human heart Christian
existence within the new, pneumatic state, and the new moral life are in-
separably connected (79, 108).

How does Gunkel comprehend this ethical work of the Spirit in detail?
First of all, he believes that Paul did not see Christian existence as a product developing organically from earlier existence. Rather, to become a
Christian means a complete break with everything that has gone before,
and becoming a καινὴ κτίσις. Christian life is hence absolutely inconceiv-
able in earthly terms; it is a miracle of God (94–95). Also the power of the
Spirit is *divine* power, that is, absolutely supernatural and never explain-
able by human powers. Consequently, humans cannot by themselves create
that mode of life which seizes the Christian – the person always remains
recipient and passive over against it (as indicated by Paul's description of
the Spirit as 'received', 'experienced' [1 Cor. 2:12; Gal. 3:4]; 'sent', 'sup-
plied' [Gal. 3:5; 4:6], etc.). On this basis Gunkel concludes that 'the power
that rules the Christian is absolutely superhuman; it is originally foreign to
the ego and thus not at all a universal human capacity, and it rules over
him so absolutely that it does not allow him to carry out his own will at all'
(93–94).[47]

Looking at this vigorous depiction of the ethical power of the Spirit in
the Christian's life one is faced with the question of how, according to
Gunkel, Paul arrived at this comprehension.

b) The experiential origin of Paul's ethical view of the Spirit. Gunkel
starts his thesis with the methodological consideration that Paul's position
concerning the Spirit can be properly understood and evaluated only when
one first considers the ideas which were available to the apostle within

---

[47] Cf. P. Wernle, *Der Christ und die Sünde bei Paulus* (Freiburg/Leipzig: J.C.B. Mohr
(Paul Siebeck), 1897), 88, 15. Nevertheless, similar to Pfleiderer, *Wernle* recognises that
this enthusiastic notion of life in the Spirit, although it is the predominant motif in Paul,
stands in tension with a different line of thought in Paul. Wernle identifies the two separate notions of ethical life as the 'indicative and the imperative' or 'an ethic of wonder
and an ethic of the will' (Wernle, *Christ*, 89; cf. the summary in Furnish, *Theology*, 245–
48).

Christian circles (9; cf. 18). In this respect, Gunkel argues against Gloël that Paul did not encounter an ethical notion of the Spirit in the teaching of Jesus or in the apostolic community. Gunkel re-enforces his statement mentioned above that the popular view only attributed certain charismatic experiences to the Spirit. Acts 6:5, 9:31, 11:24 and 13:52 demonstrate that some activities of the Spirit are not indifferent to the moral-religious sphere, but one needs to bear in mind that one is dealing here with 'a heightening of the commonplace', with *extraordinary* gifts (17–18; 77–78). Additionally, he argues that Gloël's other sources (Jn. and 1 Pet.) are post-Pauline by nature and thus more likely to be influenced by Paul than vice versa (103–104).

Also in the Old Testament, piety and morality as such are not regarded as pneumatic. Criticising Wendt, Gunkel maintains that the vast majority of Spirit-activities in the Old Testament belong to the realm of the ecstatic; the few exceptions (Isa. 11:1–2; 28:6; 32:15ff., Ezek. 36:27 [perhaps Zech. 12:10], Pss. 51:13; 143:10)[48] cannot weaken this comprehensive truth (19–20). It is 'a grave error in method' anyway to attempt to derive Paul's sphere of ideas directly from the Old Testament and consequently to ignore the apostle's origin in Judaism (76). Judaism is the real matrix of the gospel (13). And, as mentioned above, the *Jewish*-Christian community knew of no connection between the Spirit and ethics.[49]

Finally, in contrast to a number of scholars who preceded him, Gunkel does not see Paul's concept of σάρξ as a valid starting point for the search for the origin of Paul's pneumatology. The reason for this lies in the danger of this method, namely, to conceive of the Spirit in Paul as a 'concept' that merely needs defining in order to be mastered (75). The point, however, is that πνεῦμα for Paul is an *experience*. According to Gunkel, here lies the origin of Paul's ethical pneumatology: 'his experience of "the power and depth of his spiritual inspiration," by which "he felt his entire life constantly filled and driven by the power of the Spirit of Christ"'.[50]

---

[48] The first and the two last OT references were originally used by Gloël, *Geist*, 237–38, in support of Wendt's thesis. Gunkel, however, contends that the difference between these OT prophets' views and that of Paul is that for the prophets only the righteousness of the endtime is pneumatic, whereas for Paul each Christian act is pneumatic *in the present*. 'Thus the prophets hope, but Paul possesses.' Besides, the apostle neither cites nor alludes to those prophetic utterances in which the descent of the Spirit is predicted (Gunkel, *Influence*, 98–99).

[49] *Pace* Pfleiderer, also Hellenism cannot have been Paul's source (the similarities are only in form but not in content [Gunkel, *Influence*, 100–101]), nor can his Christology have been the reason for his ethical pneumatology (Gunkel, *Influence*, 115).

[50] Gunkel, *Influence*, 92 (cf. 95), quoting Pfleiderer, *Christianity*, 257 (German edition).

c) The Spirit as substance. It can be deduced from the above statement that Paul understood the Spirit as power. Indeed, Gunkel confirms at the end of his monograph that this was the primary notion of the Spirit in Paul. Nonetheless, Gunkel – following Pfleiderer – contends that for Paul the Spirit was also a substance. This is evident from the σῶμα πνευματικόν in 1 Corinthians 15:44, and from the sentiment of δόξα κυρίου as heavenly splendour in 2 Corinthians 3:18. Gunkel believes that 'this idea that the Spirit is linked to a heavenly substance is by no means specifically Pauline, nor is it specifically Christian; it is of Jewish origin' (124–26). Gunkel supports this allegation by reference to a number of early Jewish texts, most prominently *2 Baruch* 51. What is more, in his detailed interaction with Wendt he tries to demonstrate that already in the Old Testament the Spirit was comprehended as substance, after the analogy of the wind. Gunkel criticizes Wendt's methodology when he concludes from the usage of wind as an expression for the void and unreal that the Spirit was conceived of as immaterial. Such an inference would imply that the Hebrews thought of the wind as unreal and not actually existing. The fact, however, is that the wind is merely *compared* with what is void and unreal. Gunkel endorses Wendt's remark that the *tertium comparationis* is 'that the wind in its origin and continuance lacks visibility and other marks by which the reality of a thing is proved.'[51] The wind is thus compared with what is unreal. However, Gunkel makes clear that the wind itself obviously is still conceived of as existing and as material, namely, as air (see, e.g. Jer. 10:13; Ps. 135:7 [the 'storehouse' of the wind]; Job 28:25). Wind and Spirit are compared (and even named by the same term, רוח) because 'both are mighty in their effects, mysterious in their comings and goings, imperceptible to the human eye, not weighable by human measure, and not to be restrained by human strength' (60). Moreover, the underlying reason for the analogy is that

the notion of a force without any material substrate requires a highly developed capacity for abstraction which we may not assume the ancient Hebrews had. Indeed, we can say that the more vividly the Spirit's activities are experienced, and the more lively and graphically he is conceived, the more certainly the Spirit will be taken as a supersensous substance (59).

It is from here that the *Urgemeinde* as well as Paul derived their conception of the Spirit as substance.[52]

---

[51] Wendt, *Fleisch*, 18–19.

[52] Nevertheless, since Gunkel believes that the notion of substance is only a δευτέρα φροντίς for Paul, he opposes taking this concept as a starting point for a description of Pauline pneumatology (Gunkel, *Influence*, 126). Cf. H.J. Holtzmann, *Lehrbuch der Neutestamentlichen Theologie. Vol. 2*; ed. by D.A. Jülicher and W. Bauer (Tübingen: J.C.B. Mohr (Paul Siebeck), 1911²), 22, who sees the 'double nature' of Paul's thought

The publication of *Die Wirkungen*, Gunkel's revised inaugurational dissertation, lucidly demonstrated the genius of his scholarship. It was not necessarily the novelty of Gunkel's contentions but the force and clarity with which his thesis was argued that guaranteed the immense success of his first work. Pfleiderer had alleged similar claims in the three areas of contribution to Pauline scholarship which we pointed out above. Nevertheless, it was Gunkel who collected the evidence for and argued against the opponents of the view that Paul was the first to assign ethical significance to the Spirit. Gunkel also radicalized Pfleiderer's assertion of the centrality of Paul's experience for his pneumatology. And, thirdly, Gunkel supported *exegetically* the hypothesis that Paul understood the Spirit as substance.[53] Moreover, Gunkel was methodologically innovative. For instance, his emphasis on the significance of Judaism for the comprehension of Paul's (OT) background was ahead of his time.[54] Further, his call for a hermeneutic based on experience (2–8) would receive much attention (e.g. from Horn, who warns against the subjectivity of such an approach).[55] Thus,

---

(explored by Pfleiderer above) also in Paul's view of the nature of the Spirit: 'Gehört es zweifellos zu seinem Begriff des Geistes, daß er, gleich dem philonischen, im Gegensatz zu allem materiellen Dasein ganz unter die Kategorie der Kraft fällt, so kann der in Jerusalem gebildete Theologe doch nicht völlig loskommen von den Begriffen der Substantialität und Stofflichkeit.'

[53] Gunkel's attention to Paul's own expressions is to be welcomed. Nevertheless, his allegation concerning Paul's supposed material pneumatology in 1 Cor. 15:44 and 2 Cor. 3:18 is debatable (see ch. 3 above). Apart from that, at least in Gunkel's treatment of the OT understanding of the nature of the Spirit some incoherence is immediately obvious. Gunkel indicates that the points of comparison between wind and Spirit are their effects and their indifference to human measurements. Yet, he still continues his reasoning by illustrating by means of OT phraseology that wind was conceived of as substance, only to use this in support of the same contention concerning the Spirit. With this, however, he employs a different point of comparison, viz. the (physical) nature of the two entities. Furthermore, although he says that one reason for the analogy of wind and Spirit is the fact that both escape human measurements, Gunkel later quotes Scripture references which talk of the Spirit in terms of measurement, in order to strengthen his case for the material nature of the Spirit in the OT (Gunkel, *Influence*, 60–61). Consequently, Gunkel's argumentation proves unsatisfactory in this matter; nevertheless, the evidence from the OT and from Judaism requires further investigation. In this connection, also Gunkel's argument that the Hebrews did not have such a capacity for abstraction to comprehend the Spirit as having no substance needs to be dealt with. See ch. 2, section 2.1. above.

[54] Cf. W. Klatt, *Hermann Gunkel: Zu seiner Theologie der Religionsgeschichte und zur Entstehung der formgeschichtlichen Methode*; FRLANT 100 (Göttingen: Vandenhoeck & Ruprecht, 1969), 29–35. However, Gunkel did not yet work redaction-critically and hence misconstrued a historical entity ('the popular views') from a theological narrative (cf. Turner, *Power*, 26, n.18; Horn, 'Wandel', 151).

[55] Horn, *Angeld*, 14–15.

Gunkel's work was of lasting influence – the questions he raised are still discussed in the arena of Biblical pneumatology today.[56]

Nonetheless, Gunkel's thesis did not remain unchallenged. He was criticized for misrepresenting the pneumatology of the Hebrew Bible and of early Judaism concerning its ethical impact. Gunkel wrongly generalised his examples of the non-ethical activity of the Spirit and ignored the evidence that later scholars employed for proving the opposite.[57] The same was established for the *Urgemeinde*: the early Christian community also attributed ethical work to the Spirit (as argued, e.g. by Juncker).[58]

Also the nature of the Spirit's ethical sway can be questioned. While Pfleiderer's theory of two unconnected lines in Paul may not be satisfactory, Gunkel hardly seems to recognise the tension of the indicative and the imperative (110 [mentioned in passing]). Gunkel emphasizes the ethical indicative: conversion is a complete break with the past; Christians 'receive', 'experience' the Spirit given by God, they are overwhelmed by a superhuman ethical power. No room is left in this conception for human reaction or even action. But was Paul indeed so 'thoroughly supernaturalistic'? From his epistles there seems to emerge a very down-to-earth apostle who knows of struggles in the Christian life (Gal. 5:17) and who is aware of the need to encourage his fellow-disciples by the means of practical imperatives to keep in step with the Spirit's work in their lives (Gal. 5:25; Rom. 8:13; etc.).

Gunkel thus seems to have gone too far in his antagonism against idealism. This is also apparent from his resistance to developing his understanding of Pauline pneumatology from Pauline anthropology (75–76), which is

---

[56] See, for example, Menzies, *Development, passim,* who in many respects follows Gunkel's view of the development of early Christian pneumatology.

[57] After Gunkel first Sokolowski, *Geist,* 196–205, 277–79.

[58] Juncker, *Ethik. I,* 135–51. *A. Juncker* collects the main arguments which had been brought forward in critique of Pfleiderer's and Gunkel's assertion of the originality of Paul's ethical pneumatology: (1) Paul's style of writing about the ethical work of the Spirit does not give the impression he was writing something new. (2) The early Christian statement of faith that every believer receives the Spirit in baptism does not cohere with the view that the power of πνεῦμα is only expressed in extra-ordinary and ecstatic phenomena. Therefore, the early Christians must have had a different identification of what is Spirit-worked, and this was the ethical-religious dimension. (3) Judaism gives ample evidence for the correlation of Spirit and ethics. (4) Also non-Pauline writings reflect the connection of pneumatology and ethics. *Contra* Gunkel, Juncker believes that the occasional accounts of the ethical work of the Spirit (e.g. in 1 Pet. 1:2; 4:7; Hebr. 6:4–5) witness to the fact that Paul was not alone with his account of this connection. Nevertheless, Juncker, like Gloël and Bousset before him, makes clear that it was Paul's originality to promote that the Spirit is 'nicht etwa bloß ein adminiculum eines religiös-sittlichen Aufschwungs' but the creator of the *new life* (including justification, cf. 132–34). A major reason for this was Paul's conversion experience (Juncker, *Ethik. I,* 135–39).

generally to be appreciated. However, Gunkel's overemphasis on the pneumatological indicative overlooks the role of the human (spirit) altogether.[59] Apart from that, it is doubtful whether it was exclusively *Paul's* experience which energised him to develop his ethical view of the Spirit. In fact, unless one believes Paul's experience to have been fundamentally different from that of the earliest community, one would want to know why they did not promulgate the same pneumatology. By the time of the second edition of *Die Wirkungen* in 1899, however, Gunkel acknowledges that Paul's experience cannot have been the sole source for his pneumatology since 'the language of this speculation already appears in fully fixed form' (8). This is confirmed by *W. Bousset*, who two years later insisted that the early Christian belief in the indwelling of the Spirit in each individual believer was not purely an *Erfahrungssatz*, but a 'religious postulate' which originated in early Christian eschatology.[60] While Bousset agrees that Paul was the first New Testament writer to mention the ethical work of the Spirit *expressis verbis*, he objects to Gunkel, contending that Paul was nevertheless not the first to believe in this connection. Bousset gives a strong impetus to the *religionsgeschichtliche Forschung* because he particularly emphasizes Paul's debt to Hellenistic Judaism and Hellenism in general.[61]

1.4. 'Dying and Rising with Christ' as Unity of Passive and Active Ethics (A. Schweitzer)

Rejecting both Gunkel and the *religionsgeschichtliche Schule*, Friedrich Büchsel[62] and Albert Schweitzer (re-)assert the homogeneity of the early church's pneumatology as well as the continuity between Paul's ethical pneumatology and that of the Jewish Scriptures. Nevertheless, they still believe in the originality of Paul's mind. Schweitzer's influential work *The Mysticism of Paul the Apostle* (1930, transl. 1931) brought the eschatological nature as well as the theological centrality of Paul's Christ-mysticism into the focus of scholarship. Schweitzer puts forward that the history of religions method properly applied to Paul would mean binding Paul to late

---

[59] Gunkel's oversight of the anthropological spirit is noted by C.-K. Park, 'Das Verhältnis zwischen theologischem und anthropolgischem Pneumabegriff bei Paulus' (University of Hamburg: Unpublished PhD Thesis, 1982), 26.

[60] W. Bousset, 'Review of H. Weinel, *Die Wirkungen des Geistes*', *GGA* 163 (1901), 758–59.

[61] Ibid., 761–64. Cf. Reitzenstein, *Mystery-Religions*, 426–500.

[62] In his exhaustive monograph, Büchsel – similar to Bertrams – argues for the personal nature of the Spirit (Büchsel, *Geist*, 396–438). Büchsel understands the Spirit's activity as God's (*ichhafte*) *Selbstmitteilung* which is comparable with the human conscience (Büchsel, *Geist*, 400, 413, 437–38).

Apocalyptic Judaism.[63] Consequently, for Schweitzer being ἐν Χριστῷ is not merely a cultic reality as Deissmann had propounded,[64] but an eschatological reality which is experienced quasi-physically and sacramentally and brought about by the inaugurated eschatological kingdom of God. According to Schweitzer, Paul's view is new in that he connects the possession of the Spirit with the pivotal doctrine of dying and rising with Christ. As one who is already raised, the believer receives the Spirit of Christ as the new life-principle of the supernatural state which he has now entered. For Schweitzer, this dying and rising with Christ is not a metaphor but a 'quasi-physical concept'. It is the basis of ethics. This is not an ethic which is preached, like that of Jesus. Rather, Christ himself brings it into being within the believer.[65]

How does Schweitzer conceptualize the nature of this ethic? Firstly, the consequence of the union with Christ is a *new ethical state*. The possession of the Spirit indicates to the believers that they are already removed from the sphere of the flesh. Since they are 'in the Spirit' their being in the flesh is only a matter of outward appearance and not a real state of existence (167–68). The psychology of the natural human being no longer applies to them. Instead of the natural mind (νοῦς) they possess the 'mind of Christ' (1 Cor. 2:16). Unfortunately, Schweitzer sees himself unable to explain the *how* of this change. He declares that Paul gives no indication by what psychological processes the new comes into the place of the old, nor how the union of the Spirit with the natural 'inner man' comes about (296–97).

Secondly, the new state needs to be *confirmed by the believers' decision to live by the Spirit* because they cannot be in the Spirit and in the flesh at the same time. Schweitzer acknowledges that sinlessness would be the logical consequence of the new state of the believers in Christ. Their flesh has already been dealt with through dying with Christ. However, Schweitzer clarifies that this supra-mundane condition is only an accomplished fact in so far as the baptised are conscious that the limitations of the natural existence no longer apply to them, and that they should therefore not attribute an importance to them which they no longer posses. 'Really and in principle they are a new creation because the powers of death and resurrection, to the working of which they are subjected by their union with Christ, have begun their work within them. But at the same time this fact is only in progress of being realized.' By their own will be-

---

[63] A. Schweitzer, *Paul and His Interpreters: A Critical History* (London: Black, 1912), 176–77.

[64] Deissmann and Deissner had already given attention to Paulus' mysticism (Deissmann, *Formel, passim*; Deißner, *Mystik, passim*), but it was Schweitzer who managed to bring it centre-stage.

[65] Schweitzer, *Mysticism*, 294–97.

lievers should progressively make into a reality their death to the flesh and to sin as they free themselves from the thoughts and desires of the natural Ego and submit in all things to the ethical guidance of the Spirit. Through this they will show how far the dying and rising again with Christ has proceeded within them (168, 301).

Thus, while Schweitzer thinks that ethics is nothing else but the Spirit's work (294), he equally emphasizes the believer's will and decision for ethical action (296). Schweitzer concludes that this profound unity of active and passive ethics (cf. Rom. 5–8) constitutes the greatness and originality of Paul's ethics:[66]

It is only in so far as a man is purified and liberated from the world by that which he experiences and endures, that he becomes capable of truly ethical action. In the ethic of the dying and rising again with Christ passive and active ethics are interwoven as in no other. The being "not as the world" in action is the expression of the being made free from the world, through suffering and dying with Christ (302).

With this concept of the unity of active and passive ethics, Schweitzer is part of the Ernesti-Juncker era, who emphasized the interpenetration or *intima conjunctio* between divine and human activity. Schweitzer has shed new light on this relation by elucidating the eschatological nature of this union. However, Schweitzer's description of the passive and active parts of Paul's ethics sometimes appears exaggerated. Unless Schweitzer intends these as rhetorical overstatements, his system of passive and active ethics contains irreconcilable contradictions. In his explication of what should be the *passive* side of Christian ethics, Schweitzer supposes that salvation equals dying and rising with Christ. Nonetheless, Schweitzer also says that dying and rising with Christ is a process whose progress needs to be accomplished by the believer (301). Besides the contradiction of this concept of *gradual* dying and rising with Christ (cf. 167) with the statement that the believer is *already raised* (294),[67] Schweitzer here seems to overemphasize the (active) work of the believer in order to get saved. He gives too little weight to Paul's teaching on justification by grace.[68]

On the other hand, Schweitzer equally seems to undervalue human activity – his passive ethics is too passive. He believes that Christians are

---

[66] Schweitzer believes that 'the only profound ethic is one which is able, on the basis of one and the same conception, to give an ethical interpretation to all that a man experiences and suffers as well as to all that he does' (Ibid., 302).

[67] Cf. Ibid., 111–12 (112–13 in the original).

[68] Schweitzer's underestimation or even miscomprehension of the concept of justification in Paul's soteriology has been noted by many scholars (e.g. W.G. Kümmel, 'Albert Schweitzer als Paulusforscher', in W.G. Kümmel (ed.), *Heilsgeschehen und Geschichte. Vol. 2*; Gesammelte Aufsätze (Marburg: Elwert, 1978), 230). However, with E.P. Sanders and the advent of the 'New Perspective on Paul', this judgement would be reversed.

removed from the psychological processes of the natural human being. A new ontic state is automatically bestowed upon them, the flesh is 'not a real state of existence' anymore. But is this Paul's view? Is dying and rising with Christ for Paul a 'quasi-physical concept'? Are 'being in the Spirit' and 'being in the flesh' completely mutually exclusive states? The system by which Schweitzer is able to hold these seemingly contradictory statements together appears to be that of philosophical realism:[69] 'Really and in principle they are a new creation... but at the same time this fact is only in progress of being realized.' However, it is doubtful that Paul can be fathomed by this philosophy.

Apart from that, one wonders whether Paul does indeed not say or imply anything about the psychological processes by which ethical change comes about, as Schweitzer contends. Nevertheless, Schweitzer's own words (i.e., that the baptized need to be *conscious* that the limitations of the natural existence no longer apply to them, and that they should therefore *not attribute an importance to them* which they no longer posses) indicate that Schweitzer himself understands that ethical life can be furthered or even accomplished by cognitive processes (characterised by Jewett as a 'self-hypnotic act of will'[70]).

Summary and Conclusion. The conception of ethical life according to Paul as that of a *progressive development* dominated the first sixty years of critical research on the interface of Paul's ethics and pneumatology. Ernesti set the scene for this contention by introducing the idealistic concept of the Spirit of God becoming immanent to the human spirit. The interpenetration of divine and human activity is the consequence. This was then applied to the so-called fusion of the divine and human S/spirit(s).[71] Schweitzer shed new light on this interpenetration from the perspective of (a rationalistic) eschatology.

While this line of interpretation was flourishing, a serious attack on idealism was launched by Gunkel. He was able to influence subsequent students of (Pauline) pneumatology (as, e.g. Bousset and Weinel),[72] but a second hit would be necessary for idealism to loosen its grip on ethical studies of Paul, as we will see in the next section.

---

[69] Realism had already had some influence on Pfleiderer (e.g. Pfleiderer, 'πνεῦμα', 177–79; Pfleiderer, *Paulinism*, 194–95, 215–16) and more clearly on Jacoby, *Ethik*, 311, 317.

[70] Jewett, *Terms*, 76.

[71] Pfleiderer, 'πνεῦμα', 177; Jacoby, *Ethik*, 301–401; Juncker, *Ethik. I*, 139–63.

[72] H. Weinel, *Die Wirkungen des Geistes und der Geister im nach-apostolischen Zeitalter bis auf Irenäus* (Tübingen: J.C.B. Mohr (Paul Siebeck), 1899), *passim*. Cf. Bousset, 'Weinel', 753–776.

The issue raised by Pfleiderer and Gunkel concerning the nature of πνεῦμα as a physical substance remains unresolved in this era. Likewise, regarding the alleged discontinuity between Judaism and *Urgemeinde* on one side and Paul on the other, no consensus is reached. It is only from 1990 onwards that this issue would again become a point of interest in Pauline studies of Spirit and ethics.

Being somewhat influenced by rationalism (and idealism) Schweitzer started to note the importance of the believer's decision in the interplay of Spirit and ethics (cf. von Soden and Jacoby).[73] And it is this emphasis that would grant Bultmann (though against the background of existentialism) to introduce a new era of Pauline studies.

2. The Interplay of Spirit and Ethics in Paul's Theology: 1930–1990 (From Bultmann to Dunn)

2.1. *'Being in the Spirit' (Indicative) and 'Walking by the Spirit' (Imperative) Become One in the Moment of Decision (R. Bultmann)*

Intending to combat the pervasive influence of idealism (and rationalism) on the study of Paul's ethic (especially with regard to the coherence of Paul's 'indicative and imperative') Rudolf Bultmann wrote in 1924 his epoch-making article 'Das Problem der Ethik bei Paulus'.[74] He proposes that the imperative is deduced from the indicative. *Because* the Christian

---

[73] See n.8 above and Jacoby, *Ethik*, 300–317. *H. Jacoby* has employed a concept more characteristic of Paul for what Ernesti and von Soden have called before the interpenetration and fusion of divine and human ethical powers. Jacoby talks of the 'intimate faith-communion [*Glaubensgemeinschaft*] with Christ', of 'being in Christ' (Jacoby, *Ethik*, 397, 291, 401). And he also appears to do more justice to Paul's comprehension of being ἐν πνεύματι since he avoids the enthusiastic notion of the Spirit's overruling of the human will (as argued by, e.g. Gunkel). Jacoby rightly emphasizes the freedom to decide against the leading of the Spirit. However, Jacoby seems to think of only one cardinal (post-conversional) decision which determines the rest of the Christian walk. He maintains that if the Christian decides to follow the Spirit, the inception of the Spirit wrought at baptism will be succeeded by a continuous indwelling of the Spirit in the believer. But in the case of disobedience the Spirit can withdraw (Jacoby, *Ethik*, 301–302). Jacoby seems to know only of these two general states – obedience or disobedience to the Spirit. His system has no place for resistance to the Spirit in individual incidents, something that Paul may call 'quenching the Spirit' (1 Thess. 5:19).

[74] R. Bultmann, 'Das Problem der Ethik bei Paulus', *ZNW* 23 (1924), 123–40; ET: R. Bultmann, 'The Problem of Ethics in Paul', in B.S. Rosner (ed.), *Understanding Paul's Ethics: Twentieth-Century Approaches* (Grand Rapids: Eerdmans, 1995), 195–216; However, it appears that Rosner has overlooked the earlier and somewhat better translation in R. Bultmann, *The Old and the New Man in the Letters of Paul* (Richmond: Knox, 1967), 7–32. References are to the German original unless stated otherwise.

has got rid of sin through justification he should fight against sin (126). Bultmann's disagreement with the view that Paul's indicative and imperative are contradictory is based on his comprehension of justification: it is by means of *God's verdict* (which is an *event* of God's grace) that the person is made righteous. Consequently, δικαιοσύνη is not an ethical quality but an eschatological-forensic concept (128, 135, 138–39).[75] Bultmann hence talks of δικαιοσύνη as 'jenseitige[s] Heilsgut' which is only visible to the eyes of faith. 'This means that the identity of the one justified with the empirical man is something that is *believed*.'[76] However, since it is precisely this empirical man that is justified, his relation to the *Jenseits* ('Beyond') does not exist apart from or next to his concrete deeds and fate. These (ethical) deeds are not to be comprehended as 'works' on which the relation to the *Jenseits* would be founded or by which righteousness would be realized because righteousness is a present reality. Rather, ethical action takes on new meaning as obedience to God: 'the *entire* man understands himself as standing before God, and insofar as he acts he places himself at God's disposal (Rom. 6:13)' (138; 136–37). In conclusion, then, the mode of being of the justified is both fully determined by grace and fully determined by the imperative.[77] 'Wie also die im Imperativ sich aussprechende sittliche Forderung für ihn Gottes Gebot ist, so ist die der Forderung entsprechende Haltung des Gehorsams zugleich Gabe Gottes, gewirkt durch das πνεῦμα, ohne daß die Forderung ihren imperativischen Charakter verliert' (140).

Soon after the publication of his article, Bultmann was criticized by Windisch for his overemphasis on justification to the neglect of sacraments and the Spirit.[78] Perhaps partly due to this reaction, Bultmann twenty-four years later comes back to the issues raised in his 1924 article. In his *Theology of the New Testament* Bultmann now explains more fully the implications of the existentialist doctrine of justification for the function of the Spirit in the interplay of the indicative and the imperative. To this we now turn.

Bultmann sets out his presentation of 'Freedom from Sin and Walking in the Spirit' by highlighting the cardinal position of every believer as one

---

[75] Cf. R. Bultmann, 'Paul', in R. Bultmann, *Existence and Faith: Shorter Writings of Rudolf Bultmann. Selected, translated and introduced by Schubert M. Ogden* (London: Collins, 1961), 161.

[76] Bultmann, 'Problem', in Bultmann, *Man*, 25.

[77] Cf. Bultmann, 'Paul', 162, where Bultmann explains that 'God [not] merely regards the faithful "as if" he were righteous; on the contrary, by accepting me, God takes me to be a different person than I am; and if I (in faith) let go of what I am in myself, if I affirm God's judgement and understand myself in terms of him, then I really *am* a different person, namely, the one he takes me to be.'

[78] H. Windisch, 'Das Problem des paulinischen Imperativs', *ZNW* 23 (1924), 277–79.

who is constantly faced with two options, namely living κατὰ σάρκα or κατὰ πνεῦμα (Gal. 6:8; Rom. 8:12–13). This is due to the fact that sinlessness is only release from the *compulsion* of sin but not from the *possibility* of sin. From this Bultmann deduces that the imperative πνεύματι στοιχῶμεν does not contradict the indicative of justification but *results* from it: 'Clean out the old yeast so that you may be a new batch, as you really are unleavened.' (1 Cor. 5:7). Accordingly, the ζῆν πνεύματι is a *possibility* that needs to be laid hold of by στοιχεῖν πνεύματι (Gal. 5:25). To some extent Bultmann thus agrees with the sentence 'Become what you are'. However, for him this is not an idealistic process of gradual perfection. Rather, the way in which the believer becomes what he already is consists in the (individual) acts of the 'ständigen glaubenden Ergreifen der χάρις [or δικαιοσύνη] und d.h. zugleich in der konkreten, nunmehr möglichen ὑπακοή im περιπατεῖν'.[79] (cf. Rom. 6:14).

Further on in the same chapter, Bultmann attains the same interpretation of Galatians 5:25 from a different angle. According to Bultmann, πνεῦμα has a 'double reference' in Paul: it denotes first and foremost the miraculous power bestowed upon the Christian and, secondly, the norm of the Christian περιπατεῖν.[80] Bultmann explains that the first occurrence of πνεῦμα in Galatians 5:25 refers to the Spirit as power. The second occurrence refers to the norm, for it stands in place of what Paul expresses in 5:16 as κατὰ πνεῦμα. This means that the possibility newly opened by πνεῦμα of laying hold of ζωή contains by virtue of its very nature the ethical imperative to walk according to the norm of the Spirit.

---

[79] R. Bultmann, *Theologie des Neuen Testaments* (Tübingen: J.C.B. Mohr (Paul Siebeck), 1984⁹ [1948¹]), 334: 333–35. All references are to the German original.

[80] With regard to Paul's concept of the Spirit, Bultmann states that Paul uses animistic and dynamistic terminology of the Spirit interchangeably, which indicates that Paul is unconcerned with any speculative interest in the idea of the Spirit. The sporadically occurring notion of the Spirit as material (see Bultmann, 'Ethics', 209) is not really determinative for Bultmann's concept of Pauline pneumatology. This is clear, e.g. from Paul's characterisation of the law as πνευματικός (Rom. 7:14) and from the contrast of γράμμα and πνεῦμα which contradicts a material notion of the Spirit. The character of Paul's concept of πνεῦμα thus needs to be established on different grounds.

In accordance with his general method of developing theology from anthropology, Bultmann infers what Paul meant by 'Spirit' from what he understood by 'flesh'. 'As σάρξ is the quintessence of the worldly, visible, controllable and transitory, which becomes the controlling power over the man who lives κατὰ σάρκα, so πνεῦμα is the quintessence of the non-worldly, invisible, uncontrollable, eternal, which becomes the controlling power for and in him who orients his life κατὰ πνεῦμα' (Bultmann, *Theologie*, 336). Accordingly, the Pauline Spirit is the 'power of futurity' who gives the believer freedom and opens up the future, so that the believer can let herself be determined by that future (cf. Paul's eschatological terminology of ἀπαρχή [Rom. 8:23] and ἀρραβών [2 Cor. 5:5]) (Bultmann, *Theologie*, 335–36, 155–56).

Nur wenn diese Einheit von Freiheit und Gefordertsein verstanden wird – daß nämlich Freiheit Forderung begründet, und daß Forderung Freiheit aktualisiert – wird der paulinische Geistgedanke recht verstanden, d.h. aber: wenn das πνεῦμα nicht als mysteriöse, mit magischem Zwang wirkende Kraft gedacht wird, sondern als die neue Möglichkeit echt geschichtlichen Lebens, die sich dem erschließt, der sein altes Selbstverständnis preisgegeben hat, der sich mit Christus hat kreuzigen lassen, um die δύναμις τῆς ἀναστάσεως αὐτοῦ (Phl 3,10) zu erfahren (338).

Bultmann continues that the unity of power and demand is also hidden in the seemingly mythological locutions of the φρόνημα and ἐπιθυμεῖν of the πνεῦμα (Rom. 8:6, 27; Gal. 5:17), for the πνεῦμα creates a new 'willing' whose origin is not within man but within 'Gottes Heilstat – ein Wollen, das seine bestimmte Richtung hat, frei von der σάρξ, im Kampf gegen sie, geleitet durch die Forderung Gottes.'[81] This unity also solves the tension between the fact that the Spirit is, on the one hand, the gift conferred upon all Christians at baptism and that, on the other hand, it shows its operation in special deeds. The solution is to be seen in the truth that, on one side, the Spirit is the possibility of new life opened up by faith to everybody and, on the other side, this possibility needs to be appropriated by deliberate resolve.[82]

---

[81] Bultmann, *Theologie*, 338. See, however, also Bultmann's later work, R. Bultmann, 'A Reply to the Theses of J. Schniewind', in H.W. Bartsch (ed.), *Kerygma and Myth: A Theological Debate* (London: SPCK, 1953), 121, where he specifies that the Spirit is not the prime cause behind the human will, but that it operates *in* that will.

[82] Bultmann, *Theologie*, 338; R. Bultmann, 'New Testament and Mythology', in H.W. Bartsch (ed.), *Kerygma and Myth: A Theological Debate* (London: SPCK, 1953), 22.

Bultmann appears to have been unaware that a position similar to that of his 1948 *Theologie* had already been published by S. Djukanovic, *Heiligkeit und Heiligung bei Paulus* (Novi Sad: Natoševic, 1939). What *Djukanovic* writes about the interplay of Spirit and believer in Paul's ethical indicative and imperative is clearly influenced by Bultmann's 1924 and 1930 articles. In contrast to Bultmann, however, Djukanovic tries to show how already the OT did not understand קדשׁ as an (ethical) constitution but as a relational term designating separation (Ezek. 22:6; 48:8; 1 Sam. 21:5).

Djukanovic's effort to explain Paul from his own background is to be appreciated. Unfortunately, however, Djukanovic's reading of the OT seems to be influenced more by existentialism than by exegesis. In the same way as later on with Paul, he stresses that in the OT holiness is bestowed upon Israel only in the concrete relationship to God, i.e. in Israel's actual deeds. Only through obedience, God's holiness becomes salvation and grace to the people. Of the many verses which Djukanovic quotes in support of this thesis (Jonah 2:5–8; Pss. 20:3; 33:21; 77:14; 106:17) (15) only the last one could possibly be seen in positive relation to the claim. Djukanovic seems to have overlooked that separation from (i.e. in relation to) something can also be a state. The same holds true for Djukanovic's interpretation of Paul. While Djukanovic says that 'to have the Spirit means to be driven by the Spirit (Rom. 8:14), and this stands in contrast to every kind of state (*Zuständlichkeit*)' (Djukanovic, *Heiligkeit*, 47), one may ask why one could not speak of the new relationship with the Spirit at least as one of *continuity*, based on a *new standing* inaugurated by God (in fact, Djukanovic's *Doktorvater* Gaugler comes close to this latter

Bultmann has presented an innovative and coherent picture of the indicative and the imperative in the Christian life. While he has a strong emphasis on the decision of the believer to take hold of grace, he still tries to avoid the danger of comprehending this as a 'work'. Already in his 1924 article Bultmann was careful to stress that it is *the Spirit* who works the willing. This work upon the believer's will is thus the first work assigned to the Spirit by Bultmann. Every other ethical action of 'walking by the Spirit' is the Christian's laying hold of God's gift of 'being in the Spirit'. Bultmann has thus provided a more detailed analysis of the 'mechanism' of 'walking by the Spirit' than previous scholars.

Nonetheless, Bultmann has not pointed out whether this transformation of the will by the Spirit is a process, or whether it happens instantaneously upon the entry into faith. Also, he fails to indicate *how* the 'indicative-imperative' becomes reality after the decision to follow the Spirit's guiding has been made. Is this a 'second', completely supernatural act of the Spirit? Bultmann's view of the availability of the Spirit's power for the believer exhibits an extraordinary trust in the indicative. In a 'leap of faith', this power is fully actualised in a concrete situation of temptation in the Christian's life. However, is it really merely the supernatural power of the Spirit that establishes the outworking of the imperative in a particular situation? Bultmann seems to suppose that after the decision to 'walk according to the Spirit' has been taken by the believer, the victory over the particular sin has already been won. Bultmann does not know of a struggle with the power of sin *after* a first decision against sinning has been taken.

At this point we catch sight of the fundamental problem of Bultmann's ethics: it is built more upon existentialism than on Paul.[83] Bultmann fails to

---

position [E. Gaugler, 'Die Heiligung in der Ethik des Paulus', *IKZ* 2 (1925), 108–109], but he is obviously not followed by Djukanovic). Djukanovic emphasizes that Paul's pneumatological statements are two-edged: 'Der Geist ist einerseits die Existentialität der Situation der Gläubigen, der neue heilsgeschichtliche Zusammenhang, wo die Gerechtigkeit Gottes dominierende Macht ist, und andererseits dann die Existenzweise, das Wie des konkreten Lebens in der neuen Situation... Es ist also klar, daß die Wirklichkeit der Geistgemeinschaft mit nichts identisch ist, das der Mensch an sich hat. Sie ist im jenseitigen Akt Gottes begründet. Aber sie bezieht sich auf den konkreten Menschen. Sie gibt sich in seinem Tun und Wandel in seinem alltäglichen Leben der Gegenwart' (Djukanovic, *Heiligkeit*, 52; cf. 68, 99). However, it seems that Djukanovic has not escaped the danger of collapsing the indicative into the imperative. For him, the indicative does not establish a continuous relationship with God via the Spirit which would impact the believer in a lasting way. The believer will only experience change once he brings it about through his action. The indicative of the relationship-building work of the Spirit is thus 'spiritualized'; it remains in the realm of the intangible.

[83] For a similar, less brilliant model based on existentialism by one of Bultmann's contemporaries, see E. Fuchs, *Christus und der Geist bei Paulus: Eine biblisch-theologische Untersuchung* (Leipzig: Hinrichs'sche Buchhandlung, 1932), 35–73.

develop his Pauline ethics on the basis of *Paul's* historical background. He thus seems to have fallen into the trap of reading twentieth-century existentialism into Paul's Jewish-Christian mindset. Consequently, he overlooks Paul's eschatological framework of the 'now and the not yet'. Some indicatives are still reality even if the imperative is not realized. For example, if a Christian fails to walk according to the norm of the Spirit in a particular instance, this does not mean that he is not 'in the Spirit' – *contra* Bultmann, who interprets the [εἰ] ζῶμεν πνεύματι in Gal. 5:25 merely as a *possibility*[84] – or that the Spirit is not in him.

Furthermore, is justification indeed regarded by Paul as a 'forensic-eschatological' concept? Goguel raises the question whether perhaps the 'event' of grace is seen by Paul to have more of a transforming effect in the believer's life than is acknowledged by Bultmann.[85] In this sense, then, Bultmann did not entirely escape idealism: He stresses the *human* decision, talks of the 'neue Möglichkeit echt geschichtlichen Lebens, die sich dem erschließt, der sein altes Selbstverständnis preisgegeben hat'[86] and develops his pneumatology from his anthropology. Hand in hand with this goes also the existentialist emphasis on the individual. Paul's apocalyptic framework and the central role that the church-community plays in his theology is unfortunately left aside (or radically and existentially reinterpreted).

Nevertheless, Bultmann's study remains an intriguing treatment of the indicative and imperative of life in the Spirit which has influenced generations of scholars (e.g. Stalder, Schweizer and Kuss)[87] and which will need further testing in the light of Paul and his background.

---

[84] Bultmann, *Theologie*, 335.

[85] M. Goguel, *The Primitive Church* (London: Alan & Unwin, 1964), 452.

[86] Bultmann, *Theologie*, 338.

[87] Kuss, *Römerbrief. II*, e.g. 517. On the others, see below.

Bultmann was followed in his pneumatology by *H.-D. Wendland.* Wendland advances the discussion of the nature of the Spirit by highlighting the fact that the thought-through, Western separation between 'person', 'thing' or 'material world' is unknown to the NT. 'Πνεῦμα is the Spirit of Christ and with this at the same time the presence of salvation and life given by Christ, as also Christ himself gives what he is and is in what he gives. The inward [*innerweltlich*] contrast between thing and person, object and subject is of no use in Christian pneumatology' (Wendland, 'Wirken', 136–37). Wendland supports this thesis by referring to the observation made already by Bultmann, namely, that Paul employs pneumatological terminology unsystematically. In this way, Wendland argues that also 'the unsystematic' gains theological significance: our traditional, philosophically conditioned distinctions are based on the all-embracing reality of the pneuma. Dynamistic and impersonal phraseologies in Paul thus do not counteract statements like those in Gal. 4:6 or 2 Cor. 3:17. These phrases speak 'etwa von der "Gabe" oder dem "Ausgegossenwerden" des Geistes wie davon, daß er "gegeben" wird (Röm. 5,5; 2. Kor. 1,22; 5,5; 1. Thess. 4,8), um die Wirkung des Geistes im Christen und den *Gnadencha-*

Excursus 1: The Relation of Indicative and Imperative in Paul –
V.P. Furnish's Response to Bultmann

Victor Paul Furnish's work *Theology and Ethics in Paul* on the relationship of justification, sanctification and the resulting alliance of indicative and imperative has brought a
new perspective to the study of Paul's theology and ethics, challenging especially the
work of Bultmann.

1) Pneumatology. While Furnish agrees with Stalder (see next section) that Paul does
not simply equate God's Spirit with 'power', he still emphasizes that the Spirit works
with divine power and that the two concepts are therefore closely joined in the apostle's
thinking.[88]

According to Furnish, the dialectic of present and future eschatology[89] finds its focal
point in Paul's concept of the Spirit. On the one hand, for Paul the Spirit is 'the *operative
presence of God's love within men*' (Rom. 5:5) and thus represents the actual entry of the
eschaton into the present age. On the other hand, precisely because God's love is already
powerfully present and active in his Spirit, there is hope for something more (cf. Rom.
15:13), the fulfilment of salvation, the completion and perfection of God's redemptive
activity. 2 Corinthians 3:12–18 suggests that the Spirit is 'the *presentation* – construed
literally, the "making-present" – of that which belongs to another "age" and which, in
spite of its "presentation," continues to belong to that age' (132). Paul expresses this
dialectic with the help of two related metaphors, namely, ἀπαρχή (Rom. 8:23) and
ἀρραβών (2 Cor. 1:22; 5:5) (130–33).[90]

2) Justification and Sanctification. Paul's concept of justification must first of all be
understood in terms of a *relationship*. Righteousness is a restored relationship to God, not
a moral quality. Justification has a forensic-eschatological nature and the manifestation
of it in the 'now' (νυνὶ δέ, Rom. 3:21ff.) has its effects on the life of the believer (146–
47). Following Stuhlmacher, Furnish thus determines that δικαιοῦν has not only a de-
clarative but also a causative meaning in Paul.[91] The new relationship which is established upon God's initiative of grace is both reconciling and redemptive (152–53).

With regard to sanctification Furnish submits that it is not just concerned with the
'ethical', with the 'imperative', while justification would deal with the indicative. Although sanctification has a stronger ethical notion to it, this moral aspect remains secondary to its 'soteriological' reference because sanctification does not consist in a particular
moral quality which has been attained, but – as justification – in a particular relationship

---

rakter des Pneumas im Blick auf den seiner bedürftigen Menschen auszudrücken. Auch
in δύναμις liegt das Übergreifen, das Lebenschaffen des Pneuma, das sein Wesen darin
hat, daß es Gott und Mensch zur neuen Gemeinschaft (κοινωνία τοῦ πνεύματος, 2. Kor.
13:13) im Sinne des "Anteilhabens" des Menschen "am" Geist verbindet' (Wendland,
'Wirken', 137).

[88] Furnish, *Theology*, 129.

[89] Furnish believes – similarly to Schweitzer – that eschatology is the 'heuristic key to
Pauline theology as a whole, the point in which his major themes are rooted and to which
they are ultimately oriented' (Ibid., 114).

[90] Furnish denies that Paul saw the Spirit as a means by which the individual Christian
is enabled to discern God's will in the midst of decision-making situations. For these
daily situations Furnish reckons the communal context of the believer's ethical walk and
the Pauline concept of love to be of fundamental importance (Ibid., 233–35).

[91] On Stuhlmacher, see more fully ch.1, 1.2.2.2.

to God which has been given.[92] It is from this gift that the demand arises. Consequently, 'far from being the "ethical" counterpart to the "theological" doctrine of justification, the doctrine of sanctification in and of itself displays the unity of the indicative and the imperative' (153–56).

3) Indicative and Imperative. Furnish disagrees with Bultmann who sees the imperative as proceeding out of the indicative. Rather, the imperative is fully integral to the indicative as Paul's concept of obedience is included in his concept of grace. The reason why Furnish disagrees with Bultmann's formula 'Become what you are!' – apart from it being too easily misunderstood in terms of that non-Pauline idealism which Bultmann rightly rejects – is that the person who is justified has been given not just the *possibility* of a new life, but an actual and totally new existence (225). This does not mean that the believer suddenly no longer 'sins', but that he was engaged, renewed, and restored in Christ by the creative and redemptive power of God's love.

Moreover, in Christ he knows that redemption is not just deliverance from the hostile powers to which he was formerly enslaved, but freedom *for* obedience to God. For Paul, obedience is neither preliminary to the new life (as its condition) nor secondary to it (as its result and eventual fulfilment). Obedience is *constitutive* of the new life... Indeed, the apostle's exhortations seek to summon believers to that kind of *deliberate response* to God's claim without which faith forfeits its distinctive character as obedience (226–27).

Furnish rejects the idea of 'progress' in obedience if by that is meant increasing 'achievement'. Paul's preaching constantly insists that fullness of life is not attained but given, and that Christian obedience is not an expression of the believer's effort gradually to realize his own innate potentialities, but 'an ever repeated response to the ever newly repeated summons of God'. Philippians 1:25 does not speak of increasing moral achievement, but – as the subsequent exhortations show – Paul is thinking of *maintaining* the unity of the Spirit and *continuously* striving for the gospel even in the face of unsettling opposition (vv.27–28). Also, Paul's athletic or military metaphors are not designed to illustrate the need for moral progress or 'growth of character.'[93] Instead, they portray the need for *persistent* devotion to the task in spite of all hardship and danger (238–240).

Furnish presented to the scholarship of his day a fresh approach to Paul's theology and ethics. From his valuable survey of previous interpretations of Paul's ethic Furnish drew the conclusion that the relation of the indicative and imperative, the relation of 'theological' proclamation and 'moral' exhortation, is *the* crucial problem in interpreting Paul's ethic (9). And indeed, in his discussion of the indicative and the imperative, Furnish is successful in safeguarding the indicative against Bultmann's tendency to collapse it into the imperative. The actual and totally new existence of believers is grounded in the transforming relationship with God. In this regard, Furnish is to some extent a predecessor of our own relational approach developed in the present study.

---

[92] As sanctification is thus a gift of God, Rom. 6:18–22 should not be understood as if sanctification was the 'goal' (understood as an ultimate condition somehow attained) of justification. 'It is, instead, the "ever repeated" service of God, and the *goal* of justification in that it represents the meaning of God's call. Just as slavery to sin means alienation from God and thus "death", so "justification" means reconciliation with God, the fruit (καρπός) of which is sanctification (the service of God), the *telos* of which is, in turn, "eternal life" (vs. 22)' (Furnish, *Theology*, 157).

[93] *Contra* W.A. Beardslee, *Human Achievement and Divine Vocation in the Message of Paul*; SBT 31 (Naperville/London: Allenson/SCM, 1961), 68.

However, some may wonder whether Furnish was mindful enough of the other extreme, that is, paying too little attention to the imperative (see esp. 239).[94] Moreover, Furnish's innovative thesis concerning the overlap between sanctification and justification (which underlies his interpretation of the relation of indicative and imperative) has met with criticism. *S.E. Porter*'s 1993 article on 'Holiness, Sanctification'[95] recognizes Furnish as a main dialogue partner, but robustly defends the traditional model of sanctification as a consequence of justification against Furnish's critique. For example, Porter argues that in Romans 6:19–23, justification emphasizes the initial, or 'conversion', experience of the believer, but is larger than this, including the believer's life 'in Christ Jesus' (v.23). Sanctification, although it may include initiation (v.22), is the τέλος toward which the justified strive, eternal life (vv.22–23). Such a semantic distinction is also apparent in I Thessalonians, although it is in this passage between ἁγιωσύνη ('holiness': 3:13) as the 'state of being holy' and ἁγιασμός ('sanctification', 4:3, 7) as 'the process of making holy'. Paul's use of ἁγιωσύνη reflects his doctrinal assumption of the Thessalonians' status in Christ and his use of ἁγιασμός reflects his exhortation that the Thessalonians should conduct lives pleasing to God. The latter is an ongoing process, as indicated

---

[94] Further, it would need to be tested exegetically whether Furnish is right to state – in contrast to Stalder – that it is only as one resists reliance on one's own power to perform that one is free from the flesh and able to respond in obedience to God's claim. See also the critique by M. Parsons, 'Being Precedes Act: Indicative and Imperative in Paul's Writing', in B.S. Rosner (ed.), *Understanding Paul's Ethics: Twentieth-Century Approaches* (Grand Rapids: Eerdmans, 1995), 225–26.

The same potential mistake of undermining the imperative seems to be committed by *T.J. Deidun*. Although Deidun states categorically in his appendix on the indicative-imperative relationship that no solution of this issue can be true to Paul's thought which weakens either one or the other (Deidun, *Morality*, 239), his own proposition is not altogether different from that of Furnish. Deidun attributes a central role to the Spirit in the indicative-imperative-relationship, and he almost appears to belong still to the Ernesti-Schweitzer era when he says that the Christian must allow the Spirit's activity to expand in his own, so that while it is *wholly* the Spirit's activity, it is also *truly* his own (Deidun, *Morality*, 81). Nonetheless, Deidun does not regard this as a fusion. He speaks of co-operation, of the Christian's 'continuing "yes" to an activity which does not originate in himself, but which is nevertheless *already real and actual* in the core of his being' (Deidun, *Morality*, 80, italics added). However, one wonders in what sense the Spirit's activity is *already real and actual* if the Christian's co-operation is still required. At this point, being reminded of Schweitzer, we catch sight of the philosophical realism that underlies Deidun's argument: the believer's task is no more than a compliance with the activity of the Spirit, which 'has already effected – really but not definitely – and continues what the Christian is now required to do' (Deidun, *Morality*, 81). On this basis one may be slightly hesitant to agree with Deidun's paraphrase of the imperative as 'Let God be God in the core of your liberty' (Deidun, *Morality*, 243), for on Deidun's interpretation this seems to result in collapsing the imperative into the indicative ('the Christian's "new will", constantly flowing from the activity of the Spirit, is the definitely wrought indicative which *carries within itself* the christian imperative'[Deidun, *Morality*, 79–80]).

[95] S.E. Porter, 'Holiness, Sanctification', *DPL*, 397–402. It should be noted that in his own terminology, Porter prefers 'narrative ethics' to 'indicative', and 'ethical appeal' to 'imperative'.

by Paul's tone in which he expresses his desire for sanctification in Romans 6 (e.g. vv.2, 6, 11, 14, 22) and 1 Thessalonians 4 (cf. 2 Cor. 9:27; Phil. 1:6; 2:12–18; 3:12–15).[96]

2.2. The Sanctifying Work of the Spirit is the Spirit's Witness to the Believer's Acting in Faith (K. Stalder)

The most extensive study which has been written about the sanctifying work of the Spirit according to Paul is that of Kurt Stalder. His doctoral dissertation, for which he researched at the 'Christkatholisch-theologische' faculty of Bern, was published in 1962 as *Das Werk des Geistes in der Heiligung bei Paulus*. In this detailed 500–page study, Stalder endeavours to enquire into the way in which the Spirit works within Christians for their sanctification. Does the Spirit become a new disposition of the believer? Does the Spirit's entering the person destroy the person's unity or individuality? Or is sanctification a co-operation between Spirit and believer in which the Spirit enhances human ethical powers?

Stalder tries to answer these questions by looking first of all at the nature of the Spirit himself. Stalder criticizes the methodology of Bertrams' thesis,[97] for he believes it to be wrong to investigate the *work* of the Spirit without first asking about the *nature* of the Spirit because any description of the Spirit's activity presupposes a certain view of the being of the Spirit (5–8). In the second part of his book, Stalder considers Paul's understanding of sanctification in general. The third and major part of the thesis, finally, is devoted to the discussion of the Spirit's role in sanctification based on the example of Romans 8. Since Stalder's work is the only monograph which devotes itself explicitly to roughly the same questions as the present study, we will need to listen to him carefully.

1) The Spirit as a divine being. According to Stalder, the Spirit is for Paul not a personification or hypostasis of a divine attribute (such as, e.g. of power), nor is the Spirit *identified* with power since Paul refers with δύναμις merely to one of God's characteristics or to his deeds in which this character trait is demonstrated (26–35). Rather, the Holy Spirit 'ist für Paulus Gott selbst, sofern er aus sich heraustritt, um in der Kirche und ihren Gliedern sein Werk zu vollenden und von daher sogar sich selbst gegenüber für die Kirche und ihre Glieder einzustehen' (47). Stalder

---

[96] In fact, even Furnish's own understanding of obedience as 'an ever repeated response to the ever newly repeated summons of God' in practice implies the notion of growth since continual interaction with God will leave neither the individual nor the nature of the relationship unchanged.

[97] Bertrams argues that 'wenn das πνεῦμα in dem Christen wirkt, ihn zu... sittlich erhabenen Handlungen befähigt, aus ihm heraus spricht, mahnt tröstet, *so muß diese Einwirkung zuletzt auf eine göttliche Person zurückgeführt werden*' (Bertrams, *Wesen*, 159, italics added).

reaches this definition of the Spirit on the basis of verses like Galatians 4:6, Romans 8:15–16, 26–27 and 1 Corinthians 2:10–11, where 'the Spirit faces [*gegenübertreten*] God in specific action' (e.g. by praying to God within the believer) (45–46, 62–69). Nonetheless, Stalder deems it to be injudicious to talk of the Spirit as a personality (*Personalität*) since the modern linguistic usage of this term would suggest – in contrast to the wording of the Trinitarian doctrine of the 'three persons' (which is problematic as well) – that the Holy Spirit is a divine being (*Wesen*) next to and apart from God (50). When Stalder finally mentions the possibility of understanding the Spirit as substance, he admits that it would be possible that Paul comprehended the Spirit as such. Paul, however, did not go along with Stoic metaphysics resulting in a *Seinskontinuität* between God and man once the Spirit has entered an individual. Stalder adds that the conceptualisation of 'substance' was already equivocal at Paul's time. Today one is faced with the additional problem of the influence of natural science upon substance-terminology (64–67). Stalder thus prefers to use the 'unwieldy term "being"' (*Sein*)

...weil dieser Begriff eher dazu nötigt, sich immer neu zu vergegenwärtigen, was damit gemeint ist. Wir meinen aber, daß das sonst wenig differenzierte Reden von der "Substanz-Vorstellung" in den paulinischen Geistaussagen uns jedenfalls den Hinweis darauf gebe, daß der Heilige Geist bei Paulus tatsächlich nicht nur ein Gedanke, nicht nur eine Funktion und auch nicht nur ein Tun Gottes ist, sondern sein eigenes Sein hat, das göttliche Sein, aber das göttliche Sein in der Besonderung als Geist (68).

From this resolution Stalder infers that the question how the Spirit could live in the person and whether through the residence of the Spirit within man a foreign material would enter the person and destroy the internal unity, will no longer arise. 'If the Spirit has his divine being, then his dwelling within us purely designates the miracle of God's presence in us. And as a miracle this is not to be explained' (68).

What, however, does Stalder believe about the practical outworking of the relationship between Spirit and believer? Before answering this question, we will first need to have a short glance at Stalder's underlying principles concerning divine and human work in sanctification in general.

2) Ἁγιασμός as God's work and as the believer's work. Stalder refers to 1 Corinthians 6:11 as a central verse on God's sanctifying work. He asserts that the aorists indicate that one is neither dealing with imperatives nor with ideals but with 'kerygmatic' statements (*Feststellungen*). However, Stalder qualifies that these statements do not found new moral qualities which would lead automatically to ethical behaviour – otherwise there would have been no quarrels among the Corinthians. The aorists do not connote a new ontic reality; rather, Paul uses 'rechtlich-machtpolitische' or cultic language. Accordingly, ἁγιασμός as God's work does not mean that the Holy Spirit becomes a human quality. He remains God. Positively speaking, it is Stalder's fundamental belief that the work of the Spirit both in justification and sanctification is constituted by bringing the individual to a recognition of the significance of the Christ-event, that is, to the point where faith and life in justification is ventured (201–202; cf. 447).

The climax of God's gracious work of sanctification is the fact that *we* can and may do good, that we can sanctify ourselves. This leads us on to Stalder's understanding of ἁγιασμός as the believer's work. Sanctification is in that sense God's work, in that it is given to *us* to know what has been condemned to annihilation in Christ, what shape the new life should have and that *we* can live this life – no matter how much we may conceive or experience ourselves as weak or 'sinful'. 'Darum kann die Heiligung, gerade weil sie ganz und gar Gottes Werk, aber eben *dieses* Werk Gottes ist, auch durchaus als Werk des Menschen beschrieben werden' (215). Stalder concludes from this that it is mistaken to ask how far sanctification is God's work and how far that of the believer. Precisely the fact that sanctification can be described, praised and demanded as the work of the believer, demonstrates how much and how completely it is only the work of God – in Jesus Christ (215, 447).

3) The sanctifying work of the Holy Spirit illustrated by the example of Romans 8. As the final part of our summary of Stalder's view we will now turn to his contribution respecting the ethical work of Spirit and believer. For the sake of brevity we will give attention only to a few verses of Romans 8 upon which Stalder has commented.

8:5. Stalder believes that it is clear from this verse that through a miracle the Spirit brings people to the point that they freely submit themselves to the authority of the Spirit and are κατὰ πνεῦμα. It is thus a *Sein aus Entscheidung*,[98] as in the case of κατὰ σάρκα ὄντες, but the origin, power and facilitation of this decision is of an altogether different kind and quality than that of the being according to the flesh. The consequences of being κατὰ πνεῦμα are even less 'naturhaft zwangsmäßig' than those of being κατὰ σάρκα; they are 'ein kraft des Heiligen Geistes in Freiheit sich vollziehendes Bleiben und Wollen unter seiner Autorität' (424–25).

8:9. Stalder explains that, although Christians do not have the Spirit at their disposal as a natural ability, the indwelling of the Spirit has been proclaimed to them and they can expect that the Spirit will establish his position concretely. Consequently, in the situation of appeal from the law they need to take a decision, and only afterwards – and only by faith – may they recognise that the Spirit has confirmed his presence. In other words, *the Spirit is only experienced as one is acting in faith* (434–35; cf. 479).

---

[98] Stalder states that the Spirit reaches human beings in their 'Entscheidungszentrum' (centre of decision-making) (Stalder, *Heiligung*, 485; cf. 478).

8:14. Stalder interprets 'being led by the Spirit' in this verse as the Spirit driving believers to become more themselves and, listening to his directions, to do their own work to which he calls them in free responsibility. Yet more light is shed on Stalder's view of the leading of the Spirit in his paraphrase of the parallel passage in Galatians 5:16–25. Stalder asserts that Paul did not intend to say in verse 18 that the Galatians should just surrender themselves to the drive of the Spirit which would lift them to a new state in which the desires of the flesh are switched off. Rather, what Paul means is: 'The Spirit shows you that in Christ you are justified and accepted for a life pleasing to God.'

Indem ihr euch das vom Geist sagen laßt und so im Anspruch Gottes an euch euer Heil und eure Freude erkennt, werdet ihr auch die Verderblichkeit der Pläne, die aus eurem "Fleisch"-Sein kommen, durchschauen, nicht darauf eingehen wollen, erkennen, daß ihr anders leben könnt, und – sofern ihr wirklich auf den Geist hört – auch tatsächlich anders, nämlich nach dem heilsamen Geheiß Gottes leben (471).

Stalder explains Galatians 5:25 in a similar way: '*We* live in the Spirit, because it is the Spirit who lets us recognise and believe justification as our concrete reality in the freedom for God, so that we will confidently dare to live with God in obedience' (471). Furthermore, even the love of God which is poured out by the Spirit into the hearts of the believers (Rom. 5:5) is mainly the Spirit's work of making believers realize the reality of their justification and sanctification. Accordingly, it is not 'love' that loves within us, but it is *us* who shall love, as the imperatives continually need to remind us. Stalder infers from this that imperfection in love can only be due to our sluggishness and unbelief, in that we do not continually listen to the testimony of the indwelling Spirit and thus 'im Gebot der Liebe immer wieder nicht die Bestätigung unserer Rechtfertigung und die Freude des Lebens mit Gott erkennen und so es nicht wagen, ganz Gottes zu sein, obwohl wir es doch sind.'[99]

According to Stalder, Christians cannot excuse their lack of love by saying that it would not be possible to be perfect in love. On the contrary, perfection in love is the most natural for them since they have been set free from the curse of the law and have been justified and sanctified in Christ to be co-workers in the expression of the love of God to their neighbours. The Holy Spirit does not leave any chance for the discouraging thought that it would somehow not be possible to actually live in the reality of the eschatological life (472–75).

Stalder's work has provided theologians with an elaborate analysis of an area of Pauline studies that had not been treated comprehensively before. In spite of his long-winded and at times repetitive style (which has made

---

[99] Ibid., 475.

his views difficult to access and thus prevented him from being thoroughly interacted with by Pauline scholarship),[100] scholars who write about the ethical work of the Spirit are indebted to Stalder's efforts. Stalder has drawn particular attention to the function of the Spirit in sanctification as one who makes the believers aware of the kerygmatic truth of their justification and sanctification. He has liberated his readers from the misconception that a sanctified lifestyle would presuppose the infusion of supernatural spiritual power. What is more, Stalder has introduced an alertness for the practical implications of Paul's doctrine of the Spirit into his study that is unparalleled in its thoroughness.

Nevertheless, as much as this practical, or rather systematic, concern is to be appreciated, it is exactly here that the greatest danger of the book becomes evident. Unfortunately, it seems that Stalder has let these dogmatic *topoi* direct his focus more than the evidence of the Pauline text. For example, Stalder complains that the 'results' of previous studies of the nature of the Spirit have been 'nebulous' (23).[101] As a consequence, he wants to avoid speaking of the Spirit as substance. The influence of natural science has made the use of this terminology ambiguous. Stalder thus appears to be more concerned with the linguistic and paralinguistic concepts of the modern mind than he is with those of Paul. He by-passes Paul's historical context in that he does not investigate Paul's Jewish-Hellenistic background nor illustrate how, for example, the Old Testament-concept of holiness (which is treated by Stalder) is applied by Paul in his writings. Also the term which Stalder decides to use for the nature of the Spirit instead of the substance-terminology, namely, 'göttliches Sein', is not a Pauline concept.[102] One could conclude from this that the value of

---

[100] See, however, the influence which Stalder may have had on G. Haufe, 'Das Geist-motiv in der paulinischen Ethik', *ZNW* 85 (1994), 183–91.

[101] While one needs to agree with Stalder that there has been no consensus among scholars concerning Paul's concept of the nature of the Spirit one would still wish that Stalder had engaged more thoroughly with his contemporaries. *E. Schweizer*, for instance, had given new input to the discussion whether Paul understood the Spirit as power or as substance when he observed that Hellenists could think of power only in the form of a substance. In the words of Diogenes Laertius, 'All power is substantial' (7.38, 56) (E. Schweizer, 'The Spirit of Power: The Uniformity and Diversity of the Concept of the Holy Spirit in the New Testament', *Int* 6 (1952), 269; cf. Schweizer, 'πνεῦμα', 392). Schweizer further pointed out that both Greeks and Hebrews do not have a word for 'person', so that it may not be wise to use this concept with regard to Paul's understanding of the Spirit (Schweizer, 'πνεῦμα', 433–34).

[102] Cf. G. Fitzer, 'Review of K. Stalder, *Das Werk des Heiligen Geistes in der Heiligung bei Paulus*', *TZ* 20 (1964), 145: 'Ob der Begriff des Geistes als eines Seins Gottes, in dem Gott sich selbst gegenübertritt und in dem Gott aus sich heraustritt, in dem er sich selbst heiligt, in der christlichen Dogmatik gebrauchbar ist, bezweifle ich, paulinisch ist er jedenfalls nicht und muß, auf Paulus angewandt, zu Überinterpretationen führen. Das

Stalder's monograph may prove itself more by being a positive testimony 'des Glaubens und Denkens der jungen Kräfte in der altkatholischen Kirche, ihrer ökumenischen Aufgeschlossenheit, ihrer Aktivität des Glaubens und ihrer biblischen Fundierung' than by being an explanation of Paul, as Fitzer points out in his critical review.[103]

Nonetheless, Stalder has put his finger on a number of important issues regarding the relationship of pneumatology and ethics. Although Stalder did not always settle these issues on the basis of historical-critical exegesis of Paul but through dialectical theology[104] and intelligent reasoning, we will nonetheless briefly review Stalder's cardinal thesis.

Stalder is the first to argue that the work of the Spirit both in justification and sanctification constitutes the 'Geltungmachung eines Zeugnisses' and does not involve any psycho-physical effects (like the increase of ethical powers) on the person (485). With this definition Stalder undertakes an unfortunate reduction of the Spirit's work to a purely cognitive level, namely, to the impartation of rational knowledge. While the key importance of this function is not to be denied, one may raise the question

---

Heilsgeschehen wird zu einem innergöttlichen Vorgang, und die Spannung zwischen Gott und Mensch, zwischen Heil bzw. Rechtfertigung und Sünde wird aufgelöst.'

[103] Ibid., 145.

A further work which devotes itself to the study of Paul's pneumatology was published by *W. Pfister* virtually at the same time as Stalder's monograph. However, since Pfister does not seem to be guided by any specific inquiry in his research, his 'results' remain too general and lack originality (Pfister, *Paulus, passim*). The same holds true for the slightly later O. Knoch, *Der Geist Gottes und der neue Mensch: Der Heilige Geist als Grundkraft und Norm des christlichen Lebens in Kirche und Welt nach dem Zeugnis des Apostels Paulus* (Stuttgart: Katholisches Bibelwerk, 1993[2] [1975[1]]).

[104] Stalder openly acknowledges in the preface to his book his indebtedness to K. Barth and R. Bultmann. Respecting Barth's influence, philosophical-theological conceptions seem to have affected Stalder's results more than exegesis, as one may deduce, for instance, from Stalder's emphasis on the 'foreignness of the Spirit' to the believer (e.g. there is no state of 'being in the Spirit') which is strongly reminiscent of Barth's comprehension of God and the Spirit as 'completely the Other' (K. Barth, *The Epistle to the Romans* (Oxford: Oxford University Press, 1968[6] [1919[1]]), 275). Cf. the influence of Barth on Schrage's concept of the work of the Spirit in Paul's ethics (Schrage, *Einzelgebote*, esp. 84–87).

Bultmann's influence is evident in Stalder's view of justification as 'forensic-cultic', its reality being experienced only as one is acting in faith and visible exclusively to the eyes of faith. Concerning man's response of faith to God's offer of salvation, Stalder is more careful than Bultmann to avoid the trap of faith becoming a 'work'. Yet, Stalder seems to leave no room for human freedom. Stalder believes that the Spirit brings us to a point where 'we have to say yes to the new life in freedom'; only as we surrender ourselves in faith do we experience this freedom. Stalder's concept of the relation between Spirit and faith is thus one of predestination (see Stalder, *Heiligung*, 83, 444, 446–47, 453).

whether Paul does not envisage a broader field of activity of the Spirit. Indeed, Stalder himself says that the Spirit 'will establish his position concretely' as the believer decides to obey him in a specific situation (435). While Stalder does not enlarge on this effect of the Spirit, it needs to be said that Paul clearly knows of effects of the Spirit separate from the transmission of the gospel message (see, e.g., 1 Cor. 2:4; Gal. 5:22). Stalder infelicitously overlooked in his exegesis of Romans 8:13 that the Romans are supposed to put to death the deeds of the body *by the Spirit* (πνεύματι). Hence his explanation, that it is *us* with *our powers* who kill the deeds of the body and that exactly this is *completely* the work of the Spirit (454), will not suffice.[105] It seems that in Paul's presentation, *per contra*, believers are not abandoned to their own powers but should apply the concrete help of the Spirit offered in situations of temptation. Christians can 'allow' the Spirit to draw them deeper into the empowering relationship with God and the community of faith. This may imply the concept of co-operation, which Stalder vehemently opposes. Otherwise the statement that it is God who sanctifies the believer through the Spirit would become an empty shell. The believer would be the only one actively involved in the practical ethical life. In conclusion, then, it is doubtful whether the work of the Spirit is purely noetic, and, following from that, whether Paul would agree with Stalder's prime emphasis on human powers by which the believers have to 'sanctify themselves' (215).

2.3. The Eschatological Spirit Enables Obedience from the Heart and Introduces an Intense Battle with the Flesh (J.D.G. Dunn)

While the research on Pauline pneumatology thus far was dominated by German scholars, the page would turn with James D.G. Dunn. 1970 saw the publication of his dissertation *Baptism in the Holy Spirit*, which is the first academic biblical-theological treatment of the Pentecostal doctrine of Spirit-baptism as a 'second blessing'.[106] However, more important for the focal point of the present review of scholarship is his likewise influential 1975 monograph *Jesus and the Spirit*. While Dunn has extensively written

---

[105] Additionally, under the influence of his view that Christians are still in the flesh, Stalder speaks with regard to v.13 of 'killing ourselves' (Stalder, *Heiligung*, 545). This, however, seems to be an overstatement, because Stalder can speak of the work of the Spirit in the ensuing verse as that of 'driving us to become more ourselves'. Stalder does not resolve this contradiction by investigating Paul's language and conceptions.

[106] Cf. the recent issue of *Journal of Pentecostal Theology* (19/1, 2010) which is designed an appraisal and assessment of Dunn's book 40 years after it was originally published.

on Paul and the Spirit since then,[107] particularly in his *Theology of Paul the Apostle* (1998), we will focus on his 1975 monograph as this is his most comprehensive treatment of (Paul's) pneumatology, setting the agenda for his subsequent work on this matter.

In *Jesus and the Spirit*, Dunn picks up a thread that had been neglected since the days of Gunkel. He argues that Paul, on the basis of his own experience, understood the Spirit as an *inward compulsion* expressed in love (cf. Rom. 5:5). For Paul, the primary driving force in ethics was no longer obedience to a written law (coming from the outside), but obedience to an inward conviction (the law written on the heart, the law of the Spirit) shaping both motive and action (cf. 'the mind of Christ', 1 Cor. 2:16; Phil. 2:5). According to Romans 12:2, this fundamental reshaping and transformation of inner motivations and moral consciousness (νοῦς) is a process (μεταμορφοῦσθε: present tense) and leads to a spontaneous awareness of God's will in ethical decision making (δοκιμάζειν).[108] The role of the Spirit in this process cannot be degraded to some rationally construed claim of God, nor can love be reduced to a generalised ethical principle.[109] Rather, Paul and his readers had *experienced* the reality and vitality of this transformation in their own lives. Dunn believes that it was on this ground that Paul was able to promote as the distinctive element of his ethics the charismatic recognition of God's will and the inward compulsion of love.[110]

However, Dunn drastically diverges from Gunkel when he states that one only begins to understand the charismatic Spirit if one recognises him as the *eschatological Spirit* (312). With this notion Dunn wants to draw attention to the fact that a fierce warfare between Spirit and flesh is introduced at the arrival of the Spirit in a person's life (315). He contends that this conflict and suffering is the inevitable consequence of the life of the Spirit having to express itself through the body of death (327, 336). For Paul, therefore, the religious experience of the believer is characterised by paradox and continuing frustration, the believer is torn in two by conflicting desires and impulses (338, 313).

Dunn arrives at this interpretation mainly by means of his exegesis of Romans 7:14–8:25 which he regards as the *locus classicus* for compre-

---

[107] Cf. our bibliography for a list of a number of Dunn's further publications on this matter.

[108] Nonetheless, Dunn is clear that Paul's ethics is not solely enthusiastic since the law still stands as God's standard of righteousness (Dunn, *Jesus and the Spirit*, 224). Dunn's thoughts on Paul's view of the law would not much later inspire him to become one of the fathers of the 'New Perspective on Paul' (see esp. his classic, J.D.G. Dunn, 'The New Perspective on Paul', in J.D.G. Dunn, *Jesus, Paul and the Law: Studies in Mark and Galatians* (London: SPCK, 1990), 183–206).

[109] With this, Dunn speaks out against both rationalism and idealism.

[110] Dunn, *Jesus and the Spirit*, 223–25; 311; cf. Dunn, *Theology*, 430, etc.

hending Paul's view of the normal Christian life (indeed, the ἐγώ in Rom. 7 relates that Paul is speaking from the heart of his *own* experience). The difference between 7:7–25 and the rest of Romans 6–8 does not denote different conditions but the same condition viewed from different perspectives. In Romans 7, the Christian is seen predominantly in terms of flesh, law and sin, whereas Romans 8 views the Christian from the perspective of the Spirit (and the law in vv.1–8). Dunn stresses that both 'loyalties' characterise the believer as a *divided person* in the overlap of the ages, having one foot in the camp of the flesh, the other in the camp of the Spirit. As *simul justus et peccator* the believer experiences within himself a real unwillingness and antagonism against the Spirit as much as against the flesh.[111] Although Christians are ἐν πνεύματι (Rom. 8:9), they are still prone to live according to the flesh.[112]

Nonetheless, Dunn is careful enough to draw attention to the surpassing power of the Spirit, because God, 'recognizing the power of human desire, gives to those who open themselves to him a power (the Spirit) which is stronger than human desire.' The result of this 'mysterious blend of divine initiative and enabling, and human response and commitment'[113] involves two things: (1) The Christian

experiences the power of the Spirit as *the power of life beyond death*... a power which is superior to the forces of corruption and death, not in the sense that it stops them, but in the sense that it lasts through them. (2) He experiences the power of the Spirit as *the power of life out of death*... a power which enables him to put to death the attitudes and desires of life in this world, to crucify himself in his fleshness (Rom. 8.13; Gal. 5.24) even while living "in the flesh" (337–38).

The nature of the experience of the eschatological Spirit as that of death and life discloses that this is the experience of the Spirit of Christ, the experience of that death which Jesus died and of that life which Jesus lives. Dunn concludes that it is distinctive of Paul that he understands the Christian experience as *experience of Jesus* and *consciousness of Christ*, that is, as the recognition of the impress of Christ's character in Paul's experience and its outworking in the warfare between Spirit and flesh in the overlap of the ages.[114]

---

[111] Cf. Dunn, *Galatians*, 299.

[112] Dunn, *Jesus and the Spirit*, 312–18. Cf. J.D.G. Dunn, 'Rom. 7,14–25 in the Theology of Paul', *TLZ* 31 (1975), 269.

[113] Dunn, *Galatians*, 300; 315; cf. Dunn, *Romans 1–8*, 443–444, 458.

[114] Dunn, *Jesus and the Spirit*, 342. In the context of his exegesis of 2 Cor. 3:18 Dunn points out that 'the distinctive mark of the eschatological Spirit is an immediacy of relationship with God which makes the believer more like Jesus (if we may use such simple, pietistic language). Here once again then relationship with God is seen in terms of experiencing the Spirit, but once again the experienced Spirit is seen in terms of Jesus' (Dunn, *Jesus and the Spirit*, 320; cf. Dunn, *Theology*, 400). This interpretation has strong

Dunn's work on early Christian pneumatology has put new emphasis on the eschatological nature of the ethical work of the Spirit in Paul. While Schweitzer had already brought the eschatological dimension of Paul's pneumatology into focus (and Käsemann had placed the conflict between flesh and Spirit into an apocalyptic framework),[115] it was Dunn who first gave a detailed exposition of the believers' religious experience as that of life *and death* through the Spirit of Jesus. It is Dunn's strength that he can describe the severity of the continuing frustration and paradox of the Christian condition without denying that the Spirit was nevertheless experienced by Paul and the early Christians as a real ethical power.

However, Dunn may be in danger of overdrawing the severity of the struggle in the Christian life. On the one hand, Dunn terms the Spirit's leading as that of 'a power which works like a deep-rooted passion or overmastering compulsion,'[116] a formulation which seems to leave little room for the believer's own will and effort, and which certainly does not suggest a struggle in which the chances of following the Spirit are equally high as those of following the flesh.[117] On the other hand, it is exactly this ethical Spirit which introduces to the recipient a conflict of previously unknown intensity. While Dunn says in his chapter on the 'Charismatic Spirit' that it was Paul's experience of the reality and vitality of the *ethical transformation by the Spirit* that shaped his distinctively pneumatological ethics (223–25), he argues in his chapter 'The Spirit of Jesus' that Paul's spiritual experience is that of Romans 7.[118] For Dunn, Romans 7 cannot

---

parallels with the relational approach to Spirit and ethics developed in this study. However, Dunn does not major on this aspect in his overall picture of the ethical Spirit in Paul.

[115] See, e.g., Käsemann, 'Anthropology', 1–31. On Käsemann, see further ch. 1, 1.2.2.1.

[116] J.D.G. Dunn, *The Theology of Paul's Letter to the Galatians*; NT Theology (Cambridge: Cambridge University Press, 1993), 106.

[117] With regard to the flesh Dunn even seems to propose its identity with the believer's self: 'there must be that inward resolution and determined discipline to side with the Spirit *against oneself* in what is an ongoing and inescapable inner warfare' (Dunn, *Galatians*, 299). Dunn appears to underestimate that the Christian has a new identity and standing as one who is ἐν πνεύματι (Rom. 8:9; Gal. 5:24; etc.).

[118] Dunn, *Jesus and the Spirit*, 312–18. Dunn is in good company with this interpretation of Rom. 7 (e.g. Augustine, Calvin, Luther; for some modern scholars, see Dunn, 'Rom. 7,14–25', 258 n.8).

However, a long tradition of scholars has argued that Rom. 7 does *not* depict normal Christian life. E.g. W.G. Kümmel, *Römer 7 und das Bild des Menschen im Neuen Testament: Zwei Studien*; TB 53 (Munich: Kaiser, 1974 [1929[1]]), *passim*; D. Wenham, 'The Christian Life – A Life of Tension? A Consideration of Christian Experience in Paul', in D.A. Hagner and M.J. Harris (eds.), *Pauline Studies* (Exeter: Paternoster, 1980), 80–94; P. Stuhlmacher, *Paul's Letter to the Romans: A Commentary* (Edinburgh: T. & T. Clark, 1994), 114–20; S.K. Stowers, 'Romans 7.7–25 as a Speech-in-Character (προσωπο-

refer to Paul's pre-Christian experience: 'There is nothing of such anguish and frustration in other passages where he speaks explicitly of his "former life" – quite the reverse (Gal. 1.13f.; Phil. 3.4–6). Rather with Rom. 7 we listen in to a man in conflict with himself' (314). Accordingly, Dunn's interpretation almost gives the impression as if ethical living is more difficult once one has received the Spirit. Thus, if Dunn wants to remain faithful to his earlier description of the Spirit's vital ethical power (without calling it 'overmastering', though), it may be inevitable for him to allow that the ethical struggle introduced by the eschatological Spirit – of which he has made Pauline students lucidly aware – is not *as* intense as the one depicted in Romans 7.[119]

Also the struggle between flesh and Spirit mentioned in Galatians 5:16–25 appears to be less drastic and frustrating than described above. Indeed, in his important study on the ethics of Galatians, *Obeying the Truth* (1988), *John Barclay* elucidates how Paul intends to demonstrate the *sufficiency and practical value* of 'walking by the Spirit'.[120] In the face of the agitators' propagation of the necessity of the law, the Galatians had arrived at questions like 'How can we be sure that Paul's "walking in the Spirit" provides us with sufficient moral safeguards?', 'Will it match the moral standard required by God's law?'. Barclay demonstrates that, by way of answer, Paul argues that 'walking in the Spirit' excludes the 'desires of the flesh' (in 5:16). Verse 17 expounds this thought: the mutual opposition of flesh and Spirit in the conflict implies mutual exclusion and therefore ensures that the Galatians will not misuse their freedom, because 'their walk in the Spirit will set them against the flesh and thus define the moral choices they must make'.[121] The goal of the conflict of flesh and Spirit is hence not the frustration of the Spirit-inspired wishes of the believer.[122]

πoιία)', in T. Engberg-Pedersen (ed.), *Paul in his Hellenistic Context: Studies in the New Testament and its World* (Edinburgh: T. & T. Clark, 1994), 180–202; Lichtenberger, *Ich*, 266–69. Cf. 6.1. above. It is therefore methodologically precarious when Dunn calls this heavily debated passage the *locus classicus* for comprehending Paul's view of the normal Christian life.

[119] In his later *Theology of Paul the Apostle*, the emphasis on the ethical struggle inaugurated by the advent of the Spirit in the believers' lives appears to be less strong. While Dunn retains his view of Rom. 7, see his list of the blessings of the Spirit (liberty, Christian conduct, fruit, etc.) in Dunn, *Theology*, 434–39 (as opposed to the more negative statements on pp. 477, 481). See already Dunn, *Romans 1–8*, 445, where he develops the notion of the believers' *posse non peccare*.

[120] Barclay, *Truth*, 218.

[121] Ibid., 112.

[122] Barclay highlights the fact that if Paul 'is admitting here that the flesh continually defeats the Spirit's wishes, Paul is hardly providing a good reason to "walk in the Spirit"' (Ibid., 113).

Rather, Barclay concludes that 'the warfare imagery is invoked not to indicate that the two sides are evenly balanced but to show the Galatians that they are already committed *to* some forms of activity (the Spirit) *against* others (the flesh).'[123]

Summary and Conclusion. In the years after the First World War, a (second) heavy attack against the idealistic notion of ethical life was launched. The effect was to some extent an exchange of idealism for existentialism. Bultmann successfully dismantled the concept of continuous moral progression through the Spirit's immanence in the believer. He shifted the focus of attention to the issue of Paul's indicative and imperative, stressing the imperative as the realisation of the indicative. The fundamental role of human decision was brought to the fore. These emphases were then applied in more detail to the work of the Spirit in sanctification by Stalder. Stalder's dialectical pneumatology associated the Spirit with the cognitive action of making the believers aware of their salvation. The Spirit does not infuse supernatural power; rather, it is by their own powers that believers – liberated through the Spirit – have to accomplish the imperative in the struggle against sin and flesh.

However, Anglo-American scholarship on Pauline pneumatology and ethics, which only at this point (after the Second World War) really came to prominence, countered the German existentialist tradition. Furnish re-emphasized the indicative over against Bultmann's tendency to subdue it to a subjunctive. The imperative is understood as fully integral to the indicative because Paul's concept of obedience is included in his concept of grace. *Contra* Stalder, one needs to resist relying on one's own power to realize the imperative; it is the Spirit who works both willing and acting out, as Deidun stressed in application of Furnish's ethics to the realm of Paul's pneumatology.[124]

Bultmann also met with disagreement among German scholars. Käsemann and Stuhlmacher emphasized the ontological reality of the new creation (see ch. 1, 1.2.2.). Käsemann criticized Bultmann for demythologizing the Jewish-Apocalyptic perspective of Paul. In line with this latter notion (although not in reaction against Bultmann), Dunn drew attention to the warfare between Spirit and flesh which is introduced to the believer upon the reception of the Spirit. Dunn was one of the major scholars who, in the

---

It is Barclay's novelty to apprehend the Spirit–flesh antagonism as one of positive purpose, without diminishing the power of the flesh in the mutual opposition ('these are opposed *to each other*') and without equating the phrase ἃ ἐὰν θέλητε with 'what the flesh desires'.

[123] Ibid., 115.

[124] See n.94 above.

years between 1930 and 1990, gave significant weight to the role of experience in Paul's ethical pneumatology, and he was the first to give this a slightly more negative touch as he points out that the notion of struggle and moral frustration is ever present. This view of the religious existence of the believer would find a serious antagonist at the end of the twentieth century (i.e. G.D. Fee).

3. The Interplay of Pauline Pneumatology and Ethics in Recent Scholarship Since 1990 (Horn & Fee)

3.1. Developmental Approaches to the Relation of Spirit and Ethics in Pre-Pauline and Pauline Writings

In the last decade of the twentieth century the issues raised by Gunkel (and Pfleiderer) 100 years before were revisited with concentrated effort. Up to this point, Gunkel had been followed in his thesis that Paul was the first to develop a pneumatologically founded ethic by Heitmüller, Bertrams, Schweizer and a number of other scholars in Germany.[125] In 1991 this thesis was restated with new force in the British dissertation of the Pentecostal scholar Robert Menzies. Menzies argued that the Spirit in pre-Pauline pneumatology was not necessary for salvation. It was merely an empowering gift for mission as the 'Spirit of prophecy'. Endorsing Pfleiderer, Menzies maintained that it was Paul's interaction with Wisdom of Solomon 9:9–18 that precipitated his change (esp. in 1 Cor. 2:6–16).[126]

However, Gunkel and his followers were challenged respecting their assertions about pre-Pauline Judaism and Christianity. Sokolowski, Juncker, Volz, Büchsel, Davies, Vos, Suurmond, Turner, and others demonstrated that Spirit and ethics/soteriology were already connected in the Hebrew Bible, in early Judaism and in what Gunkel called the 'popular views' (cf. 5.1. above).[127] Turner refuted Menzies' position for its misinterpretation of Wisdom of Solomon 9.9–18 and 1 Corinthians 2:6–16 (Paul's 'soteriologi-

---

[125] Heitmüller, *Paulus*, 18–19; Bertrams, *Wesen*, 46–49; Schweizer, 'πνεῦμα', 409, 415–16. Cf., e.g. Kuss, *Römerbrief. II*, 560–61; Wikenhauser, *Mysticism*, 80.

[126] Menzies, *Development*, chs. 12–13. Cf. Menzies, 'Tribute', 138.

[127] Sokolowski, *Geist*, 196ff., 277ff.; Juncker, *Ethik. I*, 135–39; Volz, *Geist*, 73ff.; Büchsel, *Geist*, 133ff.; Davies, *Paul*, 117ff.; Vos, *Untersuchungen*, 34–70; J.-J. Suurmond, 'The Ethical Influence of the Spirit of God: An Exegetical and Theological Study with Special Reference to 1 Corinthians, Romans 7:14–8:30, and the Johannine Literature' (Fuller Theological Seminary: Unpublished PhD Thesis, 1983), 14ff.; Turner, 'Spirit of Prophecy and the Ethical/Religious Life', 166–90; Haufe, 'Geistmotiv', 183–91; Keener, *Spirit*, 8–10; Wenk, *Power*, chs. 2–5; et al.

cal Spirit' being based on Ezek. 36–37, not on Wis.) and the false antithesis between the 'Spirit of prophecy' and the 'soteriological Spirit'.[128]

Also in Germany the Gunkel-era received fresh attention. One year after the publication of Menzies' dissertation, Friedrich Wilhelm Horn published both his Göttingen *Habilitationsschrift, Das Angeld des Geistes* and the often overlooked article 'Wandel im Geist: Zur pneumatologischen Begründung der Ethik bei Paulus'. As we have dealt with Horn's monograph in chapter 1 (1.2.2.3.) as well as in a separate review article,[129] we will here confine ourselves to his 'Wandel im Geist'. Horn's article plays a part in the history of research because it seeks to correct Gunkel's assertion of the uniqueness of Paul's ethical pneumatology. However, as the focus of Horn's article is not on the question of *how* the Spirit empowers ethical living it will be treated in an excursus.

Excursus 2: The Limited Scope of the Connection of Spirit and Ethics in Paul – F.W. Horn's Response to Gunkel et al.

In his 1992 article 'Wandel im Geist' Horn maintains that Gunkel's thesis that Judaism did not comprehend ethical life to be induced by the Spirit should not be seen as a contrast to the views of Paul. This is the case precisely because the apostle does *not* offer a pneumatological foundation for his ethics of marriage, sexuality, slavery, work, possessions, etc. Rather, he refers to the Torah, custom, the word of Jesus, his own opinion, etc. For Horn it is thus no valid criteria of distinction when Gunkel says that, in contrast to Judaism, Paul thinks of the Spirit as the author of all Christian action.[130] Apart from that, Horn agrees with those scholars who countered Gunkel by arguing for a close connection between Spirit and ethics in pre-Pauline Judaism and Christianity.[131] Nonetheless, Horn's position is new in that he claims that Paul rather restrictively connects Spirit and ethics because 'walking in the Spirit' is not pertinent to all questions of ethics by and large. The

---

[128] Turner, *Power, passim,* Turner, *Spirit,* 107–110.

[129] Rabens, 'Development', 161–79.

[130] Horn, 'Wandel', 150.

[131] In looking at the concrete evidence, Horn appears rather confining with regard to the spreading of a pre-Pauline pneumatological ethic. Among the 'popular views' only the pre-Pauline formulae and motifs which most likely derive from the Hellenistic Jewish-Christian church give clear indication of the awareness of the Spirit ('God has given us the Spirit' [Acts 5:32; 15:8; Rom. 5:5; 11:8; 2 Cor. 1:22; 5:5; 1 Thess. 4:8, etc.]; 'You have received the Spirit' [Acts 2:33ff.; 10:47; Rom. 8:15, etc.]). Apart from that, John the Baptist's preaching did not mention the Spirit (as Q evidences); neither Jesus nor the Jerusalem church spoke about the Spirit, certainly not in paraenesis; even Paul's opponents in 2 Cor., Gal. and Phil. continue to question Paul's 'pneumatic gospel' (Ibid., 151–53). Concerning Hellenistic and Palestinian Judaism Horn affirms by means of his exemplary investigation of Wis., Philo and 1QH[a] that Spirit and ethics were connected (Horn, 'Wandel', 168, 154–62). Nevertheless, he also states that in the OT only Ezek. 36:27 gives grounds for the suggestion that the Spirit was related to ethics, whereas intertestamental Judaism does not give any hint of a pneumatological ethic (apart from *1 En.* 61.11 and *Sib. Or.* 3.582) (Horn, 'Wandel', 162).

Spirit is active exclusively in the love of one's brothers and sisters and one's neighbours (149, 170).

Horn grounds this thesis on his exegesis of the (only!) three places in which the relationship between Spirit and ethics is specifically circumscribed by Paul: 1) in the early Pauline letters, 1 Thessalonians 4:8 and 1 Corinthians 3:16; 6:19; 2) Galatians 5:13–6:10; 3) Romans 8:1–17 (163).

1) 1 Thessalonians 4:8 and 1 Corinthians 3:16; 6:19. Horn explains that the paraenetical section in 1 Thessalonians 4:8 indicates that the apostle recognized already at this early stage that sacramentally conferred holiness and empirical life do not coincide. This is evident when Paul says that 'being the temple of God' and πορνεία do not fit together (1 Cor. 6:18–19). This thought is thoroughly Jewish. The same is true for Paul's interpretation of Ezekiel 36:27 to which he alludes in 1 Thessalonians 4:8. In Ezekiel 36:27 the gift of the Spirit leads to new obedience to the law, and in 1 Thessalonians 4:8 it is aimed at the love of the brother without being critical of the law. 'Die Bruderliebe steht wie selbstverständlich an der Stelle des Gesetzesgehorsams, ist aber auch nicht einfach eine Zusammenfassung desselben. Vielmehr entspricht der Ausgrenzung vom Bereich der Unreinheit die positive Zentrierung auf die Gruppe der Brüder.'[132] Only later in Galatians 5 is this issue clarified by indicating that the love of the neighbour actually fulfils the demands of the Torah. However, this love no longer belongs to the realm of the Torah but is the fruit of the Spirit.

Horn raises the question what the gift of the Spirit implies positively for ethics. He rapidly discounts the relevance of the catalogue of *charismata* specified in 1 Corinthians 12 since it is not really ethical aspects which are mentioned there. Therefore, he concludes that only love of the neighbour and, negatively speaking, the *Ausgrenzungstendenz* in 1 Corinthians 6:18–19 are part of Paul's Spirit-ethic (163–65).

2) Galatians 5:13–6:10. Horn maintains that previous scholars have not adequately recognized that love of one's brother in Galatians 5:13–14, 6:2, 10 needs to been seen in the light of the gift of the Spirit. Against this background, love appears as the natural consequence, the 'fruit', of an 'allowing oneself to be carried along ["sich treiben lassen"] by the Spirit' (5:18). This does not render the imperative superfluous, but Paul stresses that it is *the Spirit* who establishes this walk: 'Paulus geht wie in 1.Thess. 4,8f. davon aus, daß es die Sache des Geistes Gottes ist, diese Praxis der Nächsten- und Bruderliebe zu bewirken. Ganz gleich, ob man πνεύματι στοιχῶμεν (Gal 5,25) durch "der Marschordnung des Geistes folgen" oder durch "in Übereinstimmung mit dem Geist sein" übersetzt, beidemale ist vorausgesetzt, daß der Geist selber diese Liebe vorgibt.'[133]

As Horn believes that the list of virtues in 5:22–23 is formed by traditional material and thus does not need to be taken into account, he concludes that Paul's epistle to the Galatians knows no other connection of Spirit and ethics apart from love of the neighbour as being the sign of spiritual life.[134]

3) Romans 8:1–17. In comparison with Galatians 5, Romans 8 has a stronger emphasis on the individual's ethical decision between Spirit and flesh. A *conscious orientation* κατά is required: κατὰ πνεῦμα περιπατεῖν (8:4), κατὰ πνεῦμα φρονεῖν (8:5) and κατὰ πνεῦμα ζῆν (8:12–13). Being indwelt by the Spirit (8:9–11) means being indebted to the

---

[132] Horn, 'Wandel', 165.

[133] Ibid., 167.

[134] The need of separation from every kind of impure behaviour (now for the first time designed with the term σάρξ, 5:13, 16–17, 19, 24; 6:8) continues to be stressed in Gal. (Ibid., 166–67).

Spirit. Horn explains that the concrete outworking of this happens, first of all, along the lines we are already familiar with: separation from the ungodly realm of σάρξ (8:6, 12), that is, actively killing the works of the body (8:13; cf. Gal. 5:19, 24). However, love is also (implicitly) seen as the work of the Spirit,[135] though not as explicitly as in 1 Thessalonians and Galatians (in 13:8–10 the love command occurs without pneumatological groundwork).[136]

Horn concludes that there is significant correspondence between the pneumatological ethics of the Jewish writings and Paul: (a) The person gifted with the Spirit is called to abstain from everything that might oppose the holiness of God's Spirit. (b) For Paul, life in the Spirit consists in ἀγάπη (1 Cor. 13 as explication of 12:31; Gal. 5:22), specifically in the love of the brother (1 Thess. 4:9; Gal. 6:2, 10; Rom. 12:9–11). However, Horn insists that as Paul 'die pneumatologisch begründete Sittlichkeit faktisch auf die Liebe eingrenzt, vollzieht er zugleich gegenüber den genannten Schriften des hell. Judentums, für die eine durchgehende Verhältnisbestimmung von Weisheit/Geist zu den Kardinaltugenden und zur Ethik kennzeichnend ist, *eine Einschränkung.*'[137] Paul's originality is thus not the creation of a pneumatologically founded ethic but the (reductive) conception of the Spirit's work as paving the way for love of the neighbour (168–70).

With his article 'Wandel im Geist' Horn provided new impetus to one of the major discussions raised by Gunkel's 1888 monograph. With his contention that the ethical work of the Spirit in the Hebrew Bible and in early Judaism is limited to a few places (Ezek. 36:27; 1 *En.* 61.11; *Sib. Or.* 3.582), Horn has challenged the majority opinion of scholarship. Moreover, his main thesis that Paul connects the Spirit only with love of one's neighbour but not with ethics in general is unique. However, it contradicts what he published in the same year in his *Das Angeld des Geistes.* There he reckons that the declaration 'the gift of the Spirit causes and demands sanctification' is one of the three overarching statements in the Pauline letters which are independent of the different disputes in the early and late Pauline phases.[138] Likewise, he believes that one element of the contribution of Pauline pneumatology is the concept of the Spirit as transforming

---

[135] This is implicitly suggested through the connection of 12:11 with 12:10 as well as through the semantic link of εἰρήνη (8:6) with ἀγάπη in 13:11 and Gal. 5:22. Moreover, Horn thinks that it is likely that in Romans 8:4 κατὰ πνεῦμα περιπατεῖν is aimed at love of one's neighbour (which is the fulfilment of the law, Gal. 5:14; 6:2; Rom. 13:8–10) (Ibid., 167–68).

Horn does not mention Rom. 5:5 in the context of his discussion of Romans. The reason for this is Horn's interpretation of ἀγάπη θεοῦ as a subjective genitive against the background of 5:8. Nonetheless, Horn points out that love 'als ἀγάπη θεου (Gen.subj.) oder auch als ἀγάπη εἰς ἀλλήλους nicht anders vermittelt wird als durch das Wirken des Geistes. Der Geist vergegenwärtigt die Liebe Gottes (Röm 5,5), belehrt in der Bruderliebe (1 Thess 4,8f.), läßt sie erste Frucht christlicher Existenz sein (Gal 5,22) und ist selber als "Geist der Liebe" qualifiziert (1.Kor 4,21)' (Horn, 'Wandel', 169–70). Therefore, Horn would have done well to align this verse as evidence *within Romans* for the work of the Spirit as paving the way for love of one's neighbour.

[136] Horn, 'Wandel', 167–68.

[137] Ibid., 169, italics added.

[138] Horn, *Angeld*, 385–89.

believers into δόξα (*glorificatio*).[139] This reveals a weakness with regard to his definition of ethics: it is too narrow (or otherwise inconsistent).[140]

Moreover, both early Judaism and Paul evidence a much broader connection of Spirit and ethics (see 5.1. and 6.1. above).[141] For example, regarding Paul's early pneumatology in 1 Thessalonians Horn himself writes in his monograph that the Spirit is here understood as the functional enabling for eschatological conduct *ad interim*: empowering preaching (1:5), producing joy in affliction (1:6), giving power to realize the new standing ἐν ἁγιασμῷ (4:7–8), enabling prophecy which reveals the will of God (5:19–20). The church has been given the Spirit 'da der Geist sittlich belehrt, zur Erfüllung des θέλημα θεοῦ (4,3)'.[142]

Nonetheless, it is questionable whether the Spirit is overtly linked to love in 1 Thessalonians. Horn contends that in 4:8 the gift of the Spirit is aimed at love of the brother without any notion of being critical of the law. In the context of his monograph, Horn further claims that Paul's Spirit–law antithesis is in fact only developed at a later stage of Pauline pneumatology when Paul engages with the Judaizers of 2 Corinthians and Galatians.[143] However, the fact that Paul separates 1 Thessalonians 4:8 from verse 9 with περὶ δέ works against Horn on both points.[144] This means, firstly, that Paul does not connect the Spirit with the love command. In fact, the Spirit is here actively connected with abstention from immorality (cf. the powerful connective τοιγαροῦν between vv.7 and 8).[145] Secondly, as Paul does not connect the Spirit with the love command as representation of the law, Horn's thesis that 1 Thessalonians is uncritical of the law is an argument from silence. While Horn appears correct in his conclusion that Paul develops his sharp Spirit–letter antithesis only in his conflicts with the Jewish-Christian countermission, it needs to be born in mind that the law is never mentioned in 1 Thessalonians and that therefore freedom from the law may have been taken for granted.[146]

Apart from that, Galatians also evidences a more comprehensive pneumatological ethic than Horn allows. The fact that the list of virtues in 5:22–23 may be formed by traditional material does not disqualify it as a documentation of Paul's pneumatological framework. This is especially true because Paul uses this material as a major constituent of his *persuasio*. Horn himself argues in his book that the Spirit is the Christians' help in the struggle against the flesh because 'walking by the Spirit' is the 'fruit of the Spirit'.[147]

---

[139] Ibid., 422–28.

[140] For a more comprehensive definition, see ch. 1, 1.3.

[141] See also 6.4. where it is argued that the gifts of the Spirit are presented in 1 Cor. 12 as having ethical effect.

[142] Horn, *Angeld*, 126, 131–33.

[143] Ibid., 368–69.

[144] Περὶ δέ serves Paul to introduce a new topic; see 1 Thess. 5:1; 1 Cor. 7:1, 25; 8:1; 12:1; 16:1, 12. Cf. Porter, *Idioms*, 169.

[145] Cf. Fee, *Presence*, 53.

[146] Cf. U. Wilckens, 'Zur Entwicklung des paulinischen Gesetzesverständnisses', *NTS* 28 (1982), 158. See the more comprehensive investigation of Spirit and law in 1 Thess. in Rabens, 'Development', 178–79, followed by Kim, *Perspective*, 162–63.

[147] Horn, *Angeld*, 356–66. Moreover, we have seen above (n.135) that Horn employs Gal. 5:22 to support his rather far-fetched alignment of Spirit and love in Romans 8:6. However, there is no particular connection between 'peace' and 'love' in Gal. 5:22, and Rom. 13:11, which Horn mentions as a second piece of evidence, does not mention 'peace' at all.

Moreover, when Horn submits that the gift of the Spirit implies in Galatians 'separation from every kind of impure behaviour which is for the first time designed with the term σάρξ', he needs to bear in mind that this 'impure behaviour' is not just separation from sexual impurity as mentioned in the early Paulines. Σάρξ does not equal πορνεία – the vices listed in Galatians 5:19–21 are predominantly non-sexual. Consequently, the Spirit that works against these works of the flesh (by positively producing 'fruit') affects the believers not only in the areas of ἀγάπη and abstention from πορνεία but in all ethical aspects of their lives.

Finally, Horn's contention of a development between Galatians and Romans appears to rest on shallow grounds. Horn's statement that the ethical responsibility of the self is marginalised in Galatians 5:13–6:10 seems to be contradicted by the fact that Paul addresses the ethical imperatives in this section *to the believers*. Further, Horn himself has noted in his monograph that the verbs περιπατεῖν and στοιχεῖν emphasize the responsibility of the believer.[148] Besides, it is more than questionable that the preposition κατά has such an enormous significance as if only in Romans 8 a *conscious* orientation towards πνεῦμα were required – particularly as Paul uses this formulation already in Galatians 5:17 (cf. vv.19–23).

In conclusion, Horn's 'Wandel im Geist' submits an original thesis to the history of scholarship on the matter under concern. However, it appears that the Pauline corpus (as well as Horn's own interpretation of it in his monograph) does not provide enough evidence to support the contention that Paul limited the ethical relevance of the Spirit to brotherly love and abstention from immorality.

3.2. By the Spirit Christians are Able to Resist the Temptations of the Old Aeon Without Struggle (G.D. Fee)

The most comprehensive examination of Pauline pneumatology ever undertaken is that by Gordon Fee. In 1994 Fee published his massive volume of almost a thousand pages, *God's Empowering Presence*, which is devoted to in-depth exegesis of all passages relevant to the study of the Spirit in Paul, followed by a synthesis in the second part of the book.

Fee does not interact with the debate raised by Horn two years before. Nevertheless, he touches on previous discussions when he argues afresh that Paul understood the Spirit as a *person*.[149] However, more important for our investigation is Fee's contribution to the debate on the nature of Paul's Spirit–flesh antithesis. Fee's emphasis on the supreme power of the Spirit over against that of the flesh stands in stronger contrast to the views of Dunn.[150] It is Fee's contention that Paul does not perceive Christian life as a struggle between Spirit and flesh within the human breast. This is not just due to the fact that believers are ἐν πνεύματι but simply *because Paul does not address this problem at all*. In order to comprehend how Fee

---

[148] Ibid., 358.

[149] See the summary and critique in Rabens, 'Development', 177.

[150] However, Fee does not fall into the trap of interpreting Paul as a perfectionist as Wernle, Bousset and others have done before (Wernle, *Christ*, 88, 15; Bousset, *Kyrios*, 170, 174; cf. 1.3. of this Appendix).

arrives at this thesis it is necessary to briefly look at his concept of 'flesh' in Paul.

1) Flesh as the sphere of the old aeon. In contrast to Dunn, Fee does not believe that 'the flesh' is a personal part of the believer. The flesh is the sphere of the old aeon. Dunn had put forward that the believer is 'still in all too real a sense a man of the flesh, still experiencing the dominion of sin in an integral dimension of his present existence'.[151] Fee, *per contra*, insists that Pauline language like 'according to the flesh' describes both the perspective and the behaviour of the former age that is passing away, designating believers' lives *before* and *outside of* Christ (817, cf. 819–22, 881).

2) Paul's eschatological *Spirit–flesh language* thus *does not reflect some internal struggle within the believer* (435, 514, 537–38, 547, 559, 820–21, 880). While the two aeons of Spirit and flesh currently exist side by side, the flesh has been 'decisively crippled – "killed", in Paul's language' through the death sentence by means of the death and resurrection of Christ (822; 820, 455).[152] To live according to the flesh is therefore no longer an option for believers, and one is dealing in passages like Galatians 5:24 not with wishful thinking on Paul's side but with eschatological realities (456). Fee is thus clear that none of the Pauline texts indicate that some kind of warfare is going on in the life of the believer between these two ways of existence (537, 540, 425, 431). Paul simply does not speak to that question.[153] And where it might appear as though he did, his point is rather the *sufficiency of the Spirit* (817).

---

[151] Dunn, 'Rom. 7,14–25', 269, cf. 267.

[152] Therefore, what Christians are asked to put to death are the deeds of the *body*, not the flesh since believers are no longer in the flesh (Rom. 8:13) (558). Cf. 6.3.2. See H. Ridderbos' doctoral student *E. Mauerhofer* for a similar view. However, Mauerhofer does not seem to comprehend the death of σάρξ as being of as much 'intensity' as that of the παλαιὸς ἄνθρωπος. He believes that there is an internal confrontation – also in the believer – between the human πνεῦμα and the psycho-somatic part since the latter has a 'special relation' to σάρξ as its target (Mauerhofer, *Kampf*, 173–74, 193, 208).

[153] Fee here builds on K. Stendahl, 'The Apostle Paul and the Introspective Conscience of the West', in K. Stendahl, *Paul amoung Jews and Gentiles and other essays* (Philadelphia: Fortress, 1976), 78–96. One of Fee's reasons for agreeing with Stendahl is his perception of the various imperatives of passages like Gal. 5 about the fruit of the Spirit and walking by the Spirit – they belong primarily to the believing community and not to the individual believer. Thus they have nothing to do with one's introspective conscience (883). Fee further asserts that the Spirit–flesh contrast in Paul never appears in the context of the question 'how to live the Christian life'. Rather, it appears in an argument (e.g. in Gal. 5 and Rom. 7–8) with those who have entered into the new eschatological life of the Spirit, but who are being seduced to return to the old aeon, to live on the basis of Torah observance, which for Paul is in the end only another form of life 'according to the flesh' (821).

However, all of this does not mean that the old aeon of the flesh would no longer 'be about' or that Christians do not have to resist its 'desires'. Fee thus admits that 'in that sense there is always "tension" for the Spirit person' (435).[154] He contends that because Paul is convinced that the Spirit is God's effective response to what we might describe as the 'temptability' of the Christian,[155] Paul can urge upon the Galatians the bold imperative and promise of 5:16 (435). 'What Christ and the Spirit have effected, the believer must actively participate in – by walking by, and behaving in keeping with, the Spirit' (458; cf. 436f., 457, 467). In this sense believers shall 'become what they are' by the help of the Spirit (559).

3) The praxis of walking by the Spirit. The question arises how believers can practically obey what according to Fee is Paul's basic ethical imperative: to walk by the Spirit (358). By way of answer Fee highlights, firstly, that Paul does in fact not give an answer to this question that is satisfactory in today's context.

The difference between "them" and "us" many centuries later is almost certainly at the experiential level, wherein their dynamic experience of the Spirit both at the beginning of life in Christ and in their ongoing life in the church would have made this imperative seem much more "practical" and everyday' (433).

The dynamic life of the Spirit was thus presuppositional for Paul (880). Paul therefore asks the Galatians to 'go on walking by the very same Spirit by which you came to faith and with whom God still richly supplies you' (Gal. 3:2–5) (433).

Secondly, Fee explains that since 'to walk by the Spirit' comes by way of an imperative in Galatians 5:16 (and not a passive indicative as in 5:18), it is clear that life in the Spirit is not a passive submission to a supernatural power, but it requires a conscious effort,[156] so that the indwelling Spirit can

---

[154] Nevertheless, according to Fee, one cannot speak of a tension between an ever-present 'sinful nature' and the 'indwelling Spirit'. When Paul talks about the tension between the 'already' and the 'not yet' he means the tension between the suffering and weaknesses that still mark the Christian existence in the present and the resurrection life of the future by which Christians live – and endure – the present sufferings (see, e.g. 2 Cor. 11–13) (431–32).

[155] This is not Fee's language, but it appears justified to abstract this definition of disposition from Fee's admission of some kind of tension in the life of the believer.

[156] However, for Fee this does not mean that God's people were to engage with sin in battle; rather, by the Spirit's help they are to put it to death. Again, Paul is not clear on how to do this. Fee suggests that in the light of the 'renewed mind' of Rom. 12:2 one can at least say that this action must be focused and intentional (559, n.254; cf. Fee's emphasis on Roman's imperative to '*reckoning* oneself as dead as far as sin is concerned' [6:11] [538]). But, once more, 'this does not represent a struggle for Paul; it represents experienced realities. The accent here falls decidedly on the work of the Spirit to bring it off,

accomplish his ends in one's life. It means making choices in sowing to the Spirit (Gal. 6:8), rising up and following the Spirit by walking in obedience to the Spirit's desire (433, 467, 547, 559, 563, 566).

Fee has painted a very positive and coherent picture of Christian life. He supports his evangelical-charismatic perspective with great exegetical detail and scholarly competence. His positive perspective on the Spirit's enabling of ethical life has swung the pendulum of scholarship into almost the opposite direction to that of Dunn. While both Dunn and Fee emphasize the *experience* of the eschatological Spirit as central both to Paul and his hearers, Fee comprehends this new dimension in the believers' lives as the end of internal struggles, not as the beginning of it. Fee goes further in his critique of Dunn's position than did Barclay, for Fee believes that in Paul one only finds the notion of temptation by sin but not that of internal struggle. However, it seems that precisely on this point Fee seems to go too far in what he denies and not far enough in what he affirms. The notion of being temptable appears to be much more present in Paul than Fee allows (see, e.g., 1 Cor. 10:13; Gal. 6:1, 8).[157] Apart from that, also Fee's contribution to our understanding of Spirit and flesh in Paul needs further discussion. As we provide this in section 6.3.2. of this study, we will not engage with his position at greater length at this point.

Fee believes that the experience of the Spirit in the early church is not only the reason why the recipients of Paul's epistles were very much aware of the surpassing power of the Spirit over against the flesh, but it is also the reason why Paul does not need to go into further details when he encourages them to 'walk by the Spirit'. Paul thus gives no answers to his later students who might be interested in *how* the Spirit enables ethical living. However, it seems that both points are slightly exaggerated. Firstly, if the presence and guidance of the Spirit was so much stronger in Paul's day than today, one wonders why the Galatians were tempted to return to the law. And, secondly, it is the contention of this monograph that a more detailed understanding of the practical aspects of the Spirit's transforming and empowering of ethical life can be gained by means of a focused study of the relevant passages in Paul (see esp. 6.3.3).[158]

---

not on some constant tug-of-war that believers must endure between their life in the Spirit and the pull of the flesh' (537–38). See the discussion in 6.3.2.

[157] Apart from that, in Gal. 6:1, 4 Paul appears to be less critical of 'introspection' than Fee.

[158] For a detailed model of the interaction between the self of the believer and the divine Spirit that enters her, see also Vollenweider, 'Geist', 163–92. S. *Vollenweider* distinguishes three different levels of ideas (*Vorstellungsebenen*): 1) The reception of the Spirit of Christ/God without individuating tendency (Rom. 5:5; 8:9–10, 13, 15–16; 1 Cor. 2:12; 3:16; 6:19; 2 Cor. 4:13; 11:4; 13:13; Gal. 3:2, 14; 4:6; Phil. 1:27; 2:1; 1 Thess. 4:8); 2) a certain individuation of the Spirit is perceptible in Rom. 1:9; 8:16b, 23; 1 Cor. 2:15–16;

Summary and Conclusion. The last decade of the twentieth century has become a period of concentrated interest in Paul's view of the Spirit: the two most comprehensive studies of Pauline pneumatology in the whole history of Pauline research were published in this decade. While in previous times scholars tended to read their philosophical presuppositions overtly into the few Pauline passages which they had (sometimes superficially) looked at, now the approach has become much more exegetical. In a return to many of the issues raised over 100 years ago by Gunkel, Horn now investigates Paul chronologically, first by looking at his background and then at his epistles. With regard to the connection of Spirit and ethics, he argues that Paul, in contrast to Judaism before him, restricted the work of the Spirit to love of one's brother. Also within Paul there is a development, namely, before Romans (i.e. in Gal.) Paul did not emphasize the believer's resolve to walk by the Spirit as much as in this epistle.

A more unified picture of Pauline pneumatology is presented by Fee. As a scholar with a charismatic background he approaches Paul from almost the opposite end of the spectrum to the historical-critical Horn. Like Gunkel (and in contrast to Horn), he emphasizes the importance of experience for Paul's understanding of the ethical work of the Spirit. In great exegetical depth he takes issue with Dunn and others, arguing for a very positive view of Christian life, one that could be free from internal struggle with the flesh.

5:3–4; 6:17; 7:40; 14:14–15, 32; 2 Cor. 1:22; 5:5; and, finally, 3) in a plain anthropological sense Paul seems to talk of πνεῦμα as the natural 'soul' ('*Ich*') in 1 Cor. 2:11; 7:34; 16:18; 2 Cor. 2:13; 7:1, 13, etc. (175–76).

Vollenweider argues that Paul is to be differentiated from mantic inspiration where the deity suspends the *Ichinstanz* of the individual and acts in its place. Paul rather brings to light the interference of the historical human being and the divine Spirit that enters her. 'Der eingehende göttliche Geist ersetzt also nicht das Ich als Erlebens- und Verhaltenszentrum des geschichtlichen Menschen, sondern er durchdringt es. Zugespitzt formuliert: *Das Pneuma handelt nicht anstelle unser selbst, sondern als unser Selbst*' (183). Paul can thus distinguish between Christ's words and his own advice (1 Cor. 7). And, as the case of incest in 1 Cor. 5 shows, it is possible to distance oneself from what one really ('eigentlich') is when the bestowed πνεῦμα has almost no interaction with the experiential and behavioural centre of one's self (183).

As the indwelling Spirit does not bypass the human ego but rather enlivens it, Vollenweider believes that it is impossible to escape the idea of involvement (*Mitwirkung*) of the human being – and thus of his *Ichfunktion* – in the process of new creation. However, such a synergy should not 'im Sinn neuzeitlicher Subjektivität pointiert werden, betreibt doch die Liebe als die Kraft, sich an die Stelle des anderen zu versetzen, die fortgesetzte Dezentrierung des Ichs schlechthin (1Kor 13,5)' (189). – See the critical evaluation of Vollenweider's contribution in Meier, *Mystik*, 251–53 (cf. Lehmkühler, *Inhabitatio*, 35–36).

Once again, the question of the interaction between the Spirit and the self of the believer was raised.[159] In his monograph, Horn presents a Spirit-wrought substance-ontological change of the person which brings forth ethical behaviour (see ch. 1, 1.2.2.3.). Fee, *per contra*, understands the Spirit–flesh language as divorced from anthropology; it is purely eschatological. Nonetheless, Horn and Fee have similarities in that both believe that the work of the Spirit has a strong bearing on believers in that ethical living develops almost automatically (in the case of Horn), or at least without internal struggle (in the case of Fee). Generally speaking however, no consensus on the details of the connection between Spirit and ethics in Paul has been reached in the more recent history of scholarship.[160]

4. Summary of Results and Questions

In the history of research of Pauline pneumatology *it has been established*, first of all, that Paul was not the first to develop a Spirit-based ethic. The Old Testament, early Judaism and the pre-Pauline church knew of it. Paul himself understood the whole ethical life of the Christian as walking by the Spirit. Only Horn has made a separate case here, claiming that Paul connected the Spirit only to love of one's neighbour; but his case cannot be upheld upon close scrutiny, as we have argued above. Further, since the days of Schweitzer scholarship has more and more recognised that Paul's pneumatology needs to be understood against the background of his eschatology. At the same time, the conviction that for Paul the believer's decision to actively walk by the Spirit is of fundamental importance has become a scholarly consensus.

Over the years of research on Pauline pneumatology, the method for retrieving results has become more and more that of in-depth exegesis. The primary texts for investigating the interaction of Spirit and ethics are Galatians 5–6 and Romans 8.

The last 140 years of scholarship have evidenced *diverging explanations* of the ethical work of the Spirit. At one end of the spectrum, we find the conviction that the Spirit 'drives' believers in the sense of almost overpowering them. This is the position of Gunkel, and, without the notion of overpowering, that of Deidun and Fee. It stresses the pneumatological indicative. On the other end of the scope we meet with a stronger emphasis

---

[159] Cf. Vollenweider in n.158 above.

[160] A number of investigation of Pauline pneumatology and Pauline ethics have been published since Fee. We interact with them throughout this study. However, none of these works proposes a new approach to Spirit and ethics in Paul or goes significantly beyond the positions outlined above.

on the will and the decision of the believer. Stalder (in the steps of Bultmann) understands the work of the Spirit predominantly as making believers aware of their salvation by which they are enabled to realize the ethical imperative by their *own* power. Viewed from a different perspective, life in the Spirit is on the one hand seen by Fee as without internal struggle (although not without sin), and on the other hand comprehended by Dunn (who nonetheless understands the Spirit as generating the filial obedience of the Son) as an intense battle with the flesh.

Of course, there are mediating positions between the two poles. Pfleiderer sought to encompass both lines of thought by propounding that they are found unconnectedly in Paul. However, he was not followed by scholarship by and large. Horn could be understood as arguing for both positions on a micro-scale. He believes that Paul developed from the first view (i.e. a stronger emphasis on the work of the Spirit) in Galatians to the second (i.e. a stronger emphasis on the decision of the believer) in Romans. However, Horn's main thesis of his monograph seems to side with the pneumatological indicative (though with a strong anthropological dimension). That is, Horn's model of human transformation through the reception of the *stofflich* πνεῦμα comes close to an automatism of ethical life as the result.

A number of *major issues have been left unresolved* in the course of previous research. Apart from the puzzle of the two broad lines of interpretation of the Spirit's work mentioned above, a first set of questions concerns the religious background of Paul's understanding of the relation of Spirit and ethics. Was Paul influenced by Hellenism in this regard (so Pfleiderer, Horn, Engberg-Pedersen[161] et al.)? Or was his thinking on this matter based on the Old Testament (so Wendt et al.) or early Judaism (so Gunkel et al.)?

A second set of questions regards the nature of the Spirit–flesh antithesis in Paul. Is the Christian existence one of struggle between living by the Spirit and being pulled into the opposite direction by the flesh? Related to this is the question of how to interpret Paul's metaphorical language of the Spirit entering the believer, if it is indeed metaphorical. Does it mean that the human person is totally overmastered by a foreign being? Or that the human spirit fuses with the divine? In this context, the supposed nature of the Spirit plays a significant role. Is the Spirit indeed a physical substance that transforms the individual substance-ontologically? Or should the Spirit instead be comprehended as a person (so Fee et al.)?

The interpretation of Paul's (metaphorical) language also bears on the hermeneutical inquiry raised by Pfleiderer: if there are antinomies in Paul, is it better to leave them unresolved? Or should one formulate or 'psy-

---

[161] See the recent Engberg-Pedersen, *Cosmology, passim.*

chologize' a synthesis? Likewise, in the light of Horn's work one wonders whether there is a unifying centre to the various aspects that pertain to the interplay of Spirit and believer in the domain of ethics.

It is impossible to give a satisfactory answer to all of these questions in the present study. However, our work focuses on a central question that to some extent integrates the issues raised above. Schweitzer has maintained that Paul remains silent about the psychological processes by which ethical change comes about. Similarly, Fee has argued that Paul does not unravel for the recipients of his letters *how* to walk by the Spirit because he pre-supposes their dynamic experience of life in the Spirit (Gal. 3:1–5; 5:25). Consequently, it seems to be a challenge for modern interpreters of Paul's epistles to come as close as possible to identifying the details of this pre-supposed knowledge or experience by drawing implications from the way in which Paul advises his congregations. This challenge has not yet been taken up by Pauline scholarship (Stalder's work being the only published monograph in this area). Therefore, the relational approach to Spirit and ethics developed in the main body of this monograph is able to provide a more nuanced portrayal of the interplay of the transforming and empowering work of the Spirit in Paul than that evinced by previous investigations of Pauline ethics or pneumatology.

Bibliography of Works Cited

The year number behind the publisher of a book indicates the edition of the book used in this study. For example, '... Mohr Siebeck, 2010² [2000¹]' shows that the book was originally published in 2000 but that we are using the second edition of 2010. Moreover, also if the *reprint* of a particular book employed in this study has appeared a significant amount of years after the first publication, this is usually indicated in the bibliography (e.g. '... Mohr Siebeck, 2010 [1992¹]').

Aaron, David H., *Biblical Ambiguities: Metaphor, Semantics and Divine Imagery* (BRLAJ 4; Leiden: Brill, 2001).

Aasgaard, Reidar, 'Paul as a Child: Children and Childhood in the Letters of the Apostle', *JBL* 126 (2007), 129–59.

ab Arnim, Ioannes, *Stoicorum Veterum Fragmenta*; 4 vols. (Stuttgart: Teubner, 1964).

Abegg, Martin G., Bowley, James E., Cook, Edward M., and Tov, Emanuel, *The Dead Sea Scrolls Concordance. Vol. 1,2* (Leiden/Boston: Brill, 2003).

Abelson, J., *The Immanence of God in Rabbinical Literature* (London/New York: Hermon, 1969 [1912¹]).

Adam, Jens, *Paulus und die Versöhnung aller: Eine Studie zum paulinischen Heilsuniversalismus* (Neukirchen-Vluyn: Neukirchener Verlag, 2009).

Alexander, Patrick H., Kutsko, John F., Ernest, James D., Decker-Lucke, Shirley A., and Petersen, David L. (eds.), *The SBL Handbook of Style for Ancient Near Eastern, Biblical and Early Christian Studies* (Peabody: Hendrickson, 1999).

Allen, Leslie C., *Psalms 101–150* (WBC 21; Waco: Word, 1983).

Arndt, H. W., 'Substanz; Substanz/Akzidens', *HWPh*, X, 521–32.

Arnold, E. Vernon, *Roman Stoicism: Being Lectures on the History of the Stoic Philosophy with Special Reference to its Development within the Roman Empire* (Cambridge: Cambridge University Press, 1911).

art. 'Hellenization', *DJBP*, I, 285–86.

art. 'Beziehung', in G. Wenninger (ed.), *Lexikon der Psychologie. Vol. 1* (Heidelberg: Spektrum Akademischer Verlag, 2000), 225.

Asher, Jeffrey A., *Polarity and Change in 1 Corinthians 15: A Study of Metaphysics, Rhetoric, and Resurrection* (HUTh 42; Tübingen: Mohr Siebeck, 2000).

Ashley, T. R., *The Book of Numbers* (NICOT 16; Grand Rapids: Eerdmans, 1993).

Ashton, John, *The Religion of Paul the Apostle* (London: Yale University Press, 2000).

Ashworth, Timothy, *Paul's Necessary Sin: The Experience of Liberation* (Aldershot: Ashgate, 2006).

Asting, R., *Die Heiligkeit im Urchristentum* (FRLANT 46; Göttingen: Vandenhoeck & Ruprecht, 1930).

Aune, David E., 'Human Nature and Ethics in Hellenistic Philosophical Traditions and Paul: Some Issues and Problems', in T. Engberg-Pedersen (ed.), *Paul in His Hellenistic Context* (SNTW; Edinburgh: T. & T. Clark, 1994), 291–312.

Back, Frances, *Verwandlung durch Offenbarung bei Paulus: Eine religionsgeschichtlich-exegetische Untersuchung zu 2 Kor 2,14–4,6* (WUNT II/153; Tübingen: Mohr Siebeck, 2002).

Backhaus, Knut, 'Evangelium als Lebensraum: Christologie und Ethik bei Paulus', in U. Schnelle and T. Söding (eds.), *Paulinische Christologie: Exegetische Beiträge* (*FS* H. Hübner; Göttingen: Vandenhoeck & Ruprecht, 2000), 9–31.

Baeumker, Clemens, *Das Problem der Materie in der griechischen Philosophie: eine historisch-kritische Untersuchung* (Münster: Aschendorffsche Buchhandlung, 1890).

Baldauf, Christa, *Metapher und Kognition: Grundlagen einer neuen Theorie der Alltagsmetapher* (SGBS 24; Frankfurt: Lang, 1997).

Balla, Peter, *The Child-Parent Relationship in the New Testament and its Environment* (WUNT 155; Tübingen: Mohr Siebeck, 2003).

Balz, Horst, and Schneider, Gerhard (eds.), *Exegetisches Wörterbuch zum Neuen Testament*; 3 vols. (Stuttgart: Kohlhammer, 1992²).

Barclay, John M. G., *Obeying the Truth: A Study of Paul's Ethics in Galatians* (SNTW; Edinburgh: T. & T. Clark, 1988).

–, *Jews in the Mediterranean Diaspora: From Alexander to Trajan (323 BCE – 117 CE)* (Edinburgh: T. & T. Clark, 1996).

–, 'Paul's Story: Theology as Testimony', in B.W. Longenecker (ed.), *Narrative Dynamics in Paul: A Critical Assessment* (Louisville: Westminster John Knox, 2002), 133–56.

–, 'Πνευματικός in the Social Context of Pauline Christianity', in G. Stanton, B.W. Longenecker, and S.C. Barton (eds.), *The Holy Spirit and Christian Origins: Essays in Honor of James D. G. Dunn* (Grand Rapids/Cambridge: Eerdmans, 2004), 157–67.

–, '"By the Grace of God I am what I am": Grace and Agency in Philo and Paul', in J.M.G. Barclay and S.J. Gathercole (eds.), *Divine and Human Agency in Paul and his Cultural Environment* (ECC/LNTS 335; London: Continuum, 2006), 140–57.

–, 'Manna and the Circulation of Grace: A Study of 2 Corinthians 8:1–15 ', in J.R. Wagner, C.K. Rowe, and A.K. Grieb (eds.), *The Word Leaps the Gap: Essays on Scripture and Theology in Honor of Richard B. Hays* (Grand Rapids/Cambridge: Eerdmans, 2008), 409–26.

Barcley, William B., *Christ in You: A Study in Paul's Theology and Ethics* (Lanham: University Press of America, 1999).

Barr, James, *The Semantics of Biblical Language* (Oxford: Oxford University Press, 1961).

–, 'Abba Isn't "Daddy"', *JTS* NS 39 (1988), 28–47.

Barram, Michael, *Mission and Moral Reflection in Paul* (SBL 75; New York: Lang, 2006).

Barrett, C. K., *A Commentary on the Epistle to the Romans* (BNTC; London: Black, 1957).

–, *A Commentary on the First Epistle to the Corinthians* (BNTC; London: Black, 1971²).

–, *A Commentary on the Second Epistle to the Corinthians* (BNTC; London: Black, 1982).

–, *Paul: An Introduction to his Thought* (OCT; London: Chapman, 1994).

Barth, Karl, *The Epistle to the Romans* (Oxford: Oxford University Press, 1968⁶ [1919¹]).

Barth, Markus, *Die Taufe – Ein Sakrament? Ein exegetischer Beitrag zum Gespräch über die kirchliche Taufe* (Zollikon-Zürich: Evangelischer Verlag, 1951).

Bauckham, Richard, 'Review of R.S. Kraemer, *When Aseneth Met Joseph: A Late Antique Tale of the Biblical Patriarch and His Egyptian Wife, Reconsidered*', *JTS* 51 (2000), 226–28.

Baumert, Norbert, *Die Sorgen des Seelsorgers: Übersetzung und Auslegung des ersten Korintherbriefes* (Paulus neu gelesen; Würzburg: Echter, 2007).

–, *Mit dem Rücken zur Wand: Übersetzung und Auslegung des zweiten Korintherbriefes* (Paulus neu gelesen; Würzburg: Echter, 2008).

Baumgarten, Jörg, *Paulus und die Apokalyptik: Die Auslegung apokalyptischer Überlieferungen in den echten Paulusbriefen* (WMANT 44; Neukirchen-Vluyn: Neukirchener Verlag, 1975).

Baumgarten, Joseph M., 'The Law and Spirit of Purity at Qumran', in J.H. Charlesworth (ed.), *The Bible and the Dead Sea Scrolls: The Second Princeton Symposium on Judaism and Christian Origins. Vol. 2* (Waco: Baylor University Press, 2006), 93–105.

Baur, Ferdinand Christian, *Paulus, der Apostel Jesu Christi: Sein Leben und Wirken, seine Briefe und seine Lehre – Ein Beitrag zu einer kritischen Geschichte des Urchristentums. Vol. 2* (Osnabrück: Zeller, 1867[2] [1845[1]]).

Beall, Todd S., *Josephus' Description of the Essenes Illustrated by the Dead Sea Scrolls* (SNTSMS 58; Cambridge: Cambridge University Press, 1988).

Beardslee, William A., *Human Achievement and Divine Vocation in the Message of Paul* (SBT 31; Naperville/London: Allenson/SCM, 1961).

Beardsley, Monroe C., *Aesthetics from Classical Greece to the Present: A Short History* (New York: Macmillan, 1966).

–, 'Metaphor and Falsity', *JAAC* 35 (1976), 218–22.

Beasley-Murray, G. R., *Baptism in the New Testament* (London: Macmillan, 1962).

Becker, Jürgen, 'Geschöpfliche Wirklichkeit als Thema des Neuen Testaments', in H.C. Knuth and W. Lohff (eds.), *Schöpfungsglaube und Umweltverantwortung: Eine Studie des Theologischen Ausschusses der VELKD* (ZS 26; Hannover: Lutherisches Verlagshaus, 1985), 45–100.

–, 'Die Erwählung der Völker durch das Evangelium: Theologiegeschichtliche Erwägungen zum 1. Thessalonicherbrief', in W. Schrage (ed.), *Studien zum Text und zur Ethik des Neuen Testaments* (BZNW 47; FS H. Greeven; Berlin/New York: W. de Gruyter, 1986), 82–101.

–, *Paulus: Der Apostel der Völker* (UTB 2014; Tübingen: Mohr Siebeck, 1998 [1989[1]]).

Behm, Johannes, 'μεταμορφόω', *TDNT*, IV, 755–59.

Beißer, Friedrich, 'Wann und von wem könnte der Epheserbrief verfasst worden sein?', *KD* 52 (2006), 151–64.

Belleville, Linda L., *Reflections of Glory: Paul's Polemical Use of the Moses-Doxa Tradition in 2 Corinthians 3,1–18* (JSNTSup 52; Sheffield: JSOT Press, 1991).

–, *2 Corinthians* (IVPNTCS; Downers Grove/Leicester: IVP, 1996).

–, 'Paul's Polemic and the Theology of the Spirit in Second Corinthians', *CBQ* 58 (1996), 281–304.

Bennema, Cornelis, 'The Strands of Wisdom Tradition in Intertestamental Judaism: Origins, Developments and Characteristics', *TynBul* 52 (2001), 61–82.

–, *The Power of Saving Wisdom: An Investigation of Spirit and Wisdom in Relation to the Soteriology of the Fourth Gospel* (WUNT II/148; Tübingen: Mohr Siebeck, 2002).

–, *Excavating John's Gospel: A Commentary for Today* (Delhi: ISPCK, 2005).

Berchman, Robert M., *From Philo to Origen: Middle Platonism in Transition* (BJS 69; Chico: Scholars Press, 1984).

Berger, Klaus, *Identity and Experience in the New Testament* (Minneapolis: Fortress, 2003); orig. publ.: *Historische Psychologie des Neuen Testaments* (SBS 146/147; Stuttgart: Katholisches Bibelwerk, 1991).

–, *Theologiegeschichte des Urchristentums: Theologie des Urchristentums* (UTBW; Tübingen/Basel: Francke, 1995[2]).

–, *Ist Gott Person? Ein Weg zum Verstehen des christlichen Gottesbildes* (Gütersloh: Gütersloher Verlagshaus, 2004).

Berthelot, Katell, 'Zeal for God and Divine Law in Philo and the Dead Sea Scrolls', *SPA* 19 (2007), 113–29.

Bertone, John A., *'The Law of the Spirit': Experience of the Spirit and Displacement of the Law in Romans 8:1–16* (SBL 86; New York: Lang, 2005).

Bertrams, Hermann, *Das Wesen des Geistes nach der Anschauung des Apostels Paulus: Eine biblisch-theologische Untersuchung* (NTA 4.4; Münster: Aschendorff, 1913).

Best, Ernest, *A Critical and Exegetical Commentary on Ephesians* (ICC; Edinburgh: T. & T. Clark, 1998).

Betz, H. D., Browing, D.S., Janowski, B., and Jüngel, E. (eds.), *Religion in Geschichte und Gegenwart*; 8 vols. (Tübingen: Mohr Siebeck, 1998–2005⁴).

Betz, Otto, 'Die Geburt der Gemeinde durch den Lehrer', *NTS* 3 (1956/57), 314–26.

–, 'Geistliche Schönheit', in O. Michel and U. Mann (eds.), *Die Leibhaftigkeit des Wortes* (*FS* A. Köberle; Hamburg: Furche, 1958), 71–86.

–, *Offenbarung und Schriftforschung in der Qumransekte* (WUNT 6; Tübingen: J.C.B. Mohr (Paul Siebeck), 1960).

Bieder, Werner, 'πνεῦμα, πνευματικός', *TDNT*, VI, 368–75.

–, 'Gebetswirklichkeit und Gebetsmöglichkeit bei Paulus: Das Beten des Geistes und das Beten im Geiste', *TZ* 4 (1948), 22–40.

Bird, Michael F., *The Saving Righteousness of God: Studies on Paul, Justification, and the New Perspective* (PBM; Milton Keynes/Eugene, OR: Paternoster/Wipf & Stock, 2007).

Black, Max, *Models and Metaphors: Studies in Language and Philosophy* (Ithaca: Cornell University Press, 1962).

–, 'More about Metaphor', in A. Ortony (ed.), *Metaphor and Thought* (Cambridge: Cambridge University Press, 1993²), 19–41.

Bläser, Peter, '"Lebendigmachender Geist": Ein Beitrag zur Frage nach den Quellen der paulinischen Theologie', *BEThL* 12/13 (1959), 404–13.

Blischke, Folker, *Die Begründung und die Durchsetzung der Ethik bei Paulus* (ABG 25; Leipzig: Evangelische Verlagsanstalt, 2007).

Böckler, Annette, *Gott als Vater im Alten Testament: Traditionsgeschichtliche Untersuchungen zu Entstehung und Entwicklung eines Gottesbildes* (Gütersloh: Kaiser/ Gütersloher Verlagshaus, 2000).

Bockmuehl, Markus, *The Epistle to the Philippians* (BNTC; London: Black, 1997).

–, '1QS and Salvation at Qumran', in D.A. Carson, P. O'Brien, and M.A. Seifrid (eds.), *Justification and Variegated Nomism. Vol. 1: The Complexities of Second Temple Judaism* (WUNT II/140; Tübingen: Mohr Siebeck, 2001), 381–414.

Bohak, Gideon, 'Asenath's Honeycomb and Onias' Temple', in D. Assaf (ed.), *Proceedings of the Eleventh World Congress of Jewish Studies: Jerusalem, June 22–29, 1993 – Division A: The Bible and Its World* (Jerusalem: Magnes, 1994), 163–70.

Boman, Thorlief, *Hebrew Thought Compared with Greek* (LHD; London: SCM Press, 1960).

Bornkamm, Günther, *Paulus* (Stuttgart: Kohlhammer, 1993⁷ [1969¹]).

Boschki, Reinhold, *"Beziehung" als Leitbegriff der Religionspädagogik: Grundlegung einer dialogisch-kreativen Religionsdidaktik* (Zeitzeichen 13; Ostfildern: Schwabenverlag, 2003).

Botterweck, G. Johannes, Ringgren, Helmer, and Fabry, Heinz-Josef (eds.), *Theological Dictionary of the Old Testament*; 15 vols. (Grand Rapids/Cambridge: Eerdmans, 2004).

Bousset, Wilhelm, 'Review of H. Weinel, *Die Wirkungen des Geistes*', *GGA* 163 (1901), 753–76.

–, *Kyrios Christos: A History of the Belief in Christ from the Beginnings of Christianity to Irenaeus* (New York: Abingdon, 1970); orig. publ.: *Kyrios Christos: Geschichte des Christusglaubens von den Anfängen des Christentums bis Irenaeus* (Göttingen: Vandenhoeck & Ruprecht, 1921² [1913¹]).

–, *Der erste Brief an die Korinther* (SNTG 2; Göttingen: Vandenhoeck & Ruprecht, 1917³).

–, 'J. Kroll, Die Lehren des Hermes Trismegistos', in W. Bousset, *Religionsgeschicht-liche Studien: Aufsätze zur Religionsgeschichte des Hellenistischen Zeitalters* (SNT 50; Leiden: Brill, 1979), 97–191.

Bowlby, John, *A Secure Base: Parent-Child Attachment and Healthy Human Develop-ment* (New York: Basic Books, 1988).

Boyd, Richard, 'Metaphor and Theory Change: What is "Metaphor" a Metaphor for?', in A. Ortony (ed.), *Metaphor and Thought* (Cambridge: Cambridge University Press, 1993²), 481–532.

Brandenburger, Egon, 'Die Auferstehung der Glaubenden als historisches und theolo-gisches Problem', *WD* 9 (1967), 16–33.

–, *Fleisch und Geist: Paulus und die dualistische Weisheit* (WMANT 29; Neukirchen-Vluyn: Neukirchener Verlag, 1968).

–, 'Alter und neuer Mensch, erster und letzter Adam-Anthropos', in W. Strolz (ed.), *Vom alten zum neuen Adam: Urzeitmythos und Heilsgeschichte* (VSOD 13; Freiburg: Her-der, 1986), 182–223.

Brändl, Martin, *Der Agon bei Paulus: Herkunft und Profil paulinischer Agonmetaphorik* (WUNT II/222; Tübingen: Mohr Siebeck, 2006).

Brockhaus, Ulrich, *Charisma und Amt: Die paulinische Charismenlehre auf dem Hinter-grund der frühchristlichen Gemeindefunktionen* (Wuppertal: Brockhaus, 1975).

Brodeur, Scott, *The Holy Spirit's Agency in the Resurrection of the Dead: An Exegetico-Theological Study of 1 Corinthians 15,44b–49 and Romans 8,9–13* (TGSG 14; Rome: Editrice Pontificia Università Gregoriana, 1996).

Brown, Alexandra R., *The Cross and Human Transformation: Paul's Apocalyptic Word in 1 Corinthians* (Minneapolis: Fortress, 1995).

Brown, J. A., 'Metaphorical Language in Relation to Baptism in Pauline Literature' (University of Edinburgh: Unpublished PhD Thesis, 1982).

Bruce, F. F., *The Epistle to the Galatians: A Commentary on the Greek Text* (NIGTC; Exeter/Grand Rapids: Paternoster/Eerdmans, 1982).

Brümmer, Vincent, *The Model of Love: A Study in Philosophical Theology* (Cambridge: Cambridge University Press, 1993).

Buchegger, Jürg, *Erneuerung des Menschen: Exegetische Studien zu Paulus* (TANZ 40; Tübingen: Francke, 2003).

Buck, Ross, 'Emotional Communication in Personal Relationships: A Developmental-Interactionist View', in C. Hendrick (ed.), *Close Relationships* (RPSP 10; London: Sage, 1989), 144–63.

Büchsel, Friedrich, *Der Geist Gottes im Neuen Testament* (Gütersloh: Bertelsmann, 1926).

Bultmann, Rudolf, 'γινώσκω κτλ', *TDNT*, I, 689–714.

–, 'ζάω κτλ', *TDNT*, II, 855–75.

–, 'Das Problem der Ethik bei Paulus', *ZNW* 23 (1924), 123–40.

–, 'The Problem of Ethics in Paul', in B.S. Rosner (ed.), *Understanding Paul's Ethics: Twentieth-Century Approaches* (Grand Rapids: Eerdmans, 1995), 195–216; orig. publ.: 'Das Problem der Ethik bei Paulus', *ZNW* 23 (1924), 123–40.

–, 'Paul', in R. Bultmann, *Existence and Faith: Shorter Writings of Rudolf Bultmann. Selected, translated and introduced by Schubert M. Ogden* (London: Collins, 1961), 130–72; orig. publ.: 'Paulus', in *RGG²*, IV, 1019–45.

–, *Theologie des Neuen Testaments* (Tübingen: J.C.B. Mohr (Paul Siebeck), 1984⁹ [1948¹]).

–, *Theology of the New Testament. Vol. 1* (London: SCM Press, 1952); orig. publ.: *Theol-ogie des Neuen Testaments* (Tübingen: J.C.B. Mohr (Paul Siebeck), 1984⁹ [1948¹]).

–, 'New Testament and Mythology', in H.W. Bartsch (ed.), *Kerygma and Myth: A Theo-logical Debate* (London: SPCK, 1953), 1–44; orig. publ.: 'Neues Testament und Mythodologie', in H.W. Bartsch (ed.), *Kerygma und Mythos: Ein Theologisches Gespräch* (Hamburg: Reich, 1948), 15–48.

–, 'A Reply to the Theses of J. Schniewind', in H.W. Bartsch (ed.), *Kerygma and Myth: A Theological Debate* (London: SPCK, 1953), 102–23.

–, *The Old and the New Man in the Letters of Paul* (Richmond: Knox, 1967); orig. publ.: *Der alte und der neue Mensch in der Theologie des Paulus* (Libelli XCVIII; Darmstadt: Wissenschaftliche Buchgesellschaft, 1964).

–, *Der zweite Brief an die Korinther* (KEK; Göttingen: Vandenhoeck & Ruprecht, 1976).

Buntfuß, Markus, *Tradition und Innovation: die Funktion der Metapher in der theologischen Theoriesprache* (TBT 84; Berlin/New York: W. de Gruyter, 1997).

Burchard, Christoph, 'Joseph and Aseneth: A New Translation and Introduction', *OTP*, II, 177–247.

–, *Joseph und Aseneth* (JSHRZ II/4; Gütersloh: Mohn, 1983).

–, 'The Importance of Joseph and Aseneth for the Study of the New Testament: A General Survey and a Fresh Look at the Lord's Supper', *NTS* 33 (1987), 102–34.

–, 'Der jüdische Asenethroman und seine Nachwirkung: Von Egeria zu Anna Katharina Emmerick oder von Moses aus Aggel zu Karl Kerényi', in C. Burchard, *Gesammelte Studien zu Joseph und Aseneth. Berichtigt und ergänzt herausgegeben mit Unterstützung von Carsten Burfeind* (SVTP 13; Leiden: Brill, 1996), 321–436.

–, 'Ein vorläufiger griechischer Text von Joseph und Aseneth', in C. Burchard, *Gesammelte Studien zu Joseph und Aseneth. Berichtigt und ergänzt herausgegeben mit Unterstützung von Carsten Burfeind* (SVTP 13; Leiden: Brill, 1996), 161–209; orig. publ.: in *Diehlheimer Blätter zum Alten Testament* 14 (1979), 2–53; 16 (1982), 37–39.

–, '1 Korinther 15,39–41', in C. Burchard, *Studien zur Theologie, Sprache und Umwelt des Neuen Testaments* (WUNT 107; Tübingen: Mohr Siebeck, 1998), 203–28.

Burke, Trevor J., 'The Characteristics of Paul's Adoptive-Sonship (HUIOTHESIA) Motif', *IBS* 17 (1995), 62–74.

–, 'Adoption and the Spirit in Romans 8', *EQ* 70 (1998), 311–24.

–, *Family Matters: A Socio-Historical Study of Kinship Metaphors in 1 Thessalonians* (JSNTSup 247; London: Sheffield Academic Press, 2003).

–, 'Paul's Role as "Father" to his Corinthian "Children" in Socio-Historical Context (1 Corinthians 4:14–21)', in T.J. Burke and J.K. Elliott (eds.), *Paul and the Corinthians: Studies on a Community in Conflict. Essays in Honour of Margaret Thrall* (NovTSup 109; Leiden: Brill, 2003), 95–113.

–, *Adopted into God's Family: Exploring a Pauline Metaphor* (NSBT 22; Downers Grove: IVP, 2006).

Burnett, Gary W., *Paul and the Salvation of the Individual* (BIS 57; Leiden: Brill, 2001).

Burton, Ernest de Witt, *Spirit, Soul, Flesh* (HLSLNT II/3; Chicago: University of Chicago Press, 1918).

Byrne, Brendan, S.J., *'Sons of God' – 'Seed of Abraham': A Study of the Idea of the Sonship of God of All Christians in Paul Against the Jewish Background* (AB 83; Rome: Biblical Institute, 1979).

–, 'Living Out the Righteousness of God: The Contribution of Rom 6:1–8:13 to an Understanding of Paul's Ethical Presuppositions', *CBQ* 43 (1981), 557–81.

Cage, Gary T., *The Holy Spirit: A Source Book with Commentary* (Reno: Charlotte House, 1995).

Caird, G. B., *The Language and Imagery of the Bible* (London: Duckworth, 1980).

Campbell, Douglas A., *The Quest for Paul's Gospel: A Suggested Strategy* (London: T. & T. Clark, 2005).

–, *The Deliverance of God: An Apocalyptic Rereading of Justification in Paul* (Grand Rapids/Cambridge: Eerdmans, 2009).

Campbell, J. K., 'ΚΟΙΝΩΝΙΑ and its Cognates in the New Testament', in J.K. Campbell, *Three New Testament Studies* (Leiden: Brill, 1965), 1–28; orig. publ.: *JBL* 51 (1932), 352–82.

Carson, D. A., and Moo, Douglas J., *An Introduction to the New Testament* (Leicester: Apollos, 2005²).

Carter, Timothy L., *Paul and the Power of Sin: Redefining 'Beyond the Pale'* (SNTSMS 115; Cambridge: Cambridge University Press, 2002).

Chamblin, C. K., *Paul and the Self: Apostolic Teaching for Personal Wholeness* (Grand Rapids: Baker, 1993).

Charles, R. H., *The Apocrypha and Pseudepigrapha of the Old Testament*; 2 vols. (Oxford: Clarendon Press, 1913).

Charlesworth, James H., 'The Odes of Solomon', *OTP*, II, 725–71.

–, (ed.), *The Old Testament Pseudepigrapha*; 2 vols. (New York: Doubleday, 1983, 1985).

–, *The Old Testament Pseudepigrapha and the New Testament: Prolegomena for the Study of Christian Origins* (SNTSMS/OTPNT 54; Cambridge: Cambridge University Press, 1985).

–, (ed.), *The Dead Sea Scrolls: Hebrew, Aramaic, and Greek Texts with English Translations. Vol. 2: Damascus Document, War Scroll, and Related Documents* (PTSDSSP; Tübingen/Louisville: Mohr Siebeck/Westminster John Knox Press, 1995).

–, *Critical Reflections on the Odes of Solomon. Vol. 1: Literary Setting, Textual Studies, Gnosticism, the Dead Sea Scrolls and the Gospel of John* (JSPSup 22; Sheffield: Sheffield Academic Press, 1998).

–, 'The Odes of Solomon and the Jewish Wisdom Texts', in C. Hempel, A. Lange, and H. Lichtenberger (eds.), *The Wisdom Texts from Qumran and the Development of Sapiential Thought* (BETL 159; Leuven: Leuven University Press/Peeters, 2002), 323–49.

–, *The First Christian Hymnbook: The Odes of Solomon. Translated by James H. Charlesworth* (Eugene: Cascade Books, 2009).

Chen, Diane G., *God as Father in Luke-Acts* (SBL 92; New York: Lang, 2006).

Chesnutt, Randall D., *From Death to Life: Conversion in Joseph and Aseneth* (JSPSup 16; Sheffield: Sheffield Academic Press, 1995).

–, 'Review of R.S. Kraemer, *When Aseneth Met Joseph: A Late Antique Tale of the Biblical Patriarch and His Egyptian Wife, Reconsidered*', *JBL* 119 (2000), 760–62.

Chester, Stephen, *Conversion at Corinth* (SNTW; London: T. & T. Clark, 2003).

Chevallier, Max-Alain, *Souffle de Dieu: Le Saint-Esprit dans le Nouveau Testament. Vol. 2: L'apôtre Paul etc.* (Le Point Théologique 26; Paris: Beauchesne, 1990).

Chilton, Bruce, 'God as "Father" in the Targumim, in Non-Canonical Literatures of Early Judaism and Primitive Christianity, and in Matthew', in J.H. Charlesworth and C.A. Evans (eds.), *The Pseudepigrapha and Early Biblical Interpretation* (JSPSup 14/SSEJC 2; Sheffield: Sheffield Academic Press, 1993), 151–69.

Christiansen, Ellen Juhl, 'The Consciousness of Belonging to God's Covenant and What it Entails According to the Damascus Document and the Community Rule', in F.H. Cryer and T.L. Thompson (eds.), *Qumran between the Old and New Testaments* (JSOTSup 290; Sheffield: Sheffield Academic Press, 1998), 69–97.

Christoph, Monika, *Pneuma und das neue Sein der Glaubenden: Studien zur Semantik und Pragmatik der Rede von Pneuma in Röm 8* (EUS 23/813; Frankfurt: Lang, 2005).

Coenen, Lothar, and Haacker, Klaus (eds.), *Theologisches Begriffslexikon zum Neuen Testament* (Wuppertal: Brockhaus, 1997²).

Collange, Jean François, *Énigmes de la deuxième épître de Paul aux Corinthiens: Étude exégétique de 2 Cor. 2:14–7:4* (SNTSMS 18; Cambridge: Cambridge University Press, 1972).

Collins, Raymond F., *First Corinthians* (SP 7; Collegeville: Liturgical Press, 1999).

Cotterell, Peter, and Turner, Max, *Linguistics and Biblical Interpretation* (Downers Grove: IVP, 1989).

Cox, Ronald R., *By the Same Word: Creation and Salvation in Hellenistic Judaism and early Christianity* (BZNW 145; Berlin/New York: W. de Gruyter, 2007).

Craig, Edward (ed.), *Routledge Encyclopedia of Philosophy*; 10 vols. (London: Routledge, 1998).

Cramer, Duncan, *Close Relationships: The Study of Love and Friendship* (London: Arnold, 1998).

Cranfield, C. E. B., *A Critical and Exegetical Commentary on the Epistle to the Romans. Vol. 1: Introduction and Commentary on Romans I–VIII* (ICC; Edinburgh: T. & T. Clark, 1975).

–, *A Critical and Exegetical Commentary on the Epistle to the Romans. Vol. 2: Commentary on Romans IX–XVI and Essays* (ICC; Edinburgh: T. & T. Clark, 1979).

Cross, Anthony R., 'Spirit- and Water-Baptism in 1 Corinthians 12.13', in S.E. Porter and A.R. Cross (eds.), *Dimensions of Baptism: Biblical and Theological Studies* (JSNTSup 234; London: Sheffield Academic Press, 2002), 120–48.

Das, A. Andrew, *Solving the Romans Debate* (Minneapolis: Fortress, 2007).

Davies, William D., *Paul and Rabbinic Judaism: Some Rabbinic Elements in Pauline Theology* (Philadelphia: Fortress, 1980⁴ [1948¹]).

Davis, Keith, and Todd, Michael, 'Assessing Friendship: Prototypes, Paradigm Cases and Relationship Description', in S. Duck and D. Perlman (eds.), *Understanding Personal Relationships: An Interdisciplinary Approach* (London: SAGE, 1985), 17–37.

Dawes, Gregory W., *The Body in Question: Metaphor and Meaning in the Interpretation of Ephesians 5:21–33* (BIS 30; Leiden/Boston/Cologne: Brill, 1998).

de Lacy, Phillip (ed.), *Galen, On the Doctrines of Hippocrates and Plato. Vol. 1* (CMG 5.4; Berlin: Akademie-Verlag, 1984³).

de Oliveira, Anacleto, *Die Diakonie der Gerechtigkeit und der Versöhnung in der Apologie des 2. Korintherbriefes: Analyse und Auslegung von 2 Kor 2,14–4,6; 5,11–6,10* (NA 21; Münster: Aschendorff, 1990).

Deidun, Thomas J., *New Covenant Morality in Paul* (AnBib 89; Rome: Biblical Institute Press, 1981).

Deissmann, Adolf, *Die neutestamentliche Formel 'in Christo Jesu'* (Marburg: Elwert'sche Verlagsbuchhandlung, 1892).

–, *Paul: A Study in Social and Religious History* (London: Hodder & Stoughton, 1926); orig. publ.: *Paulus: Eine kultur- und religionsgeschichtliche Skizze* (Tübingen: J.C.B. Mohr (Paul Siebeck), 1925²).

Deißner, Kurt, *Auferstehungshoffnung und Pneumagedanke bei Paulus* (Leipzig: Deichert, 1912).

–, *Paulus und die Mystik seiner Zeit* (Leipzig/Erlangen: Deichert'sche Verlagsbuchhandlung, 1921²).

DeSilva, David A., *An Introduction to the New Testament: Contexts, Methods and Ministry Formation* (Downers Grove/Leicester: IVP/Apollos, 2004).

Dey, Joseph, *ΠΑΛΙΓΓΕΝΕΣΙΑ: Ein Beitrag zur Klärung der religionsgeschichtlichen Bedeutung von Tit 3,5* (NTA 17.5; Münster: Aschendorff, 1937).

DeYoung, Patricia A., *Relational Psychotherapy: A Primer* (New York/Hove: Brunner-Routledge, 2003).

Di Fortunato, Luigi Enrico, *The Gramma – Pneuma Antithesis: An Exegetical Study of Three Pauline Texts and the Hermeneutical Value of the Antithesis Examined on the Apostle's Exposition of the Scriptures* (Zürich: Stiftung Zentralstelle der Studentenschaft der Universität Zürich, 1993).

Dibelius, Martin, *Die Geisterwelt im Glauben des Paulus* (Göttingen: Vandenhoeck & Ruprecht, 1909).

Dietzel, A., 'Beten im Geist', *TZ* 13 (1957), 12–32.

Dillon, John M., '"Orthodoxy" and "Eclecticism": Middle Platonists and Neo-Pythagoreans', in J.M. Dillon and A.A. Long (eds.), *The Question of "Eclecticism": Studies in Later Greek Philosophy* (HCS; London: UCP, 1988), 70–102.

Djukanovic, Savo, *Heiligkeit und Heiligung bei Paulus* (Novi Sad: Natošević, 1939).

Dockery, David S., 'New Nature and Old Nature', *DPL*, 628–29.

Dodd, Charles Harold, *The Interpretation of the Fourth Gospel* (Cambridge: Cambridge University Press, 1953).

–, *The Epistle of Paul to the Romans* (MNTC; London: Fontana, 1959).

Dodds, Lois A., 'The Role of the Holy Spirit in Personality Growth and Change', *JPsy-Chr* 18 (1999), 129–39.

Dreytza, Manfred, *Der theologische Gebrauch von Ruah im Alten Testament: Eine wort- und satzsemantische Studie* (Giessen/Basel: Brunnen, 1990).

Dürr, Lorenz, *Die Wertung des göttlichen Wortes im alten Testament und im antiken Orient: Zugleich ein Beitrag zur Vorgeschichte des neutestamentlichen Logosbegriffes* (MVAG 42/1; Leipzig: Hinrichs, 1938).

Duff, Paul Brooks, 'Transformed "from Glory to Glory": Paul's Appeal to the Experience of His Readers in 2 Corinthians 3:18', *JBL* 127 (2008), 759–80.

Dunn, James D. G., 'Geist/Heiliger Geist: III. Neues Testament', *RGG⁴*, III, 565–67.

–, '2 Corinthians III. 17 – "The Lord is the Spirit"', *JTS* 21 (1970), 309–20.

–, *Baptism in the Holy Spirit: A Re-examination of the New Testament Teaching on the Gift of the Spirit in Relation to Pentecostalism Today* (Philadelphia: Westminster Press, 1970).

–, *Jesus and the Spirit: A Study of the Religious and Charismatic Experience of Jesus and the First Christians as Reflected in the New Testament* (London: SCM Press, 1975).

–, 'Rom. 7,14–25 in the Theology of Paul', *TLZ* 31 (1975), 257–73.

–, *Romans 1–8* (WBC 38A; Texas: Word, 1988).

–, 'The New Perspective on Paul', in J.D.G. Dunn, *Jesus, Paul and the Law: Studies in Mark and Galatians* (London: SPCK, 1990), 183–206.

–, *The Epistle to the Galatians* (BNTC; London: Black, 1993).

–, *The Theology of Paul's Letter to the Galatians* (NT Theology; Cambridge: Cambridge University Press, 1993).

–, *The Epistles to the Colossians and to Philemon: A Commentary on the Greek Text* (NIGTC; Carlisle/Grand Rapids: Paternoster/Eerdmans, 1996).

–, *The Theology of Paul the Apostle* (Edinburgh: T. & T. Clark, 1998).

–, 'Spirit Speech: Reflections on Romans 8:12–27', in S. Soderlund and N.T. Wright (eds.), *Romans and the People of God: Essays in Honor of Gordon D. Fee on the Occasion of His 65th Birthday* (Grand Rapids/Cambridge: Eerdmans, 1999), 82–91.

–, '"Baptized" as Metaphor', in S.E. Porter and A.R. Cross (eds.), *Baptism, the New Testament and the Church: Historical and Contemporary Studies in Honour of R.E.O. White* (JSNTSup 171; Sheffield: Sheffield Academic Press, 2000), 294–310.

–, 'How are the Dead Raised? With What Body do They Come? Reflections on 1 Corinthians 15', *SwJT* 45 (2002), 4–18.

–, 'The New Perspective on Paul: Whence, What and Whither?', in J.D.G. Dunn, *The New Perspective on Paul: Collected Essays* (WUNT 185; Tübingen: Mohr Siebeck, 2005), 1–88.

–, 'Philippians 3.2–14 and the New Perspective on Paul', in J.D.G. Dunn, *The New Perspective on Paul: Collected Essays* (WUNT 185; Tübingen: Mohr Siebeck, 2005), 463–84.

–, 'Towards the Spirit of Christ: The Emergence of the Distinctive Features of Christian Pneumatology', in M. Welker (ed.), *The Work of the Spirit: Pneumatology and Pentecostalism* (Grand Rapids: Eerdmans, 2006), 3–26.

–, *Beginning from Jerusalem* (Christianity in the Making 2; Grand Rapids/Cambridge: Eerdmans, 2009).

Ebeling, Gerhard, *Dogmatik des Glaubens. Vol. 1* (Tübingen: J.C.B. Mohr (Paul Siebeck), 1987³).

Eco, Umberto, *Semiotics and the Philosophy of Language* (Advances in Semiotics; Bloomington: Indiana University Press, 1984).

–, *Die Grenzen der Interpretation* (Munich: Carl Hauser, 1992); orig. publ.: *I limiti dell'interpretazione* (Bompiani: Gruppo Editoriale Fabbri, 1990); ET: *The Limits of Interpretation* (Bloomington: Indiana University Press, 1990).

Elliger, Winfried, 'ἐν', *EWNT²*, I, 1093–96.

Elliott, Mark Adam, *The Survivors of Israel: A Reconsideration of the Theology of Pre-Christian Judaism* (Grand Rapids: Eerdmans, 2000).

Ellis, E. Earle, 'II Cor. 5:1–10 in Pauline Eschatology', *NTS* 6 (1959/60), 215.

–, *Pauline Theology: Ministry and Society* (Exeter/Grand Rapids: Paternoster Press/Eerdmans, 1989).

Emondts, Stefan, *Menschwerden in Beziehung: Eine religionsphilosophische Untersuchung der medizinischen Anthropologie Viktor von Weizsäckers* (Problemata 131; Stuttgart-Bad Cannstatt: Frommann-Holzboog, 1993).

Engberg-Pedersen, Troels, *Paul and the Stoics* (Edinburgh: T. & T. Clark, 2000).

–, 'Body Language in Paul' (19ᵗʰ British New Testament Conference, Manchester: Unpublished Paper, 2001).

–, (ed.), *Paul Beyond the Judaism/Hellenism Divide* (Louisville: Westminster John Knox Press, 2001).

–, 'Self-Sufficiency and Power: Divine and Human Agency in Epictetus and Paul', in J.M.G. Barclay and S.J. Gathercole (eds.), *Divine and Human Agency in Paul and his Cultural Environment* (ECC/LNTS 335; London: Continuum, 2006), 117–39.

–, 'A Stoic Understanding of *Pneuma* in Paul', in T. Engberg-Pedersen and H. Tronier (eds.), *Philosophy at the Roots of Christianity* (Working Papers 2; Copenhagen: The Faculty of Theology, University of Copenhagen, 2006), 101–23.

–, 'The Logic of Action in Paul: How Does He Differ from the Moral Philosophers on Spiritual and Moral Progression and Regression?', in J.T. Fitzgerald (ed.), *Passions and Moral Progress in Greco-Roman Thought* (RMCS; London: Routledge, 2008), 238–66.

–, 'Complete and Incomplete Transformation in Paul – A Philosophic Reading of Paul on Body and Spirit', in T.K. Seim and J. Økland (eds.), *Metamorphoses: Resurrection, Body and Transformative Practices in Early Christianity* (EREAMA 1; Berlin/New York: W. de Gruyter, 2009), 123–46.

–, 'The Material Spirit: Cosmology and Ethics in Paul', *NTS* 55 (2009), 179–97.

–, *Cosmology and Self in the Apostle Paul: The Material Spirit* (Oxford: Oxford University Press, 2010).

Ernesti, H. Fr. Th. L., *Die Ethik des Apostels Paulus in ihren Grundzügen dargestellt* (Braunschweig: Leibrod, 1880³ [1868¹]).

Esler, Philip F., *Conflict and Identity in Romans: The Social Setting of Paul's Letter* (Minneapolis: Fortress, 2003).

–, 'Social Identity, the Virtues, and the Good Life: A New Approach to Romans 12:1–15:13', *BTB* 33 (2003), 51–63.

Evans, Craig A., and Porter, Stanley E. (eds.), *Dictionary of New Testament Background* (Leicester/Downers Grove: IVP, 2000).

Fatehi, Mehrdad, *The Spirit's Relation to the Risen Lord in Paul: An Examination of Its Christological Implications* (WUNT II/128; Tübingen: Mohr Siebeck, 2000).

Fay, Ron C., 'Was Paul a Trinitarian? A Look at Romans 8', in S.E. Porter (ed.), *Paul and His Theology* (PS 3; Leiden: Brill, 2006), 327–45.

Fee, Gordon D., *The First Epistle to the Corinthians* (NICNT; Grand Rapids: Eerdmans, 1987).

–, *God's Empowering Presence: The Holy Spirit in the Letters of Paul* (Peabody: Hendrickson, 1994).

–, *Pauline Christology: An Exegetical-Theological Study* (Peabody: Hendrickson, 2007).

Feine, Paul, *Theologie des Neuen Testaments* (Berlin: Evangelische Verlagsanstalt, 1953[8] [1911[2]]).

Ferguson, Sinclair B., 'The Reformed Doctrine of Sonship', in N. de S. Cameron and S.B. Ferguson (eds.), *Pulpit and People: Essays in Honour of William Still on His 75th Birthday* (Edinburgh: Rutherford, 1986).

–, *Children of the Living God* (Edinburgh: Banner of Truth, 1989).

Fichtner, Johannes, 'Die Stellung der Sapientia Salomonis in der Literatur- und Geistesgeschichte ihrer Zeit', *ZNW* 36 (1937), 113–32.

–, *Weisheit Salomos* (Tübingen: J.C.B. Mohr (Paul Siebeck), 1938).

Filoramo, Giovanni, 'The Transformation of the Inner Self in Gnostic and Hermetic Texts', in J. Assmann and G.G. Stroumsa (eds.), *Transformations of the Inner Self in Ancient Religions* (SHR 83; Leiden: Brill, 1999), 137–49.

Fitzer, G., 'Review of K. Stalder, *Das Werk des Heiligen Geistes in der Heiligung bei Paulus*', *TZ* 20 (1964), 139–45.

Fitzgerald, John T., 'Paul and Friendship', in J.P. Sampley (ed.), *Paul in the Greco-Roman World: A Handbook* (Harrisburg/London: Trinity Press International, 2003), 319–43.

Fitzmyer, Joseph A., S.J., 'Glory Reflected on the Face of Christ (2 Cor 3:7–4:6) and a Palestinian Jewish Motif', *TS* 42 (1981), 630–44.

–, *Romans: A New Translation with Introduction and Commentary* (AB 33; New York/London/Sydney: Geoffrey Chapman/Doubleday, 1993).

Fletcher Brokaw, Beth, and Edwards, Keith J., 'The Relationship of God Image to Level of Object Relations Development', *JPsyTh* 22 (1994), 352–71.

Foerster, W., 'Der Heilige Geist im Spätjudentum', *NTS* 8 (1961), 117–34.

Forschner, Maximilian, *Die Stoische Ethik: Über den Zusammenhang von Natur-, Sprach- und Moralphilosophie im altstoischen System* (Stuttgart: Klett-Cotta, 1981).

Foster, Robert L., '"A Temple in the Lord Filled to the Fullness of God": Context and Intertextuality (Eph. 3:19)', *NovT* 49 (2007), 85–96.

Fowl, Stephen E., *A Commentary on Philippians* (THNTC; Grand Rapids: Eerdmans, 2005).

Fowler, Roger, *Linguistic Criticism* (Opus; Oxford: Oxford University Press, 1996[2]).

Frede, Dorothea, 'Stoic Determinism', in B. Inwood (ed.), *The Cambridge Companion to the Stoics* (CCP; Cambridge: Cambridge University Press, 2003), 179–205.

Freudenthal, Gad, *Aristotle's Theory of Material Substance: Heat and Pneuma, Form and Soul* (Oxford: Clarendon, 1995).

Fuchs, Ernst, *Christus und der Geist bei Paulus: Eine biblisch-theologische Untersuchung* (Leipzig: Hinrichs'sche Buchhandlung, 1932).

Furnish, Victor Paul, *Theology and Ethics in Paul* (Nashville: Abingdon, 1968).

–, *II Corinthians* (AB 32A; New York: Doubleday, 1984).

Gabriel, Andrew K., 'Pauline Pneumatology and the Question of Trinitarian Presuppositions', in S.E. Porter (ed.), *Paul and His Theology* (PS 3; Leiden: Brill, 2006), 347–62.

Gäckle, Volker, *Die Starken und die Schwachen in Korinth und in Rom: Zu Herkunft und Funktion der Antithese in 1Kor 8,1–11,1 und in Röm 14,1–15,13* (WUNT II/200; Tübingen: Mohr Siebeck, 2005).

Gaffin, Richard B., 'Glory, Glorification', *DPL*, 348–50.

–, '"Life-Giving Spirit": Probing the Centre of Paul's Pneumatology', *JETS* 41 (1998), 573–89.

García Martínez, Florentino, and Tigchelaar, Eibert J.C. (eds.), *The Dead Sea Scrolls Study Edition*; 2 vols. (Leiden/Cambridge: Brill/Eerdmans, 2000).

Gardner, Paul Douglas, *The Gifts of God and the Authentication of a Christian: An Exegetical Study of 1 Corinthians 8–11:1* (Lanham: University Press of America, 1994).

Garland, David E., 'The Sufficiency of Paul, Minister of the New Covenant', *CTR* 4 (1989), 21–37.

–, *2 Corinthians* (NAC 29; Nashville: Broadman & Holman, 1999).

–, *1 Corinthians* (BECNT; Grand Rapids: Baker Academic, 2003).

Gärtner, Bertil E., 'The Pauline and Johannine Idea of "To Know God" Against the Hellenistic Background', *NTS* 14 (1967), 209–31.

Gaugler, Ernst, 'Die Heiligung in der Ethik des Paulus', *IKZ* 2 (1925), 100–20.

Georgi, Dieter, *Weisheit Salomos* (JSHRZ III/4; Gütersloh: Mohn, 1980).

Gese, Hartmut, *Essays on Biblical Theology* (Minneapolis: Augsburg Publishing House, 1981); orig. publ.: *Zur biblischen Theologie: Alttestamentliche Vorträge* (Tübingen: J.C.B. Mohr (Paul Siebeck), 1977).

Giesen, Heinz, 'Söhne und Töchter Gottes kraft des Geistes: Zur ekklesialen Dimension des Christseins', in J. Eckert, M. Schmidl, and H. Steichele (eds.), *Pneuma und Gemeinde: Christsein in der Tradition des Paulus und Johannes* (FS J. Hainz; Düsseldorf: Patmos, 2001), 69–101.

Gill, Christopher, *The Structured Self in Hellenistic and Roman Thought* (Oxford: Oxford University Press, 2006).

Giora, Rachel, 'Is Metaphor Unique?', in R.W. Gibbs, Jr. (ed.), *The Cambridge Handbook of Metaphor and Thought* (Cambridge: Cambridge University Press, 2008), 143–60.

Gloël, Johannes, *Der heilige Geist in der Heilsverkündigung des Paulus: Eine biblisch-theologische Untersuchung* (Halle: Numeyer, 1888).

Glucker, John, *Antiochus and the Late Academy* (H.UAN 56; Göttingen: Vandenhoeck & Ruprecht, 1978).

Glucksberg, Sam, 'How Metaphors Create Categories – Quickly', in R.W. Gibbs, Jr. (ed.), *The Cambridge Handbook of Metaphor and Thought* (Cambridge: Cambridge University Press, 2008), 67–83.

Goguel, Maurice, *The Primitive Church* (London: Alan & Unwin, 1964); orig. publ.: *L'Eglise Primitive* (Paris: Payot, 1947).

Goldingay, John E., *Daniel* (WBC 30; Dallas: Word, 1989).

Goodenough, Erwin R., *By Light, Light: The Mystic Gospel of Hellenistic Judaism* (Oxford/New Haven: Oxford University Press/Yale University Press, 1935).

Goppelt, Leonhard, 'πίνω κτλ', *TDNT*, VI, 135–60.

Gorman, Michael J., *Cruciformity: Paul's Narrative Spirituality of the Cross* (Grand Rapids/Cambridge: Eerdmans, 2001).

Green, Joel B., *Body, Soul, and Human Life: The Nature of Humanity in the Bible* (STI; Milton Keynes: Paternoster, 2008).

Green, Joel B., and Baker, Mark D., *Recovering the Scandal of the Cross: Atonement in the New Testament and Contemporary Contexts* (Downers Grove: IVP, 2000; Carlisle: Paternoster, 2003).

Grindheim, Sigurd, 'The Law Kills but the Gospel Gives Life: The Letter–Spirit Dualism in 2. Corinthians 3.5–18', *JSNT* 84 (2001), 97–115.

Gruber, M. Margareta, *Herrlichkeit in Schwachheit: Eine Auslegung der Apologie des Zweiten Korintherbriefs 2 Kor 2,14–6,13* (FB 89; Würzburg: Echter, 1998).

Gundry, Robert H., *Sôma in Biblical Theology: With Emphasis on Pauline Anthropology* (SNTSMS 29; Cambridge: Cambridge University Press, 1976).

Gunkel, H., Zscharnack, L., Bertholet, A., Faber, H., and Stephan, H. (eds.), *Die Religion in Geschichte und Gegenwart: Handwörterbuch für Theologie und Religionswissenschaft*; 5 vols. (Tübingen: J.C.B. Mohr (Paul Siebeck), 1927–1931[2]).

Gunkel, Hermann, *The Influence of the Holy Spirit: The Popular View of the Apostolic Age and the Teaching of the Apostle Paul* (Philadelphia: Fortress Press, 1979); orig. publ.: *Die Wirkungen des heiligen Geistes nach der populären Anschauung der apostolischen Zeit und der Lehre des Apostels Paulus* (Göttingen: Vandenhoeck & Ruprecht, 1909[3] [1888[1]]).

Gunneweg, A. H. J., 'Aspekte des alttestamentlichen Geistverständnisses', in A.H.J. Gunneweg, *Sola Scriptura. Vol. I: Beiträge zu Exegese und Hermeneutik des Alten Testaments* (Göttingen: Vandenhoeck & Ruprecht, 1983), 96–106.

Gupta, Nijay K., 'The Theo-Logic of Paul's Ethics in Recent Research: Crosscurrents and Future Directions in Scholarship in the Last Forty Years', *CBR* 7 (2009), 336–61.

Hafemann, Scott J., 'Paul and His Interpreters', *DPL*, 666–79.

–, *Paul, Moses, and the History of Israel: The Letter/Spirit Contrast and the Argument from Scripture in 2 Corinthians 3* (WUNT 81; Tübingen: J.C.B. Mohr (Paul Siebeck), 1995).

–, 'The "Temple of the Spirit" as the Inaugural Fulfilment of the New Covenant within the Corinthian Correspondence', *ExAud* 12 (1996), 29–42.

Hahn, Ferdinand, *Theologie des Neuen Testaments. Band 1: Die Vielfalt des Neuen Testaments – Theologiegeschichte des Urchristentums* (Tübingen: Mohr Siebeck, 2003).

Halliday, M. A. K., *Introduction to Functional Grammar* (London: Arnold, 1985).

Halter, Hans, *Taufe und Ethos: Paulinische Kriterien für das Proprium christlicher Moral* (Freiburg: Herder, 1977).

Hamilton, Neill Q., *The Holy Spirit and Eschatology in Paul* (SJTOP 6; London: Oliver & Boyd, 1957).

Hanson, Anthony T., 'The Midrash in II Corinthians 3: A Reconsideration', *JSNT* 9 (1980), 2–28.

Harland, Philip A., 'Familial Dimensions of Group Identity: "Brothers" (Ἀδελφοί) in Associations of the Greek East', *JBL* 124 (2005), 491–513.

Harries, Karsten, 'The Many Uses of Metaphor', in S. Sacks (ed.), *On Metaphor* (Chicago: University of Chicago Press, 1981), 165–72.

Harris, Harriet A., 'Should We Say that Personhood is Relational?', *SJT* 51 (1998), 214–34.

Harris, Murray J., *Raised Immortal: Resurrection and Immortality in the New Testament* (Grand Rapids: Eerdmans, 1985).

–, *The Second Epistle to the Corinthians: A Commentary on the Greek Text* (NIGTC; Grand Rapids/Milton Keynes: Eerdmans/Paternoster, 2005).

Hartman, Lars, *'Into the Name of the Lord Jesus': Baptism in the Early Church* (SNTW; Edinburgh: T. & T. Clark, 1997).

Hartup, Willard W., 'Relationships and their Significance in Cognitive Development', in A.-N. Perret-Clermont, R.A. Hinde, and J. Stevenson-Hinde (eds.), *Social Relationships and Cognitive Development* (Oxford: Clarendon, 1985), 66–82.

Haufe, Günter, 'Taufe und Heiliger Geist im Urchristentum', *TLZ* 101 (1976), 561–66.

–, 'Das Geistmotiv in der paulinischen Ethik', *ZNW* 85 (1994), 183–91.

Hauger, Martin, 'Die Deutung der Auferweckung Jesu Christi bei Paulus', in H.-J. Eckstein and M. Welker (eds.), *Die Wirklichkeit der Auferstehung* (Neukirchen-Vluyn: Neukirchener Verlag, 2002), 31–58.

Hay, David M., 'Philo of Alexandria', in D.A. Carson, P. O'Brien, and M.A. Seifrid (eds.), *Justification and Variegated Nomism. Vol. 1: The Complexities of Second Temple Judaism* (WUNT II/140; Tübingen: Mohr Siebeck, 2001), 357–79.

–, 'Paul's Understanding of Faith as Participation', in S.E. Porter (ed.), *Paul and His Theology* (PS 3; Leiden: Brill, 2006), 45–76.

Hays, Richard B., *First Corinthians* (Int; Louisville: John Knox Press, 1997).

–, *The Moral Vision of the New Testament: Community, Cross, New Creation. A Contemporary Introduction to New Testament Ethics* (Edinburgh: T. & T. Clark, 1997).

–, 'Intertextuelle Pneumatologie: Die paulinische Rede vom Heiligen Geist', *ZNT* 25 (2010), 30–37.

Heil, John Paul, *Ephesians: Empowerment to Walk in Love for the Unity of All in Christ* (SBL 13; Leiden: Brill, 2007).

Heinze, Max, *Die Lehre vom Logos in der griechischen Philosophie* (Oldenburg: Schmidt, 1872).

Heitmüller, Wilhelm, *"Im Namen Jesu": eine sprach- u. religionsgeschichtliche Untersuchung zum Neuen Testament, speziell zur altchristlichen Taufe* (FRLANT 1/2; Göttingen: Vandenhoeck & Ruprecht, 1903).

–, *Taufe und Abendmahl bei Paulus: Darstellung und religionsgeschichtliche Beleuchtung* (Göttingen: Vandenhoeck & Ruprecht, 1903).

–, *Taufe und Abendmahl im Urchristentum* (Tübingen: J.C.B. Mohr (Paul Siebeck), 1911).

Hellemann, Wendy E., 'Philo of Alexandria on Deification and Assimilation to God', *SPA* 2 (1990), 51–71.

Hellerman, Joseph H., *The Ancient Church as Family* (Minneapolis: Fortress Press, 2001).

Hengel, Martin, *Judaism and Hellenism: Studies in their Encounter in Palestine during the Early Hellenistic Period*; 2 vols. (London: SCM Press, 1974); orig. publ.: *Judentum und Hellenismus: Studien zu ihrer Begegnung unter besonderer Berücksichtigung Palästinas bis zur Mitte des 2. Jh.s v. Chr.* (WUNT 10; Tübingen: J.C.B. Mohr (Paul Siebeck), 1969).

–, 'Qumrân und der Hellenismus', in M. Delcor (ed.), *Qumrân: Sa piété, sa théologie et son milieu* (BETL 46; Paris/Gembloux/Leuven: LUP, 1978), 333–72.

Hermann, Ingo, *Kyrios und Pneuma: Studien zur Christologie der paulinischen Hauptbriefe* (StANT 2; Munich: Kösel, 1961).

Hesse, Mary, 'Die kognitiven Ansprüche der Metaphern', in J.-P. van Noppen (ed.), *Erinnern, um Neues zu sagen: Die Bedeutung der Metapher für die religiöse Sprache* (Frankfurt: Athenäum, 1988), 128–48.

Hilberath, Bernd Jochen, *Pneumatologie* (LTh 23; Düsseldorf: Patmos, 1994).

Hill, David, *Greek Words with Hebrew Meanings: Studies in the Semantics of Soteriological Terms* (SNTSMS 5; Cambridge: Cambridge University Press, 1967).

Himmelfarb, Martha, *Ascent to Heaven in Jewish and Christian Apocalypses* (Oxford: Oxford University Press, 1993).

Hinde, Robert A., *Towards Understanding Relationships* (EMSP 18; London: Academic Press, 1979).

Hine, Virginia H., 'Pentecostal Glossolalia: Toward a Functional Interpretation', in W.E. Mills (ed.), *Speaking in Tongues: A Guide to Research on Glossolalia* (Grand Rapids: Eerdmans, 1986), 439–61.

Hoegen-Rohls, Christina, 'Κτίσις and καινὴ κτίσις in Paul's Letters', in A. Christophersen, C. Claußen, J. Frey, and B. Longenecker (eds.), *Paul, Luke and the Graeco-Roman world: Essays in Honour of Alexander J. M. Wedderburn* (JSNTSup 217; London: Sheffield Academic Press, 2002), 102–22.

Hoehner, Harold W., *Ephesians: An Exegetical Commentary* (Grand Rapids: Baker, 2002).

Hofius, Otfried, 'ἀββα', *ThBNT²*, 1721–22.

–, 'Wort Gottes und Glaube bei Paulus', in M. Hengel and U. Heckel (eds.), *Paulus und das antike Judentum: Tübingen-Durham-Symposium im Gedenken an den 50. Todestag Adolf Schlatters (19. Mai 1938)* (WUNT 58; Tübingen: J.C.B. Mohr (Paul Siebeck), 1991), 379–406.

–, 'Gesetz und Evangelium nach 2. Korinther 3', in O. Hofius, *Paulusstudien. Vol. 1* (WUNT 51; Tübingen: Mohr Siebeck, 1994²), 75–120.

Hollander, Harm W., and de Jonge, Marinus, *The Testaments of the Twelve Patriarchs: A Commentary* (SVTP 8; Leiden: Brill, 1985).

Holm-Nielsen, Svend, *Hodayot: Psalms from Qumran* (AThD 2; Aarhus: Universitetsforlaget, 1960).

Holsten, Carl, 'Die bedeutung des wortes σάρξ im lehrbegriff des Paulus (1855)', in C. Holsten, *Zum Evangelium des Paulus und des Petrus: Altes und Neues* (Rostock: Stiller'sche Hofbuchhandlung, 1868), 365–447.

Holtzmann, Heinrich Julius, *Lehrbuch der Neutestamentlichen Theologie. Vol. 2* (ed. by D.A. Jülicher and W. Bauer; Tübingen: J.C.B. Mohr (Paul Siebeck), 1911²).

Hooker, Morna D., *From Adam to Christ: Essays on Paul* (Cambridge: Cambridge University Press, 1990).

Horn, Christoph, *Antike Lebenskunst: Glück und Moral von Sokrates bis zu den Neuplatonikern* (BsR 1271; Munich: C. H. Beck, 1998).

Horn, Friedrich Wilhelm, 'Holy Spirit', *ABD*, III, 260–80.

–, *Das Angeld des Geistes: Studien zur paulinischen Pneumatologie* (FRLANT 154; Göttingen: Vandenhoeck & Ruprecht, 1992).

–, 'Wandel im Geist: Zur pneumatologischen Begründung der Ethik bei Paulus', *KD* 38 (1992), 149–70.

–, 'Zwischen Redaktionsgeschichte und urchristlicher Religionsgeschichte', in E.-M. Becker (ed.), *Neutestamentliche Wissenschaft: Autobiographische Essays aus der Evangelischen Theologie* (UTB 2475; Tübingen/Basel: Francke, 2003), 206–15.

Horrell, David G., *Solidarity and Difference: A Contemporary Reading of Paul's Ethics* (London: T. & T. Clark, 2005).

Horvath, Adam O., and Luborsky, Lester, 'The Role of the Therapeutic Alliance in Psychotherapy', *JCCP* 61 (1993), 561–73.

Hossfeld, Frank-Lothar, and Zenger, Erich, *Psalmen 51–100* (HThKAT; Freiburg: Herder, 2000).

Howard, James M., *Paul, the Community, and Progressive Sanctification: An Exploration into Community-Based Transformation within Pauline Theology* (SBL 90; New York: Lang, 2007).

Hubbard, Moyer V., 'Honey for Aseneth: Interpreting a Religious Symbol', *JSP* 16 (1997), 97–110.

–, *New Creation in Paul's Letters and Thought* (SNTSMS 119; Cambridge: Cambridge University Press, 2002).

Hübner, Hans, 'Zur Ethik der Sapienta Salomonis', in W. Schrage (ed.), *Studien zum Text und zur Ethik des Neuen Testaments* (BZNW 47; *FS* H. Greeven; Berlin/New York: W. de Gruyter, 1986), 166–87.

–, 'Der Heilige Geist in der Heiligen Schrift', *KD* 36 (1990), 181–208.

–, *Biblische Theologie des Neuen Testaments. Vol. 2: Die Theologie des Paulus und ihre neutestamentliche Wirkungsgeschichte*; 3 vols. (Göttingen: Vandenhoeck & Ruprecht, 1993).

–, 'Die Sapientia Salomonis und die antike Philosophie', in H. Hübner (ed.), *Die Weisheit Salomos im Horizont biblischer Theologie* (BThSt 22; Neukirchen-Vluyn: Neukirchener Verlag, 1993), 55–81.

–, *Die Weisheit Salomons: Liber Sapientiae Salomonis* (ATD Apokr. 4; Göttingen: Vandenhoeck & Ruprecht, 1999).

Hui, A. W. D., 'The Concept of the Holy Spirit in Ephesians and its Relation to the Pneu-
    matologies of Luke and Paul' (Aberdeen: Unpublished PhD Thesis, 1992).
Hulmi, Sini, *Paulus und Mose: Argumentation und Polemik in 2 Kor 3* (SFEG 77; Göttin-
    gen/Helsinki: Vandenhoeck & Ruprecht/Finnische Exegetische Gesellschaft, 1999).
Hultgård, Anders, *L'eschatologie des Testaments des Douze Patriarches. Vol. 1: Interpré-
    tation des textes* (AUU.HR 6; Uppsala: Almqvist & Wiksell, 1977).
Humphrey, Edith McEwan, *The Ladies and the Cities: Transformation and Apocalyptic
    Identity in Joseph and Aseneth, 4 Ezra, the Apocalypse and the Shepherd of Hermas*
    (JSPSup 17; Sheffield: Sheffield Academic Press, 1995).
–, 'On Bees and Best Guesses: The Problem of *Sitz im Leben* from Internal Evidence as
    Illustrated by *Joseph and Aseneth*', *CR.BS* 7 (1999), 223–36.
–, *Joseph and Aseneth* (GAP; Sheffield: Sheffield Academic Press, 2000).
Hurtado, Larry W., 'Does Philo Help Explain Christianity?', in R. Deines and K.-W.
    Niebuhr (eds.), *Philo und das Neue Testament: Wechselseitige Wahrnehmungen. I. In-
    ternationales Symposium zum Corpus Judaeo-Hellenisticum, 1.–4. Mai 2003, Eisen-
    ach/Jena* (WUNT 172; Tübingen: Mohr Siebeck, 2004), 73–92.
Inwood, Brad, 'Stoizismus', *DNP*, XI, 1013–18.
–, *Ethics and Human Action in Early Stoicism* (Oxford: Clarendon, 1985).
Isaacs, Marie E., *The Concept of the Spirit: A Study of Pneuma in Hellenistic Judaism
    and its Bearing on the New Testament* (London: Heythrop Monographs, 1976).
Israelstam, J., *Midrash Rabbah: Leviticus I–XIX. Translated under the Editorship of
    Rabbi H. Freedman and M. Simon* (London: Soncino, 1957).
Jackendoff, Ray, *Semantics and Cognition* (CSLS 8; London: MIT Press, 1995 [1983[1]]).
Jacoby, Hermann, *Neutestamentliche Ethik* (Königsberg: Thomas & Oppermann, 1899).
Janowski, Bernd, 'Der Mensch im alten Israel: Grundfragen alttestamentlicher Anthropo-
    logie', *ZTK* 102 (2005),
Jeremias, Joachim, *The Prayers of Jesus* (London: SCM Press, 1967).
Jervell, Jacob, *Imago Dei: Gen 1,26f. im Spätjudentum, in der Gnosis und in den pauli-
    nischen Briefen* (FRLANT 76/NF 58; Göttingen: Vandenhoeck & Ruprecht, 1960).
Jewett, Robert, *Paul's Anthropological Terms: A Study of their Use in Conflict Settings*
    (AGJU 10; Leiden: Brill, 1971).
–, 'The Question of the "Apportioned Spirit" in Paul's Letters: Romans as a Case Study',
    in G. Stanton, B.W. Longenecker, and S.C. Barton (eds.), *The Holy Spirit and Chris-
    tian Origins: Essays in Honor of James D. G. Dunn* (Grand Rapids/Cambridge: Eerd-
    mans, 2004), 193–206.
–, *Romans: A Commentary* (Hermeneia; Philadelphia/Edinburgh: Fortress/Alban, 2006).
Johnson, Luke Timothy, *Religious Experience in Earliest Christianity: A Missing Dimen-
    sion in New Testament Studies* (Minneapolis: Fortress, 1998).
–, *Among the Gentiles: Greco-Roman Religion and Christianity* (AYBRL;Yale University
    Press, 2009).
Johnston, G., '"Spirit" and "Holy Spirit" in the Qumran Literature', in H.K. McArthur
    (ed.), *New Testament Sidelights: Essays in Honor of Alexander Converse Purdy* (Hart-
    ford: HSFP, 1960), 27–42.
Jones, Larry Paul, *The Symbol of Water in the Gospel of John* (JSNTSup 145; Sheffield:
    Sheffield Academic Press, 1997).
Joyce, Paul, *Divine Initiative and Human Response in Ezekiel* (JSOTSup 51; Sheffield:
    Sheffield Academic Press, 1989).
Jüngel, Eberhard, *Paulus und Jesus: Eine Untersuchung zur Präzisierung der Frage nach
    dem Ursprung der Christologie* (HUT 2; Tübingen: J.C.B. Mohr (Paul Siebeck),
    1986[6]).
Juncker, Alfred, *Die Ethik des Apostels Paulus. Vol. 1* (Halle: Niemeyer, 1904).

Kaiser, Walter C., Jr., 'The Holy Spirit's Ministry in Personal Spiritual Development: Ephesians 5.15–21', in W. Ma and R.P. Menzies (eds.), *The Spirit and Spirituality: Essays in Honour of Russell P. Spittler* (JPTSup 24; London: T. & T. Clark, 2004), 62–68.

Kakkanattu, Joy Philip, *God's Enduring Love in the Book of Hosea: A Synchronic and Diachronic Analysis of Hosea 11,1–11* (FAT II/14; Tübingen: Mohr Siebeck, 2006).

Kamlah, Eberhard, and Klaiber, Walter, 'πνεῦμα', *ThBNT²*, 698–708.

Käsemann, Ernst, *Leib und Leib Christi: Eine Untersuchung zur paulinischen Begrifflichkeit* (BHT 9; Tübingen: J.C.B. Mohr (Paul Siebeck), 1933).

–, 'Das Abendmahl im Neuen Testament', in H. Asmussen, H. Gollwitzer, F.W. Hopf, E. Käsemann, and W. Niesel (eds.), *Abendmahlsgemeinschaft?* (BEvTh 3; Munich: Kaiser, 1937), 60–93.

–, 'Anliegen und Eigenart der paulinischen Abendmahlslehre', *EvT* 7 (1947/48), 263–83.

–, 'The Pauline Doctrine of the Lord's Supper', in E. Käsemann, *Essays on New Testament Themes* (SBT; London: SCM Press, 1964), 108–35; orig. publ.: 'Anliegen und Eigenart der paulinischen Abendmahlslehre', *EvTh* 7 (1947/48), 263–83.

–, 'On Paul's Anthropology', in E. Käsemann, *Perspectives on Paul* (London: SCM Press, 1971), 1–31; orig. publ.: 'Zur paulinischen Anthropologie', in E. Käsemann, *Paulinische Perspektiven* (Tübingen: J.C.B. Mohr (Paul Siebeck), 1969), 9–60.

–, *Commentary on Romans* (London: SCM Press, 1980); orig. publ.: *An die Römer* (Tübingen: J.C.B. Mohr (Paul Siebeck), 1973).

Keck, Leander E., 'Rethinking "New Testament Ethics"', *JBL* 115 (1996), 3–16.

–, *Romans* (ANTC; Nashville: Abingdon, 2005).

Kee, Howard Clark, 'Testaments of the Twelve Patriarchs: A New Translation and Introduction', *OTP*, I, 775–828.

Keener, Craig S., 'Family and Household', *DNTB*, 353–68.

–, *The Spirit in the Gospels and Acts: Divine Purity and Power* (Peabody: Hendrickson, 1997).

–, *1–2 Corinthians* (NCBC; Cambridge: Cambridge University Press, 2005).

Kelman, Herbert C., 'Compliance, Identification, and Internalization: Three Processes of Attitude Change', *JCR* 2 (1958), 51–60.

Kenney, Garrett C., *Translating H/holy S/spirit: 4 Models: Unitarian, Binitarian, Trinitarian, and Non-Sectarian* (Lanham: University Press of America, 2007).

Kim, Jung Hoon, *The Significance of Clothing Imagery in the Pauline Corpus* (JSNTSup 268; London: T. & T. Clark, 2004).

Kim, Seyoon, *Paul and the New Perspective: Second Thoughts on the Origin of Paul's Gospel* (Cambridge/Grand Rapids: Eerdmans, 2002).

Kirkpatrick, Lee A., and Shaver, Phillip R., 'An Attachment-Theoretical Approach to Romantic Love and Religious Belief', *PSPB* 18 (1992), 266–75.

Kittel, Gerhard, 'δόξα', *TDNT*, II, 233–53.

–, 'εἰκών', *TDNT*, II, 381–97.

Klatt, Werner, *Hermann Gunkel: Zu seiner Theologie der Religionsgeschichte und zur Entstehung der formgeschichtlichen Methode* (FRLANT 100; Göttingen: Vandenhoeck & Ruprecht, 1969).

Klauck, Hans-Josef, *Herrenmahl und hellenistischer Kult: Eine religionsgeschichtliche Untersuchung zum ersten Korintherbrief* (NTA NS 15; Münster: Aschendorff, 1986²).

Kleinknecht, Hermann, 'πνεῦμα, πνευματικός', *TDNT*, VI, 332–59.

Klinghardt, Matthias, 'Unum Corpus: Die genera corporum in der stoischen Physik und ihre Rezeption bis zum Neuplatonismus', in A. von Dobbeler (ed.), *Religionsgeschichte des Neuen Testaments* (FS K. Berger; Tübingen Francke 2000), 191–216.

Knibb, Michael A., *The Qumran Community* (CCWJCW 2; Cambridge: Cambridge University Press, 1987).

Knoch, Otto, *Der Geist Gottes und der neue Mensch: Der Heilige Geist als Grundkraft und Norm des christlichen Lebens in Kirche und Welt nach dem Zeugnis des Apostels Paulus* (Stuttgart: Katholisches Bibelwerk, 1993² [1975¹]).

Koch, Robert, *Der Geist Gottes im Alten Testament* (Frankfurt: Lang, 1991).

Koenig, John, *Charismata: God's Gifts for God's People* (BPCI; Philadelphia: Westminster Press, 1978).

–, 'The Knowing of Glory and its Consequences (2 Corinthians 3–5)', in R.T. Fortna and B.R. Gaventa (eds.), *The Conversation Continues: Studies in Paul and John in Honor of J. Louis Martyn* (Nashville: Abingdon, 1990), 158–69.

Koester, Craig R., *Symbolism in the Fourth Gospel: Meaning, Mystery, Community* (Minneapolis: Fortress, 1995).

Köhler, Ludwig, *Hebrew Man: Lectures Delivered at the Invitation of the University of Tübingen, December 1–16, 1952* (London: SCM Press, 1956).

Konstan, David, *Friendship in the Classical World* (KTAH; Cambridge: Cambridge University Press, 1997).

Koperski, Veronica, *The Knowledge of Christ Jesus my Lord: The High Christology of Philippians 3:7–11* (CBET 16; Kampen: Pharos, 1996).

Kourie, C., 'Christ-Mysticism in Paul', *The Way Supplement* 102 (2001), 71–80.

Kraemer, Ross Shephard, *When Aseneth Met Joseph: A Late Antique Tale of the Biblical Patriarch and His Egyptian Wife, Reconsidered* (Oxford: Oxford University Press, 1998).

Kraftchick, Steven J., 'Death's Parsing: Experience as a Mode of Theology in Paul', in J.C. Anderson, P. Sellew, and C. Setzer (eds.), *Pauline Conversations in Context: Essays in Honor of Calvin J. Roetzel* (JSNTSup 221; Sheffield: Sheffield Academic Press, 2002), 144–66.

Kümmel, Werner Georg, *The Theology of the New Testament: According to Its Major Witnesses, Jesus – Paul – John* (London: SCM Press, 1974).

–, *Römer 7 und das Bild des Menschen im Neuen Testament: Zwei Studien* (TB 53; Munich: Kaiser, 1974 [1929¹]).

–, 'Albert Schweitzer als Paulusforscher', in W.G. Kümmel (ed.), *Heilsgeschehen und Geschichte. Vol. 2* (Gesammelte Aufsätze; Marburg: Elwert, 1978), 215–31.

Kuschnerus, Bernd, *Die Gemeinde als Brief Christi: Die kommunikative Funktion der Metapher bei Paulus am Beispiel von 2 Kor 2–5* (FRLANT 197; Göttingen: Vandenhoeck & Ruprecht, 2002).

Kuss, Otto, *Der Römerbrief. Vol. 2 (Röm 6,11 bis 8,19)* (Regensburg: Pustet, 1963²).

Kvalvaag, Robert W., 'The Spirit in Human Beings in Some Qumran Non-Biblical Texts', in F.H. Cryer and T.L. Thompson (eds.), *Qumran between the Old and New Testaments* (JSOTSup 290; Sheffield: Sheffield Academic Press, 1998), 159–80.

Kynes, William L., 'New Birth', *DJG*, 574–76.

Ladd, George Eldon, *A Theology of the New Testament* (Grand Rapids: Eerdmans, 1993²).

LaFollette, Hugh, *Personal Relationships: Love, Identity, and Morality* (Oxford: Blackwell, 1996).

Lake, Kirsopp, 'The Holy Spirit', in F.J.F. Jackson and H.J. Cadbury (eds.), *The Beginnings of Christianity. Part I: The Acts of the Apostles. Vol. 5* (Grand Rapids: Baker, 1979 [1933¹]), 96–111.

Lakoff, George, 'The Contemporary Theory of Metaphor', in A. Ortony (ed.), *Metaphor and Thought* (Cambridge: Cambridge University Press, 1993²), 202–51.

Lambert, Michael J., and Barley, Dean E., 'Research Summary on the Therapeutic Relationship and Psychotherapy Outcome', *Psychotherapy* 38 (2001), 357–61.

Lambrecht, Jan, 'Transformation in 2 Cor 3,18', *Bib* 64 (1983), 243–54.

Lampe, Peter, 'Identification with Christ: A Psychological View of Pauline Theology', in T. Fornberg and D. Hellholm (eds.), *Texts and Contexts: Biblical Texts in Their Textual and Situational Contexts. Essays in Honor of Lars Hartman* (Oslo: Scandinavian University Press, 1995), 931–43.

Landmesser, Christof, 'Der Geist und die christliche Existenz: Anmerkungen zur paulinischen Pneumatologie im Anschluß an Röm 8,1–11', in U.H.J. Körtner and A. Klein (eds.), *Die Wirklichkeit des Geistes: Konzeptionen und Phänomene des Geistes in Philosophie und Theologie der Gegenwart* (Neukirchen-Vluyn: Neukirchener Verlag, 2006), 129–52.

Lang, Friedrich, *Die Briefe an die Korinther* (NTD 7; Göttingen: Vandenhoeck & Ruprecht, 1994[17] [1986[1]]).

–, 'Das Verständnis der Taufe bei Paulus', in J. Ådna, S.J. Hafemann, and O. Hofius (eds.), *Evangelium – Schriftauslegung – Kirche: Festschrift für Peter Stuhlmacher zum 65. Geburtstag* (Göttingen: Vandenhoeck & Ruprecht, 1997), 255–68.

Lange, Stella, 'The Wisdom of Solomon and Plato', *JBL* 55 (1936), 293–302.

Lapidge, Michael, 'Stoic Cosmology', in J.M. Rist (ed.), *The Stoics* (MTS 1; Berkeley: University of California Press, 1978), 161–85.

Lapsley, Jacqueline E., *Can these Bones Live? The Problem of the Moral Self in the Book of Ezekiel* (BZAW 301; Berlin/New York: W. de Gruyter, 2000).

Lattke, Michael, 'Die Oden Salomos: Einleitungsfragen und Forschungsgeschichte', *ZNW* 98 (2007), 277–307.

Lauha, Risto, *Psychophysischer Sprachgebrauch im Alten Testament: Eine Strukturalsemantische Analyse von לב, נפש und רוח* (AASF.DHL 35; Helsinki: Tiedeakatemia, 1983).

Laurenceau, Jean-Philippe, and Kleinman, Brighid M., 'Intimacy in Personal Relationships', in A.L. Vangelisti and D. Perlman (eds.), *The Cambridge Handbook of Personal Relationships* (Cambridge: Cambridge University Press, 2006), 637–53.

Laurentin, André, 'Le Pneuma dans la Doctrine de Philon', *ETL* 27 (1951), 390–437.

Leaney, A. R. C., *The Rule of Qumran and Its Meaning* (London: SCM Press, 1966).

Lee, Dorothy A., *The Symbolic Narratives of the Fourth Gospel: The Interplay of Form and Meaning* (JSNTSup 95; Sheffield: Sheffield Academic Press, 1994).

Lee, Michelle V., *Paul, the Stoics, and the Body of Christ* (SNTSMS 137; Cambridge: Cambridge University Press, 2006).

Leezenberg, Michiel, *Contexts of Metaphor: Semantic and Conceptual Aspects of Figurative Language Interpretation* (ILLCDS 1995–17; Amsterdam: Elsevier, 1995).

Lehmkühler, Karsten, *Kultus und Theologie: Dogmatik und Exegese in der religionsgeschichtlichen Schule* (FSÖT 76; Göttingen: Vandenhoeck & Ruprecht, 1996).

–, *Inhabitatio: Die Einwohnung Gottes im Menschen* (FSÖT 104; Göttingen: Vandenhoeck & Ruprecht, 2004).

Leisegang, Hans, *Der Heilige Geist: Das Wesen und Werden der mystisch-intuitiven Erkenntnis in der Philosophie und Religion der Griechen, I/1: Die vorchristlichen Anschauungen und Lehren vom ΠΝΕΥΜΑ und der mystisch-intuitiven Erkenntnis* (Leipzig: Teubner, 1919).

Levin, Samuel R., 'Language, Concepts, and Worlds: Three Domains of Metaphor', in A. Ortony (ed.), *Metaphor and Thought* (Cambridge: Cambridge University Press, 1993[2]), 112–23.

Levine, Lee I., *Judaism and Hellenism in Antiquity: Conflict or Confluence?* (Seattle: UWP, 1998).

Levison, John R., 'Inspiration and the Divine Spirit in the Writings of Philo Judaeus', *JSJ* 26 (1995), 271–323.

–, *The Spirit in First Century Judaism* (AGJU 29; Leiden: Brill, 1997).

–, 'Philo's Personal Experience and the Persistence of Prophecy', in M.H. Floyd and R.D. Haak (eds.), *Prophets, Prophecy, and Prophetic Texts in Second Temple Judaism* (LHB/OTS 427; New York/London: T. & T. Clark, 2006), 194–209.

–, 'The Spirit and the Temple in Paul's Letters to the Corinthians', in S.E. Porter (ed.), *Paul and His Theology* (PS 3; Leiden: Brill, 2006), 189–215.

–, *Filled with the Spirit* (Grant Rapids/Cambridge: Eerdmans, 2009).

Lewis, John G., *Looking for Life: The Role of "Theo-Ethical Reasoning" in Paul's Religion* (JSNTSup 291; London: T. & T. Clark, 2005).

Lewy, Hans, *Sobria Ebrietas: Untersuchungen zur Geschichte der antiken Mystik* (BZNW 9; Gießen: Toepelmann, 1929).

Lichtenberger, Hermann, *Studien zum Menschenbild in Texten der Qumrangemeinde* (SUNT 15; Göttingen: Vandenhoeck & Ruprecht, 1980).

–, *Das Ich Adams und das Ich der Menschheit: Studien zum Menschenbild in Römer 7* (WUNT 164; Tübingen: Mohr Siebeck, 2004).

Lietzmann, Hans, *An die Korinther I/II* (HNT 9; Tübingen: J.C.B. Mohr (Paul Siebeck), 1969⁵).

Lincoln, Andrew T., *Paradise Now and Not Yet: Studies in the Role of the Heavenly Dimension in Paul's Thought with Special Reference to his Eschatology* (SNTSMS 43; Cambridge: Cambridge University Press, 1981).

–, *Ephesians* (WBC 42; Dallas: Word, 1990).

Locke, John, *An Essay Concerning Human Understanding* (Edited with an Introduction, Critical Apparatus and Glossary by P.H. Nidditch; Oxford: Clarendon, 1975).

Löhr, Hermut, 'Paulus und der Wille zur Tat: Beobachtungen zu einer frühchristlichen Theologie als Anweisung zur Lebenskunst', *ZNW* 98 (2007), 165–88.

Lohse, Eduard, 'πρόσωπον', *TDNT*, VI, 768–79.

–, *Der Brief an die Römer* (KeK; Göttingen: Vandenhoeck & Ruprecht, 2003).

–, (ed.), *Die Texte aus Qumran: hebräisch und deutsch, mit masoretischer Punktation, Übersetzung, Einführung und Anmerkungen* (Munich: Kösel, 1981²).

Long, A. A., *Hellenistic Philosophy: Stoics, Epicureans, Sceptics* (London: Duckworth, 1974).

–, *Stoic Studies* (Cambridge: Cambridge University Press, 1996).

Long, A. A., and Sedley, D.N., *The Hellenistic Philosophers. Vol. 1: Translation of the Principal Sources, with Philosophical Commentary* (Cambridge: Cambridge University Press, 2001 [1987¹]).

Longenecker, Bruce W., *The Triumph of Abraham's God: The Transformation of Identity in Galatians* (Edinburgh: T. & T. Clark, 1998).

Longenecker, Richard N., *Galatians* (WBC 41; Dallas: Word, 1990).

Longrigg, James, *Greek Medicine From the Heroic to the Hellenistic Age – A Source Book* (London: Duckworth, 1998).

Lüdemann, Hermann, *Die Anthropologie des Apostels Paulus und ihre Stellung innerhalb seiner Heilslehre. Nach den vier Hauptbriefen* (Kiel: Universitäts-Buchhandlung, 1872).

Luz, Ulrich, 'Paul as Mystic', in G. Stanton, B.W. Longenecker, and S.C. Barton (eds.), *The Holy Spirit and Christian Origins: Essays in Honor of James D. G. Dunn* (Grand Rapids/Cambridge: Eerdmans, 2004), 131–43.

Lynch, John Patrick, *Aristotle's School: A Study of a Greek Educational Institution* (London: UCP, 1972).

Machamer, Peter, 'The Meaning of Metaphor: A Plea for Understanding', in T. Borsche, J. Kreuzer, and C. Strub (eds.), *Blick und Bild im Spannungsfeld von Sehen, Metaphern und Verstehen* (SAM III; Munich: Fink, 1998), 247–63.

Malherbe, Abraham J., 'God's New Family in Thessalonica', in L.M. White and O.L. Yarbrough (eds.), *The Social World of the First Christians: Essays in Honor of Wayne A. Meeks* (Minneapolis: Fortress Press, 1995), 116–25.

Malina, Bruce J., and Neyrey, Jerome H., *Portraits of Paul: An Archaeology of Ancient Personality* (Louisville: Westminster John Knox Press, 1996).

Malina, Bruce J., and Pilch, John J., *Social-Science Commentary on the Letters of Paul* (Minneapolis: Fortress Press, 2006).

Maloney, H. Newton, and Lovekin, A. Adams, *Glossolalia: Behavioural Science Perspectives on Speaking in Tongues* (Oxford: Oxford University Press, 1985).

Mansoor, Menahem, *The Thanksgiving Hymns* (STDJ 3; Leiden: Brill, 1961).

Marshall, I. Howard, *New Testament Theology: Many Witnesses, One Gospel* (Downers Grove: IVP, 2004).

Marshall, L. H., *The Ethics of the New Testament* (London: Macmillan, 1960).

Martin, Dale B., *The Corinthian Body* (New Haven/London: Yale University Press, 1995).

Martin, Ralph P., *2 Corinthians* (WBC 40; Dallas: Word, 1986).

Martin, Troy W., 'Paul's Pneumatological Statements and Ancient Medical Texts', in J. Fotopoulos (ed.), *The New Testament and Early Christian Literature in Greco-Roman Context: Studies in Honor of David E. Aune* (SNT 122; Leiden: Brill, 2006), 105–26.

Martinich, A. P., 'Metaphor', *REPh*, VI, 335–38.

Martyn, J. Louis, 'The Abrahamic Covenant, Christ, and the Church', in J.L. Martyn, *Theological Issues in the Letters of Paul* (SNTW; Edinburgh: T&T Clark, 1997), 161–75.

–, *Galatians: A New Translation with Introduction and Commentary* (AB 33A; New York: Doubleday, 1997).

Maschmeier, Jens-Christian, *Rechtfertigung bei Paulus: Eine Kritik alter und neuer Paulusperspektiven* (BWANT 189; Stuttgart: Kohlhammer, 2010).

Mau, Jürgen (ed.), *Plutarchi Moralia. Vol. 5.2/1* (BSGRT; Leipzig: Teubner, 1971).

Mauerhofer, Erich, *Der Kampf zwischen Fleisch und Geist bei Paulus: Ein Beitrag zur Klärung der Frage nach der Stellung des Gläubigen zur Sünde im paulinischen Heiligungs- und Vollkommenheitsverständnis* (Frutingen: Trachsel, 1980).

McAdams, Dan P., 'Motivation and Friendship', in S. Duck and D. Perlman (eds.), *Understanding Personal Relationships: An Interdisciplinary Approach* (London: SAGE, 1985), 85–105.

McCall, R. E., 'Substance', *NCE*, XIII, 766–70.

McDonnel, Kilian, and Montague, George T., *Christian Initiation and Baptism in the Holy Spirit: Evidence from the First Eight Centuries* (Collegeville: Liturgical Press, 1991).

McFague, Sallie, *Metaphorical Theology: Models of God in Religious Language* (Philadelphia: Fortress, 1982).

Meeks, Wayne A., *The Prophet-King: Moses Traditions and the Johannine Christology* (NovTSup 14; Leiden: Brill, 1967).

–, *The Origins of Christian Morality: The First Two Centuries* (New Haven: Yale University Press, 1993).

Meier, Hans-Christoph, *Mystik bei Paulus: Zur Phänomenologie religiöser Erfahrung im Neuen Testament* (TANZ 26; Tübingen: Francke, 1998).

Mell, Ulrich, *Neue Schöpfung: Eine traditionsgeschichtliche und exegetische Studie zu einem soteriologischen Grundsatz* (BZNW 56; Berlin/New York: W. de Gruyter, 1989).

Menzies, Robert P., *The Development of Early Christian Pneumatology – With Special Reference to Luke-Acts* (JSNTSup 54; Sheffield: JSOT Press, 1991).

–, 'A Fitting Tribute: A Review Essay of *The Holy Spirit and Christian Origins: Essays in Honor of James D. G. Dunn*', *Pneuma* 28 (2006), 131–40.

Metzger, Bruce M., *A Textual Commentary on the Greek New Testament* (Stuttgart: Deutsche Bibelgesellschaft, 1994²).

Michel, Otto, *Der Brief an die Römer* (KEK IV; Göttingen: Vandenhoeck & Ruprecht, 1978⁵).

Migne, J.-P. (ed.), *Patrum Aegyptiorum Opera Omnia: Praecedunt Philonis Carpasii, Asterii Amaseni, Nemesii Emeseni, Hieronymi Graeci Scripta Quae Supersunt* (PCC: SG 40; Lutetiae Parisiorum: Migne, 1863²).

Miller, George A., 'Images and Models, Similes and Metaphors', in A. Ortony (ed.), *Metaphor and Thought* (Cambridge: Cambridge University Press, 1993²), 357–400.

Miller, James C., 'The Jewish Context of Paul's Gentile Mission', *TynBul* 58 (2007), 101–15.

Mommsen, Theodor, and Watson, Alan (eds.), *The Digest of Justinian*; 4 vols. (Latin Text ed. by Th. Mommsen and P. Krueger, English Translation ed. by A. Watson; Philadelphia: University of Pennsylvania Press, 1985).

Moo, Douglas, *The Epistle to the Romans* (NICNT; Grand Rapids/Cambridge: Eerdmans, 1996).

Mooij, J. J. A., *A Study of Metaphor: On the Nature of Metaphorical Expressions, with Special Reference to Their Reference* (N-HLS 27; Oxford: North-Holland, 1976).

Morales, Rodrigo José, 'The Spirit and the Restoration of Israel: New Exodus and New Creation Motifs in Galatians' (Duke University: Unpublished PhD Thesis, 2007). [published in WUNT II/282; Tübingen: Mohr Siebeck, 2010]

Morray-Jones, C. R. A., 'Transformational Mysticism in the Apocalyptic-Merkabah Tradition', *JJS* 43 (1992), 1–31.

Motyer, Steve, '"Not Apart from Us" (Hebrews 11:40): Physical Community in the Letter to the Hebrews', *EQ* 77 (2005), 235–47.

Moule, C. F. D., *The Holy Spirit* (London: Mowbrays, 1978).

Müller, C. D., *Die Erfahrung der Wirklichkeit: Hermeneutisch-Exegetische Versuche mit besonderer Berücksichtigung alttestamentlicher und paulinischer Theologie* (Gütersloh: Mohn, 1978).

Müller, Peter, *In der Mitte der Gemeinde: Kinder im Neuen Testament* (Neukirchen-Vluyn: Neukirchener Verlag, 1992).

–, 'Gottes Kinder: Zur Metaphorik der Gotteskindschaft im Neuen Testament', *JBTh* 17 (2002), 141–61.

Munzinger, André, *Discerning the Spirits: Theological and Ethical Hermeneutics in Paul* (SNTSMS 140; Cambridge: Cambridge University Press, 2007).

Myrick, Anthony A., '"Father" Imagery in 2 Corinthians 1–9 and Jewish Paternal Tradition', *TynBul* 47 (1996), 163–71.

Neher, Martin, *Wesen und Wirken der Weisheit in der Sapientia Salomonis* (BZAW 333; Berlin/New York: W. de Gruyter, 2004).

Neugebauer, Fritz, 'Das paulinische "In Christo"', *NTS* 4 (1957/58), 124–38.

Neusner, Jacob, and Green, William Scott (eds.), *Dictionary of Judaism in the Biblical Period: 450 B.C.E. to 600 C.E.*; 2 vols. (New York: Macmillan, 1996).

Newman, Carey C., *Paul's Glory-Christology: Tradition and Rhetoric* (NovTSup 69; Leiden: Brill, 1992).

Newsom, Carol A., 'The Sage in the Literature of Qumran: The Functions of the *Maśkil*', in J.G. Gammie and L.G. Perdue (eds.), *The Sage in Israel and the Ancient Near East* (Winona Lake: Eisenbrauns, 1990), 372–82.

Neyrey, Jerome H., SJ, *Render to God: New Testament Understandings of the Divine* (Minneapolis: Fortress Press, 2004).

Nguyen, V. Henry T., *Christian Identity in Corinth: A Comparative Study of 2 Corinthians, Epictetus and Valerius Maximus* (WUNT II/243; Tübingen: Mohr Siebeck, 2008).

Nickelsburg, George W. E., *Jewish Literature Between the Bible and the Mishnah: A Historical and Literary Introduction* (Philadelphia: Fortress, 1981).

Nilsson, Martin P., *Geschichte der Griechischen Religion, II: Die Hellenistische und Römische Zeit* (Munich: Beck'sche Verlagsbuchhandlung, 1961²).

Noack, Christian, *Gottesbewußtsein: Exegetische Studien zur Soteriologie und Mystik bei Philo von Alexandria* (WUNT II/116; Tübingen: Mohr Siebeck, 2000).

Nussbaum, Martha, *Aristotle's De Motu Animalum* (Princeton: Princeton University Press, 1978).

–, *The Therapy of Desire: Theory and Practice in Hellenistic Ethics* (Princeton: Princeton University Press, 1994).

Nygren, Anders, *Commentary on Romans* (Philadelphia: Fortress Press, 1972 [1949¹]).

O'Brien, Peter T., *The Epistle to the Philippians: A Commentary on the Greek Text* (NIGTC; Grand Rapids: Eerdmans, 1991).

O'Donnel, Matthew Brook, 'Two Opposing Views on Baptism with/by the Holy Spirit and of 1 Corinthians 12.13: Can Grammatical Investigation Bring Clarity?', in S.E. Porter and A.R. Cross (eds.), *Baptism, the New Testament and the Church: Historical and Contemporary Studies in Honour of R.E.O. White* (JSNTSup 171; Sheffield: Sheffield Academic Press, 2000), 311–36.

Oegema, Gebern S., 'Das Buch der Jubiläen', in G.S. Oegema (ed.), *Unterweisung in erzählender Form* (JSHRZ IV 1,2; Gütersloh: Gütersloher Verlagshaus, 2005), 78–96.

Orr, William Fridell, and Walther, James Arthur, *1 Corinthians* (AB 32; Garden City: Doubleday, 1976).

Osiek, Carolyn, 'Relatedness', in J.J. Pilch and B.J. Malina (eds.), *Handbook of Biblical Social Values* (Peabody: Hendrickson, 1998), 176–78.

Ostmeyer, Karl-Heinrich, *Kommunikation mit Gott und Christus: Sprache und Theologie des Gebetes im Neuen Testament* (WUNT 197; Tübingen: Mohr Siebeck, 2006).

Padgett, Alan G., 'The Body in Resurrection: Science and Scripture on the "Spiritual Body" (1 Cor 15:35–58)', *WW* 22 (2002), 155–63.

Paige, Terence, 'Who Believes in "Spirit"? Πνεῦμα in Pagan Usage and Implications for the Gentile Christian Mission', *HTR* 95 (2002), 417–36.

Pannenberg, Wolfhart, *Systematische Theologie. Vol. 1* (Göttingen: Vandenhoeck & Ruprecht, 1988).

Park, Chang-Kun, 'Das Verhältnis zwischen theologischem und anthropolgischem Pneumabegriff bei Paulus' (University of Hamburg: Unpublished PhD Thesis, 1982).

Parsons, Michael, 'Being Precedes Act: Indicative and Imperative in Paul's Writing', in B.S. Rosner (ed.), *Understanding Paul's Ethics: Twentieth-Century Approaches* (Grand Rapids: Eerdmans, 1995), 217–47; orig. publ.: 'Being Precedes Act: Indicative and Imperative in Paul's Writing', *EQ* 88 (1988), 99–127.

Pascher, Joseph, *Η ΒΑΣΙΛΙΚΗ ΟΔΟΣ: Der Königsweg zu Wiedergeburt und Vergottung bei Philon von Alexandreia* (SGKA 17–3/4; Paderborn: Schöningh, 1931).

Pearson, B. A., *The Pneumatikos-Psychikos Terminology in 1 Corinthians: A Study in the Theology of the Corinthian Opponents of Paul and its Relation to Gnosticism* (SBLDS 12; Missoula: Scholars Press, 1973).

Pervo, Richard I., 'Joseph and Aseneth and the Greek Novel', *SBLSP* 112 (1976), 171–81.

Peterson, Erik, 'Der Gottesfreund: Beiträge zur Geschichte eines religiösen Terminus', *ZKG* 42 (1923), 161–202.

–, *Der erste Brief an die Korinther und Paulus-Studien* (ed. by H.-U. Weidemann; AS 7; Würzburg: Echter, 2006).

Petrenko, Ester A. G. D., '"Created in Christ Jesus for Good Works": The Integration of Soteriology and Ethics in Ephesians' (University of Durham: Unpublished PhD Thesis, 2005). [published in PBM; Milton Keynes: Paternoster, 2011]

Pfister, Willibald, OP, *Das Leben im Geist nach Paulus: Der Geist als Anfang und Vollendung des christlichen Lebens* (SF II/34; Freiburg: Universitätsverlag, 1963).

Pfleiderer, Otto, 'Das paulinische πνεῦμα: Eine exegetisch-dogmatische Studie', *ZWT* 14 (1871), 161–82.

–, *Paulinism: A Contribution to the History of Primitive Christian Theology. Vol. 1: Exposition of Paul's Doctrine* (London: Williams and Norgate, 1877); orig. publ.: *Der Paulinismus: Ein Beitrag zur Geschichte der Urchristlichen Theologie* (Leipzig: Hinrichs, 1873).

–, *Primitive Christianity: Its Writings and Teachings in their Historical Connections. Vol. 1* (Clifton: Reference Book Publishers, 1965); orig. publ.: *Das Urchristentum, seine Schriften und Lehren im geschichtlichen Zusammenhang* (Berlin: Reimer, 1902² [1887¹]).

–, *Lectures on the Influence of the Apostle Paul on the Development of Christianity. The Hibbert Lectures, Delivered in London and Oxford, 1885* (London: Williams and Norgate, 1897³).

Philip, Finny, *The Origins of Pauline Pneumatology: The Eschatological Bestowal of the Spirit upon Gentiles in Judaism and in the Early Development of Paul's Theology* (WUNT II/194; Tübingen: Mohr Siebeck, 2005).

Philonenko, Marc, *Joseph et Aséneth: Introduction, Texte Critique, Traduction et Notes* (SPB 13; Leiden: Brill, 1968).

Pinnock, Clark Harold, 'The Concept of the Spirit in the Epistles of Paul' (Manchester University: Unpublished PhD Thesis, 1963).

–, *Flame of Love: A Theology of the Holy Spirit* (Downers Grove: IVP, 1996).

Pohlenz, Max, 'Stoa und Semitismus', *JWJ* 2 (1926), 257–69.

–, *Die Stoa: Geschichte einer geistigen Bewegung. Vol. 2* (Göttingen: Vandenhoeck & Ruprecht, 1964³).

Porter, Stanley E., 'Holiness, Sanctification', *DPL*, 397–402.

–, *Idioms of the Greek New Testament* (Biblical Languages: Greek 2; Sheffield: JSOT Press, 1994²).

Prager, Karen J., *The Psychology of Intimacy* (GSPR; London: Guilford, 1995).

Preisigke, F., *Die Gotteskraft in der frühchristlichen Zeit* (PH 6; Berlin: W. de Gruyter, 1922).

Preß, Michael, *Jesus und der Geist: Grundlagen einer Geist-Christologie* (Neukirchen-Vluyn: Neukirchener Verlag, 2001).

Price, Simon, 'Delphi and Divination', in P.E. Easterling and J. Muir (eds.), *Greek Religion and Society* (Cambridge: Cambridge University Press, 1985), 128–54.

Prümm, Karl, *Diakonia Pneumatos: Der Zweite Korintherbrief als Zugang zur apostolischen Botschaft. Vol. II/1: Apostolat und christliche Wirklichkeit: Theologie des ersten Briefteils, Kap. 1–7* (Freiburg: Herder, 1960).

–, *Diakonia Pneumatos: Theologische Auslegung des zweiten Korintherbriefes. Vol. I* (Freiburg: Herder, 1967).

Pryke, J., '"Spirit" and "Flesh" in the Qumran Documents and Some New Testament Texts', *RevQ* 19 (1965), 345–60.

Puech, E., 'L'Esprit Saint à Qumrân', *SBFLA* 49 (1999), 283–97.

Pulver, Max, 'Das Erlebnis des Pneuma bei Philon', *ErJb* 13 (1945), 111–32.

Rabens, Volker, 'The Development of Pauline Pneumatology: A Response to F.W. Horn', *BZ* 43 (1999), 161–79.

–, 'Transforming Relationships: The Spirit's Empowering for Religious-Ethical Life According to the Apostle Paul' (18th British New Testament Conference, London: Unpublished Paper, 2000).

–, 'Coming Out: "Bible-Based" Identity Formation in 2 Corinthians 6:14–7:1', in U. Rembold and R.G. Czapla (eds.), *Gotteswort und Menschenrede: Die Bibel im Dialog mit Wissenschaften, Künsten und Medien* (JIG 73; Bern/Oxford/New York: Lang, 2006), 43–66.

–, 'Review of J.A. Bertone, *'The Law of the Spirit': Experience of the Spirit and Displacement of the Law in Romans 8:1–16'*, *RBL* [http://www.bookreviews.org] (2007), 1–6.

–, 'Review of M. Christoph, *Pneuma und das neue Sein der Glaubenden: Studien zur Semantik und Pragmatik der Rede von Pneuma in Röm 8'*, *RBL* [http://www.bookreviews.org] (2007), 1–5.

–, 'Geistes-Geschichte: Die Rede vom Geist im Horizont der griechisch-römischen und jüdisch-hellenistischen Literatur', *ZNT* 25 (2010), 46–55.

–, 'Begeisternde Spiritualität: Geisterfahrungen im Leben der paulinischen Gemeinden', *GlLern* 26 (2011), 133–47.

–, 'Ephesians', in M.D. Coogan (ed.), *The Oxford Encyclopedia of the Books of the Bible. Vol. 1* (New York/Oxford: Oxford University Press, 2011), 237–43.

–, 'Johannine Perspectives on Ethical Enabling in the Context of Stoic and Philonic Ethics', in J. van der Watt and R. Zimmermann (eds.), *Rethinking the Ethics of John: "Implicit Ethics" in the Johannine Writings* (Kontexte und Normen neutestamentlicher Ethik / Contexts and Norms of New Testament Ethics III; WUNT I/291; Tübingen: Mohr Siebeck, 2012), 114–39.

–, 'Power from In Between: The Relational Experience of the Holy Spirit and Spiritual Gifts in Paul's Churches', in I.H. Marshall, V. Rabens, and C. Bennema (eds.), *The Spirit and Christ in the New Testament and Christian Theology: Essays in Honor of Max Turner* (Grand Rapids: Eerdmans, 2012), 138–55.

–, 'Philo's Attractive Ethics on the 'Religious Market' of Ancient Alexandria', in P. Wick and V. Rabens (eds.), *Religions and Trade: Religious Formation, Transformation and Cross-Cultural Exchange between East and West* (DHR 5; Leiden: Brill, 2013), forthcoming.

–, 'Review of David M. Litwa, *We Are Being Transformed: Deification in Paul's Soteriology'*, *TLZ* 138 (2013), 446–48.

–, 'The Spirit in Paul's First Epistle to the Thessalonians', in K. Warrington and T.J. Burke (eds.), *A Biblical Theology of the Spirit* (London: SPCK, 2013), forthcoming.

–, 'Ethics and the Spirit in Paul (1): Religious-Ethical Empowerment through Infusion-Transformation?', *ExpTim* 125.5 (2014), forthcoming, published OnlineFirst, June 5, 2013, DOI: 10.1177/0014524613492668.

–, 'Ethics and the Spirit in Paul (2): Religious-Ethical Empowerment through the Relational Work of the Spirit', *ExpTim* 125.6 (2014), forthcoming, published OnlineFirst, June 5, 2013, DOI: 10.1177/0014524613492672.

–, '"Indicative and Imperative" as Substructure of Paul's Theology-and-Ethics in Galatians? A Discussion of Divine and Human Agency in Paul's Letter to the Churches in Galatia', in N.T. Wright, S.J. Hafemann, and M.W. Elliott (eds.), *Galatians and Christian Theology* (Grand Rapids: Baker Academic, 2014), forthcoming.

–, '*Pneuma* and the Beholding of God – Reading Paul in the Context of Philonic Mystical Traditions', in J. Frey and J.R. Levison (eds.), *Historical Contexts of the Early Christian Notion of the Spirit* (Ekstasis; Berlin/New York: De Gruyter, 2014), forthcoming.

Radice, Roberto, 'Observations on the Theory of the Ideas as Thoughts of God in Philo', *SPA* 3 (1991), 126–34.

Reinhard, Wilhelm, *Das Wirken des heiligen Geistes im Menschen nach den Briefen des Apostels Paulus: Eine biblisch-theologische Untersuchung* (FTS 22; Freiburg: Herder, 1918).

Reinhartz, Adele, 'Parents and Children: A Philonic Perspective', in S.J.D. Cohen (ed.), *The Jewish Family in Antiquity* (BJS 289; Atlanta: Scholars Press, 1993), 61–88.

Reis, Harry T., and Shaver, Phillip, 'Intimacy as an Interpersonal Process', in S.W. Duck (ed.), *Handbook of Personal Relationships: Theory, Research and Interventions* (Chichester: Wiley & Sons, 1988), 367–89.

Reitzenstein, Richard, *Hellenistic Mystery-Religions: Their Basic Ideas and Significance* (PTMS 15; Pittsburgh: Pickwick, 1978); orig. publ.: *Die hellenistischen Mysterienreligionen: Nach ihren Grundgedanken und Wirkungen* (Leipzig: Teubner, 1927³).

Richardson, Neil, *Paul's Language about God* (JSNTSup 99; Sheffield: Sheffield Academic Press, 1994).

Ricœur, Paul, *Interpretation Theory: Discourse and Surplus of Meaning* (Forth Worth: Texas Christian University Press, 1976).

–, 'The Narrative Function', *Semeia* 13 (1978), 177–202.

–, *The Rule of Metaphor: Multi-disciplinary Studies of the Creation of Meaning in Language* (London/Henley: Routledge & Kegan Paul, 1978).

Rist, John M., 'On Greek Biology, Greek Cosmology and Some Sources of Theological Pneuma', in J.M. Rist, *Man, Soul and Body: Essays in Ancient Thought from Plato to Dionysius* (CS 549; Aldershot/Brookfield: Variorum, 1996), 27–47.

Ritter, Joachim (ed.), *Historisches Wörterbuch der Philosophie*; 13 vols. (Darmstadt: Wissenschaftliche Buchgesellschaft, 1971–2007).

Robson, James Edward, 'Word and Spirit in Ezekiel' (Middlesex University: Unpublished PhD Thesis, 2004).

–, *Word and Spirit in Ezekiel* (LHB/OTS 447; London/New York: T. & T. Clark, 2006).

Rogers, Carl R., *On Becoming a Person: A Therapist's View of Psychotherapy* (Boston: Houghton Mifflin, 1961).

Rosner, Brian S., '"That Pattern of Teaching": Issues and Essays in Pauline Ethics', in B.S. Rosner, *Understanding Paul's Ethics: Twentieth-Century Approaches* (Grand Rapids: Eerdmans, 1995), 1–23.

Rüsche, Franz, 'Pneuma, Seele, Geist: Ein Ausschnitt aus der antiken Pneumalehre', *TGl* 23 (1931), 606–24.

–, *Das Seelenpneuma: Seine Entwicklung von der Hauchseele zur Geistseele – Ein Beitrag zur Entwicklung der antiken Pneumalehre* (SGKA 18/3; Paderborn: Schöningh, 1933).

Ruppert, Lothar, 'Liebe und Bekehrung: Zur Typologie des Romans Josef und Asenat', in F. Link (ed.), *Paradeigmata: Literarische Typologie des Alten Testaments. Vol. 1* (SL 5/1; Berlin: Duncker & Humbolt, 1989), 33–42.

Russel, Walter Bo, III, *The Flesh/Spirit Conflict in Galatians* (Lanham: University of America Press, 1997).

Saake, Helmut, 'Pneuma', in G. Wissowa (ed.), *Paulys Real-Encyclopädie der classischen Altertumswissenschaft. Suppl. XIV* (Stuttgart: Metzler, 1973), 387–412.

Saarinen, Risto, 'Gottes Sein – Gottes Wirken: Die Grunddifferenz von Substanzdenken und Wirkungsdenken in der evangelischen Lutherdeutung', in S. Peura and A. Raunio (eds.), *Luther und Theosis: Vergöttlichung als Thema der abendländischen Theologie* (VLAR 15; SLAG 25; Erlangen/Helsinki: Martin-Luther-Verlag/Luther-Agricola-Gesellschaft, 1990), 103–19.

Sabou, Sorin, *Between Horror and Hope: Paul's Metaphysical Language of Death in Romans 6:1–11* (PBM; Milton Keynes: Paternoster, 2005).

Sambur-sky, Samuel, *Physics of the Stoics* (London: Routledge, 1959).

Samra, James George, 'Being Conformed to Christ in Community: A Study of Maturity, Maturation and the Local Church in the Undisputed Pauline Epistles' (University of Oxford: Unpublished DPhil Thesis, 2004).

–, *Being Conformed to Christ in Community: A Study of Maturity, Maturation and the Local Church in the Undisputed Pauline Epistles* (LNTS 320; London/New York: T. & T. Clark, 2006).

Sandelin, Karl-Gustav, 'Does Paul Argue Against Sacramentalism and Over-Confidence in 1 Cor 10.1–14?', in P. Borgen and S. Giversen (eds.), *The New Testament and Hellenistic Judaism* (Aarhus: AUP, 1995), 165–82.

Sanders, E. P., *Paul and Palestinian Judaism* (London: SCM Press, 1977).

–, *Paul* (Past Masters; Oxford/New York: Oxford University Press, 1991).

Sänger, Dieter, *Antikes Judentum und die Mysterien: Religionsgeschichtliche Untersuchungen zu Joseph und Aseneth* (WUNT II/5; Tübingen: J.C.B. Mohr (Paul Siebeck), 1980).

Sarason, Barbara R., and Sarason, Irwin G., 'Close Relationships and Social Support: Implications for the Measurement of Social Support', in A.L. Vangelisti and D. Perlman (eds.), *The Cambridge Handbook of Personal Relationships* (Cambridge: Cambridge University Press, 2006), 429–43.

Sattler, Dorothea, *Beziehungsdenken in der Erlösungslehre: Bedeutung und Grenzen* (Freiburg: Herder, 1997).

Savage, Timothy B., *Power through Weakness: Paul's Understanding of the Christian Ministry in 2 Corinthians* (SNTSMS 86; Cambridge: Cambridge University Press, 1996).

Schaaf, Julius Jakob, 'Beziehung und Beziehungsloses (Absolutes)', in D. Heinrich and H. Wagner (eds.), *Subjektivität und Metaphysik: Festschrift für Wolfgang Cramer* (Frankfurt: Klostermann, 1966), 277–89.

Schäfer, Peter, 'Geist/Heiliger Geist/Geistesgaben II: Judentum', *TRE*, XII, 173–78.

Schart, Aaron, 'Die "Gestalt" YHWHs: Ein Beitrag zur Körpermetaphorik alttestamentlicher Rede von Gott', *TZ* 55 (1999), 26–41.

Schelkle, Karl Hermann, *The Second Epistle to the Corinthians* (NTSR 14; New York: Herder, 1969).

Schenk, Wolfgang, 'Wortforschung: II. Neues Testament', *TRE*, XXXVI, 335–37.

Schlatter, Adolf, *The Theology of the Apostles: The Development of New Testament Theology* (Grand Rapids: Baker, 1998); orig. publ.: *Die Theologie der Apostel* (Stuttgart: Calwer Vereinsbuchhandlung, 1922).

–, *Paulus, der Bote Jesu Christi: Eine Deutung seiner Briefe an die Korinther* (Stuttgart: Calwer Verlag, 1962³ [1931¹]).

Schlier, Heinrich, *Der Römerbrief* (HTKNT VI; Freiburg/Basel/Wien: Herder, 2002 [1977¹]).

Schnabel, Eckhard J., *Early Christian Mission. Vol. II: Paul & the Early Church* (Downers Grove/Leicester: IVP/Apollos, 2004).

–, *Der erste Brief des Paulus an die Korinther* (HTA; Wuppertal/Giessen: Brockhaus/Brunnen, 2006).

Schnackenburg, Rudolf, *Das Johannesevangelium. Vol. 4: Ergänzende Auslegungen und Exkurse* (HTKNT 4; Freiburg: Herder, 1994³ [1984¹]).

–, *Die Johannesbriefe* (HTKNT; Freiburg: Herder, 2002⁷ [1984⁷]).

Schneider, Dieter, *Der Geist des Gekreuzigten: Zur Paulinischen Theologie des Heiligen Geistes* (Neukirchen-Vluyn: Aussaat, 1987).

Schneider, Gerhard, 'Die Idee der Neuschöpfung beim Apostel Paulus und ihr religionsgeschichtlicher Hintergrund', *TTZ* 68 (1959), 257–70.

–, *Neuschöpfung oder Wiederkehr? Eine Untersuchung zum Geschichtsbild der Bibel* (Düsseldorf: Patmos, 1961).

Schnelle, Udo, *Gerechtigkeit und Christusgegenwart: Vorpaulinische und nachpaulinische Tauftheologie* (GTA 24; Göttingen: Vandenhoeck & Ruprecht, 1983).

–, *Neutestamentliche Anthropologie: Jesus – Paulus – Johannes* (Biblisch-theologische Studien 18; Neukirchen-Vluyn: Neukirchener Verlag, 1991).

–, 'Transformation und Partizipation als Grundgedanken paulinischer Theologie', *NTS* 47 (2001), 58–75.

–, *Paulus: Leben und Denken* (Berlin/New York: W. de Gruyter, 2003).

–, *Apostle Paul: His Life and Theology* (Grand Rapids: Baker Academic, 2005).

–, *Einleitung ins Neue Testament* (UTB 1830; Göttingen: Vandenhoeck & Ruprecht, 2007[6]).

Schofer, P., and Rice, D., 'Metaphor, Metonymy, and Synecdoche Revis(it)ed', *Semiotica* 21 (1977), 121–49.

Scholla, R. W., S.I., 'Into the Image of God: Pauline Eschatology and the Transformation of Believers', *Greg* 78 (1997), 33–54.

Schrage, Wolfgang, *Die konkreten Einzelgebote in der paulinischen Paränese: Ein Beitrag zur neutestamentlichen Ethik* (Gütersloh: Mohn, 1961).

–, *Ethik des Neuen Testaments* (NTD 4; Göttingen: Vandenhoeck & Ruprecht, 1989[2]).

–, *Der erste Brief an die Korinther (1Kor 1,1–6,11)* (EKKNT VII/1; Zürich/Braunschweig: Benziger/Neukirchener Verlag, 1991).

–, *Der erste Brief an die Korinther (1Kor 6,12–11,16)* (EKKNT VII/2; Zürich/Braunschweig: Benziger/Neukirchener Verlag, 1995).

–, *Der erste Brief an die Korinther (1Kor 11,17–14,40)* (EKKNT VII/3; Zürich/Braunschweig: Benziger/Neukirchener Verlag, 1999).

–, 'Schöpfung und Neuschöpfung bei Paulus in Kontinuität und Diskontinuität', *EvT* 65 (2005), 245–59.

Schreiner, Josef, 'Geistbegabung in der Gemeinde von Qumran', *BZ* 9 (1965), 161–80.

Schreiner, Thomas R., *Romans* (BECNT; Grand Rapids: Baker, 1998).

Schröter, Jens, 'Schriftauslegung und Hermeneutik in 2 Korinther 3: Ein Beitrag zur Frage der Schriftbenutzung des Paulus', *NovT* 40 (1998), 231–75.

Schulthess, Peter, 'Relation I: History', in H. Burkhardt and B. Smith (eds.), *Handbook of Metaphysics and Ontology. Vol. 2* (Analytica; Munich: Philosophica, 1991), 776–79.

Schulz, Siegfried, *Neutestamentliche Ethik* (Zürich: Theologischer Verlag, 1987).

Schweitzer, Albert, *Paul and His Interpreters: A Critical History* (London: Black, 1912).

–, *The Mysticism of Paul the Apostle* (London: Black, 1953[2] [1931[1]]); orig. publ.: *Die Mystik des Apostels Paulus* (Tübingen: J.C.B. Mohr (Paul Siebeck), 1930).

Schweitzer, Wolfgang, 'Gotteskindschaft, Wiedergeburt und Erneuerung im Neuen Testament und in seiner Umwelt' (Eberhard-Karls-Universität Tübingen: Unpublished PhD Thesis, 1944).

Schweizer, Eduard, 'πνεῦμα, πνευματικός', *TDNT*, VI, 389–451.

–, 'σάρξ κτλ', *TDNT*, VII, 119–51.

–, 'The Spirit of Power: The Uniformity and Diversity of the Concept of the Holy Spirit in the New Testament', *Int* 6 (1952), 259–78.

–, *Jesus* (London: SCM Press, 1971).

Schwöbel, Christoph, 'Human Being as Relational Being: Twelve Theses for a Christian Anthropology', in C. Schwöbel and C.E. Gunton (eds.), *Persons, Divine and Human: King's College Essays in Theological Anthropology* (Edinburgh: T. & T. Clark, 1991), 141–65.

Scott, Alan, *Origen and the Life of the Stars: A History of an Idea* (Oxford: Clarendon, 1991).

Scott, Ian W., *Implicit Epistemology in the Letters of Paul: Story, Experience and the Spirit* (WUNT II/205; Tübingen: Mohr Siebeck, 2006).

Scott, James M., *Adoption as Sons of God: An Exegetical Investigation into the Background of ΥΙΟΘΕΣΙΑ in the Pauline Corpus* (WUNT II/48; Tübingen: J.C.B. Mohr (Paul Siebeck), 1992).

–, 'The Triumph of God in 2 Cor. 2.14: Additional Evidence of Merkabah Mysticism in Paul', *NTS* 42 (1996), 260–81.

–, *2 Corinthians* (NIBCNT 8; Carlisle: Paternoster, 1998).

Scott, Walter, *Hermetica: The Ancient Greek and Latin Writings which contain Religious or Philosophic Teachings Ascribed to Hermes Trismegistus. Vol. 1* (Oxford: Clarendon, 1924).

Scroggs, Robin, *The Last Adam: A Study in Pauline Anthropology* (London: Blackwell, 1966).

Searle, John R., 'Metaphor', in A. Ortony (ed.), *Metaphor and Thought* (Cambridge: Cambridge University Press, 1993[2]), 83–111.

Sedley, David, '"Becoming like God" in the *Timaeus* and Aristotle', in T. Calvo and L. Brisson (eds.), *Interpreting the Timaeus – Critias: Proceedings of the IV Symposium Platonicum* (IPS 9; Sankt Augustin: Academia, 1997), 327–39.

Seesemann, Heinrich, *Der Begriff ΚΟΙΝΩΝΙΑ im Neuen Testament* (BZNW 14; Gießen: Töpelmann, 1933).

Segal, Alan F., *Paul the Convert: The Apostolate and Apostasy of Saul the Pharisee* (New Haven: Yale University Press, 1990).

Sekki, A. E., *The Meaning of Ruaḥ at Qumran* (SBLDS 110; Atlanta: Scholars Press, 1989).

Sellin, Gerhard, 'Die religionsgeschichtlichen Hintergründe der paulinischen "Christusmystik"', *TQ* 176 (1996), 7–27.

Shaver, Phillip R., and Mikulincer, Mario, 'Attachment Theory, Individual Psychodynamics, and Relationship Functioning', in A.L. Vangelisti and D. Perlman (eds.), *The Cambridge Handbook of Personal Relationships* (Cambridge: Cambridge University Press, 2006), 251–71.

Sheriffs, Deryck, *The Friendship of the Lord: An Old Testament Spirituality* (Carlisle: Paternoster, 1996).

–, 'The Human Need for Continuity: Some ANE and OT Perspectives', *TynBul* 55 (2004), 1–15.

Siebeck, Hermann, 'Die Entwicklung der Lehre vom Geist (Pneuma)', *ZVS* 12 (1880), 361–407.

Siegert, Folker, *Philon von Alexandrien: Über die Gottesbezeichnung "wohltätig verzehrendes Feuer" (De Deo)* (WUNT 46; Tübingen: J.C.B. Mohr (Paul Siebeck), 1988).

Simpson, J. A., and Weiner, Edmund S. C. (eds.), *The Oxford English Dictionary*; 20 vols. (Oxford: Clarendon, 1989[2]).

Slenczka, Notger, *Realpräsenz und Ontologie: Untersuchung der ontologischen Grundlagen der Transsignifikationslehre* (FSÖT 66; Göttingen: Vandenhoeck & Ruprecht, 1993).

Slezák, Thomas A., 'Platon', *DNP*, IX, 1095–109.

Smelik, Willem F., 'On Mystical Transformation of the Righteous into Light in Judaism', *JSJ* 26 (1995), 122–44.

Smith, T. C., 'Influences That Shaped the Theology of Paul', *PRSt* 25 (1998), 151–62.

Snaith, Norman H., *Distinctive Ideas of the Old Testament* (Philadelphia: Westminster, 1946).

–, *Leviticus and Numbers* (NCB; London: Nelson, 1967).

Sokolowski, Emil, *Die Begriffe Geist und Leben bei Paulus in ihrer Beziehung zueinander: Eine exegetisch-religionsgeschichtliche Untersuchung* (Göttingen: Vandenhoeck & Ruprecht, 1903).

Solmsen, Friedrich, 'Cleanthes or Posidonius? The Basis of Stoic Physics', in F. Solmsen, *Kleine Schriften. Vol. 1* (Collectanea 4/1; Hildesheim: Georg Olms Verlagsbuchhandlung, 1968), 436–60.

–, 'The vital Heat, the inborn Pneuma and the Aether', in F. Solmsen, *Kleine Schriften. Vol. 1* (Collectanea 4/1; Hildesheim: Georg Olms Verlagsbuchhandlung, 1968), 605–11.

Soskice, Janet Martin, *Metaphor and Religious Language* (Oxford: Clarendon, 1985).

–, 'Metapher und Offenbarung', in J.-P. van Noppen (ed.), *Erinnern, um Neues zu sagen: Die Bedeutung der Metapher für die religiöse Sprache* (Frankfurt: Athenäum, 1988), 68–83.

Soskice, Janet Martin, and Harré, Rom, 'Metaphor in Science', in Z. Radman (ed.), *From a Metaphorical Point of View: A Multidisciplinary Approach to the Cognitive Content of Metaphor* (PW.TS 7; Berlin/New York: W. de Gruyter, 1995), 289–307.

Spicq, Ceslaus, *Agape in the New Testament. Vol. 2: Agape in the Epistles of St. Paul, the Acts of the Apostles and the Epistles of St. James, St. Peter, and St. Jude* (London: Herder, 1965).

Sprigge, T. L. S., 'Relation III: Internal Relations', in H. Burkhardt and B. Smith (eds.), *Handbook of Metaphysics and Ontology* (Analytica; Munich: Philosophica, 1991), 781–83.

St. Clair, Michael, *Human Relationships and the Experience of God: Object Relations and Religion* (New York: Paulist Press, 1994).

Stalder, Kurt, *Das Werk des Geistes in der Heiligung bei Paulus* (Zürich: EVZ-Verlag, 1962).

Standhartinger, Angela, 'Weisheit in Joseph und Aseneth und den paulinischen Briefen', *NTS* 47 (2001), 482–501.

Stead, Christopher, *Divine Substance* (Oxford: Clarendon, 1977).

Stecher, Ludwig, *Die Wirkung sozialer Beziehungen: Empirische Ergebnisse zur Bedeutung sozialen Kapitals für die Entwicklung von Kindern und Jugendlichen* (Munich: Juventa, 2001).

Stegman, Thomas, *The Character of Jesus: The Linchpin to Paul's Argument in 2 Corinthians* (AB 158; Rome: Editrice Pontificio Instituto Biblico, 2005).

Steinmann, T., 'Substanz', *RGG*[2], II, 869.

Stendahl, Krister, 'The Apostle Paul and the Introspective Conscience of the West', in K. Stendahl, *Paul amoung Jews and Gentiles and other essays* (Philadelphia: Fortress, 1976), 78–96.

Stettler, Christian, 'The "Command of the Lord" in 1 Cor 14,37 – a Saying of Jesus?', *Bib* 87 (2006), 42–51.

Stevenson-Moessner, Jeanne, *The Spirit of Adoption: At Home in God's Family* (Louisville: Westminster John Knox Press, 2003).

Stiver, Dan R., *The Philosophy of Religious Language: Sign, Symbol, and Story* (Oxford: Blackwell, 1996).

Stockhausen, Carol Kern, *Moses' Veil and the Glory of the New Covenant: The Exegetical Substructure of II Cor. 3,1–4,6* (AB 116; Rome: Editrice Pontificio Instituto Biblico, 1989).

Stowers, Stanley K., 'Romans 7.7–25 as a Speech-in-Character (προσωποποιία)', in T. Engberg-Pedersen (ed.), *Paul in His Hellenistic Context: Studies in the New Testament and its World* (Edinburgh: T. & T. Clark, 1994), 180–202.

–, 'Does Pauline Christianity Resemble a Hellenistic Philosophy?', in T. Engberg-Pedersen (ed.), *Paul Beyond the Judaism/Hellenism Divide* (Louisville: Westminster John Knox Press, 2001), 81–102.

Straub, Jürgen, 'Personale und kollektive Identität: Zur Analyse eines theoretischen Begriffs', in A. Assmann and H. Friese (eds.), *Identitäten* (Erinnerung, Geschichte, Identität 3; S-TW 1404; Frankfurt: Suhrkamp, 1998), 73–104.

Strecker, Christian, *Die liminale Theologie des Paulus: Zugänge zur paulinischen Theologie aus kulturanthropologischer Perspektive* (FRLANT 185; Göttingen: Vandenhoeck & Ruprecht, 1999).

–, 'Zugänge zum Unzugänglichen: "Geist" als Thema neutestamentlicher Wissenschaft', *ZNT* 25 (2010), 3–20.

Strecker, Georg, *Theologie des Neuen Testaments (Bearbeitet, ergänzt und herausgegeben von Friedrich Wilhelm Horn)* (Berlin/New York: W. de Gruyter, 1996).

Strobel, August, *Der erste Brief an die Korinther* (ZBK.NT 6/1; Zürich: TVZ, 1989).

Strotmann, Angelika, *"Mein Vater bist du!" (Sir 51,10): Zur Bedeutung der Vaterschaft Gottes in kanonischen und nichtkanonischen frühjüdischen Schriften* (FTS 39; Frankfurt: Knecht, 1991).

Stuckenbruck, Earl R., 'The Spirit at Pentecost', in C.R. Wetzel (ed.), *Essays on New Testament Christianity: A Festschrift in Honor of Dean E. Walker* (Cincinnati: Standard Publishing, 1978), 90–102.

Stürmer, K., 'Das Abendmahl bei Paulus', *EvT* 7 (1947/48), 50–59.

Stuhlmacher, Peter, *Gerechtigkeit Gottes bei Paulus* (FRLANT 87; Göttingen: Vandenhoeck & Ruprecht, 1966[2]).

–, 'Erwägungen zum ontologischen Charakter der καινὴ κτίσις bei Paulus', *EvT* 27 (1967), 1–35.

–, *Paul's Letter to the Romans: A Commentary* (Edinburgh: T. & T. Clark, 1994); orig. publ.: *Der Brief an die Römer* (NTD 6; Göttingen: Vandenhoeck & Ruprecht, 1989).

–, *Der Brief an die Römer* (NTD 6; Göttingen: Vandenhoeck & Ruprecht, 1998[2]).

–, 'Hartmut Gese about "Das Alte Testament in der Johannesoffenbarung"' (University of Tübingen: Unpublished Minutes of an *Oberseminar/Sozietät* Session, 04.07.2000).

–, *Biblische Theologie des Neuen Testaments. Vol. 1: Grundlegung. Von Jesus zu Paulus* (Göttingen: Vandenhoeck & Ruprecht, 2005[3] [1992[1]]).

Sumney, Jerry L., 'Post-Mortem Existence and Resurrection of the Body in Paul', *HBT* 31 (2009), 12–26.

Suurmond, Jean-Jacques, 'The Ethical Influence of the Spirit of God: An Exegetical and Theological Study with Special Reference to 1 Corinthians, Romans 7:14–8:30, and the Johannine Literature' (Fuller Theological Seminary: Unpublished PhD Thesis, 1983).

Tengström, S., 'רוּחַ', *TDOT*, XIII, 365–96.

Theissen, Gerd, *A Theory of Primitive Christian Religion* (London: SCM, 1999).

Theobald, Michael, *Der Römerbrief* (EdF 294; Darmstadt: Wissenschaftliche Buchgesellschaft, 2000).

–, 'Angstfreie Religiosität: Röm 8,15 und 1Joh 4,17f. im Licht der Schrift Plutarchs über den Aberglauben', in M. Theobald, *Studien zum Römerbrief* (WUNT 136; Tübingen: Mohr Siebeck, 2001), 432–54; orig. publ.: in N. el-Khoury, H. Crouzel, R. Reinhard (eds.), *Lebendige Überlieferung: Prozesse der Annäherung und Auslegung* (*FS* H.-J. Vogt; Beirut/Ostfildern: Friedrich-Rückert-Verlag/Schwaben-Verlag, 1992), 321–43.

–, '*Concupiscentia* im Römerbrief: Exegetische Beobachtungen anläßlich der lutherischen Formel "simul justus et peccator"', in M. Theobald, *Studien zum Römerbrief* (WUNT 136; Tübingen: Mohr Siebeck, 2001), 250–76.

Thiselton, Anthony C., 'Realized Eschatology at Corinth', *NTS* 24 (1978), 510–26.

–, *The First Epistle to the Corinthians: A Commentary on the Greek Text* (NIGTC; Cambridge/Carlisle: Eerdmans/Paternoster, 2000).

Thom, Johan C., 'The Problem of Evil in Cleanthes' *Hymn to Zeus*', *AC* 41 (1998), 45–57.

–, 'Cleanthes' *Hymn to Zeus* and Early Christian Literature', in A.Y. Collins and M.M. Mitchell (eds.), *Antiquity and Humanity: Essays on Ancient Religion and Philosophy Presented to Hans Dieter Betz on his 70th Birthday* (Tübingen: Mohr Siebeck, 2001), 476–99.

–, *Cleanthes' Hymn to Zeus: Text, Translation, and Commentary* (STAC 33; Tübingen: Mohr Siebeck, 2005).

Thompson, Marianne Meye, '"Mercy upon All": God as Father in the Epistle to the Romans', in S. Soderlund and N.T. Wright (eds.), *Romans and the People of God: Essays in Honor of Gordon D. Fee on the Occasion of His 65th Birthday* (Grand Rapids/ Cambridge: Eerdmans, 1999), 203–16.

–, *The Promise of the Father: Jesus and God in the New Testament* (Louisville: Westminster John Knox Press, 2000).

–, *A Commentary on Colossians and Philemon* (THNTC; Grand Rapids: Eerdmans, 2005).

Thrall, Margaret E., *A Critical and Exegetical Commentary on the Second Epistle to the Corinthians. Vol. 1: Introduction and Commentary on II Corinthians I–VII* (ICC; Edinburgh: T. & T. Clark, 1994).

–, *A Critical and Exegetical Commentary on the Second Epistle to the Corinthians. Vol. 2: Commentary on II Corinthians VIII–XIII* (ICC; Edinburgh: T. & T. Clark, 2000).

Thüsing, Wilhelm, *Per Christum in Deum: Studien zum Verhältnis von Christozentrik und Theozentrik in den paulinischen Hauptbriefen* (NTA NS 1; Münster: Aschendorff, 1965).

Tibbs, Clint, *Religious Experience of the Pneuma: Communication with the Spirit World in 1 Corinthians 12 and 14* (WUNT II/230; Tübingen: Mohr Siebeck, 2007).

–, 'The Spirit (World) and the (Holy) Spirits among the Earliest Christians: 1 Corinthians 12 and 14 as a Test Case', *CBQ* 70 (2008), 313–30.

Tielemann, Teun, and Büchli, Jörg, 'Pneuma', *DNP*, IX, 1181–83.

Tilling, Chris, 'Paul's Divine-Christology: The Relation Between the Risen Lord and Believers in Paul, and the Divine-Christology Debate' (Brunel University: Unpublished PhD Thesis, 2010). [published in WUNT II/323; Tübingen: Mohr Siebeck, 2012]

Tobin, Thomas H., *Paul's Rhetoric in Its Contexts: The Argument of Romans* (Peabody: Hendrickson, 2004).

Todd, Robert B., *Alexander of Aphrodisias on Stoic Physics: A Study of the De Mixtione with Preliminary Essays, Text, Translation and Commentary* (PhA 48; Leiden: Brill, 1976).

Tolmie, D. Francois, 'Liberty – Love – the Spirit: Ethics and Ethos according to the Letter to the Galatians', in J.G. van der Watt (ed.), *Identity, Ethics, and Ethos in the New Testament* (BZNW 141; Berlin/New York: W. de Gruyter, 2006), 241–55.

Tronier, Henrik, 'The Corinthian Correspondence between Philosophical Idealism and Apocalypticism', in T. Engberg-Pedersen (ed.), *Paul Beyond the Judaism/Hellenism Divide* (Louisville: Westminster John Knox Press, 2001), 165–96.

Turner, J., 'Ontology', in J. Hastings (ed.), *Encyclopædia of Religion and Ethics. Vol. IX* (Edinburgh: T. & T. Clark, 1917), 497–99.

Turner, Max M. B., 'Spirit Endowment in Luke-Acts: Some Linguistic Considerations', *VoxEv* 12 (1981), 45–63.

–, 'The Spirit of Prophecy and the Ethical/Religious Life of the Christian Community', in M.W. Wilson (ed.), *Spirit and Renewal: Essays in Honour of J. Rodman Williams* (JPTSup 5; Sheffield: Sheffield Academic Press, 1994), 166–90.

–, *Power from on High: The Spirit in Israel's Restoration and Witness in Luke-Acts* (JPTSup 9; Sheffield: Sheffield Academic Press, 1996).

–, *The Holy Spirit and Spiritual Gifts – Then and Now* (Carlisle: Paternoster, 1999^2).

–, 'Receiving Christ and Receiving the Spirit: In Dialogue with David Pawson', *JPT* 15 (1999), 3–31.

–, '"Trinitarian" Pneumatology in the New Testament? – Towards an Explanation of the Worship of Jesus', *ATJ* 57 (2003), 167–86.

–, 'Approaching "Personhood" in the New Testament, with Special Reference to Ephesians', *EQ* 77 (2005), 211–33.

Turowski, Edmund, *Die Widerspiegelung des stoischen Systems bei Philon von Alexandreia* (Borna/Leipzig: Universitätsverlag Robert Noske, 1927).

Ulrichsen, Jarl Henning, *Die Grundschrift der Testamente der zwölf Patriarchen: Eine Untersuchung zu Umfang, Inhalt und Eigenart der ursprünglichen Schrift* (AUU.HR 10; Stockholm: Almqvist & Wiksell International, 1991).

Um, Stephen T., *The Theme of Temple Christology in John's Gospel* (LNTS 312; London: T. & T. Clark, 2006).

Vahrenhorst, Martin, *Kultische Sprache in den Paulusbriefen* (WUNT 230; Tübingen: Mohr Siebeck, 2008).

van der Watt, Jan G., *Family of the King: Dynamics of Metaphor in the Gospel according to John* (BJS 47; Leiden: Brill, 2000).

van Imschoot, P., 'L'Esprit de Jahvé, Principe de Vie Morale dans l'A. T.', *ETL* 16 (1939), 457–67.

van Unnik, Willem C., '"With Unveiled Face": An Exegesis of 2 Corinthians iii 12–18', in W.C. van Unnik, *Sparsa Collecta. Vol. 1: Evangelia, Paulina, Acta* (NovTSup 29; Leiden: Brill, 1973), 194–210; orig. publ.: *NovT* 6 (1963), 153–69.

VanderKam, James C., 'Biblical Interpretation in *1 Enoch* and *Jubilees*', in J.H. Charlesworth and C.A. Evans (eds.), *The Pseudepigrapha and Early Biblical Interpretation* (JSPSup 14/SSEJC 2; Sheffield: JSOT Press, 1993), 96–125.

–, *The Book of Jubilees* (GAP; Sheffield: Sheffield Academic Press, 2001).

Vang, Preben, 'God's Empowering Presence and the Issue of Holiness: A Relational Interpretation of Paul's Pneumatology' (Southwestern Baptist Seminary: Unpublished PhD Thesis, 1994).

Verbeke, G., *L'Évolution de la Doctrine du Pneuma: du Stoïcisme à S. Augustin* (BISPUL; Paris: Desclée de Brouwer, 1945).

Vermes, Geza, *The Complete Dead Sea Scrolls in English* (London: Penguin, 1995[4]).

Vogel, Manuel, 'Einführung', in E. Reinmuth (ed.), *Joseph und Aseneth* (SAPERE 15; Tübingen: Mohr Siebeck, 2009), 3–31.

Volf, Miroslav, *After Our Likeness: The Church as the Image of the Trinity* (SD; Grand Rapids/Cambridge: Eerdmans, 1998).

Völker, Walther, *Fortschritt und Vollendung bei Philo von Alexandrien: Eine Studie zur Geschichte der Frömmigkeit* (TU IV/4//1; Leipzig: 1938).

Vollenweider, Samuel, 'Der Geist Gottes als Selbst der Glaubenden: Überlegungen zu einem ontologischen Problem in der paulinischen Anthropologie', *ZTK* 93 (1996), 163–92.

Volz, Paul, *Der Geist Gottes und die verwandten Erscheinungen im Alten Testament und im anschließenden Judentum* (Tübingen: J.C.B. Mohr (Paul Siebeck), 1910).

von der Osten-Sacken, Peter, *Römer 8 als Beispiel der paulinischen Soteriologie* (Göttingen: Vandenhoeck & Ruprecht, 1975).

von Soden, Hermann, 'Die Ethik des Paulus', *ZTK* 2 (1892), 109–45.

von Weizsäcker, Viktor, *Der Gestaltkreis: Theorie der Einheit von Wahrnehmen und Bewegen* (Stuttgart: Thieme, 1986[5] [1940[1]]).

von Wilamowitz-Moellendorff, Ulrich, *Der Glaube der Hellenen. Vol. 2* (Berlin: Weidmannsche Buchhandlung, 1932).

Vos, Johannes S., *Traditionsgeschichtliche Untersuchungen zur Paulinischen Pneumatologie* (Assen: van Gorcum & Comp. B.V., 1973).

Wald, B., 'Substanz; Substanz/Akzidens: II.-A. Frühscholastik', *HWPh*, X, 507–10.

Wallace, Daniel B., *Greek Grammar Beyond the Basics: An Exegetical Syntax of the New Testament* (Grand Rapids: Zondervan, 1996).

Walsh, Brian J., and Keesmaat, Sylvia C., *Colossians Remixed: Subverting the Empire* (Downers Grove: IVP, 2004).

Walters, James C., 'Paul, Adoption, and Inheritance', in J.P. Sampley (ed.), *Paul in the Greco-Roman World: A Handbook* (Harrisburg/London: Trinity Press, 2003), 42–76.

Ware, James, 'Moral Progress and Divine Power in Seneca and Paul', in J.T. Fitzgerald (ed.), *Passions and Moral Progress in Greco-Roman Thought* (RMCS; London: Routledge, 2008), 267–83.

Wartenberg, Thomas E., *The Forms of Power: From Domination to Transformation* (Philadelphia: Temple University Press, 1990).

Watson, Francis, 'The Two Roman Congregations: Romans 14:1–15:13', in K.P. Donfried (ed.), *The Romans Debate* (Edinburgh: T. & T. Clark, 1991[2]), 201–15.

Way, David V., *The Lordship of Christ: Ernst Käsemann's Interpretation of Paul's Theology* (OTM; Oxford: Clarendon, 1991).

Webster, John, 'Christology, Imitability and Ethics', *SJT* 39 (1986), 309–26.

Wedderburn, A. J. M., *Baptism and Resurrection: Studies in Pauline Theology against its Graeco-Roman Background* (WUNT 44; Tübingen: J.C.B. Mohr (Paul Siebeck), 1987).

–, *The Reasons for Romans* (Edinburgh: T. & T. Clark, 1988).

–, 'Pauline Pneumatology and Pauline Theology', in G. Stanton, B.W. Longenecker, and S.C. Barton (eds.), *The Holy Spirit and Christian Origins: Essays in Honor of James D. G. Dunn* (Grand Rapids/Cambridge: Eerdmans, 2004), 144–56.

Weidemann, Hans-Ulrich, 'Zur Einführung', in E. Peterson, *Der erste Brief an die Korinther und Paulus-Studien* (ed. by H.-U. Weidemann; AS 7; Würzburg: Echter, 2006), XV–XCVI.

Weinel, Heinrich, *Die Wirkungen des Geistes und der Geister im nach-apostolischen Zeitalter bis auf Irenäus* (Tübingen: J.C.B. Mohr (Paul Siebeck), 1899).

Weinrich, Harald, *Sprache in Texten* (Stuttgart: Klett, 1976).

Weiß, Bernhard, *Lehrbuch der biblischen Theologie des Neuen Testaments* (Berlin/ Stuttgart: Hertz/Cotta'sche Buchhandlung, 1903[7] [1868[1]]).

Weiss, Johannes, *Earliest Christianity: A History of the Period A.D. 30–150*; 2 vols. (New York: Harper, 1959); orig. publ.: *Das Urchristentum*, 1917; ET: *The History of Primitive Christianity*; 2 vols. (New York: Wilson-Erickson, 1937).

–, *Der erste Korintherbrief* (KEK 5; Göttingen: Vandenhoeck & Ruprecht, 1970[9] [1910[9]]).

Weiss, Johannes, and Baumgarten, Otto, *Die Schriften des Neuen Testaments* (Göttingen: Vandenhoeck & Ruprecht, 1907[2]).

Weissenrieder, Annette, 'Der Blick in den Spiegel: II Kor 3,18 vor dem Hintergrund antiker Spiegeltheorien und ikonographischer Abbildungen', in A. Weissenrieder, F. Wendt, and P.v. Gemünden (eds.), *Picturing the New Testament: Studies in Ancient Visual Images* (WUNT II/193; Tübingen: Mohr Siebeck, 2005), 313–43.

Welker, Michael, *God the Spirit* (Minneapolis: Fortress, 1994); orig. publ.: *Gottes Geist: Theologie des Heiligen Geistes* (Neukirchen-Vluyn: Neukirchener Verlag, 1992).

Wendland, Heinz-Dietrich, 'Das Wirken des Heiligen Geistes in den Gläubigen nach Paulus', in E. Schlink and H. Volk (eds.), *Pro Veritate: Ein theologischer Dialog* (FS L. Jaeger and W. Stählin; Münster: Aschendorffsche Verlagsbuchhandlung, 1963), 133–56; orig. publ.: in *ThLZ* 77 (1952), 457–70.

–, *Vom Leben und Handeln der Christen: Eine Betrachtung zu Römer 6* (Stuttgart: Calwer Verlag, 1972).

Wendt, Hans Heinrich, *Die Begriffe Fleisch und Geist im biblischen Sprachgebrauch* (Gotha: Berthes, 1878).

Wenham, David, 'The Christian Life – A Life of Tension? A Consideration of Christian Experience in Paul', in D.A. Hagner and M.J. Harris (eds.), *Pauline Studies* (Exeter: Paternoster, 1980), 80–94.

–, *Paul: Follower of Jesus or Founder of Christianity?* (Grand Rapids: Eerdmans, 1995).

Wenk, Matthias, *Community-Forming Power: The Socio-Ethical Role of the Spirit in Luke-Acts* (JPTSS 19; Sheffield: Sheffield Academic Press, 2000).

Wernle, Paul, *Der Christ und die Sünde bei Paulus* (Freiburg/Leipzig: J.C.B. Mohr (Paul Siebeck), 1897).

White, Michael J., 'Stoic Natural Philosophy (Physics and Cosmology)', in B. Inwood (ed.), *The Cambridge Companion to the Stoics* (CCP; Cambridge: Cambridge University Press, 2003), 124–52.

Whiteley, Denys Edward Hugh, *The Theology of St Paul* (Oxford: Blackwell, 1974^2).

Wikenhauser, Alfred, *Pauline Mysticism: Christ in the Mystical Teaching of St. Paul* (Freiburg/Edinburgh-London: Herder/Nelson, 1960); orig. publ.: *Die Christusmystik des Apostels Paulus* (Freiburg: Herder, 1956^2).

Wilckens, Ulrich, 'Zur Entwicklung des paulinischen Gesetzesverständnisses', *NTS* 28 (1982), 154–90.

Wili, W., 'Die Geschichte des Geistes in der Antike', *EvJ* 13 (1945), 49–93.

Williams, Daniel Day, *The Spirit and the Forms of Love* (LCT; Digswell Place: Nisbet, 1968).

Williams, Guy, *The Spirit World in the Letters of Paul the Apostle: A Critical Examination of the Role of Spiritual Beings in the Authentic Pauline Epistles* (FRLANT 231; Göttingen: Vandenhoeck & Ruprecht, 2009).

Willis, Wendell L., 'Bibliography: Pauline Ethics, 1964–1994', in E.H. Lovering and J.L. Sumney (eds.), *Theology and Ethics in Paul and His Interpreters: Papers in Honor of Victor Paul Furnish* (Nashville: Abingdon, 1996), 306–19.

Willoughby, H. R., *Pagan Regeneration: A Study of Initiations in the Graeco-Roman World* (Chicago: University of Chicago Press, 1929).

Windisch, Hans, 'Das Problem des paulinischen Imperativs', *ZNW* 23 (1924), 265–81.

–, *Der zweite Korintherbrief* (KEK NT 6; Göttingen: Vandenhoeck & Ruprecht, 1924^9).

Winston, David, *The Wisdom of Solomon: A New Translation with Introduction and Commentary* (AB 43; Garden City/New York: Doubleday, 1981).

–, 'Philo's Ethical Theory', in W. Haase (ed.), *Principat* (ANRW II.21.1; Berlin/New York: W. de Gruyter, 1984), 372–416.

–, 'The Sage as Mystic in the Wisdom of Solomon', in J.G. Gammie and L.G. Perdue (eds.), *The Sage in Israel and the Ancient Near East* (Winona Lake: Eisenbrauns, 1990), 383–97.

–, 'Philo's Mysticism', *SPA* 8 (1996), 74–82.

–, 'Judaism and Hellenism: Hidden Tensions in Philo's Thought', in G.E. Sterling (ed.), *The Ancestral Philosophy: Hellenistic Philosophy in Second Temple Judaism. Essays of David Winston* (BJS 331/SPM 4; Providence: Brown Judaic Studies, 2001), 181–98.

Witherington III, Ben, *Conflict and Community in Corinth: A Socio-Rhetorical Commentary on 1 and 2 Corinthians* (Grand Rapids/Carlisle: Eerdmans/Paternoster, 1995).

Witherington III, Ben, and Ice, Laura Michaels, *The Shadow of the Almighty: Father, Son, and Spirit in Biblical Perspective* (Grand Rapids: Eerdmans, 2002).

Wolff, Christian, *Der zweite Brief des Paulus an die Korinther* (THKNT 8; Berlin: Evangelische Verlagsanstalt, 1989).

–, *Der erste Brief des Paulus an die Korinther* (THKNT 7; Berlin: Evangelische Verlagsanstalt, 2000^2).

Wolfson, Harry Austryn, *Philo: Foundations of Religious Philosophy in Judaism, Christianity and Islam. Vol. 2: Structure and Growth of Philosophic Systems from Plato to Spinoza* (London: Harvard University Press, 1982 [1947¹]).

Wolter, Michael, *Theologie und Ethos im frühen Christentum: Studien zu Jesus, Paulus und Lukas Michael Wolter* (Wissenschaftliche Untersuchungen zum Neuen Testament; Tübingen: Mohr Siebeck, 2009).

Wrede, William, 'Paulus', in K.H. Rengstorf (ed.), *Das Paulusbild in der neueren deutschen Forschung* (WdF 24; Darmstadt: Wissenschaftliche Buchgesellschaft, 1969), 1–97; orig. publ.: in *Religionsgeschichtliche Volksbücher. Vol. 1* (Halle: Gebauer-Schwetschke, 1904).

Wright, John H., SJ, 'Spirit and Matter: An Essay in Theology, Philosophy and the Natural Science', in M.J. Himes and S.J. Pope (eds.), *Finding God in all Things: Essays in Honor of Michael J. Buckley, S.J.* (New York: Crossroad, 1996), 127–39.

Wright, Nicholas Thomas, *The Climax of the Covenant: Christ and the Law in Pauline Theology* (Edinburgh: T. & T. Clark, 1991).

–, *The Resurrection of the Son of God. Christian Origins and the Questions of God* (London: SPCK, 2003).

Wülfing von Martitz, Peter, 'υἱοθεσία', *TDNT*, VIII, 397.

Yamauchi, Edwin M., 'Gnosis, Gnosticism', *DPL*, 350–53.

Yarbrough, O. Larry, 'Parents and Children in the Jewish Family of Antiquity', in S.J.D. Cohen (ed.), *The Jewish Family in Antiquity* (BJS 289; Atlanta: Scholars Press, 1993), 39–59.

–, 'Parents and Children in the Letters of Paul', in L.M. White and O.L. Yarbrough (eds.), *The Social World of the First Christians: Essays in Honor of Wayne A. Meeks* (Minneapolis: Fortress Press, 1995), 126–41.

Yates, John W., *The Spirit and Creation in Paul* (WUNT II/251; Tübingen: Mohr Siebeck, 2008).

Yonge, C. D., *The Works of Philo* (Peabody: Hendrickson, 1995³).

Young, Edward J., *My Servants the Prophets* (Grand Rapids: Eerdmans, 1953).

Young, Frances, and Ford, David F., *Meaning and Truth in 2 Corinthians* (Grand Rapids: Eerdmans, 1988).

Zahl, Paul Francis Matthew, *Die Rechtfertigungslehre Ernst Käsemanns* (CThM 13; Stuttgart: Calwer Verlag, 1996).

Zeller, Dieter, *Der Brief an die Römer* (RNT 6; Regensburg: Pustet, 1985).

–, 'La Métamorphose de Jésus comme Épiphanie (Mc 9,2–8)', in A. Marchadour (ed.), *L'Évangile exploré: Mélanges offerts à Simon Légasse à l'occasion de ses soixante-dix ans* (LD 166; Paris: Les Éditions du Cerf, 1996), 167–86.

–, *Der erste Brief an die Korinther* (KEK 5; Göttingen: Vandenhoeck & Ruprecht, 2010).

Ziener, Georg, *Das Buch der Weisheit* (WB-KK 12; Düsseldorf: Patmos-Verlag, 1970).

Zimmerli, Walther, *Ezechiel* (HAT I/13; Tübingen: J.C.B. Mohr (Paul Siebeck), 1955²).

Zimmermann, Christiane, *Die Namen des Vaters: Studien zu ausgewählten neutestamentlichen Gottesbezeichnungen vor ihrem frühjüdischen und paganen Sprachhorizont* (AJEC 69; Leiden: Brill, 2007).

Zimmermann, Ruben, 'Einführung: Bildersprache verstehen oder Die offene Sinndynamik der Sprachbilder', in R. Zimmermann, *Bildersprache verstehen: Zur Hermeneutik der Metapher und anderer bildlicher Sprachformen* (Übergänge 38; Munich: Fink, 2000), 13–54.

–, 'Jenseits von Indikativ und Imperativ: Zur "impliziten Ethik" des Paulus am Beispiel des 1. Korinterbriefs', *TLZ* (2007), 260–84.

Index of References

Hebrew Bible

New Testament

Early Jewish Literature

Graeco-Roman Literature

Early Christian Literature

Index of Authors

Index of Subjects

CPSIA information can be obtained at www.ICGtesting.com
Printed in the USA
LVOW04s0818110115

422314LV00001B/1/P

9 781451 472202